# 8000
## awesome
## things
you should know

# 8000
## awesome
## things
### you should know

First published in 2007 by Miles Kelly Publishing Ltd
Harding's Barn, Bardfield End Green, Thaxted, Essex, CM6 3PX, UK

This edition printed in 2010

6 8 10 9 7 5

EDITORIAL DIRECTOR  Belinda Gallagher
ART DIRECTOR  Jo Brewer
COVER DESIGNERS  Candice Bekir, Simon Lee
SENIOR DESIGNER  Simon Lee
ASSISTANT EDITOR  Lucy Dowling
EDITORIAL ASSISTANT  Carly Blake
PICTURE RESEARCH MANAGER  Liberty Newton
PRODUCTION MANAGER  Elizabeth Collins
REPROGRAPHICS  Anthony Cambray, Liberty Newton, Ian Paulyn
ASSETS MANAGER  Bethan Ellish

ISBN 978-1-84810-219-4

Printed in China

British Library Cataloguing-in-Publication Data
A catalogue record for this book is available from the British Library

All images are from the Miles Kelly Archives

Made with paper from a sustainable forest

www.mileskelly.net
info@mileskelly.net

www.factsforprojects.com

Self-publish your
children's book

buddingpress.co.uk

# CONTENTS

# DINOSAURS 18–75

# PREHISTORIC LIFE 76–133

# SHARKS 134–191

# INSECTS 192–249

# BIRDS 250–307

# MAMMALS 308–365

# ANCIENT HISTORY 366–423

# MODERN HISTORY 424–481

# Introduction

This incredible reference resource provides knowledge, fascination and inspiration on every page. Its 800 subject panels contain facts that will inform, amaze and entertain. You can read about dinosaurs, sharks, mammals, ancient and modern history and much much more. Learn hundreds of new fascinating facts such as these:

• *The full name of Tyrannosaurus is Tyrannosaurus rex, which means 'King of the tyrant reptiles'.*

• *Sharks range in size from about the size of a banana to bigger than a bus.*

• *The giraffe's black tongue is almost half a metre long and is used to grip vegetation and pull it into its mouth.*

• *The Emperor Trajan went to a gladiator contest that lasted 117 days and involved 10,000 gladiators.*

Read on to discover the other 7996 facts in *8000 More Things You Should Know*.

# Using this book

*8000 More Things You Should Know* is divided into eight broad areas. On each double-page spread there are three or four subject panels. Each panel contains ten key facts and is identified with a highlighted subject symbol. Look at each individual section contents to find out what they mean.

The subjects are organized so that you will find interest and variety throughout the book. Use the subject symbols, contents page and the index to navigate.

Headings tell you which of the eight areas of the book you are in.

Ten key facts are provided in each subject panel. There are 800 panels making 8000 facts in all.

## Chima

- Although relate sharks or rays. T cartilaginous fish
- Various types of ghost sharks, spo
- Chimaeras grow but most are sma Many chimaeras h make up a large pa
- Feeding on small f chimaeras usually
- Chimaeras are so c a combination of di
- Like some sharks, c front of their dorsal

▶ A ratfish (a type of c seabed. Chimaeras are f and the Antarctic.

## Sharks a

- Sharks have been arou humans have.
- It's a p

## Babies

- As far as we know, fema which their babies hatched
- The time between eggs out is called the incubatio
- Incubation periods for by weeks or months for today's reptiles.
- Many fossils of adult hadrosaur) have been and hatchlings (just-
- Fossils of Maiasaura

▲ Some fo the process Dinosaur

So

## Pack-hunters

- Dinosaurs were reptiles, but no reptiles today hunt in packs in which members cooperate with each other.
- Certain types of crocodiles and alligators come together to feed where prey is abundant, but they do not coordinate their attacks.
- Fossil evidence suggests that several kinds of meat-eating dinosaurs hunted in groups or packs.
- Sometimes the fossils of several individuals of the same type of dinosaur have been found in one place, suggesting the dinosaurs were pack animals.

- The fossil bones of some plant-eating dinosaurs have been found with many tooth marks on them, apparently made by different-sized predators, which may have hunted in packs.
- Tyrannosaurus may have been a pack-hunter.

- In southwest Montana, USA, the remains of three or four Deinonychus were found near the fossils of a much larger plant-eater named Tenontosaurus.
- One Deinonychus probably would not have attacked a full-grown Tenontosaurus, but a group of three or four might have.

▲ The raptors could probably hunt alone, but also bring down larger prey in packs, as hyaenas or lions do today.

★ STAR FACT ★
Some meat-eaters may have had fairly large brains, enabling them to hunt as a group.

## Ceratopsians

- Ceratopsians were large plant eaters that appeared less than 90 million years ago.
- Most ceratopsian fossils come from North America.
- 'Ceratopsian' means 'horn-face', after the long horns on their snouts, eyebrows or foreheads.
- Most ceratopsians had a neck shield or frill that swept sideways and up from the back of the head to cover the upper neck and shoulders.

- Well-known ceratopsians included Triceratops, Styracosaurus, Centrosaurus, Pentaceratops, Anchiceratops, Chasmosaurus and Torosaurus.
- The neck frills of some ceratopsians, such as that of Chasmosaurus, had large gaps or 'windows' in the bone.
- In life, the windows in the neck frill of a ceratopsian were covered with thick, scaly skin.
- Ceratopsians had no teeth in the fronts of their hooked, beaklike mouths.
- Using rows of powerful cheek teeth, ceratopsians sheared their plant food.

★ STAR FACT ★
Torosaurus had the longest skull of any land animal ever, at about 2.5 m from the front of the snout to the rear of the neck frill.

▶ Centrosaurus was a Late Cretaceous 'horn-face', about 6 m long.

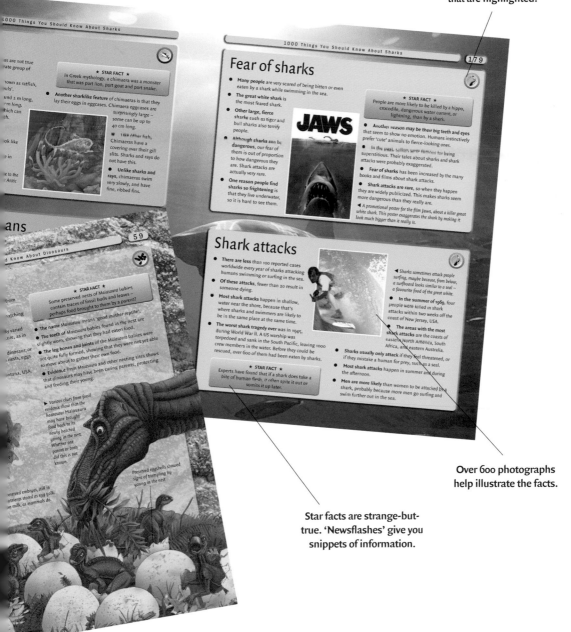

**Subject symbols appear on every panel. Look for the ones that are highlighted.**

...as are not true
...rate group of

...own as ratfish,
...uls'.

...und 2 m long,
...rm long,
...hich can
...th.

...ook like
...e in
...e to the
...Arctic

★ STAR FACT ★
In Greek mythology, a chimaera was a monster that was part lion, part goat and part snake.

• Another sharklike feature of chimaeras is that they lay their eggs in eggcases. Chimaera eggcases are surprisingly large – some can be up to 40 cm long.

❋ Like other fish, Chimaeras have a covering over their gill slits. Sharks and rays do not have this.

❋ Unlike sharks and rays, chimaeras swim very slowly, and have fine, ribbed fins.

# Fear of sharks

• Many people are very scared of being bitten or even eaten by a shark while swimming in the sea.
• The great white shark is the most feared shark.
• Other large, fierce sharks such as tiger and bull sharks also terrify people.
• Although sharks can be dangerous, our fear of them is out of proportion to how dangerous they are. Shark attacks are actually very rare.
• One reason people find sharks so frightening is that they live underwater, so it is hard to see them.

★ STAR FACT ★
People are more likely to be killed by a hippo, crocodile, dangerous water current, or lightning, than by a shark.

• Another reason may be their big teeth and eyes that seem to show no emotion. Humans instinctively prefer 'cute' animals to fierce-looking ones.
• In the past, sailors were famous for being superstitious. Their tales about sharks and shark attacks were probably exaggerated.
• Fear of sharks has been increased by the many books and films about shark attacks.
• Shark attacks are rare, so when they happen they are widely publicized. This makes sharks seem more dangerous than they really are.

◀ A promotional poster for the film Jaws, about a killer great white shark. This poster exaggerates the shark by making it look much bigger than it really is.

★ STAR FACT ★
Some preserved nests of Maiasaura babies contain traces of fossil buds and leaves – perhaps food brought to them by a parent?

...ly varied
...ure, as in
...dinosaur, or
...nests, eggs
...ntana, USA.

• The name Maiasaura means 'good mother reptile'.
• The teeth of Maiasaura babies found in the nest are slightly worn, showing that they had eaten food.
• The leg bones and joints of the Maiasaura babies were not quite fully formed, showing that they were not yet able to move about to gather their own food.
• Evidence from Maiasaura and other nesting sites shows that dinosaurs may have been caring parents, protecting and feeding their young.

▶ Various clues from fossil evidence show that the hadrosaur Maiasaura may have brought food back to its newly hatched young in the nest. Whether one parent or both did this is not known.

Preserved eggshells showed signs of trampling by young in the nest

...eserved embryos, still in
...utrients stored as egg yolk,
...e milk, as mammals do.

# Shark attacks

• There are less than 100 reported cases worldwide every year of sharks attacking humans swimming or surfing in the sea.
• Of these attacks, fewer than 20 result in someone dying.
• Most shark attacks happen in shallow, water near the shore, because that's where sharks and swimmers are likely to be in the same place at the same time.
• The worst shark tragedy ever was in 1945, during World War II. A US warship was torpedoed and sank in the South Pacific, leaving 1000 crew members in the water. Before they could be rescued, over 600 of them had been eaten by sharks.

★ STAR FACT ★
Experts have found that if a shark does take a bite of human flesh, it often spits it out or vomits it up later.

◀ Sharks sometimes attack people surfing, maybe because, from below, a surfboard looks similar to a seal – a favourite food of the great white.

• In the summer of 1969, four people were killed in shark attacks within two weeks off the coast of New Jersey, USA.
• The areas with the most shark attacks are the coasts of eastern North America, South Africa, and eastern Australia.
• Sharks usually only attack if they feel threatened, or if they mistake a human for prey, such as a seal.
• Most shark attacks happen in summer and during the afternoon.
• Men are more likely than women to be attacked by a shark, probably because more men go surfing and swim further out in the sea.

**Over 600 photographs help illustrate the facts.**

**Star facts are strange-but-true. 'Newsflashes' give you snippets of information.**

# DINOSAURS

## MEAT-EATING DINOSAURS

## HERBIVOROUS DINOSAURS

## DINOSAURS' ANATOMY

## LIFESTYLE AND BEHAVIOUR

## WHERE THEY LIVED

## FOSSIL FINDS

# Age of Dinosaurs

● **The Age of Dinosaurs** corresponds to the time period that geologists call the Mesozoic Era, from about 248–65 million years ago.

● **The Mesozoic Era** is divided into three shorter time spans – the Triassic, Jurassic and Cretaceous Periods.

● **In the Triassic Period**, 248–208 million years ago, the dinosaurs began to evolve.

● **During the Jurassic Period** – about 208–144 million years ago – the dinosaurs reached their greatest size.

● **The Cretaceous Period** is when dinosaurs were at their most varied – about 144–65 million years ago.

● **In the Triassic Period**, all the continents were joined in one supercontinent – Pangaea.

| MYA | ERA | PERIOD | |
|---|---|---|---|
| 80 | | | |
| 100 | | CRETACEOUS | |
| 120 | | | |
| 140 | MESOZOIC | 136 MYA | AGE OF REPTILES |
| 160 | | JURASSIC | |
| 180 | | | |
| 200 | | 193 MYA | |
| 220 | | TRIASSIC 225 MYA | |

◀ Dinosaurs ruled the land for 160 million years – longer than any other animal group.

● **In the Jurassic Period**, the supercontinent of Pangaea separated into two huge land-masses – Laurasia in the north and Gondwana in the south.

● **In the Cretaceous Period**, Laurasia and Gondwana split, and the continents as we know them began to form.

● **In the Mesozoic Era**, the major land-masses gradually moved across the globe in a process known as 'continental drift'.

● **The joining and separating** of the continents affected which kinds of dinosaurs lived where.

# Legs and posture

● **All dinosaurs had four limbs.** Unlike certain other reptiles, such as snakes and slow-worms, they did not lose their limbs through evolution.

● **Some dinosaurs**, such as massive, plant-eating sauropods like *Janenschia*, stood and walked on all four legs nearly all the time.

● **The all-fours method** of standing and walking is called 'quadrupedal'.

▲ The small plant-eater Hypsilophodon *was a bipedal dinosaur, walking and running on its two larger back legs.*

● **Some dinosaurs**, such as nimble, meat-eating dromaeosaurs like *Deinonychus*, stood and walked on their back limbs only. The front two limbs were used as arms.

● **The back-limbs-only method** of standing and walking is called 'bipedal'.

● **Some dinosaurs**, such as hadrosaurs like *Edmontosaurus*, could move on all four limbs or just on their back legs if they chose to.

● **The two-or-four-legs method** of standing and walking is called 'bipedal/quadrupedal'.

● **Reptiles** such as lizards and crocodiles have a sprawling posture, in which the upper legs join the body at the sides.

● **Dinosaurs** had an upright posture, with the legs directly below the body.

● **The more efficient upright posture** and gait may be one major reason why dinosaurs were so successful compared to other animals of the time.

# Fabrosaurs

- **Fabrosaurs** were small dinosaurs that lived towards the beginning of the Jurassic Period, about 208–200 million years ago.

- **The group was named** from *Fabrosaurus*, a dinosaur that was itself named in 1964, from just the fossil of a piece of lower jaw bone, found in southern Africa.

- **Lesothosaurus** was a fabrosaur, the fossils of which were found in the Lesotho region of Africa, near the *Fabrosaurus* fossil. It was named in 1978.

- **The lightly built** *Lesothosaurus* was only 1 m long from nose to tail-tip, and would have stood knee-high to an adult human.

- **Lesothosaurus** had long, slim back legs and long toes, indicating that it was a fast runner.

- **The teeth and other fossils** of *Lesothosaurus* show that it probably ate low-growing plants such as ferns.

- **Lesothosaurus's teeth** were set inwards slightly from the sides of its skull, suggesting it had fleshy cheek pouches for storing or chewing food.

- **Lesothosaurus** may have crouched down to rest on its smaller front arms when feeding on the ground.

- **Lesothosaurus** probably lived in herds, grazing and browsing, and then racing away at speed from danger.

- **Some experts believe** that *Lesothosaurus* and *Fabrosaurus* were the same, and that the two sets of fossils were given different names.

◀ *Lesothosaurus's head and neck were small in relation to its body.*

# Ancestors

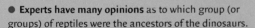

- **Experts have many opinions** as to which group (or groups) of reptiles were the ancestors of the dinosaurs.

- **The earliest dinosaurs** appeared in the Middle Triassic Period, about 230–225 million years ago, so their ancestors must have been around before this.

- **Very early dinosaurs** walked and ran on their strong back limbs, so their ancestors were probably similar.

★ STAR FACT ★
Creatures similar to *Euparkeria* or *Lagosuchus* may have given rise to the first dinosaurs.

- **The thecodonts** or 'socket-toothed' group of reptiles may have been the ancestors of the dinosaurs.

- **A thecodont's teeth** grew from roots fixed into pit-like sockets in the jaw bone, as in dinosaurs.

- **Some thecodonts** resembled sturdy lizards. Others evolved into true crocodiles (still around today).

- **The ornithosuchian thecodonts** became small, upright creatures with long back legs and long tails.

- **The smaller thecodonts** included *Euparkeria*, at about 60 cm long, and *Lagosuchus*, at about 30 cm long.

- **Euparkeria and Lagosuchus** were fast-moving creatures that used their sharp claws and teeth to catch insects.

◀ *The early reptile Dimetrodon was a pelycosaur, not a dinosaur.*

# Prosauropods

● **The prosauropods** were the first really big dinosaurs to appear on Earth. They were plant-eaters that thrived about 230–180 million years ago.

● **Prosauropods** had small heads, long necks and tails, wide bodies and four sturdy limbs.

● **One of the first prosauropods** was *Plateosaurus*, which lived about 220 million years ago in present-day France, Germany, Switzerland and other parts of Europe.

● **Plateosaurus** usually walked on all fours, but it may have reared up on its back legs to reach high leaves.

● **Plateosaurus** was up to 8 m in total length, and weighed about 1 tonne.

● **Another prosauropod** was *Riojasaurus*. Its fossils are 218 million years old, and come from Argentina.

● **Riojasaurus** was 10 m long and weighed about 2 tonnes.

● **Anchisaurus** was one of the smallest prosauropods, at only 2.5 m long and about 30 kg. It lived in eastern North America about 190 million years ago.

● **Fossil evidence** suggests that 5-m-long *Massospondylus* lived in southern Africa and perhaps North America.

● **The sauropods** followed the prosauropods and were even bigger, but had the same basic body shape, with long necks and tails.

◀ Riojasaurus *was South America's first big dinosaur.*

# Horns

● **A dinosaur's horns** got bigger as the animal grew – they were not shed and replaced each year like the antlers of today's deer.

● **Each horn** had a bony core and an outer covering of horny substance formed mainly from keratin.

● **Horns** were most common among the plant-eating dinosaurs. They were probably used for self-defence and to defend offspring against predators.

● **The biggest horns** belonged to the ceratopsians or 'horn-faces', such as *Triceratops*.

★ STAR FACT ★
Dinosaurs may have used their horns to push over plants or dig up roots for food.

● **In some ceratopsians**, just the bony core of the horn was about 1 m long, not including the outer sheath.

● **The ceratopsian** *Styracosaurus* or 'spiked reptile' had a series of long horns around the top of its neck frill, and a very long horn on its nose.

● **Horns may have been used** in head-swinging displays to intimidate rivals and make physical fighting less likely.

● **In battle**, male dinosaurs may have locked horns in a trial of strength, as antelopes do today.

● **Armoured dinosaurs** such as the nodosaur *Panoplosaurus* had horn-like spikes along the sides of its body.

◀ Styracosaurus's *frill horns had bony centres.*

# Tyrannosaurus

● **Tyrannosaurus** is not only one of the most famous of the dinosaurs, but also one about which a great deal is known. Several discoveries have revealed fossilized bones, teeth, whole skeletons and other remains.

● **Tyrannosaurus** lived at the very end of the Age of Dinosaurs, about 68–65 million years ago.

● **The full name** of Tyrannosaurus is Tyrannosaurus rex, which means 'king of the tyrant reptiles'.

● **The head** of Tyrannosaurus was 1.2 m long and had more than 50 dagger-like teeth, some longer than 15 cm.

● **Tyrannosaurus** fossils have been found at many sites in North America, including Alberta and Saskatchewan in Canada, and Colorado, Wyoming, Montana and New Mexico in the USA.

★ STAR FACT ★
Tyrannosaurus, when fully grown, was about 12–13 m long and stood taller than a two-decker bus. It weighed 6–7 tonnes.

● **The arms and hands** of Tyrannosaurus were so small that they could not pass food to its mouth, and may have had no use at all.

● **Recent fossil finds** of a group of Tyrannosaurus, includes youngsters, suggesting that they may have lived as families in small herds.

● **Tyrannosaurus** may have been an active hunter, pounding along at speed after its fleeing prey, or it may have been a skulking scavenger that ambushed old and sickly victims.

● **Until the 1990s,** Tyrannosaurus was known as the biggest meat-eating dinosaur, and the biggest meat-eating animal ever to walk the Earth, but its size record has been broken by Giganotosaurus.

▲ The huge skull of Tyrannosaurus was deep from top to bottom, but relatively narrow from side to side. The jaw hinged at the rear of the head, giving a vast gape when the mouth was open.

Curved neck allowed head to face forwards

Two-fingered 'hand'

Deep chest probably gave great stamina

Three-toed foot

Thick, heavy, muscular base to tail

▶ Tyrannosaurus's massive, powerful rear legs contrasted greatly with its puny front limbs or 'arms'. As it pounded along, its thick-based tail balanced its horizontal body and the head, which was held low. The rear feet were enormous, each set of three toes supporting some 3–4 tonnes.

# Raptors

- **'Raptors'** is a nickname for the dromaeosaur group.

- **'Raptor'** is variously said to mean 'plunderer', 'thief' or 'hunter' (birds of prey are also called raptors).

- **Dromaeosaurs** were medium-sized, powerful, agile, meat-eating dinosaurs that lived mainly about 110–65 million years ago.

- **Most dromaeosaurs** were 1.5–3 m from nose to tail, weighed 20–60 kg, and stood 1–2 m tall.

- **Velociraptor** lived 75–70 million years ago, in what is now the barren scrub and desert of Mongolia in Central Asia.

- **Like other raptors,** *Velociraptor* probably ran fast and could leap great distances on its powerful back legs.

- **The dromaeosaurs** are named after the 1.8-m long *Dromaeosaurus* from North America – one of the least known of the group, from very few fossil finds.

- **The best-known raptor** is probably *Deinonychus.*

- **The large mouths of dromaeosaurs** opened wide and were equipped with many small, sharp, curved teeth.

> ★ STAR FACT ★
> On each foot, a dromaeosaur had a large, curved claw that it could swing in an arc to slash through its victim's flesh.

◀ *Velociraptor, the 'speedy thief', was a typical dromaeosaur. Fossils of it were found in Central Asia.*

# Tails

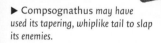

▶ Compsognathus *may have used its tapering, whiplike tail to slap its enemies.*

- **All dinosaurs** evolved with tails – though some individuals may have lost theirs in attacks or accidents!

- **The length of the tail** relative to the body, and its shape, thickness and special features, give many clues as to how the dinosaur used it.

- **The longest tails,** at more than 17 m, belonged to the giant plant-eating sauropods such as *Diplodocus.*

- **Some sauropods** had a linked chain of more than 80 separate bones inside the tail – more than twice the usual number.

- **A sauropod** may have used its tail as a whip to flick at enemies.

- **Many meat-eating dinosaurs** that stood and ran on their back legs had thick-based tails to counterbalance the weight of their bodies and heads.

- **Small, fast, agile meat-eaters,** such as *Compsognathus,* used their tails for balance when leaping and darting about.

- **The meat-eater** *Ornitholestes* had a tail that was more than half of its 2-m length, and was used as a counterbalance-rudder to help it turn corners at speed.

- **The armoured dinosaurs** known as ankylosaurs had two huge lumps of bone at the ends of their tails, which they swung at their enemies like a club.

- **The tails of the duck-billed dinosaurs** (hadrosaurs) may have been swished from side to side in the water as an aid to swimming.

# Gobi Desert

- **The Gobi** covers much of southern Mongolia and parts of northern China. During the Age of Dinosaurs, it was a land of scrub and scattered trees.

▲ The Gobi's fossil sites are far from any towns.

- **The first fossil-hunting expeditions** to the Gobi Desert took place in 1922–25, organized by the American Museum of Natural History.

- **The 1922–25 Gobi expeditions** set out to look for fossils of very early humans, but instead found some amazing dinosaur remains.

- **The first fossil dinosaur eggs** were found by the 1922–25 expeditions.

- **Velociraptor, Avimimus and Pinacosaurus** were discovered in the Gobi.

- **Russian fossil-hunting trips** into the Gobi Desert in 1946 and 1948–49 discovered new types of armoured dinosaurs, duck-billed dinosaurs, and the huge meat-eater *Tarbosaurus*.

- **More expeditions** to the Gobi in the 1960s–70s, especially to the fossil-rich area of the Nemegt Basin, found the giant sauropod *Opisthocoelicaudia* and the helmet headed *Prenocephale*.

- **Other dinosaurs** found in the Gobi include the ostrich-dinosaur *Gallimimus* and the strong-beaked 'egg thief' *Oviraptor*.

- **The inhospitable Gobi** can be -40°C in winter and 40°C in summer.

- **Despite the harsh conditions**, the Gobi Desert is one of the most exciting areas in the world for finding dinosaur fossils.

# Brachiosaurus

- **Relatively complete** fossil remains exist of *Brachiosaurus*.

- *Brachiosaurus* was a sauropod – a huge plant-eater.

- **At 25-m long** from nose to tail, *Brachiosaurus* was one of the biggest of all dinosaurs.

- **Fossils** of *Brachiosaurus* have been found in North America, east and north Africa, and also possibly southern Europe.

- **Estimates of the weight** of *Brachiosaurus* range from about 30 to 75 tonnes.

- *Brachiosaurus* lived about 150 million years ago, and may have survived until 115 million years ago.

- **The name** *Brachiosaurus* means 'arm reptile' – it was so-named because of its massive front legs.

- **With its huge front legs and long neck**, *Brachiosaurus* could reach food more than 13 m from the ground.

- **The teeth** of *Brachiosaurus* were small and chisel-shaped for snipping leaves from trees.

- *Brachiosaurus's* nostrils were high on its head.

▶ *Brachiosaurus had similar body proportions to a giraffe, but was more than twice as tall and 50 times heavier.*

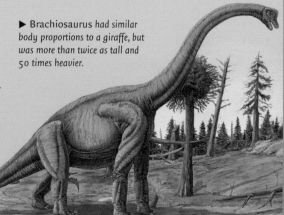

# Europe

- **The first dinosaur fossils** ever discovered and given official names were found in England.

- **One of the first almost complete dinosaur skeletons** found was that of

▲ The dots indicate dinosaur fossils found in Europe.

the big plant-eater *Iguanodon*, in 1871, in southern England.

- **Some of the most numerous early fossils found** were those of *Iguanodon*, discovered in a coal mine in the Belgian village of Bernissart in 1878.

- **About 155–150 million years ago**, Solnhofen in southern Germany was a mosaic of lush islands and shallow lagoons – ideal for many kinds of life.

- **In sandstone** in the Solnhofen region of Germany, fossils of amazing detail preserved the tiny *Compsognathus* and the first known bird, *Archaeopteryx*.

- **Fossils** of tiny *Compsognathus* were found near Nice in southern France.

- **Many fossils** of the plant-eating prosauropod *Plateosaurus* were recovered from Trossingen, Germany, in 1911–12, 1921–23 and 1932.

- **Some of the largest fossil dinosaur eggs**, measuring 30 cm long (five times longer than a hen's egg), were thought to have been laid by the sauropod *Hypselosaurus* near Aix-en-Provence in southern France.

- **The Isle of Wight** off southern England has provided so many dinosaur fossils that it is sometimes known as 'Dinosaur Island'.

- **Fossils** of *Hypsilophodon* have been found in eastern Spain, and those of *Camptosaurus* on the coast of Portugal.

# Names: 1

- **Every dinosaur has a scientific name**, usually made up from Latin or Greek, and written in *italics*.

- **Many dinosaur names** end in *-saurus*, which some say means 'reptile' and others say means 'lizard' – even though dinosaurs were not lizards.

- **Dinosaur names** often refer to a feature that no other dinosaur had. *Baryonyx*, for example, means 'heavy claw', from the massive claw on its thumb.

- **The medium-sized meat-eater** *Herrerasaurus* from Argentina was named after Victorino Herrera, the farmer who first noticed its fossils.

- **Many dinosaur names are real tongue-twisters**, such as *Opisthocoelicaudia*, pronounced 'owe-pis-thowe-see-lee-cord-ee-ah'.

- *Opisthocoelicaudia* means 'posterior tail cavity', and refers to the joints between the backbones in the tail.

- **Some dinosaurs** were named after the place where their fossils were found. Minmi was located near Minmi Crossing in Queensland, Australia.

- **Some dinosaur groups** are named after the first-discovered or major one of its kind, such as the tyrannosaurs or stegosaurs.

- **The fast-running ostrich-dinosaurs' name**, ornithomimosaurs, means 'bird-mimic reptiles'.

◀ *Herrerasaurus was named after the Andean farmer who found it.*

---

★ **STAR FACT** ★
*Triceratops*, or 'three-horned face', is one of the best known dinosaur scientific names.

# Monsters

- **Dinosaurs** can be measured by length and height, but 'biggest' usually means heaviest or bulkiest.

- **Dinosaurs were not the biggest-ever living things** on Earth – some trees are more than 100 times their size.

- **The sauropod dinosaurs** of the Late Jurassic were the biggest animals to walk on Earth, as far as we know.

- **Sauropod dinosaurs** may not have been the biggest animals ever. Today's great whales, and perhaps the massive, flippered sea reptiles called pliosaurs of the Dinosaur Age, rival them in size.

- **For any dinosaur,** enough fossils must be found for a panel of scientists to be sure it is a distinct type, so

they can give it a scientific name. They must also be able to estimate its size. With some giant dinosaurs, not enough fossils have been found.

- **Supersaurus** remains found in Colorado, USA, suggest a dinosaur similar to *Diplodocus*, but perhaps even longer, at 35 m.

- **Seismosaurus** fossils found in 1991 in the USA may belong to a 40-m long sauropod.

- **Ultrasaurus** fossils found in South Korea suggest a dinosaur similar to *Brachiosaurus*, but smaller.

- **Ultrasaurus** fossils from the USA suggest a dinosaur similar to *Brachiosaurus*, but possibly even bigger.

- **Argentinosaurus** from South America may have weighed 100 tonnes or more.

*Long neck for reaching high leaves*

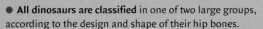

▲ *Seismosaurus is known from few fossils.*

# Hips

- **All dinosaurs are classified** in one of two large groups, according to the design and shape of their hip bones.

- **One of the two large groups of dinosaurs** is the Saurischia, meaning 'reptile-hipped'.

- **In a saurischian dinosaur,** the lower front pair of rod-shaped bones in the pelvis project down and forwards.

- **All meat-eating dinosaurs** belonged to the Saurischia.

- **The biggest dinosaurs,** the plant-eating sauropods, belonged to the Saurischia.

- **The second of the two groups of dinosaurs** is the Ornithischia, meaning 'bird-hipped'.

★ STAR FACT ★
One way experts assign a dinosaur to a main group is by the structure of its hip bones.

- **In an ornithischian dinosaur,** the lower front pair of rod-shaped bones in the pelvis, called the pubis bones, project down and backwards, lying parallel with another pair, the ischium bones.

- **All dinosaurs** in the group Ornithischia, from small *Heterodontosaurus* to huge *Triceratops*, were plant-eaters.

- **In addition to hips,** there are other differences between the Saurischia and Ornithischia, such as an 'extra' bone called the predentary at the front tip of the lower jaw in ornithischians.

◄ *Saurischian ('reptile-hipped') bones.*

▶ *Ornithischian ('bird-hipped') bones.*

# Ostrich-dinosaurs

- **'Ostrich-dinosaurs'** is the common name of the ornithomimosaurs, because of their resemblance to today's largest bird – the flightless ostrich.

- **Ostrich-dinosaurs** were tall and slim, with two long, powerful back legs for very fast running.

- **The front limbs** of ostrich-dinosaurs were like strong arms, with grasping fingers tipped by sharp claws.

- **The eyes of ostrich-dinosaurs** were large and set high on the head.

- **The toothless mouth** of an ostrich-dinosaur was similar to the long, slim beak of a bird.

- **Ostrich-dinosaurs** lived towards the end of the Cretaceous Period, about 100–65 million years ago, in North America and Asia.

◀ *Ostrich-dinosaurs such as Dromiceiomimus were probably the fastest runners of their time, speeding along at 60–70 km/h.*

- **Fossils** of the ostrich-dinosaur *Struthiomimus* from Alberta, Canada, suggest it was almost 4 m in total length and stood about 2 m tall – the same height as a modern ostrich.

- **The ostrich-dinosaur** *Gallimimus* was almost 6 m long and stood nearly 3 m high.

- **Ostrich-dinosaurs probably ate** seeds, fruits and other plant material, as well as small animals such as worms and lizards, which they may have grasped with their powerful clawed hands.

- **Other ostrich-dinosaurs** included *Dromiceiomimus*, at 3–4 m long, and the slightly bigger *Ornithomimus*.

# Sauropelta

- **Sauropelta** was a nodosaur – a type of armoured dinosaur.

- **The name** *Sauropelta* means 'shielded reptile', from the many large, conelike lumps of bone – some almost as big as dinner plates – on its head, neck, back and tail.

- **The larger lumps of bone** on *Sauropelta* were interspersed with smaller, fist-sized bony studs.

- **Sauropelta** had a row of sharp spikes along each side of its body, from just behind the eyes to the tail. The spikes decreased in size towards the tail.

- **Sauropelta** was about 7.5 m long, including the tail, and its bulky body and heavy, bony armour meant it probably weighed almost 3 tonnes.

▶ *Sauropelta was heavily armoured and protected on its upper side, but not on its belly.*

**★ STAR FACT ★**
*Sauropelta lived 110–100 million years ago, in present-day Montana and Wyoming, USA.*

- **The armour** of *Sauropelta* was flexible, almost like lumps of metal set into thick leather, so the dinosaur could twist and turn, but was unable to run fast.

- **Strong, sturdy, pillarlike legs** supported *Sauropelta's* great weight.

- **Sauropelta** probably defended itself by crouching down to protect its softer belly, or swinging its head to jab at an enemy with its long neck spines.

- **Using its beaklike mouth,** *Sauropelta* probably plucked its low-growing plant food.

# Fossil formation

● **Most of the information** we know, or guess, about dinosaurs comes from fossils.

● **Fossils are the remains of once-living things** that have been preserved in rocks and turned to stone, usually over millions of years.

● **Not just dinosaurs,** but many kinds of living things from prehistoric times have left fossils, including mammals, birds, lizards, fish, insects and plants such as ferns and trees.

● **The flesh, guts and other soft parts** of a dead dinosaur's body were probably eaten by scavengers, or rotted away, and so rarely formed fossils.

● **Fossils usually formed** when a dinosaur's remains were quickly covered by sediments such as sand, silt or mud, especially along the banks of a river or lake, or on the seashore.

● **The sand or other sediment** around a creature or plant's remains was gradually buried deeper by more

sediment, squeezed under pressure, and cemented together into a solid mass of rock.

● **As the sediment turned to rock,** so did the plant or animal remains encased within it.

● **Information about dinosaurs** comes not only from fossils, but also from 'trace' fossils. These were not actual parts of their bodies, but other items or signs of their presence.

● **Trace fossils** include egg shells, footprints, marks made by claws and teeth, and coprolites – fossilized dinosaur droppings.

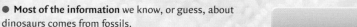

**❶** *Animal dies and is covered by water*

**❷** *Animal's soft parts are scavenged or rot away*

▶ *Fossil formation is a very long process, and extremely prone to chance and luck. Only a tiny fraction of animals that ever lived have left remains preserved by this process. Because of the way fossils are formed, animals that died in water or along banks and shores were most likely to become fossilized. It is very rare to find all the parts of an animal arranged as they were in life. Much more often, parts have been separated, jumbled, broken, crushed and distorted.*

**❸** *Sand, mud or other sediments cover the hard parts, such as the shell teeth or bones*

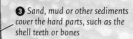

**❺** *Erosion (wearing away) of upper rock layers exposes the fossil, which is now solid stone*

**❹** *More layers build up as the minerals in the shell and other hard parts turn to rock*

# Stegosaurus

- **Stegosaurus** was the largest of the stegosaurs group.

- **Fossils** of *Stegosaurus* were found mainly in present-day Colorado, Utah and Wyoming, USA.

- **Stegosaurus**, like most of its group, lived towards the end of the Jurassic Period, about 150 million years ago.

- **The mighty** *Stegosaurus* was about 8–9 m long from nose to tail-tip and probably weighed more than 2 tonnes.

- **The most striking feature** of *Stegosaurus* were the large roughly triangular bony plates along its back.

- **The name** *Stegosaurus* means 'roof reptile'. It was given this name because it was first thought that its 80-cm long bony plates lay flat on its back, overlapping slightly like the tiles on a roof.

- **It is now thought** that the back plates of *Stegosaurus* stood upright in two long rows.

▶ Stegosaurus's *shorter front limbs meant that it ate low-growing plants.*

- **The back plates** of *Stegosaurus* may have been for body temperature control, allowing the dinosaur to warm up quickly if it stood side-on to the sun's rays.

- **Stegosaurus's** back plates may have been covered with brightly coloured skin, possibly to intimidate enemies – they were too flimsy for protection.

- **Stegosaurus's** tail was armed with four large spikes, probably for swinging at enemies in self defence.

# Great meat-eaters

- **The large meat-eating dinosaurs** belonged to a general group known as the 'carnosaurs'.

- **All carnosaurs** were similar in body shape, and resembled the fearsome *Tyrannosaurus*.

- **Tarbosaurus** was very similar to *Tyrannosaurus*. It lived at the same time, 70–65 million years ago, but in Asia rather than North America.

- **Some experts believe** that *Tarbosaurus* was an Asian version of the North American *Tyrannosaurus*, and both should have been called *Tyrannosaurus*.

- **The carnosaur** *Albertosaurus* was about 8–9 m long and lived 75–70 million years ago, in present-day Alberta, Canada.

◀ Albertosaurus *had bony ridges on its eyebrows.*

> ★ STAR FACT ★
> *Giganotosaurus* lived about 100 million years ago in today's Argentina, South America.

- **Spinosaurus** was a huge carnosaur from North Africa, measuring 12 m long and weighing 4–5 tonnes. It had tall, rodlike bones on its back, which may have been covered with skin, like a 'sail'.

- **Daspletosaurus** was a 9-m long carnosaur that lived at the end of the Age of Dinosaurs in Alberta, Canada.

- **Biggest of all the carnosaurs** was *Giganotosaurus*, the largest meat-eater ever to walk the Earth.

- **Giganotosaurus** was up to 16 m long and weighed at least 8 tonnes.

◀ The Asian Tarbosaurus *was almost identical to* Tyrannosaurus.

# Claws

- **Like reptiles today**, dinosaurs had claws or similar hard structures at the ends of their digits (fingers and toes).

- **Dinosaur claws** were probably made from keratin – the same hard substance that formed their horns, and from which our own fingernails and toenails are made.

- **Claw shapes and sizes** relative to body size varied greatly between dinosaurs.

- **In many meat-eating dinosaurs** that ran on two back legs, the claws on the fingers were long and sharp, similar to a cat's claws.

- **A small, meat-eating dinosaur** such as *Troodon* probably used its finger claws for grabbing small mammals and lizards, and for scrabbling in the soil for insects and worms.

- **Larger meat-eating dinosaurs** such as *Allosaurus* may have used their hand claws to hold and slash their prey.

- **Huge plant-eating sauropods** such as *Diplodocus* had claws on its elephant like feet that resembled nails or hooves.

- **Many dinosaurs** had five clawed digits on their feet, but some, such as *Tyrannosaurus*, had only three clawed toes on each foot to support their weight.

- **Some of the largest dinosaur claws** belonged to *Deinocheirus* – its massive finger claws were more than 35 cm long.

- *Deinocheirus* was probably a gigantic ostrich-dinosaur that lived in the Late Cretaceous Period in Mongolia. Only parts of its fossil hands and arms have been found, so the rest of it remains a mystery.

◀ The long, relatively sharp finger claws of *Troodon* were used for extracting small prey and for self defence.

# Asia

- **Hundreds of kinds of dinosaurs** have been discovered on the continent of Asia.

- **In Asia**, most of the dinosaur fossils that have been found so far were located in the Gobi Desert, in Central Asia, and in present-day China. Some were also found in present-day India.

- **Remains of the huge plant-eating sauropod** *Titanosaurus* were uncovered near Umrer, in central India.

- *Titanosaurus* was about 12 m long and weighed 5–10 tonnes.

- *Titanosaurus* lived about 70 million years ago, and was very similar in shape to its close cousin of the same time, *Saltasaurus*, from South America.

- **Fossils** of the sauropod *Barapasaurus* were found in India. They date from the Early Jurassic Period, about 180 million years ago.

- *Barapasaurus* was 18 m long and probably weighed more than 20 tonnes.

- **Fossils** of the dinosaur *Dravidosaurus*, from the stegosaur group, were found near Tiruchirapalli in southern India.

- *Dravidosaurus* was about 3 m in total length. It lived much later than other stegosaurs, in the Late Cretaceous Period about 70 million years ago.

- *Dravidosaurus* had bony plates sticking up from its back, like *Stegosaurus*.

▲ Dinosaur fossil finds span this vast continent.

# Coelophysis

- **Coelophysis** was a small, agile dinosaur that lived early in the Age of Dinosaurs, about 220 million years ago.

- **A huge collection of fossils** of Coelophysis was found in the late 1940s, at a place now known as Ghost Ranch, New Mexico, USA.

- **Hundreds** of Coelophysis were preserved together at Ghost Ranch – possibly a herd that drowned as the result of a sudden flood.

- **Coelophysis** was almost 3 m in total length.

- **The very slim, lightweight build** of Coelophysis meant that it probably weighed only 25–28 kg.

- **Coelophysis** belonged to the group of dinosaurs known as coelurosaurs. It probably ate small animals such as insects, worms and lizards.

- **Long, powerful back legs** allowed Coelophysis to run fast.

- **The front limbs** of Coelophysis were like arms, each with a hand bearing three large, strong, sharp-clawed fingers for grabbing prey.

- **Coelophysis** means 'hollow form'. It was so-named because some of its bones were hollow, like the bones of birds, making it lighter.

- **Coelophysis** had many small, sharp teeth in its narrow, birdlike skull.

◀ Coelophysis *would have stood almost waist-high to a person as it darted about on its long back legs.*

# Dinosaur fossil-hunters

- **Many dinosaurs** were found in the USA in the 1870s–90s by Othniel Charles Marsh and Edward Drinker Cope.

- **Marsh and Cope** were great rivals, each one trying to find bigger, better and more dinosaur fossils than the other.

- **The rivalry between Marsh and Cope** extended to bribing people to smash each other's fossils with hammers, planting fake fossils, and damaging food, water and other supplies at each other's camps in the Mid-West.

**Edward Drinker Cope**
**(1840–97)**

**Othniel Charles Marsh**
**(1831–99)**

> ★ **STAR FACT** ★
> One of the first great fossil-hunters in the USA was Joseph Leidy, who found *Troodon* in 1856.

- **Cope and Marsh found and described** about 130 new kinds of dinosaurs between 1877 and 1897.

- **Joseph Tyrrell** discovered fossils of *Albertosaurus* in 1884, in what became a very famous dinosaur region, the Red Deer River area of Alberta, Canada.

- **Lawrence Lambe** found and described many North American dinosaur fossils, such as *Centrosaurus* in 1904.

- **German fossil experts** Werner Janensch and Edwin Hennig led expeditions to east Africa in 1908–12, and discovered *Brachiosaurus* and *Kentrosaurus*.

- **From 1933** Yang Zhong-jiang (also called CC Young) led many fossil-hunting trips in various parts of China.

- **José Bonaparte** from Argentina has found many fossils in that region, including *Carnotaurus* in 1985.

# Size

- **The biggest dinosaurs** were the sauropods such as *Brachiosaurus* and *Argentinosaurus* – but working out how heavy they were when they were alive is very difficult.

- *Brachiosaurus* is known from many remains, including almost complete skeletons, so its length can be measured accurately.

- **A dinosaur's weight** is estimated from a scaled-down model of its skeleton 'fleshed out' with muscles, guts and skin on the bones, using similar reptiles such as crocodiles for comparison.

- **The size of a dinosaur** model is measured by immersing it in water to find its volume.

- **The volume of a model dinosaur** is scaled up to find the volume of the real dinosaur when it was alive.

> ★ STAR FACT ★
> The weights and volumes of reptiles alive today are used to calculate the probable weight of a dinosaur when it was alive.

- **The sauropod** *Apatosaurus* is now well known from about 12 skeletons, which between them have almost every bone in its body.

- **Different experts** have 'fleshed out' the skeleton of *Apatosaurus* by different amounts, so estimates of its weight vary from 20 tonnes to more than 50 tonnes.

- **The length of** *Apatosaurus* is known accurately to have been 21 m in total.

- **Fossils of a dinosaur called** *Brontosaurus* were found to be identical to those of *Apatosaurus*, and since the name *Apatosaurus* had been given first, this was the name that had to be kept – so, officially, there is no dinosaur called *Brontosaurus*.

Long neck allowed head to browse in treetops

▲ It is thought that despite its massive size, Apatosaurus would have been able to trot surprisingly quickly on its relatively long legs.

Massive, heavy tail to swing at attackers

▶ Reconstruction of Argentinosaurus is based on relatively few of its own bones, combined with other bones from similar sauropod dinosaurs.

Human-sized meat-eaters present little threat

# Heterodontosaurus

- **Heterodontosaurus** was a very small dinosaur at only 1.2 m in length (about as long as a large dog), and would have stood knee-high to a human.

- **Heterodontosaurus** lived about 205–195 million years ago, at the beginning of the Jurassic Period.

- **Probably standing partly upright** on its longer back legs, Heterodontosaurus would have been a fast runner.

- **Fossils** of Heterodontosaurus come from Lesotho in southern Africa and Cape Province in South Africa.

> ★ STAR FACT ★
> The name Heterodontosaurus means 'different-toothed reptile'.

- **Most dinosaurs had teeth of only one shape** in their jaws, but Heterodontosaurus had three types of teeth.

- **The front teeth** of Heterodontosaurus were small, sharp and found only in the upper jaw. They bit against the horny, beak-like lower front of the mouth.

- **The four middle teeth** of Heterodontosaurus were long and curved, similar to the tusks of a wild boar, and were perhaps used for fighting rivals or in self-defence.

- **The back or cheek teeth** of Heterodontosaurus were long and had sharp tops for chewing.

- **Heterodontosaurus** probably ate low-growing plants such as ferns.

▶ Tiny and slim, Heterodontosaurus looked outwardly similar to mini-meat-eaters such as Compsognathus.

# Speed

- **The fastest-running dinosaurs** had long, slim, muscular legs and small, lightweight bodies.

- **'Ostrich-dinosaurs'** were probably the speediest dinosaurs, perhaps attaining the same top speed as today's ostrich – 70 km/h.

- **The main leg muscles** of the ostrich-dinosaur Struthiomimus were in its hips and thighs.

- **The hip and leg design** of ostrich-dinosaurs meant that they could swing their limbs to and fro quickly, like those of a modern racehorse.

- **Large, powerful, plant-eating dinosaurs** such as the 'duck-bill' Edmontosaurus may have pounded along on their huge back legs at 40 km/h.

- **Plant-eaters** such as Iguanodon and Muttaburrasaurus may have trotted along at 10–12 km/h for many hours.

- **Some experts think** that the great meat-eater Tyrannosaurus may have been able to run at 50 km/h.

- **Other experts think** Tyrannosaurus was a relatively slow runner at 30 km/h (almost as fast as a human sprinter).

- **The slowest dinosaurs** were giant sauropods such as Brachiosaurus, which probably plodded at 4–6 km/h (about human walking speed).

- **Today's fastest runner**, the cheetah, would beat any dinosaur with its maximum burst of speed of more than 100 km/h.

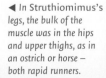

◀ In Struthiomimus's legs, the bulk of the muscle was in the hips and upper thighs, as in an ostrich or horse – both rapid runners.

# Allosaurus

- *Allosaurus* was a huge meat-eating dinosaur, almost as big as *Tyrannosaurus*.
- *Allosaurus* was about 11–12 m in total length.
- **The weight** of *Allosaurus* is variously estimated at 1.5–4 tonnes.
- **The head** of *Allosaurus* was almost 1 m long, but its skull was light, with large gaps or 'windows' that would have been covered by muscle and skin.
- *Allosaurus* could not only open its jaws in a huge gape, but it could also flex them so that the whole mouth became wider, for an even bigger bite.
- *Allosaurus* lived about 155–135 million years ago, during the Late Jurassic and Early Cretaceous Periods.
- **Most** *Allosaurus* fossils come from the states in the American Midwest.

★ STAR FACT ★
The remains of 60 *Allosaurus* were found in the Cleveland-Lloyd Dinosaur Quarry, Utah, USA.

◀ *Allosaurus* almost rivalled *Tyrannosaurus* in size, but lived 70 million years earlier.

- *Allosaurus* may have hunted the giant sauropod dinosaurs such as *Diplodocus*, *Camarasaurus* and *Brachiosaurus*.
- **Fossils** of *Allosaurus* were identified in Africa, and a smaller or 'dwarf' version was found in Australia.

# Armour

- **Many kinds of dinosaurs** had protective 'armour'.
- **Some armour** took the form of bony plates, or osteoderms, embedded in the skin.
- **A dinosaur with armour** might weigh twice as much as a same-sized dinosaur without armour.

- **Armoured dinosaurs** are divided into two main groups – the ankylosaurs and the nodosaurs.
- **The large sauropod** *Saltasaurus* had a kind of armour.
- *Saltasaurus* had hundreds of small, bony lumps, each as big as a pea, packed together in the skin of its back.
- **On its back**, *Saltasaurus* also had about 50 larger pieces of bone the size of a human hand.
- *Saltasaurus* is named after the Salta region of Argentina, where its fossils were found.
- **Uruguay** provided another site for *Saltasaurus* fossils.
- *Saltasaurus* was 12 m long and weighed about 3–4 tonnes.

◀ *Ankylosaurus's tail club was nearly 1 m across.*

# Carnotaurus

- The big, powerful, meat-eating *Carnotaurus* is in the carnosaur group of dinosaurs.

- *Carnotaurus* fossils come mainly from the Chubut region of Argentina, South America.

- *Carnotaurus* lived about 100 million years ago.

- A medium-sized dinosaur, *Carnotaurus* was about 7.5 m in total length and weighed up to 1 tonne.

- The skull of *Carnotaurus* was relatively tall from top to bottom and short from front to back, compared to other carnosaurs like *Allosaurus* and *Tyrannosaurus*, giving it a snub-snouted appearance.

- The name *Carnotaurus* means 'meat-eating bull', referring partly to its bull-like face.

- *Carnotaurus* had two curious, cone-shaped bony crests or 'horns', one above each eye, where the horns of a modern bull would be.

- Rows of extra-large scales, like small lumps, ran along *Carnotaurus* from its head to its tail.

- Like *Tyrannosaurus*, *Carnotaurus* had very small front limbs that could not reach its mouth, and may have had no use.

- *Carnotaurus* probably ate plant-eating dinosaurs such as *Chubutisaurus*, although its teeth and jaws were not especially big or strong.

◀ The fossils of Carnotaurus *were first discovered in 1985.*

# Ankylosaurs

- Ankylosaurs had a protective armour of bony plates.

- Unlike the armoured nodosaurs, ankylosaurs had a large lump of bone at the ends of their tails, which they used as a hammer or club.

- One of the best-known ankylosaurs, from the preserved remains of about 40 individuals, is *Euoplocephalus*.

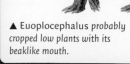

▲ Euoplocephalus *probably cropped low plants with its beaklike mouth.*

- *Euoplocephalus*, or 'well-armoured head', had bony shields on its head and body, and even had bony eyelids. Blunt spikes ran along its back.

- The hefty *Euoplocephalus* was about 7 m long and weighed 2 tonnes or more.

- *Euoplocephalus* lived about 75–70 million years ago in Alberta, Canada and Montana, USA.

- Specimens of *Euoplocephalus* are usually found singly, so it probably did not live in herds.

- The ankylosaur *Pinacosaurus* had bony nodules like chain-mail armour in its skin, and rows of blunt spikes from neck to tail.

- Ankylosaurs had small, weak teeth, and probably ate soft, low-growing ferns and horsetails.

★ STAR FACT ★
*Pinacosaurus* was about 6 m long and lived in Asia some 80–75 million years ago.

# Herbivores

- **Hundreds of kinds of dinosaurs** were herbivores, or plant-eaters. As time passed, the plants available for them to eat changed or evolved.

- **Early in the Age of Dinosaurs**, during the Triassic Period, the main plants for dinosaurs to eat were conifer trees, gingkoes, cycads and the smaller seed ferns, ferns, horsetails and club-mosses.

- **A few cycads** are still found today. They resemble palm trees, with umbrella-like crowns of long green fronds on top of tall, unbranched, trunklike stems.

- **In the Triassic Period**, only prosauropod dinosaurs were big enough or had necks long enough to reach tall cycad fronds or gingko leaves.

- **In the Jurassic Period**, tall conifers such as redwoods and 'monkey-puzzle' trees became common.

- **The huge, long-necked sauropods** of the Jurassic Period would have been able to reach high into tall conifer trees to rake off their needles.

- **In the Middle Cretaceous Period**, a new type of plant food appeared – the flowering plants.

> ★ **STAR FACT** ★
> Gingkoes are still found today in the form of the maidenhair tree, with fan-shaped leaves.

- **By the end of the Cretaceous Period** there were many flowering trees and shrubs, such as magnolias, maples and walnuts.

- **No dinosaurs ate grass**, because grasses did not appear on Earth until 30–20 million years ago, long after the dinosaurs had died out.

Barosaurus, 26 m long and 25–30 tonnes

◄ During the warm, damp Jurassic Period, plants thrived in most areas, covering land that previously had been barren. Massive plant-eaters such as Barosaurus thrived on the high-level fronds, needles and leaves of towering tree-ferns, gingkoes and conifers.

# Triceratops

- **Many fossil remains** of *Triceratops* have been found. It is one of the most studied and best known dinosaurs.

- *Triceratops* was the largest of the plant-eating ceratopsians, or 'horn-faced' dinosaurs.

- *Triceratops* lived at the very end of the Age of Dinosaurs, 67–65 million years ago.

- **Fossils of 50 or so** *Triceratops* have been found in North America, though no complete skeleton has been found.

- *Triceratops* was about 9 m long and weighed 5–6 tonnes – as big as the largest elephants of today.

- **As well as a short nose horn** and two long eyebrow horns, *Triceratops* also had a wide, sweeping frill that covered its neck like a curved plate.

- **The neck frill** of *Triceratops* may have been an anchor for the dinosaur's powerful chewing muscles.

- **Acting as a shield**, the bony neck frill of *Triceratops* may have protected it as it faced predators head-on.

- *Triceratops'* neck frill may have been brightly coloured, to impress rivals or enemies.

- **The beak-like front** of *Triceratops'* mouth was toothless, but it had sharp teeth for chewing in its cheeks.

◄ *The beak, head and neck frill of Triceratops made up almost a quarter of its length.*

# Earliest dinosaurs

- **The first known dinosaurs** appeared about 230–225 million years ago, in the Middle Triassic Period.

- **The earliest dinosaurs** were small-to-medium meat-eaters with sharp teeth and claws. They ran quickly on their two longer back legs.

- **Fossils** of *Herrerasaurus* date from 228 million years ago and were found near San Juan in Argentina, South America.

- *Herrerasaurus* was about 3 m in total length, and probably weighed some 90 kg.

- **At about the same time and in the same place** as *Herrerasaurus*, there lived a similar-shaped dinosaur named *Eoraptor*, at only 1.5 m long.

- **The name** *Eoraptor* means 'dawn plunderer' or 'early thief'.

- *Staurikosaurus* was a meat-eater similar to *Herrerasaurus*. It is known to have lived about the same time, in present-day Brazil, South America.

- *Procompsognathus* was another early meat-eater. It lived in the Late Triassic Period in Germany.

- *Pisanosaurus* lived in Argentina in the Late Triassic Period, and was only 1 m long. It may have been a plant-eater similar to *Lesothosaurus*.

◄ *Staurikosaurus was about 2 m in total length.*

**★ STAR FACT ★**
*Eoraptor* and *Herrerasaurus* hunted small animals such as lizards, insects and mammal-like reptiles.

# Smallest dinosaurs

● **One of the smallest dinosaurs** was *Compsognathus*, which lived during the Late Jurassic Period, 155–150 million years ago.

● **Fossils** of *Compsognathus* come from Europe, especially southern Germany and southeastern France.

● *Compsognathus* was slim, with a long, narrow tail. It probably weighed less than 3 kg.

● **Each hand** of *Compsognathus* had two clawed fingers, and each foot had three long, clawed running toes, with another toe (the first or big toe) placed higher up in the 'ankle' region.

● *Compsognathus* had small teeth that were sharp and curved. It probably darted through the undergrowth after insects, spiders, worms and similar small prey.

▼ *Very few fossils of* Compsognathus *have been found. They mainly belong to two individuals, one from Var, France, and the other from Bavaria, Germany. The larger specimen was about 1.2 m long, and was presumably an adult.*

● **Two other very small dinosaurs** were *Heterodontosaurus* and the 1-m long fabrosaur *Lesothosaurus*.

● **The smallest fossil dinosaur specimens** found to date are of *Mussaurus*, which means 'mouse reptile'.

● *Mussaurus* was a plant-eating prosauropod similar to *Plateosaurus*, which lived in the Late Triassic Period in South America.

● **The fossils of** *Mussaurus* measure just 20 cm long – but these are the fossils of babies, just hatched from their eggs. The babies would have grown into adults measuring 3 m long.

# Africa

- **The first major discoveries** of dinosaur fossils in Africa were made from 1907, at Tendaguru in present-day Tanzania, east Africa.

- **Discoveries at Tendaguru** in east Africa included the giant sauropod *Brachiosaurus*, the smaller *Dicraeosaurus*, and the stegosaur-like *Kentrosaurus*.

- **Remains** of the massive sauropod *Cetiosaurus* were uncovered in Morocco, north Africa.

- *Camarasaurus*, a 20-tonne plant-eater, is known from fossils found in Niger, as well as from European and North American fossils.

- **Fossils** of the huge, sail-backed meat-eater *Spinosaurus* come from Morocco and Egypt.

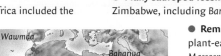

▲ In Africa, as elsewhere, fossils are easier to find in places with bare, rocky soils.

- **The sail-backed plant-eater** *Ouranosaurus* is known from remains found in Niger.

- **Many sauropod fossils** were uncovered at sites in Zimbabwe, including *Barosaurus* and *Vulcanodon*.

- **Remains** of the medium-sized plant-eating prosauropod *Massospondylus* were extracted from several sites in southern Africa.

- **Fossils** thought to belong to the small prosauropod *Anchisaurus* were found in southern Africa, the only site for this dinosaur outside North America.

- **During the 1908–12 fossil-hunting expedition** to Tendaguru, more than 250 tonnes of fossil bones and rocks were carried by people for 65 km to the nearest port, for transport to Germany.

# Mamenchisaurus

- *Mamenchisaurus* was a massive plant-eating dinosaur, a sauropod similar in appearance to *Diplodocus*.

- **The huge** *Mamenchisaurus* measured about 25 m from nose to tail tip.

- **The weight of** *Mamenchisaurus* has been estimated at 20–35 tonnes.

- *Mamenchisaurus* lived during the late Jurassic Period, from 160 to perhaps 140 million years ago.

- **The hugely long neck** of *Mamenchisaurus* had up to 19 vertebrae, or neckbones – more than almost any other dinosaur.

- *Mamenchisaurus* fossils were found in China.

- **The name** *Mamenchisaurus* is taken from the place where its fossils were discovered – Mamen Stream.

- *Mamenchisaurus* may be a close cousin of other sauropod dinosaurs found in the region, including *Euhelopus* and *Omeisaurus*.

- *Mamenchisaurus* may have stretched its vast neck high into trees to crop leaves, or – less likely – it may have lived in swamps and eaten soft water plants.

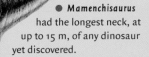

- *Mamenchisaurus* had the longest neck, at up to 15 m, of any dinosaur yet discovered.

◀ The joints between the fossil bones of Mamenchisaurus's 15-m long neck show that the neck was not very flexible.

# Deinonychus

- **Deinonychus** is one of the best-known members from the group of meat-eaters known as raptors.

- **The Middle Cretaceous Period**, about 115–100 million years ago, is when *Deinonychus* thrived.

- **Fossils** of *Deinonychus* come from the American

Midwest, mainly from Montana and Wyoming.

- **Deinonychus** was about 3 m long from nose to tail and weighed 60–70 kg, about the same as an adult human.

- **When remains of Deinonychus were dug up** and studied in the 1960s, they exploded the myth that dinosaurs were slow, small-brained and stupid.

- **Powerful, speedy and agile**, *Deinonychus* may have hunted in packs, like today's lions and wolves.

- **Deinonychus** had large hands with three powerful fingers, each tipped with a dangerous sharp claw.

- **On each foot**, *Deinonychus* had a massive, scythelike claw that it could flick in an arc to slice open prey.

- **The tail** of *Deinonychus* was stiff and could not be swished.

- **Deinonychus** and other similar dromaeosaurs, such as *Velociraptor*, were the basis for the cunning and terrifying raptors of the *Jurassic Park* films.

◀ Deinonychus *would often attack prey much larger than itself.*

# Myths

- **Dinosaurs were the only animals alive** during the Age of Dinosaurs – false, there were many kinds of creatures, from worms, insects and fish to other kinds of reptiles.

- **Dinosaurs flew in the air** – false, although other reptiles called pterosaurs did fly.

- **Dinosaurs lived in the sea** – false, although other reptiles such as ichthyosaurs and plesiosaurs did.

- **Mammals appeared** on Earth after the dinosaurs died out – false. Small mammals lived all through the Age of Dinosaurs.

- **A single kind of dinosaur** survived all through the Age of Dinosaurs – false. A few kinds may have lived for 10, 20 or even 30 million years, but none came close to 160 million years.

> ★ STAR FACT ★
> Dinosaurs and humans fought each other – false. The last dinosaurs died out more than 60 million years before humans appeared.

- **Dinosaurs were huge lizards** – false. Dinosaurs were reptiles, but not members of the lizard group.

- **Dinosaurs gave birth to babies** – false. As far as we know, dinosaurs laid eggs.

- **All dinosaurs were green** – false, probably.

- **Dinosaurs live on today** – false ... unless you've found one!

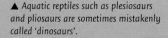

▲ Aquatic reptiles such as plesiosaurs and pliosaurs are sometimes mistakenly called 'dinosaurs'.

# Reconstructions

● **No complete fossilized dinosaur**, with all its skin, muscles, guts and other soft parts, has yet been found.

● **Most dinosaurs are reconstructed** from the fossils of their hard parts – chiefly teeth, bones, horns and claws.

● **The vast majority of dinosaurs** are known from only a few fossil parts, such as several fragments of bones.

● **Fossil parts** of other, similar dinosaurs are often used in reconstructions to 'fill in' missing bones, teeth, and even missing heads, limbs or tails.

● **Soft body parts** from modern reptiles such as lizards are used as a guide for the reconstruction of a dinosaur's muscles and guts, which are added to the fossils.

> ★ STAR FACT ★
> 'Sue', the part-mummified *Tyrannosaurus*, was sold in 1997 for more than $8.3 million to the Field Museum, Chicago, USA.

● **On rare occasions**, remains are found of a dinosaur body that dried out rapidly so that quite a few parts were preserved as mummified fossils.

● **One of the best-known**, part-mummified dinosaur fossils is 'Sue', a specimen of *Tyrannosaurus* found in 1990 in South Dakota, USA.

● **'Sue' is the biggest** and most complete preserved *Tyrannosaurus* ever found.

● **'Sue'** was a female *Tyrannosaurus*. It was named after its discoverer, fossil-hunter Susan Hendrickson of the Black Hills Institute of Geological Research.

▼ At a fossil site or 'dig', scientists record every stage of excavation with measurements, maps, photographs and sketches.

Fossil 'bones' on display are usually lightweight copies in GRP (glass-reinforced plastic)

▶ Some fragile fossils are wrapped in plaster bandages. These harden to support and protect the remains so that they can be moved.

Frame supports upper body

▶ This early reconstruction shows an ornithopod dinosaur similar to Iguanodon in a fairly upright, kangaroolike pose. As their knowledge increases, dinosaur experts change their views about how dinosaurs stood, walked and ran. Modern reconstructions tend to show Iguanodon on the move with its body almost horizontal.

Mini model shows fleshed-out appearance in life at much smaller scale

# Male and female

- **In many living reptiles,** females are larger than males.
- **In dinosaur fossils,** the shapes of the hip bones and head crests can indicate if the creatures were male or female.
- **Head crest fossils** of different sizes and proportions belonging to the hadrosaur (duck-billed dinosaur) *Lambeosaurus* have been found.
- **Some** *Lambeosaurus* had short, rounded main crests with small, spikelike spurs pointing up and back.
- **Other** *Lambeosaurus* had a large, angular main crest with a large spur pointing up and back.

★ STAR FACT ★
In *Parasaurolophus* specimens, some head crests were twice as long as others – probably a male-female difference.

- **The head crest differences** in *Lambeosaurus* fossils may indicate that males and females looked different.
- **Remains of the hadrosaur** *Corythosaurus* show two main sizes of head crest, perhaps one belonging to females and the other to males.
- **New studies** in the variations of head crests led to more than 8 different species of dinosaurs being reclassified as one species of *Corythosaurus*.
- **In dinosaurs and other animals,** differences between the sexes – either in size or specific features – is known as sexual dimorphism.

◀ *The large, angular head crest shows this is a male* Corythosaurus.

# Herds

- **When the fossils of many individuals** of the same type are found together, there are various possible causes.
- **One reason why** individuals of the same dinosaur type are found preserved together is because their bodies were swept to the same place by a flood.
- **A group of individuals** of the same type may have died in the same place if they had lived there as a group.
- **There is much evidence** that various dinosaur types lived in groups or herds, examples being *Diplodocus*, *Triceratops* and *Iguanodon*.
- **Some fossil groups** include dinosaurs of different ages, from newly hatched babies to youngsters and adults.
- **Fossil footprints** suggest some dinosaurs lived in herds.
- **Footprints** of a plant-eating dinosaur were found with the prints of a meat-eater to one side of them – perhaps evidence of a hunter pursuing its victim.

▶ *A mixed-age herd would have left similar footprints of different sizes.*

★ STAR FACT ★
At Peace River Canyon, British Columbia, Canada, some 1700 footprints were found.

- **Sometimes** the footprints of many dinosaurs of the same type are found together, suggesting a herd.
- **Sometimes larger footprints** are found to the sides of smaller ones, possibly indicating that adults guarded their young between them.

# Stegosaurs

● **Stegosaurs** were a group of plant-eating dinosaurs that lived mainly during the Late Jurassic Period, 160–140 million years ago.

● **Stegosaurs are named after** the best-known of their group, *Stegosaurus*.

● **Stegosaurs are often called** 'plated dinosaurs', from the large, flat plates or slabs of bone on their backs.

● **Stegosaurs** probably first appeared in eastern Asia, then spread to other continents, especially North America and Africa.

★ STAR FACT ★
The back plates of *Kentrosaurus* were leaf- or diamond-shaped to about halfway along its back, and spike-shaped on its hips and tail.

● **The stegosaur** *Kentrosaurus* was about 5 m long and weighed an estimated 1 tonne.

● **The name** *Kentrosaurus* means 'spiky reptile'.

● ***Kentrosaurus*** lived about 155–150 million years ago in east Africa.

● **Most stegosaurs had no teeth** at the fronts of their mouths, but had horny beaks, like those of birds, for snipping off leaves.

● **Most stegosaurs chewed** their food with small, ridged cheek teeth.

◀ The back plates of Kentrosaurus were taller and narrower than those of Stegosaurus.

# Cousins: Air

● **Many flying creatures** lived during the Age of Dinosaurs, especially insects such as flies and dragonflies, and also birds.

● **The main flying reptiles** during the Age of Dinosaurs were the pterosaurs, or 'winged reptiles'.

● **Hundreds of different kinds** of pterosaurs came and went through almost the entire Age of Dinosaurs, about 220–65 million years ago.

● **The arms of a pterosaur** resembled wings – a light, thin, stretchy wing membrane was held out mainly by the finger bones, especially the fourth finger.

▲ The wings of Quetzalcoatlus were as long as those of a four-seater airplane.

● **Pterosaurs** are sometimes called pterodactyls, but *Pterodactylus* was just one kind of pterosaur.

● ***Pterodactylus*** had a wing span of 1–2 m. It lived 150–140 million years ago in southern Germany.

▲ Pteranodon had a long projection on the back of its head.

● **Some pterosaurs**, such as *Pterodactylus*, had very short tails, or no tail at all.

● **The pterosaur** *Rhamphorhynchus* had a long, trailing tail with a widened, paddle-shaped end.

● **Fossils** suggest that some pterosaurs, such as *Sordes*, had fur, and may have been warm-blooded, agile fliers rather than slow, clumsy gliders.

● **The biggest pterosaur**, and the largest flying animal ever, was *Quetzalcoatlus*. Its 'beak' was longer than an adult human, and its wings were almost 12 m across.

# Noses

- **Dinosaurs breathed** through their mouths and/or noses, like many other creatures today.

- **Fossil dinosaur skulls** show that there were two nose openings, called nares, in the bone.

- **A dinosaur's two nasal openings**, or nares, led to nasal chambers inside the skull, where the smell organs were located.

- **Some meat-eaters**, especially carnosaurs such as *Allosaurus* and *Tyrannosaurus*, had very large nasal chambers and probably had an excellent sense of smell.

- **In most dinosaurs** the nasal openings were at the front of the snout, just above the upper jaw.

- **In some dinosaurs**, especially sauropods such as *Mamenchisaurus* and *Brachiosaurus*, the nasal openings were higher on the skull, between the eyes.

- **Fossils** show that air passages led from the nasal chambers rearwards into the head for breathing.

- **The nasal openings** in a dinosaur's skull bone led to external openings, or nostrils, in the skin.

- **New evidence** from animals alive today suggests that a dinosaur's nostrils would have been lower down than the nares (the openings in the skull bone), towards the front of the snout.

▶ The nasal openings of *Baryonyx* were towards the front of its snout, rather than at the tip.

# Nests and eggs

- **There are hundreds of discoveries** of fossil dinosaur eggs and nests, found with the parent dinosaurs.

- **Eggs and nests** are known of the pig-sized plant-eater *Protoceratops*, an early kind of horned dinosaur.

- **Many** *Protoceratops'* nests were found in a small area, showing that these dinosaurs bred in colonies.

- **Protoceratops'** nests were shallow, bowl-shaped pits about 1 m across, scraped in the dry, sandy earth and surrounded by low walls.

- **At the** *Protoceratops* **site**, it was discovered that new nests had been made on top of old ones, showing that the colony was used again year after year.

- **The female** *Protoceratops* laid a clutch of 20 or so tough-shelled, sausage-shaped eggs.

- *Protoceratops'* eggs were probably covered with earth and incubated by the heat of the sun.

- **Nests and eggs** of the small plant-eater *Orodromeus* have been found in Montana, USA.

- **In each nest** about 20 *Orodromeus* eggs were arranged neatly in a spiral, starting with one in the centre and working outwards.

- *Protoceratops* arranged its eggs neatly in its nest, in a circle or spiral shape resembling the spokes of a wheel.

▶ Most dinosaur eggs were elongated and had tough, flexible shells, like stiff leather.

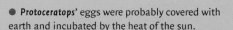

▶ *Protoceratops* was about 1.8 m long.

# Names: 2

● **More than 100 kinds of dinosaurs** have been named after the people who first discovered their fossils, dug them up, or reconstructed the dinosaur.

● **The very large duck-bill (hadrosaur)** *Lambeosaurus* was named after Canadian fossil expert Lawrence Lambe.

● **Lawrence Lambe** worked mainly during the early 1900s, and named one of his finds *Stephanosaurus*.

● **In the 1920s**, *Stephanosaurus* was re-studied and renamed, along with *Didanodon*, as *Lambeosaurus*, in honour of Lambe's great work.

● **The full name** of the 'heavy-claw' meat-eater *Baryonyx* is *Baryonyx walkeri*, after Bill Walker, the discoverer of its massive claw.

★ **STAR FACT** ★
Australian *Leaellynasaura* was named after Lea Ellyn, the daughter of its discoverers.

◀ *The first fossil find of Baryonyx was its huge thumb claw.*

● **Part-time fossil-hunter** Bill Walker found the claw of *Baryonyx* in a clay pit quarry in Surrey, England.

● **Some dinosaur names** are quite technical, such as *Diplodocus*, which means 'double beam' – it was named for its tail bones, which have two long projections like a pair of skis.

● **The 4-m long plant-eater** *Othnielia*, related to *Hypsilophodon*, was named after the late 19th-century American fossil-hunter Othniel Charles Marsh.

● **Parksosaurus**, a 2.5-m long plant-eater related to *Hypsilophodon*, was named in honour of Canadian dinosaur expert William Parks.

# Diplodocus

● **Diplodocus** was a huge plant-eating dinosaur belonging to the group known as the sauropods.

● **Diplodocus** lived during the Late Jurassic Period, about 155–145 million years ago.

● **The first discovery** of *Diplodocus* fossils was in 1877, near Canyon City, Colorado, USA.

● **The main fossils** of *Diplodocus* were found in the Midwest of the USA, in Colorado, Utah and Wyoming.

● **At an incredible 27 m** or more in length, *Diplodocus* is one of the longest dinosaurs known.

● **Although so long**, *Diplodocus* was quite lightly built – it probably weighed 'only' 10–12 tonnes!

● **Diplodocus** probably swung its tiny head on its enormous neck to reach fronds and foliage in the trees.

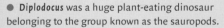

● **The teeth** of *Diplodocus* were slim rods that formed a comblike fringe only around the front of its mouth.

● **Diplodocus** may have used its comblike teeth to strip leaves from twigs and swallow them without chewing.

▶ Diplodocus *was long but light for a sauropod, weighing 'only' about 10 tonnes.*

● **Diplodocus's** nostrils were so high on its skull (almost above its eyes) that experts once thought it had a trunk like an elephant's.

# Colours

- **No one knows** for certain what colours dinosaurs were.

- **There are several good fossil specimens** of dinosaur skin, but all of them are stone coloured, because fossils are living things that have turned to stone.

- **Some experts believe** that dinosaurs were similar in colour to crocodiles – dull greens and browns.

- **Dinosaurs** that were dull greens and browns would have been well camouflaged among trees, rocks and earth.

- **According to some experts**, certain dinosaurs may have been bright yellow, red or blue, and possibly striped or patched, like some of today's lizards and snakes.

- **Some dinosaurs** may have been brightly coloured to frighten off predators or to intimidate rivals at breeding time.

- **The tall 'sails'** of skin on the backs of the plant-eater *Ouranosaurus* and the meat-eater *Spinosaurus* may have been for visual display, as well as for (or instead of) temperature control.

- **The large, bony back plates** on stegosaurs may have been used for colourful displays to rivals.

- **The large neck frills** of horned dinosaurs such as *Triceratops* were possibly very colourful and used for display.

- **Recent finds** of dinosaur skin and scales with microscopic ridges and patterns on their surface may show how the scales reflected light, and so what colour they would have appeared.

◄ *Like all reconstructions from fossils, the colours of featherered dinosaur* Caudipteryx *are intelligent guesswork.*

# Ornitholestes

- *Ornitholestes* was a smallish meat-eating dinosaur in the group known as coelurosaurs.

- **The name** *Ornitholestes* means 'bird robber' – experts who studied its fossils in the early 1900s imagined it chasing and killing the earliest birds.

- *Ornitholestes* lived about 150 million years ago, at the same time as the first birds.

- **Present-day Wyoming, USA,** was the home of *Ornitholestes*, a continent away from the earliest birds in Europe.

- **Only one specimen** of *Ornitholestes* has been found, along with parts of a hand at another site.

- *Ornitholestes* was about 2 m long from nose to tail-tip.

★ STAR FACT ★
According to some experts, *Ornitholestes* may have had a slight ridge or crest on its nose. Other experts disagree.

- **Slim and lightweight**, *Ornitholestes* probably weighed only about 12–15 kg.

- **The teeth** of *Ornitholestes* were small and well-spaced, but also slim and sharp, well suited to grabbing small animals for food.

- *Ornitholestes* had very strong arms and hands, and powerful fingers with long claws, ideal for grabbing baby dinosaurs newly hatched from their eggs.

◄ Ornitholestes *relied for survival on speed and its good senses of sight and smell.*

# Duck-bills

- **'Duck-bills'** is the common name for the group of dinosaurs called hadrosaurs.

- **Hadrosaurs were big plant-eaters** that walked mainly on their two large, powerful rear legs.

- **Hadrosaurs** were one of the last main dinosaur groups to appear on Earth, less than 100 million years ago.

- **Hadrosaurs were named after** *Hadrosaurus*, the first dinosaur of the group to be discovered as fossils, found in 1858 in New Jersey, USA.

- **Most hadrosaurs had wide mouths** that were flattened and toothless at the front, like a duck's beak.

- **Huge numbers of cheek teeth** filled the back of the hadrosaur's mouth, arranged in rows called batteries. They were ideal for chewing tough plant food.

- **Some hadrosaurs** had tall, elaborate crests or projections of bone on their heads, notably *Corythosaurus*, *Tsintaosaurus*, *Saurolophus* and *Parasaurolophus*.

- **Hadrosaurs that lacked bony crests** and had low, smooth heads included *Anatosaurus*, *Bactrosaurus*, *Kritosaurus* and *Edmontosaurus*.

- **The name** *Hadrosaurus* means 'big reptile'.

▶ *Parasaurolophus may have had a 'web' of brightly coloured skin extending from its bony head crest to the back of its neck – perhaps part of a visual display for mating, herd dominance or gaining territory. Alternatively, the bony crest may have lacked skin and simply projected upwards and backwards like a pole.*

Possible inflatable bag of skin on snout and forehead

Tall, relatively narrow tail with muscular tail base to swish tail from side to side

★ STAR FACT ★
*Edmontosaurus* may have had a loose bag of skin on its nose that it blew up like a balloon to make a honking or trumpeting noise – perhaps a breeding call.

▲ *Asian Saurolophus was about 12 m long – larger than its North American counterparts. It also had a relatively larger, horn-like head crest, which may have supported a balloon-like pouch of skin that the dinosaur could inflate to make a trumpeting call.*

Powerful rear legs for rapid walking and trotting

# Warm or cold blood?

- **If dinosaurs were cold-blooded** and obtained heat only from their surroundings, like reptiles today, they would have been slow or inactive in cold conditions.

- **If dinosaurs were warm-blooded**, like birds and mammals today, they would have been able to stay warm and active in cold conditions.

- **Some time ago** experts believed that all dinosaurs were cold-blooded, but today there is much disagreement.

- **One type of evidence** for warm-bloodedness comes from the detailed structure of the insides of very well-preserved fossil bones.

- **The inside structure** of some fossil dinosaur bones is more like that of warm-blooded creatures than reptiles

▲ *The detailed microscopic structure inside bones can give clues as to warm- or cold-bloodedness.*

- **Certain small, meat-eating dinosaurs** may have evolved into birds, and since birds are warm-blooded, these dinosaurs may have been, too.

- **In a 'snapshot' count** of dinosaur fossils, the number of predators compared to prey is more like that in mammals than in reptiles.

- **Some dinosaurs** were thought to live in herds and raise families, as many birds and mammals do today. In reptiles, such behaviour is rare.

- **Most dinosaurs stood upright** on straight legs, a posture common to warm-blooded creatures, but not to other, cold-blooded reptiles.

- **If dinosaurs had been warm-blooded**, they would probably have needed to eat at least 10 times more food than if they were cold-blooded, to 'burn' food energy and make heat.

# Eustreptospondylus

- **Eustreptospondylus** was a large meat-eater that lived in present-day Oxfordshire and Buckinghamshire, in central southern England.

- **Eustreptospondylus** lived about 165 million years ago.

- **In the 1850s**, a fairly complete skeleton of a young *Eustreptospondylus* was found near Wolvercote, Oxford, but was named as *Megalosaurus*, the only other big meat-eater known from the region.

- **In 1964**, British fossil expert Alick Walker showed that the Wolvercote dinosaur was not *Megalosaurus*, and gave it a new name, *Eustreptospondylus*.

- **Eustreptospondylus** means 'well curved, or true reversed, backbone'.

- **A full-grown** *Eustreptospondylus* measured about 7 m in total length.

- **Eustreptospondylus** is estimated to have weighed a massive 200–250 kg.

- **In its enormous mouth**, *Eustreptospondylus* had a great number of small, sharp teeth.

- **Eustreptospondylus** may have hunted sauropods such as *Cetiosaurus* and stegosaurs, two groups that roamed the region at the time.

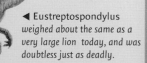

◀ *Eustreptospondylus weighed about the same as a very large lion  today, and was doubtless just as deadly.*

★ STAR FACT ★
For more than 100 years, the fossil *Eustreptospondylus* from near Oxford was known by the name *Megalosaurus*.

# Pachycephalosaurs

- **The pachycephalosaurs** are named after one of the best-known members of the group, *Pachycephalosaurus*.
- *Pachycephalosaurus* means 'thick-headed reptile', due to the domed and hugely thickened bone on the top of its skull – like a cyclist's crash helmet.
- **Pachycephalosaurs** were one of the last dinosaur groups to thrive. They lived 75–65 million years ago.

- **Pachycephalosaurs were plant-eaters** that stood up and ran on their longer back legs.
- *Pachycephalosaurus* was about 4.5 m long from nose to tail, and lived in the American Midwest.
- *Stegoceras*, also from the American Midwest, was about 2.5 m long with a body the size of a goat.
- *Homalocephale*, another pachycephalosaur, was about 3 m long and had a flatter skull. It lived in east Asia.
- **Pachycephalosaurs** may have defended themselves by lowering their heads and charging at their enemies.
- **At breeding time**, the males may have engaged in head-butting contests, as some sheep and goats do today.

Extra thick skull bone

◀ Typical of its group, Pachycephalosaurus had a thickened layer of bone on the top of its head.

# Baryonyx

- **Baryonyx** was a large meat-eating dinosaur that lived about 120 million years ago.
- **The first fossil find** of *Baryonyx* was its huge thumb claw, discovered in Surrey, England, in 1983.
- **The total length** of *Baryonyx* was 10–11 m.
- **Baryonyx** had a slim shape and long, narrow tail, and probably weighed less than 2 tonnes.
- **The head** of *Baryonyx* was unusual for a meat-eating dinosaur in having a very long, narrow snout, similar to today's slim-snouted crocodiles.
- **The teeth** of *Baryonyx* were long and slim, especially at the front of its mouth.
- **The general similarities** between *Baryonyx* and a crocodile suggest that *Baryonyx* may have been a fish-eater.
- **Baryonyx** may have lurked in swamps or close to rivers, darting its head forwards on its long, flexible neck to snatch fish.
- **The massive thumb claw** of *Baryonyx* may have been used to hook fish or amphibians from the water.
- **The long thumb claw** of *Baryonyx* measured about 35 cm in length.

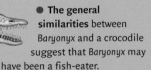

▶ Fossils of Baryonyx were found associated with remains of fish scales, suggesting this dinosaur was a semi-aquatic fish-catcher.

# Footprints

- **Thousands of fossilized dinosaur footprints** have been found all over the world.

- **Some dinosaurs left footprints** when they walked on the soft mud or sand of riverbanks. Then the mud baked hard in the sun, and was covered by more sand or mud, which helped preserve the footprints as fossils.

- **Some fossil footprints** were made when dinosaur feet left impressions in soft mud or sand that was then covered by volcanic ash, which set hard.

- **Many footprints** have been found together in lines, called 'trackways'. These suggest that some dinosaurs lived in groups, or used the same routes regularly.

- **The distance between same-sized footprints** indicates whether a dinosaur was walking, trotting or running.

> ★ **STAR FACT** ★
> Hadrosaur footprints 135 cm long and 80 cm wide were found near Salt Lake City, Utah, USA.

- **Footprints of big meat-eaters** such as *Tyrannosaurus* show three toes with claws, on a forward-facing foot.

- **In big plant-eaters** such as *Iguanodon*, each footprint shows three separate toes, but less or no claw impressions, and the feet point slightly inwards.

- **In giant plant-eating sauropods**, each footprint is rounded and has indentations of nail-like 'hooves'.

- **Some sauropod footprints** are more than 1 m across.

◀ *The relative positions of footprints indicate how a dinosaur stood or moved.*

# Archosaurs

- **Archosaurs** were a very large group of reptiles that included the dinosaurs as one of their subgroups.

- **Other archosaur subgroups** included thecodonts, flying reptiles called pterosaurs, and crocodiles.

- **The thecodonts** included a smaller reptile group, the ornithosuchians – possibly the dinosaurs' ancestors.

- **One of the most dinosaur-like of the archosaurs** was the thecodont *Ornithosuchus*.

- **The 4-m long** *Ornithosuchus* stood almost upright.

- *Ornithosuchus* fossils were found in Scotland.

- **Sharp-toothed** *Ornithosuchus* was probably a powerful predator.

- **Features** in *Ornithosuchus's* backbone, hips and feet indicate that it was almost certainly not a dinosaur.

- **The archosaur** *Longisquama* was a lizard-like reptile only 15 cm long, with tall scales forming a V-shaped row along its back.

- **Archosaur means 'ruling reptile'**, and archosaurs did indeed rule the land, swamps and skies for over 170 million years.

▶ *Ornithosuchus had a mix of features, both non-dinosaur (hips, back plates) and dinosaur (legs, skull).*

# Teeth

- **Some of most common fossil remains** of dinosaurs are their teeth – the hardest parts of their bodies.

- **Dinosaur teeth** come in a huge range of sizes and shapes – daggers, knives, shears, pegs, combs, rakes, filelike rasps, crushing batteries and vices.

- **In some dinosaurs**, up to three-quarters of a tooth was fixed into the jaw bone, so only one-quarter showed.

- **The teeth of plant-eaters** such as *Iguanodon* had angled tops that rubbed past each other in a grinding motion.

- **Some duck-bill dinosaurs** (hadrosaurs) had more than 1000 teeth, all at the back of the mouth.

- **Like modern reptiles**, dinosaurs probably grew new teeth to replace old, worn or broken ones.

- **Individual teeth** were replaced at different times.

- **Some of the largest teeth** of any dinosaur belonged to 9-m long *Daspletosaurus*, a tyrannosaurlike meat-eater.

- **Some of** *Daspletosaurus*'s teeth were 18 cm long.

▼ *The shape, number and layout of teeth indicate what food a dinosaur ate.*

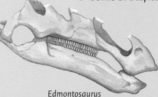

Apatosaurus

Tyrannosaurus

Edmontosaurus

# Plateosaurus

- **Plateosaurus**, a prosauropod, was one of the first really big dinosaurs to appear, some 220 million years ago.

- **The name** Plateosaurus means 'flat reptile'.

- **Groups of** Plateosaurus have been found at various sites, including one in Germany and one in France.

- **Plateosaurus** used its many small, serrated teeth to crop and chew plant food.

- **Plateosaurus** had very flexible, clawed fingers, which it perhaps used to pull branches of food to its mouth.

- **Plateosaurus** could bend its fingers 'backwards', allowing it to walk on its hands and fingers, in the same posture as its feet and toes.

- **Plateosaurus's thumbs** had especially large, sharp claws, perhaps used as weapons to jab and stab enemies.

- **Fossil experts** once thought that Plateosaurus dragged its tail as it walked.

- **Experts today** suggest that Plateosaurus carried its tail off the ground, to act as a balance to its head, long neck and the front part of its body.

- **Plateosaurus** was one of the earliest dinosaurs to be officially named, in 1837, even before the term 'dinosaur' had been invented.

◄ *Plateosaurus may have reared up to chomp on leaves 2–3 m above the ground.*

# Growth and age

- **No one knows for sure** how fast dinosaurs grew, how long they took to reach full size, or how long they lived.

- **Most estimates** of dinosaur growth rates and ages come from comparisons with today's reptiles.

- **Some reptiles today** continue to grow throughout their lives, although their growth rate slows with age.

- **Dinosaurs** may have grown fast as youngsters and slower as adults, never quite stopping until they died.

- **Estimates for the age of a full-grown meat-eater** such as *Tyrannosaurus* range from 20 to more than 50 years.

- **Full-grown, small meat-eaters** such as *Compsognathus* may have lived to be only 3–10 years old.

- **A giant sauropod** probably lived to be 50 years old, or even over 100 years old.

- **Like many reptiles today**, a dinosaur's growth rate probably depended largely on its food supply.

- **Dinosaurs** probably ate a lot and grew fast when food was plentiful, and slowed down when food was scarce.

- **During its lifetime**, a big sauropod such as *Brachiosaurus* would have increased its weight 2000 times (compared to 20 times in a human).

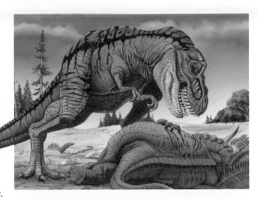

▶ *Tyrannosaurus may have taken 20–50 years to reach adult size.*

# Cousins: Land

▶ Protosuchus, *a North American crocodile, lived 200 million years ago.*

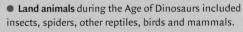

- **Land animals** during the Age of Dinosaurs included insects, spiders, other reptiles, birds and mammals.

- **Dinosaurs** had many large, fierce, reptile enemies.

- **One of the biggest** non-dinosaur land reptiles was *Deinosuchus* (or *Phobosuchus*), a type of crocodile.

- ***Deinosuchus*** lived in the Late Cretaceous Period, in present-day Texas, USA.

- **The fossil skull** of *Deinosuchus* measures about 2 m long, much bigger than any crocodile of today.

- **The first mammals** appeared on Earth at about the same time as the early dinosaurs.

- **Various kinds of mammals** survived all through the Age of Dinosaurs, although none grew larger than a pet cat.

- **One of the first mammals** known from fossils is *Megazostrodon*, which resembled a shrew of today.

- ***Megazostrodon*** was just 12 cm long and its fossils, from 220–210 million years ago, come from southern Africa.

- **If Deinosuchus's body** was in proportion to its skull, it would have been 15 m long!

# Anchisaurus

- **Anchisaurus** was a prosauropod, a plant-eater with a small head, long neck and long tail.

- **Although officially named as a dinosaur** in 1912, *Anchisaurus* had in fact been discovered almost 100 years earlier.

- **Anchisaurus** was very small and slim compared to other prosauropods, with a body about the size of a large dog.

- **Fossils** of *Anchisaurus* date from the Early Jurassic times.

- **The remains of** *Anchisaurus* were found in Connecticut and Massachusetts, eastern USA, and in southern Africa.

- **With its small, serrated teeth**, *Anchisaurus* probably bit off the soft leaves of low-growing plants.

> ★ **STAR FACT** ★
> Remains of *Anchisaurus* were the first fossils of a dinosaur to be discovered in North America in 1818.

- **To reach leaves** on higher branches, *Anchisaurus* may have been able to rear up on its back legs.

- **Anchisaurus** had a large, curved claw on each thumb.

- **The thumb claws** of *Anchisaurus* may have been used as hooks to pull leafy branches towards the mouth, and/or as weapons for lashing out at enemies and inflicting wounds.

◀ *The main body of Anchisaurus was about the size of a pet dog such as a labrador.*

# Cousins: Sea

- **Placodont reptiles** lived mainly during the Triassic Period. They were shaped like large salamanders or turtles, and probably ate shellfish.

- **The placodont** *Placodus* was about 2 m long and looked like a large, scaly newt.

- **The nothosaurs** were fish-eating reptiles of the Triassic Period. They had small heads, long necks and tails, and four flipper-shaped limbs.

- **Fossils** of the 3-m long nothosaur *Nothosaurus* have been found across Europe, Asia and Africa.

▼ *Plesiosaurus was 2.5 m long, and was one of many plesiosaurs to thrive in Jurassic seas.*

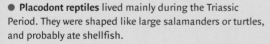

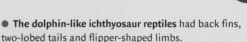

- **The dolphin-like ichthyosaur reptiles** had back fins, two-lobed tails and flipper-shaped limbs.

- **Many kinds of ichthyosaurs** thrived in the seas during the Triassic and Jurassic Periods, although they had faded away by the middle of the Cretaceous Period.

- **One of the biggest ichthyosaurs** was *Shonisaurus*, which measured up to 15 m long.

- **The plesiosaurs** were fish-eating reptiles of the Mesozoic Era, with small heads, tubby bodies, four flipper-shaped limbs and short, tapering tails.

- **The plesiosaur** *Elasmosaurus* was up to 14 m long, with more than half of this length being its extraordinarily long, snakelike neck.

> ★ **STAR FACT** ★
> One of the biggest meat-eaters ever was the short-necked plesiosaur *Liopleurodon*, at possibly 20 m long and weighing 50 tonnes.

# Dino-birds: 1

- **The earliest known bird** for which there is good fossil evidence, and which lived during the Age of Dinosaurs, is Archaeopteryx.

- **Archaeopteryx** lived in Europe during the Late Jurassic Period, about 155–150 million years ago.

- **At about 60 cm long** from nose to tail tip, Archaeopteryx was about the size of a large crow.

- **Archaeopteryx** resembled a small, meat-eating dinosaur in many of its features, such as the teeth in its long, beaklike mouth, and its long, bony tail.

> ★ STAR FACT ★
> Archaeopteryx was covered with feathers that had the same detailed designs found in feathers covering flying birds today.

- **In 1951,** a fossilized part-skeleton was identified as belonging to a small dinosaur similar to *Compsognathus*, but in the 1970s it was re-studied and named *Archaeopteryx* – showing how similar the two creatures were.

- **Three clawed fingers** grew halfway along the front of each of Archaeopteryx's wing-shaped front limbs.

- **The flying muscles** of Archaeopteryx were anchored to its large breastbone.

- **Archaeopteryx** probably flew, but not as fast or as skilfully as today's birds.

- **Archaeopteryx** probably fed by swooping on prey, running to catch small creatures such as insects and worms, or perhaps even by scavenging carrion.

Long tail with tail backbones

Three clawed 'fingers' midway along front of wing

Flight feathers suited to agile manoeuvres in the air

Teeth in long, light jaws (all birds lack teeth today)

▲ Archaeopteryx could probably glide well, swoop and turn as it pursued flying prey such as dragonflies. However, its long, strong legs suggest that it was also an able walker and runner. So it may have chased victims such as baby lizards and cockroaches on the ground.

# Skin

- **Several fossils of dinosaur skin** have been found, revealing that dinosaurs had scales, like today's reptiles.

- **As in crocodiles**, the scales of a dinosaur were embedded in its thick, tough, leathery hide, rather than lying on top of its skin and overlapping, as in snakes.

- **When the first fossils** of dinosaur skin were found in the mid 1800s, scientists thought they were from giant prehistoric crocodiles.

- **Fossil skin** of the horned dinosaur *Chasmosaurus* has been found.

- ***Chasmosaurus*** had larger bumps or lumps, called tubercles, scattered among its normal-sized scales.

- **Samples of fossil skin** belonging to the duck-bill hadrosaur *Edmontosaurus* have been found.

- ***Edmontosaurus*** was covered in thousands of small scales, like little pebbles, with larger lumps or tubercles spaced among them.

> ★ **STAR FACT** ★
> Many dinosaur scales were roughly six-sided, like the cells in a bee's honeycomb.

- **Various specimens** of fossil skin show that the scales of *Iguanodon*-type dinosaurs were larger than those of same-sized, similar duck-bill dinosaurs.

- **Scaly skin** protected a dinosaur against the teeth and claws of enemies, accidental scrapes, and the bites of small pests such as mosquitoes and fleas.

◀ Fossil skin, such as this piece from Edmontosaurus, is a relatively rare find.

# Camarasaurus

- ***Camarasaurus*** is one of the best known of all big dinosaurs, because so many almost-complete fossil skeletons have been found.

- ***Camarasaurus*** was a giant plant-eating sauropod.

- ***Camarasaurus*** lived during the Late Jurassic Period, about 155–150 million years ago.

- **The famous American fossil-hunter** Edward Drinker Cope gave *Camarasaurus* its name in 1877.

- **The name** *Camarasaurus* means 'chambered reptile', because its backbones, or vertebrae, had large, scoop-shaped spaces in them, making them lighter.

- **The huge** *Camarasaurus* was about 18 m long.

- **Compared to other sauropods**, such as *Diplodocus*, *Camarasaurus* had a relatively short neck and tail, but a very bulky, powerful body and legs.

- **North America, Europe and Africa** were home to *Camarasaurus*.

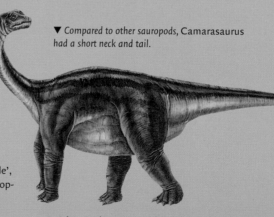

▼ Compared to other sauropods, Camarasaurus had a short neck and tail.

- **A large, short-snouted, tall head**, like that of *Brachiosaurus*, characterized *Camarasaurus*.

- **A fossil skeleton** of a young *Camarasaurus* was uncovered in the 1920s, and had nearly every bone in its body lying in the correct position, as they were in life – an amazingly rare find.

# Could dinosaurs live again?

- **The Jurassic Park movies** showed dinosaurs being recreated as living creatures in the modern world.

- **The instructions**, or genes, of all animals, including dinosaurs, are in the form of the genetic substance known as DNA (de-oxyribonucleic acid).

- **In Jurassic Park**, dinosaur DNA came not from dinosaur fossils, but from mosquitoes that had sucked the blood of living dinosaurs, and then been preserved.

- **Scientists** in Jurassic Park combined the DNA of dinosaurs with DNA from living amphibians such as frogs.

- **Tiny bits of DNA** have been recovered from fossils formed in the Age of Dinosaurs.

- **The bits of dinosaur DNA found so far** represent a tiny amount of the DNA needed to recreate a living thing.

- **Most scientists** doubt that living dinosaurs could really be made from bits of fossilized DNA.

- **Plants today** might not be suited to 'modern' dinosaurs.

- **'Modern' dinosaurs** might die from today's diseases.

- **The task of recreating** a living dinosaur from tiny fragments of DNA has been compared to writing all the plays of Shakespeare starting with couple of words.

◀ *The heroes of Jurassic Park find a sick Triceratops.*

# Oviraptor

- ***Oviraptor*** was an unusual meat-eater from the dinosaur group known as theropods.

- **Fossils of** *Oviraptor* were found in the Omnogov region of the Gobi Desert in Central Asia.

- **From beak to tail-tip**, *Oviraptor* was about 2 m long.

- ***Oviraptor*** lived during the Late Cretaceous Period about 85–75 million years ago.

- ***Oviraptor*** was named 'egg thief' because the first of its fossils was found lying among the broken eggs possibly of another dinosaur *Protoceratops*.

- **The mouth of** *Oviraptor* had no teeth. Instead, it had a strong, curved beak, like that of a parrot or eagle.

- **On its forehead**, *Oviraptor* had a tall, rounded piece of bone, like a crest or helmet, sticking up in front of its eyes.

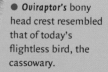

- ***Oviraptor's*** bony head crest resembled that of today's flightless bird, the cassowary.

- ***Oviraptor*** may have eaten eggs, or cracked open shellfish with its powerful beak.

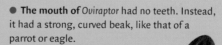

★ **STAR FACT** ★
*Oviraptor* had two bony spikes inside its mouth that it may have used to crack eggs when it closed its jaws.

◀ *Oviraptor's unusual features included its parrot-like beak.*

# Pack-hunters

● **Dinosaurs were reptiles,** but no reptiles today hunt in packs in which members cooperate with each other.

● **Certain types of crocodiles and alligators** come together to feed where prey is abundant, but they do not coordinate their attacks.

● **Fossil evidence** suggests that several kinds of meat-eating dinosaurs hunted in groups or packs.

● **Sometimes** the fossils of several individuals of the same type of dinosaur have been found in one place, suggesting the dinosaurs were pack animals.

● **The fossil bones** of some plant-eating dinosaurs have been found with many tooth marks on them, apparently made by different-sized predators, which may have hunted in packs.

● *Tyrannosaurus* may have been a pack-hunter.

● **In southwest Montana, USA,** the remains of three or four *Deinonychus* were found near the fossils of a much larger plant-eater named *Tenontosaurus*.

● **One** *Deinonychus* probably would not have attacked a full-grown *Tenontosaurus*, but a group of three or four might have.

> ★ STAR FACT ★
> Some meat-eaters may have had fairly large brains, enabling them to hunt as a group.

◀ *The raptors could probably hunt alone, but also bring down larger prey in packs, as hyaenas or lions do today.*

# Ceratopsians

● **Ceratopsians** were large plant-eaters that appeared less than 90 million years ago.

● **Most ceratopsian fossils** come from North America.

● **'Ceratopsian' means 'horn-face',** after the long horns on their snouts, eyebrows or foreheads.

● **Most ceratopsians** had a neck shield or frill that swept sideways and up from the back of the head to cover the upper neck and shoulders.

● **Well-known ceratopsians** included *Triceratops, Styracosaurus, Centrosaurus, Pentaceratops, Anchiceratops, Chasmosaurus* and *Torosaurus*.

● **The neck frills of some ceratopsians,** such as that of *Chasmosaurus*, had large gaps or 'windows' in the bone.

● **In life,** the windows in the neck frill of a ceratopsian were covered with thick, scaly skin.

● **Ceratopsians** had no teeth in the fronts of their hooked, beaklike mouths.

● **Using rows of powerful cheek teeth,** ceratopsians sheared their plant food.

▶ *Centrosaurus was a Late Cretaceous 'horn-face', about 6 m long.*

> ★ STAR FACT ★
> *Torosaurus* had the longest skull of any land animal ever, at about 2.5 m from the front of the snout to the rear of the neck frill.

# Babies

● **As far as we know**, female dinosaurs laid eggs, from which their babies hatched.

● **The time between** eggs being laid and babies hatching out is called the incubation period.

● **Incubation periods** for dinosaur eggs probably varied by weeks or months depending on the temperature, as in today's reptiles.

● **Many fossils** of adult Maiasaura (a duck-bill dinosaur, or hadrosaur) have been found, together with its nests, eggs and hatchlings (just-hatched babies).

● **Fossils of** Maiasaura come mainly from Montana, USA.

---

★ STAR FACT ★
Some preserved nests of *Maiasaura* babies contain traces of fossil buds and leaves – perhaps food brought to them by a parent?

---

● **The name** *Maiasaura* means 'good mother reptile'.

● **The teeth of** *Maiasaura* babies found in the nest are slightly worn, showing that they had eaten food.

● **The leg bones and joints** of the *Maiasaura* babies were not quite fully formed, showing that they were not yet able to move about to gather their own food.

● **Evidence** from *Maiasaura* and other nesting sites shows that dinosaurs may have been caring parents, protecting and feeding their young.

▶ *Various clues from fossil evidence show that the hadrosaur Maiasaura may have brought food back to its newly hatched young in the nest. Whether one parent or both did this is not known.*

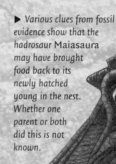

▲ Some fossil dinosaur eggs contain preserved embryos, still in the process of development. They use nutrients stored as egg yolk. Dinosaurs did not suckle their babies on milk, as mammals do.

Some eggs were still not hatched

Preserved eggshells showed signs of trampling by young in the nest

# Dinosaur eyes

● **No fossils have been found of dinosaur eyes**, because eyes are soft and squishy, and soon rot away after death, or are eaten by scavengers.

● **The main clues** to dinosaur eyes come from the hollows, or orbits, in the skull where the eyes were located.

● **The orbits** in fossil dinosaur skulls show that dinosaur eyes were similar to those of reptiles today.

● **The 6-m long sauropod** *Vulcanodon* had tiny eyes relative to the size of its head.

● **Small-eyed dinosaurs** probably only had good vision in the daytime.

● **The eyes** of many plant-eating dinosaurs, such as *Vulcanodon*, were on the sides of their heads, giving them all-round vision.

● **The small meat-eater** *Troodon* had relatively large eyes, and it could probably see well even in dim light.

● ***Troodon's*** eyes were on the front of its face and pointed forwards, allowing it to see detail and judge distance.

● **Dinosaurs that had large bulges**, called optic lobes, in their brains – detectable by the shapes of their skulls – could probably see very well, perhaps even at night.

> ★ **STAR FACT** ★
> The plant-eater *Leaellynasaura* had large optic lobes, and probably had good eyesight.

◀ *Leaellynasaura had very large eyes for the size of its skull, suggesting it was active at dusk or at night.*

# Coprolites: Dino-dung

● **Coprolites** are the fossilized droppings, or dung, of animals from long ago, such as dinosaurs.

● **Dinosaur coprolites** are not soft and smelly – like other fossils, they have become solid rock.

● **Many thousands** of dinosaur coprolites have been found at fossil sites all over the world.

● **Cracking or cutting open** coprolites sometimes reveals what the dinosaur had recently eaten.

● **Coprolites** produced by large meat-eaters such as *Tyrannosaurus* contain bone from their prey.

◀ *Fossilized droppings are no longer squishy or smelly.*

> ★ **STAR FACT** ★
> One of the largest dinosaur coprolites found measures 44 cm long and was probably produced by *Tyrannosaurus*.

● **The microscopic structure** of the bones found in coprolites shows the age of the prey when it was eaten. Most victims were very young or old, as these were the easiest creatures for a predator to kill.

● **Coprolites produced by small meat-eaters** such as *Compsognathus* may contain the hard bits of insects, such as the legs and wing-cases of beetles.

● **Huge piles of coprolites** found in Montana, USA, were probably produced by the large plant-eater *Maiasaura*.

● ***Maiasaura*** coprolites contain the remains of cones, buds and the needlelike leaves of conifer trees, showing that these dinosaurs had a tough diet.

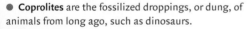

# Scelidosaurus

- **Scelidosaurus** was a medium-sized armoured dinosaur, perhaps an early member of the group called the ankylosaurs.

- **Fossils of** *Scelidosaurus* have been found in North America, Europe and possibly Asia.

- **Scelidosaurus** lived during the Early Jurassic Period, about 200 million years ago.

- **From nose to tail**, *Scelidosaurus* was about 4 m long.

- **Scelidosaurus** probably moved about on four legs, although it could perhaps rear up to gather food.

- **A plant-eater**, *Scelidosaurus* snipped off its food with the beaklike front of its mouth, and chewed it with its simple, leaf-shaped teeth.

- **Scelidosaurus** is one of the earliest dinosaurs known to have had a set of protective, bony armour plates.

- **A row of about 50 bony plates**, or scutes, stuck up from *Scelidosaurus*'s neck, back and tail.

- **Scelidosaurus** had rows of conical bony plates along its flanks, resembling limpets on a rock.

- **Scelidosaurus** was described in 1859, and named in 1863, by Richard Owen, who also invented the name 'dinosaur'.

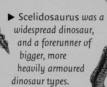

▶ Scelidosaurus *was a widespread dinosaur, and a forerunner of bigger, more heavily armoured dinosaur types.*

# Australia

- **In the past 40 years**, some of the most exciting discoveries of dinosaur fossils have come from Australia.

- **Remains of the large plant-eater** *Muttaburrasaurus* were found near Muttaburra, Queensland.

- **Muttaburrasaurus** was about 7 m long and similar in some ways to the well-known plant-eater *Iguanodon*.

- **Fossils of** *Rhoetosaurus*, a giant plant-eater, were found in 1924 in southern Queensland.

- **The sauropod** *Rhoetosaurus* was about 17 m long and lived 170 million years ago.

- **Near Winton, Queensland**, more than 3300 footprints show where about 130 dinosaurs once passed by.

- **One of the major new fossil sites** in Australia is 'Dinosaur Cove', on the coast near Melbourne, Victoria.

★ **STAR FACT** ★
Dinosaur Cove is difficult to reach, and many of the fossils are in hard rocks in the middle of sheer cliffs with pounding waves far beneath.

- **Fossil-rich rocks** at 'Dinosaur Cove' are part of the Otway-Strzelecki mountain ranges, and are 120–100 million years old.

- **Remains** found at 'Dinosaur Cove' include *Leaellynasaura* and a smaller version of the huge meat-eater *Allosaurus*.

Muttaburra
Winton
Roma
Inverloch　Dinosaur Cove

◀ *Many exciting fossils have been found in Australia over the past 40 years – many found nowhere else.*

# Sauropods

- **The sauropods** were the biggest of all the dinosaurs.

- **The huge plant-eating sauropods** lived mainly during the Jurassic Period, 208–144 million years ago.

- **A typical sauropod** had a tiny head, a very long neck and tail, a huge, bulging body and four massive legs, similar to those of an elephant, but much bigger.

- **Sauropods** included the well-known *Mamenchisaurus*, *Cetiosaurus*, *Diplodocus*, *Brachiosaurus* and *Apatosaurus*.

- **Rebbachisaurus** fossils were found in Morocco, Tunisia and Algeria.

- **Rebbachisaurus** lived 120 million years ago.

- **Cetiosaurus** was about 18 m long and weighed 30 tonnes.

- **Cetiosaurus**, or 'whale reptile', was so-named because French fossil expert Georges Cuvier thought that its giant backbones came from a prehistoric whale.

- **Cetiosaurus** was the first sauropod to be given an official name, in 1841 – the year before the term 'dinosaur' was invented.

- **The first fossils** of *Cetiosaurus* were found in Oxfordshire, England, in the 1830s.

◀ Sauropods could browse in tree-tops.

# Dinosaur feet

- **Dinosaur feet differed**, depending on the animal's body design, weight and lifestyle.

- **A typical dinosaur's front feet** had metacarpal bones in the lower wrist or upper hand, and two or three phalanges bones in each digit (finger or toe), tipped by claws.

- **The rear feet** of a typical dinosaur had metatarsal (instead of metacarpal) bones in the lower ankle.

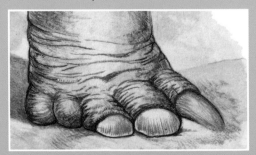

▲ Each foot of Apatosaurus supported more than 5 tonnes.

★ STAR FACT ★
The dinosaur group that includes all the meat-eaters, both large and small, is named the theropods, or 'beast feet'.

- **Some dinosaurs had five toes** per foot, like most other reptiles (and most birds and mammals).

- **Sauropods** probably had feet with rounded bases supported by a wedge of fibrous, cushion-like tissue.

- **Most sauropods** had claws on their first three toes, and smaller, blunter 'hooves' on the other two toes.

- **Ostrich-dinosaurs** such as *Gallimimus* had very long feet and long, slim toes for fast running.

- **Many fast-running dinosaurs** had fewer toes, to reduce weight – *Gallimimus* had three toes per back foot.

- **The dinosaur group** that includes *Iguanodon*, duck-billed dinosaurs, *Heterodontosaurus* and many other plant-eaters is named the ornithopods, or 'bird feet'.

# Extinction

- **All dinosaurs on Earth** had died out, or become extinct, by 65 million years ago.

- **Many other reptiles**, such as pterosaurs and plesiosaurs, and many other animals and plants disappeared with the dinosaurs, in a 'mass extinction'.

- **A possible cause** of the mass extinction was a new kind of disease that swept across the land and seas.

- **The mass extinction** of the dinosaurs and other animals may have been due to a series of huge volcanic eruptions that filled the air with poisonous fumes.

- **Climate change** is another possible cause of the mass extinction – perhaps a period of global warming that lasted for a few hundred years, or even longer.

▼ *We can only guess at the havoc caused when a massive meteorite hit Earth 65 million years ago. Whether this was the main cause of the mass extinction, or the 'last straw' following other problems, is not clear from evidence found so far.*

> ★ STAR FACT ★
> Scientists found a huge crater – the Chixulub Crater – under sea-bed mud off the coast of Yucatan, Mexico. This could be where a giant meteorite hit Earth 65 million years ago.

- **One theory** for the mass extinction is that a giant lump of rock from space – a meteorite – hit Earth.

- **A giant meteorite** 10 km across smashing into Earth would have set off earthquakes and volcanoes, and thrown up vast amounts of dust to darken the skies.

- **Skies darkened by dust for one year or more** would mean the death of many plants, and so the death of plant-eating animals, and consequently the meat-eaters.

- **One great puzzle** about the disappearance of the dinosaurs is why similar reptiles, such as crocodiles, lizards and turtles, survived.

# Dilophosaurus

- **Dilophosaurus** was a large meat-eating dinosaur in the group known as the ceratosaurs.

- **About 200 million years ago**, *Dilophosaurus* roamed the Earth in search of prey.

- **Fossils** of *Dilophosaurus* were found in Arizona, USA, and possibly Yunnan, China.

- **The remains** of *Dilophosaurus* in Arizona, USA, were discovered by Jesse Williams, a Navajo Native American, in 1942.

- **Studying the fossils** of *Dilophosaurus* proved very difficult, and the dinosaur was not given its official name until 1970.

- **Dilophosaurus** measured about 6 m from its nose to the end of its very long tail.

- **The name** *Dilophosaurus* means 'two ridged reptile', from the two thin, rounded, bony crests on its head, each shaped like half a dinner plate.

- **The crests** of *Dilophosaurus* were too thin and fragile to be used as weapons for head-butting.

- **Brightly coloured skin** may have covered *Dilophosaurus's* head crests, as a visual display to rivals or enemies.

◄ *The fearsome Dilophosaurus was one of the first large meat-eating dinosaurs. It gained the nickname 'terror of the Early Jurassic'.*

> ★ STAR FACT ★
>
> *Dilophosaurus* probably weighed about 500 kg – as much as the biggest polar bears today.

# Mysteries

- **Some dinosaurs have been named** on very scant evidence, such as a single bit of fossil bone, or just one tooth or claw.

- **The small meat-eater** *Troodon* was named in 1856 on the evidence of a single tooth.

- **The first tooth** of *Troodon* was found in the Judith River region of Montana, USA.

- **At first**, the tooth of *Troodon* was thought to have come from a lizard such as a monitor lizard.

▶ *Deinocheirus, known only from a few fossil pieces of arm and hand, may have been an ostrich-dinosaur like this – but as tall as a giraffe.*

- **In the early 1900s**, more *Troodon*-like teeth were found in Alberta and Wyoming, and were believed to have come from a pachycephalosaur or 'bone-head' dinosaur.

- **In the 1980s**, a fuller picture of *Troodon* was built up by putting its teeth together with other fossils, including bones.

- **Only parts of the hands and arms** of *Deinocheirus* have been found. They were discovered in Mongolia, Central Asia, in the 1970s.

- **It is possible** that *Deinocheirus* was a gigantic ostrich-dinosaur, perhaps as tall as a giraffe, at 5–6 m.

- **Therizinosaurus**, or 'scythe reptile', was a huge dinosaur known only from a few parts of its limbs. It lived in the Late Cretaceous Period in Mongolia, Central Asia.

- **A mysterious fossil claw** was found, thought possibly to belong to *Therizinosaurus*, and measuring about 90 cm around its outer curve.

# Psittacosaurus

- **Psittacosaurus** was a plant-eater in the group known as the ceratopsians, or horn-faced dinosaurs.

- **Living in the Middle Cretaceous Period,** *Psittacosaurus* walked the Earth about 115–110 million years ago.

- **Psittacosaurus** was named in 1923 from fossils found in Mongolia, Central Asia.

- **Fossils** of *Psittacosaurus* have been found at various sites across Asia, including ones in Russia, China and Thailand.

- **The rear legs** of *Psittacosaurus* were longer and stronger than its front legs, suggesting that this dinosaur may have

reared up to run fast on its rear legs, rather than running on all four legs.

- **Psittacosaurus** measured about 2 m long.

- **On each foot** *Psittacosaurus* had four toes.

- **The name** *Psittacosaurus* means 'parrot reptile', after the dinosaur's beak-shaped mouth, like that of a parrot.

- **Inside its cheeks**, *Psittacosaurus* had many sharp teeth capable of cutting and slicing through tough plant material.

◀ *Psittacosaurus had two small ridges or horns, one on each cheek.*

> ★ **STAR FACT** ★
> Fossil evidence shows that when newly hatched from their eggs, baby *Psittacosaurus* were hardly longer than a human hand.

# Beaks

- **Several kinds of dinosaurs** had a toothless, beak-shaped front to their mouths.

- **Beaked dinosaurs** included ceratopsians (horn-faces) such as *Triceratops*, ornithopods such as *Iguanodon* and the hadrosaurs (duck-bills), stegosaurs, segnosaurs, ankylosaurs (armoured dinosaurs) and fast-running ostrich-dinosaurs.

- **Most beaked dinosaurs** had chopping or chewing teeth near the backs of their mouths, in their cheeks, but ostrich-dinosaurs had no teeth.

- **A dinosaur's beak** was made up of the upper (maxilla) and the lower (mandible) jaw bones.

- **Ornithischian (bird-hipped) dinosaurs** had what is called a 'predentary' bone at the front tip of the lower jaw.

> ★ **STAR FACT** ★
> Some of the largest beaks in relation to body size belonged to *Oviraptor* and *Psittacosaurus*.

- **Ceratopsian (horn-faced) dinosaurs** had a 'rostral' bone at the front tip of the upper jaw.

- **In life**, the bones at the front of a dinosaur's jaw would have been covered with horn, which formed the outer shape of the beak.

- **Dinosaurs almost certainly** used their beaks for pecking, snipping, tearing and slicing their food.

- **Dinosaurs may have** used their beaks to peck fiercely at any attackers.

◀ *Ornithomimus's long, toothless jaws would have been covered by horny beak.*

# Massospondylus

- **Massospondylus** was a medium-sized plant-eater belonging to the group known as the prosauropods.

- **Africa and perhaps North America** were home to *Massospondylus*, about 200 million years ago.

- **In total**, *Massospondylus* was about 5 m long, with almost half of this length being its tail.

- **The rear legs** of *Massospondylus* were bigger and stronger than its front legs, so it may have reared up to reach high-up food.

▶ All day, *Massospondylus* would have been kept busy eating to fuel its bulky body.

- **The name** *Massospondylus* means 'huge backbone'.

- **Fossils of more than 80** *Massospondylus* have been found, making it one of the best-studied dinosaurs.

- **Massospondylus** had a tiny head compared to its large body, and it must have spent many hours each day gathering enough food to survive.

- **The front teeth** of *Massospondylus* were surprisingly large and strong for a plant-eater, with ridged edges more like meat-eating teeth.

- **The cheek teeth** of *Massospondylus* were too small and weak for chewing large amounts of plant food, so perhaps the dinosaur's food was mashed mainly in its stomach.

- **In the 1980s**, some scientists suggested that *Massospondylus* may have been a meat-eater, partly because of the ridged edges on its front teeth.

# Stomach stones

- **Some dinosaur fossils** are found with unusually smooth, rounded stones, like seashore pebbles, jumbled up among or near them.

- **Smoothed pebbles** occur with dinosaur fossils far more than would be expected by chance alone.

- **Smooth stones** are mainly found with or near the remains of large plant-eating dinosaurs, especially those of prosauropods such as *Massospondylus*, *Plateosaurus* and *Riojasaurus*, sauropods such as *Brachiosaurus* and *Diplodocus*, the parrot-beaked *Psittacosaurus* and the stegosaurs.

- **Some plant-eating dinosaurs** may have used smooth stones to help process their food.

▶ Gastroliths range from pea- to football-sized.

- **The smoothed pebbles** associated with dinosaur remains are known as gastroliths, gastric millstones or gizzard stones.

- **Gastroliths** were stones that a dinosaur found on the ground and deliberately swallowed into its stomach.

- **In the dinosaur's stomach**, gastroliths acted as 'millstones', crushing and churning plant food, and breaking it down into a soft pulp for better digestion.

- **As gastroliths churned and rubbed** inside a dinosaur's guts, they became very rounded, smoothed and polished.

- **Gastroliths as small as a pea** and as large as a football have been found.

- **Gastroliths may be the reason why** many big plant-eaters, especially sauropods, had no chewing teeth – the mashing was done inside the guts.

# Migration

- **Almost no land reptiles today** go on regular, long-distance journeys, called migrations.

- **Over the past 30 years**, scientists have acquired evidence that some dinosaurs regularly migrated.

- **Evidence for migrating dinosaurs** comes from the positions of the continents at the time. In certain regions, cool winters would have prevented the growth of enough plants for dinosaurs to eat.

- **Fossil evidence suggests** that some plants stopped growing during very hot or dry times, so some dinosaurs would have had to migrate to find food.

- **The footprints or tracks** of many dinosaurs travelling in herds is possible evidence that some dinosaurs migrated.

- **Dinosaurs that may have migrated** include *Centrosaurus* and *Pachyrhinosaurus*, sauropods such as *Diplodocus*, and ornithopods such as *Iguanodon* and *Muttaburrasaurus*.

- **One huge fossil site** in Alberta, Canada, contains the fossils of about 1000 *Pachyrhinosaurus* – perhaps a migrating herd that got caught in a flood.

- **In North America**, huge herds of *Centrosaurus* migrated north for the brief sub-Arctic summer, when plants were abundant, providing plentiful food.

- **In autumn**, *Centrosaurus* herds travelled south again to overwinter in the forests.

> ★ STAR FACT ★
> Migrating *Centrosaurus* may have walked 100 km a day.

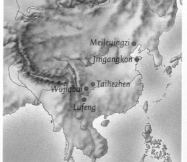
◄ *Pachyrhinosaurus may have migrated.*

# China

- **For centuries**, dinosaur fossils in China were identified as belonging to folklore creatures such as dragons.

- **The first dinosaur fossils** studied scientifically in China were uncovered in the 1930s.

- **Because of China's political isolation in the past**, many dinosaur fossils found there remained unknown to scientists in other countries.

- **From the 1980s**, dinosaur discoveries in almost every province of China have amazed scientists around the globe.

- **A few exciting dinosaur finds** in China have been fakes, such as part of a bird skeleton that was joined to the part-skeleton of a dinosaur along a natural-looking crack in the rock.

- **Some better-known Chinese finds** of dinosaurs include *Mamenchisaurus*, *Psittacosaurus*, *Tuojiangosaurus* and *Avimimus*.

> ★ STAR FACT ★
> Of all the world's countries, probably only the USA has more fossil dinosaurs than China.

- **Remains** of the prosauropod *Lufengosaurus* were uncovered in China's southern province of Yunnan, in 1941.

- **China's** *Lufengosaurus* lived during the Early Jurassic Period, and measured about 6–7 m long.

- **Many recently found fossils** in China are of feathered dinosaurs.

Meileyingzi
Jingangkou
Wujiabai
Taihezhen
Lufeng

◄ *Recent fossil finds in China are causing scientists to change many long-held ideas.*

# South America

● **Many of the most important discoveries** of dinosaur fossils in the last 30 years were made in South America.

● **Dinosaur fossils have been found** from the north to the south of the continent, in the countries of Colombia, Peru, Chile, Brazil, Uruguay and Argentina.

● **Most dinosaur fossils in South America** have been found on the high grassland, scrub and semi-desert of southern Brazil and Argentina.

★ **STAR FACT** ★
Some of the biggest of all dinosaurs, including the largest meat-eater *Giganotosaurus* and the vast sauropod *Argentinosaurus* come from Argentina.

● **Some of the earliest known dinosaurs,** such as *Herrerasaurus* and *Eoraptor,* lived more than 225 million years ago in Argentina.

● **Some of the last dinosaurs,** such as the sauropods *Saltasaurus* and *Titanosaurus,* lived in Argentina.

● **Fossils of the meat-eating predator** *Piatnitzkyosaurus* come from Cerro Condo in southern Argentina.

● **Piatnitzkyosaurus** was similar to the great predator *Allosaurus* of North America, but at 4–5 m long was less than half its size.

● **Like many dinosaurs in Argentina,** *Piatnitzkyosaurus* lived during the Middle Jurassic Period.

● **Remains of about 10 huge** *Patagosaurus* sauropods were found in the fossil-rich region of Chubut, Argentina, from 1977.

▼ *The high, windswept, stony, grassy plains of southern Argentina are especially rich in Jurassic and Cretaceous fossils, including those of the vast plant-eating sauropods Argentinosaurus. The plains slope upwards to the west, finally reaching the foothills of the Andes, where sun, wind and rain constantly erode the rocks and reveal new remains.*

Cerro Rajada
El Breté
Santa Maria
Ischigualasto
Neuquen
Cerro Condor
Santa Cruz

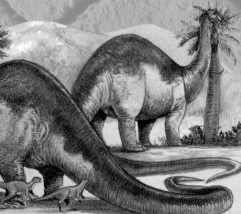

▲ Dinosaur fossils found in South America since the 1970s reveal unique kinds of meat-eaters, the biggest predatory dinosaurs, some of the earliest members of the dinosaur group, and possibly the largest of all dinosaurs.

# Tuojiangosaurus

- **Tuojiangosaurus** was a member of the group called plated dinosaurs, or stegosaurs.

- **The first nearly complete dinosaur skeleton** to be found in China was of a *Tuojiangosaurus*, and excellent fossil skeletons are on display in several Chinese museums.

- **The name** *Tuojiangosaurus* means 'Tuo River reptile'.

- **Tuojiangosaurus** lived during the Late Jurassic Period, about 155 million years ago.

- **Tuojiangosaurus** was 7 m long from nose to tail-tip.

- **The weight of** *Tuojiangosaurus* was probably about 1 tonne.

- **Like other stegosaurs**, *Tuojiangosaurus* had tall slabs or plates of bone on its back.

- **The back plates of** *Tuojiangosaurus* were roughly triangular and probably stood upright in two rows that ran from the neck to the middle of the tail.

- **Tuojiangosaurus** plucked low-growing plant food with the beak-shaped front of its mouth, and partly chewed the plant material with its leaf-shaped, ridge-edged cheek teeth.

- **On its tail**, *Tuojiangosaurus* had four long spikes arranged in two Vs, which it could swing at enemies to keep them at a distance or inflict wounds.

◄ Tuojiangosaurus had about 15 pairs of tall plates along its neck, back and tail.

# Head crests

- **Many dinosaurs** had lumps, bumps, plates, bulges, ridges or other shapes of bone on their heads, called head crests.

- **Head crests** may have been covered with brightly coloured skin in life, for visual display.

- **Meat-eaters with head crests** included *Carnotaurus* and *Dilophosaurus*.

- **The dinosaurs with the largest** and most complicated head crests were the hadrosaurs.

- **The largest dinosaur head crest** was probably a long, hollow, tubular shape of bone belonging to the hadrosaur *Parasaurolophus*.

- **The head crests of hadrosaurs** may have been involved in making sounds.

- **Some years ago** the hadrosaur *Tsintaosaurus* was thought to have a very unusual head crest – a hollow tube sticking straight up between the eyes, like a unicorn's horn.

- **The so-called head crest of** *Tsintaosaurus* is now thought to be the fossil part of another animal, and not part of *Tsintaosaurus* at all.

- **Tsintaosaurus** is now usually known as *Tanius*, a hadrosaur with a small crest or no crest at all!

▲ Dilophosaurus was one of the few meat-eaters with a large head crest.

★ STAR FACT ★
The head crests of some large *Parasaurolophus*, perhaps full-grown males, reached an incredible 1.8 m in length.

# Sails

● **Long, bony extensions**, like rods or spines, stuck up from the backs of some dinosaurs.

● **In life**, a dinosaur's bony extensions may have held up a large area of skin, commonly called a back sail.

● **Dinosaurs with back sails** included the huge meat-eater *Spinosaurus* and the large plant-eater *Ouranosaurus*.

● *Spinosaurus* and *Ouranosaurus* both lived over 100 million years ago.

● **Fossils of** *Spinosaurus* and *Ouranosaurus* were found in North Africa.

▶ *Apart from its sail, Ouranosaurus was similar to its close cousin, the plant-eater Iguanodon.*

▲ *Spinosaurus was almost as large as Tyrannosaurus.*

● **The skin** on a dinosaur's back sail may have been brightly coloured, or may even have changed colour, like the skin of a chameleon lizard today.

● **A dinosaur's back sail** may have helped to control its body temperature.

● **Standing sideways** to the sun, a back sail would absorb the sun's heat and allow the dinosaur to warm up quickly, ready for action.

● **Standing in the shade**, a back sail would lose warmth and help the dinosaur to avoid overheating.

● **The bony back rods** of *Spinosaurus* were up to 1.6 m tall.

# North America

● **North America** is the continent where most dinosaur fossils have been found.

● **Most dinosaur fossils** in North America come from the dry, rocky 'badlands' of the

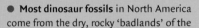
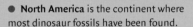

▲ *Coelophysis was discovered in New Mexico, USA, in about 1881. In the late 1940s, another expedition found dozens of skeletons in a mass dinosaur grave.*

Midwest region, which includes Alberta in Canada, and the US states of Montana, Wyoming, Utah, Colorado and Arizona.

● **Fossils of the most famous dinosaurs** come from North America, including *Allosaurus*, *Tyrannosaurus*, *Diplodocus*, *Triceratops* and *Stegosaurus*.

● **Several fossil-rich sites** in North America are now national parks.

● **The US Dinosaur National Monument**, on the border of Utah and Colorado, was established in 1915.

● **The Cleveland-Lloyd Dinosaur Quarry** in Utah contains fossils of stegosaurs, ankylosaurs, sauropods and meat-eaters such as *Allosaurus*.

● **Along the Red Deer River** in Alberta, a large area with thousands of dinosaur fossils has been designated the Dinosaur Provincial Park.

● **Fossils found in Alberta** include those of the meat-eater *Albertosaurus*, armoured *Euoplocephalus* and the duck-bill *Lambeosaurus*.

● **The Dinosaur Provincial Park** in Alberta is a United Nations World Heritage Site – the same status as the pyramids of ancient Egypt.

● **A huge, 20-m long plant-eater** was named *Alamosaurus* after the famous Battle of the Alamo in Texas in 1836.

# Iguanodon

- **Iguanodon** was a large plant-eater in the dinosaur group known as ornithopods.

- **Numerous fossils** of *Iguanodon* have been found in several countries in Europe, including England, Belgium, Germany and Spain.

- **Iguanodon** measured about 9 m from nose to tail.

- **It is estimated** that an *Iguanodon* weighed about the same as a large elephant – 4–5 tonnes.

- **Iguanodon** lived during the Early to Middle Cretaceous Period, 140–110 million years ago.

- **Iguanodon** probably walked and ran on its large, powerful back legs for much of the time, with its body held horizontal.

- **A cone-shaped spike** on *Iguanodon*'s thumb may have been a weapon for jabbing at rivals or enemies.

> ★ STAR FACT ★
> *Iguanodon* was one of the very first dinosaurs to be given an official scientific name, in 1825.

- **The three central fingers** on *Iguanodon*'s hands had hooflike claws for occasional four-legged walking.

- **The fifth or little finger** of *Iguanodon* was able to bend across the hand for grasping objects, and was perhaps used to pull plants towards the mouth.

▲ Iguanodon is *very well known from many fossils.*

# Hibernation

- **Dinosaurs may have gone into an inactive state** called hibernation during long periods of cold conditions, as many reptiles do today.

- **Dinosaurs** such as the small plant-eater *Leaellynasaura*, found at 'Dinosaur Cove', Australia, may have had to hibernate due to the yearly cycle of seasons there.

- **Dinosaur Cove, Australia**, was nearer the South Pole when dinosaurs lived there, 120–100 million years ago.

▶ Leaellynasaura *may have slept through the cold season, perhaps protected in a cave or burrow.*

- **The climate** was relatively warm 120–100 million years ago, with no ice at the North or South Poles.

- **Dinosaurs at Dinosaur Cove, Australia**, would have had to cope with long hours of darkness during winter, when few plants grew.

- **Australia's Dinosaur Cove dinosaurs** may have hibernated for a few months each year to survive the cool, dark conditions.

- **The eyes and brain shape** of *Leaellynasaura* from Dinosaur Cove, Australia, suggest that this dinosaur had good eyesight.

- **Leaellynasaura** may have needed good eyesight to see in the winter darkness, or in the dim forests.

- **Dinosaur fossils** have been found in the Arctic region near the North Pole.

- **Arctic dinosaurs** either hibernated during winter, or migrated south to warmer regions.

# Sounds

- **Few reptiles today make sounds**, except for simple hisses, grunts and coughs.

- **Fossils suggest that dinosaurs** made a variety of sounds in several different ways.

- **The bony, hollow head crests** of duck-bills (hadrosaurs) may have been used for making sounds.

- **The head crests of some hadrosaurs** contained tubes called respiratory airways, used for breathing.

- **Air** blown forcefully through a hadrosaur's head crest passages could have made the whole crest vibrate.

- **A hadrosaur's vibrating head crest** may have made a loud sound like a honk, roar or bellow – similar to an elephant trumpeting with its trunk.

▼ Dinosaurs, such as this Cetiosaurus, may have made sounds to keep in touch with other members of their herd, to frighten away enemies, to intimidate rivals and to impress potential mates at breeding time.

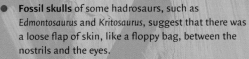

- **Fossil skulls** of some hadrosaurs, such as *Edmontosaurus* and *Kritosaurus*, suggest that there was a loose flap of skin, like a floppy bag, between the nostrils and the eyes.

- **Kritosaurus** may have inflated its loose nasal flap of skin like a balloon to make a honking or bellowing sound, as some seals do today.

◄ In a battle between predator and prey, Tyrannosaurus may have been startled or even warned off by the trumpeting of Parasaurolophus. The effect of the sudden noise on the predator may have given the plant-eating hadrosaur time to escape. Its noise may also have summoned members of its herd, for massed defence against the huge meat-eater.

Tyrannosaurus may have been startled by the noise of its prey

Long, hollow crest may have resonated to make a loud call

★ STAR FACT ★

By blowing through models of hadrosaur head crests, a wide range of sounds can be made – a bit like those of brass and wind instruments!

Powerful rear legs used for kicking in self defence

Tail used for lashing out

# Nodosaurs

- **Nodosaurs** were a subgroup of armoured dinosaurs, in the main ankylosaur group.

- **The nodosaur subgroup** included *Edmontonia*, *Sauropelta*, *Polacanthus* and *Nodosaurus*.

- **Nodosaurs were slow-moving**, heavy-bodied plant-eaters with thick, heavy nodules, lumps and plates of bone in their skin for protection.

- **Most nodosaurs lived** during the Late Jurassic and the Cretaceous Periods, 150–65 million years ago.

- ***Edmontonia*** lived in North America during the Late Cretaceous Period, 75–70 million years ago.

- ***Edmontonia*** was about 7 m long, but its bony armour made it very heavy for its size, at 4–5 tonnes.

★ STAR FACT ★
Like many nodosaurs, *Edmontonia* and *Polacanthus* probably had long, fierce spikes on their shoulders, used to 'spear' enemies.

- **Along its neck, back and tail** *Edmontonia* had rows of flat and spiky plates.

- **The nodosaur** *Polacanthus* was about 4 m long and lived 120–110 million years ago.

- **Fossils** of *Polacanthus* come from the Isle of Wight, southern England, and perhaps from North America, in South Dakota, USA.

◀ *Edmontonia, one of the last dinosaurs, was covered in many sharp lumps of bone that gave it some protection from its enemies.*

# Inventing the 'dinosaur'

- **When fossils of dinosaurs were first studied** by scientists in the 1820s, they were thought to be from huge lizards, rhinoceroses or even whales.

- **The first dinosaur** to be given an official name was *Megalosaurus*, by English clergyman William Buckland in 1824.

- **Fossils of dinosaurs** were found and studied in 1822 by Gideon Mantell, a country doctor in Sussex, southern England.

- **In 1825**, Englishman Gideon Mantell named his creature *Iguanodon*, because its fossil teeth were very similar in shape to, but larger than, the teeth of the iguana lizard.

- **In the late 1830s**, British scientist Richard Owen realized that some fossils did not belong to lizards, but to an as yet unnamed group of reptiles.

- **In 1841–42**, Richard Owen invented a new name for the group of giant prehistoric reptiles – Dinosauria.

- **The name 'dinosaur'** means 'terrible reptile'.

- **Life-sized models** of several dinosaurs were made by sculptor Waterhouse Hawkins in 1852–54.

- **Hawkins' models** were displayed in the gardens of the Crystal Palace Exhibition in London, and caused a public sensation – the first wave of 'Dino-mania'.

- **The three main dinosaurs** of the Dinosauria in the 1840s were *Iguanodon*, the big meat-eater *Megalosaurus* and the nodosaur *Hyaelosaurus*.

◀ *Megalosaurus was the first dinosaur to be given an official scientific name, even though the term 'dinosaur' had not yet been invented.*

# Brains

- **There is a broad link** between the size of an animal's brain compared to the size of its body, and the level of intelligence it shows.

- **Some fossil dinosaur skulls** have preserved the hollow where the brain once was, revealing the approximate size and shape of the brain.

- **In some cases** a lump of rock formed inside a fossil skull, taking on the size and shape of the brain.

- **The tiny brain** of Stegosaurus weighed about 70–80 g, while the whole dinosaur weighed up to 2 tonnes.

- **The brain** of Stegosaurus was only 1/25,000th of the weight of its whole body (in a human it is 1/50th).

- **Brachiosaurus's** brain was perhaps only 1/100,000th of the weight of its whole body.

- **The brain of the small meat-eater** Troodon was about 1/100th the weight of its whole body.

▶ Troodon may have been fairly 'intelligent' for a dinosaur.

- **The brain-body size comparison** for most dinosaurs is much the same as the brain-body size for living reptiles.

- **Small and medium sized meat-eaters** such as Troodon may have been as 'intelligent' as parrots or rats.

- **It was once thought** that Stegosaurus had a 'second brain' in the base of its tail! Now this lump is thought to have been a nerve junction.

# Segnosaurs

- **Little is known** about the segnosaur group of dinosaurs – the subject of much disagreement among experts.

- **Segnosaurs** are named after almost the only known member of the group, Segnosaurus.

- **The name** Segnosaurus means 'slow reptile'.

- **Segnosaurus** lived during the Mid to Late Cretaceous Period, about 90 million years ago.

- **Fossils** of Segnosaurus were found mainly in the Gobi Desert

in Central Asia in the 1970s. The dinosaur was named in 1979 by Mongolian scientist Altangerel Perle.

- **Segnosaurus** had a narrow head and probably a toothless, beaklike front to its mouth.

- **Experts have variously described** Segnosaurus as a predatory meat-eater, a swimming or wading fish-eater, a rearing-up leaf-eater, or even an ant-eater.

- **Different experts have said** Segnosaurus was a theropod, a prosauropod and an ornithopod.

- **Some scientists have suggested** that Segnosaurus was a huge dinosaur-version of today's anteater that ripped open the nests of termites and ants with its powerful claws.

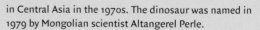

▶ Segnosaurus remains a mystery – even its diet is hotly debated by the experts.

> ★ STAR FACT ★
> Segnosaurus was a sizeable dinosaur, probably about 6 m long and standing 2 m tall.

# Dino-birds: 2

- **Fossils found during the last 20 years** show that some dinosaurs may have been covered with feathers or fur.

- **Sinosauropteryx** was a small, 1-m long meat-eater that lived 135 million years ago in China.

- **Fossils** of Sinosauropteryx show that parts of its body were covered not with the usual reptile scales, but with feathers.

- **The overall shape** of Sinosauropteryx shows that, despite being feathered, it could not fly.

- **The feathers** of Sinosauropteryx may have been for camouflage, for visual display, or to keep it warm – suggesting it was warm-blooded.

- **Avimimus** was a small, light dinosaur. Its fossils come from China and Mongolia, and date from 85–82 million years ago.

- **The 1.5-m long** Avimimus had a mouth shaped like a bird's beak for pecking at food.

- **The fossil arm bones** of Avimimus have small ridges of the same size and shape as the ridges on birds' wing bones, where feathers attach.

- **In modern science**, any animal with feathers is a bird, so some experts say that feathered dinosaurs were not actually dinosaurs or even reptiles, but birds.

- **Some experts say** that birds are not really a separate group of animals, but a subgroup of dinosaurs that lives on today, and they should be regarded as feathered dinosaurs.

▲ Avimimus may have evolved feathers for warmth or for camouflage.

# After dinosaurs

- **The Age of Dinosaurs** came to a fairly sudden end 65 million years ago. We know this from rocks and fossils, which changed dramatically at that time.

- **The Cretaceous Period** ended 65 million years ago.

- **There are no dinosaur fossils** since 65 million years ago.

- **Many animal groups**, including fish, crocodiles, turtles, lizards, birds and mammals, survived the extinction that took place 65 million years ago.

- **Birds and mammals** in particular underwent rapid changes after the dinosaurs disappeared.

- **Within 10 million years** of the dinosaurs' demise, bats, primates, armadillos, hoofed mammals and rodents such as rats had all appeared.

- **The land mammal** that came closest to rivalling the great size of the dinosaurs was Indricotherium, also known as Baluchitherium.

- **Indricotherium** was 8 m long, 5 m tall and weighed perhaps 25 tonnes.

- **Indricotherium** was less than half the size of the biggest dinosaurs.

▶ Indricotherium was three times bigger than elephants of today.

★ STAR FACT ★
Some people believe that dinosaurs may still be alive today, deep in tropical forests or in remote valleys – but no firm evidence exists.

# PREHISTORIC LIFE

# Prehistoric time

- **Time since Earth** formed is split into units called eras, which are in split into periods. Some periods split into epochs. These units relate to the formation of rock layers.

- **The Precambrian Era** ran from 4600–542 million years ago (mya). It saw the beginning of sea life. In the Cambrian Period (542–490 mya) vertebrates appeared.

- **In the Ordovician Period** (490–435 mya) plants spread to land. In the Silurian Period (435–410 mya) the first jawed fish appeared. Upright plants grew on land.

- **The Devonian Period** (410–355 mya) saw the arrival of bony fish. Trees and insects appeared on land.

- **The Carboniferous Period** (355–298 mya) was the time of great tropical forests and the first land vertebrates.

- **Reptiles ruled land** in the Permian Period (298–250 mya).

- **The Triassic Period** (250–208 mya) saw the rise of the dinosaurs and the first mammals. In the Jurassic Period (208–144 mya) reptiles ruled land, sea and sky.

- **In the Cretaceous Period** (144–65 mya) flowering plants appeared. The dinosaur died out.

- **The Tertiary Period** (65–1.6 mya) saw the rise of mammals. Temperatures cooled.

- **The Quaternary Period** (1.6 mya–present) has seen the most recent ice ages and the rise of humans.

▼ *Many animals and plants died out 65 mya, but other groups such as fish, insects, birds and mammals survived.*

# Earliest plants

- **The first living things** on Earth were single-celled bacteria and blue-green algae.

- **Blue-green algae** emerged around 3500 mya.

- **Although it is not a plant**, blue-green algae contains chlorophyll and was the first living thing to photosynthesize (make energy from sunlight).

- **Photosynthesis** also produces oxygen. Over millions of years, the blue-green algae produced enough oxygen to enable more complex life forms to develop.

- **True algae**, which are usually regarded as plants, developed around 1000 mya.

- **By about 550 mya**, multi-celled plants had begun to appear, including simple seaweeds.

◄ *Lichens such as these are made up of an alga and fungus. Early lichens – like modern-day ones – grew on rocks and, over time, eroded part of the rock and helped form soil.*

- **Algae and lichens** were the first plants to appear on land.

- **Bryophyte plants** (mosses and liverworts) emerged on land around 440 mya. Bryophytes are simple green seedless plants.

- **Bryophytes cannot grow high** above the ground because they do not have strengthened stems, unlike vascular plants, which emerged later.

★ STAR FACT ★
Liverworts grew on mats of blue-green algae, which trapped nitrogen from the air. They used this nitrogen to grow tissues.

# Vascular plants

- **Vascular plants** are more suited to living on drier land than mosses and liverworts.

- **They have branching stems** with tubelike walls that carry water and nutrients.

- **These stems and walls** also mean the plants can stand tall. Vascular plants have spores (reproductive cells, like seeds) – the taller the plant the more widely it can disperse its spores.

- **One of the first known** vascular plants was *Cooksonia*. It was about 5 cm tall, with a forked stem.

- **Scientists called palaeontologists** discovered fossil remains of Cooksonia in Wales. Palaeontologists study fossils of prehistoric plants and animals to see how they lived and evolved.

- **One site where lots** of vascular plant fossils have been found is Rhynie in Scotland.

- **The plants at Rhynie** would have grown on the edges of pools in the Early Devonian Period (about 400 mya).

- **One plant fossil found** at Rhynie is *Aglaophyton*, which stood around 45 cm high.

- **Aglaophyton** had roots and tissues that supported the stem. It also had water-carrying tubes and stomata (tiny openings) that allowed air and water to pass through.

- **Land plants** were essential in providing conditions for animals to make the transition from sea to land. They created soil, food and cover for shelter.

◀ *The Cooksonia plant had forked stems ending in spore-filled caps. The earliest examples of Cooksonia have been found in Ireland, dating to around 430 mya.*

# Ferns

- **Ferns are flowerless**, spore-producing plants, with roots, stems, and leaves called fronds.

- **They developed from** the earliest vascular plants, such as *Cooksonia*.

- **Ferns first appeared** in the Devonian Period (410–355 mya).

- *Cladoxylon* was an early, primitive fern. It had a main stem, forked branches and leaves, and fan-shaped structures that contained spores.

- **During the Carboniferous Period** (355–298 mya), ferns became some of the most abundant plants on Earth.

▼ *The underside of a fern frond (leaf), dotted with spore cases. Some types of ferns look exactly the same now as they did more than 200 mya.*

★ STAR FACT ★
Ferns remain successful plants today – there are over 12,000 living varieties.

- **Prehistoric ferns** would have looked similar to modern ones, but they could grow much larger. Large ferns are called tree-ferns.

- **Sometimes palaeontologists** find many fossilized fern spores in a single layer of rock. These 'fern spikes' show that there were a lot of ferns around at a particular time.

- **There is a major fern spike** from rock layers that are around 65 million years old, when many other plants had died out, along with dinosaurs and other animals. This fern spike shows that ferns were not affected by the extinctions.

- **Ferns are great survivors** – after volcanic eruptions, they are the first plants to grow again in a landscape.

# Clubmosses

● **Clubmosses are covered** with tiny spiral-patterned leaves. Near the top of the stem are club-shaped structures that produce spores.

● **Clubmosses started to grow** in the Devonian Period (410–355 mya).

● **Early clubmosses** included *Baragwanathia* and *Sawdonia*.

● **Another early clubmoss** was *Asteroxylon*. It had forked branches with tiny leaves called leaflets.

● **By the Late Devonian Period**, clubmosses evolved into bigger forms and produced the first tree-sized plants, such as *Lepidodendron*.

● *Lepidodendron* **trees** could grow more than 30 m high. The diameter of their trunks could be over 2 m.

● *Lepidodendron* **grew** all over the world in the Carboniferous Period (355–298 mya).

● **It produced large spores** inside cone-shaped containers.

● **Some clubmosses** survive to this day, including *Lycopodium*.

◀ Fossilized Lepidodendron bark shows that the trunks of these giant clubmosses were covered in diamond-shaped patterns. Lepidodendron leaves could be up to 1 m long, and its roots stretched out for up to 12 m.

# Gymnosperms

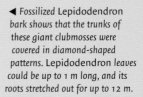

● **Gymnosperms** are plants that produce exposed seeds on the surface of structures such as cones. The word gymnosperm comes from two Greek words: *gymnos*, meaning 'naked', and *sperma*, meaning 'seed'.

● **They first appeared** about 370 mya. Like ferns, they probably developed from early plants such as *Cooksonia*.

● **Gymnosperms grew well** in the damp, tropical forests of the Carboniferous Period (355–298 mya).

● **Varieties of gymnosperm** include conifers, cycads and seed-ferns.

● **Cycads** are plants with feathery tops. They were more common in prehistoric times than today.

▶ These modern pine cones each surround many individual seeds. When the seeds are ripe, the cones open so that the seeds can fall out. Early gymnosperms had less sophisticated seed containers, which consisted of forked branches that loosely held the seeds in place.

● **One type of cycad** is the maidenhair tree, *Gingko biloba*. It still grows in towns and cities, but is now very rare in the wild.

● **One extinct gymnosperm** is *Glossopteris*, which some palaeontologists believe is the ancestor of later flowering plants.

● **Together with ferns and horsetails** (a type of herb), gymnosperms dominated landscapes during the Mesozoic Era (250–65 mya).

● **In the Jurassic Period** (208–144 mya), plant-eating dinosaurs ate their way through huge areas of coniferous forest.

● **In response,** conifers developed tough leaves, sharp needles and poisons.

# Angiosperms

- **Angiosperms** are flowering plants. They produce seeds within an ovary, which is contained within a flower. The word comes from the Greek terms *angeion*, meaning 'vessel', and *sperma*, meaning 'seed'.

- **Angiosperms** first appeared about 140 mya.

- **The earliest evidence** of flowering plants comes from the fossil remains of leaves and pollen grains.

- **Plant experts** used to think that magnolias were one of the first angiosperms, but now they think that an extinct plant called *Archaefructus* was older. It lived about 145 mya.

- **Fossil remains** of *Archaefructus* were discovered in northeast China in the mid to late 1990s.

▶ An Archaefructus plant, which some scientists think is the earliest-known example of an angiosperm. The Archaefructus fossil, which may be around 145 million years old, has a number of angiosperm features including enclosed seeds and flowers.

- **By 100 mya**, angiosperms had developed into dozens of families of flowering plants, most of which still survive.

- **By 60 mya**, angiosperms had taken over from gymnosperms as the dominant plants on Earth.

- **The start of the Tertiary Period** (65 mya) saw a rise in temperatures that produced the right conditions for tropical rainforests.

- **It was in the rainforests** that angiosperms evolved into many, many different types of plants.

- **Angiosperms** were so successful as they grew quickly, they had extensive roots to anchor them and take up water and nutrients, and they could grow in a wide range of environments .

# Forests

- **The Carboniferous Period** (355–298 mya) was the time of the greatest forests on Earth.

- **The damp climate** of this period suited forests, as did the huge number of swamps in which many trees grew.

- **Carboniferous forests** contained huge clubmosses, growing up to 50 m tall, as well as tree-ferns and primitive conifers, such as *Archaeopteris*.

- **The huge numbers of enormous trees** in this period produced the highest levels of oxygen there has ever been on Earth.

- **Dead forest trees** fell and formed mats of rotting wood, which over time turned into peat.

- **Layers of sandstone or other rock** formed over the peat. The pressure of these new layers eventually caused the peat to dry and harden into coal.

◀ Two plant-eating dinosaurs (Jobaria left, and Janenschia right) eating leaves in forests of the late Jurassic Period (159–144 mya). These forests had developed millions of years earlier, in the Carboniferous Period.

- **Coal deposits are** rich sources of fossilized animals.

- **In later periods**, following the Carboniferous Period, plant-eating dinosaurs ate huge areas of forest.

- **Forests were home** to many prehistoric animals, including the first mammals, such as *Megazostrodon* and *Morganucodon*, which hid from predators amongst the trees.

- **By the Tertiary Period** (65–1.6 mya), forests contained many more deciduous (leaf-shedding) trees, such as magnolias, than evergreens, such as conifers.

# Grasslands

▶ Etosha National Park, Namibia, South Africa. Grasses did not appear on Earth until around 50 mya. Their ability to withstand drought, fire and grazing are part of the reason why they spread so successfully across the world.

● **In the Oligocene Epoch** (37–24 mya), the Earth's climate became cooler, causing the ice cap covering Antarctica to increase in size.

● **As a result**, tropical rainforests began to decline and grasslands became increasingly common.

● **Grasslands** are called many things in different parts of the world: plains, savannahs, steppes, veldt and prairies.

● **The change from one ecosystem** to another, such as forest to grassland, is called succession. It is a continual process and in central Australia, for example, prehistoric grasslands have been succeeded by desert.

● **Grasses provided** an abundant source of food.

● **Grasses can be cropped** without destroying the plant itself, so they provide animals with a constant supply of food.

● **Grasses are tougher** than forest plants. This meant that plant eaters had to develop strong teeth and better digestive systems.

● **The open nature of grasslands** meant that mammals had to become faster runners, too – to chase after prey or to escape predators.

● **About 11,000 years ago** temperatures began to rise and many grasslands dried out. Lush, mixed grasses gave way to much coarser grasses and scrub – or to desert.

● **This change led** to the extinction of many prehistoric herbivores, such as camel and horse species.

# The first invertebrates

● **An invertebrate** is an animal that does not have a spinal column. Invertebrates were the first animals to live on Earth, in the seas.

● **The first animal-like** organisms that fed on other organisms or organic matter were single-celled and sometimes called protozoans.

● **Only prehistoric protozoans** with hard parts survive as fossils. The earliest fossils are around 700 million years old.

● **One of the earliest fossils** of a multi-celled animal is around 600 million years old. This is a creature called *Mawsonites*, which may have been a jellyfish or worm.

◀ *Charnia was a prehistoric animal that grew in feather-like colonies attached to the seabed, like living sea pens.*

● **Most of the earliest** invertebrate fossils are from extinct groups of animals.

● **Some of these animals** had segmented bodies that looked a bit like quilts.

● **One such invertebrate** is *Spriggina*, which is named after Reg Sprigg, a geologist. He discovered its fossilized remains near Ediacara in southern Australia in 1946.

● **Palaeontologists have unearthed** the fossils of many other jellyfish-like invertebrates from Ediacara.

● **Another famous invertebrate** discovery was made by Roger Mason, an English schoolboy, in 1957. This was the fossil of *Charnia*, an animal similar to a living sea pen.

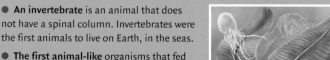

★ STAR FACT ★

*Spriggina* has a curved, shieldlike end to one part of its body. Some palaeontologists think this was its head, while others think it was an anchor that secured it to the sea bed.

# More early invertebrates

- **The early, quilted invertebrates** were extinct by the beginning of the Cambrian Period (542–490 mya).

- **Palaeontologists** regard their extinction as a loss that compares with the death of the dinosaurs at the end of the Cretaceous Period (around 65 mya).

- **Small, shelled invertebrates** emerged in the Early Cambrian Period.

- **These creatures included** the archaeocyathids, which had bodies that were like two cups, one inside the other.

- **Living animals** that most closely resemble archaeocyathids are sponges and corals.

- **Other small**, shelled invertebrates included animals such as *Tommotia* and *Latouchella*. They may have been early molluscs, the ancestors of snails and clams.

- **Tommotia and Latouchella** left behind fossils of their shells, which have strange-looking horns and tubes on the surface.

- **Other Early Cambrian invertebrates**, such as wormlike creatures, did not live in shells. Once predators began to appear, they would have made easy pickings.

- **Invertebrates therefore evolved** defences against hunters, such as a tough exoskeleton (outer skeleton).

- **Another defence was hiding**. Many invertebrates, from worms to arthropods, began to burrow into the sea floor.

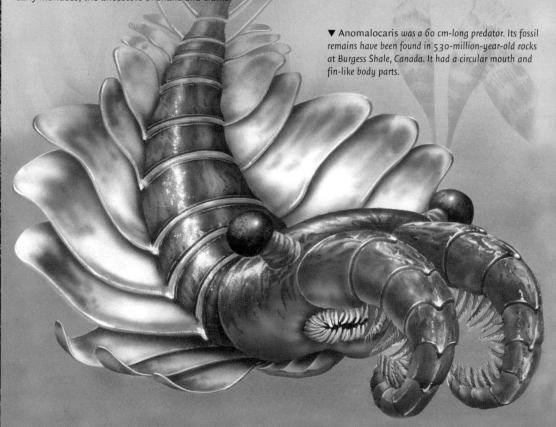

▼ Anomalocaris was a 60 cm-long predator. Its fossil remains have been found in 530-million-year-old rocks at Burgess Shale, Canada. It had a circular mouth and fin-like body parts.

# Molluscs and graptolites

- **Modern molluscs** include gastropods (slugs, snails and limpets), bivalves (clams, oysters, mussels and cockles) and cephalopods (octopuses, squids and cuttlefish).

- **Modern and prehistoric molluscs** represent one of the most diverse animal groups ever to have lived.

- **The first molluscs were tiny** – the size of a pinhead. They appeared in Cambrian Period, about 542 mya.

- **The first cephalopod molluscs** emerged towards the end of the Cambrian Period, around 490 mya.

- **One early cephalod** was *Plectronoceras*, which had a horn-shaped shell divided into different chambers.

- **Graptolites** had tentacles that they used to sieve food particles from water or the seabed.

- **Gastropod molluscs** (snails and slugs) were one of the first groups of animals to live on land.

- **Snails and slugs** are limited to where they can live on land as they require moist conditions.

▶ This snail is a mollusc. It has a muscular foot, a head with eyes and tentacles and a shell. Today there are more than 100,000 species of molluscs but many more times this number lived in the past. Their shells make good fossils, and some types evolved quickly, so their changing shapes are used as 'marker fossils' to date rocks.

- **Cephalopods** are the most highly developed of all molluscs. Squids and octopuses evolved big brains, good eyesight, tentacles and beaklike jaws.

- **Graptolites** are an extinct group of molluscs that lived in string-like communities, like lines. Graptolite means 'written stone' because the fossils of the lines of these creatures resemble scrawled handwriting.

# Ammonites

▶ A rock containing an ammonite fossil, displaying the shell's different chambers. The innermost chamber was the home of a newborn ammonite. As it grew, it built a bigger chamber and moved into it.

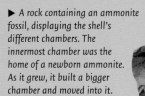

- **Ammonites** belong to the cephalopod group of molluscs.

- **They were once widespread** in the oceans, but, like the dinosaurs, died out at the end of the Cretaceous Period (about 65 mya).

- **The number of ammonite fossils** that have been found proves how plentiful these animals once were.

- **Ammonites were predators** and scavengers. They had good vision, long seizing tentacles and powerful mouths.

- **Their mouths consisted of** sharp beaks, poisonous glands and a tooth-covered tongue.

- **Ammonites had** multi-chambered shells that contained gas and worked like flotation tanks, keeping the creatures afloat.

- *Stephanoceras* was an ammonite with a spiral, disc-shaped shell, 20 cm across. It was very common in the seas of the Mesozoic Era (250–65 mya).

- **The closest living relative** of ammonites is the nautilus, a cephalopod that lives near the seabed.

- **People once thought** that ammonite fossils were the fossils of curled-up snakes.

- **Builders have traditionally set** ammonite fossils into the walls of buildings for decoration.

# Worms

- **Worms** are invertebrates that usually have long, soft, slender bodies.

- **They were among the earliest** multi-celled animals to live in the prehistoric seas.

- **The soft bodies of worms** means that they do not make good fossils.

- **Much of our knowledge** of prehistoric worms comes from trace fossils, which include tracks, tunnels and the impressions of their bodies in fine-grained rocks.

- **The tracks and trails** of early worms show that they were mobile creatures, which probably grazed the microbes that covered the sea floor.

- **The 530 million-year-old** mudstone deposits of the Burgess Shale, Canada contain fossil impressions of worms.

- **Some of the Burgess Shale worms** like *Canadia* and *Burgessochaeta*, had thousands of hairlike bristles.

- *Canadia* is an annelid worm. The body is divided into segments. It is thought that millipedes and other arthropods evolved from annelids.

- **Some types of worms**, such as serpulid worms, secrete tubes, which they live in and which contain durable minerals.

- **Remains of serpulids' tubes** are common in rocks of the Mesozoic and Cenozoic Eras (250 mya to the present).

▶ Ottoia, a sea worm whose fossil remains were discovered at Burgess Shale. Ottoia lived in burrows on the seabed, and fed by filtering food from the water.

# Trilobites

- **Trilobites** belonged to the invertebrate group called arthropods – animals with segmented bodies and hard outer skeletons.

- **Trilobite means** 'three lobes'. Trilobites' hard outer shells were divided into three parts.

- **The first trilobites** appeared about 530 mya. By 500 mya, they had developed into many different types.

- **Trilobites had compound eyes**, like insects' eyes, which could see in many different directions at once.

- **Some trilobites** could roll up into a ball, like some woodlice do today. This was a useful means of protection.

- **Trilobites had long**, thin, jointed legs. They moved quickly over the seabed or sediment covering it.

- **Trilobites moulted** by shedding their outer skeletons. Most trilobite fossils are the remains of shed skeletons.

- **One of the largest trilobites** was *Isotelus*, which grew up to 44 cm long.

- **Trilobites could also be** much smaller, such as *Conocoryphe*, which was about 2 cm long.

- **Trilobites became extinct** around 250 mya – along with huge numbers of other marine animals.

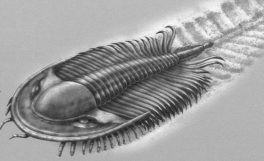

▲ Conocoryphe trilobites lived in the seas of the Mid-Cambrian Period, about 530 mya. It was one of the smaller trilobites.

# Pterygotus

● **Pterygotus** was an enormous water scorpion that grew up to 2.3 m long.

● **Fossils of Pterygotus** have been found in rocks of the Silurian Period (435–410 mya).

● **Pterygotus** was a fearsome hunter, equipped with large eyes and long claws.

● **It had two huge claws** (called chelicerae) for grasping prey, two paddles for swimming, and eight legs for chasing victims over the seabed and digging them up from the sediment.

● **Pterygotus belonged** to the group of invertebrates known as eurypterids (water scorpions).

● **Eurypterids** lived between 490 and 250 mya.

● **Not all eurypterids were giants** – some were only 10 cm long.

★ STAR FACT ★
Dolphins swim by beating their tails up and down – which is how palaeontologists think *Pterygotus* swam.

● **They were not true scorpions**, because their tail parts (called the opisthosoma) served as swimming paddles, not stinging weapons.

● **Pterygotus' opisthosoma** was long and ended in a flattened paddle. Palaeontologists think it swam by beating this paddle up and down.

▼ Pterygotus, which was bigger than a human, was the largest arthropod (an animal with a segmented body and a hard outer skeleton) ever to have lived.

# Insects, centipedes and millipedes

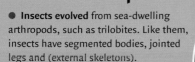

● **Insects evolved** from sea-dwelling arthropods, such as trilobites. Like them, insects have segmented bodies, jointed legs and (external skeletons).

● **The first land-living insects** appeared in the Devonian Period (410–355 mya).

● **Insects made the transition** to breathing air on land by developing small tubes called tracheae in their bodies.

● *Rhyniella* was the first known land insect. It was a springtail – an insect still alive today, which eats rotting plants and flips itself into the air if disturbed.

● *Latzelia* was an early centipede that lived on forest floors in the Carboniferous Period (355–298 mya).

● *Latzelia* **had poisonous fangs**, which it used to kill worms and other insects.

◀ The evolution of winged, pollinating insects such as these honey bees is linked to the evolution of flowering plants. Bees, as well as other flying insects, help these plants to spread by carrying pollen from the male part of one flower to the female part of another as they feed off nectar.

● **Insects were the first animals** to achieve flight. Early flying insects had stiff wings, which stuck out from their bodies – similar to dragonflies' wings.

● **The Cretaceous Period** (144–65 mya) saw a big rise in the number of flying insects, because of the emergence of flowering plants.

● **Many flowering plants** rely on flying insects to spread their pollen, while flying insects, such as bees, rely on flowers for food (nectar and pollen).

● **Beelike insects** date back to the Late Cretaceous Period, while modern bees first appeared around 30 mya.

# Monster mini-beasts

● **The biggest insects** ever known lived in the forests of the Carboniferous Period (355–298 mya).

● **The size of flying insects** increased with the size of trees. One explanation for this is that they needed to fly higher to feed on the insects that lived in the tall trees.

● *Meganeura* was the biggest winged insect, with a wingspan of 70 cm. It was 15 times the size of a dragonfly.

● **Like modern dragonflies**, *Meganeura* was unable to fold back its wings when it was resting.

● **The Carboniferous forests** were also home to enormous millipedes. They are known to palaeontologists because of fossilized traces of their footprints. Some of these millipedes might have been as long as a human is tall.

● **Some millipedes** had poisonous fangs. A human-sized, poisonous millipede must have been a terrifying predator.

● **Mega-insects did not live** only in the Carboniferous Period. *Formicium giganteum* was a giant ant that lived about 45 mya.

▶ Like this modern-day dragonfly, Meganeura had large eyes that allowed it to spot the movements of potential prey.

● **Worker giant ants** grew up to 3 cm long, but queens were nearly 6 cm, with a wingspan of 13 cm – bigger than some small birds!

● *Formicium giganteum's* closest living relative is the red wood ant.

★ STAR FACT ★
Another huge Carboniferous dragonfly is known as the 'Bolsover dragonfly', since its remains were discovered in Bolsover, England. It was the size of a seagull.

# Pikaia

- Pikaia was a small, wormlike creature that is thought to be the ancestor of all backboned animals.

- **Its fossil remains** were found in the 530 million-year-old mudstone deposits of the Burgess Shale in Canada.

- Pikaia was the first-known chordate, an animal with a supporting rod, called a notochord, along its back. All vertebrates belong to this group, as well as marine animals called tunicates and acraniates.

- Pikaia **was 5 cm long** with a notochord (stiffening rod) running along its body – a kind of primitive spine that gave its body flexibility.

- **The notochord** allowed the animal's muscles to work against it, and the animal's body organs to hang from it.

- Pikaia **is similar** to a modern creature called *Branchiostoma*, a small, transparent creature that lives in sand on the seabed.

◀ Pikaia *looked a little like an eel with tail fins. The stiff rod that ran along its body developed, in later animals, into the backbone.*

- **As it lacked a bony skeleton**, a backbone, ribs, paired fins and jaws, Pikaia was not really a fish.

- **Pikaia was a more complex creature** than many other animals found in the Burgess Shale. It suggests that other complex creatures must have lived before it, although there is no fossil evidence for this.

- **The head of the** Pikaia was very primitive, with a pair of tentacles, a mouth and a simple brain (a swelling of the nerve cord) for processing information.

- **Pikaia swam** in a zig-zag fashion, similar to sea snakes.

# Jawless fish

- **The first fish appeared** in the Late Cambrian Period, about 500 mya.

- **These fish had permanently** gaping mouths – as they had no jaws they could not open and close their mouths.

- **Early fish were called** agnathans, which means 'jawless'.

- **Agnathans ate by** sieving plankton through their simple mouth opening, as well as scooping up algae on the seabed.

▲ *Early jawless fish such as* Hemicyclaspis, *could swim much farther and quicker than most invertebrates. This meant they could more easily search for and move to new feeding areas.*

**★ STAR FACT ★**
*Hemicyclaspis* had eyes on top of its head. This suggests it lived on the seabed, and used its eyes to keep a lookout for predators above.

- **Among the oldest** complete agnathan fossils are *Arandaspis*, which comes from Australia, and *Sacabambaspis*, which comes from Bolivia.

- *Hemicyclaspis* was another agnathan. It was a very flat fish, with a broad head shield and a long tail.

- **Later jawless fish** had more streamlined, deeper bodies and eyes at the front of their heads. This suggests they were not restricted to the seabed.

- **Most jawless fish** died out by the end of the Devonian Period (around 350 mya).

- **Living relatives of agnathans** include lampreys and hagfish, which have soft bodies and look like eels. Like agnathans, they are also jawless.

# Jawed fish

● **The first jawed fish** emerged in the Early Silurian
Period (about 430 mya).

● **Palaeontologists** call jawed fish
acanthodians, from the Greek word
*akantha*, meaning 'thorn' or 'spine'.

● **Jaws and teeth** meant acanthodians
could eat a greater variety of food and
defend themselves more effectively.

● **Jaws and teeth allowed** acanthodians
to become predators.

● **Acanthodians' jaws** evolved from gill
arches in the pharynx, the tube that runs
from the mouth to the stomach.

● **Gill arches** are bony rods and muscles that surround
the gills, the breathing organs of a fish.

● **As acanthodians developed jaws**, they developed
teeth, too.

● **The earliest fish teeth** were conelike shapes along the
jaw, made out of bone and coated with hard enamel.

● **The teeth of early acanthodians** varied. In some
species they were sharp and
spiky, in others they were like
blades while in others they
resembled flat plates.

◄ Climatius, *a type of acanthodian
or jawed fish, that lived around
400 mya. Another name for
acanthodians is 'spiny sharks' –
although they were not sharks, many
had spines on the edges of their fins.*

# Placoderms

● **Placoderms** were jawed fish that
had bony plates covering the front
part of the body.

● **They appeared** in the Late
Silurian Period (415 mya) and were
abundant in the seas of the
Devonian Period (410–355 mya).

● **Placoderm means 'plated skin'.** The plating provided
protection against predators.

● **Most placoderms** ranged in length from 30 cm to 10 m.

● **The two groups** of placoderms were arthrodires and
antiarchs.

● **Arthrodires** could turn their head in many directions.

● **Arthrodires had powerful jaws** and sharp teeth.

● **Antiarchs were smaller** than arthrodires. Like
arthrodires, the head and front part of its body were
covered in bony plates.

▲ Bothriolepis *had eyes on top of its head. Its mouth was lined
by cutting plates situated under the head. This lead
palaeontologists to believe that it was a bottom-dwelling feeder.*

● **Antiarchs also had a pectoral** (front end) fin connected
to its head plates. Palaeontologists think they might have
used this fin as a leg, to help it move over the seabed.

# Sharks

◀ Hybodus was a blunt-headed prehistoric shark that lived between 250 and 125 mya, in the time of the dinosaurs. It looked quite similar to modern sharks, but had different jaws.

● **The earliest-known** shark fossils come from rock layers of the Early Devonian Period (410–355 mya).

● **Sharks belong to the group** known as cartilaginous fish, which also includes rays and skates. Their skeletons are made from cartilage, not bone.

● *Cladoselache* was a prehistoric shark, which could grow up to 2 m long.

● *Cladoselache* **appears to have been** quite similar to a modern shark – it had a streamlined body, a pair of dorsal (back) fins and triangular-shaped pectoral (front end) fins.

● **Early sharks hunted squid,** small fish and crustaceans.

● *Stethacanthus* **was a prehistoric shark** that looked nothing like a modern one. It had an anvil-shaped projection above its head, which was covered in teeth.

● *Stethacanthus* **lived** during the Carboniferous Period (355–298 mya).

● **Sharks are at the top of the food chain** in modern seas, but this was not the case during the Devonian Period.

● **Placoderms,** such as *Dunkleosteus*, dwarfed even the biggest sharks.

▲ This modern blue shark, is a fast swimmer and a fierce hunter. The main features of sharks – from their tightly packed, needle-sharp teeth to their streamlined shape – have changed little over 400 million years.

> ★ STAR FACT ★
> Prehistoric sharks' jaws were fixed to the side of their skull, while modern sharks' jaws hang beneath their braincase, which gives them a more powerful bite.

# Bony fish

- **Bony fish** have internal skeletons and external scales made of bone.

- **They first appeared** in the Late Devonian Period (around 360 mya).

- **Bony fish evolved** into the most abundant and varied fish in the seas.

- **There are two types** of bony fish – ray-finned fish and lobe-finned fish.

- **There were plenty of** prehistoric lobe-finned fish, but only a few species survive today. They belong to one of two groups – lungfish or coelacanths.

- **Amphibians** – and, ultimately, reptiles and mammals – evolved from lobe-finned fish.

▶ *This modern-day coelacanth is a direct descendant of the lobe-finned bony fish that lived 350 mya. Coelacanths were thought to be extinct until a fisherman caught one off the coast of South Africa in 1938.*

- **Ray-finned fish** were so-called because of the bony rays that supported their fins. Most early ray-finned fish were small, ranging in size from about 5 cm to 20 cm long.

- *Rhadinichthys* **and** *Cheirolepis* were two early ray-finned fish. They were small predators, equipped with good swimming ability and snapping jaws.

- **Around 250 mya,** ray-finned fish lost many of the bony rays from their fins. The fins became less stiff and more flexible – and the fish became better swimmers.

- **New types of** ray-finned fish, called teleosts, also developed more symmetrical tails and thinner scales.

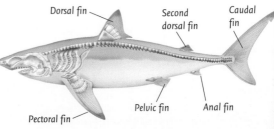

# Fins

- **The earliest fish** did not have fins. The first fish to have them were acanthodians (jawed fish).

- **Acanthodians** were the first fish predators. Fins gave them manoeuvrability – needed for chasing their prey.

- **Fins let fish** make quick or subtle changes in direction.

- **They also help fish** to stay afloat and counter gravity, since their bones and muscles are denser than water.

- **This explains why** most agnathans (jawless fish), which lacked fins, lived on the bottom of seas – it meant they did not have to struggle against gravity.

- **Pectoral fins**, at the front end of a fish, help to keep it level and counteract its tendency to pitch forward at the front because of the weight of the head.

- **Dorsal fins**, on a fish's back, and pelvic and anal fins at its rear, stop it from rolling over.

- **The first acanthodians** to have fins had a pair of dorsal fins, a single anal fin beneath the tail and a varying number of pairs of fins on their undersides.

- **Later bony fish** developed pairs of fins that were borne by lobes, or projections, of bone and muscle. They were called lobe-finned fish.

- **The fins of lobe-finned fish** evolved into the limbs of amphibians.

Dorsal fin · Second dorsal fin · Caudal fin · Pelvic fin · Anal fin · Pectoral fin

▲ *The skeleton of a great white shark. On its back is a large dorsal fin followed by a much smaller one. On its front are pairs of pectoral and pelvic fins. The caudal fin, the shark's tail, is used for propulsion and steering.*

# From fins to limbs

- **The first land animals with** backbones were tetrapods. They had legs to move around in search of food.

- **Tetrapods** evolved from lobe-finned fish.

- **Fossil skeletons** of the lobe-finned fish *Eusthenopteron* show that the organization of bones in its front and rear fins was similar to the arrangement of limbs in tetrapods.

- *Eusthenopteron* used its fins as legs to move over land.

- **The lobe-finned fish** *Panderichthys*, could more effectively use fins as limbs than *Eusthenopteron*. *Panderichthys* more tetrapod than fish.

- **The front fins** in lobe-finned fish connected to a shoulder girdle, while the rear fins connected to a hip girdle. These girdles connected to the backbone.

- **These hip and shoulder connections** meant that limbs of future tetrapods were connected to a skeleton, which stopped the limbs pressing on the inside of the body .

- **Tetrapods** developed heads that were separated from their shoulders and joined instead by a neck.

- **Necks** allowed animals to bend down to feed, reach up for food, and turn around to see.

◀ *Eusthenopteron used its fins to move out of the water. Its name means 'good strong fin'.*

# Tetrapods

▶ *Eogyrinus was an amphibious tetrapod that lived around 310 mya. It grew up to 4.5 m long and had a skull similar to a crocodile's and a body similar to an eel's.*

- **Tetrapod means** 'four-legged'. Early tetrapods were amphibians – animals that lived in water and on land.

- **The first tetrapods** emerged in the Late Devonian Period (about 360 mya).

- **They lived in shallow freshwater lakes** and rivers. They developed limbs and lungs to cope with the waters drying out and this enabled them to move to new habitats.

- **The size of tetrapods** increased during the Carboniferous Period (355–298 mya). This may have been because there was more oxygen in the atmosphere, produced by the huge Carboniferous forests.

- **Tetrapods adapting to the land** had to face a range of challenges such as greater temperature variations than in water, and more ultraviolet radiation from the Sun.

- **The early tetrapods** were called labyrinthodonts, because of their labyrinth-like tooth structure. These animals include *Ichthyostega*, *Eogyrinus* and *Diadectes*.

- *Diadectes* is the earliest plant-eating vertebrate known. At 3 m long it had small jaws with blunt teeth.

- **Modern amphibians** can be less than 10 cm long, while early tetrapods could grow up to 2 m.

- **Like their living relatives**, frogs, early tetrapods laid eggs in water that hatched into tadpoles.

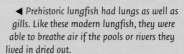

# Breathing air

- **Fish breathe oxygen** in water through their gills. When a fish is out of the water, these gills collapse.

- **For creatures to adapt** to living on land, they had to develop air-breathing lungs.

- **Tetrapods** were not the first creatures to develop lungs – this step was taken by lobe-finned fish.

- **Lungfish** are lobe-fins that still exist today. They live in hot places and, when rivers dry out, bury themselves in mud and breathe through lungs.

- **Early tetrapods**, such as *Ichthyostega* and *Acanthostega*, had gills and lungs, which suggests they could breathe in both air and water.

- **Later tetrapods breathed through gills** when they were first born, but, like modern frogs and newts, their gills shrank when they got older and were replaced by lungs.

◀ *Prehistoric lungfish had lungs as well as gills. Like these modern lungfish, they were able to breathe air if the pools or rivers they lived in dried out.*

- **Modern amphibians** also take in oxygen through their skin, which is soft and moist.

- **Early tetrapods had tougher skin**, so were unable to breathe through it.

- **Breathing through skin** limits an animal's size, which is why modern amphibians are much smaller than many of their prehistoric ancestors.

★ **STAR FACT** ★
Animals could only evolve to live on land because of the work of plants over millions of years, producing oxygen that became part of Earth's atmosphere.

# Acanthostega

▶ *Acanthostega may have evolved from lobe-finned fish. It had a number of fishlike features such as gills and lungs, as well as tail fin.*

- *Acanthostega* was one of the earliest tetrapods. It had a fishlike body, which suggests it spent most of its life in water.

- **Its fossil remains** were found in rock strata dating from the Late Devonian Period (around 370 mya).

- *Acanthostega's* **body** was about 1 m long.

- **It had a wide tail**, which would have been useful for swimming but inconvenient for moving on land.

- **Its legs were well-developed**, however, with eight toes on the front feet and seven on the rear ones.

- **The number of toes** on its feet surprised palaeontologists – they had previously thought all tetrapods had five toes.

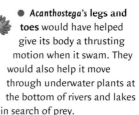

- *Acanthostega's* **legs and toes** would have helped give its body a thrusting motion when it swam. They would also help it move through underwater plants at the bottom of rivers and lakes in search of prey.

- *Acanthostega* had a flattened skull, and its eye sockets were placed close together on the top of its head.

- **A complete but jumbled-up** *Acanthostega* **fossil** was discovered in hard rock in Greenland. Palaeontologists had to work very carefully to prise the fossil from the rock.

★ **STAR FACT** ★
*Acanthostega* had fishlike gills for breathing water as well as lungs for breathing air.

# Ichthyostega

- **Ichthyostega** was another early tetrapod. Like *Acanthostega*, it was discovered in Greenland in rock that was 370 million years old.

- **Its body was around 1 m long.** Palaeontologists think it was probably covered in scales.

- **Ichthyostega had a flat head,** a long snout, large jaws and teeth.

- **Its body was barrel shaped**. It had short, strong legs and a fishlike tail.

- **This tetrapod ate small fish** and shellfish, but would have been prey for large fish.

- **Ichthyostega had a skull** that was completely solid apart from its eye sockets. This meant that there were no holes around which jaw muscles could attach.

- **Without proper jaw muscles**, Ichthyostega and other early tetrapods could do little more than snap their jaws open and shut.

- **Like Acanthostega**, Ichthyostega was more suited to swimming than walking. It used its legs for paddles, and its tail for manoeuvrability.

- **Ichthyostega also used its limbs** and feet for holding onto plants and digging for shellfish.

- **Ichthyostega and Acanthostega** show how animals were slowly adapting from a life in water to one on land.

▼ Scientists think that Ichthyostega's shape and behaviour were similar to that of seals. Like seals, it could probably tuck its limbs alongside its body when swimming. On land, it might have used its forelimbs to drag the rest of its body over the ground.

# Temnospondyls

◀ *Gerrothorax was an aquatic temnospondyl of the Late Triassic Period (215–208 mya). Like most other temnospondyls, it was a predator.*

● **Other temnospondyls,** such as *Paracyclotosaurus* and *Cyclotosaurus*, had rounder bodies and thinner heads with powerful teeth and jaws.

● *Gerrothorax, Paracyclotosaurus* and *Cyclotosaurus* were suited to water habitats. Other temnospondyls show more adaptations for land.

● **Temnospondyls** were a group of tetrapods that emerged in the Carboniferous Period (355–298 mya). They were some of the biggest early tetrapods.

● *Gerrothorax* was a temnospondyl. It grew up to 1 m or more long and had a flattened body shape and a very wide, flat head, with eyes on top.

● *Gerrothorax* **looked a little like** an enormous tadpole. It probably spent most of its time in water rather than on land.

● **Its flat body shape** suited a life spent hunting by lying at the bottom of swamps and ambushing passing fish.

● **One temnospondyl** that had a land-adapted body was the sturdily built *Cacops*, which grew to about 40 cm long.

● **A much bigger land-living** temnospondyl was *Eryops*, which grew to about 2 m in length.

● **Temnospondyls** were the most successful land predators of their day.

● **They were all destined for extinction,** however. Temnospondyls were not the ancestors of reptiles – this role belonged to smaller tetrapods.

# Lepospondyls

● **Lepospondyls** were another group of early tetrapods. Like temnospondyls, they first appeared between 350 and 300 mya.

● **Lepospondyls were small animals,** often about the size of modern-day newts (10–15 cm long).

● **Their backbones differed** from temnospondyls' backbones.

● **Lepospondyls also had simpler teeth** and fewer bones in their skulls than temnospondyls.

● *Diplocaulus* was a lepospondyl with strange wing shapes, which looked a bit like a boomerang, protruding from its skull.

▲ *One theory about Diplocaulus' strange skull shape is that it was a form of defence, and difficult for any predator to swallow. Another idea is that it helped Diplocaulus move through the water, like a hydrofoil.*

● **It lived in the Mid Permian Period** (about 275 mya).

● **One *Diplocaulus* fossil** found in the USA was 0.8 m long.

● *Diplocaulus* **lived in freshwater streams**. Its oddly shaped head probably increased its manoeuvrability in the water, like the rudder on a submarine.

● **Lepospondyls** were controversial creatures. Some palaeontologists argue that they were the ancestors of modern amphibians.

> ★ STAR FACT ★
> At least one lepospondyl, *Ophiderpeton*, reversed the trend of the tetrapods by losing all its legs so that it resembled an eel.

# Frogs and salamanders

- **Modern amphibians**, such as frogs, toads, salamanders and newts, belong to the group called the lissamphibians.

- **Lissamphibians** evolved between the Late Carboniferous and Early Triassic Periods (300–240 mya).

- **Triadobatrachus lived** in the Early Triassic Period, in Madagascar and was 10 cm long.

- **Triadobatrachus had a froglike skull.** Compared to earlier amphibians, it had a shortened back, with fewer spinal bones, and a shortened tail.

▶ Triadobatrachus *was the earliest-known frog.*

- **Evolution did not stop** with *Triadobatrachus* – modern frogs have even fewer spinal bones and no tail at all.

- **Triadobatrachus' hind legs** were the same size as its front legs. Modern frogs have longer hind legs for hopping.

- **Karaurus** is the first known salamander. It lived in the Late Jurassic Period (around 150 mya) in Kazakhstan. It was 19 cm long, with a broad skull.

- **More modern-looking** frog and salamander fossils have been discovered in Messel, Germany. They date from the Early Eocene Epoch (around 50 mya).

- **Some Messel frog fossils** have their legs bent, as if they were in mid-hop. There are even tadpole fossils.

# First reptiles

- **Reptiles evolved** from amphibians during the Carboniferous Period (355–298 mya).

- **Unlike amphibians**, which live near and lay their eggs in water, reptiles are more adapted to life on land.

- **Compared to amphibians**, reptiles had better limbs for walking, a more effective circulatory system for moving blood around their bodies, and bigger brains.

- **They also had more powerful jaw muscles** than amphibians and would have been better predators. Early reptiles ate millipedes, spiders and insects.

- **One of the earliest reptiles** was a small creature called *Hylonomus*, which lived in the Mid Carboniferous Period.

- **Hylonomus** lived in forests on the edges of lakes and rivers. Fossil remains of this reptile have been found inside the stumps of clubmoss trees.

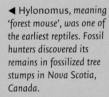

◀ Hylonomus, *meaning 'forest mouse', was one of the earliest reptiles. Fossil hunters discovered its remains in fossilized tree stumps in Nova Scotia, Canada.*

- **Another early reptile** was *Paleothyris*. Like *Hylonomus*, it was about 20 cm long, and had a smaller head than amphibians.

- **One animal that represents** a staging post between amphibians and reptiles is *Westlothiana lizziae*, which was discovered in Scotland in the 1980s.

- **Westlothiana lizziae** lived in the Early Carboniferous Period (about 340 mya).

- **At first palaeontologists thought** that *Westlothiana lizziae* was the oldest reptile. But its backbone, head and legs are closer to those of an amphibian.

# Eggs

- **Reptiles' eggs** are a major evolutionary advance over amphibians' eggs.

- **Early amphibians**, like modern ones, laid their eggs in water. This is because their eggs were covered in jelly (like modern frogspawn) and would dry out on land.

- **Reptiles evolved eggs** that were covered by a shell. This meant they could lay them on land and they would not dry out.

- **Shelled eggs** meant that reptiles did not have to return to water to lay them.

- **Another advantage** was that reptiles could hide their eggs on land. Eggs laid in water are easy pickings for hungry animals.

- **Reptiles' embryos** complete their growth phases inside eggs – when they hatch they look like miniature adults.

- **In contrast**, baby amphibians hatch from eggs as larvae, such as tadpoles. They live in water and breathe with gills before they develop lungs and can live on land.

- **Reptile shells are hard**, and protect the growing reptile embryos. They also provide them with food while they develop.

- **During the evolution** from amphibians to reptiles, some tetrapods laid jelly-covered eggs on land.

- **A number of living amphibians** lay jelly-covered eggs on land, including some tropical frogs and mountain salamanders.

◀ *A female snake protecting her eggs. Eggs laid on land are easier to protect than those laid in water.*

# Skulls

- **The jaws of reptiles** are another feature that shows the evolutionary progression from amphibians.

- **Amphibians' jaws** are designed to snap but not to bite together tightly.

- **In contrast**, reptiles had more jaw muscles and could press their jaws together firmly. This meant they could break insect body casings and chew tough plant stems.

- **By the Late Carboniferous Period** (about 300 mya), reptiles developed openings in their skulls, behind the eye socket. These allowed room for more jaw muscles.

- **Four types of reptile skull** developed. Each belonged to a different type of reptile.

- **Anapsids had no openings** in their skull other than the eye sockets.

★ STAR FACT ★
Plants developed tough stems and leaves, spines and poisons to protect themselves frum hungry reptiles.

- **Euryapsids had one opening** high up on either side of the skull. Sea reptiles, such as ichthyosaurs, were euryapsids, but this group has no surviving relatives.

- **Synapsids** had one opening low down on either side of the skull. Mammals are descended from this group.

- **Diapsids had two openings** on either side of the skull. Dinosaurs and pterosaurs were diapsids; so too are birds and crocodiles.

◀ *Varanosaurus was a synapsid reptile that lived in the Early Permian Period, about 290 mya. There are important similarities between the skulls of synapsid reptiles and mammals.*

# Synapsids

- **Synapsids** were a group of reptiles that had a pair of openings on their lower skull, behind the eye socket, to which their jaw were attached.

- **Synapsids are the ancestors** of mammals, which explains why they are sometimes called 'mammal-like reptiles'.

- **These reptiles** first appeared in the Late Carboniferous Period (about 310 mya). They were dominant animals in the Permian and Triassic Periods (298–208 mya).

- **The first synapsids** are called pelycosaurs. They were heavy-bodied and walked a bit like modern-day crocodiles.

- *Dimetrodon* and the *Edaphosaurus* – both of which had long, fanlike spines on their backs – were pelycosaurs.

- **Later synapsids** are called therapsids. The earliest ones had bigger skulls and jaws than pelycosaurs, as well as longer legs and shorter tails.

◀ *Diictodon was a mammal-like reptile that lived about 260 mya. A plant eater and a burrower, it was an advanced form of a synapsid known as a dicynodont.*

- **Later therapsids** are split into subgroups – dicynodonts and cynodonts. Dicynodont means 'two dog teeth' – cynodont means 'dog tooth'.

- **Dicynodonts were herbivores**. Most had rounded bodies and beaks that they used to cut plant stems.

- **Cynodonts were carnivores**. They used different teeth for different tasks – for stabbing, nipping and chewing.

- **Cynodonts were the most mammal-like** of all reptiles. Some had whiskers and may have been warm-blooded.

# Dimetrodon

- *Dimetrodon* was an early synapsid reptile called a pelycosaur.

- **It was a carnivore**, and was one of the first land animals that could kill creatures its own size (about 3.5 m long).

- *Dimetrodon* had a tall, skinny fin – a bit like a sail – running along its backbone. This fin was formed by a row of long spines that grew out of separate vertebrae.

- **Blood flowing** inside this sail would have been warmed by the early morning sun and carried to the rest of the body. The sail could also have radiated heat out, preventing overheating.

- **As a result**, *Dimetrodon* would warm up more quickly than other reptiles, so it could hunt them while they were still sluggish, cold or asleep.

- *Dimetrodon* had a deep skull and sharp, dagger-like teeth of different sizes. Its name means 'two shapes of teeth'.

▶ *As well as allowing its body to quickly warm up or cool down, Dimetrodon's large fin might have helped it to attract mates or ward off rivals.*

- **In contrast** with other sail-backed pelycosaurs such as the herbivore *Edaphosaurus*, *Dimetrodon* had lightly built limbs and was a fairly fast mover.

- *Dimetrodon* was one of the dominant land predators between 280 and 260 mya.

- **After that time**, however, other reptiles, known as archosaurs, began to eclipse *Dimetrodon* because they were even bigger and better hunters.

- *Dimetrodon* was extinct by the beginning of the Triassic Period (about 250 mya).

# Moschops

- **Moschops** was a later synapsid reptile called a therapsid. It belonged to a group of reptiles called dinocephalians (meaning 'terrible heads'), because it had a very big skull.

- **It was a plant eater**, and was probably preyed upon by large flesh-eating dinocephalians, such as *Titanosuchus*.

- **Moschops lived** in the Permian Period (298–250 mya) in southern Africa.

- **It grew up to 5 m long**. It had a squat body and a short tail. Stocky limbs held it well off the ground.

- **Moschops had many** peglike, chisel-edged teeth, which were adapted for biting and uprooting plant matter.

- **Its back sloped downwards** from the front, rather like a giraffe's.

◄ The bones on the top of Moschops' skull could be up to 10 cm thick – enough to withstand the blows from head-butting rivals or enemies.

- **It had enormous limb girdles** for both its front and rear legs, to support its heavy weight.

- **Moschops had a high skull** with an extremely thick bone on top, which it may have used to head-butt its rivals or enemies.

- **Its skull bones** became thicker as it got older. This thickening of the skull is called pachyostosis.

- **While Moschops' skull** was very big, its brain was not. 'Bone head' might be a good nickname for it!

# Cynognathus

- **Cynognathus** was a therapsid reptile called a cynodont.

- **It lived** in the Early to Mid Triassic Period (250–220 mya).

- **Cynognathus was the size** of a large wolf, and weighed between 40 and 50 kg.

- **Its skull was about 40 cm long**, and its total body length was around 2 m.

- **Like modern wolves**, *Cynognathus* was an active predator.

- **Cynognathus had** some very mammal-like features. Palaeontologists think it may have been warm-blooded, may have had hair on its skin, and may have given birth to live young.

- **One of the many features** *Cynognathus* had in common with mammals was a bony palate that separated the mouth from the nasal cavity, and allowed it to breathe as it ate.

◄ Cynognathus means 'dog jaw'. Like other synapsid reptiles, it had strong muscles for opening and closing its jaws, which made it a powerful killer.

- **Its teeth were similar** to a dog's. It had incisors (front teeth) for cutting, canines (teeth next to incisors) for piercing and molars (cheek teeth) for slicing.

- **The legs were designed** for fast running – they were tucked underneath and close to its body unlike the legs of Moschops, which stuck out more at the sides.

- **Fossil skeletons of Cynognathus** have been found in South Africa. Palaeontologists think that it favoured hunting in dry, desert-like areas.

# Crocodilians

- **The first crocodile-like reptiles** were called eosuchians, meaning 'dawn crocodiles'. They appeared in the Permian Period (298–250 mya).

- **The first true crocodiles** appeared at the end of the Triassic Period (about 215 mya). They were called protosuchians, and lived in pools and rivers.

- **Protosuchus** had a short skull and sharp teeth, and would have looked quite like a modern crocodile.

- **Other early crocodiles,** such as Terrestrisuchus, looked less like modern crocodiles.

- **Terrestrisuchus** had a short body and long legs. Its name means 'land crocodile', as it may have been more at home on land than in water.

- **The next group of crocodilians** to evolve were the mesosuchians, which lived in the sea.

- **One subgroup** of mesosuchians, the eusuchians, are the ancestors of modern crocodiles.

- **Metriorhynchus** was a marine mesosuchian. It had flippers instead of limbs, and sharp, fish-stabbing teeth. It lived in the Late Jurassic Period (around 150 mya).

- **Deinosuchus** was an eusuchian. It was thought to be the largest-ever crocodile at 11 m long until a recent discovery of a Sarchosuchus fossil estimated to measure 15 m.

▼ Fossils of Protosuchus have been discovered in Arizona, dating to around 200 mya. Although similar to living crocodiles in many ways, its legs were much longer.

★ STAR FACT ★
Modern crocodiles are living fossils.
They look similar to the crocodiles that
were alive 100 mya.

# Archosaurs

- **The archosaurs** (meaning 'ruling reptiles') dominated land, seas and skies in the Mesozoic Era (250–65 mya).

- **Archosaurs** included crocodilians, dinosaurs and the flying reptiles called pterosaurs.

- **Archosaurs are the ancestors** of modern birds and crocodiles.

- **Archosaurs were diapsid reptiles** – they had two openings in the skull to which jaw muscles were attached, which meant their jaws werevery powerful.

- **The first archosaurs** appeared in the Permian Period (around 255 mya). They would have looked like lizards, but with shorter bodies and longer legs and necks.

- **One early archosaur** was *Chasmatosaurus*. It had a large, heavy body, and probably spent most of its time hunting in rivers.

◄ *Chasmatosaurus was an early archosaur and a forerunner of the dinosaurs. It lived about 250 mya and grew up to 2 m long.*

- **Lagosuchus** was another early archosaur. Some palaeontologists think it might have been the direct ancestor of the dinosaurs.

- **Lagosuchus was very small.** It was about 30 cm long and weighed about 90 g. It had a slender body, and ran on its hind legs.

- **The name *Lagosuchus*** means 'rabbit crocodile' – palaeontologists think it may have moved by hopping.

> ★ STAR FACT ★
> Like many later dinosaurs, some early archosaurs were bipedal (two-legged walkers), leaving their arms free.

# Placodonts

- **After adapting** so well to life on land, some groups of reptiles evolved into water-dwelling creatures.

- **Placodonts were early aquatic** (water-living) reptiles. They lived in the Mid Triassic Period (240–220 mya).

- **The name placodont** means 'plate tooth'. These reptiles had large cheek teeth that worked like large crushing plates.

- **Placodonts appeared** at about the same time as another group of aquatic reptiles, called nothosaurs.

- **They had shorter,** sturdier bodies than the nothosaurs but, like them, did not survive as a group for a very long time.

- **Placodus was a placodont.** It had a stocky body, stumpy limbs, and webbed toes for paddling. It may have had a fin on its tail.

- ***Placodus* means 'flat tooth'.** It probably used its flat teeth, which pointed outwards from its mouth, to prise shellfish off rocks.

- ***Psephoderma*** was a turtle-like placodont. Its body was covered in a shell, which in turn was covered by hard plates.

- ***Psephoderma* also had** a horny beak, like a turtle's, and paddle-shaped limbs.

- ***Henodus*** was another turtle-like placodont. It also had a beak, which it probably used to grab molluscs from the sea bed.

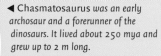

◄ *Placodus was 2 m long, and probably used its sticking-out front teeth to scrape up molluscs from the seabed. Its platelike side teeth would then make short work of crunching the molluscs.*

# Nothosaurs

- **Nothosaurs** were another group of reptiles that returned to live in the seas.

- **Nothosaurus was**, as its name implies, a nothosaur. Its neck, tail and body were all long and flexible.

- **Its total length** was about 3 m and its approximate weight was 200 kg.

- **Impressions left** in some *Nothosaurus* fossils show that it had webs between its toes.

- **Nothosaurus' jaw** had many sharp, interlocking teeth, which would have crunched up the fish and shrimps on which it fed.

- *Ceresiosaurus* was another nothosaur. Palaeontologists think it swam by swaying its body and tail from side to side, like a fish.

- *Ceresiosaurus* means 'deadly lizard'. It was bigger than *Nothosaurus* at 4 m in length and 90 kg in weight.

★ **STAR FACT** ★
*Nothosaurus* had nostrils on the top of its snouts, which suggests that it came to the water's surface to breathe, like crocodiles.

- **Nothosaurs emerged** in the middle of the Triassic Period (250–208 mya), but were extinct by the end of it.

- **The place left** by the extinct nothosaurs was taken by the plesiosaurs – another group of marine reptiles, but ones that were better adapted to life in the seas.

◄ **Nothosaurus** *was an aquatic reptile that could use its webbed feet to move over land. The long-necked nothosaurs may be ancestors of plesiosaurs.*

# Ichthyosaurs

- **Ichthyosaurs** looked similar to sharks, which are fish, and to the later dolphins, which are mammals. When one type of animal evolves to look like another, scientists call it convergence.

- **Unlike plesiosaurs**, which relied on their paddles to propel them forwards, ichthyosaurs swayed their tails from side to side, like fish.

- **Hundreds of complete skeletons** of the ichthyosaur *Ichthyosaurus* have been discovered. This reptile could grow up to 2 m long, and weighed 90 kg.

- *Ichthyosaurus* had large ear bones, which it may have used to pick up underwater vibrations caused by prey.

- **Some fossilized skeletons** of *Ichthyosaurus* and other ichthyosaurs have embryos (unborn infants) inside. This shows that ichthyosaurs gave birth to live young, as opposed to laying eggs.

★ **STAR FACT** ★
The first *Ichthyosaurus* fossil was found in 1811 by the English fossil-hunter Mary Anning. It took seven years before scientists identified the skeleton as that of a reptile.

- **One of the largest ichthyosaurs** was *Shonisaurus*, which was 15 m long and weighed 15 tonnes.

- **Ichthyosaurs were plentiful** in the Triassic and Jurassic Periods (250–144 mya), but became rarer in the Late Jurassic and in the Cretaceous Periods (144–65 mya).

- **Ichthyosaur means** 'fish lizard'.

- **Fossil-hunters have found** ichthyosaur remains all over the world – in North and South America, Europe, Russia, India and Australia.

◄ *Fossils of prehistoric marine reptiles such as Ichthyosaurus created a sensation in the early 19th century because fossil hunters discovered them before they had found any dinosaur remains.*

# Plesiosaurs

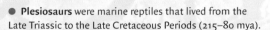

- **Plesiosaurs** were marine reptiles that lived from the Late Triassic to the Late Cretaceous Periods (215–80 mya).

- **They were better suited** to marine life than nothosaurs or placodonts. Their limbs were like paddles, which moved their bodies through water.

- **Many plesiosaurs** had long necks, small heads, strong jaws and sharp teeth.

- **The diet** included fish, squid and pterosaurs (flying reptiles), which flew above the water.

- **The first** *Plesiosaurus* **fossil** was discovered at Lyme Regis, England in the 19th century. The fossil is 2.3 m long.

- **Plesiosaurus** was not a fast swimmer. It used its flipper-like limbs to move through the water but it had a weak tail that could not propel it forward very powerfully.

- **Elasmosaurus**, the longest plesiosaur, lived in the Cretaceous Period (144–65 mya). It grew up to 14 m long and weighed up to 3 tonnes.

- **One group of plesiosaurs** were known as pliosaurs. They had shorter necks, much larger heads and huge jaws and teeth.

- **Research suggests** that plesiosaurs may have caught prey with quick, darting head movements.

▼ Elasmosaurus *had a 5 metre-long neck—as long as three people lying head to toe.*

> ★ **STAR FACT** ★
> One large pliosaur was *Rhomaleosaurus*, another was *Liopleurodon*. Both could grow up to 15 m long.

Pteranodon

# Mosaurs

● **Mosasaurs** were a group of large sea reptiles. They first between 160 and 120 mya.

● **Mosasaurs were diapsid reptiles,** which included dinosaurs and pterosaurs. Other large sea reptiles belonged to the euryapsids group.

● **Mosasaurs** have living relatives. These include monitor lizards, such as the Komodo dragon.

● **The best-known mosasaur** is *Mosasaurus*, which could be up to 10 m long and 10 tonnes in weight.

● **The teeth of** *Mosasaurus* were cone-shaped, each with different cutting and crushing edges. They were the most advanced teeth of any sea reptile.

● **So distinctive are** *Mosasaurus'* **teeth** that palaeontologists have identified its tooth marks on fossils of the giant turtle *Allopleuron*.

◀ Mosasaurus *was a fast swimmer. It had an enormous tail and huge paddle-shaped limbs.*

● **The jaws of a** *Mosasaurus* were found in a mine in Maastricht, the Netherlands, in 1780. The fossil disappeared in 1795 when France invaded, but turned up in Paris.

● **Scientists first thought** the jaws were from a prehistoric whale or crocodile, not a giant lizard.

● *Mosasaurus* **means** 'lizard from the River Meuse', as it was found in Maastricht, through which the river Meuse flows.

● **In 1998,** more than 200 years after the discovery of the first *Mosasaurus* fossil, palaeontologists found the remains of another *Mosasaurus* in the same location – St Pietersburg quarry in Maastricht.

# Rhamphorhynchoids

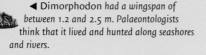

◀ Dimorphodon *had a wingspan of between 1.2 and 2.5 m. Palaeontologists think that it lived and hunted along seashores and rivers.*

● **The earliest pterosaurs** (flying reptiles) were the rhamphorhynchoids. They first appeared in the Late Triassic Period (around 220 mya).

● **Rhamphorhynchoids** had long tails that ended in a diamond-shaped vane, like a rudder.

● **Their tails** gave them stability in flight, which meant they could soar and swoop effectively.

● **One of the first** rhamphorhynchoids – and first flying vertebrates – was *Peteinosaurus*.

● **Well-preserved fossils** of *Peteinosaurus* have been found near Bergamo in Italy.

★ **STAR FACT** ★
Fossil-hunters have found *Rhamphorhynchus* fossils alongside those of the early bird *Archaeopteryx*, in Solnhofen, Germany.

● **They reveal** *Peteinosaurus'* **sharp**, cone-like teeth, and suggest it ate insects, which it caught in the air.

● **In contrast**, another early rhamphorhynchoid, *Eudimorphodon*, had fangs at the front of its mouth and smaller spiked ones behind. This suggests that it ate fish.

● *Dimorphodon* was a later rhamphorhynchoid from the Early Jurassic Period (208–180 mya). It had a huge head that looked a bit like a puffin's.

● One of the last rhamphorhynchoids to appear was *Rhamphorhynchus*, in the Late Jurassic Period (160 mya).

# Pterodactyls

- **Pterodactyls** are a later group of pterosaurs (flying reptiles) than the rhamphorhynchoids.

- **They lived in the Late Jurassic** through to the Late Cretaceous Periods (160–65 mya).

- **Pterodactyls** lacked the long, stabilizing tail of rhamphorhynchoids, but were more effective fliers, able to make quicker turns in the air.

- **They were also much lighter** than rhamphorhynchoids, because their bones were hollow.

- **The pterodactyl** *Pterodactylus* and the rhamphorhynchoid *Rhamphorhynchus* were roughly the same size, but *Pterodactylus* weighed between 1 and 5 kg, while *Rhamphorhynchus* weighed 10 kg.

- **Some of the largest pterodactyls,** such as *Pteranodon*, appeared in the Late Cretaceous Period and had a wingspan of 7 m.

- **Unlike earlier flying reptiles,** *Pteranodon* had no teeth. Instead, it used its long, thin beak to scoop up fish.

◀ *Pterodactylus was a small pterosaur that lived next to the sea. It fed on fish and shellfish.*

- **Pteranodon also had** a pelican-like pouch at the bottom of its mouth – it probably used this to store fish before swallowing them.

- **Pteranodon weighed about 16 kg.** This was heavier than earlier pterodactyls, and suggests it was probably a glider rather than an active flyer.

- **Pteranodon** had a long crest on its head, which may have worked as a rudder during flight.

# Quetzalcoatlus

- *Quetzalcoatlus* was the largest known flying animal of any kind ever to have lived.

- It had a **wingspan** of 15 m – the size of a small aeroplane!

- It was also the **heaviest flying reptile**, weighing 86 kg. Its bulk suggests that it was not a brilliant flyer, and instead glided as much as possible.

- **Its name comes from** an Aztec word meaning 'feathered serpent'. Quetzalcoatl was the Aztec god of death and resurrection.

- *Quetzalcoatlus* had long, narrow wings, jaws without teeth, and a long, stiff neck.

◀ *Quetzalcoatlus belonged to a family of pterosaurs called the azhdarchids, which had giant wingspans, long necks and toothless beaks. The name 'azhdarchid' comes from the Uzbek word for a dragon.*

- **Palaeontologists** were amazed when they discovered the fossil bones of *Quetzalcoatlus* – they did not think a flying creature could be that large.

- **The discovery of these bones** in inland areas, suggests *Quetzalcoatlus* may have flown over deserts like a vulture.

- **Some palaeontologists** say that *Quetzalcoatlus* was not like a vulture as its beak was not designed for ripping at the bodies of dead animals.

- **Another puzzle** is how *Quetzalcoatlus* could lift itself off the ground to fly.

★ **STAR FACT** ★
A student, Douglas Lawson, discovered *Quetzalcoatlus*' bones in the Big Bend National Park, Texas, in 1971.

# Flight

▶ Birds' skeletons, such as this modern-day pigeon's, are built for flight. The bones are lightweight and often hollow, the finger bones in the wing are joined to provide greater strength and the ribs, backbone and breastbone form a secure cage that supports powerful wings.

● **Pterosaurs** (flying reptiles) evolved wings that consisted of a stretched membrane (a piece of thin skin).

● **The fourth finger** of flying reptiles was extremely long, and held up the wing membrane.

● **Flying reptiles** had an extra flap of skin, between the shoulder and wrist, that gave added stability in flight.

● **The forelimbs grew longer** and developed into wings.

● **They also developed feathers**, which possibly evolved from the scales of their reptile ancestors.

● **Flying birds have asymmetrical feathers**, with longer barbs on one side of the shaft than the other. This helps to lift them up and allows them to fly. Flightless birds have symmetrical feathers – which is why they cannot fly.

● **One theory** of how birds and reptiles developed flight is that as they ran along the ground, they flapped their arms to give them stability. Over time, these arms developed into wings.

● **Another theory** is that some animals glided between trees searching of food. They then developed wings.

● **Feathered bird wings** survive injury better than the more fragile skin wings of flying reptiles could have done. This may suggest why birds have outlived pterosaurs.

> ★ STAR FACT ★
> The reason why palaeontologists are confident that *Archaeopteryx*, the first known bird, could fly is because it had asymmetrical feathers.

# Archaeopteryx

◀ *Archaeopteryx is the first known flying bird, but it would not have been a very efficient flyer because of its primitive skeleton and long tail.*

> ★ STAR FACT ★
> The chick of the hoatzin bird, which lives in Venezuela and Guyana, has claws on each wing that are very similar to *Archaeopteryx*'s. It uses them to climb and cling onto trees.

● *Archaeopteryx* is the earliest known flying bird.

● **It lived** in the Late Jurassic Period (159–144 mya).

● **Roughly** the size of a magpie – it would have weighed about 270 g and had a wingspan of approximately 60 cm.

● **Probably eight identified** *Archaeopteryx* fossils have been found, ranging from almost a whole skeleton to just one feather, all of them preserved in limestone, in Solnhofen, southern Germany.

● **The fossils reveal** that *Archaeopteryx* had feathers and that, like modern birds, they were asymmetrical – one side was thicker than the other.

● **Archaeopteryx was therefore capable of flight,** but could not fly long distances as it lacked a suitable skeleton.

● **Like carnivorous dinosaurs,** *Archaeopteryx* had jaws with teeth, and forelimbs that had separate fingers with claws.

● **Archaeopteryx looks so similar** to a small dinosaur that one museum labelled its *Archaeopteryx* fossil as such for decades until someone realized it had feathers.

● **Archaeopteryx was a tree-dwelling creature.** The big toe at the end of its hind legs pointed backwards, allowing it to grip branches.

# Confuciusornis

- **Confuciusornis** was the first-known bird to have a true birdlike beak.

- **It lived** in the Late Jurassic to Early Cretaceous Periods (around 150–120 mya).

- **Unlike the slightly older Archaeopteryx,** which had a mouth filled with teeth, *Confuciusornis*, had a toothless beak, like modern birds.

- **This beak had an upwards curve** – a fact that has led palaeontologists to argue about this bird's diet. Some think it ate seeds and others that it hunted fish.

▶ A male Confuciusornis. Scientists think that males had long tail feathers, but females had much shorter tails.

- **Confuciusornis** was approximately 60 cm long.

- **It had lightweight bones**, a deep chest and a short, rudder-like tail. All of this means it was probably a better flyer than *Archaeopteryx*.

- **Like Archaeopteryx,** it had a backwards-pointing big toe on its hind feet, which suggests it lived in trees.

- **The remains of Confuciusornis** were discovered at the Liaoning Fossil Beds, in northeast China, in the mid 1990s.

- **The Liaoning Fossil Beds** were the site of a prehistoric lake. Fossil-hunters have found so many *Confuciusornis* fossils at this site that the bird probably lived in large colonies on the lakeshore.

- **Confuciusornis** means 'Confucius bird'. It is named after the ancient Chinese philosopher Confucius.

# Terror birds

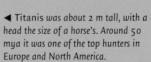

- **After the dinosaurs** became extinct (about 65 mya), huge flightless birds – known as terror birds – seized the opportunity to become the dominant predators of their day.

- **Gastornis** was one such terror bird. It had an enormous head and powerful legs, like those of its dinosaur ancestors, so it could outrun its prey.

- **Some experts believe** that *Gastornis* is the ancestor of ducks, geese and other related birds.

- **Even though these birds were huge,** they were quick light-footed runners as they had hollow bones.

- **The diets of terror birds** included small and medium-sized mammals, such as rodents and horses.

- **During the Late Eocene** and Oligocene Epochs (40–24 mya), big carnivorous mammals became more powerful and better hunters and so more dominant, taking over.

◀ Titanis was about 2 m tall, with a head the size of a horse's. Around 50 mya it was one of the top hunters in Europe and North America.

- **However, in South America,** which was cut off from North America and the rest of the world for much of the Tertiary Period (65–1.6 mya), terror birds managed to stay dominant for longer.

- **One South American terror bird** was *Phorusrhacus*, which grew up to 1.5 m tall.

- **Titanis was another** South American terror bird, and the biggest of all – it was 2.5 m tall and weighed 150 kg.

- **Unlike other flightless birds** *Titanis* had clawed fingers at the end of its fore-limbs. It probably used these for seizing its prey.

# Other flightless birds

★ STAR FACT ★

*Dinornis* was a type of moa bird. The only survivor of this group is the kiwi.

● **Most prehistoric flightless birds** were giants, but not all of them were terror birds.

● **Shuvuuia**, which lived about 8o mya, was an early, flightless bird. Like the terror birds, it was very large.

● **Shuvuuia was about 1 m high**. It probably fed on insects and small reptiles.

● **The name Shuvuuia** comes from the Mongolian word for 'bird'. It lived on the plains of Central Asia and had the long, thin legs of a fast runner.

● **For a long time**, palaeontologists thought that *Shuvuuia* was a reptile, but in fact its skull is much more similar to a modern bird's than a reptile's.

● **Much later giant birds** grew to incredible sizes. *Dinornis* was the tallest flightless bird ever at 3.5 m tall.

▶ *These living flightless birds are descendants of prehistoric flightless birds. The collective name for flightless birds is ratites.*

Cassowary

Kiwi

● **Dinornis lived in New Zealand**. It first appeared about 2 mya and survived until 300 years ago!

● **At 450 kg,** *Aepyornis* was the heaviest bird ever to have lived. It lived on the island of Madagascar between 2 million and 500 years ago.

● **Both Dinornis and Aepyornis** were herbivores. Their diet consisted of seeds and fruit.

# Water birds

★ STAR FACT ★

The skull of *Presbyornis* most closely resembles that of the living Australian duck *Stictonetta*.

● **Ichthyornis** was a prehistoric seagull, which first appeared in the Late Cretaceous Period (85–65 mya).

● **It was similar in size** to a modern seagull, but had a much larger head and a beak full of very sharp teeth.

● **Presbyornis** was a prehistoric duck. Like *Ichthyornis*, it evolved in the Late Cretaceous Period and was abundant in the Early Tertiary Period (65–40 mya).

● **Presbyornis was much bigger** than a modern duck – it stood between 0.5 m and 1.5 m tall.

● **It had much longer legs** than its modern relative and so may have been a wading bird rather than a diving bird.

● **Presbyornis lived** in large flocks on lake shores, like modern flamingos.

▶ Some experts believe that *Palaelodus was a prehistoric flamingo that lived in France about 26 mya.*

● **Osteodontornis was a huge flying** bird, with a wingspan up to 5.2 m across.

● **It lived in the Miocene Epoch** (24–5 mya), and would have flown over the North Pacific Ocean.

● **Osteodontornis** had a long bill, lined with toothlike bony spikes. Its diet probably included squid, seized from the surface of the sea.

# Land birds

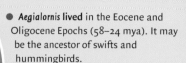

▶ Parrot fossils date back to at least 20 mya.

● **Land birds** are flying birds that fly in the skies over land and hunt or feed on the ground, unlike water birds.

● **Fossils of prehistoric land birds** are rare because their bones were light and would not have fossilized well.

● **As a result**, there are big gaps in palaeontologists' knowledge of the evolution of many species of birds. However, there are some species they do know about.

● **Archaeopsittacus** was an early parrot of the Late Oligocene Epoch (28–24 mya).

● **Ogygoptynx** was the first-known owl. It lived in the Palaeocene Epoch (65–58 mya).

● **Aegialornis lived** in the Eocene and Oligocene Epochs (58–24 mya). It may be the ancestor of swifts and hummingbirds.

● **Gallinuloides** was an early member of the chicken family. Fossils have been found in Wyoming, USA, in rock strata of the Eocene Epoch (58–37 mya).

● **The earliest-known vultures** lived in the Palaeocene Epoch (65–58 mya).

● **The earliest-known hawks**, cranes, bustards, cuckoos and songbirds lived in the Eocene Epoch.

★ **STAR FACT** ★
Neocathartes was an early vulture-like bird. There are similarities between its skeleton and that of storks, which suggests vultures and storks are closely related.

# Argentavis

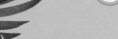

▶ The colossal Argentavis, whose fossils were discovered in 1979, is an ancestor of North American turkey vultures.

● **Argentavis** was an enormous bird of prey – the largest one ever discovered.

● **Its wingspan** was more than 7 m across, which is double the size of the largest modern living bird, the wandering albatross.

● **Individual** Argentavis feathers were up to 1.5 m long!

● **Argentavis lived** between 8 and 6 mya.

● **It looked similar** to a modern vulture, and may have had a similar scavenging lifestyle.

● **Its huge size and weight** (up to 80 kg) suggests that it was more of a glider than an active flier.

● **Argentavis was possibly bald-headed**, with a ruff of feathers around its neck, much like a modern vulture or a condor.

● **It had a large, hooked beak,** which was probably more effective at grabbing hold of prey than its feet.

● **Argentavis means** 'bird of Argentina' and it is so-called because its remains were first discovered there.

● **Argentavis belonged** to a family of extinct flying birds called teratorns.

# Rise of the mammals

● **The earliest mammals** were small, shrewlike creatures that appeared in the Late Triassic Period (220–208 mya).

● **After their initial emergence,** mammals developed little in the two periods following the Triassic, Jurassic and Cretaceous Periods (208–65 mya).

● **This is because dinosaurs dominated the land** at this time. Mammals had to remain small and hidden to avoid becoming prey.

● **It was only after dinosaurs became extinct** around 65 mya, that mammals started to evolve into larger and more varied forms.

● **Mammals (and birds)** have bigger brains than reptiles, and are also warm-blooded.

● **These abilities meant** that mammals could be adaptable – something that ensured their success in the changing climates of the Tertiary and Quaternary Periods (65 mya to the present).

● **The rise of mammals** to the top was not instant – during the Early Tertiary Period, (65–58 mya), the major killers were the giant flightless terror birds.

● **During the Eocene Epoch,** (58–37 mya), mammals became the most dominant animals on land.

● **Eocene mammals** also took to the air in the form of bats – and the seas in the form of whales – and later, dolphins and seals.

● **Mammals have been** – and still are – the most adaptable of all backboned animals.

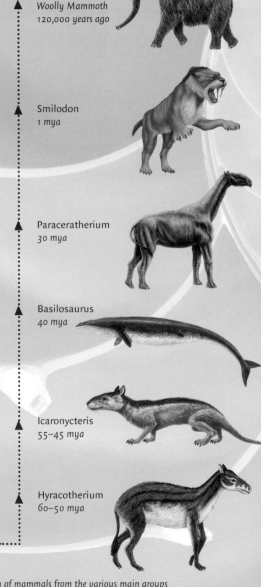

Woolly Mammoth
120,000 years ago

Smilodon
1 mya

Paraceratherium
30 mya

Basilosaurus
40 mya

Icaronycteris
55–45 mya

Megazostrodon
220 mya

Plesiadapis
60 mya

Hyracotherium
60–50 mya

▲ This timeline shows a selection of mammals from the various main groups like whales, primates, horses and elephants. Many kinds of mammals came and went during prehistory, and the ones that are alive today are a relatively limited selection of all the mammals that have ever existed on Earth.

# Early mammals

- **Megazostrodon** was one of the first true mammals. It appeared at the end of the Triassic Period (about 220 mya).

- **It was a shrewlike insectivore** (insect-eater) and about 12 cm long. It had a long body that was low to the ground and long limbs that it held out to the side in a squatting position.

- **Eozostrodon** was another very early mammal, which emerged about the same time as *Megazostrodon*.

- **It had true mammalian teeth**, including two different sorts of cheek teeth – premolars and molars – which were replaced only once during its lifetime.

- **Its sharp teeth suggest** it was a meateater, and its large eyes suggest that it hunted at night.

- **A further early mammal** was *Morganucodon*. It too had premolars and molars and chewed its food in a roundabout motion, rather than the up-down motion of reptiles.

▲ Like other small, early mammals, Megazostrodon *was probably a nocturnal animal, coming out to hunt at night.*

- **Sinoconodon** was another early mammal that lived in the Early Jurassic Period (about 200 mya).

- **These early mammals** also had three middle ear bones, which made their hearing more sensitive than reptiles.

- **They also had whiskers**, which suggests they had fur, which in turn suggests they were warm-blooded.

- **All mammals** are warm-blooded, which means they maintain a constant body temperature. Fur helps some mammals to keep warm – at night, for instance.

# Offspring

- **Mammals developed** a different way of producing young, compared to reptiles and birds, which lay eggs.

- **Instead, most mammals are viviparous,** which means they give birth to live young.

- **One mammal group**, the monotremes, defies this rule by laying eggs. There are five surviving monotremes – the duck-billed platypus and four species of echidna.

- **After the young of mammals are born**, their mothers feed them milk, produced in their mammary glands.

- **The word 'mammal'** comes from the mammary glands – the part of female mammals' bodies that secretes milk.

- **The first mammals**, such as *Megazostrodon*, *Eozostrodon* and *Morganucodon* grew a single set of milk teeth, which suggests that the young fed on breast milk.

- **Milk teeth are temporary teeth** that grow using the nutrients provided by milk, and prepare the jaw for later teeth.

- **Mammals can be divided** into three groups depending on how they rear their young – placentals, marsupials and monotremes.

- **In placental mammals**, the offspring stays inside its mother's body, in the womb, until it is a fully developed baby – at which point it is born.

- **Marsupial mammals give birth** to their offspring at a much earlier stage. The tiny infants then develop fully in their mothers' pouch, called a marsupium.

◄ Marsupial mammals, such as this kangaroo and its joey (infant), give birth at an earlier stage than other mammals.

# Rodents

- **In terms of numbers**, variety and distribution, rodents are the most successful mammals that have ever lived.

- **Squirrels**, rats, guinea pigs, beavers, porcupines, voles, gophers and mice are all types of rodent.

- **Rodents have been** – and still are – so successful because they are small, fast-breeding and able to digest all kinds of foods, including substances as hard as wood.

- **The first-known rodent** was *Paramys*, which appeared about 60 mya.

- **Paramys was a squirrel-like rodent** that could climb trees. It was 60 cm long, and had a long, slightly bushy tail.

- **Modern squirrels evolved** from *Paramys* 38 mya. These mammals have one of the longest ancestries we know of.

▶ Platypittamys *was a prehistoric, ratlike rodent. Rodents became plentiful during the Oligocene Epoch (37–24 mya).*

- **Another early rodent** was *Epigaulus*, which was a gopher with two horns.

- **Epigaulus was 26 cm long** and lived in North America in the Miocene Epoch (24–5 mya). It probably used its horns for defence or digging up roots.

- **Prehistoric rodents could be massive.** *Castoroides* was an early beaver that was over 2 m long – almost the size of a black bear.

> ★ STAR FACT ★
> Rabbits and hares are descended from rodents. Modern hares first appeared around 5 mya.

# Carnivores

- **The first carnivorous mammals** ranged in size from the catlike *Oxyaena* to the wolflike *Mesonyx*.

- **In the Late Eocene Epoch** (around 40 mya) large carnivores appeared, such as *Andrewsarchus*.

- **Modern carnivores** are descended from a separate group called miacids.

- **Carnivores belong** to the order Carnivora. This order had two subgroups – the fissipeds, which include the cat and dog families and the pinnipeds (seals, sea lions and walruses). Many classification schemes put pinnipeds in their own group, separate from fissiped carnivores.

▶ Potamotherium *was a carnivore, very similar to modern-day otters. It hunted fish in rivers and streams.*

> ★ STAR FACT ★
> Allodesmus was a prehistoric seal. It had flippers, large eyes and spiky teeth, which it used to impale slippery fish.

- **During the Oligocene Epoch** (37–24 mya), fissipeds began to replace creodonts as the dominant carnivores.

  - **Fissipeds** were smart, fast, and deadly. They were the only predators that could catch fast-running herbivores.

  - **Faster mammals evolved** in the Oligocene Epoch as forests changed to open woodlands, with more space to run after, and from, other creatures.

  - **Carnivores gradually developed** bigger brains, more alert senses, sharper claws and teeth, and stronger jaws and limbs.

- **Pinnipeds** are carnivorous mammals that, like whales and dolphins, reinvaded the seas.

# Herbivores

- **The first specialist herbivores** (plant eaters) appeared in the Late Palaeocene Epoch (around 60 mya).

- **They ranged in size** from the equivalent of modern badgers to pigs.

- **These herbivores** foraged for food on forest floors.

- **It was not until** the very end of the Palaeocene Epoch (58 mya) that the first large herbivores evolved.

- **Large herbivores emerged** before large carnivores. They must have had a peaceful life – for a while!

- **Uintatherium was a large early herbivore.** It was the size of a large rhinoceros.

- **Uintatherium had three pairs of** bony knobs protruding from its head. Males had long, strong canine teeth, which they used if attacked.

- **The growth of grasslands** and the decline of forests in the Miocene Epoch (24–5 mya) speeded up changes to herbivores' bodies.

- **They could** outrun carnivores in open spaces. They also developed better digestive systems to cope with the new, tough grasses.

- **The most important requirements** for a herbivore are complex teeth and digestive systems to break down plant food and release its energy.

◀ A mother Uintatherium and her baby. This strange-looking creature was the largest land animal of its time. Its head was covered in horns and it had small tusks.

# Cats

- **Cats are the fastest** most intelligent hunters, with the sharpest claws and teeth.

- **Cats evolved along two lines.** One extinct group is the sabre-tooths, which included *Smilodon*.

- **Sabre-tooths preyed on** large, heavily-built animals with thick hides, which explains their long canine teeth.

- **The other group of cats** is the felines, which are the ancestors of modern cats, from lions to pet cat.

- **Felines were faster** than the sabre-tooths, which became extinct as their prey was able to outrun them. The felines continued to be successful hunters.

- **One prehistoric feline** was *Dinictis*, a puma-sized cat that lived in the Oligocene Epoch (37–24 mya).

- **A later feline** was *Dinofelis*, which lived between 5 and 1.4 mya.

- **Dinofelis** means 'terrible cat'. It , had strong front legs that it used to press down on its prey before stabbing with its teeth.

- **Dinofelis' diet** included baboons, antelope and australopithecines – our human ancestors.

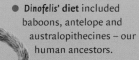

◀ *Dinictis was a fissiped carnivore and member of the cat family, which lived about 30 mya.*

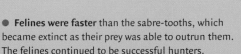

# Dogs

- **Early dogs hunted** in a similar way to modern wild dogs – in packs.

- **Dogs developed long snouts**, which gave them a keen sense of smell, and forward-pointing eyes, which gave them good vision.

- **Dogs also developed a mixture of teeth** – sharp canines for stabbing, narrow cheek teeth for slicing and, farther along the jaw, flatter teeth for crushing.

- **These different teeth** meant that dogs could eat a variety of different foods, including plants, which they might have had to eat if meat was in short supply.

▶ *A pack of Hesperocyon dogs, tracking the scent of their prey. Organized hunting is an example of dogs' intelligence.*

★ **STAR FACT** ★
Hunting in packs allowed *Hesperocyon* to catch large animals that it would not have been able to kill on its own.

- **One of the ancestors of dogs**, as well as bears, was the bear-dog *Amphicyon*. Its name means 'in-between dog'. It lived between 40 and 9 mya.

- **Fossils footprints of *Amphicyon*** show that it walked like a bear with feet flat on the ground.

- **Hesperocyon** was an early dog, living between 37 and 29 mya.

- **Hesperocyon was the size of a small fox.** It had long legs and jaws, forward-pointing eyes and a supple, slender body.

# Andrewsarchus

- **Andrewsarchus** is one of the largest meat-eating land mammals that has ever existed.

- **It lived in Asia** in the Late Eocene Epoch (around 40 mya).

- **No complete *Andrewsarchus* skeleton** has ever been found – only its skull, which measured 83 cm long.

- **Palaeontologists have built up** an impression of the rest of the animal's body from knowledge of its skull, and its relation to the earlier, bearlike *Mesonyx*.

- **If their impression is correct,** *Andrewsarchus* was 5 m long.

- **It had long, strong jaws,** which it used to eat a variety of foods.

- **Andrewsarchus was a scavenger** and an omnivore.

- **It belonged to a group** of mammals known as mesonychids.

- **Fossil-hunters have found** most mesonychid remains near prehistoric rivers and coasts, suggesting that this was where they lived and hunted.

★ **STAR FACT** ★
*Andrewsarchus* means 'Andrew's flesh-eater'. It was named after the naturalist, explorer and writer Roy Chapman Andrews (1884–1960).

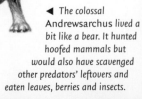

◀ *The colossal Andrewsarchus lived a bit like a bear. It hunted hoofed mammals but would also have scavenged other predators' leftovers and eaten leaves, berries and insects.*

# Smilodon

- **Smilodon** was a terrifying predator that belonged to a group of cats called sabre-tooths.

- **It lived between** 1 million and 11,000 years ago in North and South America.

- **One of Smilodon's most distinctive features** was its huge, curved canine teeth, which could be up to 25 cm long. It could also open its jaws to an angle of about 90 degrees!

- **The first sabre-tooth** was *Megantereon*. It lived about 30 mya.

- **Smilodon** was only a little larger than a big lion, but was around twice its weight at 200 kg.

- **Its 'design' was more like a bear's** than a modern cat's – it had very powerful forelegs, a thick neck, and a short spine.

- **Because of its shorter spine** and heavier build, *Smilodon* was not as fast as feline cats (the ancestors of modern cats). But it made up for this with its power and its teeth.

- **Smilodon preyed on** large and slow-moving creatures, such as prehistoric bison, mammoths, giant camels and ground sloths.

- **Smilodon was a top predator**, with no real enemies and no direct competitors – until the emergence of modern humans.

▼ Smilodon *was a fearsome predator. It became extinct because it was not fast enough to catch the quick-running mammals that evolved at the end of the last ice age, about 11,000 years ago.*

★ STAR FACT ★
*Smilodon's* large canines were very delicate. They could break when stabbing thick-skinned animals, such as bison.

# Paraceratherium

- **Paraceratherium** is the largest land mammal to have lived.

- **It was a gentle giant**, which could be as tall as 5.5 m at the shoulder.

- **Paraceratherium** belonged to the group of mammals called perissodactyls – hoofed mammals with an odd number of toes.

- **It was also an early rhinoceros**, but unlike its living relatives, had no horns on its snout.

- **Remains of this huge beast** have been discovered in Europe and Central Asia, where it lived between 30 and 16 mya.

- **Until recently** this beast was known as *Indricotherium*, but it is now more commonly known as *Paraceratherium*.

- **Paraceratherium** had long front legs and a long neck, which it used like a giraffe to reach leaves on the high branches of trees.

◀ Also known as Indricotherium, *Paraceratherium was a giant, long-necked rhinoceros. Although it was massively heavy, long legs indicate that Paraceratherium was capable of running.*

- **Males were larger than females,** and had heavier heads with more dome-shaped skulls.

- **In comparison with the rest of its body,** *Paraceratherium's* skull was quite small.

> ★ STAR FACT ★
> Male *Paraceratherium* could be as heavy as
> 30 tonnes – four times the weight of a
> modern elephant!

# Megatherium

- **Megatherium** was a giant ground sloth – an extinct type of sloth that lived about 5 mya.

- **Megatherium was** 7 m tall. It had strong arms and massive claws, which it used to pull down branches and uproot trees.

- **It had short hind legs** and a powerful tail that it used for extra support when it stood up on its rear legs to reach the tallest branches.

- **Megatherium walked** on its knuckles on its forelimbs and on the side of its feet on its hind legs.

- **The size of Megatherium** would have put off predators, but it also had very tough skin as extra defence.

- **The remains of ground sloth skin** found in caves in South America show that its was made even stronger by tiny lumps of bone.

◀ Megatherium, meaning 'great beast' was identified and named by the French naturalist Georges Cuvier (1769–1832).

- **Megatherium lived in parts of South America,** such as present-day Bolivia and Peru.

- **When South America became joined** to North America about 3 mya, *Megatherium* spread northwards.

- **Megatherium is thought to have become extinct** 11,000 years ago, but some people in Argentina claim it lived until 400 years ago. If so, it is likely that humans killed off the last of these giants.

> ★ STAR FACT ★
> Megatherium belonged to a group
> of mammals called edentates, which lacked
> front teeth.

# Glyptodonts

▶ Glyptodon, *means 'grooved tooth'. It was named by the English scientist Richard Owen (1804–1892) from fossilized bones that the English naturalist Charles Darwin (1809–1882) brought back with him from South America.*

● **Glyptodonts** were giant armadillos that lived in South America between 5 million and 11,000 years ago.

● **They had domelike shells** and armoured tails that ended in a spiked club.

● **Their tail also served** as an extra support when they reared up on their hind legs – either to defend themselves against attackers or to mate.

● **They also had powerful jaws** and huge cheek teeth that were constantly replaced, unlike most other mammals.

★ STAR FACT ★
Glyptodonts' armour and tails were similar to those of ankylosaur dinosaurs. This is another example of evolutionary convergence – when separate groups of animals develop similar characteristics.

● **This meant** that glyptodonts could chew through the toughest plants without wearing down their teeth.

● **Glyptodon was a 3 m-long glyptodont.** Like other glyptodonts it did not have front teeth.

● **Doedicurus was an even bigger glyptodont.** It weighed 1400 kg and was 4 m long – the size of a big car!

● **Doedicurus is** the most heavily-armoured planteater ever to have lived. A sledgehammer would have made little impression on its massive, bony shell.

● **The body armour and weaponry** of glyptodonts were designed to protect them against predators such as *Thylacosmilus* (see pages 154–155).

# Bats

★ STAR FACT ★
Bats are the only mammals that are known to have reached Australia after it became isolated from the rest of the world around 40 mya.

● **Icaronycteris** is the earliest-known bat. Its fossil remains are between 55 and 45 million years old.

● **Despite its age**, *Icaronycteris* looked similar to a modern bat. It had large ears, which it may used as a sonar, like modern bats.

● **One difference from modern bats** was that *Icaronycteris'* tail was not joined to its legs by flaps of skin.

● **Palaeontologists think** that there must have been earlier, more primitive-looking bats from which *Icaronycteris* evolved.

● **The chance of finding** earlier prehistoric bat fossils is very small – like birds, bats have very fragile skeletons that do not fossilize well.

● *Icaronycteris* ate insects. Palaeontologists know this because they have found insect remains in the part of the fossil where its stomach would have been.

● *Icaronycteris* fossils have been found in North America.

● **The fossil remains** of another prehistoric bat, *Palaeochiropteryx*, have been found in Europe.

● **Like** *Icaronycteris*, this bat seems to have been an insectivore (insect eater).

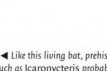

◀ *Like this living bat, prehistoric bats such as Icaronycteris probably used sonar to sense nearby objects and hunt for prey. Bats use sonar by making a high-pitched sound and then listening to its echoes.*

# Marsupials

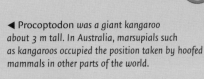

- **Marsupials** are mammals that give birth to offspring at an early stage in their development – when they are tiny.

- **After being born**, the infant crawls through its mother's fur to a pouch called the marsupium, where it stays, feeding on milk, until it is big enough to leave.

- **The first marsupials** probably evolved in North America and then spread to South America and Australia.

- *Alphadon*, meaning 'first tooth', was an early marsupial that emerged 70 mya. It lived in North and South America.

- *Alphadon* **was 30 cm long** and weighed 300 gm. It would have lived in trees, using its feet to climb and fed on insects, fruit and small vertebrates.

- **When Australia became isolated** from the rest of the world about 40 mya, its marsupials continued to evolve – unlike the rest of the world, where they died out.

◀ *Procoptodon was a giant kangaroo about 3 m tall. In Australia, marsupials such as kangaroos occupied the position taken by hoofed mammals in other parts of the world.*

- **Marsupials continued** to exist in South America, which was also isolated from the rest of the world, during much of the Tertiary Period (65–1.6 mya).

- **But when South America** became reconnected with North America, about 3 mya, the arrival of placental mammals from the north led many marsupials to become extinct.

- **Today, there are only two** surviving groups of marsupials in the Americas: the opossums found throughout America and the rat opossums found in South America.

- Australia has many living marsupials, from kangaroos to koalas. However it had a much greater marsupial population in the Tertiary Period – we know this from fossil sites such as Riversleigh in northwest Queensland.

# Thylacosmilus

- *Thylacosmilus* was a carnivorous marsupial. It belonged to a family of South American marsupials called the Borhyaenidae, all of whom had large skulls and teeth.

- **It lived and hunted** on the grassy plains of South America in the Pliocene Epoch (5–1.6 mya).

- *Thylacosmilus* **was about** the size of a modern jaguar, growing up to 1.2 m long and weighing about 115 kg.

- **There are some amazing similarities** between *Thylacosmilus* and the sabre-tooth cats, such as *Smilodon*.

- *Thylacosmilus* **also had** long, upper canine teeth, which it used to stab its prey.

- **Like** *Smilodon*, *Thylacosmilus* had powerful shoulder and neck muscles, and it could press its huge canines down with great force.

- **This is remarkable** as the sabre-tooths were placental mammals that evolved in North America and *Thylacosmilus* was a marsupial that evolved in South America at a time when the two continents were not connected.

- **It is example** of evolutionary convergence – when separate animal groups develop similar characteristics.

- **The teeth of** *Thylacosmilus*' grew throughout its life.

- *Thylacosmilus* **became extinct** after the land bridge between North and South America was re-established. It could not compete with the more powerful carnivores that arrived from the north.

◀ *Thylacosmilus had much in common with sabre-tooth cats, but it had some differences too. Unlike true cats, it was a marsupial, its teeth never stopped growing and it could not retract its claws.*

# Elephant evolution

- **Elephants and their ancestors** belong to an order of animals called Proboscidea, meaning 'long-snouted'.
- **The ancestors of elephants** appeared around 40 mya. They were trunkless and looked a bit like large pigs.
- **Moeritherium** is the earliest known ancestor. It is named after Lake Moeris in Egypt, where its fossils were found.
- **It was 3 m long** and weighed 200 kg, and probably spent much of its life in rivers or lakes, like a hippo.

> ★ STAR FACT ★
> Mammoths were giant elephants. The first mammoth was possibly *Stegodon*, which had very long tusks and lived in Asia and Africa.

- **The next step in the development** of elephants was taken by *Phiomia*, which lived about 36 mya.
- **Phiomia had a trunk** as well as two pairs of tusks.
- **Phiomia is the first-known** of a group of elephants called mastodonts. Its shoulder height was up to 2.4 m.
- **One group of elephants** that descended from *Phiomia* were the deinotheres, which had one pair of enormous downward curving tusks in the lower jaw.
- **Other groups that evolved** from mastodonts were true elephants (resembling living elephants) and mammoths, which appeared in the Pliocene Epoch (5–1.6 mya).

◀ The hippopotamus-like Moeritherium. The American palaeontologist Henry Fairfield Osborn (1857–1935) described it as 'a missing link' between elephants and other mammals.

# Platybelodon

▶ It *was thought Platybelodon ate soft water plants. Recent research on its fossilized tusks suggests that it ate tougher plant material.*

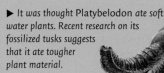

- **Platybelodon** was an early – but not the first – member of a group of prehistoric elephants called mastodonts.
- **It lived about 25 mya** in the cold northern regions of Europe, Asia and North America.
- **Platybelodon's lower jaw** ended in two very wide, flat tusks – like a pair of spades.
- **Platybelodon is called** 'shovel-tusker', because palaeontologists think it used its tusks as a shovel to scoop up plants.

> ★ STAR FACT ★
> The first elephants lived in Africa but – as discoveries of Platybelodon fossils have shown – they migrated to Europe, Asia and then North America.

- **It also had flat cheek teeth**, sharp front teeth, and a very wide trunk.
- **This mastodont** had a pair of tusks on its upper jaw, too. They slotted into an indentation near the top of its lower tusks when the mouth was closed.
- **Platybelodon** weighed between 4 and 5 tonnes.
- **The time period** in which *Platybelodon* lived was quite short compared to other animals, and other species of elephant in particular.
- **This is because** *Platybelodon* was a specialized feeder and vulnerable to any climate change that would affect the plants it ate.

# Woolly mammoth

● **Woolly mammoths** (scientific name *Mammuthus primigenius*) lived between 120,000 and 6000 years ago.

● **They lived on the steppes of Russia and Asia** and the plains of North America during the ice ages of the Quaternary Period (1.6 mya to the present).

● **To survive these cold places**, woolly mammoths were designed for warmth and insulation.

● **Their woolly coats** were made up of two layers of hair – an outside layer of long, coarse hairs, and a second layer of densely packed bristles.

● **They also had very tough skins** – up to 2.5 cm thick – beneath which was a deep layer of fat.

> ★ STAR FACT ★
> People often think the woolly mammoth had red hair, but in fact this colour was a chemical reaction that happened after the animal died.

● **Male woolly mammoths** could grow up to 3.5 m long and 2.9 m high at the shoulder, and weigh up to 2.75 tonnes.

● **They had long tusks** that curved forward, up and then back. They used their tusks to defend themselves against attackers and – probably – to clear snow and ice to reach low-lying plants.

● **Some cave paintings** by Cro-Magnon humans clearly depict woolly mammoths.

● **Many excellently preserved woolly mammoth** remains have been discovered in the permanently frozen ground of Siberia.

▼ *In 1994, scientists discovered DNA, or genetic material, in the fossil remains of a woolly mammoth. They found that it was nearly identical to the DNA of living elephants.*

# Columbian mammoth

- **The Columbian mammoth** (scientific name *Mammuthus columbi*) was an even bigger than the woolly mammoth.

- **Its coat was not thick** like the woolly mammoth's, and it lived in warm areas, such as North America and Mexico.

- **The Columbian mammoth grew** up to 4.2 m high at the shoulder, and weighed over 10 tonnes – the equivalent of 130 adult humans!

- **It ate more than** 350 kg of food and drank about 160 litres of water each day.

- **It used its trunk** for feeding, as well as for moving and breaking things.

- **This trunk was like an extra arm**. It had two finger-like projections at the end, which could grab hold of objects.

- **Its tusks grew** up to 5 m long. It used these for fighting rival mammoths and defending itself against predators.

- **Some scientists think** the Columbian mammoth was the same species as the imperial mammoth (scientific name *Mammuthus imperator*). The imperial mammoth was one of the largest mammoths to have lived, estimated to have stood 4.8 m high at the shoulder.

- **Both the Columbian** and the imperial mammoths lacked thick coats and lived in relatively warm climates.

- **The imperial mammoth's tusks** were much more twisted than those of the Columbian mammoth.

◄ *Early humans hunted the Columbian mammoth, a fact known from finds of tools and building materials made out of the mammoth's bone.*

# The first horses

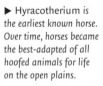

► *Hyracotherium is the earliest known horse. Over time, horses became the best-adapted of all hoofed animals for life on the open plains.*

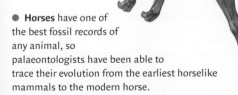

- **Horses** have one of the best fossil records of any animal, so palaeontologists have been able to trace their evolution from the earliest horselike mammals to the modern horse.

- **Hyracotherium is the first-known horse**. It lived in forests in North America and Europe in the Late Palaeocene and Early Eocene Epochs (60–50 mya).

- **Another name for Hyracotherium** is *Eohippus*, which means 'dawn horse'.

- **Hyracotherium was the size of a fox**. It had a short neck, a long tail and slender limbs. It also had three toes on its hind feet and four toes on its front feet.

- **Mesohippus** was one of the next horses to evolve after *Hyracotherium*, between 40 and 25 mya. Its name means 'middle horse'.

- **Mesohippus had longer legs** than *Hyracotherium* and would have been a faster runner.

- **It would also have been** better at chewing food, because its teeth had a larger surface area.

- **An improved chewing ability** was important for horses and other plant-eaters as forests gave way to grasslands, and more abundant but tougher plants.

- **Mesohippus had also evolved** three toes on its front feet to match the three on its hind feet.

- **As horses evolved**, they migrated from North America and Europe to Asia, Africa and South America.

# Later horses

- **Merychippus** lived between 11 and 5 mya. It was the size of a pony.

- **It was the first horse** to eat only grass, and – to help it reach the grass – had a longer neck and muzzle (snout) than earlier horses.

- **Merychippus' middle toe** had also evolved into a hoof, although this hoof did not have a pad on the bottom, unlike modern horses.

- **The legs** were designed for outrunning carnivores. Its upper leg bones were shorter than previous horses, the lower leg bones were longer.

- **Shorter upper leg bones** meant that the horse's main leg-moving muscles could be packed in at the top of the leg – which translates into a faster-running animal.

- **Hipparion**, which means 'better horse', was a further advance on *Merychippus*. It had thinner legs and more horse-like hooves.

- **Hipparion lived** between 15 and 2 mya.

◀ The pony-sized Hypohippus *lived around the same time as Merychippus, between 17 and 11 mya. Unlike later horses it had three spreading toes, which helped it walk on the soft ground of the forests where it lived.*

- **Pliohippus** was an even more advanced horse. The side toes that *Hipparion* still had, had vanished on *Pliohippus*, making it the first one-toed horse.

- **Pliohippus' teeth** were similar to those of modern horses – they were long and had an uneven surface for grinding up grass.

- **Equus**, the modern horse and the latest stage in the evolution of the animal, first appeared around 2 mya.

# Whales

- **Basilosaurus** which first appeared about 40 mya, closely resembled whales we are familiar with today, more so than its ancestors *Pakicetus* and *Ambulocetus*.

- **It was also enormous!** It measured between 20 and 25 m long – the same as three elephants standing in a row.

- **It had a variety of teeth** in its mouth – sharp teeth at the front for stabbing, and saw-edged teeth at the back for chewing.

- **Basilosaurus ate large fish**, squid, and other marine mammals.

- **There were some big differences** between *Basilosaurus* and modern whales. For a start, it had a slimmer body.

- **It also lacked a blowhole**, a nostril on the top of modern whales' heads that they breathe out of when they come to the surface. Instead, *Basilosaurus* had nostrils on its snout.

- **Prosqualodon did have a blowhole** and was a more advanced whale than *Basilosaurus*. It lived between 30 and 20 mya.

▲ The prehistoric whale Basilosaurus, *which means 'king of the lizards', was so named because the first person to examine its remains thought it was a gigantic plesiosaur – a prehistoric marine reptile.*

- **It may have been the ancestor** of toothed whales, a group that includes sperm whales, killer whales, beaked whales and dolphins.

- **Prosqualodon looked similar** to a dolphin. It had a long, streamlined body and a long, narrow snout, which was full of pointed teeth.

> ★ STAR FACT ★
> *Cetotherium* was a prehistoric baleen whale that first appeared 15 mya. Instead of teeth, these whales had hard plates in their mouths called baleen that filtered plankton and small fish.

# The first whales

● **The very first whales** looked nothing like the enormous creatures that swim in our oceans today.

● **Ambulocetus**, one of the first members of the whale family, looked more like a giant otter. It lived about 50 mya.

● **Ambulocetus means** 'walking whale', and it spent more time on land than in water.

● **It would, however,** have been a good swimmer. Fossil remains show that *Ambulocetus* had webbed feet and hands.

● **An even earlier whale ancestor** than *Ambulocetus* was *Pakicetus*, which lived about 52 mya.

● **Pakicetus** is named after the country Pakistan, where a fossil of its skull was found in 1979.

● **Pakicetus was around** 1.8 m long. *Ambulocetus*, at 3 m, was bigger.

● **Palaeontologists think** that whales evolved from carnivorous hoofed mammals called mesonychids.

● **Around 40 mya,** the first true whales, which swam only, evolved from their half-walking, half-swimming ancestors.

> ★ STAR FACT ★
> Only the back of *Pakicetus*' skull and part of its lower jaw have been found. From this, however, palaeontologists can tell it was not able to dive very deeply.

▼ *Pakicetus could run and swim well. It probably lived alongside rivers and streams and hunted animals both in and out of the water.*

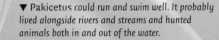

# Megaloceros

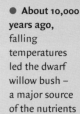

▶ Scientists used to believe that, because Megaloceros' antlers were so big, they could only have been used for display purposes – to scare off rivals. In the 1980s however, research proved that these antlers were used for fighting.

● **Megaloceros** is one of the largest species of deer ever to have lived. Adult males were 2.2 m long, 2 m tall at the shoulders and weighed 700 kg.

● **It lived** between 400,000 and 9000 years ago.

● **Megaloceros is known as** the Irish elk as a large number of its fossils have been found in Ireland in peat bogs.

● **Megaloceros lived all over Europe**, the Middle East, China and North America, too.

● **It had a broader**, flatter snout than modern deer, which suggests it was a less fussy eater and just ate plant food in huge quantities.

● **Like modern deer**, Megaloceros males shed their antlers and grew another pair every year. For antlers as big as Megaloceros', this required a huge intake of nutrients.

● **About 10,000 years ago,** falling temperatures led the dwarf willow bush – a major source of the nutrients Megaloceros needed to grow its antlers – to decline.

● **This food shortage** is one theory as to why Megaloceros became extinct.

● **Another theory is** that early humans, who greatly prized Megaloceros' antlers, hunted it to extinction.

---

**★ STAR FACT ★**
Megaloceros was a fast runner – it could move at around 80 km/h. It used this turn of speed to escape from predators such as wolves.

---

# Early primates

▶ The early primate Plesiadapis had a long tail and claws on its fingers and toes – unlike later monkeys and apes, which had nails.

● **The primates** are a group of mammals that include lemurs, monkeys, apes and humans.

● **Primates have a much greater range** of movement in their arms, legs, fingers and toes than other mammals.

● **They also have a more acute sense of touch** because their fingers and toes end in flat nails, not curved claws – so the skin on the other side evolved into a sensitive pad.

● **The ancestors of primates** were small insectivorous (insect-eating) mammals that looked like shrews.

● **The first known primate** was Plesiadapis, which lived about 60 mya in Europe and North America. It was a squirrel-like tree climber.

● **More advanced primates** developed about 10 million years later. They looked a bit like modern lemurs.

● **Notharctus** was one of these lemur-like primates. It ate leaves and fruit, was about 40 cm long, and had a grasping thumb to grip well to branches.

● **More advanced** primates include Smilodectes and Tetonius. They had larger brains and eyes and longer tails than Plesiadapis.

● **These animals were ancestors** of tarsiers, lemurs and lorises, but not higher primates – the monkeys, apes and humans.

● **One early monkey** was Mesopithecus, which lived 8 mya. It was similar to modern monkeys, but had a longer tail.

# Apes

▼ The early ape *Dryopithecus* stood about 1 m tall. It had the largest brain for its size of any mammal and flourished in open grassland regions in Africa, Asia and Europe.

● **Dryopithecus was a chimp-like ape** that evolved after *Proconsul* and lived in the Miocene Epoch (24–5 mya). It may have stood on two legs but climbed using all four.

● **Ramapithecus was an ape** that lived in the Middle and Late Miocene Epoch. It is now thought to be part of the chain of evolution of Asian apes and is possibly an ancestor of the orang-utan.

● **Australopithecines** were a further step in the evolution from apes to humans. *Australopithecines* (meaning 'southern apes') walked on two legs.

● **The biggest-ever ape** was *Gigantopithecus*, which lived in China until around 1 mya. It may have been up to 2.5 m tall and weighed 300 kg.

> ★ STAR FACT ★
> *Proconsul* was named in 1927 after Consul, a performing chimpanzee that appeared on stage smoking a pipe and riding a bicycle.

● **Apes are primates** that have more complex brains than monkeys and no tails. Hominids (early humans) evolved from apes.

● **Aegyptopithecus** was one of the ancestors of apes. It lived in Egypt in the Oligocene Epoch (37–24 mya). It was small and had a short tail.

● **Proconsul**, which lived between 23 and 14 mya, was an early ape. Its body size varied from that of a small monkey to that of a female gorilla, and had a larger brain than *Aegyptopithecus*.

● **Proconsul was a fruit eater**. Palaeontologists think that it walked on four limbs with part of its weight supported by the knuckles of its hands, like modern chimpanzees and gorillas.

● **Two lines of apes developed** after *Proconsul*. From one line came gibbons and orang-utans, from the other chimpanzees, gorillas and humans.

▶ The enormous Gigantopithecus could probably stand on its hind legs to reach food.

# Walking upright

- **Hominidae** is the human family of ourselves, our ancestors and prehistoric relatives.
- **Hominid fossils** demonstrate their evolution from apes that walked on all fours.
- **Hominid spines** developed an S-shaped curve so that the hips supported the weight of the upper body.
- **Hominid heads** evolved to sit on top of the spine, while apes' heads sit at the front.

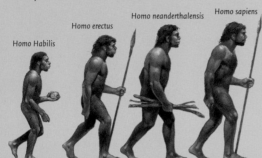

Homo Habilis · Homo erectus · Homo neanderthalensis · Homo sapiens

- **Hominids'** have flat feet to support the body on the ground. Apes have curved toes for climbing.
- **Hominid leg bones** became longer and straighter than those of apes, so they could walk greater distances.
- **Walking on two legs** helped hominids cover greater distances in the open grasslands of Africa.
- **It also let them** to see above tall grasses, an advantage when looking for food or keeping a lookout for danger.
- **Upright walking** freed the arms to do other things, such as carrying babies or food.

◀ *Walking upright was one of the most important developments in the history of hominids.*

# Offspring

- **Human parents** look after their young for a longer period than any other animal.
- **A close bond** between parents and young is also a feature of modern primates – and would have been for prehistoric primates, too.
- **This is because humans and primates** have small numbers of infants compared to many other animals, and females are pregnant for longer.
- **There is also a longer period** of upbringing during which time offspring learn survival and social skills.
- **The pelvises of early hominids** were wide, which meant that their offspring were quite large when they were born.
- **Like modern humans**, later hominids – from *Homo ergaster* on – had smaller pelvises, which meant that their babies were smaller and less developed when born.

◀ *A female orang-utan and infant. Primates have closer relationships with their young than other animals. Unlike monkeys and apes, human babies cannot move around independently after birth and are very dependent on their mothers.*

- **Smaller and less developed babies** require more care and protection – as a result, childcare became an even bigger concern for hominids.
- **This change led to other ones.** Hominid groups increased in size, so that the responsibility for childcare could be spread.
- **There was also more cooperation** between males and females and they began to pair-up in partnerships.
- **Such partnerships** were mutually beneficial – the female could look after the offspring while the male provided food. In turn, the male could be certain that the offspring was his own.

# Early hominids

● **One of the earliest-known** hominids (early humans) is *Ardipithecus ramidus*, which lived about 4.5 mya.

● **It would have looked similar** to a chimpanzee except for one major difference, *Ardipithecus ramidus* walked on two legs.

● **It lived in woods**, sleeping in trees at night, but foraging on the ground for roots during the day.

● **An adult *Ardipithecus ramidus* male** was about 1.3 m tall and 27 g in weight.

● **Archaeologists discovered** the teeth, skull and arm fossils of *Ardipithecus ramidus* in Ethiopia in 1994.

● **In 2001,** archaeologists in Ethiopia found the remains of an even older hominid, *Ardipithecus ramidus kadabba*, which lived between 5.6 and 5.8 mya.

◀ Ardipithecus ramidus. *Scientists gave it its name from the Afar language of Ethiopia – 'ardi' means 'ground' while 'ramid' means 'root' – words that express its position at the base of human history.*

● **The fossils of *Ardipithecus ramidus kadabba*** are similar to those of *Ardipithecus ramidus*, so it is possible both are closely related.

● **Some scientists argue,** however, that *Ardipithecus ramidus kadabba* is closer to an ape than a hominid.

● *Australopithecus anamensis* is a later hominid. Its fossils date to between 4.2 and 3.9 million years old.

● **A fossil of one of *Australopithecus anamensis*' knee-joints** shows that it shifted its weight from one leg to the other when it moved – a sure sign that it walked on two legs.

# Sahelanthropus tchadensis

● **In 2002,** French archaeologists announced the discovery of a new species called *Sahelanthropus tchadensis*. It may be a missing link between apes and early hominids.

● **The archaeologists discovered** a near-complete fossil skull of *Sahelanthropus tchadensis*, which has been dated to between 7 and 6 million years old.

● **They also found the fossils** of two pieces of jawbone and three teeth.

● **The French team** found the skull not in East Africa, like all the other early hominids, but in Chad, central Africa.

● **Finding the skull in Chad** indicates that early hominids ranged well beyond East Africa, where scientists previously believed all early hominids lived.

● **The skull was nicknamed** *Toumaï*, meaning 'hope of life' in Goran, an African language.

● **Despite its great age,** *Sahelanthropus tchadensis*' skull suggests that it had a surprisingly human face, which protruded less than apes.

▶ *The skull of* Sahelanthropus tchadensis. *Some people believe that this is the remains of the oldest hominid of all.*

● *Sahelanthropus tchadensis* also had heavy ridges for its eyebrows. Some archaeologists believe that, because of this, it was closer to an ape than a hominid, since female apes have similar heavy ridges.

● **Like later hominids,** *Sahelanthropus tchadensis* had small canine teeth and did not grind its teeth in the same way as apes.

● *Sahelanthropus tchadensis* lived alongside a diverse range of animals. Other fossil finds in the same region include more than 700 types of fish, crocodiles and rodents.

# Australopithecus afarensis

- **Australopithecus afarensis** was an early hominid that lived 3.5 mya.
- **Its brain** was the size of a modern chimpanzee's, and it had the short legs and long arms of modern apes.
- **Australopithecus afarensis** was 90 to 120 cm in height.
- **Like other australopithecines**, it walked on two legs. This was the most efficient way for it to move in search of food.
- **It had a wider pelvis** and shorter legs than modern humans. This may have made it a more efficient walker than modern humans.
- **Australopithecus afarensis** ate seeds, fruits, nuts and occasionally meat.
- **These hominids had a brief childhood,** reaching adulthood at the age of 11 years old. They lived for a maximum of 50 years.

- ◀ Australopithecus afarensis spent its days on the ground, foraging for food, but at night may have slept in trees.
- **Fossil footprints of Australopithecus afarensis** show that their feet were similar to ours.
- **The first fossils of Australopithecus afarensis** to be discovered belonged to a female. They were found in 1974, at Hadar in Ethiopia.

★ STAR FACT ★
Johanson and Gray named the female 'Lucy' after the Beatles' song 'Lucy in the Sky with Diamonds', which they listened to on the day of their discovery.

# Homo habilis

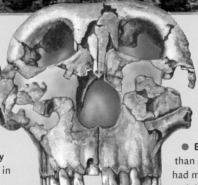

- **Homo habilis** is one of the earliest-known members of the genus Homo, to which we also belong.
- **Homo habilis** lived between 2.4 and 1.6 mya.
- **The archaeologists Louis and Mary Leakey** first discovered its remains at Olduvai Gorge in Tanzania, in 1961.
- **Fossils of Homo habilis' skulls** have since been found around Lake Turkana in Kenya, one of the richest sites for hominid fossils in the world.
- **The skulls show** that Homo habilis had a flat face with prominent cheekbones, similar to australopithecines, which it would have lived alongside.
- **Homo habilis was much more ape-like** than its successor, Homo ergaster. It had fur and lacked any form of language.

- ◀ The first Homo habilis skull found by Louis and Mary Leakey in Tanzania. Homo habilis had a bigger brain than any previous hominid.
- **But it did have a bigger brain** than any australopithecine. It also had more flexible hands and straighter, more sensitive fingers.
- **Homo habilis** means 'handy man' – it could use its hands to gather fruit and crack nuts. It also created the first stone tools.
- **A fully grown Homo habilis male** was around 1.5 m tall and weighed about 50 kg.

★ STAR FACT ★
Homo habilis used stone tools to crack open animal bones so it could eat the nutritious marrow inside.

# Homo ergaster

● **Homo ergaster** was the first 'human-looking' early human. It first appeared about 1.9 mya.

● **Adult males** grew to approximately 170 cm tall, with long, slender limbs and a straight spine.

● **Homo ergaster** was the first smooth-skinned hominid, unlike its hairy ancestors. Like us it cooled down by sweating, not panting, which is how earlier hominids cooled themselves.

● **It was also the first hominid** to have a protruding nose – previous hominids merely had nostrils on the surface of their face.

● **Homo ergaster** was generally a scavenger, although it would hunt and kill older or weaker animals.

● **Scientists know that it ate a lot of meat** because one of the skeletons that have been found shows evidence of a bone disease caused by eating too many animal livers.

● **Fossil remains of** *Homo ergaster* were first discovered in 1975. The most complete skeleton was found in 1984.

● **The skeleton belonged to a teenage boy** named Nariokotome Boy after the site in Lake Turkana, Kenya, where it was found.

● **The structure of Nariokotome Boy's bones** suggest that he was much stronger than modern humans.

● **Homo ergaster** was the first hominid to travel beyond Africa. One place where its remains have been found is Dmanisi, in the Republic of Georgia, near Russia.

▼ Homo ergaster *was different from any previous hominid. It was taller, with a face that was more lightly built and had smaller cheek teeth.*

# Homo erectus

- **Homo erectus** may be a descendant of Homo ergaster.

- **It was almost identical** to its immediate ancestor, except that it had thicker skull bones and a more protruding eyebrow ridge.

- **Homo erectus and Homo ergaster** lived alongside each other for 2 million years.

- **While Homo ergaster became extinct** about 600,000 years ago, Homo erectus survived until less than 50,000 years ago.

- **Like its ancestor,** Homo erectus spread beyond Africa and settled in Europe and Asia.

- **In the 19th century,** Eugène Dubois found Homo erectus fossils on the island of Java. He was a palaeoanthropologist (someone who studies hominid fossils).

- **In the 1930s,** archaeologists discovered more than 40 Homo erectus skeletons in China.

◀ Stone hearths in caves that were used by Homo erectus prove that it had mastered fire. Fire provided warmth, light, protection and the means to cook food.

- **The archaeologists also found evidence** that Homo erectus used fire and practised cannibalism!

- **For a long time,** people called the human to which the Chinese fossils belonged 'Peking Man'. It was much later that palaeoanthropologists realized it was, in fact, Homo erectus.

> ★ STAR FACT ★
> The 'Peking Man' fossils disappeared at the beginning of the World War II and have never been found. They were confiscated by Japanese troops just when they were about to be shipped to the USA.

# Homo heidelbergensis

- **Homo heidelbergensis** lived between 600,000 and 250,000 years ago in Africa and Europe.

- **It was the first hominid** to settle in northern Europe.

- **Homo heidelbergensis** had a body like ours, but it had a heavier jaw, a flat nose and thick eyebrow ridges.

- **The teeth of Homo heidelbergensis** were 50 percent longer than ours.

- **They also had a thicker covering of enamel,** which suggests that it ate tough animal flesh and maybe used its teeth for gripping objects.

- **Towards the end of its existence,** Homo heidelbergensis would have lived alongside Neanderthals.

- **Homo heidelbergensis** is named after the city of Heidelberg in Germany. It was near there that one of the hominid's jawbones was found in 1907.

◀ Homo heidelbergensis used stones, wooden spears and even stone blades to catch food.

- **The greatest find of Homo heidelbergensis' fossils** was made in the Atapuerca hills of northern Spain, in 1976. Archaeologists discovered the remains of 32 individuals.

- **In the mid 1990s,** archaeologists unearthed Homo heidelbergensis bones, tools and animal carcasses in England. The carcasses had been stripped of their meat.

> ★ STAR FACT ★
> Unlike the Neanderthals that came later, there is no evidence that Homo heidelbergensis buried its dead.

# Homo neanderthalensis

- **Homo neanderthalensis** – or Neanderthals – lived between 230,000 and 28,000 years ago across Europe, Russia and parts of the Middle East.

- **Homo neanderthalensis** means 'man from the Neander Valley', which is the site in Germany where the first of its fossil remains were found in 1865.

- **Neanderthals are our extinct cousins** rather than our direct ancestors .

- **They were about 30 percent heavier** than modern humans.

- **Neanderthals' shorter, stockier bodies** were suited to life in Europe and Russia during the ice ages of the Pleistocene Epoch (1.6 million to 10,000 years ago).

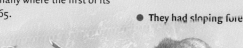

- **They had sloping foreheads** and heavy brow ridges.

- **They buried their dead,** cooked meat and made tools

- **Neanderthals made the first spears** tipped with stone blades.

- **For about 10,000 years** Neanderthals lived beside modern humans in Europe, before becoming extinct.

◀ *Early humans had to face many natural dangers, such as cave bears.*

# Homo floresiensis

- **In 2004,** Australian palaeoanthropologists discovered a new species of human, *Homo floresiensis,* which lived on the Indonesian island of Flores between 95,000 and 13,000 years ago.

- **The remains of seven** specimens have been found.

- **The most complete** skeleton is that of a female. Study of of its leg bone shows that it walked upright.

- **Before the discovery** it was thought *Homo sapiens* had been the sole remaining human species since the disappearance of Neanderthals 30,000 years ago.

- **Palaeoanthropologists nicknamed** *Homo floresiensis* 'hobbit man' because of its tiny size. It was about one metre tall.

- **Its small brain size** does not seem to have reflected its intelligence – *Homo floresiensis* was a skilled toolmaker.

- **Flores, off the coast of Asia,** has been an island for over a million years. Being small represents an adaptation to living on an island, where resources were limited.

◀ Two *Homo floresiensis* hunters prepare to attack a pygmy elephant. The discovery of this new species of human challenges our ideas of human evolution.

- **Some people believe** that this human species evolved into a smaller creature to cope with its island habitat.

- **Local people** have told stories of little hairy people, *ebu gogo,* meaning 'grandmother who eats anything'.

- **Homo floresiensis was a hunter.** It preyed on the pygmy elephant. Both *Homo floresiensis* and the pygmy elephant seem to have become extinct after a volcanic eruption 12,000 years ago.

# Homo sapiens

- **Homo sapiens** means 'wise man'. They appeared in Africa 150,000 years ago. Humans belong to this species.

- **The first Homo sapiens** outside Africa appeared in Israel, 90,000 years ago.

- **By 40,000 years ago,** Homo sapiens had spread to many parts of the world.

- **The humans** that settled in Europe are Cro-Magnons. They dressed in furs and hunted with spears and nets.

- **Cro-Magnons** had a basic language and culture, which included wall paintings.

- **They were similar to modern humans,** but with slightly bigger jaws and noses and more rounded braincases.

◄ Cave painting, cooking and toolmaking are all features of early Homo sapiens. They different from other human species, having a higher forehead and a more prominent chin.

- **Homo sapiens probably arrived** in North America about 30,000 years ago.

- **They would have crossed the Bering land bridge** – formed by shrunken sea levels – from present-day Siberia to present-day Alaska.

- **The earliest-known human culture** in North America is that of the Clovis people, which is thought to be 11,500 years old.

- **Modern humans have** evolved only slightly from the earliest Homo sapiens.

# Brains and intelligence

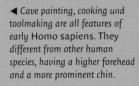

- **Primates,** from which hominids descended, had bigger brains in relation to body size than other mammals.

- **Primates developed larger brains** – and more intelligence – as living in trees required balance, coordination and skilful use of hands and feet.

- **Once hominids' brains started getting bigger,** their skulls began to change. Bigger brains led to the development of foreheads.

- **Homo habilis' brain** was 50 percent bigger than its predecessors, with a capacity of 750 ml.

- **Its brain structure** was different to that of earlier hominids. It had bigger frontal lobes – parts of the brain linked to problem-solving.

- **Homo habilis used its greater intelligence** find meat, which it scavenged from animals kills.

- **Meat gave hominids** bigger brains. Breaking down plant food uses lots of energy. Eating fewer plants allowed more energy for the brain.

- **Homo ergaster had an even bigger brain,** with a capacity of around 1000 ml. It used its intelligence to read animal tracks – a key development in hunting.

- **The brain** of Homo erectus became larger during its existence. About 1 mya its brain capacity was 1000 ml; 500,000 years later it was 1300 ml.

- **Our brain** capacity is 1750 ml.

*Australopithecus afarensis*

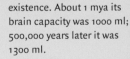

Homo habilis

◄ Brain size is linked to intelligence, but what makes humans and our ancestors intelligent is our brain's complex structure.

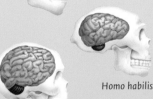

Homo sapien

# Tools

- **The greatest number of** *Homo habilis* tools has been found in the Olduvai Gorge in Tanzania. They include rocks that were used as hammers, flakers, choppers and scrapers.

*Stone tool*

- **Homo habilis used** these tools to cut meat and, especially, to scrape open animal bones to eat the marrow inside.

- **The stone tools** used by *Homo habilis* are crude and basic. This hominid was the first toolmaker, but, hardly surprisingly, it was not a skilled one.

- **But making these early stone tools** was still a challenging task – the toolmaker needed to strike one rock with another so that it would produce a single, sharp flake rather than shattering into many pieces.

- **Toolmaking requires considerable intelligence.** It involves the use of memory, as well as the ability to plan ahead and to solve abstract problems.

- **Homo ergaster's tools** were more advanced. It made tear-drop shaped, symmetrical hand axes called 'Acheulean axes', after the place in France where similar axes have been discovered from a later period.

- **Neanderthals made** sharp flakes of stone, called Levallois flakes, which were placed on the end of spears.

- **This method required** great precision and dexterity. While modern humans have a broader range of skills, they would be hard pushed to make such tools.

- **Modern humans developed** the greatest variety of tools. Cro-Magnon tools include knives, spearpoints and engraving tools.

- **Cro-Magnon humans** also began to make tools from materials other than stone, including wood, bones, antlers and ivory.

# Hunting

- **Homo erectus** was one of the earliest human hunters. Earlier hominids may have hunted small or lame animals, but mainly scavenged other animals' kills.

- **Homo erectus** drove animals into traps using fire. They made handaxes to kill animals or butcher them once dead.

- **The Neanderthals** excelled at hunting – a skill they developed during the ice ages of the Pleistocene Epoch (1.6–0.01 mya).

- **Hunting developed** not only provided food, but also clothing and materials for tools.

- **Neanderthals used nets or spears** to catch fish. They also hunted seals.

- **In the 1990s,** finds of Neanderthal weapons in England showed the range of its hunting tools. They include axes, knives, and blades.

- **As well as hunting meat,** hominids gathered fruits, vegetables and nuts.

- **Another Neanderthal site**, at Schöningen in Germany, had the remains of nine polished wooden spears, made from a spruce tree.

- **Each spear** was over 2 m long, and was designed to be thrown like a javelin.

- **Homo sapiens developed new weapons** for hunting, including the bow and arrow, the blowpipe and the boomerang.

◄ *Early humans developed more sophisticated methods of hunting, including weapons, traps and fire.*

# SHARKS

## SHARK ANATOMY

## HOW SHARKS LIVE

## SHARK SPECIES

## SHARKS AND PEOPLE

## SHARK SCIENCE

# All about sharks

- **Sharks are a type of fish.** They live and breathe underwater and are brilliant swimmers.

- **All sharks are carnivores,** which means they eat other animals. Many are fierce hunters.

- **Sharks are found in seas and oceans** and in a few rivers too.

- **There are about** 400 different species of shark.

- **A species is the name for a particular type of shark** or other living thing. Sharks of the same species can mate and have young.

- **Most sharks have long bodies,** triangle-shaped fins and lots of sharp teeth.

◀ *A great white shark on the prowl. Many sharks hunt and eat other types of fish, as well as all kinds of sea creatures.*

- **Sharks range in size** from about the size of a banana to bigger than a bus.

- **Sharks are closely related to other fish called rays** and skates. They are similar to sharks but usually have much flatter bodies.

- **Sharks have existed** for almost 400 million years.

- **Most sharks are not dangerous.** Only a few species have been known to attack humans.

# Shark shapes

- **A typical shark** has a long, narrow, torpedo-shaped body, designed for moving quickly through the water.

- **All sharks,** even unusually shaped ones, have the same basic body parts: a head with eyes, nostrils and a mouth, a body, a tail and fins.

- **A body shape designed for speed,** like a shark's, is called a 'streamlined' shape. It allows water to move past it easily with very little resistance or 'drag'.

- **The tip of a shark's nose** is called the snout. Most sharks' snouts are pointed, like the tip of a bullet.

- **A shark's mouth** is usually a long way back underneath its snout.

> ★ **STAR FACT** ★
> Some sharks can change shape. Swell sharks inflate their bodies with water or air to make themselves bigger and rounder.

- **Hammerhead sharks** get their name because their heads are shaped like wide, flat hammers.

- **Angel sharks** have wide, spread-out fins that look like an angel's wings.

- **Engineers sometimes study** sharks' fins and bodies to determine the best shapes for aeroplane wings or boat hulls.

- **Some large fish,** such as tuna, are shaped like sharks.

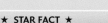

◀ *Due to the strange shape of their heads, hammerhead sharks are probably the easiest to recognize of all sharks.*

# Shark sizes

◄ Although sharks vary greatly in size, most of them have similar torpedo-shaped bodies that enable them to cut through water at speed.

- The whale shark is the biggest living shark. It can reach a maximum size of 18 m – as long as two buses end-to-end.

- The biggest shark ever, *Megalodon*, is now extinct. Scientists think it may have weighed almost twice as much a whale shark.

- The biggest sharks are gentle creatures that filter tiny food particles from the water.

- The biggest hunting shark is the great white shark.

- A great white shark's mouth can measure up to 40 cm across.

- Most sharks are medium-sized, measuring between 1 m and 3 m in length.

- The smallest sharks are the spined pygmy shark and the dwarf lanternshark. They would fit on two pages of this book.

- The average size for a shark is very similar to the size of a human.

- Although some sharks are small, most are bigger than other types of fish.

- Sharks aren't the biggest animals in the sea. Some whales are bigger – but they are mammals, not fish.

▲ This is a whale shark, the biggest shark of all. It swims along with its mouth wide open in order to collect food from the water.

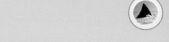

# Inside a shark

> ★ STAR FACT ★
> The insides of a shark's intestines, or guts,
> are spiral-shaped. Because of this, some
> sharks have spiral-shaped droppings!

- **Sharks are vertebrates** – they have a skeleton with a backbone. Many types of animals, including all fish, reptiles, birds and mammals, are vertebrates.

- **Sharks' skeletons** are not made of bone, but of cartilage (see bendy bones).

- **Sharks have thick layers of muscles** just under their skin. They are used to move the body from side to side as it swims.

- **Most of a shark's vital organs** are in a cavity in the middle of its body. Sharks have many of the same organs as other animals.

- **Sharks' livers** contain a lot of oil. Oil is lighter than water, so this helps it to float.

- **A shark's stomach is stretchy**. It can expand so that the shark can consume large amounts of food quickly.

- **Just like humans**, sharks have a heart that pumps blood around their bodies.

- **Most sharks are cold-blooded**, which means their blood is the same temperature as the water around them.

- **A few sharks are warm-blooded** – they can heat their blood to be warmer than their surroundings. This helps them to swim faster and move into cooler water to hunt.

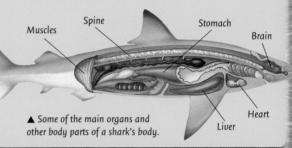

Muscles · Spine · Stomach · Brain · Heart · Liver

▲ Some of the main organs and other body parts of a shark's body.

# Bendy bones

- **Cartilage** is the white or pale blue, rubbery, bendy substance that sharks' skeletons are made of.

- **A shark's bendy skeleton** gives it flexibility, helping it to twist and turn in the water.

- **Although human skeletons** are made of bone, they have a small amount of cartilage too. It can be felt in the bendy tip of the nose.

- **Cartilage can also be found in meat**. It's the tough, chewy substance that's usually called 'gristle'.

- **As well as being very flexible**, cartilage is lighter than bone, giving sharks lots of strength without making them heavy.

- **Most other fish have bones** instead of cartilage. They are called 'bony fish', while sharks, rays and skates are known as 'cartilaginous fish'.

- **Sharks' fins and tails** contain hundreds of thin rods of cartilage, which stiffen them and give them their shape.

> ★ STAR FACT ★
> Some sharks are so flexible, they can bend right
> around and touch their tails with their snouts.

- **A shark's spine and skull** are harder than the rest of its skeleton. They need to be stronger to hold the body together and protect the brain.

- **Sharks have simpler skeletons** than most other bony fish, with fewer ribs and other parts.

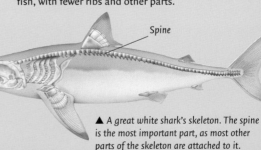

Spine

▲ A great white shark's skeleton. The spine is the most important part, as most other parts of the skeleton are attached to it.

# Shark skin

- **Sharks don't have scales**, like other fish. Instead their skin is covered with tiny, hard points called denticles.

- **The word 'denticle'** means 'little tooth' – because denticles are very similar to teeth.

- **Denticles make a shark's skin** feel very rough to the touch. Some swimmers have been badly scratched just from brushing against a shark.

- **Denticles have two uses:** they protect the shark from enemies and help it to slide through the water.

- **Denticles range** from microscopic in size to about 5 mm across.

- **The shape of denticles varies** on different parts of a shark's body, and from one shark species to another.

◄ Along with its streamlined shape, the denticles on a shark's skin helps it to slide smoothly through the water.

- **Denticles on the side** of a shark are the sharpest – ensuring fast movement through the water.

- **Sharks also release** a slimy substance from their skin, to make their bodies move through the water even faster.

- **Large sharks have very thick skin** – thicker than a human finger.

★ STAR FACT ★
Shark skin is so rough that in the past it was used to make a type of sandpaper, called shagreen.

# Tails and fins

- **A typical shark** has up to seven fins, not including its tail. Fins help sharks to swim and cut through water.

- **The big fin on a shark's back** is called the dorsal fin. It's the one that can be seen sticking out of the water in shark films. A shark's dorsal fin stops its body swinging from side to side while swimming.

- **A shark's tail** is also known as its 'caudal fin'. The anal fin is just in front of the tail.

- **A shark's tail is made up of** two points called lobes – an upper lobe and a lower lobe.

★ STAR FACT ★
Without their fins, sharks wouldn't be able to stay the right way up. They would roll over in the water.

- **There are two large pectoral fins** near the front of a shark's body, a bit like arms. The shark uses them to steer while swimming.

- **Epaulette sharks** use their pectoral fins like legs to 'crawl' along the seabed.

- **In parts of Asia**, people use sharks' fins to make a special kind of soup.

- **Thresher sharks** can be recognized by their very long upper tail lobes.

- **A whale shark's pectoral fin** can be a massive 2 m long – that's as big as a bed!

Anal fin

Dorsal fin

Pectoral fin

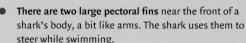

◄ Hammerhead sharks have very long dorsal fins.

# Spikes and spines

- **Many prehistoric sharks** had sharp spines in front of their dorsal fins. Scientists think these may have helped to hold the fins up.

- **Today**, only a few sharks have spines, spikes or sharp horns on their bodies. They usually use them to fight off attackers.

- **Some dogfish sharks** and horn sharks have two sharp 'fin spines' in front of their dorsal fins, which can inflict a painful wound.

- **The spined pygmy shark** is the only shark that has just one spine, not two or none.

- **Stingrays**, which are related to sharks, have poisonous stings in the middle of their tails.

- **Smaller sharks** are more likely to have spines. They are most at risk of being eaten, so they need defences that will deter their enemies from biting them.

- **Spiny dogfish** coil themselves right around their enemies to stab them with their spines.

- **Shark spines** are made of modified, extra-large denticles.

- **Saw sharks** have long, saw-shaped snouts, edged with sharp teeth.

- **A sawfish** is a type of ray, and is closely related to sharks. Its sharp, spiky snout can grow to almost 2 m long.

◀ *Saw sharks have small, sharp spikes along their long snouts. They use their snouts to slash at fish or to dig for prey in the seabed.*

# Shark vision

- **Most sharks** have big eyes and good eyesight. They mainly use it to spot their prey.

- **Sharks need to be able to see well** in the dark, as there is limited light underwater.

- **Many sharks** have a layer called the *tapetum lucidum* at the back of their eyes. It collects and reflects light, helping them to see, even in the gloomy darkness.

- **The *tapetum lucidum*** (Latin for 'bright carpet') makes sharks' eyes appear to glow in the dark.

- **Some sharks** have slit-shaped pupils, like a cat's.

- **Scientists think** sharks can probably see in colour.

- **Some very deepwater sharks** have small eyes and poor eyesight. The deepest oceans are so dark, many animals living there rely on other senses instead.

- **Sharks have a third eye**, called a pineal eye, under the skin in their foreheads. It can't see as well as a normal eye, but it can sense daylight.

★ **STAR FACT** ★
Most sharks never close their eyes. Some have special see-through eyelids that protect their eyes without cutting out any light. Others just roll their eyes up into their head to protect them.

- **The shy-eye shark** gets its name because when it is caught, it covers its eyes with its tail to shield them from the light.

▶ *A close-up of a tiger shark's eye, showing a special eyelid called the nictitating membrane. This closes over the eye when the shark is about to bite, to protect it from being damaged.*

# Sensing sounds

- **Sharks have ears**, but they're very hard to spot. Their openings are nothing more than tiny holes, just behind the shark's eyes.

- **If you think you can see a shark's ears**, you're probably looking at its spiracles, which can look a bit like ears, but are in fact used for breathing.

- **In the sea**, sound travels in the form of vibrations rippling through the water. Sharks hear by sensing these vibrations.

- **Inside a shark's ear** is a set of looping, fluid-filled tubes called the 'labyrinth'.

- **Sharks hear** using tiny microscopic hairs inside the labyrinth. Vibrations travel through the fluid, moving the hairs, which send signals to the shark's brain.

◀ Scientists and tourists sometimes use cages to safely get close to sharks.

- **A shark's hearing** is its best long-distance sense. Some sharks can hear sounds from several kilometres away.

- **Sharks are best at hearing low sounds**, such as the noise made by an injured animal underwater.

- **Ears also help sharks** to keep their balance. Movements of the fluid inside their ears tell them which way up they are.

- **Some sharks can recognize** the clanking sound of shark-watching cages. When they hear it, sharks may try to find the cages, in the hope of being fed.

> ★ STAR FACT ★
> Although sharks can hear sounds, they rarely make a noise.

# Touch and taste

- **Like us**, sharks can feel things that touch their skin. They can also feel things that are nearby, from the ripples they make as water flows around them.

- **Like humans**, sharks have nerve endings all over their skin that can feel pressure, temperature and pain.

- **Sharks also have an extra sense organ** called the 'lateral line'. This is a long tube running down each side of a shark's body, under its skin.

- **As a shark swims**, ripples in the water pass into the lateral line through tiny holes in the skin. Hairs inside the lateral line sense the ripples, and send signals to the shark's brain.

- **All fish**, not just sharks, have lateral lines.

> ★ STAR FACT ★
> A shark can sense a turtle, octopus or other prey from up to 20 m away.

- **Sharks use their sense of touch** to navigate. They can 'feel' where obstacles are, even if they can't see them.

- **Sharks have taste buds** inside their mouths.

- **As well as tasting the food they eat**, sharks can taste chemicals dissolved in the water. This helps them to find prey and avoid pollution.

- **Some sharks have fleshy 'whiskers'** on their snouts, called barbels. These can sense the location of food on the seabed.

The lateral line

◀ The lateral line runs down the side of the shark's body, from its gills to its tail.

# Sensing smells

- **The sense of smell** is the most important sense for most sharks.

- **As a shark swims**, water constantly flows into the nostrils on its snout, and over the scent-detecting cells inside them.

- **Sharks can smell blood in water**, even if it's diluted to one part in ten million. That's like one drop of blood mixed into a small swimming pool.

- **A shark can smell an injured animal** up to 1 km away.

- **The biggest part of a shark's brain** is the olfactory lobe – the part used for processing smells.

- **The great white shark** has biggest olfactory lobe of all – which means it probably has the best sense of smell of any shark.

- **Swimmers have been known to attract sharks** just by having a tiny scratch on their skin.

- **Sharks use their nostrils** for smelling, not breathing.

- **A shark homes in on a scent** by zig-zagging its snout from side to side. It moves towards the side where the smell is strongest.

▼ *A great white shark hunting, trying to detect traces of blood from injured fish or other animals. The water flows into the nostrils at the front of its snout as it swims along.*

> ★ STAR FACT ★
> In one experiment, a scientist plugged a shark's nostril. It swam around in a circle!

# The sixth sense

- **A shark has six senses**. Besides vision, hearing, touch, taste and smell, sharks can also sense the tiny amounts of electricity given off by other animals.

- **To detect electricity**, a shark has tiny holes in the skin around its head and snout. They're called the 'ampullae of Lorenzini'.

- **Ampullae** are a type of Roman bottle. The ampullae of Lorenzini get their name because of their narrow-necked bottle shape.

- **Each ampulla** contains a jelly-like substance, which collects electric signals.

- **All animals** give off tiny amounts of electricity when their muscles move. Electricity doesn't travel well through air, but it travels well through water.

- **A shark's ampullae of Lorenzini** can sense animals within a range of about one metre.

- **Some sharks** use their electrical sense to find prey that's buried in the seabed.

- **A fierce hunting shark** such as a tiger shark has up to 1500 ampullae of Lorenzini.

- **Stefano Lorenzini** was an Italian anatomist (body scientist) who studied the ampullae of Lorenzini.

◀ Each ampulla looks like a tiny hole. Beneath the surface of the skin it opens into a wider bottle shape.

# Smart sharks

- **Most sharks** have big brains for their body size and are probably smarter than many bony fish.

- **Almost all of a shark's brain** is used for processing information from the senses.

- **The brain parts** used for learning and thinking are quite small in sharks.

- **In relation to their body size**, hammerhead sharks have the biggest brains.

- **In captivity**, some sharks have learned to do simple tasks in exchange for a reward.

- **Experiments with lemon sharks** show they can recognize different shapes and colours.

- **Some sharks are brighter than others**. Fast hunters such as great whites are the most intelligent. Slow-moving bottom-feeders like carpet sharks are less smart.

- **Scientists used to think** all sharks had little intelligence. They have only recently started to learn about how their brains work.

- **Sharks can be trained** to fetch rubber rings, just like a dog fetching a stick.

◀ A scalloped hammerhead, one of the smartest sharks. Hammerhead sharks are fast, fierce hunters. They also spend time in groups and scientists think they have simple social systems.

# How sharks breathe

- **Like most animals,** sharks need to take in oxygen to make their bodies work.

- **Like other fish,** sharks breathe underwater using gills in their throats.

- **Most sharks have five pairs of gills.** Each gill is made up of a set of hair-like filaments full of blood vessels.

- **Many sharks have extra breathing holes** called spiracles, just behind their eyes, that take in water for the shark to breathe.

- **Sharks do not have lungs** – their gills do the same job that lungs do in humans.

- **As a shark swims,** water flows into its spiracles or mouth and past the gills, where oxygen is taken out of the water into the shark's bloodstream.

- **The water flows out again through the gill slits** – the lines you can see on the sides of a shark's neck.

> ★ STAR FACT ★
> Sea water contains just one percent oxygen gas – much less than air, which is 21 percent oxygen.

◀ *The five gill slits on this silky shark's throat are clearly visible.*

- **Some fast sharks,** such as mako sharks, have to swim continuously so that water flows over their gills and they can breathe. If they stop, water stops flowing past their gills and they suffocate.

- **Slow-moving sharks** such as the Port Jackson shark are able to pump water across their gills using the muscles of their mouth and neck, so they can stop for a rest and still keep breathing.

# How sharks swim

> ★ STAR FACT ★
> If sharks don't keep swimming, they gradually sink onto the seabed.

- **A shark's main swimming organ** is its tail. A shark thrashes its tail to push itself through the water.

- **Sharks use their pectoral and pelvic fins** to help them steer and swim upwards and downwards.

- **The fastest shark** is the shortfin mako shark, which has been recorded swimming at over 55 km/hour.

- **Most sharks** have an everyday cruising speed of around 8 km/hour.

- **Sharks normally swim** with a regular rhythm. They don't dart around like most bony fish do.

- **Other bony fish** have a swim bladder – a gas-filled organ that keeps them afloat. Sharks don't have swim bladders, so they are slightly heavier than water.

- **Many sharks swim** in a figure-of-eight pattern when they are annoyed.

- **Sharks are streamlined** so they can swim very quietly.

- **Some sharks swallow air** to help them to float better.

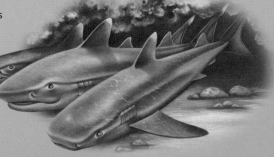

▶ *White-tip reef sharks often stop swimming to rest on the seabed. As they are heavier than water, they have to start swimming again if they want to move off the seabed.*

# Shark teeth

- **A hunting shark,** such as a great white or a tiger shark, has several rows of teeth.

- **A shark's gums** are like a conveyor belt. The rows of teeth constantly move slowly forwards. Gradually the front row wears out, and a new row replaces them.

- **Only the two front rows of teeth** are used for biting. The rest are just lining up to replace them.

- **In a lifetime,** some sharks will get through 30,000 teeth altogether.

▲ A great white shark stretches its mouth wide open, revealing its sharp, triangle-shaped teeth.

- **You can sometimes find** sharks' old, used teeth washed up on beaches.

- **Shark's teeth** really are as sharp as razors. Each tooth has serrated edges, with tiny, sharp points on them, like a saw, for cutting through meat.

- **The biggest shark teeth** belong to the great white shark. They can grow to over 6 cm long.

- **Some sharks,** such as smooth-houndsharks, don't have sharp biting teeth. Instead they have hard, flat plates in their mouths for grinding up crabs and shellfish.

- **The sand tiger shark** has the deadliest-looking teeth – but they are only used for catching small fish.

◄ A tiger shark's teeth have very sharp, serrated edges, like a sharp knife. This helps the teeth to cut through flesh.

# What sharks eat

- **Most sharks** eat many different kinds of animals.
- **Big, fast hunting sharks**, such as great whites and bull sharks, feed on large fish (including other sharks), as well as seals, turtles, octopuses, squid, seabirds and other sea creatures.
- **Many smaller sharks**, such as dogfish sharks, hunt smaller fish, octopuses and squid.
- **Slow-moving sharks**, such as nurse sharks, angel sharks and carpet sharks, crunch up crabs, shrimps and shellfish that they find on the seabed.

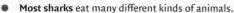

▼ Hammerhead sharks prey on other sharks, rays, bony fish, crabs and lobsters, octopuses and squid.

- **Filter-feeders** are sharks that feed on plankton – tiny floating animals and plants – which they filter out of the water.
- **There are hardly any animal species** in the sea that aren't part of the diet of one shark or another.
- **Tiger sharks are well-known for eating anything** they can find, including objects that aren't food, such as tin cans.
- **After being eaten**, food stays in a shark's stomach for up to three days.
- **Most sharks don't eat every day.** Some big hunters can go without food for months.

> ★ STAR FACT ★
> Sharks generally prefer the taste of fish, seals and turtles to the taste of humans.

# How sharks hunt

- **Most sharks are nocturnal** – which means they hunt at night, or crepuscular – which means they hunt at dusk.
- **Before attacking**, some sharks 'bump' their prey with their snouts, probably to see if it's something edible.
- **When about to bite**, a shark raises its snout and thrusts its jaws forward, so that its teeth stick out.
- **Some sharks shake their prey** from side to side to rip it apart.
- **Sharks don't usually chew** – they tear their prey into chunks or just swallow it whole.
- **Some sharks will attack** animals that are much bigger than themselves.
- **Sometimes**, lots of sharks are attracted to a source of food, and they all jostle to eat it at the same time. This is known as a 'feeding frenzy'.

◀ This great white is taking a bite out of a piece of meat dangled from a boat. Although it isn't hunting, you can see it is thrusting its teeth forward to attack.

- **Most hunting sharks** prefer prey that's weak or helpless, because it's easier to catch. That's why sharks are good at smelling blood – it tells them when an animal is injured.
- **Many sharks give their prey a fatal bite**, then leave it to bleed to death. They then return to feed on the body.

> ★ STAR FACT ★
> Sharks have very strong jaws. They can bite other animals in half – even those with tough shell, such as turtles.

# Filter-feeding

- **The biggest sharks of all** – whale sharks, basking sharks and megamouths – eat the smallest prey – plankton. These sharks are the filter-feeders.

- **Plankton** is made up of small sea creatures such as shrimps, baby crabs and squid, little fish and tiny free-floating plants. It drifts along with the currents.

- **Filter-feeding sharks** have 'gill rakers'. These are special comblike bristles in their throats that sieve plankton out of the water.

- **Gill rakers** are coated in sticky mucus to help plankton to stick to them.

*Plankton*

- **Filter-feeding sharks swallow the plankton** they have collected, while the water they have sieved escapes from their gills.

◀ *Whale sharks are filter-feeders. Although they are huge, they feed on some of the tiniest animals in the sea – plankton.*

- **Filter-feeders have massive mouths** so they can suck in as much water as possible.

- **To collect a kilogram of plankton**, a shark has to filter one million litres of water.

- **In one hour**, a whale shark filters around 2 million litres of water, and collects 2 kg of food.

- **Whale sharks** sometimes suck in shoals of little fish, such as sardines, that are also busy feeding on plankton.

- **Some other big sea creatures** – such as the blue whale, the world's biggest animal – are also filter-feeders.

# Scavenging

**★ STAR FACT ★**
In Australia in 1935, a tiger shark vomited up a human arm. The shark had not killed anyone but had scavenged the arm after a murder victim had been cut up with a knife and thrown into the sea.

- **Scavenging** means feeding on other hunters' leftovers or on animals that are dying or already dead.

- **Almost all sharks** will scavenge if they can't find other food.

- **Some sharks**, such as the Greenland shark and the smooth dogfish, get a lot of their food by scavenging.

- **Sharks in deep water** often feed on dead sea creatures that sink down from higher levels.

- **Sharks are much more likely to eat people** who have already drowned than they are to attack living people.

- **Sharks scavenge humans' food too** – especially waste food that's thrown overboard from ships.

- **Sharks sometimes eat fish** caught in fishing boats' nets before they can be pulled to the surface.

- **Great white sharks love to scavenge** – especially on the bodies of dead whales.

- **Scavenging is kind of natural recycling**. It keeps the oceans clean, and makes sure leftovers and dead animals are rapidly recycled rather than left to slowly decompose.

◀ *Sharkwatchers make use of the great white's scavenging behaviour, drawing it close to their boat using a chunk of meat attached to a line.*

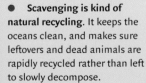

# Lighting up

- **Some sharks** can glow in the dark.

- **When animals give off light,** it's known as bioluminescence, which means 'living light'.

- **Glowing sharks** are often found in the deepest, darkest oceans.

- **Some deep-sea glowing sharks,** such as the velvet belly shark, may use their lights to illuminate their surroundings and help them see their prey.

- **Lanternsharks** have glowing dots around and inside their mouths. This may attract small fish and lure them into the shark's mouth.

- **Some sharks that live at medium depths** have glowing undersides. This makes them hard to see from below, as their light bellies match the light coming down from the sea surface.

◄ Lanternsharks get their name from the glowing lights on their bodies, which help them to attract prey.

- **Sharks may use bioluminescence to communicate.** For example, green dogfish sharks feed in groups. Their light patterns may help them to find each other.

- **Glowing lights** may also help sharks to find a mate of their own species in the darkness of the deep ocean.

- **Bioluminescence** is made in tiny organs in the skin called 'photophores'. In a photophore, two chemicals are combined, creating a reaction that gives off light.

- **Some other animals** have bioluminescence too. They include deep sea fish such as the anglerfish, as well as fireflies and some types of worms.

# Staying safe

- **Smaller sharks** make a tasty snack for other animals, so they need to defend themselves against predators such as killer whales, dolphins and porpoises.

- **The biggest sharks are rarely eaten** by other sea creatures, but they can still be hunted by humans.

- **Sharks are good at hiding.** They slip in between rocks, or into caves to escape from their enemies.

- **When in danger,** some sharks swim in a jerky, random manner to confuse their attacker.

- **Thresher sharks** use their tails to fight off predators, as well as for attacking their own prey.

> ★ STAR FACT ★
> As another way to put off attackers, sharks can turn their stomachs inside out and vomit up their latest meal. Some predators eat the vomit instead of the shark.

- **Swell sharks** can inflate their bodies while in a small space between rocks. This wedges the shark into the space so that it can't be pulled out by a predator.

- **Sharks' skin** acts like armour, making it hard for predators to bite them.

- **Sharks with spines** can often put a predator off by giving it a sharp stab.

- **Most sharks are scared of humans.** If they hear divers, they will usually swim away quickly.

◄ When great whites feel threatened, they open their mouths wide to show off their sharp teeth.

# Sharks in disguise

- **Many sharks** can disguise themselves to look like their surroundings. This is called 'camouflage'.

- **Camouflage** is a good way to hide from enemies, but it can also be used to help sharks sneak up on their prey without being seen.

- **Many small sharks**, such as zebra sharks, epaulette sharks and wobbegongs, have brown or grey patterns to help them blend in with coral and seaweed.

- **Sharks are often darker** on their top half and paler on their bottom half. This is called countershading.

- **A shark with countershading** viewed from below will blend with the brightly lit sea surface. Seen from above, it blends with the murky depths.

- **Some wobbegong sharks** have barbels that look like seaweed around their mouths. The fake seaweed tricks fish to come close so the wobbegong can catch them.

- **Angel sharks** have very flat, smooth bodies. When they lie on the sandy seabed they become almost invisible.

- **The shovelnose shark** or guitarfish (really a type of ray) disguises itself by burying itself under the seabed, with only its eyes sticking out.

- **The cookie-cutter shark** uses patches of light on its skin to attract hunting fish, seals or whales to come close – then the cookie-cutter takes a bite out of them.

- **When leopard sharks are young**, they have spots to help them hide. As they get older and bigger they don't need so much protection, and the spots fade.

◀ *A silvertip shark demonstrates the countershading that many sharks have – pale skin on the underside, and darker skin above.*

# Loners and groups

- **Many sharks**, such as whale sharks and bull sharks, are solitary. This means that they like to live alone.

- **Sharks don't live in families**. They meet up to mate, but a mating pair do not live together. Their young do not live with them either.

- **Some sharks form groups** with other members of their species. White-tip reef sharks, for example, often rest together in small groups of about ten individuals.

- **Sharks may form groups** because there's safety in numbers. A group of sharks are less likely to be attacked than a single shark.

- **Hammerhead sharks** prefer to live in groups. They travel in shoals of hundreds of sharks.

★ STAR FACT ★
Groups of nurse sharks sometimes relax by lying in a heap on the seabed.

- **Being in a group** may help sharks to find a mate.

- **Some species**, such as lemon sharks, form single-sex groups of just males or just females. Scientists are not sure why.

- **Porbeagle sharks** have been seen playing together in groups of about 20.

- **Great whites** are usually solitary, but scientists have found that they sometimes hunt in pairs.

◀ *Hammerheads are happy to spend time swimming together in huge shoals.*

# Meeting and mating

- **Like most animals**, sharks have to mate in order to reproduce.

- **Mating happens** when a male and a female of the same species meet up, and the male gives the female some cells from his body. This allows her to make new young inside her body.

- **Nurse sharks**, blue sharks and many other species have special mating areas in shallow parts of the sea.

- **In other species**, such as white-tip reef sharks, the females release pheromones to help the males find them.

- **Male sharks** sometimes bite female sharks to show they want to mate with them.

- **Female sharks** often have thicker skin than males so that being bitten during courtship doesn't harm them.

- **When sharks mate**, the male uses two body parts called claspers to deliver cells into an opening in the female's body, called the cloaca.

- **Sharks often wind their bodies** around each other when they are mating.

- **Sharks don't mate very often**. In most species, they only reproduce only once every two years.

▼ Male white-tip reef sharks sometimes spend time resting in shallow water during the day. If they smell a pheromone scent from a female telling them she's looking for a mate, they will try to find her.

# Communication

- **Animals don't have complicated languages** like humans do – but they can still communicate.

- **When they are close together**, sharks can 'talk' using body language. They make different postures, just as humans show their feelings by making faces.

- **For example**, when a shark is annoyed or frightened, it arches its back, raises its snout, and points its pectoral fins down.

- **Sharks also release special scents** called pheromones to send messages to other sharks. These can indicate if a shark is looking for a mate or feeling agitated.

- **Many other animals use pheromones too**, including moths, bees, pigs, deer, and humans.

★ STAR FACT ★
One shark kept in captivity could detect the minute electrical current caused by corroding metal near its tank.

- **When sharks live in a group**, the strongest ones usually become the leaders. They will sometimes have fights with the other sharks to show their dominance.

- **Bioluminescence** (lighting up) helps some sharks to communicate. It can help a shark recognize another shark of the same species in the dark.

- **Sharks may also be able to recognize each other** from the ripples their bodies make as they swim.

- **A few shark species** can make sounds. Swell sharks can make a barking noise, but experts are not sure if it's a way of 'talking'.

◀ This shark is displaying aggression. Its raised snout, arched back and lowered fins mean it's ready to attack.

# Shark eggs

- **Many sharks** have young by laying eggs, as most bony fish do. Sharks that do this are called 'oviparous' sharks.

- **Bullhead**, dogfish, horn, zebra and swell sharks are all oviparous sharks.

- **A typical shark** lays between 10 and 20 eggs at a time.

- **A mother shark** doesn't guard her eggs. She lays them in a safe place, such as between two rocks or under a clump of seaweed, then leaves them to hatch.

- **Sharks' eggs** are enclosed in protective egg cases. The egg cases come in many shapes, including tubes, spirals and pillow shapes.

★ STAR FACT ★
Catsharks' eggs have sticky strings on them that wind around seaweed, holding the eggs secure.

- **When the female first lays her eggs**, their cases are soft, but when they come in contact with the seawater, they get harder.

- **Like a chicken's egg**, a shark egg contains a yolk that feeds the baby as it grows bigger.

- **Inside the egg**, a shark baby grows for between six and ten months before hatching.

- **You can sometimes find empty shark eggcases** washed up on beaches. They're known as 'mermaid's purses'.

◀ A fully formed Port Jackson shark emerges from its spiral-shaped egg case.

# Shark young

- **Not all sharks lay eggs**. Some give birth to live young instead. They're called 'viviparous' or 'ovoviviparous' sharks.

- **In ovoviviparous sharks**, such as basking sharks, the young grow inside eggs, but hatch while they are still inside the mother's body, before being born.

- **In viviparous sharks**, such as hammerheads, there are no eggs. The babies grow inside the mother's body from the start.

- **Young sharks** are called pups.

- **When a shark pup is born alive**, it usually slips out of its mother's body tail-first.

- **Most shark pups** look like smaller versions of their parents, but with a narrower body shape and stronger colours.

▶ *Tiger shark pups are usually born at the end of spring or the beginning of summer. There can be between 10 and 80 pups in a litter.*

- **Some species**, such as sand tiger sharks, have just two pups in a litter.

- **Whale sharks** are thought to be able to give birth to up to 300 pups at a time.

- **Shark parents** don't look after their babies. Once a pup is born, or hatches from its egg, it has to look after itself.

- **In sand tiger sharks** and several other species, the biggest, strongest pups eat the others while they are still inside their mother's body.

# Growing up

- **Sharks grow slowly**. It can take a pup up to 20 years to grow into an adult.

- **Blue sharks are among the fastest growers**. A blue shark pup grows about 30 cm longer every year.

- **As shark pups are small**, predators often try to eat them. The biggest danger comes from other adult sharks. Sometimes, pups even get eaten by adults of their own species.

- **For every ten shark pups born**, only one or two will survive to be adults.

- **Many types of shark pups** live in 'nursery areas' – shallow parts of the sea close to the shore, where there are plenty of hiding places to shelter in and smaller sea creatures to feed on.

- **Sharks are born** with a full set of teeth, so they can start hunting for their own food straight away. Unlike the young of birds, humans, dogs and cats, shark pups are never fed by their parents.

- **Young sharks eat things** such as small fish, shrimps and baby octopuses.

- **A typical shark** lives for around 25 to 30 years, although some species, such as whale sharks and dogfish sharks, may live for 100 years or more.

- **When a shark dies**, scientists are able to tell how old it is by counting growth rings in its spine – like the rings inside tree trunks.

- **Even when they reach adulthood**, sharks don't stop growing. They just grow more slowly.

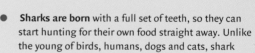

◀ *As a baby shark grows, it feeds on the yolk from its egg. This is a lanternshark pup with its yolk.*

# Shark companions

- There are several types of sea creatures that like to hang around sharks. They include some fish species, and many parasites that feed on a shark's skin, blood or insides.

- **Small crablike creatures** called copepods attach themselves to a shark's eyes, gills, snout or fins. They nibble the shark's skin or suck its blood.

- **Sea leeches** bite sharks on their undersides and suck their blood.

- **Barnacles** are tiny sea creatures with shells. They fix themselves to rocks, boats, and large animals such as whales and sharks.

- **Whale sharks** sometimes try to get rid of skin parasites by rubbing themselves against boats.

- **Inside their bodies**, many sharks have parasites such as tapeworms. They live in a shark's gut and feed on its food.

- **Pilot fish** swim alongside sharks to hitch a ride on the shark's slipstream – the currents it makes in the water.

- **Sometimes a shark** and another species can help each other. This kind of relationship between two animals is called 'symbiosis'.

- **Remoras or 'shark suckers'** are fish that attach themselves to sharks using suction pads on their heads. They hitch a ride on the shark's body and feed on scraps of food left over by the shark.

> ★ STAR FACT ★
> Sharks open their mouths to let tiny cleaner wrasse fish nibble lice and dead skin from between their teeth. As the wrasse are helping the sharks, they don't get eaten.

▼ A silvertip shark with a much smaller fish swimming along in its slipstream.

# Where sharks live

- **Sharks are found** in seas and oceans all around the world.

- **Sharks are almost all marine fish** – which means they live in the salty sea rather than in fresh water.

- **Just a few shark species** such as bull sharks and Ganges sharks can survive in fresh water, and swim out of the sea into rivers and lakes.

- **Sharks are most common around coasts.** Many species like to live in shallow sandy bays, near coral reefs, or in the medium-deep water a few miles from the shore.

◀ Hammerheads often swim close to the seabed, searching for buried fish and shellfish.

- **Coral reefs and seaweed forests** are a good home for young sharks. They provide them with food and shelter.

- **Sharks that live out in the open ocean**, such as blue sharks, are known as pelagic sharks.

- **Many types of sharks** spend most of their time on the ocean floor. They're called benthic sharks.

- **Many sharks like warm waters**, but a few, such as the Greenland shark, live in cold water around the Arctic.

- **Sharks are hardly ever found** in the Southern Ocean around Antarctica – probably because it's too cold for them there.

> ★ STAR FACT ★
> Epaulette sharks are often found in rock pools. They can move from one pool to another across dry land, by dragging themselves with their strong pectoral fins.

# Sharks at home

- **Most sharks** don't have a fixed home. They swim anywhere they like, looking for food or a mate.

- **Sharks don't build nests**, dig burrows, or make any other kind of shelter.

- **A territory** is an area that a wild animal marks out for itself and guards against rivals.

- **Many animals are territorial**, but scientists are still trying to find out how territorial sharks are.

- **Some shark species** seem to have a territory that they patrol and guard.

- **White-tip reef sharks** stay in the same area for several months or years, although they don't defend it like a true territory.

- **Some sharks**, such as horn sharks, pick a special nursery area to lay their eggs in.

> ★ STAR FACT ★
> The Portuguese shark has been found in depths of 2640 m – deeper than any other shark.

- **Some shark species**, such as nurse sharks, use underwater sea caves as a place to rest during the day.

- **Some sharks have special preferences** about where they live. The Galapagos shark is only found around groups of small oceanic islands.

▶ A nurse shark rests quietly in a cave in a coral reef. Many sharks use caves as hiding places.

# Long-distance travel

- **Many types of sharks** travel long distances in the course of their lives.

- **As all the world's seas and oceans** are connected, it's easy for sharks to cover huge distances.

- **Dogfish sharks** that have been tagged and released back into the sea can be located over 8000 km away from where they were first caught.

- **Migrating** means moving around, usually from season to season, according to a regular pattern.

- **The longest migrations** are made by blue sharks. They follow the Gulf Stream current across the Atlantic from the Caribbean Sea to Europe, then swim south along the African coast, then cross the Atlantic again to return to the Caribbean.

- **Blue sharks** can cover over 6000 km in one year.

- **Sharks sometimes migrate** in order to mate in one part of the sea, then move far away to another area to lay their eggs somewhere safer.

- **Another reason for sharks to migrate** is to follow shoals of fish as they move around the oceans, in order to feed on them.

- **Scientists think sharks** may use their ampullae of Lorenzini to detect the Earth's magnetic field, helping them to navigate over long distances.

- **Many sharks,** like spined pygmy sharks, spend the daytime in deep water, but swim up to the surface at night. This is called vertical migration.

▼ *This dogfish shark has been tagged by scientists so that they can keep track of how far it travels.*

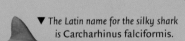

# Types of shark

- **Scientists divide the 400 species** of sharks into eight large groups, called orders, and around 30 smaller groups, or families.

- **Arranging sharks into groups,** or 'classifying' them, helps scientists to study them and identify them.

- **Scientists often disagree** about how to classify sharks, so there are several different ways to do it.

- **Shark orders and families** have long scientific names. For example, goblin sharks belong to the Mitsukurinidae family, in the order Lamniformes.

- **Some shark groups** have common names too. The Lamniformes, for example, are also known as mackerel sharks.

- **Each shark species** has its own scientific name, which is written in Latin. For example, the great white shark is *Carcharodon carcharias*.

▼ *The Latin name for the silky shark is Carcharhinus falciformis.*

- **Scientists decide** which group a shark belongs to by looking at things like its body shape, markings and behaviour.

- **Sometimes,** very different-looking sharks can belong to the same group. Huge whale sharks and small, slender epaulette sharks are both in the same order.

- **Some sharks** have several different names. For example, the sand tiger shark is also known as the sand shark, the ragged-tooth shark, or the grey nurse shark.

- **There may still be unknown types of sharks** that scientists have not yet discovered.

# Great white sharks

- **The great white** is the most famous of all sharks.
- **Belonging to the mackerel shark group**, great white sharks are fast, fierce hunters.
- **A typical great white shark** is around 4 to 5 m long – slightly longer than a car.
- **The biggest great whites** on record were over 7 m long.

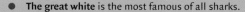

★ **STAR FACT** ★
Scientists do not know exactly how great whites reproduce, where they migrate to or how long they live.

- **Great white sharks** are often found in medium-warm waters such as those around Australia and Japan.
- **They sometimes attack humans**, but great whites much prefers to eat fish, seals and sealions.
- **Great white sharks are not white all over**. They are grey on top, with a pale grey or creamy underside.
- **When swimming**, great whites will sometimes stick their heads out of the water, or leap high into the air.
- **It is difficult** to keep a great white in captivity. If they are put into an aquarium, they only live for a few days.

◄ *Great whites have massive, powerful jaws and huge teeth, ideal for ripping viciously into their prey.*

# Mako sharks

◄ *The shortfin mako is the faster of the two species of mako shark.*

- **There are two species of mako** – the shortfin and the longfin. The longfin has longer pectoral fins.
- **The name 'mako'** comes from the Maori name for the shark, mako-mako – which means 'man-eater'. Makos are common around New Zealand, the home of the Maori people. They are also found in oceans all around the world.
- **Swift and fierce makos** are strong, muscular hunting sharks that can swim at great speed.
- **Makos are closely related** to great white sharks and live and hunt in a similar way. They will sometimes attack humans but they usually eat fish.
- **Makos have long, graceful bodies** and pointed snouts.
- **Makos are known for their vivid colours**. They are dark purplish-blue on top and silvery-white underneath.
- **Makos grow** up to 4 m long.
- **Mako sharks' teeth** are very narrow and pointed to help them grab slippery fish in their jaws.
- **People often fish for makos** as a sport and they are also caught to use as food.
- **Makos are also known as** bonito sharks or blue pointers.

# Thresher sharks

- **There are three species of thresher** – the common, the pelagic, and the bigeye thresher.

- **Thresher sharks** are easily recognized by their extremely long tails. The upper lobe, or part, of a thresher's tail can be up to 50 percent of the shark's whole body length.

- **Including the tail**, threshers can grow up to 6 m long.

- **Threshers use their amazing tails** to round up shoals of small fish such as sardines or herrings. Then they stun the fish by beating (or 'threshing') them with their tails, before eating them.

- **Although threshers are big**, their mouths are small so they only eat small prey.

- **Threshers hardly ever attack humans.** But they have been known to injure fishermen by hitting them with their tails.

▼ *Thresher sharks use their enormous tails by sweeping them from side to side. Because the tail is so long, its sweeping or 'threshing' movements can hit dozens of fish at once.*

★ STAR FACT ★
Thresher sharks have a reputation for being very cunning. Because of this, the ancient Greeks and Romans called them 'fox sharks'.

- **Common threshers** are the best-known and are often seen near the shore.

- **Pelagic threshers** get their name because they prefer to stay in the pelagic zone – the open sea, away from the shore.

- **Bigeye threshers** often live deep down in the sea. Their eyes are up to 10 cm across.

*The thresher's teeth are small and triangle-shaped, but they are very sharp*

*The thresher's tail can be up to 3 m long*

# Sandtiger sharks

- **A typical sand tiger shark** is around 3.2 m long.

- **Sand tiger sharks** are not closely related to tiger sharks. They belong to a different order, and are more closely related to makos and great whites.

- **Sand tiger sharks don't have stripes** – they have brownish spots instead.

- **They are called sand tiger sharks** because they swim over the sandy seabed, and because of their large teeth.

- **Sharks often circle their prey** before closing in for the kill.

- **Sandtiger sharks are not very dangerous** to humans.

- **The diet of sand tiger sharks** is mainly fish and sometimes they kill and eat bigger animals such as sealions.

**★ STAR FACT ★**
Sand tiger sharks have been known to approach divers who are spear-fishing, and grab the fish off their spears.

- **When hunting,** sand tiger sharks sometimes work in groups, surrounding a shoal of fish and feeding on them together, in a 'feeding frenzy'.

- **Sand tigers are popular in aquariums**, as they look exciting and survive well in captivity.

◄ *Sandtiger sharks can hold air in their stomachs so they can stay afloat without moving.*

# Porbeagle sharks

- **To help porbeagle sharks swim faster** they have a second keel (ridge) on their tails.

- **Like great white sharks**, porbeagles are grey on top and white underneath. Porbeagles also have a white mark on the dorsal fin.

- **Porbeagle sharks** grow up to 3 m long.

- **Cooler seas** are the preferred habitat of porbeagle sharks.

- **Porbeagles can make their bodies warmer** than their surroundings. This helps them to stay warm in their chilly habitat.

- **Porbeagle sharks used to be known as** mackerel sharks.

- **The diet of porbeagles** is mostly fish and squid. They will chase shoals of mackerel long distances.

- **Porbeagles are aggressive** and can attack people. However, these are very rare, because people don't usually swim in cold water.

- **Porbeagle sharks are among the few fish** that are known to play. They will roll over and over at the sea surface and wrap themselves in seaweed.

- **The name 'porbeagle'** is thought to be a combination of porpoise (which the porbeagle resembles) and beagle, a dog known for its determination and toughness.

▶ *A porbeagle shark chasing mackerel, its favourite food.*

# Basking sharks

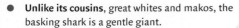

- **Unlike its cousins**, great whites and makos, the basking shark is a gentle giant.

- **The basking shark** is the second-biggest shark in the world, after the whale shark. It grows up to 9 m long – as long as five people lying end-to-end.

- **Basking sharks are filter-feeders**, and eat by sieving tiny animals, known as plankton, out of the water as they swim along.

- **Basking sharks are not interested** in eating humans – as they don't have big teeth for biting or chewing.

- **Basking sharks get their name** because they appear to 'bask', or lie in the sun, close to the surface of the sea. When they do this they are probably feeding.

◄ Krill are like tiny prawns. They are just one of the many small sea animals that make up the basking shark's diet of plankton.

- **Basking sharks will sometimes leap** right out of the water, and then flop back down with an enormous splash.

- **Other names for basking sharks** are bone sharks, elephant sharks, bigmouth sharks, or sunfish – because people used to think basking sharks enjoyed lying in the sun.

- **Occasionally** basking sharks have been seen swimming in large groups of 50 or more.

- **People used to catch basking sharks** and collect the oil from their livers to use as lamp fuel. Because basking sharks are so big, one basking shark liver could provide a huge amount of lamp oil.

> ★ STAR FACT ★
> Basking sharks have huge livers that weigh up to 2000 kg.

# Goblin sharks

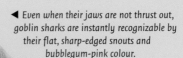

- **With incredibly long, flattened, pointed snouts**, goblin sharks look very strange. They can stick their jaws right out of their heads.

- **The goblin shark's long snout** looks like a weapon – but in fact scientists think it helps the shark find prey using its sense of electrical detection.

- **Goblin sharks** have pale pink skin which is much softer and flabbier than the skin of most sharks.

- **When its jaws are not pushed forward**, the goblin shark looks fairly similar to other sharks.

- **When it is about to catch prey**, a goblin shark thrusts its jaws out so far they look like a second snout.

- **Goblin sharks feed on fish**, squid and crustaceans such as crabs and lobsters.

◄ Even when their jaws are not thrust out, goblin sharks are instantly recognizable by their flat, sharp-edged snouts and bubblegum-pink colour.

- **A goblin shark has sharp teeth** at the front of its mouth for grabbing prey and smaller teeth at the back of its mouth for chewing.

- **Most goblin sharks** are between 1 m to 2 m long.

- **As goblin sharks are rarely caught** scientists still don't know much about them.

> ★ STAR FACT ★
> Goblin sharks probably got their name because of their strange appearance – although they don't really look like goblins!

# Crocodile sharks

- **Scientists** are still trying to find out more about the little-known crocodile shark.
- **When fully grown** crocodile sharks are quite small – around 1 m long.
- **The crocodile shark** has huge eyes compared to its body size. They take up almost half its head.
- **Female crocodile sharks** always give birth to four babies at a time.
- **Small fish**, squid and shrimps are the main diet of the crocodile shark.
- **Humans have only known about** crocodile sharks since 1936, when one was discovered in a fish market in Japan.

★ STAR FACT ★
Crocodile sharks cause problems for humans by biting through undersea communications cables.

- **The crocodile shark's name** comes from its Japanese name, mizuwani, meaning 'water crocodile'. It is so named because it has pointed teeth and snaps its jaws like a crocodile.
- **Crocodile sharks don't attack people**, but if caught they often bite fishermen on the hand.
- **One of the crocodile shark's closest relatives** is the megamouth shark – even though they're very different in size and feeding habits.

◀ Its *big teeth and large eyes make it look threatening, but the crocodile shark is no bigger than an average-sized dog.*

# Megamouth sharks

- **One of the most recently** discovered sharks is the megamouth. It is probably one of the rarest sharks.
- **The first known megamouth** was caught in 1976, off the islands of Hawaii.
- **The megamouth grows** to over 5 m long. It has a very thick, rounded, heavy body and a huge head.
- **Megamouth sharks are filter-feeders**. They feed at night, cruising along near the ocean surface with their mouths wide open to filter plankton out of the water.

▶ *It's easy to see how the megamouth got its name. Its mouth is so big, an armchair could fit inside it.*

★ STAR FACT ★
Less than 20 megamouth sharks have ever been found.

- **During the day,** a megamouth swims down to depths of 200 m or deeper.
- **The megamouth** gets its name because its mouth is so big – up to 1.3 m wide.
- **The scientific name** of the megamouth is *Megachasma pelagios*, which means 'huge yawner of the open sea'.
- **The mouth** of the megamouth shark is right at the front of its snout, not underneath as in most sharks.
- **Megamouths have been caught** around the world in the Pacific, Atlantic and Indian Oceans.

# Tiger sharks

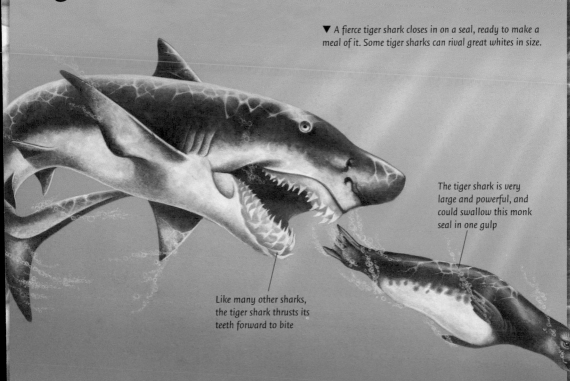

▼ A fierce tiger shark closes in on a seal, ready to make a meal of it. Some tiger sharks can rival great whites in size.

The tiger shark is very large and powerful, and could swallow this monk seal in one gulp

Like many other sharks, the tiger shark thrusts its teeth forward to bite

- **One of the most dangerous sharks in the sea** is the tiger shark. It will attack almost anything, including humans.

- **Tiger sharks are usually** about 3 m long, but they can grow to 6 m.

- **Young tiger sharks** have stripes to camouflage them and protect them from predators. As a tiger shark gets older, its stripes fade.

- **Tiger sharks have massive heads** with a blunt snout, large eyes and a wide mouth.

- **The diet of tiger sharks** consists of fish, seals, sealions, turtles, shellfish, crabs, seabirds, dolphins, crocodiles, squid and jellyfish. They also take bites out of bigger animals such as whales.

- **Tiger sharks have even been seen** eating other tiger sharks.

- **Many unusual objects,** such as oil drums, tin cans, glass bottles, clothes, rubber tyres, coal, cushions and tools, and even pieces of armour have been found in the stomachs of tiger sharks.

- **The tiger shark** is found in most of the world's warmer seas and oceans.

- **Tiger sharks sometimes swim** into the mouths of rivers.

> ★ STAR FACT ★
> Tiger sharks might eat metal objects because they give off a slight electrical signal, which the shark can detect with its electrical sense. It probably mistakes them for living things.

# Bull sharks

- **Bull sharks** are powerful, ferocious and aggressive hunting sharks.

- **The bull shark gets its name** because its body is thick, stocky and muscular, like a bull.

- **Like the tiger shark**, the bull shark belongs to a family of sharks called requiem sharks.

- **Requiem sharks** probably got their name because of the French word for shark, *requin*.

- **Bull sharks are not especially long** – they usually grow to between 2 to 3 m.

- **Bull sharks are among the few sharks** that can survive in fresh water. They swim hundreds of kilometres up rivers such as the Mississippi, the Amazon and the Zambezi.

- **One group of bull sharks** lives in Lake Nicaragua, a huge lake in Central America.

- **Bull sharks are often known by other names**, depending on where they live – such as the Zambezi river shark or the Nicaragua shark.

- **The bull shark is very dangerous**, and often lurks in shallow water where humans swim.

- **Bull sharks have attacked humans so often**, some experts think they may be the most dangerous sharks of all.

◀ A bull shark swims along in shallow water with a remora fish below it.

# Blue sharks

- **One of the fastest sharks** in the sea, blue sharks can reach a top speed of almost 30 km/h.

- **Sleek, slim and graceful,** the body of the blue shark is around 4 m long.

- **The blue shark really is blue**. It's a deep, silvery indigo on top, with a paler underside.

- **The migration route** of the blue shark is notoriously long. They travel right across oceans, making trips of 3000 km or more.

- **A blue shark can travel** more than 60 km in a day.

- **The blue shark was once** one of the most common sharks, and they are found in almost every part of every ocean. Its population is now falling fast because so many have been caught by humans.

◀ Blue sharks have very slender, flexible bodies, with long snouts and long, narrow fins.

- **Blue sharks are fished for food**, but many more are caught by accident by hooks or nets meant for tuna and swordfish.

- **Experts have estimated** that 6 million blue sharks are caught and killed every year.

- **Blue sharks eat mostly squid**, although they will try any kind of fish or other sea creature.

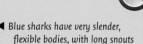

---

★ **STAR FACT** ★
Blue sharks don't normally attack people, but they have been reported to go into feeding frenzies to attack the survivors of sunken ships.

# White-tip sharks

- **There are two quite different sharks** that have the name 'white-tip' – the white-tip reef shark and the oceanic white-tip shark.

- **The white-tip reef shark** is a common shark about 1.5 m long.

- **Distinctive white tips** on their tails and dorsal fins make white-tip reef sharks easily recognizable.

- **Swimmers and divers** often spot white-tip reef sharks because they inhabit in coral reefs, sea caves and shallow water during the day.

- **Warm seas** such as the Persian Gulf and the waters around Australia and the Pacific islands are home to many white-tip reef sharks.

- **White-tip reef sharks go hunting** at night for squid and octopus.

- **White-tip reef sharks rarely bother people,** except to steal fish from fishing spears.

- **The oceanic white-tip shark** is a large, fast hunting shark, around 3 m long. It lives in the open oceans.

- **The oceanic white-tip shark sometimes,** but not always, has a white or pale grey mark on its dorsal fin.

- **Oceanic white-tips can be dangerous.** They are attracted to shipwrecks and plane wrecks in the sea, and may attack the survivors.

▶ A white-tip reef shark in its favourite habitat, a shallow coral reef. The white tips on its fins and tail make it easy to identify.

# Black-tip sharks

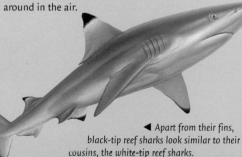

- **A medium-sized shark,** the black-tip reef shark is around 1.5 m long.

- **Like its cousin** the white-tip, the black-tip reef shark likes warm, shallow water.

- **Black-tip reef sharks** have black marks on the tips of all their fins.

- **Black-tips are sometimes** known as 'black sharks'.

- **The black-tip reef shark** has long, slender teeth ideally suited to snapping up its main prey – fish that live around coral reefs.

- **Scuba divers** often encounter black-tip reef sharks, but they're rarely aggressive – although they have been known to bite people's legs and feet.

- **Another shark, the spinner shark,** is also known as the black-tip shark. It's a completely different species from the black-tip reef shark, and grows to about 2 m long.

- **The black-tip or spinner shark** also has black tips on all its fins.

- **Spinner sharks get their name** because they sometimes leap out of the water and spin around in the air.

> ★ STAR FACT ★
> Since the Suez Canal was built, black-tip reef sharks have swum through it from the Red Sea, and now live in the Mediterranean Sea too.

◀ Apart from their fins, black-tip reef sharks look similar to their cousins, the white-tip reef sharks.

# Bonnethead sharks

- **Bonnetheads** are a type of hammerhead shark.

- **This shark's head** looks less like a hammer, and more like a rounded bonnet or shovel shape.

- **Bonnetheads** are the smallest hammerheads, averaging around 1 m long.

- **Bonnetheads form huge groups** – sometimes there can be thousands of them in a school.

- **The bonnethead shark** is often found in shallow bays and river estuaries. They mainly eat crabs, shrimps and other crustaceans.

- **Scientists think bonnetheads** have complex social systems, with different members of a group having different levels of importance.

- **Bonnetheads are also called bonnet sharks**, bonnetnose sharks, or shovelheads.

- **Fishermen have to be careful** if they grab a bonnethead by the tail, as it can reach up and bite their hand.

- **The scalloped bonnethead** is another type of hammerhead shark. Its bonnet-shaped head has curved or scallop-shaped lines on it.

◀ A bonnethead shark swallows a ray it has just found part-buried in the sand.

★ STAR FACT ★
Dominant bonnethead sharks keep other individuals in their place with behaviour such as head-shaking, jaw-snapping and butting.

# Hammerhead sharks

- **Hammerhead sharks** are probably the strangest-looking sharks of all. Their heads really do look like the ends of hammers.

- **A hammerhead's head** is extremely wide. The shark's eyes are at either end of the 'hammer', making them a very long way apart.

◀ A hammerhead shark's head is a wide, flat, oblong shape that looks like a hammer when seen from above.

- **Experts think hammerheads' heads** may help them to find food by spreading out their ampullae of Lorenzini (electrical detectors) over a wide area.

- **Seen from the side**, a hammerhead looks similar to a normal shark, as the 'hammer' is so flat and streamlined.

- **There are nine species of hammerhead**. They include great, scalloped, smooth, wingheads and bonnethead sharks.

- **The great hammerhead** is the biggest. It can reach 6 m long and has been known to attack humans.

- **Hammerheads go hunting alone** at night for fish, squid, octopuses, crabs and stingrays.

- **By day**, hammerheads often swim in large groups.

- **Hammerheads have unusually long dorsal fins**. They are often seen swimming with their dorsal fins sticking out of the water.

- **The winghead shark has the widest head** of any shark. It can measure as much as half the shark's body length.

# Lemon sharks

★ STAR FACT ★

When a male and female lemon shark meet up to mate, they swim along side by side, so closely that they can look like a two-headed shark.

▶ Lemon sharks really are lemon in colour. This helps to distinguish them from bull sharks, which are their close relatives.

- **The lemon shark** gets its name from its yellowish colour, especially on the underside.

- **Lemon sharks are fish-eating sharks** related to tiger and bull sharks.

- **Lemon sharks grow** up to 3 m long.

- **People sometimes confuse** lemon sharks with bull sharks, as they have a similar shape.

- **Apart from the colour**, you can tell a lemon shark because its two dorsal fins are almost the same size (in most sharks, the first dorsal fin is much bigger).

- **Lemon sharks survive** very well in captivity and might be seen in an aquarium or sealife centre.

- **Since lemon sharks can be kept in tanks**, scientists often use them for experiments.

- **When lemon sharks are young**, they eat small fish, sea worms and shrimps. As they get older, they feed on seabirds, rays and lobsters.

- **Lemon sharks have been found with stings** from stingrays embedded in their mouths.

# Houndsharks

- **There are over 30** different species of houndsharks.

- **Houndsharks** are a family of smallish sharks around 1.5 m long.

- **Most types of houndsharks** live on shallow seabeds, feeding on shellfish, crabs and lobsters.

- **Most houndsharks have flat teeth** used for crushing their prey.

- **Houndsharks** belong to a different shark order to dogfish and dog sharks.

- **Whiskery sharks** are a type of houndshark with barbels – finger-like organs on their snouts that look like whiskers. They help the shark feel its way along the seabed

- **The tope shark** is a houndshark with a pointy snout. It's also called the vitamin shark because it used to be hunted for its liver oil that was used as a health food.

◄ The leopard shark is one of the most distinctive of all sharks. They are between 1 to 2 m long.

- **The leopard shark** is an unmistakable species of houndshark. It gets its name from the beautiful leopard-like spots on its back.

- **Soupfin sharks** are houndsharks too. They get their name because their fins are used to make shark's fin soup – although other sharks are used for this too.

- **Gummy sharks** are another type of houndshark – named because they seem to have have no teeth. Like other houndsharks, they simply have flat, grinding teeth instead of sharp ones.

# Weasel sharks and catsharks

- **You can spot a weasel shark** because it looks as if it's had a bite taken out of its tail. This is actually a natural dent in the tail called the 'precaudal pit'.

- **Weasel sharks are a type of small shark** just over 1 m long.

- **There are several different species of weasel sharks,** including the hooktooth, the sickelfin weasel and the snaggletooth.

- **Catsharks** are a separate shark family from weasel sharks. There are over 40 catshark species.

- **Catsharks are less than 1 m in length** and eat small fish and crabs.

- **Catsharks get their name** because their eyes look like a cat's.

- **The lollipop catshark** is an unusual catshark with a very large head.

- **Many catsharks have beautiful markings.** The draughtboard shark, for example, is a catshark with dark and light checkerboard markings, while the chain shark has skin patterns that look like silver chains.

- **Shy-eye sharks** and swell sharks are both types of catsharks.

- **The false catshark** is not a catshark at all. At 3 m long, it's much bigger than a real catshark, and was given its name by mistake.

◄ Weasel sharks are related to bull and lemon sharks, and have a typical shark shape.

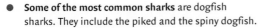

# Dogfish sharks

- **Some of the most common sharks** are dogfish sharks. They include the piked and the spiny dogfish.

- **There is a huge family** of dogfish sharks, containing around 80 different species.

- **Dogfish sharks usually have spines** in front of their dorsal fins and they have no anal fin at all.

- **Dogfish sharks range in size** from less than 20 cm long to over 6 m long.

- **Millions of dogfish sharks** are caught every year – for their meat but also for their fins, oil and skin.

- **Spiny dogfish sharks are ground up** to be made into garden fertilizer.

> **★ STAR FACT ★**
> In America, spiny dogfish used to be caught, dried and burnt as a fuel.

- **Spiny dogfish often cause problems** for fishermen. They tear up fishing nets and eat the fish and steal lobsters from lobster pots.

- **Many species of dogfish sharks** swim together in groups.

- **Dogfish sharks** may have got their name because they form packs, like dogs. In the past, any common type of plant or animal used to be given the name 'dog' – like the dog rose, for example.

◀ *A group of dogfish sharks on the prowl. They sometimes form schools of hundreds or even thousands of individuals.*

# Greenland sharks

> **★ STAR FACT ★**
> A reindeer was once found inside a dead Greenland shark's stomach.

- **The biggest type of dogfish shark** is the Greenland shark. It grows up to 6.5 m in length.

- **Greenland sharks** like cold water. They live in the north Atlantic, around Greenland, Iceland and Canada, and can stand temperatures as low as 2°C.

- **Gurry shark and sleeper shark** are other names for the greenland shark.

- **The Greenland is known as** the sleeper shark because it is sluggish and swims very slowly.

- **Luminescent copepods** (tiny sea creatures) live in the eyes of the greenland shark. They make the shark's eyes glow in the dark, which may help it by luring prey towards it.

- **Greenland sharks eat fish**, squid, seals and sealions, as well as scavenging on the dead bodies of whales.

- **In summer**, greenland sharks swim up to the surface to find food, but they spend the rest of their time swimming at depths of 1500 m.

- **Inuit people** caught Greenland sharks on lines through iceholes. They used the skin to make boots and the teeth for knife blades.

- **Fresh Greenland shark meat** is poisonous, but can be eaten safely if it is boiled several times.

◀ *Greenland sharks are unusual in choosing to live in the deep, icy waters of the arctic – most sharks prefer shallow, warm seas.*

# Dwarf and pygmy sharks

- **The smallest sharks in the world** are dwarf and pygmy sharks. The spined pygmy shark and the dwarf dogshark are both around 18 to 20 cm long.

- **The pygmy shark** or slime shark is around 25 cm long.

- **Sharks this small** are harmless to humans.

▶ *Working as a group, spined pygmy sharks can attack a fish much larger than themselves.*

- **The spined pygmy shark** lives as deep as 2000 m down during the day, but at night it swims up to hunt in shallower water about 200 m deep.

- **The dwarf dogshark** is also found at great depths – as deep as 1000 m.

- **Dwarf and pygmy sharks** all have luminous undersides.

- **Although dwarf and pygmy sharks are small**, they hunt just like many larger sharks, snapping up fish, shrimps and octopuses.

- **The spined pygmy shark** was first discovered in 1908, off the coast of Japan. We now know it lives all around the world. It is also called the cigar shark, because of its size, slim shape and dark colour.

- **Dwarf and pygmy sharks** are hard to keep in captivity, as they prefer very deep water.

# Prickly and bramble sharks

- **Almost all sharks** have rough skin, but the skin of prickly and bramble sharks is really rough.

- **The bramble shark** is a deepwater shark that has large, thornlike spikes scattered unevenly all over its body.

- **A bramble shark's spikes** are made of extra-large, extra-sharp denticles.

- **Bramble sharks grow** to about 3 m long.

- **Although they are large**, bramble sharks are rarely seen. This is because they live in deep water and are quite shy.

▼ *A bramble shark has the prickliest, roughest skin of any shark. Its whole body is scattered with sharp, thorny spikes.*

- **The prickly shark** is a relative of the bramble shark. It looks similar, but has smaller prickles.

- **Prickly sharks grow** to around 4 m long.

- **Prickly dogfish** belong to a separate family. They have deep bodies, and very rough skin rather than long prickles.

- **Though their skin is tough and prickly**, prickly dogfish have strangely soft, spongy lips.

# Cookie-cutter sharks

▲ Cookie-cutters open their mouths wide to bite circular lumps out of their prey. They rarely kill their victims.

- **Cookie-cutter sharks** are strange, deep water sharks that are found around the world.

- **There are two species**, the cookie-cutter and the large-tooth cookie-cutter.

- **The large-tooth cookie-cutter** is the smaller of the two, but it has bigger teeth. Its teeth are bigger in relation to its body size than those of any other shark.

- **Cookie-cutters belong** to the dogfish shark family.

- **Cookie-cutter sharks are brown** in colour, with greenish eyes.

- **Instead of eating whole animals**, cookie-cutters take bites out of much bigger sea creatures such as big sharks and whales.

- **To feed**, a cookie-cutter shark attaches itself to its prey by sucking with its mouth. Then it swivels its sharp teeth around in a circle until it has cut out a lump of flesh.

- **Cookie-cutters themselves are not big** – only around 50 cm long. Because they don't need to catch or kill their prey, they can feed on animals that are many times larger than they are.

- **Many sharks**, dolphins, porpoises and whales have permanent, round scars left by cookie-cutters.

▶ A close-up view of a cookie-cutter shark's unusual mouth and teeth.

★ STAR FACT ★
Cookie-cutters have been known to take bites out of parts of submarines and undersea cables.

# Carpet sharks

- **The carpet sharks** are a varied group of more than 30 different species of sharks.

- **Many carpet sharks** are less than 1 m long, but this group also includes the whale shark, the biggest shark of all.

- **Carpet sharks live** in warm tropical seas, like those around Australia, Indonesia and Arabia, and usually live in shallow waters around reefs and sandbars.

- **Carpet sharks like to lie still** on the seabed. Many of them have a slightly flattened body shape that helps them to camouflage themselves on the ocean floor.

- **Most carpet sharks** feed on seabed-dwelling prey such as crabs, shellfish, octopuses and sea worms.

- **Many carpet sharks** have beautiful speckled markings. They were named because these often resemble patterned carpets or tapestries.

- **Collared carpet sharks** can change colour to match their surroundings.

- **Epaulette sharks** are a type of carpet shark. They get their name because they have dark patches on their 'shoulders' – like epaulettes (cloth flaps) on a jacket.

- **Long-tailed carpet sharks** have extra-long tails, with long, fine fins that resemble fronds of seaweed.

- **The barbelthroat carpet shark** has barbels – fleshy finger shapes used for feeling things – on its throat. Only one example of this breed has ever been found.

▼ The massive whale shark belongs to the carpet shark group. Its relatives include tiny carpet sharks such as the epaulette shark.

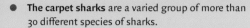

# Wobbegongs

- **Wobbegongs** belong to the carpet shark family.

- **The name 'wobbegong'** was given to these sharks by the Australian Aborigine people. Wobbegongs are often found in shallow, sandy water around the coast of Australia.

- **Wobbegongs can be quite large** – some, like the tasselled wobbegong, growing up to 4 m long.

- **Wobbegong have wide, flattened bodies** to help them hide on the seabed.

- **A typical wobbegong** has lots of barbels around its mouth.

- **The frilled wobbegong's barbels** are branched and frilly.

- **The tasselled wobbegong** has tassel-like barbels right around its face like a beard.

- **Wobbegong sharks**, also known as wobbies, feed on smaller fish and on other sea creatures such as crabs, octopuses and squid.

- **Wobbegongs have very strong jaws**, and can easily bite off a person's hand or foot.

- **Wobbegongs sometimes attack people** who accidentally step on them. For this reason, they have a reputation as being dangerous, although they are not interested in eating humans and rarely attack unless threatened.

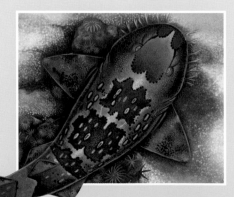

◄ A wobbegong shark lying in wait for prey on the seabed, disguised among seaweed and coral.

# Nurse sharks

- **The carpet shark group** includes nurse sharks, although unlike most carpet sharks they don't have carpet-like markings.

- **Nurse sharks** are usually brownish-grey, and sometimes have a few spots.

- **During the day**, nurse sharks often lie around on the seabed in groups.

- **At night**, nurse sharks wake up and go hunting.

- **Nurse sharks can reach** 4 m long, but most are nearer 3 m in length.

- **Nurse sharks have two barbels** hanging down underneath their noses. They use them to smell and feel their way along the seabed as they search for prey.

> ★ STAR FACT ★
> Divers sometimes grab nurse sharks' tails, hoping for a ride. The sharks don't like this and may turn around and bite.

- **Crabs, lobsters and sea urchins** are the preferred food of nurse sharks. They have flat, grinding teeth for crushing up shells.

- **If a nurse shark bites you**, it hangs on with a clamplike grip that's painful (though not deadly), and it can be almost impossible to dislodge them.

- **As they survive well in aquariums**, nurse sharks are often used in shark intelligence experiments.

◀ *A diver creeps close to a nurse shark hiding in a gap in a coral reef.*

# Blind sharks

- **The carpet shark group** includes the blind shark. This shark is not actually blind at all.

- **When they are caught** and pulled out of the water, blind sharks close their eyes tightly and appear to have no eyes.

- **Blind sharks live** off the coast of Australia and are often found in shallow water near the shore. They hide in caves or crevices during the day and hunt at night.

- **There are two species of blind shark**. One is simply known as the blind shark, while the other is called Colclough's shark or the bluegray carpet shark.

- **The blind shark is yellow underneath** and brownish on top, with pale spots.

- ◀ Blind sharks can see perfectly well in their natural habitat.

- **At 1.3 m in length**, the blind shark is slightly bigger than Colclough's shark, which is just under 1 m long.

- **Young blind sharks** have dark stripes or bands across their bodies, which fade as they grow older.

- **Colclough's shark**, as its other name suggests, is blueish-grey in colour.

- **Both types of blind shark** feed by snuffling along the seabed for cuttlefish, shellfish and crabs.

- **Blind sharks have large spiracles**. These help them breathe even when their snouts are buried in the muddy seabed to find food.

# Tawny and zebra sharks

> ★ STAR FACT ★
> The tawny shark has a powerful suck. It can use its mouth to suck prey such as fish and octopuses out of their hiding places.

- **Part of the carpet shark group**, tawny and zebra sharks are related to nurse, blind and whale sharks.

- **At 3 m in length**, the tawny shark is quite large. It lives in warm tropical seas close to the shore.

- **The tawny shark** is also known as the spitting shark because it spits out water as a defence if captured.

- **After spitting**, the tawny shark is said to grunt. It is one of the few sharks thought to make a noise.

- **The zebra shark** is another medium-sized carpet shark that grows up to 3 m long.

- **Distinctive dark and pale stripes** give zebra sharks their name – but they only have these when they are young. As they become adults, the stripes separate into blotches.

- **A zebra shark's egg cases** are a deep purplish-brown and have tufts of hair on them to help them lodge firmly among rocks and seaweed.

- **Like thresher sharks**, zebra sharks have very long tails.

- **Zebra sharks have long, hard ridges** running all the way down the backs and sides of their bodies. This helps divers to recognize them immediately.

◄ This adult zebra shark shows how some of its spots were once connected to form stripes.

# Whale sharks

- **The carpet shark group** also includes the whale shark.

- **Closest relatives of the whale shark** are wobbegongs and nurse sharks – not other filter-feeders like basking sharks and megamouths.

- **Whale sharks are the biggest sharks** in the world. Their average length is 10 to 12 m long – as long as a six or seven adult humans lying end-to-end.

- **The filter-feeding whale shark** sieves tiny plankton out of the water.

- **To feed**, whale sharks swim along with their massive mouths streched wide. A whale shark's mouth can be 1.5 m across.

- **A whale shark has around 3000 tiny teeth**, but it doesn't use them to eat with. Instead, it uses bristles in its gills to trap its food.

- **Whale sharks are covered** with pale stripes and spots.

▲ As a whale shark cruises along it sometimes swallows larger fish such as tuna, which can grow to 4 m long.

- **Scientists think** some whale sharks could live to be 100 years old or more.

- **Whale sharks might look dangerous**, but they're harmless to humans.

> ★ STAR FACT ★
> A whale shark's skin is around 10 cm thick, making it the thickest skin in the world.

# Hornsharks

- **The relatively small hornshark** has its own order, or shark group. It reaches 1.0 m to 1.5 m in length.

- **Hornsharks get their name** because they have poisonous spines, or horns, in front of both their dorsal fins.

- **Because of their large, rounded heads**, hornsharks are also called bullhead sharks.

- **Hornsharks have piglike snouts** and large lumps above their eyes that look like eyebrows.

◀ Hornsharks use the sharp spines near their fins to defend themselves against any predators that try to catch them.

- **Crabs and sea urchins are** the preferred food of hornsharks.

- **Hornsharks are only found** in the Pacific and Indian Oceans.

- **After laying**, the female hornshark takes each egg case in her mouth and jams it into a rock crevice to keep it safe. The eggcases are spiral-shaped.

- **Spines from hornsharks** are sometimes made into jewellery.

- **The Port Jackson shark** is a type of hornshark, named because it was discovered living in the bay of Port Jackson, Australia.

> ★ STAR FACT ★
> Some hornsharks have red-stained teeth because of all the sea urchins they eat.

# Angel sharks

- **The angel shark order** contains about ten species of sharks. They get their name because of their wide, winglike fins.

- **Monkfish** is another name for angel sharks, because people used to think their fins looked like a monk's robes.

- **Another name for angel sharks** is sand devils, because they lie on the seabed and sometimes bite people who tread on them.

- **Angel sharks have very flattened bodies**. Most are around 1.5 m long.

- **The biggest angel shark** is the Japanese angel shark, which reaches 2 m long. It is hunted for food and was once also used to make shagreen (sharkskin sandpaper).

◀ Angel sharks an be very hard to spot in its preferred habitat – the shallow, sandy seabed.

- **By burying themselves on the sandy seabed**, angel sharks are hidden from passing fish and shellfish. They leap out to catch their prey with their small but sharp teeth.

- **An angel shark can lie in wait** for over a week until the right food comes past.

- **Like wobbegongs** and other bottom-dwelling sharks, angel sharks are camouflaged with spotted, speckled skin patterns.

- **In some countries**, angel sharks are served as a delicacy in expensive restaurants, where they are always called monkfish.

- **Angel sharks are viviparous** – they give birth to live babies. There are usually around ten pups in a litter.

# Saw sharks

★ STAR FACT ★

Saw sharks aren't usually seen near the shore.
They prefer to live at depths of up to 400 m.

- **Part of an order of five species of shark**, saw sharks have flat heads and long, saw-shaped snouts.

- **A saw shark's snout is called a rostrum**. It is pointed and has teeth of various sizes, called rostral teeth, sticking out all the way around it.

- **At around 1 m in length**, saw sharks are relatively small.

- **For their size**, saw sharks' 'saws' are very long compared to other sharks' snouts. The snout of a longnose saw shark can make up half its total body length.

- **Saw sharks use their saws** for digging up prey such as shellfish from the seabed. Then they slash and jab at the prey before eating it.

- **The two long barbels** halfway along its snout help the saw shark feel its way along the seabed.

- **People sometimes eat saw sharks** in Japan and Australia.

- **Most saw sharks are grey**, but one species, the Japanese saw shark, is a muddy brown.

- **Saw sharks should not be confused** with sawfish, which are a type of ray.

▼ A saw shark hunting for food using its snout and sensitive barbels, which can feel, smell and taste its fishy prey.

# Frilled sharks

- **The frilled shark** is the only species in its family.

- **A strange-looking shark**, the frilled shark has big, frilly gill slits – the first pair reach right around its head like a collar.

- **The long, thin body of the frilled shark** reaches up to 2 m in length.

- **Frilled sharks** only have one dorsal fin, instead of two as in most sharks. This fin is positioned far back towards the shark's tail.

- **Because of its snakelike appearance**, the frilled shark is sometimes mistaken for an eel or a sea snake.

- **Found in the cold, deep water of the Pacific** and Atlantic Oceans, frilled sharks feed on octopuses and squid.

◀ The frilled shark is an extremely rare shark species.

- **With three sharp points** on each tooth, frilled sharks have very unusual teeth. This is one of the features that is used to identify this rare shark.

- **Frilled sharks** have six gill slits on each side. Only a few sharks have more than five (including the frilled shark's relatives, six-gill and seven-gill sharks, and the six-gill saw shark).

- **Scientists have found** that after female frilled sharks mate, they are pregnant for as long as three years.

- **People used to think** that the frilled shark had been extinct for millions of years, as it was only known from ancient fossils. Living frilled sharks were first discovered in the late 19th century.

# Shark relatives

- **Sharks are closely related** to two other groups of fish – the batoids and the chimaeras.

- **The batoids** include rays, skates and sawfish.

- **Batoids range from plate-sized skates** to giant manta rays more than 8 m across.

- **There are more than 500 species of batoids** – more than there are species of sharks.

- **Most batoids have wide, flat heads and bodies**, and long tapering tails. They look similar to some types of sharks, such as angel sharks.

- **Like some sharks**, batoids spend most of their time on the seabed.

- **Batoids feed on** bottom-dwelling sea creatures such as clams, shrimps and flatfish.

- **Because sharks are often difficult to catch** and keep in captivity, scientists often study batoids instead. They are so similar to sharks that they can provide clues to how sharks live.

- **Chimaeras** are a group of fish that are like sharks in some ways and more like bony fish in other ways.

- **Like sharks**, batoids and chimaeras have light, flexible skeletons made of cartilage, instead of having bones like other fish.

▼ An electric ray, a type of batoid, resting on the seabed. Its eyes are on the top of its body.

# Rays

- **Close relatives of sharks**, rays are a type of batoid.

- **With their huge winglike fins**, some ray species wider than they are long.

- **A ray swims** using rippling motions of its fins and looks as if it is 'flying' along.

- **Many rays have a long, whiplike tail.** Unlike sharks, they don't use their tails to push themselves through the water.

- **Rays live in seas and oceans** all around the world, from shallows near the shore to seabeds 3000 m deep.

- **Rays have eyes on the tops of their heads** and large spiracles to breathe through. This enables them to see and breathe without difficulty, even while lying flat on the seabed.

- **Most rays are ovoviviparous** – they give birth to live young that have hatched from eggs inside their mothers' bodies.

- **Many rays are solitary** and like to live alone. However some, like golden cow-nosed rays, form huge groups of thousands of individuals.

- **Some rays**, such as the mangrove stingray and the huge manta ray, can leap right out of the water.

- **All rays are carnivores.** Some hunt for fish or shellfish, while others are filter-feeders.

▶ Two different ray species: the huge manta ray, which has a dark upper side and a paler underside, and the smaller spotted eagle ray, which has a white underside and spots on top.

# Types of rays

- **The biggest ray of all** is the manta ray. It is usually about 7 m wide by 7 m long (including the tail). The biggest are nearly 9 m wide.

- **The manta ray is a filter-feeder**, like the basking and whale sharks. It sucks in seawater and filters tiny plankton out of it.

- **Stingrays have a poisonous spine** (or sometimes two or three) in the middle of their tails. They are used mainly to defend themselves against attackers.

- **River stingrays**, unlike other rays, live in fresh water. They are found in rivers in Africa and South America, especially the river Amazon.

◀ Gill arches in the manta ray's mouth filter food from the water.

- **Round stingrays** have almost completely round, flat bodies, like dinner plates.

- **Electric rays can generate electricity** to give other animals a powerful electric shock. It can be used to put off predators, or to stun prey.

- **Short-nose electric rays** include some of the smallest rays, at less than 20 cm across.

- **The blind electric ray** is almost completely blind. It relies on its sense of electrical detection, which works like radar, to find prey.

- **Spotted eagle rays** are covered with beautiful pale spots on a dark background.

---

**★ STAR FACT ★**
Stingray stings have often been used around the world to make pointed weapons.

# Sawfish

▲ A sawfish snout is the same width all the way along, with a gently curved tip.

- **Another type of ray** is the sawfish.

- **Sawfish get their name** from their long, sawlike snouts, which are edged with sharp teeth like the teeth on a saw.

- **The green sawfish** grows to over 7 m long – longer than a great white shark.

- **The saw can account** for up to one-third of a sawfish's whole length.

- **Like rays**, sawfish have flattened bodies, but they look more like sharks than most rays do.

- **A sawfish uses its saw** to poke around for prey on the seabed and to slice into shoals of fish.

- **When young sawfish are born**, their snouts are soft and enclosed in a covering of skin. This protects the inside of the mother's body from being injured by the sharp teeth. After birth, the protective skin soon falls off and the saw becomes harder.

- **The large-tooth sawfish** sometimes swims up rivers in Australia.

- **Although sawfish look quite like saw sharks**, they are not the same at all. Sawfish are much bigger. They also have longer saws for their body size and no barbels.

> ★ STAR FACT ★
>
> Some sailors used to think sawfish sawed holes in boats in order to eat the passengers – but there is no evidence for this.

# Skates

- **A relative of sharks**, skates are similar to rays, but they tend to have a straighter edges to the front of their pectoral fins and shorter tails.

- **Most types of skate** live in deep water, as far as 3000 m down.

- **Skates usually lie on the seabed** waiting for prey such as crabs and shrimps to come close.

- **As its mouth is on its underside**, the skate does not lunge at its prey. Instead it swim over it and grasps it from above.

◄ The common skate can be recognized by its unusually long and pointed snout.

- **Like some sharks**, skates lay eggs with protective cases around them.

- **Skate eggcases** have stiff spikes on them to help them stick into the seabed, and a sticky coating so that they soon become covered with sand or pebbles as a form of camouflage.

- **Skates are a very popular food** with people – especially the fins, which are called 'skate wings'.

- **The largest skates** include common and barndoor skates. They can reach 2 m to 3 m long (about the size of a large door).

- **The Texas skate** has two big spots, one on each wing. This may be a disguise that helps protect the skate by making it look like the eyes of a larger animal.

> ★ STAR FACT ★
>
> Sailors used to collect skates, dry them, twist them into strange shapes and sell them as miniature sea monsters.

# Chimaeras

- **Although related to sharks**, chimaeras are not true sharks or rays. They belong to a separate group of cartilaginous fish.

- **Various types of chimaeras** are also known as ratfish, ghost sharks, spookfish and even 'ghouls'.

- **Chimaeras grow** to a maximum of around 2 m long, but most are small, from 60 cm to 100 cm long. Many chimaeras have very long tails, which can make up a large part of their body length.

- **Feeding on small fish** and octopuses, chimaeras usually live on the seabed.

- **Chimaeras are so called** because they look like a combination of different types of fish.

- **Like some sharks**, chimaeras have a spine in front of their dorsal fin.

▶ A ratfish (a type of chimaera) swimming close to the seabed. Chimaeras are found in the waters of the Arctic and the Antarctic.

> **★ STAR FACT ★**
> In Greek mythology, a chimaera was a monster that was part lion, part goat and part snake.

- **Another sharklike feature** of chimaeras is that they lay their eggs in eggcases. Chimaera eggcases are surprisingly large – some can be up to 40 cm long.

- **Like other fish**, Chimaeras have a covering over their gill slits. Sharks and rays do not have this.

- **Unlike sharks and rays**, chimaeras swim very slowly, and have fine, ribbed fins.

# Sharks and humans

- **Sharks have been around** for much longer than humans have.

- **It's a natural instinct** for people to be scared of sharks, as some of them are fierce hunters.

- **However**, people are more dangerous to sharks than the other way around.

- **Some sharks**, such as Greenland sharks and angel sharks, are among the easiest fish to catch with a hook or fishing spear.

- **People hunt sharks** for all kinds of useful products such as sharkskin leather and liver oil.

- **People in the Pacific islands** used shark teeth to make tools and weapons as long as 5000 years ago.

> **★ STAR FACT ★**
> The word 'shark' is sometimes used to mean a ruthless person or a thief.

- **In the 5th century BC**, the ancient Greek historian Herodotus wrote about how sharks attacked sailors when ships sank during battles at sea.

- **The ancient Greek scientist Aristotle** studied sharks and was one of the first to notice that they were different from other fish.

- **Sharks are sometimes described** as vicious killers, but they only kill in order to survive.

◀ This photographer is using an underwater camera to get the best possible photo of a great white shark.

# Fear of sharks

- **Many people** are very scared of being bitten or even eaten by a shark while swimming in the sea.

- **The great white shark** is the most feared shark.

- **Other large, fierce sharks** such as tiger and bull sharks also terrify people.

- **Although sharks can be dangerous**, our fear of them is out of proportion to how dangerous they are. Shark attacks are actually very rare.

- **One reason people find sharks so frightening** is that they live underwater, so it is hard to see them.

★ STAR FACT ★
People are more likely to be killed by a hippo, crocodile, dangerous water current, or lightning, than by a shark.

- **Another reason may be their big teeth and eyes** that seem to show no emotion. Humans instinctively prefer 'cute' animals to fierce-looking ones.

- **In the past**, sailors were famous for being superstitious. Their tales about sharks and shark attacks were probably exaggerated.

- **Fear of sharks** has been increased by the many books and films about shark attacks.

- **Shark attacks are rare**, so when they happen they are widely publicized. This makes sharks seem more dangerous than they really are.

◄ A promotional poster for the film Jaws, about a killer great white shark. This poster exaggerates the shark by making it look much bigger than it really is.

# Shark attacks

- **There are less** than 100 reported cases worldwide every year of sharks attacking humans swimming or surfing in the sea.

- **Of these attacks**, fewer than 20 result in someone dying.

- **Most shark attacks** happen in shallow, water near the shore, because that's where sharks and swimmers are likely to be in the same place at the same time.

- **The worst shark tragedy ever** was in 1945, during World War II. A US warship was torpedoed and sank in the South Pacific, leaving 1000 crew members in the water. Before they could be rescued, over 600 of them had been eaten by sharks.

★ STAR FACT ★
Experts have found that if a shark does take a bite of human flesh, it often spits it out or vomits it up later.

◄ Sharks sometimes attack people surfing, maybe because, from below, a surfboard looks similar to a seal – a favourite food of the great white.

- **In the summer of 1969**, four people were killed in shark attacks within two weeks off the coast of New Jersey, USA.

- **The areas with the most shark attacks** are the coasts of eastern North America, South Africa, and eastern Australia.

- **Sharks usually only attack** if they feel threatened, or if they mistake a human for prey, such as a seal.

- **Most shark attacks** happen in summer and during the afternoon.

- **Men are more likely** than women to be attacked by a shark, probably because more men go surfing and swim further out in the sea.

# Survival stories

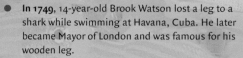

- **In 1749**, 14-year-old Brook Watson lost a leg to a shark while swimming at Havana, Cuba. He later became Mayor of London and was famous for his wooden leg.

- **Rodney Fox** was grabbed by a great white while taking part in a spear-fishing contest in Australia in 1963. His body was bitten right open, but he survived and went on to become a shark expert.

- **A great white shark** bit off undersea photographer Henri Bource's leg while he was diving off Australia in 1964. He was soon back at work in the same job, and four years later another shark bit his artificial leg!

- **In 1996**, surfer Joey Hanlon was attacked by a great white while surfing in California, USA. The shark bit into his torso, but he recovered after being given over 300 stitches.

- **Another surfer**, John Forse, was on his surfboard in Oregon, USA in 1998 when a great white shark grabbed his leg and pulled him deep underwater. He escaped by hitting the shark's dorsal fin until it let go.

> ★ STAR FACT ★
> In 2004, while snorkelling in Australia, Luke Tresoglavic was bitten by a small wobbegong that refused to let go. Tresoglavic had to swim to shore and drive to get help with the shark still attached to his leg.

- **13-year-old Bethany Hamilton** had her left arm bitten off by a tiger shark while surfing in Hawaii in 2003. She was surfing again within months.

- **Fishermen often get bitten** on the hands by sharks they have caught. Most of these shark bites are minor and go unreported.

- **Shark attack survivors** are often left with huge semicircular scars from the shark's teeth.

- **Today, shark attack victims** are more likely to survive than they used to be, thanks to fast boats and modern treatments such as blood transfusions.

▼ *Great whites are curious about unfamiliar objects in the sea, and they will nearly always investigate because they are constantly on the lookout for food.*

# Shark safety

- **Humans have developed** several ways to try to stay safe from shark attacks.

- **Swimming beaches** in shark areas are sometimes surrounded with strong nets to keep sharks out.

- **Chainmail diving suits** protect divers from sharks' teeth, but the body can still be crushed by a bite.

- **Some ships carry shark screens** – floating sacks that shipwreck survivors can climb inside. The screen disguises a person's shape and hides their scent, making them less likely to attract sharks.

- **Anti-shark weapons** can be used to scare sharks away. They include electrical prods that confuse a shark's electrical sense, and bangsticks, which are like underwater guns.

- **Some people have tried** to banish sharks by releasing chemicals they don't like the smell of into the water.

- **Some divers** wear striped diving suits for camouflage, so that it's harder for sharks to see them.

> ★ STAR FACT ★
> If you are ever attacked by a shark, you may be able to scare it off by punching its snout.

- **You shouldn't swim in a shark zone** if you have a cut or wound on your body. The blood could attract sharks.

- **If you see a large shark** when you're in the sea, the safest thing to do is to stay calm, avoid splashing about, and swim steadily towards the shore.

▲ *A great white shark showing how deadly its bite could be as it mouths the bars of an underwater shark-watching cage.*

# Dangerous sharks

- **The great white shark** is often thought to be the most dangerous shark because it is most often identified in shark attacks. This is because it is easy to recognize. It is blamed for up to half of all serious shark attacks.

- **As well as biting humans**, great whites have been known to attack small boats.

- **Why are great whites so deadly?** It may be partly because they love eating seals and sealions, which look similar to humans in size and shape. The sharks simply get confused and attack the wrong prey.

- **Many experts think** bull sharks are actually more dangerous than great whites – but they are not well-known as killers because they are harder to identify.

- **After bull sharks attack**, they often escape unseen.

- **Not all dangerous sharks are fast hunters.** Nurse sharks and wobbegongs are usually placid and sluggish – but they can bite suddenly and hard if disturbed or annoyed.

- **Sharks with spines**, such as horn and dogfish sharks, are not deadly but often inflict painful injuries on people.

- **Stingrays**, which are related to sharks, can be killers – a few people die every year from their venom.

- **Sharks often bite** then swim away fast, making it hard to tell what species they are.

- **Huge basking sharks and manta rays**, though they don't bite, can be dangerous if they leap out of the water and land on a small boat.

# Harmless sharks

- **The vast majority of shark species** are not interested in eating humans and never attack them.

- **Many sharks**, such as pygmy and zebra sharks, are so small they could not kill or eat a human even if they wanted to.

- **Most sharks can bite**, but will only do so if they themselves are attacked, caught or threatened.

- **Filter-feeders** such as whale sharks have very big mouths, but their throats are narrow, so they can't swallow a human.

- **Whale sharks** are often very friendly. They let snorkellers come close and even touch them.

- **Even big, dangerous sharks** such as the great white can get used to humans and become friendly enough to be stroked and tickled.

- **Harmless sharks** such as basking sharks are sometimes killed because they are mistaken for great whites or other dangerous sharks.

- **At some aquariums and sealife centres**, visitors can pay to climb into the tank with non-dangerous sharks.

- **Many shark scientists**, experts and photographers spend huge amounts of time with sharks without ever getting bitten.

- **Some people even keep small sharks** at home in fishtanks, although this is very difficult to do.

▼ Although basking sharks are a massive 10 m in length, they are completely harmless.

# Shark fishing

- **Important species for fishing** include thresher sharks and various types of dogfish.

- **Most of the sharks** caught are used as food, though sharks have many other uses too.

- **Smaller sharks** such as the lesser spotted dogfish are caught by trawlers – boats that drag, or trawl huge fishing nets along behind them.

- **Flat, bottom-dwelling sharks** such as angel sharks can be caught by a diver using a fishing spear to stab through the shark onto the seabed.

- **Sea anglers go fishing** for sharks as a sport. Many coastal tourist resorts have special boats that take tourists sportfishing for sharks and other large fish. Sharks caught for sport are often thrown back alive.

▼ Sharks are often caught in nets intended for fish such as tuna. Bycatch (unwanted catch) accounts for a significant proportion of shark fatalities.

- **Sport fishermen** like to catch fast-swimming species, such as mako sharks, because they struggle a lot when they are hooked and so provide the most entertainment.

- **Whale sharks and other species** are sometimes hunted for their fins. After the fins are cut off, the rest of the shark is thrown back into the sea to die.

- **Millions of sharks** are caught by accident every year in nets meant for other sea creatures, such as squid.

- **Sharks are often caught** and killed just because there is a small risk that they might bite someone.

- **Humans catch** around 100 million sharks every year.

# Sharks as food

- **Sharks are a nutritious food** because their flesh is very lean and full of protein. It often tastes good, too.

- **However, many people don't like the idea** of eating sharks, so when they are sold as food, sharks' names are often changed to things such as 'grayfish' or 'huss'.

- **In Japan** you can buy canned shark, smoked shark and shark fishcakes.

- **Raw shark** is eaten as part of traditional Japanese sashimi dishes.

- **Shark's-fin soup**, popular in Asia, is made by boiling shark fins to extract the gluey cartilage rods, which are the soup's main ingredient.

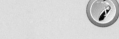

▶ *Shark liver oil has long been thought to have nutritional properties. Vitamin pills made from the oil are believed to help heal wounds and prevent flu.*

> ★ STAR FACT ★
> In Iceland, people eat dried, slightly rotted Greenland shark – a dish known as hakarl.

- **In the UK**, fish and chips is a popular takeaway meal. This fish is often a shark, the spiny dogfish – sold as 'rock salmon'.

- **Parts of sharks** are often made into health food supplements – such as shark liver oil tablets, which contain E and A vitamins. Some people even believe that eating shark can give you a shark's strength and courage, but there is no evidence for this.

- **Some types of Muslims** do not eat sharks as their religion forbids them to eat fish without scales.

- **Shark flesh goes off very fast**. It has to be eaten when fresh, or preserved by canning, smoking or pickling soon after being caught.

# More uses for sharks

- **Polished shark skin leather** was once used to cover books and scientific objects such as telescopes.

- **Some species**, such as the spotted wobbegong, are still hunted for their skin. It's made into things such as shoes and handbags.

- **The ancient Greeks** used burnt angel shark skin to treat skin diseases, and shocks from electric rays as a painkiller during operations.

- **Squalene is an oil that is extracted from shark livers**. It is used in cosmetics, perfume, skin care and pharmaceutical products. It can take up to 3000 shark livers to produce one tonne of squalene.

- **Shark liver oil** is also used in some candles and paints.

- **Shark cartilage** is used to make a medicine for treating burns.

> ★ STAR FACT ★
> Shagreen – shark leather that still has its rough denticles – was used in the past to make non-slip grips for sword handles.

- **A type of medicine for heart disease** is made from chemicals extracted from sharks' blood.

- **Scientists have worked out** how to use shark corneas (the transparent protective covering in front of the eye) to make cornea transplants for humans.

- **Sharks' teeth** are often made into necklaces and other jewellery.

◀ *A handbag made from shark skin leather. Sharks that are hunted for their skin are usually species with beautiful mottled or speckled markings, such as the carpet shark.*

# Shark tourism

- **People like to get close to sharks** because they are exciting and fiersome.

- **In coastal areas** around the world, tourists pay to see real sharks in their natural habitat.

- **Ecotourism** is tourism that helps preserve wild habitats and species. Some of the money paid by the ecotourists is used for conservation work.

- **Cage-diving** allows people to view dangerous sharks. They are lowered into the sea inside a metal cage.

- **People can view great whites** in Australia and South Africa.

- **People swim with sharks**. You can go on dives and snorkelling trips to see species such as reef and whale sharks.

- **On shark-feeding tours**, tourists go diving to the seabed, where a guide uses frozen fish to attract species such as white-tip reef sharks.

- **Sharks attract visitors** to sealife centres and aquariums, where you can often walk through the shark tank in an underwater tunnel.

- **Undersea photographers** use special underwater cameras to take pictures of tourists with sharks as part of the experience.

◀ *A diver has a close encounter with a great white shark while cage-diving.*

# Sharks in captivity

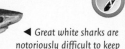

- **Most shark species are** difficult to keep in captivity. They need tanks with lots of space.

- **For a shark to survive** in captivity the water has to have conditions that exactly match the shark's natural habitat.

- **For this reason**, many aquariums only keep sharks that come from their own local area. The further a shark is from home, the harder it is to recreate the conditions it is used to.

- **Sand tiger, lemon sharks and smaller sharks** do better in captivity than other species of shark.

- **Captive sharks** can suffer from diseases such as goitre, caused by a lack of the minerals they need to stay healthy.

- **Sharks in captivity** seem to eat less than those in the wild. In captivity they do not expend so much energy in finding food or in day-to-day living.

◀ *Great white sharks are notoriously difficult to keep in captivity, as they seem to go off their food when they are in a tank.*

- **The tiger shark** is one of the few large, fierce sharks to have survived a long time in captivity. They have been kept in aquariums for up to five years.

- **To be transported** from the wild to an aquarium, sharks have to be carried in special holding tanks that are transported on trucks or planes.

- **In 1998**, a group of sandbar sharks died in an aquarium in the UK after getting too cold when their flight was delayed at Amsterdam airport.

# Sharks in trouble

> ★ STAR FACT ★
> Many shark species are so hard to study that scientists have no idea how many of them are left in the sea.

- **There are far fewer sharks** than there used to be. The numbers of many species are falling fast. Some are in danger of dying out.

- **This is mainly because** of human activities such as hunting and fishing.

- **Overfishing** may mean that shark populations can't recover. Porbeagle sharks have been overfished.

- **In the second half of the 20th century**, shark fishing increased as shark meat, shark's-fin soup became more popular.

- **Sharks are also in demand** because other fish such as cod have become scarce, having also been overfished.

- **Many sharks are killed** when they get caught in nets put up to protect swimmers from shark attacks.

- **Sharks caught for sport** are usually released, but often die from exhaustion soon afterwards.

- **Because sharks grow slowly** and don't bear many young, it is especially hard for a species to build up its numbers again after being overfished.

- **Sharks are at the top of the food chain**. Poisonous chemicals from pollution collect in sea creatures. When sharks eat their prey, the poison builds up in their bodies. Scientists think this may make sharks ill and make it harder for them to reproduce.

◀ *Shark pups are very vulnerable while they are in their egg cases, and many do not survive into adulthood. This makes it difficult for shark populations to recover from over-fishing.*

# Endangered species

- **An endangered species** is in danger of dying out and becoming extinct.

- **When a species becomes extinct**, all the members of that species die and it can never exist again.

- **Scientists try to find out** if a shark species is at risk by counting the sharks seen in a particular area and measuring how much this changes over time.

- **Experts found** that sandbar shark sightings on America's east coast fell by 20 percent over 20 years. The sandbar shark is now endangered.

- **Well-known sharks** that are endangered include great white, whale and basking sharks.

- **Most sharks** are endangered because of overfishing.

- **International organizations** such as the IUCN (International Union for the Conservation of Nature and Natural Resources) compile lists of which species are endangered.

- **According to the IUCN** over 50 shark species are now endangered.

- **Some sharks and shark relatives** are threatened when natural coastlines and estuaries are developed and built on. This destroys nursery areas where sharks lay eggs or bear their young.

- **The Ganges shark**, found in the river Ganges in India, is one of the most endangered sharks.

◀ *Great whites are one species that are known to be in danger of dying out. There are several international campaigns to try to save them.*

# Shark beliefs and folklore

- **Throughout history**, people have believed all sorts of things about sharks. Many unproved shark beliefs still survive to this day.

- **Sailors used to say** sharks could smell a dead body and followed a ship if someone on board had died. Scientists today think this may be true.

- **Sailors also used to believe** that sharks liked eating humans and would go out of their way to find them. In fact, this isn't true at all.

- **In the past**, many peoples around the world worshipped shark gods .

- **People from the Solomon Islands**, in the Pacific Ocean, believed that the spirits of people who had died lived on in sharks.

◀ Sharks are common in the waters around the Pacific island of Fiji. Local people have many beliefs and customs relating to sharks.

- **The Solomon Islanders** even used to make human sacrifices to sharks to keep the shark-spirits happy.

- **In Vietnam**, the whale shark is known as ca ong or 'Sir Fish'. It was once worshipped there .

- **Sharks rarely get diseases**, so many people believe eating shark products can protect against illness. There is no scientific evidence for this.

- **In Fiji in the Pacific Ocean**, people used to catch sharks and kiss their stomachs. This was believed to make the sharks harmless.

- **In Europe**, catching a shark used to be considered good luck, especially if it was female.

# Shark myths and legends

- **There are many myths and legends** involving sharks, most of them from places where sharks are common.

- **Hawaiian legends** tell of a shark king and a shark queen who controlled all the other sharks in the sea.

- **In one Hawaiian myth**, a god threw a shark into the sky, where it formed the constellations.

- **In a legend** of the Warrau people of South America, a man arranged for his mother-in-law to be eaten by a shark. As punishment his own leg was bitten off and became the constellation of Orion's Belt.

▶ Jonah was thought to have been trapped in the belly of the great fish for three days.

- **Another Hawaiian story** tells how a shark king married a human woman. They had a son, who grew up to find he could turn himself into a shark.

- **The Bible** tells how the prophet Jonah was swallowed by a 'great fish'. In most translations this is a whale, but some people think it might have meant a shark.

- **The ancient Greek writer Aristotle** developed a theory that sharks had to roll upside-down in order to bite. This isn't true, but the myth lived on for centuries.

- **In legends from the South Pacific**, 'shark men' were sharks that could take human form and come ashore.

- **Old Japanese legends** also featured a terrifying god called the shark man.

★ STAR FACT ★
When China and Japan fought each other in the Second World War, the Chinese painted sharks on their planes to scare the Japanese.

# Saving sharks

- **Some sharks are now endangered**, and people have started working to try to save them.

- **Ecotourism** helps to save sharks by encouraging local people not to kill sharks, as they can make money from them as tourist attractions.

- **Some shark-fishing countries** have imposed quotas to limit how many sharks fishermen can catch.

- **Governments** can ban the killing of some sharks altogether. The UK has passed a law making it illegal to catch or disturb a basking shark.

- **Some countries have set up** marine wildlife reserves where harming wildlife is banned.

- **Conservation charities** such as WWF (The WorldWide Fund for Nature) work to educate people to help them avoid killing sharks unnecessarily.

★ **STAR FACT** ★

Some scientists are worried that diving with sharks makes them less scared of humans, which could put sharks at greater risk.

- **By banning trade** in shark products, governments can stop some people from killing sharks.

- **To help protect sharks**, people should avoid buying products such as shark's-fin soup.

- **Some shark charities** will let you 'adopt' a shark. You pay a fee and receive information about a shark living in a protected area. The money goes towards conservation campaigns.

▼ *Some sharks take an interest in diving cages, and seem to become more tame when they have contact with humans.*

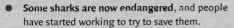

# Sharks in art, books and films

- **Ancient peoples** made images of sharks. Maori artists made carvings of sharks from wood and bone.

- **Ancient aboriginal rock art** depict sharks, along with other animals important to the early Aborigines.

- **In 1778**, American artist John Singleton Copley painted a famous picture of Brook Watson being attacked by a shark.

- **In his 1851 novel** *Moby Dick*, Herman Melville described a character almost losing his hand to a shark, even though it had been killed and dragged on board.

- **Another famous novel**, *20,000 Leagues Under the Sea* by Jules Verne, features man-eating sharks.

- **The best-known shark novel** is *Jaws*, by Peter Benchley, published in 1974. It tells of a great white shark attacking swimmers off the east coast off the USA.

- **In 1975**, *Jaws* was made into a film by Steven Spielberg. It broke box-office records and is still one of the biggest-grossing films of all time.

- **Much of** *Jaws* was filmed using a 7 m-long artificial shark, known as Bruce.

- **There were three film sequels to Jaws**, including a 3D version. The audience wore special 3D spectacles that made the shark appear to come out of the screen towards them.

- **In a later shark movie**, *Deep Blue Sea* (1999), the shark sequences were partly created using computer animation.

◀ *A still from the shark film Deep Blue Sea. It tells the story of a group of scientists who use genetic engineering to create super-intelligent sharks – which then turn against their captors.*

# Shark science

- **We know relatively little about sharks**. Scientists are trying to find out more about them.

- **The study of sharks** is sometimes called elasmobranchology.

- **Knowing more about sharks** – things such as how they breed and what they need to survive – will help us to conserve them and stop shark species from dying out.

- **To find out how sharks live**, scientists have to study them in the wild. This is called 'fieldwork'.

- **Scientists also catch sharks** so they can study them in captivity. This lets them look closely at how sharks swim, eat, breed and behave in other ways.

- **In laboratories**, scientists study things such as sharks' blood, skin and cartilage to find out how their bodies work.

- **Some scientists study sharks' cells** to try to find out why they get so few diseases. This information could help to make new medicines.

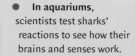

- **In aquariums**, scientists test sharks' reactions to see how their brains and senses work.

- **Governments and wildlife charities** sometimes pay scientists to study sharks.

▲ *Denticles are incredibly hard and strong, but still flexible enough to allow great mobility. Scientists are interested in the possibilities of recreating the effects of denticles for human use.*

# Shark scientists

- There are many different types of scientists who work with sharks.

- **Biologists** are scientists who study living things. Many shark scientists are marine biologists – which means they study sea life.

- **Zoologists** are scientists who study animals, and ichthyologists are scientists who study fish. These scientists also work with sharks.

- **Other scientists** study shark genes and DNA – the instructions inside cells. Scientists who study genes and DNA are called geneticists.

- **Palaeontologists** study fossils. Shark fossils are very important in revealing how sharks evolved. Some scientists specialize in studying just shark fossils.

- **Oceanographers** study the sea. They know about habitats and how sharks live with other animals.

◄ This diver is wearing the latest diving equipment. This allows scientists to study sharks close-up in their natural habitats.

- **Most shark scientists** work for universities or research centres such as the Woods Hole Oceanographic Institute in Massachusetts, USA.

- **One of today's most famous shark scientists** is American zoologist Dr. Eugenie Clark. She has studied shark behaviour and deep-sea sharks.

- **The famous French undersea expert** Jacques Cousteau was one of the first people to study sharks underwater. He invented scuba diving equipment, which scientists still use when studying sharks.

- **If you'd like to be a shark scientist**, it will help if you pick subjects such as biology and chemistry at school, and study biology or zoology at university.

# Studying sharks

- **To learn more about sharks**, scientists need ways of finding, following and catching them.

- **Most shark scientists** have to be strong and good at diving.

- **Scientists** often use diving cages or protective chainmail suits to get close to sharks.

- **They can also study sharks** such as great whites without going in the water, using cameras on the ends of long poles.

◄ Studies of reef sharks often begin by tracking mature females to gain data on breeding times and to locate habitat sites for newborn pups.

- **Scientists tag sharks** by attaching a tag saying where and when the shark was last seen. The same shark may then be found again somewhere else, giving scientists clues about shark movements.

- **A camera** can be attached to a shark to record its travels. The strap holding the camera gradually dissolves, and the camera floats to the surface to be collected.

- **To follow sharks**, scientists radio-track them. They catch a shark and attach a transmitter that gives out radio signals. Wherever the shark goes, they can pick up the signals and work out the shark's location.

- **Some shark scientists** dissect dead sharks to find out about their bodies or what they have eaten recently.

- **To tag or track a shark**, scientists have to catch it using a net or trap. They may drug it so that they can attach the transmitter or tag safely.

- **Scientists have to be careful** when working with live sharks, as they may get bitten by a shark that is not happy about being caught.

# Early sharks

- **Sharks first evolved** about 380 million years ago. That means they were around long before the dinosaurs.

- **Sharks' basic body shapes** and behaviour have hardly changed since they first appeared.

- **Experts think sharks evolved** from ancient types of fish that had no jawbones.

- **Sharks appeared** long before many other kinds of fish that are alive today, such as salmon and goldfish.

- **One of the earliest sharks of all** was *Cladoselache*, which lived 370 million years ago. It was around 1.5 m long, and had 3-pointed teeth, just as frilled sharks do now.

- *Stethacanthus*, which lived about 350 million years ago, was a strange-looking shark with a platform of denticles on top of its first dorsal fin.

◀ *A fossilized Megalodon tooth (left) compared to a tooth from a modern great white shark.*

- *Hybodus* **lived about 160 million years ago**. Like many modern sharks, it had both sharp cutting teeth and flat, blunt, chewing teeth.

- **The biggest shark ever** was probably *Megalodon*. It first appeared about 20 million years ago. Scientists think it looked like a great white shark, only bigger –maybe 20 m in length (as long as two buses).

- **Of course**, these prehistoric sharks didn't have these names when they were alive, as there were no humans around to name them. Their names have been given to them by modern scientists.

- **Sharks survived** a huge mass extinction 65 million years ago, which wiped out other creatures such as dinosaurs and ammonites.

# Shark fossils

- **A fossil is a record** of the shape of an animal, or part of an animal, preserved in rock.

- **A fossil forms** when an animal dies and is gradually covered by earth. Over a very long time, the sand or mud hardens into rock. The animal rots away, but its shape is left behind, and may get filled in with minerals to leave a 'model' of the animal.

- **Often**, only the hardest parts of an animal, such as its skeleton, get fossilized.

- **Because sharks have soft cartilage skeletons**, there are few whole shark fossils. Many shark fossils only show teeth or fins.

- **Scientists use shark fossils** to find out what sharks looked like long ago and how they lived. They often use tooth fossils to guess how big an entire shark was.

- **Shark fossils are often found** on land in places that used to be seas millions of years ago.

- **Some of the best shark fossil areas** are in parts of the USA, such as California, Maryland and Oklahoma.

- **Palaeontologists** go searching for fossils at sites and dig, cut or chip them out of the rocks. Then they take them back to a lab to clean them and study them.

- **Fossils show** that some sharks that are alive today are very similar to ones that lived millions of years ago.

- **Fossils are often displayed** at museums and fossil shops.

◀ *A palaeontologist at work. They have to be very careful when they dig delicate fossils out of the ground.*

# Shark discoveries and mysteries

- **Shark scientists** are still finding out new things about sharks, and puzzling over unanswered questions.

- **Shark experts** sometimes disagree strongly about shark facts. They meet up at conferences where they share their discoveries and hold debates.

- **For example**, some experts think the prehistoric shark *Megalodon* died out over a million years ago, while others say it lived until 10,000 years ago.

- **No one knows** why basking sharks seem to disappear at certain times of year.

- **The dwarf lanternshark** was discovered in 1985. New species of sharks are still being found.

- **Scientists don't always find new shark species** in the sea. Instead, they are often found in fish markets or reported by local people.

- **In 2004**, scientists found that Greenland sharks eat giant squid. Before this, only sperm whales were thought to eat these creatures.

- **In 2002**, scientists worked out how to test the DNA in shark's-fin soup to see which species it contains. This helps to stop people hunting protected sharks.

- **Scientists studying whale sharks** found that they don't just eat plankton. Sometimes they wait for other fish to lay their eggs so that they can eat them.

- **Scientists studying shark's fins** in 2001 found they sometimes contain very high levels of mercury, which comes from from pollution in seawater.

▲ Most of what we know about prehistoric sharks such as Hybodus *comes from studying the fossilized remains of their teeth.*

# Shark records

- **The most widespread shark** is the blue shark, found in most of the world's seas and oceans.

- **The brightest luminescent shark** is the cookie-cutter. Its glow is as bright as a reading lamp.

- **More than ten shark species** share the title of rarest shark, as they are known from only one specimen. They include two types of angel shark, the Taiwan angel shark and the ocellated angel shark.

- **The flattest-bodied sharks** are angel and wobbegong sharks.

- **The bigeye thresher shark** has the biggest eyes in relation to its body size than any other shark.

◄ *The great white shark is the largest of the predatory sharks.*

- **The shortfin mako** makes the highest leaps. It can jump more than 5 m out of the water.

- **The whale shark** has the most pups at once – as many as 300.

- **The fussiest eaters of the shark world** are bullhead sharks. The diet of some bullheads consists of just sea urchins.

- **The common thresher shark** has the longest tail compared to its body size.

- **The great white shark** has had more books written and films made about it than any other shark.

# INSECTS

## INSECT WORLD

## ANTS, BEES AND WASPS

## BUTTERFLIES AND MOTHS

## FLIES, BEETLES AND BUGS

## COCKROACHES, CRICKETS AND GRASSHOPPERS

## OTHER INSECTS

# Evolution

- **Insects are small animals** that belong to a class called Insecta. They are part of the phylum (group) called Arthropoda.

- **Arthropods** include crustaceans (crabs and their relatives), myriapods (centipedes and millipedes), and arachnids (spiders, mites and scorpions), as well as insects.

- **Some whole insects** were trapped and fossilized in amber (pine tree resin).

- **Some species of insects,** such as dragonflies or stoneflies, are so successful at surviving that they have not changed much over millions of years.

- **Entomologists have divided** all the insects discovered so far into 32 groups or orders.

- **The study of insects** is known as entomology.

◀ Trapped in sticky tree resin millions of years ago, this delicate insect was beautifully preserved as the soft resin turned into hard amber.

- **New species of insects** are constantly evolving as insects adapt themselves to their living conditions.

- **Fossils of insects** are sometimes preserved in rocks. These fossils are often only fragments of various insect body parts.

- **It is difficult to find** insect fossils because the soft bodies of insects decay quickly and do not become fossilized.

- **The oldest fossils** of tiny wingless insects were found to be 380 million years old.

# Insect fact file

- **There are over one million** different species of insects, compared to just one human species.

- **Insects are successful survivors** because of their powerful exoskeletons, their ability to fly and their minute size.

- **Some insects can fly** for long distances. Some butterflies migrate thousands of kilometres to avoid bad weather.

- **Cockroaches have been living on Earth** for around 300 million years. Today's cockroaches look very similar to those living hundreds of millions of years ago.

- **Insects serve** as the largest source of food for other animals.

- **Fairyflies are the smallest insects** in the world. They are only 0.2 mm – about the size of a full stop.

- **Scientists have discovered the fossils** of a dragonfly that lived around 300 million years ago. Its wingspan was as big as a seagull.

◀ Moths and butterflies, such as this swallowtail butterfly, together make up one of the largest groups of insects. There are ten times more moths than butterflies.

- **People have domesticated silkworms** for so long that these insects do not exist in the wild anymore.

- **Insects are cold-blooded animals,** so their growth and development depends upon how hot or cold the weather is.

- **Scientists have developed 'insect robots'** that copy the agility of real insects. These robots are used to explore dangerous areas, such as minefields and the surface of other planets. Robots are not nearly as agile as real insects, but mimic the way they move.

# Insect firsts

● **Insects made the first paper!** Paper wasps chew the bark of some plants and add saliva to make a type of paper. This 'paper' is used for building nests.

● **Insects such as the dragonfly** were the first ever fliers on Earth.

● **Insects were the first animals** to use sound to communicate. Bees use buzzing sounds to warn about danger, indicate the presence of food and convey various other types of information.

● **Cicadas and crickets** have been captured and reared by humans for the beautiful sound they make.

● **Dragonflies are known to hover**, like modern day helicopters, over their prey.

> ★ **STAR FACT** ★
> Insects were the first doctors! Some insects produce toxins to combat and treat infections and diseases that occur in their bodies.

▶ *Butterflies were among the first pollinating insects.*

● **Termites made the first ever colonies** where the inhabitants all had different jobs. There are queens, soldiers and workers in termite colonies.

● **Insects were the first to** 'tame' other animals. Ants 'tame' the larvae of some butterflies and aphids and extract a type of sugary liquid called honeydew from them.

● **Dragonflies invented** 'fast food' long before humans! They hold prey with their legs and eat while flying.

● **Insects used the techniques of camouflage** and ambush for defence and attack long before humans used them in military operations.

# Insects and people

▶ *People began to domesticate bees about 3000 years ago. Today, most domesticated honeybees are kept in beehives containing removable frames. The bees store honey in the upper frames, which the beekeeper removes to harvest the honey.*

● **Insects were always** of great importance to human civilizations. People rear insects such as silkworms and honeybees to obtain important materials from them, such as silk, honey and wax.

● **Archaeologists have discovered** prehistoric cave paintings that show scenes of honey collection and the extraction of honey from beehives.

● **Many insects,** such as mosquitoes and bed bugs, feed on human blood.

● **Japanese Samurai warriors** painted intricate butterfly patterns on weapons and flags to symbolize nobility.

● **Many stories, songs and poems** have been written about different insects in different cultures of the world.

● **Many people eat insects** such as termites, cicadas and leafcutter ants, and consider them to be delicacies.

● **Deadly diseases** such as the Bubonic plague were transmitted to humans from tiny insects such as fleas, and caused millions of deaths.

● **Doctors used to insert maggots** in wounds to eat dead flesh and disinfect the wounds by killing bacteria.

● **Many insects feed on agricultural pests** and help farmers.

● **Some insects can be pests** and can destroy crops and fields and cause serious damage.

# Sacred insects

▶ Images of scarab beetles were often carved on ancient Egyptian precious stones and jewellery. The carvings were thought to bring luck and ward off evil.

- **Ancient Egyptians worshipped** an array of beetles and other creepy crawlies, such as centipedes and scorpions.

- **The scarab or the dung beetle** was associated with the creator-god, Atum. This beetle was believed to have come into being by itself, from a ball of dung.

- **The wings of the jewel bug** are metallic green, purple and golden in colour. It is another insect revered by the ancient Egyptians.

- **Egyptians used amulets** with motifs of insects, such as locusts, beetles and flies, for good luck.

- **Egyptians believed that honey** could protect them from evil spirits.

- **Motifs of butterflies** have been discovered on ancient tombs and jewellery.

- **Some Moslems believe** that a praying mantis in the praying posture offers prayers towards Mecca.

- **Tiny black ants** are revered by some Hindus in India.

- **The ancient Chinese** regarded cicadas as a symbol of immortality and rebirth.

> ★ STAR FACT ★
> Honeybees were believed to be the tears of the Egyptian Sun-god, Ra.

# Anatomy

- **The segmented body** of an insect is divided into three parts: head, thorax (middle section) and abdomen (rear section).

- **All insects have six legs** that are joined to the thorax. They usually have either one or two pairs of wings, which are also joined to the thorax.

- **All insects have an exoskeleton** – a strong outer skeleton that protects the insect's body.

- **The muscles and delicate organs** of insects are enclosed and protected within this exoskeleton.

- **All insects have two antennae on their head.** These are used to sense smell, touch and sound.

- **The head also contains** mouthparts that are adapted to different feeding methods, such as chewing, biting, stabbing and sucking.

Antenna
Compound eye
Head
Thorax
Wing
Leg
Abdomen

◀ This diagram of a honeybee shows the main parts of an insect's body. A honeybee has two pairs of wings.

- **The digestive and reproductive systems** of insects are contained in the abdomen.

- **Insects have an open circulatory system** without lots of tubes for carrying blood. The heart of an insect is a simple tube that pumps greenish-yellow blood all over the body.

- **Insects breathe** through special openings on the side of the body called spiracles.

- **Insects have tiny brains,** which are just collections of nerve cells fused together. The brain sends signals to control all the other organs in the body.

# Moulting

● **Moulting is the shedding of the hard exoskeleton** periodically because it does not stretch as the insect grows bigger. All insects moult during the early stages of their life.

● **Insects swallow air** or water or use blood pressure to expand their body, causing the exoskeleton to split.

● **A soft new exoskeleton** is exposed when the insect gets rid of its old one. The new exoskeleton is bigger in size and allows the insect to expand.

● **The new exoskeleton hardens** and becomes darker in colour.

● **Insects normally moult** five to ten times in a lifetime.

> ★ **STAR FACT** ★
> A caterpillar grows about 2000 times bigger than its size at the time of its birth. If a 3 kg human baby grew at the same rate, the baby would weigh as much as a bus in a month.

▶ A young adult dragonfly emerges during its moult. After resting, it will pump blood into its short wings to spread them out to their full adult size.

● **A silverfish** can moult up to 60 times in a lifetime.

● **The larval stage** between moults is known as an instar.

● **Moulting takes a long time** and the insect is vulnerable to predatory attacks during this period. Most insects moult in secluded areas.

● **Other animals,** such as snakes and spiders, also moult in order to grow.

# Defence

● **As well as camouflage** and mimicry, insects also use other strategies to protect themselves from predators.

● **Some caterpillars and larvae** have special glands that secrete poison when they are attacked. Predatory birds soon learn to avoid them.

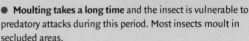

◀ This katydid could escape from the formidable claws of a desert scorpion by shedding a leg and flying away.

● **Ants, bees and wasps** can deliver stings to an attacker. These insects pump in venom and cause pain and irritation.

● **Stick insects and weevils** are known to 'play dead' when attacked. They keep very still and the attacker leaves the insects alone because most predators do not eat dead prey.

● **Some butterflies,** such as the monarch butterfly, are poisonous and cause the attacking bird to vomit if it eats the butterfly.

● **Some insects, such as katydids,** shed limbs if an attacker grabs them by the leg. This process is known as autotomy.

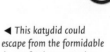

● **The bombardier beetle** has special glands, which enable it to spray boiling hot poisonous fluids at an attacker.

● **Moths, grasshoppers and mantids** show the bright colours on their hind wings to startle a predator. These are called flash colours.

● **Stink glands** present in some bugs release obnoxious and repelling smells that predators cannot tolerate.

● **When alarmed,** ants raise their abdomen. This sends a signal to other ants in the colony, and all the other ants raise their abdomens too.

# Camouflage and mimicry

- **Insects use defence strategies**, such as camouflage and mimicry, to protect themselves from predators. Killer insects sometimes use the same strategies to catch their prey.

- **Some insects cleverly hide themselves** by blending in with their surroundings. This is known as camouflage.

- **Some harmless insects** mimic (imitate) harmful insects in appearance and behaviour to fool predators into leaving them alone.

- **Hoverflies have yellow-and-black stripes** on their bodies, which makes them resemble stinging insects such as wasps or hornets. so predators avoid them.

- **The larvae of some butterflies** resemble bird droppings, or even soil.

- **Some moths imitate dangerous wasps and bees** in behaviour and sound. Their buzz startles predators.

- **Stick insects** and praying mantids appear to be the twigs and leaves of plants. They blend into their environment so well that they are often missed by predators.

▶ *The hornet moth has a yellow-and-black striped body, making it look like a large wasp called a hornet. It even behaves like a hornet. Predators avoid hornet moths because they look as if they might sting.*

Hornet

- **Monarch butterflies** are bitter-tasting and poisonous, so birds do not eat them. Viceroy butterflies have orange and black wings similar to those of monarch butterflies. Birds avoid viceroy butterflies because they think that they are poisonous as well.

- **Adults and caterpillars** of some moths and butterflies have large eyelike spots to scare away predatory birds.

Hornet moth

- **The velvet ant** is actually a wasp. It resembles an ant and can easily attack ant nests with this disguise.

# Stings

- **Insects that belong** to the Hymenopteran order, such as ants, bees and wasps, are the most familiar stinging insects.

- **A stinging insect** has special organs that secrete venom (poison) and a sharp sting or teeth to inject venom into the victim.

- **The venom** can have a paralyzing effect on the prey. It can also damage tissues and cause pain. Hornet venom is the most potent.

- **Insect venom consists of** enzymes, proteins and chemicals known as alkaloids.

- **Some insects,** such as mosquitoes, do not sting. They puncture the skin surface in order to suck up blood. Such insects can spread various diseases, such as malaria.

- **Insects sting** for two purposes – to catch prey and to defend themselves from predators.

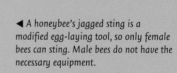

◀ *A honeybee's jagged sting is a modified egg-laying tool, so only female bees can sting. Male bees do not have the necessary equipment.*

- **Honeybees sting only once** and die soon after that. Their jagged stings remain stuck in their victim's skin, which tears out the honeybee's insides.

- **Wasps sting their victims** many times over because their stings are smooth and can be pulled out of the victims and used again.

- **Ants normally sting** as well as bite. They inject formic acid when they sting.

> ★ **STAR FACT** ★
> Ant venom glands have evolved to produce a chemical called pheromones, which the ants use to communicate.

# Habitats

- **Insects have adapted themselves** to survive in almost every habitat on Earth, including some with extreme climates.

- **Entomologists have discovered** certain species of insect that live on volcanic lava and others that survive in cold polar regions.

- **Most insects live in** tropical regions where the warm temperatures are most suitable for their growth and development.

- **Insects can live** in the freshwater of ponds, lakes, streams, rivers, and even muddy pools and small waterholes.

- **Some insect species** can live very deep underwater while others need to come to the surface to breathe in air.

- **Many insects lay their eggs** in water and their larvae thrive underwater. These insects fly out to live in the air when they become adults.

- **The larvae of house-flies** grow up in animal manure and household waste.

- **Some insects can survive** on the surface of ponds of crude oil. They feed on other insects that fall into the oil.

- **Some insects can survive** on man-made food sources, such as glue, paint, clothes and paper. They make their homes in our homes.

> ★ STAR FACT ★
> Around 97 percent of the insect world lives on the land or in freshwater. Very few insects can survive in the sea.

▼ Temperate woodlands are home to a rich variety of insects because of the range of food and shelter available. The numbers and species of insect living in woodlands vary with the seasons and the types of trees dominating the woodlands.

Key
1. Elm beetle
2. Furniture beetle
3. Flower bug
4. Shield bug

# Winter survival

- **Insects use various methods** to survive cold winters. Many go into a deep sleep called hibernation. Their body temperature falls to just above that of the surroundings and vital body processes slow down.

- **Some insects go into a dormant state** called diapause. They stop developing and growing. Diapause is most common among moth pupae.

- **Some insects spend winter** in swellings (galls), that they cause on plants. Galls provide these insects with food and shelter.

- **Beetles and ants** may burrow deep furrows in the ground and keep themselves warm inside them.

- **Ladybirds cluster together** in huge numbers when they hibernate.

- **Some species of beetle** store fat in their bodies to keep themselves warm.

◀ Many insects find safe places in which to survive the winter. Peacock butterflies have a chemical 'antifreeze' that helps to stop their body fluids freezing during cold weather.

- **Some butterflies and moths** survive the winter by hibernating in tree holes or caves. They may hibernate for months before emerging in spring or summer.

- **Some insects survive** the winter as eggs, which only start to develop the following spring.

- **Some insects replace the water content** in their body with glycerol, which works as an antifreeze.

- **Honeybees stay inside their hives** during cold weather. They vibrate their wings or cluster together to keep warm.

# Migration

- **Insects migrate** great distances in search of suitable living and breeding conditions. They often migrate when the weather changes or when food becomes scarce.

- **Migrating insects** may land in some places and lay a large number of eggs before moving on.

- **Insects migrate in two ways**, which are known as homeostatic and dynamic migration.

- **Homeostatic migration** is when insects pass through a defined path and return the same way. In dynamic migration, insects use the wind or tides to decide their path.

- **Monarch butterflies** migrate across continents, covering a distance of more than 3000 km.

- **Pilots have spotted** migrating butterflies at an altitude of 1200 m.

★ **STAR FACT** ★
Migrating butterflies such as the painted lady do not return to their home ground, but the next generation does.

- **Butterflies sometimes travel** in huge groups. Most of the older butterflies cannot withstand the journey and die on the way.

- **Locusts migrate across farmlands** in large swarms in their search for greener pastures.

- **Army ants** do not build permanent nests because they constantly migrate in search of food.

◀ Every autumn, monarch butterflies fly from the northern areas of North America to the warmth of Florida, California and Mexico. In spring, new generations of monarchs make the long return journey north again.

# Ants

● **Ants are one of the most** successful insects on Earth. There are more than 9000 different species.

● **The study of ants** is known as myrmecology. People sometimes rear ants in elaborate ant farms.

● **Ants belong to an order of insects** known as Hymenoptera. Bees and wasps also belong to this group.

● **Entomologists believe** that ants evolved from wasps millions of years ago.

● **Ants are social insects** and live in huge colonies. These colonies consist of the queen ant, female workers and male ants.

● **An ant can lift a weight** that is 20 to 50 times more than its own body weight.

▶ *When ants find food, they form a chemical trail of pheromones so that other ants can find their way from the nest to the food source.*

● **In ant colonies,** the different ants divide themselves into groups that perform various tasks. Some ants are cleaners, some take care of the young while others gather food or defend the nest.

● **Ants are intelligent.** Experts have discovered that ant brains can function as fast as a powerful computer.

● **Ants spray formic acid** on predators as a form of defence. People used to obtain this acid by boiling ants.

★ **STAR FACT** ★
Birds allow ants to crawl on their bodies and spray them with formic acid. Known as anting, this gets rid of parasites from their feathers.

# More ants

● **Most ants live in anthills** made of mounds of soil, sand and sticks, but some nest in trees.

● **Anthills consist** of different chambers and tunnels. Each chamber is used for different purposes, such as food storage, nurseries or resting areas.

● **Not all ants live in anthills.** Army ants are nomadic in nature. They carry their eggs and young with them while travelling and set up temporary camps.

● **The queen** is the largest ant in the colony. When she matures, she flies off to find a place to build a new colony.

● **Queen ants** nip off their wings once they find a place to breed. Smaller worker ants also have wings.

● **Worker ants** take care of the eggs. At night, they carry the eggs into deep nest tunnels for protection. In the morning, the workers carry the eggs back to the surface.

◀ *Tailor, or weaver, ants make nests out of leaves or similar materials sewed together with silk produced by the larvae.*

● **Male ants** die shortly after mating with the queen ant.

● **Ants have two stomachs.** One stomach carries its own food while the other carries food that will be shared with other ants. This is called the crop.

● **Ants communicate** with the help of their feelers (antennae). They also leave scent trails behind them to let the other ants know where exactly to find the food source.

● **Each ant colony** has a unique smell that helps the members to identify each other. This also helps the ants to detect an intruder in the nest.

# Army ant

- **Army ants** constantly migrate in search of food. They can attack and enslave ants living in other colonies.

- **Army ants march only at night** and stop to camp in the morning.

- **Army ants are nomadic** in nature, and do not build permanent nests.

- **Temporary nests** are formed by army ants while the queen lays her eggs. The ants cling onto each other and form the walls and chambers.

- **Army ants are voracious eaters.** They march in swarms of up to one million ants and eat nearly 50,000 insects in a single day!

- **These ants eat insects,** birds and small animals that cross their path. Army ants can even eat a horse.

★ STAR FACT ★
A queen army ant can lay up to 4 million eggs in one month.

- **Army ants have simple** and not compound eyes like other ant species. However, worker army ants are blind.

- **Army ants have not evolved** (changed) much in the last 100 million years.

- **Some people allow army ants** to march into their homes and clear them of insects and other pests.

▼ The army ants of tropical America march in columns. To cross gaps, some of the ants form bridges with their bodies, allowing the rest of the army to swarm over them. The worker ants also link up to form chains that surround the queen and young.

# Leafcutter ant

- **Leafcutter ants** cut out bits of leaves from plants and carry them back to their underground nest.

- **Leafcutter ants cannot digest** leaves. They feed on a fungus that is specially grown by them.

- **The cut leaf pieces** are used to fertilize fungus farms that are grown inside the ant nest. There can be several farms in a single nest.

- **A queen leafcutter ant** can produce about 15 million offspring during her lifetime.

- **Leafcutter ants divide themselves** into workers and soldiers. The soldiers are bigger, and they protect the nest.

- **Small worker ants** take care of the young and the nest, while the bigger worker ants collect pieces of leaves.

- **In some species of leafcutter ant,** tiny workers ride on the pieces of snipped leaves. They protect the larger workers from flies that try to lay their eggs on them.

- **Leafcutter ants are usually found** in tropical rainforests.

- **Leafcutter ants are eaten** in some cultures. They are a rich source of protein.

- **Leafcutter ants do not sting,** but they can bite.

◀ Leafcutter ants in Central and South American rainforests often cut leaves 50 to 200 m away from their nest. Each leaf fragment can take two or three minutes to cut and is many times bigger than the tiny ant.

# Weaver ant

▶ Weaver ants joining leaves together to make their nest.

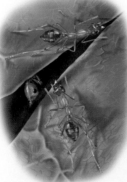

- **Weaver ants** build their colonies in the treetops, using live green leaves.

- **The larvae of weaver ants** secrete a sticky silklike substance. Adult ants use the larvae like glue sticks.

- **A team of adult worker weaver ants** holds two leaves together. Another worker holds the larva in its mandibles (mouthparts) and uses the silky secretion to stick the leaves together.

- **A colony can contain** about 150 weaver nests in 20 different trees. The queen ant's nest is built in the centre of the colony. It is made with extra silk and is feathery in appearance.

- **The larger worker** (soldier) ants protect the nest. Smaller workers take care of various chores inside the nest.

- **Weaver ants are carnivores** and feed on body fluids from small, soft bodied insects. Some species also feed on honeydew.

- **For 2000 years,** the Chinese have used weaver ants to control pests in their fields.

- **Weaver ants do not sting** but they can inflict very painful bites if provoked. When they bite, weaver ants squirt formic acid into the wound, which causes even more pain.

- **Some caterpillars and spiders** camouflage themselves as weaver ants and attack weaver ant nests. The spiders may even smell like weaver ants.

> ★ STAR FACT ★
> Weaver ants are eaten in Eastern cultures.
> The oil extracted from these ants is often
> used as sweeteners in food.

# Bees

- **There are approximately** 20,000 species of bee. Some live alone but over 500 species are social and live in colonies.

- **Bees are small** – only 2 to 4 cm in length. They have hairs and a sting to protect them. The hairs also help them to collect pollen.

- **Bees are usually black** or grey in colour but can also be yellow, red, green or blue.

- **Bees feed on pollen and nectar** from flowers. Pollen contains protein and nectar provides energy.

- **Social bees secrete wax** to build their nests. A honeybee colony may contain 3000 to 40,000 bees. It consists of a single queen bee, female workers and male drones.

- **The male drones do not have stings** and their function is to mate with the queen bee. The queen lays about 600 to 700 eggs every day.

◄ Honeybee workers crowd around their queen. The workers stroke and lick the queen to pick up scents called pheromones, which pass on information.

- **Bees have five eyes.** They have two compound eyes and three simple eyes, or ocelli. Bees cannot see red but they can see ultraviolet light, which is invisible to us.

- **A normal bee's lifespan** ranges from five to six weeks but a queen bee can live up to five years.

- **Bees communicate with other bees** about the distance, direction and quantity of the food source through a unique combination of dance and sounds.

- **A honeybee attacks** to protect itself or its colony. Once a bee stings, it leaves behind its sting and venom in the victim's body. As the bee pulls away from the victim, it dies when its organs are pulled out of its abdomen.

# Bee behaviour

- **Bees have two kinds of mouthparts.** The first, found in honeybees, is adapted for sucking. The other is adapted for biting. This is found in carpenter bees.

- **The antennae are the organs** of touch and smell. Bees use them to detect flower fragrances and to find nectar.

- **Bees can rarely distinguish** sweet and bitter tastes but can identify sour and salty tastes. Bees use their front legs, antennae and proboscis for tasting.

- **Bees have no ears,** but they can sense vibrations through their sensitive hairs.

- **Bees do not sleep at night,** although they remain motionless.

- **Wild bees nest underground** or in tree holes, caves or under houses. Honeybees also live in hives constructed by people.

◄ Bees are important because they carry pollen from flower to flower so that seeds can grow.

- **Social bees** live in large colonies of queens, males and workers. Males do not help in the organization and other activities of the colony.

- **When a colony becomes overcrowded,** some of the bees fly to a new location. This is called swarming.

- **The queen bee lays eggs** and male bees fertilize the queen bee. Worker bees perform various tasks, such as cleaning the cells, keeping the young warm, feeding larvae and collecting food for the colony.

- **The queen bee secretes pheromones,** which inhibit the development of worker bees into queens. Once she lays eggs, the fertilized eggs become female worker bees and the unfertilized eggs become male bees.

# Bee nests

- **Social bees make complex nests,** which consist of a number of cells, often built in flat sheets called combs.

- **Social bees** make cells of wax. However, honeybees are the only species that makes prominent honeycombs. People sometimes keep honeybees in hives for their honey.

- **Honeycombs** are divided into three sections. The upper section is used for storing honey, the middle section for storing pollen. The lower section holds eggs and young.

- **The hexagonal shape** of the honeycomb cells allows the maximum amount of honey to be stored using the least amount of wax.

- **Social bees use their nests** to raise their eggs, larvae and pupae – their brood. Some also use their nests to prepare and store honey for the winter.

- **Bees use 'bee glue'** (propolis), a sticky tree resin, to strengthen and repair their nests.

- **Bees use water** as a coolant to maintain an optimum temperature of 35°C in a beehive.

- **Male drones** have bigger cells than the female workers in a honeybee hive.

- **A bumblebee queen** builds her nest in a hole in the ground.

- **Stingless bees** build saclike combs made from a mixture of resin and wax called cerumen. The combs are held together by propolis in the hollows of trees, rocks and walls.

▶ A honeybee hive showing some of the cells used for storing pollen, honey eggs or developing larvae.

# Honey

- **Honey** is a natural, unrefined sweetener, which is an alternative to sugar.

- **Every 100 g of honey** provides 319 kcal of energy.

- **Bees collect the nectar** of flowers, and other plant secretions, and turn it into honey. It is then altered chemically into different types of sugars and stored in the comb cells.

- **The honey in a honeycomb** includes matured nectar, pollen, bee saliva and wax granules.

- **Honey mainly contains** moisture, sugars and minerals. Several trace elements, such as calcium, phosphorous, magnesium, iron, silica and vitamin C, are also present.

- **Honey is considered** to be the only source of food that has all the energy and protein reserves necessary to sustain life.

◀ A natural honeycomb, showing the double layer of six-sided cells constructed by the bees to store honey. The honeycomb is used in the winter as food for the larvae and other members of the colony.

- **The colour and flavour of honey** depends upon the climate and the flowers from which the nectar has been collected.

- **Honey serves as an important source** of medicines because of its mild laxative, bactericidal, sedative, antiseptic and alkaline characteristics.

- **Honey extracted from wild beehives** can be dangerous if the nectar is obtained from poisonous flowers.

- **Honey is used in a fluid medium** in the preservation of the cornea (layer at the front of the eye).

# Bumblebee

● **Bumblebees are hairy.** They are black, yellow or orange in colour and up to 25 mm long. They are most common in temperate regions.

● **Bumblebees live** in small colonies of between 50 to 600 bees.

● **Bumblebees build their nests** on the ground in grassy hollows or deserted nests. The chambers are spherical with one exit. The cells inside are capsule shaped.

● **The queen bumblebee** lays her eggs in wax cups inside the nest. The wax is secreted by her abdominal glands.

● **Only the young queen bumblebees** survive the winter. The rest of the bees in the colony die.

◀ The bee combs the pollen from its body and packs it tightly into the pollen baskets (long, stiff bristles) on its back legs.

● **Bumblebees regulate their body temperature** using their body hair. The queens hibernate in winter and emerge in the spring to lay eggs and start a new colony.

● **Bumblebees are low fliers** and move slowly around the flowers.

● **Bumblebees help to pollinate plants,** such as red clover. Their long tongue enables them to reach deep inside flowers.

● **In summer,** the bumblebee workers fan their wings to cool the developing young. The buzzing sound of fanning is so loud that it can be heard from a distance.

> ★ STAR FACT ★
> Bumblebees do not produce large quantities of honey. They store honey just for feeding themselves and their young.

# Carpenter bee

● **Carpenter bees** are named after their habit of drilling into wood for building nests.

● **Blue-black or metallic in colour,** carpenter bees resemble large bumblebees.

● **Carpenter bees** are found all over the world, especially in areas where woody plants flourish. They are common in forested regions of the tropics.

● **Carpenter bees are solitary** in nature and do not live in colonies.

● **Male carpenter bees** have white-coloured faces or white markings and females have black-coloured faces.

● **Males do not have a sting** but they do guard the nest. The females do have stings but are very docile and do not sting unless in danger.

> ★ STAR FACT ★
> Adult carpenter bees hibernate during the winter. They remain in their wooden nest, surviving on stored honey and pollen.

◀ A carpenter bee is about 20 to 25 mm long. It is less hairy than a bumblebee, with short hairs on its abdomen or none at all.

● **Female carpenter bees** nest in their wooden tunnels. They prefer weathered, unpainted, bare wood. In these tunnels, carpenter bees drill holes, where they lay eggs in individual cells and store enough food for the larvae to grow. There is only a single entrance to each tunnel.

● **People take preventive measures,** such as spraying pesticides, to keep carpenter bees away from their home and gardens.

# Honeybee

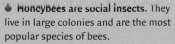

- **Honeybees are social insects.** They live in large colonies and are the most popular species of bees.

- **Some well-known species** of honeybee are Italian bees, Carniolan (Slovenian) bees, Caucasian bees, German black bees and Africanized honeybees.

- **In a honeybee colony,** different groups of bees carry out different tasks. A colony is made up of a queen bee, female workers and male drones.

- **Queen bees** are sexually productive and responsible for laying eggs that develop into drones and worker bees.

- **Worker bees** have a sharp sting, pollen baskets, wax secreting glands and a honey sac for collecting honey. The wax is used to build sheets of cells called combs.

- **Honeybees are the biggest producers of honey.** This is why they are the species most domesticated by humans.

◀ Honeybees have a hairy thorax and an abdomen with orange-yellow rings separating the segments.

- **Worker bees build the nest** as well as collect pollen and nectar for food. They are also responsible for maintaining the nursery temperature at 34°C, which is ideal for hatching the eggs and rearing the larvae.

- **Drones do not have a sting.** Their sole function is to mate with the queen, and they die after mating. During the winter, they are driven out by the workers to die.

- **Honeybees** have an amazing mode of communication among themselves – dancing. Dr Karl Von Frisch won the Nobel Prize for deciphering the bee dance.

- **Honeybees are susceptible** to various diseases and attacks by parasites. Parasite and virus attacks may cause paralysis in bees.

# Leafcutter bee

- **Leafcutter bees are named** after their habit of cutting pieces of leaf to make a protective casing for their eggs. They nest in the soil or hollow plant stems.

- **They have hair** on their back, which helps them collect pollen.

- **Most leafcutter bees** are solitary, and females construct individual nests. Males are smaller than females and have hairy faces.

- **The female bee** builds her nest from leaf pieces. Once a cell is ready, she stores pollen and honey inside, lays an egg and closes the cell with a disk of leaf. Then she repeats the sequence until the entire nest is complete.

- **Individual female leafcutter bees** do all the work. They select the nesting place, construct cells, lay the eggs and rear the larvae.

- **Leafcutter bees are docile** with a mild sting. They use the sting to defend themselves.

◀ A female leafcutter bee snips off a piece of leaf with her sharp jaws. She will roll up the leaf fragment and carry it between her legs as she flies back to her nest.

- **It is possible** for leafcutter bees to harm plants because of their habit of constructing nests with plant leaves.

- **Leafcutter bees help some plants,** such as alfalfa, with pollination. They do this by carrying the pollen from one plant to another.

- **The predators of the leafcutter bee** include wasps, velvet ants and some species of blister beetle.

---

**★ STAR FACT ★**
The average lifespan of a female leafcutter bee is two months and in this time, she lays 30 to 40 eggs.

# Wasps

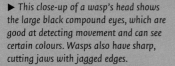

▶ This close-up of a wasp's head shows the large black compound eyes, which are good at detecting movement and can see certain colours. Wasps also have sharp, cutting jaws with jagged edges.

● **Wasps belong to the Hymenopteran order,** as do bees and ants. They have hard exoskeletons and their bodies are divided into head, thorax and abdomen. They all have transparent wings and two compound eyes.

● **Wasps are solitary** as well as social insects. Social wasps live in huge colonies while solitary wasps live alone. There are about 17,000 species of wasps, but only about 1500 species are social.

● **Wasp nests can be simple or complex.** Some nests are just burrows in the ground while others are built with mud and twigs and can have many cells and tunnels.

★ STAR FACT ★
When disturbed, female wasps can sting.

● **Each nest has at least one queen wasp** as well as workers and males.

● **Not all wasps build nests.** Some wasps such as cuckoo wasps, lay eggs in the nests of other bees and other wasps.

● **Other species of wasp** lay their eggs in stems, leaves, fruits and flowers instead of building nests.

● **Adult wasps feed on nectar,** and fruit and plant sap while the larvae feed on insects.

● **Many species of wasp** are parasitic in nature, which means that they live part of their lives as parasites inside other insects. The larvae of such wasps feed on other insects and sometimes eat plant tissues.

● **Wasps are helpful for controlling pests,** such as caterpillars.

# Hornet

● **Hornets belong to the order** Hymenoptera and the Vespidae family. They have dark brown and yellow stripes all over their body.

● **Hornets are known for their ferocious nature** and painful sting. They are huge, robust wasps and are social in nature.

● **Social hornets form huge colonies** that can contain about 25,000 individuals.

● **Hornets can build their nest anywhere** – at a height or even on the ground. They insulate their nests with layers of 'paper'.

● **These insects chew plant fibre** and mix it with saliva to form a papery paste, which they use to build nests. The nest is spherical, with an entrance at the bottom and is divided into many tiers inside. These tiers have hexagonal cells, in which the young ones are raised.

● **Hornets build the largest nests** of all wasps. A hornet nest can be 122 cm long and 91 cm in circumference.

▶ Hornets can be 30 mm in length. They can be distinguished from wasps by their larger size and deeper yellow colour.

● **Hornet colonies die out in one year.** No member of the colony survives the winter except the female hornets that have mated.

● **Abandoned hornet nests** provide shelter to other insects during the winter.

● **Some insects have stripes,** which resemble those of hornets. These ward off predators, which mistake harmless insects for hornets.

★ STAR FACT ★
Hornets are known to chase their tormentors. Hence the saying 'never stir a hornet's nest'.

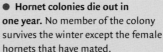

# Gall wasp

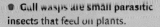

● Gall wasps are small parasitic insects that feed on plants.

● **These insects are named** after their habit of causing the formation of a tumour-like growth in plants, known as galls.

● **Galls are an abnormal growth** of plant tissues and leaves. Some of them look like greenish apples or berries on leaves.

● **Galls are formed when** a female gall wasp injects her eggs into a plant. When the eggs hatch, the larvae release some chemicals, which causes the plant to cover them with soft tissues in the form of a gall.

● **Galls can be either** spongy or hollow inside.

● **Gall wasp larvae** feed on the gall and pupate inside it. Adult gall wasps emerge from the gall either by boring a hole or by bursting it through the surface.

◀ *Gall wasps are usually about 2 to 8 mm long. Their shiny abdomen is oval in shape and their wings have few veins.*

● **Different types of galls,** such as leaf, flower, seed and stem galls, are caused by different species of gall wasp.

● **A gall is like a nursery** for one or more species of gall wasp.

● **A species of gall wasp,** known as a fig wasp, causes the formation of seed galls inside wild figs and in the process, pollinates them. No other insect pollinates wild figs.

● **Gall wasps are very selective** about the plants on which they lay their eggs. For instance, some gall wasps lay their eggs on figs, while others prefer roses.

▼ *Female fig wasps lay eggs on flowers inside immature figs. The eggs develop into larvae, pupae and adults. Adult females emerge and fly off to find other figs in which to lay their eggs. The wingless male wasps die without ever leaving the fig.*

# Paper wasp

▶ *Wasps do not store food in their nests as the cells face downwards.*

● **Paper wasps** are reddish-brown in colour and have yellow stripes on their body.

● **They are social insects** and live in small colonies of 20 to 30 insects. After the queen wasp mates, she builds a nest made of six-sided cells. The nests are mostly built in the spring.

● **Paper wasps chew plant fibre,** which they mix with their saliva to build their nests.

● **A few queen paper wasps** build a nest together. The most powerful queen dominates and leads the colony, while the others become workers.

● **Some paper wasp nests** look like inverted umbrellas, so these insects are also known as 'umbrella wasps'.

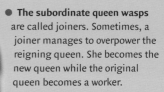

● **The subordinate queen wasps** are called joiners. Sometimes, a joiner manages to overpower the reigning queen. She becomes the new queen while the original queen becomes a worker.

● **Unlike other wasps,** bees and ants, queen paper wasps closely resemble the worker wasps.

● **Adult paper wasps** feed only on nectar while the young larvae feed on chewed insects.

● **Sometimes, army ants** invade paper wasp nests and destroy the entire colony.

★ **STAR FACT** ★
The Chinese were inspired by the humble paper wasp to invent paper.

# Parasitic wasps

● **Parasitic wasps lay their eggs** inside other wasps, spiders and insects, such as bees, caterpillars and aphids.

● **Female parasitic wasps** inject their eggs into the body of their host using an ovipositor (egg-laying tube). Once the eggs hatch, the larvae eat their way out of the host.

● **Parasitic wasps can lay as many as** 3000 eggs inside a single host insect.

● **Some parasitic wasps** are known for infesting moth and butterfly caterpillars. They are helpful for controlling the caterpillar populations in fields.

● **Some tiny wasps** specialize in parasitizing insect eggs. The eggs of these wasps can multiply into many cells and almost 150 wasps of the same sex can hatch from a single egg.

● **The smallest insect,** the fairyfly, is an egg parasite wasp. A fairyfly measures only about 0.2 mm.

● **A parasitic wasp can be infested** by a smaller parasitic wasp, which in turn can be infested by another wasp. This phenomenon is known as hyperparasitism.

● **Unlike other social wasps and bees,** parasitic wasps do not sting.

● **Aphids that serve as hosts** for parasitic wasps appear puffy and hard. They are known as aphid mummies, and die once the wasp larvae are ready to pupate.

● **Parasitic wasps are useful to us** because their hosts are pest insects.

◀ *The Ichneumon wasp has larvae that grow and develop inside their living host, only killing the host when they are nearly fully grown and ready to pupate.*

# Velvet ant

- **These wasps resemble** huge hairy ants, which is why they are known as velvet ants.

- **Velvet ants are usually** red, brown or black in colour.

- **Found in dry areas,** velvet ants are densely covered with long, whitish hair. When it is too hot to venture outside, velvet ants burrow underground or climb into plants.

- **Male velvet ants** have wings and cannot sting. Females, on the other hand, do not have wings and can sting. They move about on the ground like ants and their sting can be quite painful.

- **Velvet ants have a tough outer covering,** which protects them against bee and wasp stings.

- **Female velvet ants** move swiftly and are often found searching for the burrows of solitary bees and wasps.

- **Velvet ants lay eggs** in the nests of bees and other wasps and are parasitic in nature.

- **The larva of the velvet ant** emerges before the eggs of its host hatch. It eats its host's eggs as well as its larvae.

- **Velvet ants make a squeaky noise** if they are attacked or captured.

- **The sting of the velvet ant** is powerful and people used to believe it could kill a cow. This, however, is not true.

◀ *The females lay their eggs in bumblebee nests and the velvet ant larvae feed on the bee larvae.*

# Butterfly lifestyle

- **Butterflies do not have** a mouth or teeth to chew their food. Instead they have a strawlike structure called a proboscis, which helps them suck nectar.

- **A butterfly's wings** are covered with microscopic scales, which overlap like roof tiles.

- **Butterflies are active** during the day and fly only in the daytime. Some tropical butterflies also fly at night.

- **Adult butterflys lay eggs on plants.** The eggs hatch into caterpillars, or larvae. The caterpillar develops into a pupa or chrysalis and finally matures into a butterfly.

- **Caterpillars grow at a tremendous rate.** They shed their skin (moult) occasionally as the skin does not expand with their growth.

- **Most caterpillars moult four or five times** before they enter the pupa or chrysalis stage.

- **Butterflies do not have lungs.** Instead, they breathe through small holes in their abdomen, which are called spiracles.

- **In some species,** the caterpillars have stinging hairs containing poisons, which cause pain when touched.

- **Some male butterflies** have scent pockets on their wings, which disperse pheromones.

- **Some butterflies migrate** in order to avoid bad weather, overcrowding, or to find a new place to live.

▲ *A butterfly drinking nectar from a flower using its proboscis.*

# Butterfly features

● **Butterflies are beautiful insects** that belong to the order Lepidoptera. About 28,000 species of butterfly have been identified so far.

● **The earliest butterfly fossils** can be traced back to the Cretaceous Period, 130 million years ago.

● **Butterflies can live anywhere in the world** except in cold regions, such as Antarctica. They cannot withstand cold weather and have to maintain a body temperature above 30°C.

● **Like other insects,** butterflies have an exoskeleton, a hard outer covering that protects the body. A butterfly's body is also divided into three sections – head, thorax and abdomen. All butterflies have a pair of compound eyes.

● **The average lifespan of butterflies** is 20 to 40 days but some species can survive up to 10 months while others last only three to four days.

▼ *Butterflies, such as this small postman butterfly, usually hold their wings upright when they rest. Moths usually spread their wings out or fold them flat.*

▼ *All butterflies have similarly shaped bodies, but the markings on their wings depend on their habitat. This comma butterfly, with its ragged wings and mottled colour, is well-camouflaged as a dead leaf, which protects it from predators.*

Head

Thorax                    Abdomen

● **Butterflies only consume liquid food,** such as flower nectar and liquids from rotten fruits or vines. Some feed on liquid animal waste.

● **Butterflies protect themselves from predators,** such as birds, lizards, bats and spiders, by mimicry and camouflage.

● **After bees,** butterflies are the second largest pollinators of crops.

● **Some butterflies can be destructive too.** Cabbage white butterflies feed on cabbages and can destroy entire crops.

---

★ **STAR FACT** ★
Male butterflies attract the females by dancing around them. This is called a 'courtship dance'. While dancing, males secrete pheromones, a chemical scent that stimulates mating.

# Tortoiseshell butterfly

● **Tortoiseshell butterflies** are brightly coloured and are found all over the world. They are one of the most common butterflies in the UK.

● **Tortoiseshell butterflies can also be found** in the hill forests of Asia and northern USA.

● **Adult tortoiseshell butterflies** feed on fruit juices or the nectar from flowers, such as daisy and aster.

● **Female tortoiseshell butterflies** are larger than the male butterflies.

● **After mating,** a female tortoiseshell butterfly lays her eggs in batches of 60 to 100 on young nettle leaves.

● **The eggs hatch after about 10 days** and the caterpillars spin a web over the nettle's growing tip. Tortoiseshell caterpillars live in groups and feed on the nettle leaves.

◀ *Tortoiseshell butterflies have a long life as adults, surviving for about 10 months.*

● **Tortoiseshell caterpillars** grow to about 2 cm in length in a month. They are black, with two yellow lines along their sides.

● **Tortoiseshell butterfly pupae** are greyish brown and have metallic spots.

● **Tortoiseshell butterflies** used to be known as the 'devil's butterfly' in Scotland.

★ STAR FACT ★
Tortoiseshell butterflies hibernate during the winter. Adults often hibernate in houses and sheds and can be spotted in the open between March and October, while caterpillars are seen between May to August.

# Red admiral butterfly

★ STAR FACT ★
Red admiral butterflies prefer woods, gardens, parks, marshes and fields. During migration, these butterflies can be found in almost any habitat, from the tundra in Canada to subtropical countries near the Equator.

● **The red admiral butterfly** is easy to recognize. It is black with red bands and white markings on the wings.

● **Red Admirals are easily found** in gardens, orchards and woodlands across Europe, North America and Asia.

● **Adult red admiral butterflies** feed on flowers and rotting fruits, while caterpillars feed on nettle plants.

● **This species is known** for its migratory behaviour. Red admiral butterflies cannot survive cold winters. Once the winter sets in, they migrate to warmer places.

● **The red admiral has a very erratic,** rapid flight. Unusually for a butterfly, it sometimes flies at night.

◀ *The red admiral butterfly's name comes from its bright, 'admirable' colours.*

● **Female red admiral butterflies** lay their eggs on nettle leaves. After seven days, the caterpillar emerges and folds leaves around itself to make a protective tent. The leaves are held together with silk threads and the caterpillar feeds inside its leaf shelter.

● **The caterpillars** are black to greenish-grey in colour and have a yellow line running along each side.

● **Adult red admiral butterflies may hibernate** in winter, storing enough fat in their bodies for survival.

● **Red admiral butterflies feed on tree sap,** rotting fruit, bird droppings. and the nectar of plants, such as common milkweed, red clover, aster and alfalfa.

# Monarch butterfly

- **Monarch butterflies** are found all over the world, except in the cold regions. They are black and orange in colour and have a wingspan ranging up to 10 cm.

- **Monarch butterflies use their body colour** to frighten off their enemies. The orange colour is considered a warning sign. They can also blend easily with the surroundings.

- **Monarch caterpillars feed on milkweed plants,** retaining the sap in their bodies even when they mature into butterflies. Birds attempting to eat monarchs dislike the taste and spit them out.

- **Monarchs are beneficial for crops** as they eat milkweed plants, which are weeds.

- **Monarch caterpillars are brightly coloured,** with white spots around the margin of their wings. They are voracious eaters.

- **Male monarch butterflies** have dark spots called scent scales on their hind wings. Females do not have scent scales.

- **A monarch butterfly takes approximately one month** to mature from an egg into an adult butterfly. Adult monarch butterflies feed on flower nectar and water.

- **They are long distance migratory insects** and can migrate over 3200 km. Monarch butterflies guide themselves during migration using the position of the Sun and the magnetic field of the Earth.

- **Habitat destruction and changes caused by logging** are constant threats to monarch butterflies. Spraying of pesticides for weed control kills milkweed plants. This endangers the habitat and food source for these butterflies.

▲ Canadians call this butterfly 'King Billy' because its orange and black colours are the same as those of King William of Orange, who was king of Great Britain from 1689–1702.

▲ The white spots on the head and thorax of monarch butterflies act as an extra warning signal, which emphasizes to birds and reptiles that this butterfly tastes horrible.

★ STAR FACT ★
Monarch butterflies from northern USA and Canada migrate to the Sierra Madre Mountains, west of Mexico City, Mexico in the winter. The location was first discovered in 1975.

# Bhutan glory butterfly

- **Bhutan glory butterflies** are found in Bhutan and north-eastern parts of Asia.

- **These butterflies prefer to live** in grass fields and undisturbed forests.

- **The wings of Bhutan glory butterflies** are black and measure about 9 to 11 cm.

- **Bhutan glory butterflies breed twice a year** from May to June and from August to October.

- **Very little is known** about the life history of Bhutan glory butterflies.

- **Experts believe** that these insects probably feed on the poisonous Indian birthwort plant.

- **Bhutan glory butterflies protect themselves** from predators by absorbing poison from the plants they feed on.

- **These butterflies fly at altitudes** of 1700–3000 m in the mountains.

- **Bhutan glory butterflies were collected** in large numbers in the past. Now, their numbers have been greatly reduced and they are very rare to spot.

- **Bhutan glory butterflies are now listed** as an endangered and protected species.

◀ At rest, the Bhutan glory butterfly hides its colourful back wings with its front wings so it is well camouflaged. If disturbed, this butterfly quickly opens and shuts it wings, exposing its bright orange markings. These sudden flashes of colour may confuse a predator and allow the butterfly time to escape.

# Painted lady butterfly

**★ STAR FACT ★**
Painted lady butterflies do not survive in winter. They die in the cold weather.

- **The painted lady butterfly** is also known as the thistle butterfly, as its caterpillar feeds mostly on thistle plants, and as cosmopolite because it is found worldwide.

- **The painted lady is one of the best-known** butterflies in the world.

- **Painted lady butterflies are mostly found** in temperate regions across Asia, Europe and North America.

▶ The painted lady butterfly has white marks on the black tips of its front wings.

- **These butterflies are primarily** black, brown and orange in colour. They have a wingspan of 4 to 5 cm.

- **Female painted lady butterflies lay eggs** on plants, such as thistles. After three to five days, they hatch into caterpillars. The caterpillars transform into pupae and finally emerge as colourful adult butterflies.

- **The caterpillar, or larva,** lives in a silky nest woven around the plant on which it feeds.

- **Adult painted lady butterflies feed on nectar** from flowers, such as aster, cosmos, ironweed and joe-pye weed.

- **An adult painted lady butterfly lives** for only two weeks.

- **Painted lady butterflies are strong fliers** and long-distance migrants. They can travel thousands of kilometres, sometimes with thousands of individuals flying together.

# Birdwing butterfly

- **Female Queen Alexandra's birdwing butterflies** are the world's largest butterflies. They have a wingspan of about 26 cm!

- **Birdwing butterflies belong to** the swallowtail group of butterflies. The butterflies have tails on their hind wings, like the wings of a swallow.

- **Male birdwing butterflies** are brightly coloured with yellow, pale blue and green markings.

- **Female birdwing butterflies** have cream and chocolate brown markings on their wings.

- **Predators avoid birdwing butterflies** because they are poisonous and taste bad. Birdwing caterpillars feed on the pipevine plants and absorb poisons from these plants.

- **A birdwing butterfly lives** for about seven months.

> ★ STAR FACT ★
> Queen Alexandra's birdwing butterflies were named in honour of the wife of King Edward VII of England.

- **The birdwing butterfly is listed** as an endangered species. People are not allowed to hunt this insect.

- **The golden birdwing** and southern birdwing are some of the cousins of the Queen Alexandra's birdwing butterfly.

- **Birdwing butterflies are found** in tropical areas. The best time to spot these butterflies is in the early morning when they collect nectar from flowers.

◀ The beautiful Rajah Brooke's birdwing soars high in the rainforest canopy from Malaysia through to Sumatra and Borneo.

# Apollo butterfly

- **Apollo butterflies** are mostly found in hilly regions of Spain, central Europe, southern Scandinavia and Asia. Some live above an altitude of 4000 m and rarely descend to lower levels.

- **Apollo butterflies are cream in colour** with red and yellow eyespots on their wings. They are frail-looking butterflies but survive harsh weather conditions.

- **Habitat destruction** has made Apollo butterflies extremely rare. They are now an endangered species, protected by law in many countries.

- **The breeding season** of Apollo butterflies lasts from July to August. The female lays hundreds of eggs.

- **An adult Apollo butterfly** has a lifespan of a week.

- **Apollo caterpillars feed on** stonecrop plants.

◀ This mountain butterfly has a wingspan of 50 to 100 mm and a furry body to protect it from the cold.

- **Female butterflies lay round,** white eggs. The eggs usually hatch in the months of August and September.

- **These caterpillars moult five times** in their lifetime.

- **Attempts are being made** to save Apollo butterfly populations by means of habitat management measures, reduction of insecticide use and observation of their behaviour during the time they are on the wing.

> ★ STAR FACT ★
> Adult butterflies use their proboscis, a kind of sucking tube, to feed on nectar from flowers, such as the thistle.

# Peacock butterfly

◀ Peacock butterflies use the false eyes on their wings to scare predators away.

● **Peacock butterflies** are named after their large, multi-coloured spots, which look like the 'eyes' on a real peacock's feathers. Adult peacock butterflies are light to dark brown in colour and have purplish-black lines.

● **These butterflies live** in temperate areas of Europe and Asia. They are commonly found in England and Wales.

● **Adult peacock butterflies** love to be around orchards, gardens and other places that have lots of flowers. They feed on the flower nectar of thistles, lavender and buddleia and also suck juices from overripe fruits.

● **Peacock caterpillars** feed on nettle plants.

● **Peacock butterflies live in groups.** They have a single brood in a year. Adults hibernate through the winter and emerge in the spring. They die after laying eggs.

● **Female peacock butterflies lay** up to 500 eggs. The caterpillars emerge after one to two weeks.

● **Fully grown caterpillars** are about 4 cm long. They have black-and-white spots and long black dorsal spines.

● **The pupae are** greyish-brown, with metallic gold spots.

● **The lifespan of a peacock butterfly** is relatively long and can even last up to one year.

# Viceroy butterfly

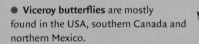

● **Viceroy butterflies** are mostly found in the USA, southern Canada and northern Mexico.

● **They have black and orange patterns** with white spots on their wings.

● **These butterflies are found** in meadows, marshes and swamps and other wet areas with trees, such as willow, aspen and poplar.

● **There are usually two or three generations** of viceroy butterflies born in each breeding season.

● **Viceroy butterflies mate** in the afternoon. The female butterfly lays her eggs on poplar and willow leaves.

● **These eggs hatch** and the viceroy caterpillars feed on the leaves of trees such as willow and poplar.

● **The caterpillars are white** and olive brown.

● **Adult viceroy butterflies feed on** the liquids from decaying fungi, dung and other animal waste.

◀ The viceroy has a faster wingbeat than the monarch butterfly and also glides with its wings held horizontally, not held at an angle like the monarch.

● **Predators often mistake**  **viceroy butterflies** for monarch butterflies, and avoid eating them. Viceroy butterflies are not poisonous.

# Moths

● **Moths make up about 90 percent** of the insects that belong to order Lepidoptera, which also includes butterflies. Insects that belong to this order have scaly wings.

● **Moths feed on nectar** as well as other plant juices. Some moths do not feed as adults because they do not have mouthparts.

● **In some species of moth,** the females do not have wings.

● **Most moths** are active only at night.

● **Like butterflies,** some moths, such as hawk-moths, migrate long distances.

● **Some moths have large spots** on their wings. From a distance, these spots resemble the eyes of a fearsome animal and scare away potential predators.

◀ The Polyphemus moth has striking eyespots on its back wings and is named after the one-eyed giant of Greek myths.

● **Moths are masters** of mimicry and camouflage.

● **Some moths can be mistaken for** bird droppings when they lie still on the ground. This helps them to escape the eyes of predatory birds.

● **Species of moths known as clothes moth** are quite unusual. The larvae of these moths are destructive in nature and feed on different types of natural fabrics, such as wool, cotton, linen and even on fur, feathers and hair.

★ STAR FACT ★
Tiger moths produce supersonic sound just like bats. These moths are known for their awful taste and bats avoid eating them.

# Death's head hawk-moth

● **Death's head hawk-moths** belong to a group called sphinx moths, and are found in Africa, Asia and Europe.

● **This moth is named after** a peculiar mark, which is visible on its thorax. The mark looks like a skull.

● **Death's head hawk-moths steal honey** from bees' nests, which is why they are also known as 'bee robbers'.

● **At any point in its growth stage,** a death's head hawk-moth is capable of producing a loud squeaking sound to scare its predators away.

● **These moths force air** out of their strong, thick proboscis to make this squeaky sound.

● **Females lay single eggs** on different plants. They prefer to lay their eggs on potato and brinjal plants.

● **The caterpillars have a horn on their tail end** and are also known as hornworms.

● **To pupate,** the caterpillars make a mud cell deep in the soil and smoothe it by pushing their head against the wall of the cell.

▲ The caterpillars of Death's head hawk-moths reach 12.5 cm when fully grown and make a clicking sound if disturbed.

● **Death's head hawk-moths find it difficult** to survive harsh winters and migrate to warmer places.

★ STAR FACT ★
The strange mark on the thorax of the death's head hawk-moth has given rise to many superstitions. In ancient times the presence of this moth was considered a sign of death.

# Atlas moth

- **Atlas moths belong** to the group of emperor moths and are known for their large size. They are named because the patterns on their wings look like maps.

- **Atlas moths are the largest moths,** with a wingspan of 24 to 30 cm. When they fly, they are often mistaken for birds.

- **Atlas moths are found** in forests in south-east Asia.

- **The tips of their wings** are hooked and have patterns on them, which helps to scare predators away.

- **Females are much larger and heavier** than the males, and their antennae are less hairy.

- **Females lay eggs under leaves.** These eggs hatch into greenish caterpillars, which feed on leaves.

- **Adults do not have mouthparts** so they cannot eat. They live for just two weeks and die soon after mating.

◀ *Giant Atlas moths have transparent triangles in the middle of each wing where the coloured scales are missing. These shiny patches may confuse predators by reflecting the light.*

- **Males have large feathery antennae.** These antennae are capable of sensing pheromones released by female atlas moths from a distance of several kilometres.

- **The caterpillars have fleshy projections** all over their bodies, and can grow up to 12 cm in length.

> ★ STAR FACT ★
> Atlas moth cocoons hang from trees like fruits. These cocoons are used to produce a type of silk in Asia, known as Fagara silk.

# Swallowtail moth

- **Swallowtail moths** belong to the family geometridae of the order Lepidoptera.

- **Swallowtail moths** are strikingly unusual and can be mistaken for butterflies. They have slender bodies, thin legs and a short proboscis.

- **These moths** sometimes fly during the day.

- **Swallowtail moths** are very large in size and are found mainly in tropical countries.

- **In June and July,** swallowtail moths are widespread and common in Europe and parts of Asia.

- **Not much is known** about the life history of swallowtail moths.

- **Some of the nocturnal species** have eyespots at the tip of their short pointed hind wings.

◀ *This large moth has broad wings, like a butterfly, but flies rapidly.*

- **These eyespots give an impression** of a false head at the rear side of the moth, which protects it from predators. Therefore, during the day, these moths always rest on the upper side of leaves.

- **The size and marks** on the bodies differ in male and female swallowtail moths.

> ★ STAR FACT ★
> Swallowtail moths derive their names from their resemblance to swallowtail butterflies. Their hindwings have a tail similar to that of swallowtail butterflies.

# Hummingbird hawk-moth

- **Hummingbird hawk-moths** belong to the hawk-moth group and are found all over the world.

- **Unlike other hawk-moths,** these moths fly during the day and can be easily spotted hovering over flowers in gardens and parks.

- **Brownish in colour,** hummingbird hawk-moths have black-and-white spots all over their body and their hind wings are orange.

- **These moths have a brown,** white-spotted abdomen with tufts of hair at the tip.

- **Like other butterflies and moths,** hummingbird hawk-moths have long, tubelike mouthparts that are coiled and tucked under their head.

- **These moths use their long tongue** to collect nectar from flowers.

- **The caterpillar is slender and colourful.** It has a horned tail, which gives it a fearsome look.

- **The moth pupates** in leaf litter (dead leaves, bits of bark, and other dead plant matter lying on the ground), and weaves a very thick cocoon.

- **People often mistake this moth** for a hummingbird because it hovers over flowers and sucks nectar from them, like a hummingbird.

- **Hummingbird hawk-moths** hibernate in winter to survive the cold weather.

▼ The broad body of this robust little hawk-moth shows that it is a powerful flier. It holds its body still while hovering in front of flowers, beating its wings so fast that they are almost invisible. The rapidly beating wings produce a high-pitched hum, like the wings of a hummingbird.

# Lobster moth

- **Lobster moths** belong to the group of moths known as prominent moths.

- **These moths are commonly found** in deciduous forests in Europe and Asia.

- **The wingspan of lobster moths** is about 5.5 to 7 cm.

- **Males are often attracted** to light, but females are not.

▶ *A lobster moth caterpillar confuses predators by suddenly changing shape. It raises its head and tail over its body (making it look like a tiny lobster) and waves a pair of filaments at the end of its abdomen. Lobster moth caterpillars can also squirt formic acid over their predators.*

- **This moth appears in two colour forms** – one with light front wings and one with dark front wings.

- **Lobster moths move in a way** that resembles the movements of ants.

- **The unusual shape of lobster moth caterpillars** often confuses their predators and scares them away.

- **As an act of defence,** the caterpillar curls back its large head and raises its legs in the air to startle small birds.

- **The caterpillar constructs a silken cocoon** and pupates in it.

> ★ **STAR FACT** ★
> Lobster moths are so-called as their larvae have six wiry, elongated legs and a swollen tale like a lobster.

# Peppered moth

- **Peppered moths** belong to a group of moths known as geometrid moths.

- **These moths are delicate insects** and have long legs and a slender body.

- **Peppered moth caterpillars** do not have any legs in the middle of their body. They hold onto branches with their first two pairs of specialized limbs called prolegs and a clasper at their tail end.

- **The antennae of male peppered moths** are feathery, and are longer thn those of the females.

- **Males are smaller and more slender** in comparison with the larger and heavier female peppered moths.

- **There are two varieties of peppererd moths;** a paler coloured variety, speckled with salt and pepper (black-and-white) marks while the other is coal-black in colour.

- **Peppered moths are nocturnal** and usually rest on barks of lichen-covered trees during the day.

◀ *The pale form of the peppered moth is more easily seen against dark backgrounds. The wingspan is 50 to 60 mm.*

- **Peppered moth caterpillars camouflage themselves** by resembling a twig.

- **During the Industrial Revolution,** the barks of many trees became blackish-grey in colour due to air pollution. Dark-coloured peppered moths blended with this environment and matched the colour of the tree bark. Paler peppered moths stood out as targets for birds and other predators so more dark-coloured moths survived.

> ★ **STAR FACT** ★
> Peppered moth caterpillars are known as inchworms because they move their bodies in a looping fashion as though they are measuring the earth.

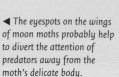

# Moon moth

- **Moon moths** belong to the group known as Emperor moths. They live all over the world, but are mostly seen in tropical countries.

- **Moon moths have a white body** and maroon legs.

- **The wings of the moon moth** are bright green in colour. The colour of female moon moths is brighter than that of the males.

- **Moon moths have a wingspan** of about 10 to 13 cm and their tail is almost 8 cm long.

- **The hind wings of males** are longer than the females'. In overall size, male moon moths are smaller than females.

- **An adult female** lays about 250 eggs at a time, on walnut leaves. The eggs resemble seeds with grey specks on them.

- **Adult moon moths** have no mouthparts and do not eat anything. They do not live for more than a week.

◀ *The eyespots on the wings of moon moths probably help to divert the attention of predators away from the moth's delicate body.*

- **Moon moths make their cocoons in leaves.** The silk of the cocoon does not shine and is brown in colour.

- **Moon moth caterpillars** are bright green in colour and are beautifully segmented, with some white hairs.

> ★ STAR FACT ★
> Moon moths are also called 'lunar moths' because of marks on their wings that look like a new moon.

# Vinegar fly

- **Vinegar flies** are tiny insects and measure about 2 mm in length.

- **Vinegar flies are also called pomace flies** because they are attracted by the sour smell of pomace, which is the liquid squeezed from fruit or seeds.

- **These insects have large red eyes** and their bodies are brownish yellow in colour.

- **Vinegar flies are not strong fliers** and can cover only short distances but these lightweight insects are easily carried along by the wind.

- **Vinegar flies are used extensively** for genetic research because their cells are strikingly similar to those of humans. Around 60 percent of their genes match with those of humans.

◀ *Adult vinegar flies live for just two weeks, feeding on nectar and other sugary solutions.*

- **A female vinegar fly** can lay around 200 eggs if conditions are suitable.

- **The eggs laid by female vinegar flies** are not easily visible to the human eye. These eggs are normally found near decaying and fermented fruits and vegetables.

- **The larvae feed on fermented food materials.** They pupate and develop into adult flies in four to five days.

- **Several generations can be produced** in a couple of weeks, which is why these insects are suitable for scientific studies.

- **Vinegar flies are considered pests** because they can transmit germs and diseases from decaying food materials.

# Horse fly

- **Horse flies** are strong-bodied flies with colourful patterns on their bodies.

- **Horse flies suck and feed** on the blood of humans and animals. These insects get their names, such as deer flies or moose flies, depending on the animal they feed on.

- **There are about** 25,000 species of horse fly.

- **Horse flies have compound eyes,** which are very prominent and occupy the entire surface of head in the males.

- **Colourful patterns** on the compound eyes are caused by the refraction of light. There are no pigments present in the eyes.

- **The mouthparts of these insects** consist of a short powerful, piercing organ capable of penetrating tough skin. If undisturbed, horse flies can suck blood from their host for as long as half an hour.

- **After mating,** females lay their eggs on plant and rock edges near water. The eggs are creamy white in colour.

- **Female horse flies bite other animals** to suck blood before they reproduce. Male horse flies do not bite. They feed mainly on flower nectar and plant sap.

- **Horse fly larvae** feed on soft-bodied insects and other small animals. They can become cannibalistic if there is a lack of food.

- **While biting and sucking blood** from animals, horse flies can transmit diseases such as anthrax.

◀ Horse flies are among the fastest flying insects, reaching maximum speeds of 39 km/h. Unlike most other flies, their flight can be silent, allowing females to sneak up on their prey.

# Crane fly

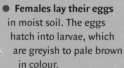

▶ The long, thin legs of a crane fly are often twice as long as its body. Crane flies can also be recognized by the V-shaped groove on the top of their thorax.

- **Crane flies** belong to order Diptera and are closely related to mosquitoes.

- **These long-legged insects** are also known as 'daddy long legs'. Their legs are weakly attached to their body and often break off.

- **Some of the larger species of crane fly** have legs that are as long as 2.5 cm.

- **Crane flies have extremely narrow wings.** They have a thin body and long legs and resemble large mosquitoes. These insects cannot bite.

- **Crane flies are nocturnal insects** and remain inactive in the day.

- **Females lay their eggs** in moist soil. The eggs hatch into larvae, which are greyish to pale brown in colour.

- **The larvae of crane flies** feed on dead and decaying matter. Some species also feed on other small insects and others eat plant roots.

- **Crane fly larvae are also known as** leatherjackets because of their tough, brown skin. They are often used as fishing bait.

- **Farmers dislike the larvae** of these insects because they damage the roots and turf of grain fields and grass crops.

- **A rare species of crane fly** does not have wings. These insects are found in Hawaii.

# House-fly

● **House-flies** belong to the order Diptera and are one of the most common insects.

● **House-flies have small projections** below their front wings known as halteres. Halteres are modified hind wings, which are used for landing and balancing.

● **House-flies feed on liquid food** and do not bite animals and other insects. The mouthparts of a house-fly are like a sponge, which absorbs liquid food.

● **House-flies will vomit** a portion of their last feed onto new food particles. This makes new food easier to digest.

● **Most of the time,** house-flies do not eat all the food and leave some particles behind. These remaining food particles can spread a variety of diseases.

● **House-flies are considered** to be the most dangerous vector. A vector is an organism which carries disease-causing micro-organisms from host to host.

● **House-flies have compound eyes,** and each eye has 4000 individual lenses. They cannot see the colour red.

★ STAR FACT ★
House-flies are known to spread forty serious diseases. A single fly harbours as many as 500 million on its body surface and legs.

◀ Sticky pads and sharp claws enable house-flies to walk upside down with ease. Fine hairs on the tip of a house fly's legs also enable it to 'taste' liquids.

● **Female house-flies** can lay more than 600 to 1000 eggs in a lifetime, but most offspring do not survive to reproduce.

● **Common house-flies** are normally found wherever there is human activity. They thrive on the waste materials left behind by humans and other animals.

# Mosquito

● **Mosquitoes are the only flies** of the order Diptera that have scaly wings.

● **Most female mosquitoes** have to feed on the blood of other animals to reproduce. They need the protein extracted from blood for the development of their eggs.

● **The eggs float on water** and hatch to produce aquatic larvae known as wrigglers.

● **The larvae cannot breathe underwater** and 'hang' from the water's surface to take in air.

● **Mosquito larvae pupate** in the water itself. The pupa is not completely immobile. It can change position according to the light and wind conditions in its environment.

● **Adult male mosquitoes** feed on nectar and other plant fluids. Only female mosquitoes feed on blood.

◀ A female mosquito uses her needle-like mouthparts to pierce a victim's skin and suck up a blood meal. She injects a salivary fluid to keep the blood flowing and stop it from clotting.

● **Male mosquitoes cannot bite.** Their mouthparts are modified for sucking only.

● **Mosquitoes have infrared vision.** They can sense the warmth of other insects and animals.

● **Dragonflies feed on mosquitoes** and are also known as mosquito hawks. Dragonfly nymphs also feed on mosquito larvae.

● **Mosquitoes are known to spread many infectious diseases,** such as yellow fever and dengue fever. The female Anopheles mosquito spreads malaria.

# Firefly

- **Fireflies are actually a type of beetle.** They are also known as lightning bugs.

- **Fireflies grow** up to 2.5 cm in length and live for three to four months. Female fireflies live longer than males.

- **Fireflies have a special organ** under their belly, which emits flashes of green or yellow light.

- **The light is known as 'cold light'.** This process of producing light is also known as bioluminescence. No other insects can produce light from their own bodies.

- **Fireflies emit only light energy.** A light bulb emits only 10 percent of the energy as light. The remaining 90 percent is emitted as heat energy.

- **Female fireflies and their larvae** are carnivorous and feed on snails, slugs and worms. Most male fireflies don't eat but some feed on pollen and nectar.

★ STAR FACT ★
Some female fireflies fool males of other species by flickering their light. When the males come closer to mate, the females eat them.

- **Male and female fireflies** emit light to attract mates.

- **Fireflies are nocturnal in nature.** They live on plants and trees during the day and are active at night.

- **Some female fireflies** are wingless and are also known as glow-worms.

◀ A female firefly signals to a mate with her glowing tail.

# Goliath beetle

- **The Goliath beetle** is one of the largest and heaviest insects in the world. Males are as heavy as an apple.

- **Goliath beetles grow up to** 12 cm and weigh about 115 g.

- **Found in many colours,** most Goliath beetles have black and white spots on their wings.

- **Goliath beetles used to be found** only in Africa. Today, however, these insects can be found in almost all parts of the world.

- **Males have a horn-shaped structure** on their heads. They often fight each other with their horns.

- **Goliath beetles are good fliers.** They produce a low, helicopter-like whir while flying.

- **By feeding on dead plant and animal tissues,** Goliath beetles help to keep the environment clean.

- **A fossil of the oldest Goliath beetle** dates is almost 300 million years old.

- **Scientists believe that Goliath beetles,** like some other insects, were much larger in prehistoric times. This may because there was more oxygen in the air long ago.

▶ The male Goliath beetle would only just fit on your hand! Adult beetles cannot grow, which means that Goliath beetles also have giant larvae.

★ STAR FACT ★
The Goliath beetle is named after the Biblical giant, Goliath.

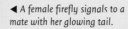

# Bombardier beetle

- **Bombardier beetles** are ground beetles. They have a black body and yellow-spotted wings.

- **The wing covers of bombardier beetles** are fused together. They cannot fly but they are very fast runners.

- **Bombardier beetles have an interesting defence strategy.** Two separate chambers within the beetle's body contain chemicals – hydrogen peroxide and hydroquinone.

- **These chemicals fuse together** to form a noxious toxin, which causes irritation.

- **The temperature of this toxic liquid** is 100°C. It is squirted out from the beetle's body straight away, otherwise it would explode.

▶ The bombardier beetle can twist the end of its abdomen to squirt out a poisonous spray. This gives the insect time to escape.

- **Bombardier beetles use a cannon-like body part** in their abdomen to spray the liquid at their predators.

- **The liquid evaporates** after it is sprayed, forming a gas that temporarily blinds the enemy, while the bombardier beetle runs away.

- **Bombardier beetles spend most of their time** in rotting wood and lay eggs on plant remains and other decomposing matter.

- **These beetles are scavengers** and come out at night. Their larvae are carnivorous and feed on other insects.

★ STAR FACT ★
The bombardier beetle inspired Germans to use jet propulsion to spray noxious toxins on their enemies during World War II.

# Tiger beetle

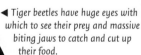

- **Tiger beetles are usually shiny metallic colours,** such as green, black and purple. They often have stripes just like tigers.

- **The smallest tiger beetles** live in Borneo and measure up to 6 mm. The largest tiger beetles live in Africa and are as large as 44 mm.

- **Tiger beetles are found in** sandy areas and are usually active during the day. There are some species that come out at night.

- **Tiger beetles are good fliers** and will fly in a zigzag pattern if a predator approaches. They are also very fast runners.

◀ Tiger beetles have huge eyes with which to see their prey and massive biting jaws to catch and cut up their food.

- **These insects are predatory in nature.** Once they locate their prey, they pounce on it and use their jaws to tear it into pieces.

- **Tiger beetles taste awful** and their predators avoid eating them.

- **Female tiger beetles lay their eggs** in burrows in the ground. The burrow can be almost 0.5 m deep.

- **The larvae of tiger beetles** have a pair of powerful and large jaws, which are used to capture small insects.

- **Some species of tiger beetles** are endangered or nearing extinction. This is because of the lack of undisturbed sandy areas in which they can breed.

★ STAR FACT ★
In Borneo, a type of locust mimics tiger beetles to save itself from its predators.

# Diving beetle

● **Diving beetles** have an oval body, which is brown or black in colour. Their wings are shiny and look metallic green when light reflects off their body. Diving beetles are commonly found in ponds and other still water.

● **A diving beetle has strong hairy legs,** which it uses like the oars of a rowing boat to push its body forwards while swimming

● **These insects cannot breathe underwater** and have to come to the water's surface to breathe air. They store this air under their wing covers.

● **Diving beetles often fly at night** in search of new ponds.

● **The beetles locate new ponds** with the help of the light that reflects from water surfaces. They often get confused with light that is reflected from a glass surface and mistake it for water.

● **The female diving beetle** is much bigger in size than the male beetle.

● **Females make small slits** in a plant stem and lay their eggs inside.

● **The larvae float on the surface** of the pond and move to the shore to pupate.

● **The larvae are known as 'water tigers'** because they can attack and bite other insects. They can even eat tadpoles and small fish.

● **Diving beetles feed on** other water insects, small fishes and tadpoles.

▼ The great diving beetle has a flattened, streamlined body, which helps it to swim rapidly. It moves its back legs together, rather than alternately like most other water beetles. When the beetle stops swimming, it floats to the surface of the water.

# Stag beetle

- **Stag beetles** are usually brown or black in colour but there are some species that are bright green and red.

- **These beetles live in damp wooded areas,** especially near oak woodlands.

- **Stag beetles have mandibles** (jaws), which look similar to the antlers of a stag.

- **Males have long and ferocious looking jaws.** The jaws of females are not as long as those of the males.

- **Males use their antlers** to attract females. They rarely use their jaws to fight.

- **At dusk, male stag beetles** fly in search of females to mate. They often get misguided by bright lights.

> ★ **STAR FACT** ★
> Stag beetles are also known as 'pinching bugs' because they can nip with their jaws and draw blood from people.

- **The larvae of these insects** feed on rotten wood and plant remains.

- **The larvae take a long time** to develop into mature adults because their food is not nutritious.

- **Adult stag beetles** feed on the sap of trees.

◀ *Lesser stag beetles have smaller jaws than the larger elephant or giant stag beetles. Stag beetles are one of the 20,000 species in the scarab beetle superfamily.*

# Rhinoceros beetle

- **Rhinoceros beetles** are believed to be proportionally the strongest creatures on Earth. They can carry about 850 times their own weight.

- **These beetles** can grow up to 13 cm in length.

- **The preferred habitat of rhinoceros beetles** is tropical rainforests where the vegetation is thick and there is plenty of moisture in the atmosphere.

- **Rhinoceros beetles are named after** the horns on their head, which resemble spikes.

- **Only males have horns.** The larger the horn, the better are their chances of winning a mate's attention.

- **The horns are very strong** and can pierce through the exoskeletons of insects.

- **Rhinoceros beetles do not use their horns** for defending themselves from predators. They use them to fight other males for food and to attract female beetles for mating.

◀ *This rhinoceros beetle has two horns, but some have three, or even five, horns. The very tough exoskeleton protects the beetle's body like a suit of armour.*

- **Rhinoceros beetles are nocturnal** in nature and almost all their hunting and feeding activities take place at night.

- **These beetles help to keep the jungle clean** and feed on plant sap and rotten fruits that have fallen on the ground.

- **Rhinoceros beetles are known to be fierce fighters.** Natives in some parts of Thailand hold beetle fighting competitions to watch these beetles fight.

# Ladybird beetle

● **Ladybird beetles,** or ladybugs, were named after the Virgin Mary, because in early religious paintings she was often shown wearing a red clock. They were known as 'beetle of Our Lady' during the Medieval period.

● **Ladybirds are almost circular in shape.** They are bright pink, orange or red with black and red or orange spots. The number of spots may vary from species to species. Ladybirds are found in temperate and tropical regions all over the world.

● **These beetles are one of the most beneficial insects** because they feed on insect pests that damage crops.

● **Ladybirds are sometimes bred** on a large scale and are then introduced into farms or greenhouses to get rid of pests. However, some species of ladybirds are herbivorous and are considered pests themselves.

● **These insects are easily mistaken** for leaf beetles because of their similar colouring and spots.

● **When disturbed,** ladybirds secrete a foul smelling fluid, which causes a stain. This is called reflex-bleeding.

● **Both adults and larvae eat aphids, scale insects and** other soft-bodied insects.

● **Ladybird larvae do not have wings.** They are metallic blue in colour with bright yellow spots all over their body. Their bright colour warns birds not to eat them.

● **The halloween ladybird** is a pumpkin-orange coloured beetle found in the USA during late October. It is named after Halloween because it is often seen during this festival.

● **Adult ladybirds hibernate** in huge clusters in densely vegetated areas, usually at high altitudes.

▼ *The bright colours of adult ladybirds warn predators that they taste horrible and are best left alone. Hidden under the brightly coloured wing cases are two delicate wings.*

# True bugs

- **True bugs belong** to the suborder Heteroptera of the order Hemiptera. There are at least 55,000 different kinds of bugs.

- **These bugs generally** have two pairs of wings. The first pair is partially hard and protects the delicate membrane-like second pair of wings.

- **Some bugs do not have wings** while the nymphs of all bugs are wingless.

- **True bugs have compound eyes** and mouthparts that are adapted for sucking and piercing.

- **Bugs undergo incomplete metamorphosis.** There is no pupal stage and the bugs grow into adults by moulting repeatedly. The nymphs resemble the adult bugs.

- **Bugs survive on land,** in air, on the surface of water and even under water.

- **Bugs feed on plant and animal juices.** There are some bugs, such as bed bugs, which are parasites. They live by sucking blood from other animals.

▲ A true bug is an insect with piercing and sucking mouthparts, which are tucked beneath the head when not in use.

- **Some bugs give out a bad odour.** This is a defence strategy.

- **Carnivorous bugs** are predatory and help to control pests while herbivorous bugs are a threat to crops. Bugs can also be cannibalistic.

- **Some people** cultivate certain species of bugs to obtain dyes from them, while others relish bugs as food.

# Assassin bug

★ STAR FACT ★
The saliva of assassin bugs can cause temporary blindness in humans.

- **Assassin bugs** are black, brown or bright red and black.

- **The wings of assassin bugs** lie flat on their abdomen. They have long legs, which are adapted for running.

- **Assassin bugs are predatory.** They grab their prey and 'assassinate' it by injecting venom. This venom is so powerful that caterpillars, which are several times larger than assassin bugs, can be killed in a few seconds.

- **The venom paralyzes the prey** and partially dissolves and disintegrates it. The bug then sucks the liquid food.

▶ An assassin bug may take several days to eat a large victim. Its front legs have powerful muscles for holding prey.

- **Assassin bugs have a powerful curved beak,** which is used for sucking the blood of other insects, larger animals and even humans.

- **Male and female assassin bugs** are similar in appearance but sometimes the females don't have wings.

- **Assassin bugs give out a pungent smell** and have a poisonous bite, to protect them from predators.

- **An assassin bug's bite** can be painful and can transmit germs and diseases. These bugs are known to spread a disease called Chagas' disease.

- **A species of assassin bug,** known as the masked assassin bug, camouflages itself by sticking dirt to its body.

# Squash bug

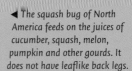

- **Squash bugs** are named for squash. They are a threat to squash and other related plants. They can usually be found in colours ranging from brown to black.

- **Some squash bugs** have leaflike extensions on their hind legs. This makes them look like dead leaves, which helps with camouflage. These bugs are called leaf-footed bugs.

- **With their powerful beaks,** squash bugs can easily pierce and suck fluids from plants and insects.

- **Squash bugs have scent glands** that emit a pungent smell. However, the odour is not as strong as that of stink bugs.

◄ The squash bug of North America feeds on the juices of cucumber, squash, melon, pumpkin and other gourds. It does not have leaflike back legs.

- **A few squash bugs** feed on both plants and insects, and some are strictly vegetarian.

- **While feeding,** the squash bug injects a toxic substance into the plant. As a result, the plant wilts and dies.

- **Squash bugs lay their eggs** in clusters on plants. The eggs are oval, flattish or elongated in shape.

- **The nymphs that hatch from these eggs** resemble black ants and moult four to five times before maturing into adults.

- **Farmers consider squash bugs** to be dangerous pests and adopt various measures to get rid of them.

★ STAR FACT ★
A rice field affected by squash bugs can be smelt from a considerable distance away.

# Cicada

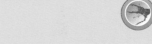

► Cicada eggs hatch into wingless nymphs. Most cicadas spend between one and three years as nymphs.

- **Cicadas** belong to the order Homoptera and are related to true bugs.

- **Most species of cicada** are found in deserts, grasslands and forests.

- **Cicadas have large and colourful wings.** They hold their wings in a slanting position over their abdomen, like a tent.

- **Cicadas emit a sound** similar to that of a knife grinder, a railway whistle and even to fat spitting in an overheated pan.

- **Male cicadas sing loudly to attract females,** with the help of special drumlike membranes called timbals. Female cicadas do not produce any sound because their timbals are not developed.

★ STAR FACT ★
In Borneo, Malaysia and many other areas of the South Pacific, people eat cicadas.

- **Large swarms of cicadas** attract birds, which feast on these insects.

- **Female cicadas lay their eggs** on plants and tree twigs. When the eggs hatch, the nymphs fall to the ground. The nymphs live underground for many years, feeding on the roots of plants. Later, they emerge from the ground, climb up trees and then moult.

- **Adult cicadas do not live as long as the nymphs.** They only survive a few weeks.

- **A species of cicada known as the periodical cicada** is found in America. It emerges from under the ground every 13 or 17 years. These insects are one of the longest-lived in the world.

# Spittlebug

- **Spittlebugs** are different shades of yellow and brown. They have a triangular head, red eyes and spotted wings.

- **Spittlebugs have a froglike appearance** and are also known as froghoppers. They are good jumpers but rarely fly, although they do have wings.

- **Adult spittlebugs** have rather large heads in comparison with their small bodies.

- **They are named after** the frothy mass secreted by the nymphs, sometimes known as cuckoo-spit.

- **Cuckoo-spit** protects the spittlebug nymphs from predators.

- **Spittlebug nymphs** are hard to spot as they are often hidden in a frothy mass on leaves.

- **The froth also helps the nymphs** to control their temperature and even prevents them from losing moisture and drying out.

- **Some spittlebug nymphs** form delicate tubes about 10 to 12 mm in length. They attach these tubes along the sides of twigs and live there after filling them with spittle.

- **Spittlebugs are considered to be pests** as they feed on the sap of plants.

◀ Spittlebug nymphs produce 'cuckoo spit' by giving off a sticky liquid and blowing it into a frothy mass of white bubbles. As well as hiding the nymph from predators, these bubbles also protect the young bug from the drying effects of the sun.

# Aphid

- **Aphids are related to cicadas.** They can be found in green, red or brown colours and are also known as greenflies.

- **They have a large abdomen** with two slender tubes called cornicles attached to it. The cornicles secrete wax.

- **Aphids with wings are weak fliers,** but they can cover great distances with the help of air currents.

- **Many aphids live underground** and suck sap from roots. Sometimes, they depend upon ants to carry them through tunnels in the soil and leave them out on fresh roots.

- **Aphids produce honeydew,** because they cannot digest all the plant sugar they eat. The honeydew is clear and sweet but it becomes black because a fungus grows on it.

- **Ants feed on the honeydew.** In return, the ants protect the aphids from their predators and even take them into their ant nests during bad weather.

- **Aphids breed in huge numbers.** An aphid can produce up to 100 young at a time.

- **Some aphids lay eggs** but some can reproduce without mating. These aphids give birth to live young .

- **Some aphids secrete strands of a waxlike substance** from their cornicles.

- **Aphids can cause damage to plants.** Their saliva causes plant leaves to fold and curl and even form galls.

◀ The cornicles are clearly visible on the abdomens of these aphids. The fluid they produce from these tubes may help to protect them from predators.

# Mealybug

- **Mealybugs are small insects** up to 3 mm long and are found in huge clusters on leaves, twigs and tree bark. They are also called coccids.

- **Females do not usually have wings,** eyes or legs and remain immobile on plants. They are always covered in a white sticky coating of their own secretion. This protective coating looks like cornmeal.

- **Males do not have mouthparts.** However, they have wings and can fly.

- **Female mealybugs never lay their eggs in the open.** The eggs are attached to their bodies. However, some species of mealybugs can give birth to live young.

- **The flat, oval larvae crawl** about quite actively at first, but soon lose their legs and cover themselves with their mealy secretions.

- **A male mealybug's hind wings** are modified into tiny structures called halteres.

- **Mealybugs feed on the sap extracted from the plant tissues** and are considered to be pests of citrus trees and greenhouse plants.

- **Mealybugs can harm plants in many ways.** Galls can form on plants, or their stems can become twisted and deformed.

▲ Mealybug nymphs do not usually move after their first moult. They stay in one place, joined to plants only by their sucking mouthparts.

- **Mealybugs produce a sugary substance** known as honeydew. Ants often visit these insects for this sweet-tasting secretion.

- **Beetles, lacewings and caterpillars** prey on mealybugs.

◀ Male mealybugs usually have a pair of wings, well-developed legs and antennae and no mouthparts. Females are often wingless and legless, with reduced antennae.

# Leafhopper

● **Leafhoppers** related to cicadas. They have a distinct leaflike shape and colour and are easy to recognize.

● **Leafhoppers can survive** in almost any part of the world. They are terrestrial bugs and can be found in deserts as well as in marshy and moist places.

● **Strong fliers,** leafhoppers are also capable of jumping considerable distances.

● **If these insects feed on plants,** they can cause the leaves to curl and affect the plant's growth.

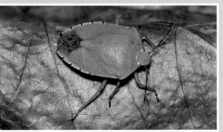

▶ *Leafhoppers are very common jumping insects that look rather like a narrow version of an adult spittlebug, or froghopper. They are tiny insects, only 2 to 15 mm long.*

● **Leafhoppers are considered to be pests** and can cause damage to crops.

● **Leafhoppers search for their mates** by making special mating calls.

● **Females lay their eggs** in slits made in plant stems. The eggs can remain dormant for a month. In some species, the eggs can even remain dormant for a year.

● **Like aphids,** leafhoppers produce honeydew from the excess plant sap that they feed on.

● **These bugs communicate** with each other by producing low frequency sounds, which humans cannot hear.

● **Birds, reptiles and large insects,** such as wasps, are a threat to leafhoppers.

# Stinkbug

● **Stinkbugs have glands** on their undersurface, from which they secrete a fluid. This fluid has a foul odour, which is why these insects are called stinkbugs.

◀ *In some stinkbugs, the thorax extends down the back to form a protective shield, which almost covers the abdomen. These stinkbugs are also called shield bugs.*

● **Their scent affects** many animals and protects the bug from predators.

● **Stinkbugs can be found in many colours,** such as green, grey, brown, red, black and yellow. They are one of the most notorious pests found in farmlands and orchards.

● **Some species of stinkbugs** produce a loud sound to defend themselves.

● **Stinkbugs have a compound** called glycerol in their blood. This prevents their blood from freezing in winter.

● **Many species of stinkbug** are active during the day, while others are nocturnal, especially the dark-coloured species, which live in thick grass or under leaves.

● **Stinkbugs normally feed on the sap from flowers,** leaves and fruits, which is why they destroy crops.

● **Male and female stinkbugs** are very similar in appearance, but the male is much smaller.

● **Stinkbug nymphs do not have wings** but adult stinkbugs are very good at flying.

★ STAR FACT ★
In some parts of Mexico, India and Africa, stinkbugs are relished as a source of food.

# Water boatman

- **Water boatmen** are aquatic insects and are usually found in ponds and other freshwater bodies, such as canals and ditches.

- **Water boatmen have powerful, hairy legs** and are named after their habit of using their legs as oars to 'row' themselves through the water.

- **Most species of water boatman can fly,** but they often cling to water plants or live at the bottom of ponds.

- **Water boatmen do not have gills** and have to come to the surface to breathe.

- **Hairs on the body trap air bubbles.** This helps water boatmen to stay under water for long periods.

- **Water boatmen feed on algae,** plants and decaying animal matter.

- **Water boatmen find their food** on the bottom of ponds, canals and ditches, using their shovel-like front legs to scrabble it up.

▶ *Water boatmen are not buoyant enough to float, so when they stop swimming, they sink to the bottom.*

- **Some males rub their legs together** to make squeaky sounds that attract females.

- **The females lay their eggs under water.** The young nymphs that hatch from the eggs resemble adult water boatmen (without wings) but they moult five times before they become winged adults.

> ★ **STAR FACT** ★
> People in Mexico dry water boatmen eggs and eat them. In some countries, water boatmen are also sold as bird food.

# Backswimmer

- **Backswimmers** spend almost their entire life floating in an upsidedown position in ponds. They use their legs like oars.

- **These insects fly from one pond** to another in search of food.

- **While floating,** backswimmers identify direction with the help of light.

- **The underside** of backswimmers is dark in colour while the top of the body is light. The dark colour helps to hide the backswimmer from predators.

- **Backswimmers come to the water surface for air.** They carry a bubble of air under their belly, which helps them to stay underwater for a long time.

- **Backswimmers feed on other water insects,** worms and tadpoles.

◀ *Backswimmers are shaped like boats, with a keel along their back. As they swim on their backs, the keel points downwards, like the keel on a boat. The bubble of air held beneath the body makes the insect float to the surface if it stops swimming.*

- **Also known as the water bees,** the backswimmer's bite is painful. It can even bite humans.

- **Backswimmers look very similar** to water boatmen. However, water boatmen float the right way up and feed mainly on plants. Backswimmers, in contrast, are predators.

- **When attacking,** backswimmers inject toxins into their prey. This has a chemical reaction, which kills the prey.

- **Some species of backswimmers** are known to hibernate. During winter, these insects are found moving under the surface of frozen water.

# Giant water bug

- **Giant water bugs** are like snorkellers. They have flaplike back legs to help them swim fast and special breathing tubes that resemble a snorkel.

- **By lying still in the water,** giant water bugs camouflage themselves so that they look like dead leaves.

- **These insects can fly** but they can survive only for about 15 minutes if they are taken out of water.

- **Giant water bugs hold their prey** with their claws and inject venom to paralyze it. Their mouthparts help them to pierce and suck fluid.

◄ Giant water bugs have large claws and a powerful bite. They are fierce hunters that feed on tadpoles, fish and other insects.

- **Giant water bugs store air** between their abdomen and their wings.

- **Giant water bugs help to control** the mosquito population by feeding on mosquito larvae.

- **Males carry fertilized eggs on their backs** for about 10 days. They take care of the eggs until they hatch.

- **Giant water bugs are also known as 'toe biters'** because they may bite the toes of people wading.

- **In some Asian countries,** giant water bugs are considered a tasty snack.

★ STAR FACT ★
Female giant water bugs lay their eggs on the backs of the males. They secrete a waterproof glue to stick the eggs onto the male's back.

# Water strider

- **Water striders are often found** floating on still water and slow moving streams. They are one of the few insects that can survive in the sea and have even been found floating on the surface of the Pacific Ocean.

- **Water striders** (pond skaters) seldom go underwater. Their long legs help them to skate across the water.

- **These insects have six legs.** The front two are short and are mainly used to grasp prey.

- **Water striders have long, slender, hairy legs,** which end in a pad of water-repellent hairs so they do not break the surface of the water.

- **Some adults have wings,** while others are wingless.

- **Adults hibernate throughout winter** and mate in the spring.

★ STAR FACT ★
Water striders are also known as Jesus bugs because of their ability to walk on water.

- **Water striders feed on insects** that fall into the water and aquatic insects that come to the surface to breathe.

- **Water striders communicate** by making vibrations and ripples on the water's surface.

- **Water striders move very quickly** and can run across water. If they were as big as humans, they would move as fast as a jet plane.

◄ The thin legs of a water strider help to spread its weight. The surface of the water bends into dips around the end of each leg, but does not break.

# Cockroach

● **Cockroaches** belong to the order Blattodea of class Insecta. There are about 4000 known species of cockroaches. Some well-known cockroaches are oriental black beetles and croton bugs.

● **Cockroaches are found everywhere,** especially in bat caves, peoples' homes, under stones, in thick grass and on trees and plants. The cockroaches found in caves are usually blind.

● **These insects can be winged or wingless.** Adult cockroaches can be 1 to 9 cm long. They are nocturnal and prefer dark and damp places.

● **Cockroaches are swift creatures** and can run extremely fast. Their legs are adapted for quick movement. They have flat and oval bodies that help them to hide in narrow cracks in walls and floors.

● **Most cockroach species are omnivorous.** Their main food is plant sap, dead animals and vegetable matter but they will even eat shoe polish, glue, soap and ink.

● **Adults can live for up to two years.** Males and females are very similar in appearance but males have a pair of bristle-like styli.

★ **STAR FACT** ★
The name cockroach comes from the Spanish word cucaracha. These insects adapt quickly to changes in the environment and can even survive a nuclear explosion.

● **In some species,** females release pheromones or produce a hissing sound and wave their abdomen to attract male cockroaches.

● **Females can lay up to 30 to 40 eggs at a time** and can reproduce four times in a year. They store the eggs in a brownish egg case called an ootheca. The cockroach can either carry this egg case along with her or hide it somewhere. The young cockroaches are called nymphs.

● **Cockroaches play an important role** in balancing the environment by digesting a wide range of waste substances. They decompose forest and animal waste matter. At the same time, household cockroaches can contaminate food and spread diseases among humans.

▼ *Cockroaches are not dirty creatures. They work hard to keep themselves clean in order to preserve a coating of wax and oils that prevents them from drying out. It is the bacteria they carry that makes them dangerous.*

# Madagascan hissing cockroach

● **Madagascan hissing cockroaches** are found on the island of Madagascar, off the south-east coast of Africa. They are large, wingless and famous for the hissing sound they make.

● **These cockroaches are chocolate brown,** with dark orange marks on their abdomen. Adults can grow to 10 cm in length.

● **A male cockroach** can distinguish between familiar males and strangers from the sound that they make.

● **Males look different from the females.** They have a large, hornlike structure behind their heads and hairy antennae.

● **These cockroaches feed on dead animal matter,** waste food or ripe fruits.

● **Females produce 30 to 60 eggs.** The eggs are stored in an egg sac. The eggs hatch into nymphs.

● **The nymphs of hissing cockroaches** moult six times before maturing into adult cockroaches. During moulting, the skin of a cockroach splits down the back and the cockroach wriggles out.

● **Newly moulted cockroaches** are whitish but their colour darkens within hours. Hissing cockroaches live for 2 to 5 years.

● **Madagascan hissing cockroaches** are easily bred.

◀ Hissing cockroaches hiss by pushing air thorugh breathing holes in their sides.

# Oriental cockroach

● **Oriental cockroaches** are seasonal insects and can be most easily spotted during the spring and summer. They are found in places such as damp basements, drains, leaky pipes and kitchen sinks.

● **These cockroaches** are dark brown or black in colour so they are sometimes called 'black beetles'. Adults can grow up to 3.5 cm in length.

● **This cockroach is sometimes called** the 'shad roach' because its young appear in large numbers when shad (a fish) are swimming into fresh waters to breed.

● **Males have short wings** but females are wingless.

● **Females do have small wing stubs.** This is what makes them different from their nymphs.

● **A female can produce 5 to 10 egg cases** (oothecae) in her lifetime. Each egg case contains about ten eggs.

● **Young cockroach nymphs** hatch from the egg cases in 6 to 8 weeks and mature in 6 to 12 months. Adult cockroaches can live for up to one year.

◀ The head of this male oriental cockroach is almost hidden under the large hard collar (pronotum) at the front of the thorax. The cerci at the end of the abdomen are important sensory organs.

● **These cockroaches can enter homes** through sewer pipes, air ducts or any other opening.

● **Unlike other pest cockroaches,** oriental cockroaches do not have sticky pads on their feet and cannot climb slippery or smooth surfaces.

# Death's head cockroach

- Death's head cockroaches are large insects. They measure 5 to 8 cm in length. These cockroaches are mostly found in the Americas.

- This cockroach is named after the markings on its thorax, which look like skulls or vampires.

- This insect is also known as the palmetto bug or giant death's head cockroach.

- Death's head cockroaches live mostly in tropical forests or bat caves but they are also sometimes found in buildings.

- Cockroaches are scavengers and are active at night.

◄ A fast runner, the death's head cockroach lives on the ground, searching through leaf litter or bat droppings for scraps of food.

- Death's head cockroaches are brownish in colour with yellow and black marks on their body. While adults are beautifully coloured, the nymphs are dark in colour, although newly moulted nymphs are whitish.

- The wings are very long and cover their abdomen. The nymphs are wingless.

- Females carry the eggs inside their bodies and give birth to live young that hatch from the eggs.

- Decaying plant and animal matter are the favourite food of these cockroaches.

> ★ STAR FACT ★
> Death's head cockroaches make good pets and are popular among cockroach lovers.

# Crickets

- Crickets belong to the order Orthoptera and closely resemble grasshoppers. They are found nearly everywhere.

- Crickets have flattened bodies, long antennae and measure up to 5 cm. All crickets have wings.

- These insects make sounds that attract females and warn rival males to keep away.

- Crickets produce these sounds by rubbing the bases of their forewings.

- Crickets feed on crops, vegetables, plants, small animals, clothes and each other.

- Some species of crickets are considered to be pests because they can eat crops.

> ★ STAR FACT ★
> The ancient Chinese conducted 'cricket matches' in which crickets would wrestle with each other.

▶ All crickets have wings, but some cannot fly.

- Crickets are nocturnal and have keen hearing and sight. Compound eyes help crickets see in many directions at once. Their hearing organs are found on their front legs.

- Females have long ovipositors to lay eggs. They carry the eggs until they find a safe place for the eggs to hatch.

- In some parts of the world, crickets are thought to be a sign of good luck.

# Cave cricket

- **Cave crickets** are named after their habit of living in caves and other dark and damp places.

- **These crickets are also found in wells,** rotten logs, hollow trees and under damp leaves and stones.

- **These insects are also known as cave crickets** because they have a hump on their back.

- **Long hind legs** give cave crickets a spider-like appearance. They are good jumpers.

- **Cave crickets are brown in colour** and have long antennae. They do not have wings.

- **These insects cannot chirp or make sounds** because they are wingless. Crickets normally produce a high-pitched sound by rubbing their wings together.

- **Cave crickets are omnivorous** and feed on decaying organic matter, plants and vegetables.

- **In the spring,** females lay their eggs in soil. The nymphs and adults spend the winter in sheltered areas.

- **Cave crickets can damage articles** stored in boxes, garages and laundry rooms, as they love to live in cool and damp places.

- **Cave crickets are sometimes troublesome** in buildings and homes, especially in basements.

▼ The long, sensitive antennae of the cave cricket help it to find its way around in the dark.

# Field cricket

- **Field crickets** are usually found in green fields and forested areas.

- **These insects are either black or brown** in colour and measure about 2.5 cm in length.

- **Spiky projections** called cerci are located on their abdomens.

- **Field crickets are omnivorous** and feed on plant seeds, smaller insects and fruits. Some species become cannibalistic if there is a shortage of food.

- **Males attract female crickets** by chirping and dancing. They perform a courtship dance before mating. The high-pitched sounds they make are heard from early spring to autumn.

- **Field crickets** are very active at night.

◄ The antennae of the field cricket are longer than its body. It has shorter front wings than those of a grasshopper.

- **Females usually lay** about 50 eggs at a time. They can lay up to 400 eggs in their lifetime.

- **Eggs are stored** in the female's ovipositor until she finds damp soil, where the eggs are deposited.

- **Field crickets do not usually survive the winter,** although their eggs can withstand harsh weather conditions.

- **Frogs, birds and other insects** feed on field crickets.

# Katydid

- **Katydids** are usually green-coloured insects. They are 5 to 6 cm in length and have two pairs of wings.

- **These insects can be found** in grasslands, fields and rainforests.

- **The eardrums of katydids** are located on their front legs.

- **Katydids have long hind legs and antennae.** Their antennae help them search for food. Their long back legs help them to make powerful jumps.

- **Katydids can fly short distances** and feed on willow leaves, rosewood and citrus trees.

- **The males of various species** produce different sounds to communicate with members of their own species and with males of other species.

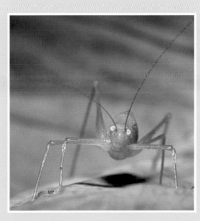

◀ Katydids are well camouflaged as they rest among leaves during the day. Some tropical species even have fake leaf veins and chewed leaf edges to their wings to make them look even more like real leaves.

- **Females respond to mating calls** by singing a soft 'song'.

- **The female lays her eggs in bark,** on twigs or on leaves. The eggs hatch into nymphs within three months. The total lifespan of katydids is about one year.

- **Katydids** are nocturnal.

★ STAR FACT ★
Katydids are named after their loud calls that sound like 'Katy-did-Katy-didn't'.

# Grasshoppers

- **Grasshoppers are green or brown in colour.** Some species change colours in different seasons. They have six legs and a pair of compound eyes and wings.

- **Found almost everywhere,** grasshoppers prefer to live in green fields, meadows and forest areas.

- **There are three main types of grasshoppers** – long-horned, short-horned and pygmy.

- **Grasshoppers make a loud noise** during the mating season to attract a mate and scare rivals.

- **After mating,** the female lays eggs in low bushes or digs a hole in the soil to deposit eggs from her ovipositor.

- **Grasshoppers are herbivorous.** They feed on a variety of plants.

- **These insects are a threat to crops.** A large group of grasshoppers can destroy an entire crop.

★ STAR FACT ★
When captured, grasshoppers spit a brown liquid to protect themselves from their predators.

- **Flies, spiders, toads and reptiles** prey on grasshoppers and even eat their eggs.

- **In some parts of the world,** grasshoppers are considered a delicacy. They are ground into a meal, and sometimes fried or roasted and dipped in honey.

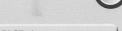

◀ When a grasshopper is at rest, the wide, delicate, back wings are folded like a fan underneath the long, narrow front wings. The front wings are lifted up to allow the flying wings to spread out when the grasshopper flies.

# Bush cricket

- **Bush crickets** are so-called as they usually live on the bark of trees and shrubs in forests.

- **Bush crickets have flat bodies.** These insects are actually grasshoppers, and they are also known as long-horned grasshoppers.

- **These crickets are found in different colours** – from green to brown or even grey. They have underwings that are usually red and black in colour.

- **Bush crickets sing at night** and each species has a distinct song.

- **Bush crickets produce** a high-pitched chirping sound.

- **Unlike grasshoppers,** bush crickets produce sound by rubbing their forewings. Their ears are situated on their front legs.

- **Male bush crickets** are aggressive in nature and fiercely defend their territory.

- **The female lays her eggs** in the bark of trees and in leaf-stalks.

- **Sometimes, when the eggs are laid** in the tissue of living plants, they are transported to other countries with the plants.

- **Unlike grasshoppers,** females do not cover their eggs with an egg-pod (hard shell-like covering).

◀ Most species of bush cricket are omnivorous and feed on leaves, flowers, fruits and other insects.

# Locust

- **Locusts** are found all over the world except in cold regions. They are dark brown in colour and their average length is 2.5 cm.

- **Locusts live in fields,** open woods or arid areas.

- **These insects are migratory** and can travel great distances. Locusts can be highly destructive of crops. A large swarm can consume 3000 tons of green plants in a single day.

- **Locusts can breed very quickly** compared to other insects. Some well-known species are the desert locust, the red-legged locust and the Carolina locust.

◀ Locusts can fly for up to 20 hours at a time.

- **Females lay their eggs** in soil. The nymphs are small and wingless. A female locust can lay 20 eggs at a time.

- **Locusts feed** on crops, weeds, grass or other plants.

- **Locusts have two phases.** In the solitary phase, locusts don't breed in large numbers. In the gregarious phase, the insect reproduces and grows quickly in the presence of an abundant food supply.

- **In the gregarious phase,** the locusts accumulate in large numbers. As a result, their habitat is not sufficient to support them, so they migrate in search of new feeding ground. This phenomenon is called swarming.

- **In some tribal groups,** dried locusts are eaten as food.

★ STAR FACT ★
A locust swarm may occupy 26 to 777 sq km. Such swarms cast a shadow on the ground and appear like a huge black cloud.

# Stick insect

● Stick insects belong to the order Phasmatodea. They look like leafless sticks and branches and are also called walkingsticks.

● **These insects are green or brown in colour** and spend their time clinging to trees, plants and shrubs.

● **Stick insects are excellent** at camouflaging themselves.

● **Some tropical species** of stick insect have spines on their legs, which blend with the thorns of plants. If threatened, they can stab their enemies. They also change their colour like chameleons.

● **Stick insects are active at night,** and feed on foliage.

● **Females are larger than the males.** Males can fly but the females can only glide.

● **Females produce pheromones to attract males.** They scatter their eggs randomly or hide them in order to protect them.

● **Asiatic stick insects** are the longest stick insects, measuring more than 30 cm.

● **Stick insects are the only insects** that can regenerate lost legs. If old limbs are cut off they can grow new ones.

▶ If a stick insect is disturbed, it may suddenly drop to the ground or lose one of its legs to avoid capture. Many are wingless, but those with wings may flash their brightly coloured back wings to startle a predator.

> ★ STAR FACT ★
> Stick insects lie motionless and pretend to be dead to save themselves from their predators. This is called catalepsis.

# Leaf insect

● **Leaf insects** belong to the order Phasmatodea and are most common in south-east Asia.

● **These insects have a unique appearance.** Their bodies are flat, irregular in shape and resemble a leaf. These insects are about 10 cm in length and sometimes have brown or yellow patches on their body.

● **Females are much larger** than males. They do not have hind wings and cannot fly but they have leaflike forewings.

● **The female can lay eggs** without mating with the male. This is called parthenogenesis.

● **A female scatters her eggs** on the ground. The eggs have a hard outer shell and resemble seeds, so predators do not feed on them.

> ★ STAR FACT ★
> Leaf insects are leafy green in colour and are popularly known as walking leaves.

● **The eggs of the leaf insect** hatch in the spring.

● **Leaf insects are herbivorous,** feeding only on plant leaves.

● **Rodents, birds and other insects** feed on leaf insects.

● **Leaf insects are good at camouflage** and hiding from predators. They move very slowly and mimic the foliage on which they live.

◀ This leaf insect would be very hard for predators to spot among green leaves, as long as it remained completely still.

# Damselfly

● **Damselflies** belong to the order Odonata and suborder Zygoptera. They have long, slender bodies and four long wings. They are weak fliers and timid predators.

● **These insects are the beautiful,** slender cousins of dragonflies but are not as ferocious. They have compound eyes and excellent eyesight.

● **Damselflies are usually found near water** and their nymphs live in the water until they mature into adults.

● **Mosquitoes, midgets, gnats and small water insects** are the preferred food of damselflies.

● **Damselfly nymphs have external gills** on the tip of their abdomen for breathing underwater. In dragonfly nymphs, these gills are internal.

● **Males and females mate during flight** or over shallow water. While mating, a male carries a female around to allow her to collect sperm from the front of his abdomen.

● **After mating,** females deposit their eggs in and around water.

● **The lifespan of a damselfly** is around one year but it can live up to two years.

● **During winter,** damselflies hibernate to survive the cold weather.

> ★ STAR FACT ★
> Damselflies capture their prey with the help of their legs, folding them like a basket to form a trap. Once the insect is trapped it is transferred to the damselfly's mouth.

◀ The large compound eyes of a damselfly bulge out to the side. Damselflies also have long legs, which they use to hold insects captured in flight. Their legs are not suited to walking.

# Dragonfly

● **Dragonflies** are named for their fierce jaws, which they use for catching prey.

● **These insects can grow** up to 12 cm in length. They have long, slender bodies with two pairs of veined wings.

● **Larger dragonflies are called hawkers** while the smaller ones are called darters. Dragonflies have huge compound eyes, which cover their entire head.

● **Adult dragonflies survive on land** but their nymphs live underwater. They cannot survive harsh winters.

● **The lifespan of a dragonfly** ranges from six months to more than seven years.

● **Dragonflies mate** while they fly. The female dragonfly then deposits her eggs in water or inside water plants.

● **A female dragonfly** lays up to 100,000 eggs at a time. These eggs hatch into nymphs. These nymphs feed on fish, tadpoles and other small aquatic animals.

● **Dragonflies are beneficial to humans.** They prey on mosquitoes, flies and many small insects that are pests.

● **Experts have found dragonfly fossils** that are more than 300 million years old. These prehistoric dragonflies were as big as crows.

▶ *Each one of a dragonfly's wings can moves independently. This makes the dragonfly a very versatile flyer, able to hover, turn at 90 degree angles, dart backwards and forwards and come to a sudden stop.*

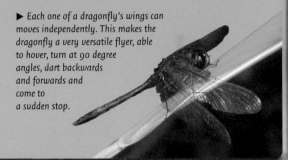

# Praying mantis

● **Praying mantises** belong to the order Mantodea. These insects are closely related to cockroaches.

● **The praying mantis** is named for its posture. It holds its front legs together as if it were praying.

● **They can grow** up to 6.5 cm in length and have triangular heads that can turn in a full circle. They are generally green or brown in colour.

● **Praying mantises are camouflaged** as protection against predators. Their body colour blends with their environment. A species called the Asiatic rose mantis looks like flower petals.

● **Females are larger than the males.** They lay their eggs inside an egg case (ootheca) during the autumn.

● **Females secrete** a sticky substance to attach their eggs to plant stems. Nymphs hatch in the spring or summer.

◀ *A praying mantis moves its front legs rapidly to grab its prey. Sharp spines stop the prey from escaping.*

● **Praying mantises are carnivorous** and feed on insects. They can even attack small reptiles and birds, and can also become cannibalistic.

● **This insect silently stalks its prey** before attacking. While feeding, it holds its prey with its front legs.

● **Praying mantises are useful to humans.** They protect crops by feeding on pests. Sometimes farmers buy them for pest control. They are often kept as pets, even though large praying mantises can hurt people.

# Antlion

- **Antlions** are named after the larva's habit of feeding on ants and other insects. Adult antlions feed on pollen or nectar or do not feed at all.

- **Antlions resemble dragonflies.** They both have long slender bodies and four delicate wings. However, unlike dragonflies, antlions are nocturnal in nature.

- **These insects are found in damp areas** where vegetation is thick. Antlions are also found near riverbeds.

- **Some antlion larvae** make a pit in the sand by moving around in a spiral path and throwing out sand.

- **While making the pit,** the larva leaves behind squiggly doodles on the sand. For this reason, antlions are also known as doodlebugs.

▲ An antlion larva waits at the bottom of its pit trap for an unsuspecting insect to fall down into its pincer-like jaws.

▼ The stout, clubbed antennae of adult antlions are very different from the short, thin antennae of dragonflies.

- **The larva then waits inside the pit** and feeds on insects that fall into it. When the prey struggles to escape, the larva throws sand on it to make it fall back down into the pit.

- **Once the larva has sucked the body juices** of its victim, the remains of the insect are thrown out of the pit. These larvae are voracious eaters and can eat even adult antlions when food is scarce.

- **An antlion larva** secretes silk and pupates inside a cocoon made of soil and silk.

- **Unlike the larva of other insects,** an antlion larva secretes silk from the tip of its abdomen instead of its mouth.

> ★ STAR FACT ★
> Antlion larvae have a peculiar appearance. Their shape has inspired the creation of monsters in many Hollywood science fiction movies.

# Mantisfly

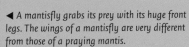

- **Mantisflies** are named after their folded pair of front legs, which look like those of praying mantises. Although these insects look similar, they are not related.

- **These insects are not common** and are found in tropical regions.

- **Mantisflies, along with lacewings and antlions,** belong to the order Neuroptera.

- **Mantisflies lay their rose-coloured eggs** on slender plant stalks.

- **The mantisfly has a complicated development cycle.** It has two growth stages as a larva and two more stages as a pupa.

◄ A mantisfly grabs its prey with its huge front legs. The wings of a mantisfly are very different from those of a praying mantis.

- **The larva of one species of mantisfly is** a parasite of wolf spiders. A larva enters a cocoon and preys upon the egg or young. The larva pierces the egg or spider with its pointed mouthparts and feeds on it.

- **The larva then pupates** inside the spider's cocoon.

- **The parent spider** watches over the cocoon, unaware of the presence of the parasite mantisfly.

- **Some mantisflies** mimic wasps and bees for protection.

- **Mantisflies are as predatory** as praying mantises and have similar feeding habits.

# Lacewing

- **Lacewings** are delicate green or brown insects, which are named after their thin, translucent, lacelike wings.

- **These insects have long,** threadlike antennae and their eyes are bright golden yellow or brown in colour.

- **Birds and other predators** avoid lacewings because they give off a pungent odour similar to garlic.

- **Lacewings are not good fliers** because their wings are too weak to support their weight for long distances.

- **A lacewing lays a large number of eggs** at a time. The eggs are white and are glued to a twig or leaf.

- **Lacewing larvae feed on small insects.** They eat a lot of aphids (greenfly) in a day and are sometimes used to control the population of aphids in crop fields.

- **The larvae of lacewings** are sometimes reared commercially to get rid of pests. Apart from aphids, these larvae feed mealybugs, leafhoppers, caterpillars, moths and other insects.

- **Lacewing larvae have 'jaws',** which they use to suck the body fluids of the prey after injecting it with paralyzing venom.

- **Many species of adult lacewings** do not eat other insects. Instead, they feed on nectar, pollen and honeydew.

- **Some lacewing larvae** build camouflage from debris, including the skin and other remains of their prey.

◄ A lacewing has two pairs of wings. When it rests, it holds its wings together like a roof over its body.

# Stonefly

- **Stoneflies** are an ancient order of insects which has been around for nearly 300 million years.

- **Stonefly nymphs** cling to stones in clear mountain streams or lakes. They are eaten by fish and are also used as models for artificial fish bait.

- **Some stonefly nymphs** breathe through gills near their legs. Others obtain oxygen through their body surface

- **Adult stoneflies** live on land. However, they never wander too far from water, and spend their time crawling over stones. Stoneflies live for two to three years.

- **Female stoneflies deposit their eggs** in deep water. To prevent the eggs from floating away, they attach them to rocks with a sticky secretion.

- **A stonefly nymph resembles an adult** but does not have wings and its reproductive organs are not as well developed.

- **Fishes often attack** female stoneflies when they try to deposit their eggs in streams.

▶ *The flat body of a stonefly nymph helps to stop it being washed away as it clings to stones at the bottom of streams.*

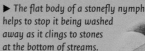

- **Stonefly nymphs feed** on underwater plants. Some species are carnivorous and feed on aquatic insects. Most adults feed on algae and pollen.

- **Stoneflies are sensitive to water pollution.** Experts use these insects to study the level of water purity.

> ★ STAR FACT ★
> Some male stoneflies attract females by drumming their abdomen against a hard surface. They are popularly known as 'primitive drummers' for this reason.

# Scorpionfly

- **Scorpionflies** are a small group of insects with dark spots on their two pairs of membranous wings. These primitive insects have been around for 250 million years.

- **The rear body part** of some males is curled upwards, similar to a scorpion's. Only males resemble scorpions.

- **Adult scorpionflies have modified mouthparts.** They have a long beak pointing downwards.

- **Scorpionflies feed** on live as well as dead insects. Some also feed on pollen, nectar and plants.

- **They are predators** and often steal their food from spiders' webs. Scorpionflies catch their prey with their hind legs.

- **While mating,** a male scorpionfly secretes a sweet, sticky secretion, on which the female scorpionfly feeds.

> ★ STAR FACT ★
> During the mating season, a male scorpionfly offers the female a gift. This courtship gift can be a dead insect or a drop of his saliva.

- **A female scorpionfly lays her eggs** in wooden crevices and soil. The eggs hatch and the larvae live and pupate in loose soil or waste material.

- **Scorpionfly larvae** feed on dead and rotten plant and animal matter. Some larvae also feed on small insects.

- **Scorpionflies are considered** helpful because they keep the environment clean by feeding on dead insects.

◀ *The most distinctive feature of scorpionflies is their elongated head with a long 'beak', which ends in biting jaws.*

# Silverfish

- **The silverfish** is a primitive insect, which belongs to the order Thysanura.

- **These insects are soft-bodied and do not have wings.** Silverfish have a longish body with three tail filaments.

- **Silverfish are silver or brown** and move very swiftly.

- **Silverfish prefer to live** in dark, humid places. They are mostly found in moist, warm places, such as kitchens and baths.

- **These insects feed on flour,** glue, paper, leftover food and even clothes. Silverfish can easily survive for months without food.

- **Silverfish can destroy books** and are considered to be indoor pests.

- **Silverfish mate** in a unique way. A male spins a silk thread and deposits his sperm on it. The female then picks up the sperm and uses it to fertilize her eggs.

- **A female silverfish can lay up to 100 eggs** in her lifetime. After mating, she deposits clusters of her eggs in cracks or crevices.

- **Even after maturing into adults,** these insects continue to moult. They can live for two to eight years.

- **Silverfish are generally harmless to humans,** but they can contaminate food.

◄ Silverfish are named after the shiny scales that cover their carrot-shaped body (bottom right). They belong to a group of insects called bristletails because their abdomen ends in a bristly tail.

# Springtail

- **Springtails** belong to the order Collembola.

- **Springtails are wingless insects** measuring up to 5 mm in length. Unlike most other insects, springtails do not have compound eyes.

- **These insects have a springlike organ,** known as a furcula, under their abdomen. It helps them to leap high into the air.

- **Springtails do not have a respiratory system.** They breathe through their cuticle (hard skin).

- **Even though springtails can jump,** they normally crawl from one place to another.

- **Decaying vegetable matter,** pollen, algae and other plants are the preferred food of springtails.

- **Springtails prefer to live in soil** and moist habitats. However they can survive almost anywhere in the world including Antarctica and Arctic regions.

- **A female springtail lays** approximately 90 to 150 eggs in her lifetime.

- **The lifespan of a springtail** is one year or less.

▼ Springtails live in moist places because their bodies dry out easily. They are usually a grey or brown colour, sometimes with mottled colours for camouflage.

★ STAR FACT ★
Springtails are also called snow fleas as they can survive in extreme cold. They are active even in freezing weather.

# BIRDS

# The world of birds

- **There are more than 9000 species** of birds.
- **One of the most widespread** of all birds is the osprey, which is found nearly all over the world.
- **More than a third of all known bird species** live and breed in South and Central America.

▲ *Ospreys make a large nest at the top of a tree or on a cliff. They feed mostly on fish, which they snatch up with their feet.*

- **A species** is a particular type of bird. Birds of the same species can mate and have young, and these themselves can have offspring.
- **The 9000 bird species** are organized into about 180 families. Species in a family share certain characteristics such as body shape.
- **Bird families** are organized into 28 or 29 larger groups called orders. Largest is the perching bird order, with more than 5000 bird species.
- **The wandering albatross** is one of the longest-lived birds. Individuals may live as long as 50 years.
- **The red-billed quelea** is probably the most common wild bird. There are thought to be at least 1.5 billion.
- **The largest bird**, the ostrich, weighs almost 80,000 times more than the smallest, the bee hummingbird.
- **All birds** lay hard-shelled eggs, in which their young develop. If a mother bird had young that developed inside her body instead, she would be too heavy to fly.

# Cormorants and anhingas

- **The four species of anhinga** also called darters all live in freshwater in tropical parts of the world.
- **The flightless cormorant** lives on two of the Galapagos Islands. Its tiny wings are useless for flight, but it is an expert swimmer.
- **The feathers** of cormorants and darters lack waterproofing and quickly get soaked through. This makes the birds heavier in water and better able to dive for fish.
- **After diving for food**, cormorants stand on a rock with their wings outstretched to dry.

▶ *The cormorant's long, hooked beak is an ideal shape for catching fish, its main food.*

- **In parts of Asia**, fishermen use cormorants to catch fish – the birds dive for the fish but do not swallow them.
- **Cormorant colonies** may number 100,000 birds or more. Their droppings, known as guano, are collected and used as fertilizer.
- **The biggest species** of cormorant, the great cormorant, is up to 1 m long.
- **A great cormorant eats** 15 percent of its body weight in fish a day. That's like an adult human eating more than 80 hamburgers a day.
- **The American darter**, or snake bird, swims with its neck held in a snakelike curve above the water's surface.

★ STAR FACT ★
Cormorants can dive to an incredible 50 m or more in their hunt for fish.

# Ducks

- **The female eider duck** lines her nest with soft down feathers that she pulls from her breast. Humans use the feathers, too, to make quilts and sleeping bags.

- **Torrent ducks** live by fast-flowing streams in South America's Andes mountains. When new ducklings hatch, they leap straight into the swirling waters.

- **There are more than 100 duck species**, living all over the world, except Antarctica.

- **Steamer ducks** get their name from their habit of paddling over water with their wings as well as their feet, at speeds of up to 28 km/h.

- **Ducks have been domesticated** for more than 2000 years for their meat and eggs.

- **Ducks** feed on fish, shellfish, leaves and seeds.

- **Like cuckoos**, the black-headed duck lays its eggs in the nests of other birds, such as herons.

- **The merganser** has a serrated beak like the blade of a bread knife, to help it hold slippery fish.

- **The wood duck** was hunted nearly to extinction in the 19th century for the male's colourful feathers, which were used as fishing flies and hat decorations.

- **The red-breasted merganser** is one of the fastest-flying birds. It can reach speeds of more than 65 km/h – and possibly even 100 km/h.

▼ The beautiful wood duck breeds in North America.

# Hoopoes and relatives

- **Rollers** have a spectacular courtship flight, rolling and somersaulting as they dive towards land.

- **The eight insect-eating woodhoopoe species** live in forests in central and southern Africa.

- **A light, coin-shaped mark** on each wing of the broad-billed roller is the reason for its other common name – 'dollar bird'.

- **The cuckoo-roller** lives only in Madagascar and the Comoros

Islands, where it catches chameleons and insects.

- **Groups of woodhoopoes** make loud calls and rocking movements, and pass bark to each other, in a display of territorial ownership.

- **The 16 or so species of roller** and ground roller live in southern Europe, Asia, Africa and Australia.

- **The broad-billed roller** catches winged termites in the air. A roller will eat as many as 800 termites an evening.

- **If threatened** by birds of prey, the hoopoe hides by flattening itself on the ground with its wings and tail spread out.

- **The hoopoe** was a symbol of gratitude in ancient Egyptian hieroglyphics. The Egyptians believed that the hoopoe comforted its parents in their old age.

- **The hoopoe lines its nest** with animal excrement, perhaps so that the smell will keep enemies away!

◀ With its decorative crest and striking plumage, the hoopoe is easy to recognize. It lives in Europe, Asia and Africa.

# Starlings

- **The male wattled starling** loses his head feathers in the breeding season. Scientists investigating cures for human baldness are researching the bird's ability to regrow its head feathers each year.

- **When kept in captivity**, hill mynahs mimic human speech, but wild birds do not imitate the calls of other bird species, only the calls of other hill mynahs.

- **The largest starlings** are up to 43 cm long and weigh just over 100 g.

- **European starlings** feed their young on caterpillars, earthworms and beetle grubs, and may make 400 feeding trips a day.

- **Male starlings** bring fresh green leaves to the nest, which release a substance that deters parasites.

- **The Brahminy starling** has a brushlike tip on its tongue, used for collecting pollen and nectar.

- **There are about 113 species of starling** in Europe, Africa and Asia. Starlings have also been introduced into Australasia and North America.

- **Some 100 years ago**, 60 pairs of European starlings were released in New York. Fifty years later, starlings were one of the most common birds in the USA.

- **Locusts** are the favourite food of the rose-coloured starling. Large flocks fly to wherever they are plentiful.

▶ *The male starling has glossy, iridescent plumage. The female is much plainer, with brownish feathers.*

> ★ STAR FACT ★
> In some cities, flocks of as many as 1 million starlings gather for the night.

# The structure of birds

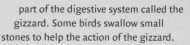

- **Birds are the only creatures** to have feathers. These keep them warm and protected from the weather and allow them to fly.

- **Like mammals, fish and reptiles**, a bird is a vertebrate animal – it has a backbone.

- **Birds** have a body temperature of 40°C to 44°C – higher than other warm-blooded animals.

- **A bird's bones** have a honeycomb structure. The bones are so light that they account for only about five percent of its total weight.

- **Birds** do not have teeth. Instead their food is ground down by a part of the digestive system called the gizzard. Some birds swallow small stones to help the action of the gizzard.

- **A bird's nostrils** are usually at the base of the beak, but in the kiwi, which has a better sense of smell than most birds, they are at the tip.

- **Birds' muscles** make up 30–60 percent of their total weight. The biggest are the flight and leg muscles.

- **Small birds** have about 15 neck vertebrae, while the mute swan has 23. (Mammals have only seven).

- **The skeleton** of a bird's wings has bones similar to those in the hand and arm of mammals, but there are much reduced bones for only three fingers not five.

- **The heart rate** of a tiny hummingbird reaches an astonishing 615 beats a minute.

▲ *Thrushes are adaptable birds, able to feed on fruit as well as insects. Many have beautiful songs.*

# Swifts

- **Once a young swift** has left its nest, it may not come to land again until it is about two years old and ready to breed. In this time it may fly 500,000 km.

- **The edible-nest swiftlet** makes a nest of its own spit (saliva) and a few feathers on a cave wall. Birds nest soup made from this nest is considered a delicacy in China.

- **Swifts** do almost everything in the air. They eat, drink, court and even mate on the wing.

- **There are about 74 species of swifts** found all over the world, except in the very far north and south.

- **The largest swift**, the white-naped swift, is about 25 cm long and weighs 175 g – about the weight of a lemon.

- **Trials with ringed birds** have shown that a

common swift that has only just left the nest can fly from London to Madrid in three days.

- **A swift's legs** and feet are so small and weak that it cannot move on the ground. It must land on a cliff ledge or building so it can launch itself into the air again.

- **The cave swiftlet** finds its way in totally dark caves by using a form of echolocation.

- **The African palm swift** glues its nest to the underneath of a palm leaf with its own spit, and glues its eggs to the nest. The parents cling on with their claws while incubating the clutch.

- **When a swift regurgitates** a mouthful of food for its young to eat, it may contain as many as 1000 tiny insects and spiders.

◀ *The Eurasian swift is seen in Europe in the summer, swooping overhead on sunny days. It flies to tropical Africa for the winter.*

# Partridges and relatives

- **The Himalayan snowcock** (partridge family) lives on the lower slopes of the Himalayas, where its grey and white feathers hide it among rocks and snow.

- **Tiny quail chicks** are born with their eyes open and their bodies covered in warm, downy feathers. They can follow their mother within one hour of hatching.

- **A mother quail** helps her chicks to learn how to find food by pointing at food items with her beak.

- **At about 50 cm long**, the vulturine guineafowl is the largest of the six species of guineafowl. It lives in Africa and eats fallen fruit.

- **The female red-legged partridge**

lays one clutch of eggs for her mate to incubate, and another to incubate herself.

- **The partridge family** includes more than 90 species of partridges and francolins. They feed mainly on seeds.

- **In parts of Europe and North America**, partridges are reared in captivity and then released and shot for sport.

- **The helmeted guineafowl**, originally from Africa, was domesticated in Europe more than 2500 years ago.

- **A group of partridges** is called a 'covey'. A covey usually contains a family of male, female and young, plus a few other birds.

- **The grey partridge** lays the largest clutch of any bird – on average about 19 or 20 eggs, but some birds lay as many as 25.

◀ *The crested wood partridge lives in woodland and forest in Southeast Asia. It feeds on insects, snails, fruit and seeds.*

# Birds of paradise

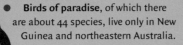

- **Birds of paradise**, of which there are about 44 species, live only in New Guinea and northeastern Australia.
- **The king of Saxony** bird of paradise has two 50 cm head plumes decorated with small, sky-blue squares, so unusual-looking they were first thought to be fake.
- **The magnificent riflebird** gets its name from its loud whistling call, which sounds like a passing bullet.
- **The Female bird** makes a cup or dome-shaped nest and lays 1–2 eggs.
- **During courtship**, the blue bird of paradise hangs upside-down from a branch with his splendid blue feathers and tail plumes spread over his head.
- **Fruit and insects** are the main foods of

▲ *The blue bird of paradise is one of the rarer birds of the species.*

> ★ STAR FACT ★
> The tail feathers of the male ribbon-tailed bird of paradise are up to 1 m long.

the birds of paradise. Some also eat leaves and buds.

- **New Guinea tribesmen** traditionally wear bird of paradise feathers in their head-dresses.
- **During the early 19th century**, 100,000 bird of paradise skins were sold each year in Europe for hat and dress decorations.
- **The first bird of paradise skins** brought to Europe from New Guinea did not have feet, so some people thought the birds never landed.

▶ *The male king bird of paradise has long tail feathers for display.*

# Geese and swans

- **Whooper, trumpeter and mute swans** are among the heaviest flying birds, weighing up to 16 kg.
- **Snow geese** breed in the Arctic tundra, but fly south to spend the winter months around the Gulf of Mexico – a journey of some 3500 km.
- **The black swan** makes a nest of sticks and other plant material in shallow water and lays up to six eggs. Both parents help to incubate the eggs.
- **Geese** feed mostly on leaves, and can eat as many as 100 blades of grass in one minute.
- **Tundra swans** mate for life, returning year after year to the same nesting site. They usually make their nest on marshland and lay 3–5 eggs.
- **Although quieter than other swans**, the mute swan is not really

> ★ STAR FACT ★
> Bar-headed geese have been seen flying near the top of Mount Everest, at 8848 m high.

mute, but makes many snorting and hissing calls.

- **The Hawaiian goose** is the world's rarest goose. Fifty years ago there were only about 30 left. Now it is protected and numbers are increasing.
- **Red-breasted geese** often make their nests near those of peregrines and buzzards. This gives them protection, and they don't seem to get attacked by the birds of prey.
- **Male swans** are known as 'cobs', females as 'pens' and baby swans are called 'cygnets'.

▼ *Swans generally stay faithful to one mate.*

# Tyrant flycatchers

- **The tyrant flycatcher family** includes at least 300 species of birds. They range from northern Canada through the USA to the tip of South America.

- **Not all flycatchers** feed only on insects. The great kiskadee dives into water for fish and tadpoles, as well as catching flying insects in the air.

- **The vermilion flycatcher** is one of the few brightly coloured flycatchers. The male has bright red plumage, which it shows off in his courtship display.

- **In 1976**, ornithologists – bird-watchers – in Peru found a previously unknown flycatcher, which they named the cinnamon-breasted tody-tyrant. It lives only in cloud forests on a few mountain peaks in Peru.

- **The royal flycatcher** is a plain, brownish bird, but it has an amazing crest of feathers on its head that it sometimes unfurls and shows off. Males have red crests and females yellow or orange crests.

- **Smallest of all the tyrant flycatchers** is the short-tailed pygmy tyrant, at only 6.5 cm long. It lives in northern South America.

▶ *The vermilion flycatcher brings a flash of colour to the desert and dry scrub of the southwestern USA, Central America and tropical South America.*

- **The eastern phoebe** makes a nest of mud mixed with grass and plant stems. The female lays 3–7 eggs, and incubates them for 14–16 days. The young leave the nest when they are about 17 days old.

- **The boat-billed flycatcher** has a larger beak than other flycatchers, and eats frogs and other small animals, as well as insects.

- **Some flycatchers**, including the great crested flycatcher, line their nests with snakeskins that have been cast off.

▲ *The tyrant flycatchers are the largest bird family in North and South America. Shown here are: (1) the buff-breasted flycatcher, (2) the lesser flycatcher and (3) the great-crested flycatcher.*

★ STAR FACT ★
Well-known for its fierce behaviour, the eastern kingbird (a flycatcher) attacks larger birds that dare to approach its territory, sometimes even landing on their backs.

# Nightjars and relatives

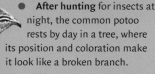

- **After hunting** for insects at night, the common potoo rests by day in a tree, where its position and coloration make it look like a broken branch.

- **The 12 species of frogmouth** live in the rainforests of Southeast Asia and Australia.

- **The common poorwill** (nightjar family) is one of the few birds known to hibernate. It sleeps in a rock crevice.

- **The bristle-fringed beak** of the nightjar opens very wide to help it snap up moths and beetles at night.

- **The oilbird** is the only bird to feed on fruit at night. Its excellent sense of

◀ *The potoo lives in forests and woodlands in Mexico and Central and South America.*

> ★ STAR FACT ★
> So as not to give themselves away by their droppings, potoos squirt out their faeces so that they land well away from their perches.

smell helps it find the oily fruits of palms and laurels in the dark.

- **Oilbird chicks** put on so much weight from their rich diet that they may weigh much more than their parents when they are only a couple of months old.

- **There are about 70 species of nightjars**, found in most warmer parts of the world except New Zealand and southern South America.

- **The oilbird** nests in dark caves, and uses echolocation.

- **An old name** for nightjars is goatsuckers, because people mistakenly thought they saw the birds feeding on goats' milk, when in fact they were snapping up insects disturbed by the animals.

# Oystercatchers and relatives

- **The oystercatcher** uses its strong, bladelike beak to prise mussels off rocks and open their shells.

- **Oystercatcher chicks** stay with their parents for up to one year while they learn how to find and open shellfish.

- **The Egyptian plover** (courser family) buries its eggs in sand and leaves them to be incubated by the warmth of the sun. The parents sit on the eggs at night and if the weather is cool.

- **The cream-coloured courser** has pale, sandy feathers that help to keep it hidden in its desert home.

- **The 17 species in the courser and pratincole family**

▶ *The common oystercatcher breeds in Europe and Asia, but spends the winter in South Africa and southern Asia.*

live in southern Europe, Asia, Africa and Australia.

- **The common pratincole** nests on sand or rocks, and lays 2–4 mottled, well-camouflaged eggs. The parents take turns to incubate the eggs for 17–18 days.

- **The nine species in the thick-knee family** include the stone curlew and the dikkop. These long-legged birds usually feed at night on insects, worms and shellfish.

- **The thick-knees** get their common name from the knobbly joints on their legs – actually between the ankle and shin bones.

- **If the Egyptian plover's chicks** get too hot, the parent birds soak their own belly feathers with water and give their young a cooling shower.

- **The pygmy seed-snipe** of southern South America blends in with the plains landscape so well that it is almost invisible when it crouches on the ground.

# Fairy-wrens and relatives

- **The 26 species of fairy-wrens live in Australia and New Guinea, where they forage for insects on the ground.**

- **Young fairy-wrens** often stay with their parents and help them raise the next brood of young. Pairs with helpers can raise more young than those without.

- **The rock warbler** makes its nest in a dark cave or mine-shaft, attaching the nest to the walls with spiderwebs.

- **During its courtship display,** the male superb fairy-wren may present his mate with a yellow flower petal.

- **If a predator** comes too close to a fairy-wren's nest, the parent birds make a special 'rodent run' away from the nest, squeaking and trailing their tails to confuse and distract the enemy.

- **The 50 or so species of thickhead** live in rainforests and scrub in Southeast Asia and Australasia.

- **The white-throated gerygone's** nest hangs from a eucalyptus branch and is made from bark strips and plant fibres woven together with spiderwebs.

- **The hooded pitohui** (thickhead family) is one of the very few poisonous birds known. Its feathers and skin contain a poison that protects it from predators.

- **The Australasian warbler** family includes 65 species of gerygone, thornbills and scrubwrens.

- **The golden whistler** is probably the most variable of birds – the 70 or more races all have slightly different feather patterns or beak shapes.

◄ *The male superb fairy-wren is easily recognized by the bright blue plumage around its head and neck.*

# Beaks and feet

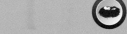

- **No bird** has more than four toes, but some have three and the ostrich has only two.

- **Four-toed birds** have different arrangements of toes: in swifts, all four point forwards; in most perching birds, three point forwards and one backwards; and in parrots, two point forwards and two backwards.

- **A beak** is made up of a bird's projecting jaw bones, covered in a hard horny material.

- **The hyacinth macaw** has one of the most powerful beaks of any bird, strong enough to crack brazil nuts.

- **Webbed feet** make all waterbirds efficient paddlers.

- **The Australian pelican** has the largest beak of any bird, at up to 50 cm long.

> ★ STAR FACT ★
> A baby bird has a spike called an 'egg-tooth'
> on its beak for breaking its way out of its egg.

- **Nightjars** have the shortest beaks, at 8–10 mm long.

- **A bird stands** on the tips of its toes – the backward bending joint halfway down its leg is the ankle joint.

- **A bird's beak** is extremely sensitive to touch. Birds that probe in the ground for food have extra sensory organs at the beak tip.

▼ *When a chick is ready to hatch, it makes a tiny hole in the shell with its 'egg-tooth' – a process called 'pipping' – and then struggles its way out.*

*First tiny hole*

*Egg cracks*  *Chick appears*

*Chick breaks free of egg*

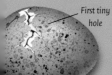

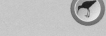

# Divers and grebes

- **The great crested grebe** is best known for its amazing courtship dance, during which male and female perform a series of movements in water and exchange pieces of weed.

- **At 90 cm long,** the white-billed diver is the largest of the four species of diver.

- **The short-winged grebe** lives on lakes high in the mountains of Peru and Bolivia, and cannot fly. It basks in the sun to warm its body after the cold nights.

- **Divers feed only on fish,** which they catch underwater. The great northern diver can dive

◀ *The great crested grebe lives in parts of Europe, Asia, Africa and Australasia.*

★ STAR FACT ★
Grebes have up to 20,000 feathers to keep their bodies warm and dry as they dive for food.

as deep as 20 m or more below the water's surface.

- **In the 19th century,** the breast feathers of grebes were used to make muffs to keep ladies' hands warm.

- **There are about 20 species of grebes** (three flightless). They live near freshwater lakes and marshes.

- **Divers** are so specialized for diving and swimming that adult birds cannot walk upright on land.

- **Grebes** feed on fish, insects and shellfish. They also swallow moulted feathers, which may help them to regurgitate waste such as fish bones and keep their gut free of parasites.

- **The great crested grebe** makes a nest of water plants floating near the water's edge. It lays 3–6 eggs, which both male and female incubate.

# Falcons

- **The peregrine** is the fastest bird, diving through the air at 180 km/h to catch prey.

- **The peregrine's hunting technique** is so exacting that only one in ten attacks is successful.

- **At up to 60 cm long,** the gyr falcon is the largest of the falcon family, and can catch ducks and hares.

- **The common kestrel** hovers above the ground on fast-beating wings while it searches for small mammals.

- **Falconets and pygmy falcons** are the smallest birds of prey. The Philippine falconet is only 15 cm long.

- **Falcons** have adapted well to city life – kestrels hover above rubbish bins to watch for mice, and peregrines dive down between New York skyscrapers.

- **Eleonora's falcon** is named after a 14th-century

★ STAR FACT ★
Kestrels can see ultra-violet light, which reflects off the urine a rodent uses to mark its tracks.

Sardinian princess, who brought in laws to protect it.

- **The earliest known records** of falconry come from 2nd-century BC China.

- **In winter,** both male and female kestrels spend about a quarter of their day hunting. But when the female is incubating eggs, the male hunts for longer.

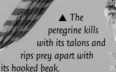

▲ *The peregrine kills with its talons and rips prey apart with its hooked beak.*

# Parrots

- **The only flightless parrot** is the New Zealand kakapo or owl parrot, which is now extremely rare.

- **The palm cockatoo** has an amazing courtship display. The male bird holds a stick in its foot and makes a loud drumming noise by beating the stick against the side of a tree.

- **At about 85 cm long**, the scarlet macaw of South and Central America is one of the largest of the parrot family.

- **Unlike most parrots**, the kea of New Zealand eats meat as well as fruit and insects. It feasts on carrion – animals that are already dead – and also hunts young shearwaters in their burrows.

- **Macaws nest in tree holes** high in rainforest trees. The female lays two eggs which her mate helps to incubate. The young macaws stay with their parents for up to two years.

- **The little blue-crowned hanging parrot** gets its name from its strange habit of hanging upside down from a branch when at rest.

- **Macaws** swallow beakfuls of clay from riverbanks. The clay may help to protect the birds from the effects of some plants and seeds that they eat, many of which are poisonous to other creatures.

- **There are about 350 species in the parrot order**, including birds such as macaws, budgerigars, lories and cockatoos. They live in Central and South America, Africa, southern Asia and Australasia.

- **As early as 400 BC**, a Greek author wrote of owning a pet parrot – a bird that could speak words in both Indian and Greek!

> ★ STAR FACT ★
> The pattern of feathers on each side of the red-and-green macaw's face is unique – no two birds look identical.

▶ *With its bright red feathers, the scarlet macaw is one of the most beautiful of all the parrots. It can fly at up to 56 km/h as it searches the rainforest for fruit, nuts and seeds to eat.*

# Bird senses

- **Almost all birds** have excellent sight, and most depend on their eyes for finding food.

- **A bird's outer ear** consists of a short tube leading from the eardrum to the outside. In most birds the ear openings are just behind the jaw.

- **A barn owl's hearing** is so good that it can detect and catch prey in complete darkness without using its eyes at all.

- **A chicken** has only 24 tastebuds and a starling about 200 – a human has 9000.

- **An eagle** can spot prey from as much as 1.6 km above the Earth.

- **A starling's eye** is as much as

▲ With its amazing hearing, the barn owl hunts mice and other small rodents at night.

15 percent of the total weight of its head. A human's eye is only one percent of the head weight.

- **An ostrich's eye**, at 5 cm in diameter, is larger than any other land animal's eye.

- **Birds** are ten times more sensitive to changes of pitch and intensity in sounds than humans. They can detect sounds of 1/200 second.

- **Kiwis have poor sight** and depend more on their sense of smell for finding many food items, such as earthworms, at night.

- **Albatrosses** have a good sense of smell. In experiments, they have been attracted to food from a distance of 30 km.

# Terns and skimmers

- **The noddy**, a species of tern, gets its name from its habit of nodding its head during its courtship display.

- **The black skimmer's beak** has a flattened lower part that is longer than the upper part. The bird flies over water with the lower part of its beak just below the surface, ready to snap up prey.

- **The 42 or so species of terns** are found all over the world, mostly along coasts.

- **Arctic terns** are long-lived birds, known to survive to 27 – and sometimes even 34 – years of age.

- **Most terns eat fish**, squid and shellfish, but marshland terns also eat insects and frogs.

▼ The Arctic tern has a long, forked tail, short red legs and a cap of black feathers on its head.

★ STAR FACT ★
The Arctic tern makes a round-trip migration from the Arctic to Antarctica and back – a record distance of more than 32,000 km.

- **At up to 59 cm long**, the Caspian tern is the largest of the terns, and one of the most widespread.

- **The fairy tern** does not make a nest. Instead, it balances its one egg on a tree branch and manages to sit on it without knocking it off.

- **Most terns mate for life**. Even if they don't stay together all year round, pairs meet up when they return to breeding sites.

- **There are only three species of skimmers**. most live in coastal areas of tropical Africa, Southeast Asia and North and South America.

# Weavers and relatives

- **The sociable weaver** nests in groups of up to 300 birds. The huge nest is made of sticks and grass, and may measure 4 m deep and weigh up to 1000 kg. Each pair of birds has its own hole in the nest.

- **Desert-living sociable weavers** use their nest all year round for shelter from sun, wind and cold. At night, when temperatures drop, the nest holes stay 20°C warmer than the outside air.

- **Whydah birds** do not make their own nests, but lay their eggs in the nests of other birds, usually waxbills.

▶ *When the male cape weaver has finished making a nest, it calls to the female.*

- **Young whydahs** make the same sounds and have the same mouth markings as their foster parents' own young, and because of this they get fed.

- **The baya weaver** makes a beautiful nest of woven grass and leaves that it hangs from a tree or roof.

- **In the breeding season**, the male paradise whydah grows 28 cm long tail feathers – almost twice the length of its body – for display in flight.

- **Most weavers** have short, strong beaks that they use for feeding on seeds and insects.

  - **The red bishop** mates with three or four females, who all nest in his territory.

  - **The red-vented malimbe** (a weaver) feeds mainly on the husks of oil palm nuts.

> ★ STAR FACT ★
> As many as 500 pairs of red-billed queleas may nest together in one acacia tree.

# Plovers and lapwings

- **The wrybill**, a New Zealand plover, has a unique beak that curves to the right. The bird sweeps its beak over sand to pick up insects.

- **If a predator** comes near a killdeer's nest, the bird moves away, trailing a wing to look as though it is injured. The predator, seeing what it thinks is an easy victim, follows the killdeer which, once far enough away, flies off.

- **Kentish plover chicks** have markings like the stones and pebbles of their nest site. If danger threatens, the chicks flatten themselves on the ground and are almost impossible to see.

▶ *The wrybill breeds on New Zealand's South Island, but overwinters on North Island.*

- **There are 60 or so species of plovers** and lapwings around the world.

- **Female dotterels** lay clutches of eggs for several males, which incubate the eggs.

- **To attract females**, the male lapwing performs a spectacular rolling, tumbling display flight in the air.

- **Spur-winged plovers** are often seen close to crocodiles in Africa and Asia – they may feed on small creatures that the crocodiles disturb.

- **The lapwing** is also known as the peewit.

- **Golden plovers** have been recorded flying at more than 113 km/h.

> ★ STAR FACT ★
> Many plovers pat the ground with their feet to imitate the sound of rain. This attracts worms to the surface, where they are snapped up.

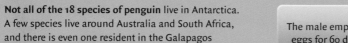

# Penguins

- **Not all of the 18 species of penguin** live in Antarctica. A few species live around Australia and South Africa, and there is even one resident in the Galapagos Islands on the equator.

- **Penguins have wings,** but cannot fly. They spend as much as 85 percent of their time in water, where they use their wings like flippers to help push themselves through the water.

- **The king penguin** has been known to dive down to 250 m in search of prey.

- **An emperor penguin** may travel at least 900 km on one feeding expedition.

*An emperor penguin stands about 110 cm high*

◀ *An emperor chick spends the first two months of its life on its parent's feet, protected from the cold by a pouch of skin. If it falls off, it freezes to death in seconds.*

> ★ STAR FACT ★
> The male emperor penguin incubates his mate's eggs for 60 days, eating nothing and losing as much as 45 percent of his body weight.

- **Like many other penguins,** gentoos nest in a simple scrape on the ground, but they surround it with a ring of pebbles. A courting gentoo shows its mate an example of the sort of pebbles it will provide.

- **The emperor penguin** keeps its egg warm on its feet, where it is covered by a fold of skin. The temperature there stays at 36°C, despite the freezing surroundings.

- **Penguins** eat fish, squid and shellfish. They have spiny tongues to help them hold on to slippery prey.

- **A dense covering** of three layers of feathers keeps penguins warm. An emperor penguin has about 12 feathers per square cm of his body.

- **Penguins** usually swim at 5–10 km/h, but can reach speeds of up to 24 km/h.

*Emperor penguin chick*

▲ *Emperor penguins are highly streamlined, allowing them to dive to depths of 500 m when they hunt. They can stay underwater for more than fifteen minutes, using their strong flippers to propel them forward.*

# Bird song and calls

- **Birds** make two sorts of sounds – simple calls, giving a warning or a threat, and the more complicated songs sung by some males at breeding time.

- **Birds' songs** have a definite dialect. The songs of a group of chaffinches in one area, will sound slightly different from those of a group somewhere else.

- **A songbird** reared in captivity away from its family produces a weak version of its parents' song, but cannot perform the whole repertoire.

- **Gulls and parrots** do not sing, but they do make various calls to attract mates or warn off enemies.

- **A bird sings** by vibrating the thin muscles in its syrinx – a special organ in its throat.

- **A sedge warbler** may use at least 50 different sounds in its songs.

- **Male and female boubou shrikes** sing a duet together, performing alternate parts of the song.

- **Songbirds** may make as many as 20 calls; gulls make only about ten.

- **Birds** make other sounds, too. During courtship flights, male woodpigeons make a loud clapping with their wings.

◄ The chaffinch is the commonest of Europe's finches.

> ★ STAR FACT ★
> A baby songbird starts to learn to sing about 10 days after it hatches, and continues to learn for about 40 days.

# Shrikes and vangas

- **If it has plenty of prey**, such as lizards, frogs or insects, the northern shrike will store items for later by impaling them on a thorn bush or barbed wire fence.

- **Shrikes** are also known as 'butcher birds', because of their habit of hanging prey in trees.

- **The 14 species of vanga** live only on Madagascar and the neighbouring Comoros Islands.

- **The fiscal shrike** is an aggressive bird that kills other birds that come near it.

- **During its courtship display**, the male puffback (a shrike) fluffs up the long feathers on its lower back like a powder puff.

▲ The beautiful crimson-breasted shrike often uses strips of acacia bark to build its nest.

- **There are 65 species of shrikes** found in Africa, Europe, Asia and North America, as well as 72 species of cuckoo-shrikes and nine species of helmet shrikes.

- **All shrikes** have powerful hooked beaks that they use for killing insects, lizards and frogs.

- **The call of the brubru shrike** sounds just like a phone ring.

- **The loggerhead shrike** makes a nest of twigs and grass in a thorny bush or tree, where the female incubates 5–7 eggs.

- **The sickle-billed vanga** uses its long, curved beak to probe bark for insects. It hangs upside down by its claws while it feeds.

# Tits

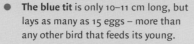

- **The blue tit** is only 10–11 cm long, but lays as many as 15 eggs – more than any other bird that feeds its young.

- **The largest of the tits** is the Asian sultan tit, at about 22 cm long and 30 g in weight – twice the size of most tits.

- **The penduline tit** makes an amazing nest woven from plant fibres and suspended from the end of a twig. The walls of the nest may be 2.5 cm thick.

- **There are about 50 species of true tits** found in Europe, Africa, Asia and North America. There are also seven species of long-tailed tits and ten species of penduline tits.

◄ *Agile little blue tits and their relatives can often be seen clinging to wire bird feeders in gardens during the winter.*

★ STAR FACT ★
The willow tit may bury up to 1000 nuts and seeds a day, to eat later when food is scarce.

- **The black-capped chickadee** gets its name from its call, which sounds like a 'chick-a-dee-dee', and is one of the most complex of any bird songs.

- **The female great tit** lays 8–13 eggs, each of which is about ten percent of her body weight.

- **Great tits** hatch blind and helpless, and are fed by their parents for about three weeks. The parents may make 1000 feeding trips a day to the young.

- **The long-tailed tit** makes its nest from feathers and moss that it collects – one nest may contain as many as 2000 feathers in all.

- **The long-tailed tit** is only about 14 cm long, and more than half of its length is its tail feathers.

# Pigeons and sandgrouse

- **The passenger pigeon** was once one of the most common birds in North America – one flock was 480 km long and 1.6 km wide. But overhunting made the birds rare, and the last passenger pigeon died in captivity in 1914.

- **Both male and female pigeons** can make a milky substance in their crops that they feed to their young.

- **Wood pigeons** feed on leaves, seeds, nuts, berries and some insects, but those living near humans also eat bread and food scraps.

- **At about 74 cm long** (nearly as big as a turkey), the Victoria crowned pigeon of New Guinea is the largest member of its family.

- **Pigeon 'races'** are held

▲ *Sandgrouse usually have grey or brownish feathers with mottled patterns that blend with their desert surroundings.*

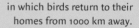

in which birds return to their homes from 1000 km away.

- **The 16 or so species of sandgrouse** live in southern Europe, Africa and parts of Asia.

- **One adult sandgrouse** was found to have 8000 seeds in its crop.

★ STAR FACT ★
A male sandgrouse soaks his belly feathers at a desert waterhole, then flies back to his nest so the chicks can drink from his plumage.

- **In Christianity**, a dove is often used to symbolize the Holy Spirit. Doves are often released as a gesture of peace and goodwill.

- **There are more than 300 species of pigeon**, and they occur all over the world, except in the far north and Antarctica.

# Hawks and harriers

- **The female sparrowhawk** is almost twice the size of the male. At breeding time she defends the nest while the more agile male brings the family food.

- **The marsh harrier** flies close to the ground searching for mice, rats, frogs, rabbits and even fish. When it sights prey, it swoops down, seizes the victim in its sharp talons and tears it apart with its beak.

- **Tiny spines** on the underside of the black-collared hawk's toes help it catch and hold slippery fish prey.

- **The African harrier hawk** likes to feed on baby birds. It has long, double-jointed legs that allow it to reach into other birds' nests and grab the chicks.

- **There are about 66** species of hawks and harriers, including goshawks and sparrowhawks.

- **Young goshawks** first leave the nest at about 40 days old and start to fly at about 45 days. By 50 days or so they can hunt for themselves, and by 70 days they can manage without their parents.

- **The largest hawk** is the northern goshawk, which is up to 60 cm long and weighs as much as 1.3 kg.

- **Fledgling goshawks** 'play' as a way of practising their hunting skills.

- **About 95 percent** of the northern harrier's diet is mice.

- **The smallest hawk** is the African little sparrowhawk, which is only about 25 cm long.

◄ *The sparrowhawk preys mostly on other birds, ranging in size from tits to pheasants.*

# Rails and bustards

▼ *The great bustard, with its 2.5 m wingspan, lives on the plains, steppes and farmland of Europe and Asia, feeding mainly on insects.*

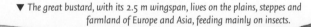

- **The weka** is a flightless rail that lives in New Zealand. Its diet includes seeds, fruit, mice, eggs and insects, and it also scavenges in rubbish bins.

- **Female great bustards** are much smaller and lighter than males, weighing only about 5 kg.

- **The world's smallest flightless bird**, the Inaccessible Island rail, weighs only 35 g – about the same as a small tomato. It lives on Inaccessible Island in the South Atlantic Ocean.

- **There are more than 130 species of rails** found all over the world, including many small islands. The family includes moorhens, coots and crakes, as well as rails.

- **The takahe**, a large flightless rail, is now extremely rare and lives only in South Island, New Zealand.

- **The 22 species of bustard** live in Africa, southern Europe, Asia and Australia.

- **Fights between Asian watercocks** (a type of rail) are staged for sport in some parts of Asia.

- **Coots** are the most aquatic of all the rails. They dive in search of plants and water insects to eat.

- **The female moorhen** makes a nest of dead leaves at the water's edge. The male helps incubate the 5–11 eggs.

> ★ STAR FACT ★
> The great bustard of southern Europe and Asia is the world's heaviest flying bird. The male weighs up to 18 kg.

# Prehistoric birds

- **The earliest known bird** is *Archaeopteryx*, which lived 155 million years ago. It had feathers like a modern bird but teeth like a reptile.

- *Ichthyornis* was a seabird with long, toothed jaws. It lived alongside dinosaurs in the Late Cretaceous period.

- **Although it could fly,** *Archaeopteryx* could not take off from the ground, and probably had to climb a tree before launching itself into the air.

- **Scientists believe** that birds evolved from lightly built dinosaurs such as *Compsognathus*, which ran on two legs.

- **The dodo** stood 1 m tall and lived on the island of Mauritius. It became extinct in the 17th century.

- *Aepyornis*, a 3 m tall ostrich ancestor from Madagascar, probably became extinct in the 17th century.

- **The eggs** of Aepyornis, or elephant bird may have weighed as much as 10 kg – more than nine times the weight of an ostrich egg today.

- **The tallest bird ever** was the moa (*Dinornis*) of New Zealand. It was a towering 3.5 m tall.

- **The great auk** first lived two million years ago. It became extinct in the mid 19th century after being overhunted for its fat, which was burned in oil lamps.

- **An early member** of the vulture family, *Argentavix* of South America had an amazing 7.3 m wingspan.

◄ *Archaeopteryx had a wingspan of about 50 cm. Its name means 'ancient wing'.*

# Waxwings and relatives

- **The waxwing** gets its name from the red markings like drops of wax at the tips of its wing feathers.

- **Palmchats** nest in palm trees. One nest may house 30 pairs of birds, each with its own tunnel entrance to the outside.

- **The silky flycatcher** feeds mostly on mistletoe berries, passing out the seeds.

*Prominent crest*

◄ *Bohemian waxwings will strip a bush clean of its berries before moving on.*

> ★ **STAR FACT** ★
> When courting, a male bohemian waxwing gives the female a gift – a berry or ant larva.

- **The bohemian waxwing** makes a nest of twigs, moss and grass, usually in a conifer tree. The female incubates 4–6 eggs, while the male keeps her fed.

- **Adult cedar waxwings** store berries in their crops, or throat pouches, and regurgitate them for their young.

- **The male silky flycatcher** builds a nest for his mate's eggs, and does most of the incubation.

- **Adult waxwings** eat mainly berries, but feed their young on insects for the first two weeks of their lives.

- **The single species of palmchat** is found on the islands of Haiti and the Dominican Republic in the Caribbean.

- **Cedar waxwings** have been seen sitting in rows on a branch passing a berry from one bird to the next until one of them swallows it!

# True and harpy eagles

- **The most powerful of all eagles,** the South American harpy eagle hunts prey that may weigh more than itself, such as large monkeys and sloths.

- **The Philippine eagle** is one of the rarest of all birds of prey. Twenty years ago there were only about 200 birds. Now they are strictly protected, and there is a captive breeding programme to increase numbers.

- **The golden eagle** makes a bulky nest of sticks and branches that may measure as much as 2 m high and 1.5 m across often called the eyrie.

- **A harpy eagle** weighs over 8 kg, has a wingspan of more than 2 m, and talons the size of a bear's claws.

- **True eagles** are also known as booted eagles, because their legs are covered with feathers down to their toes.

- **Verreaux's eagle** lays two eggs, but the first chick to hatch usually kills the younger chick.

- **At up to 96 cm long,** the martial eagle is the largest African eagle. It feeds on mammals such as hyrax and young antelope, and on other birds, including guineafowl and even storks.

★ **STAR FACT** ★
A eaglet weighs only 85 g when it hatches, but by the time it reaches adulthood the bird weighs about 7 kg.

- **A young martial eagle** is fed by its parents for about 60 days, by which time is has a full covering of feathers and is able to tear up prey for itself.

- **The golden eagle** usually has a hunting territory of about 260 sq km.

Hooked beak
for tearing
apart its prey

Large eyes – the eagle
has excellent eyesight

Tapering wing
feathers increase lift
so the eagle can soar
for long periods

Long curved talons

▶ Golden eagles lay two eggs, but one chick
usually dies. At first the mother keeps the
surviving chick warm while the male finds food,
but as the chick grows larger, both parents are
kept busy supplying it with food.

# Turkeys and grouse

- **Male wild turkeys** of the USA, Mexico and Central America can weigh up to 8 kg.

- **At 87 cm long**, the western capercaillie is the biggest of the 17 species of grouse. The female is only 60 cm long.

▲ Wild turkeys usually feed on the ground, but they are strong flyers over short distances.

- **In winter**, the spruce grouse feeds mainly on the buds and needles of pine trees.

- **An adult turkey** has about 3500 feathers.

- **The 17 species of grouse** live in North America, Europe and northern Asia.

- **Wild turkeys** are not fussy eaters. They feed on seeds, nuts, berries, leaves, insects and other small creatures.

- **To attract females** and challenge rival males, the ruffed grouse makes a drumming sound with its wings.

- **At the start of the breeding season**, foot-stamping dances are performed by groups of male prairie chickens at their traditional display areas.

- **The ruffed grouse** lays 9–12 eggs. When the young hatch, the female shows them where to find food.

# Mockingbirds and relatives

- **Mockingbirds** are so-called because they imitate the calls of other bird species – as many as 36 in all.

- **The alpine accentor** breeds high in the mountains, and has been seen nesting at 8000 m in the Himalayas.

- **As well as mockingbirds,** the 32 species in the family includes birds such as catbirds, thrashers and tremblers. The live in North and South America.

- **The brown trembler**, a resident of some Caribbean islands, gets its name from its habit of shaking its body from time to time.

- **The 13 accentor species** live in mountainous parts of northern Africa, Europe and Asia.

▶ The northern mockingbird is the best mimic in its family, usually copying the sounds made by other bird species.

- **'Mimic of many tongues'** is the meaning of the northern mockingbird's scientific name, *Mimus polyglottus*.

- **The grey catbird** lines its cup-shaped nest of sticks, leaves and grasses with pine needles and even hair. The female lays 3–5 eggs, and incubates them for 12–13 days.

- **The brown thrasher** scatters dead leaves with its beak as it searches on the ground for its insect prey.

- **The catbird** gets its name from its strange, catlike call.

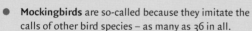

# Wrens and babblers

- **The white-necked rockfowl** (babbler family) makes a mud nest on the roof of caves. It sometimes builds onto old wasps' nests.

- **The cactus wren** builds its nest among the spines of the chola cactus. Few enemies will brave the spines to steal the wren's eggs or young.

- **At about 23 cm long**, the black-capped donacobious of South America is the largest of the wren family.

- **The only species** of the babbler family to live in North America is the wren-tit, while 256 species are found in Asia, Africa and Australasia.

- **The tuneful song** of the red-billed leiothrix (babbler family) makes it a popular cage bird in China.

- **Although common in west Africa**, the pale-breasted thrush-babbler is so good at hiding on the forest floor, where it searches for insects, that it is rarely seen.

- **A male wren** courts a mate by building up to 12 nests. The female chooses one in which to lay her eggs.

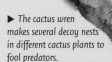

▶ The cactus wren makes several decoy nests in different cactus plants to fool predators.

- **The winter wren** usually lays 5–8 eggs, and incubates them for 14–17 days. The young stay in the nest for 20 days.

- **Brightly coloured patches** of bare skin on the head are a distinguishing feature of rockfowl (babbler family).

- **Most wrens** live in Europe, Asia, Africa and North America.

# Caring for young

- **Many baby birds** are blind, naked and helpless when they hatch, and have to be cared for by their parents.

- **The young of ducks and geese** hatch with a covering of feathers, and can find food hours after hatching.

- **A young golden eagle** has grown feathers after 50 days and learned to fly after 70, but stays with its parents for another month while learning to hunt.

> ★ STAR FACT ★
> In a colony of thousands of terns, baby terns can recognize the call of their own parents.

- **A young bird** is known as a fledgling from the time it hatches until it is fully feathered and can fly.

- **A young pelican** feeds by putting its head deep into its parent's large beak and gobbling up any fish it finds.

- **A swan** carries its young on its back to keep them safe.

- **To obtain food** from its parent, a young herring gull has to peck at a red spot on the parent's beak. The adult gull then regurgitates food for the chick to eat.

- **Shearwaters** feed their young for 60 days, then stop. After a week the chicks get so hungry that they take to the air to find food for themselves.

- **In three weeks**, a new-born cuckoo gets 50 times heavier.

◀ Bokmakierie shrike chicks are born blind, but can see by four days old.

# Ostriches and emus

- **The ostrich** is the largest of all birds alive today. It stands 2.5 m tall and weighs about 130 kg – more than twice as much as an average human.

- **The male emu** incubates his mate's clutch of eggs for eight weeks, during that time he does not eat or drink. He lives on the stores of body fat that it has built up during the previous months.

- **In Southwest Asia**, the shells of ostrich eggs are believed to have magical powers, and are sometimes placed on the roofs of houses as protection from evil.

- **Ostriches don't really bury their heads** in the sand. But if a female is approached by an enemy while sitting on her nest on the ground, she will press her long neck flat on the ground, to appear less obvious.

- **The largest bird in Australia** is the emu, which measures 2 m tall and weighs as much as 45 kg. Like the ostrich, it cannot fly.

> **★ STAR FACT ★**
> The ostrich cannot fly, but is a very fast runner. It can speed along at 60 km/h – as fast as a racehorse.

- **An ostrich feather** was used as a symbol of justice in ancient Egypt.

- **Seeds, fruits, flowers and plant shoots** are the emu's main sources of food, but it also eats some insects and small animals.

- **The male ostrich** makes a shallow nest on the ground and mates with several females, all of whom lay their eggs in the nest. The chief female incubates the eggs during the day, and the male takes over at night.

- **Ostrich chicks** have many enemies, including jackals and hyenas, and only 15 percent are likely to survive until their first birthday.

The male has black feathers on its back; females and young birds have brown feathers

The long, flexible neck is bare skinned

Long, strong legs for running

▲ The ostrich lives in Africa in dry grassland areas, where it often has to run for long distances in search of food.

# Migration

- **Migration** is generally the journey made twice a year between a summer breeding area, where food is plentiful, and a wintering area with a good climate.

- **Many migrating birds** have to build up fat stores to allow them to fly non-stop for many days without food.

- **A migrating bird** can fly across the Sahara Desert in 50–60 hours without stopping to 'refuel'.

- **Birds find their way** by observing landmarks, the patterns of stars and the position of the setting sun. They also use their sense of smell and monitor the Earth's magnetic field.

- **Most birds** that migrate long distances fly at night.

- **The snow goose** migrates nearly 5000 km south from Arctic Canada at an altitude of 9000 m.

- **Before migration was studied**, some people thought swallows simply spent the winter asleep in mud.

- **Even flightless birds migrate.** Emus make journeys on foot of 500 km or more, and penguins migrate in water.

- **Every year** at least five billion birds migrate from North to Central and South America.

- **The Arctic tern** spends the northern summer in the Arctic and migrates to the Antarctic for the southern summer, enjoying 24 hours of daylight in both places.

▼ *Geese migrate in huge flocks, but pairs stay together within the flock.*

# Finches and relatives

- **The crossbill** gets its name from its crossed beak, specially shaped for extracting seeds from pine cones.

- **The beaks** of some crossbills cross to the left, while those of others cross to the right.

- **Canaries** were first domesticated in the early 16th century, from the island canary of the Canary Islands, the Azores and Madeira.

- **The male American goldfinch** brings

▲ *Wild canaries have duller plumage than their bright yellow domestic relatives.*

the female food while she incubates the 4–6 eggs.

- **The bullfinch** feeds on fruit buds in spring and it can pluck as many as 30 buds in a minute.

- **The kernels** of cherry stones and olive stones are a favourite food of the strong-beaked hawfinch.

- **The goldfinch** uses its slender beak like tweezers to take seeds from between the spines of a teasel head.

- **Finches are small birds**, ranging from 4–19 cm long and weighing up to 100 grams.

- **Siskins and goldfinches** have long been popular as cage birds, and are now rare in many areas.

★ STAR FACT ★
Although the hawfinch weighs only 50 g, its beak can exert a pressure of 45 kg.

# Cranes and trumpeters

- **The whooping crane** is one of the world's most endangered birds, with only about 300 surviving in 1995.

- **The crowned crane**, which has a fine crest of yellow feathers, performs a spectacular courtship display that involves leaping 2 m into the air.

- **The three species of trumpeter** live in tropical rainforests. All make a loud trumpeting call – hence their name.

- **In China and Japan** the crane symbolizes long life and good luck.

- **At about 1.5 m long**, the Sarus crane of India, Southeast Asia and northern Australia is one of the largest members of the crane family.

▶ The handsome crowned crane lives in Africa, usually around swamps and marshland.

- **The limpkin** is a relative of the cranes and the only member of its family. It has a long, curved beak, which it uses to remove snails from their shells.

- **Trumpeters** spend most of their time on the ground in search of fruit, nuts and insects, but they roost in trees.

- **The sandhill crane** makes a nest of plant material on the ground. The female lays two eggs, which both parents help to incubate. Soon after hatching, the young leave the nest.

- **Siberian cranes** have been known to live more than 80 years – one captive male even fathered chicks at the age of 78!

- **The 14 or so species of crane** live all over the world, in North America, Africa, Europe, Asia and Australia.

# Bowerbirds

- **Male bowerbirds** build bowers of twigs and other plant material to attract females. They decorate their creations with berries and shells, and some perform dances in front of their bowers.

- **The Vogelkop gardener bowerbird** builds a hutlike structure big enough for a person to crawl into.

- **Male bowerbirds' bowers** are not built as a place for the

◀ The male spotted bowerbird spends much of its time looking after its bower.

female to lay eggs and rear young. The females build their own, more practical nests.

- **The forests** of New Guinea and northern and eastern Australia are home to the 18 or so species of bowerbird.

- **At about 36 cm long**, the great grey bowerbird of northern Australia is the largest of the family.

- **Bowerbirds** feed on fruit, berries, seeds, insects and other small creatures.

- **A female bowerbird** cares for her 1–3 chicks alone.

- **The male regent bowerbird** paints its bower yellow using a mix of spit and the juice of crushed leaves.

- **Catbirds** are members of the bowerbird family. They get their name from their catlike calls.

# Feathers

- **Feathers** are made of a protein called keratin. Human hair and nails are also made of keratin.

- **Feathers grow** at a rate of 1–13 mm a day.

- **The ruby-throated hummingbird** has only 940 feathers, while the whistling swan has 25,216.

- **A bird's feathers** are replaced once or twice a year in a process called 'moulting'.

- **Feathers** keep a bird warm, protect its skin, provide camouflage, and may also attract mates.

- **In most birds**, a third of the feathers are on the head.

- **The longest feathers ever known** were 10.59 m long, and belonged to an ornamental chicken.

- **The feathers** that cover a bird's body are called contour feathers. Down feathers underneath provide extra warmth.

- **The 7182 feathers** of a bald eagle weighed 677 g, more than twice as much as the bird's skeleton.

- **Birds** spend time every day 'preening' – cleaning and rearranging their feathers with their beaks.

▲ *The peacock has the most ornate feathers of any bird.*

▶ *The plumage of the little hummingbird gleams with iridescence.*

# Antbirds and tapaculos

- **Antbirds** follow columns of army ants as they march over the forest floor, perching just above the ground to seize other insects as they flee from the ants.

- **The 230 or so species of antbird** live in Mexico, Central and South America.

- **The 30 species of tapaculos** are insect-eating birds that live in dry scrub and the cool mountain forests of South America.

- **Antbirds** mate for life.

- **During the courtship ritual** of the ocellated antbird, the male presents the female with an item of food.

- **Antbirds have white spots** on their back feathers, which they use to signal

★ **STAR FACT** ★
An antbird rubs a mouthful of ants over its feathers to clean them. The formic acid from the ants kills any lice and mites in the feathers.

warnings to each other. They show the spots in particular patterns according to the message – like a sort of Morse code.

- **Antbird species** range from 10–38 cm long, and have differently shaped beaks to suit their food.

- **Some larger species of antbirds** have a special 'tooth' inside the beak that helps them chew food.

- **Most antbirds** do not fly much and have poorly developed wings, but their legs are strong, for running and perching.

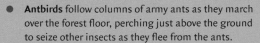

◀ *Female antbirds are often brownish or greenish in colour. Males usually have dark grey plumage with white markings.*

# Swallows and martins

- **There are about 80 species of swallows and martins** found all over the world. Most migrate between breeding grounds and wintering areas.

- **The sand martin** digs a 120 cm long nesting burrow in river banks.

- **Swallows** catch their insect food in the air as they fly.

- **Only discovered in 1968**, the white-eyed river martin spends the winter in reedbeds on Lake Boraphet in Thailand.

- **Purple martins** often nest in old woodpecker holes or in nest-boxes. The female incubates the 4–5 eggs

▼ The house martin often lives near people, making its nest under the eaves of buildings or under bridges or other structures.

alone, but the male helps feed the young.

- **There is an old saying** that the weather will be good when swallows fly high, but bad when swallows fly low. This is based on fact – in wet weather, insects tend to stay nearer the ground, so their predators – the swallows – do the same.

- **Adult swallows** will carry a mass of crushed insects, squashed in a ball in the throat, back to their young. A barn swallow may take 400 meals a day to its chicks.

- **Sand martins** breed in the northern hemisphere, migrating south in the winter in flocks of thousands.

- **In most swallow species** males and females are alike, but in the rare blue swallow the female has a short tail, while the male's is long and forked.

> ★ STAR FACT ★
> The ancient Romans used swallows as messengers to carry news of the winners of chariot races to neighbouring towns.

# Snake and sea eagles

- **The bald eagle** performs an amazing courtship display, in which male and female lock their claws together and tumble through the air towards the ground.

- **The short-toed eagle** kills a snake with a bite to the back of the head, instantly severing the backbone.

- **The white-tailed sea eagle** snatches fish from the water in its powerful talons.

- **The bald eagle** was chosen as the national emblem of the USA in 1782, and appears on most of the gold and silver coins in the USA.

- **Spikes** on the underside of its toes help the African fish eagle hold

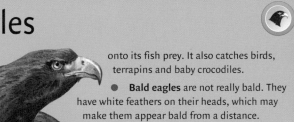

onto its fish prey. It also catches birds, terrapins and baby crocodiles.

- **Bald eagles** are not really bald. They have white feathers on their heads, which may make them appear bald from a distance.

- **The bateleur**, a snake eagle, may fly as much as 300 km a day in search of food.

- **Snake eagles** eat snakes, and have short, strong toes ideal for tackling their writhing victims.

- **The name 'bateleur'** means 'tumbler' or 'tightrope walker' in French, and refers to the rocking, acrobatic movements that the bird makes in flight.

- **There are only about 40 pairs** of the Madagascar fish eagle left in the world.

◄ Steller's sea eagle lives along Asia's coasts and rivers, preying mostly on salmon.

# Rainforest birds

- **Male and female eclectus parrots** of the Amazon rainforest have very different plumage. The male bird is mostly bright green, while the female is red with a blue underside.

- **The crowned eagle** lives in African rainforests, where it feeds on monkeys and other mammals such as mongooses and rats.

- **The king vulture** of South America is the only vulture to live in rainforest. As well as feeding on carrion, it also kills mammals and reptiles.

- **The sunbittern** lives along river banks in the rainforests of South America, feeding on frogs, insects and other creatures.

- **With its abundance** of flowers, leaves, fruits and insects all year round, a rainforest is the ideal home for many different kinds of birds.

- **The muscovy duck**, now familiar in farmyards and parks in many parts of the world, originally came from the rainforests of Central and South America.

- **Large, flightless cassowaries** live in the rainforests of New Guinea, where people hunt them to eat.

- **The spectacled eagle owl** of South America has rings of white feathers around its eyes. Its call resembles the hammering sound made by woodpeckers.

- **The rare Cassin's hawk eagle** lives in African rainforests, and hunts squirrels and other birds.

> ★ STAR FACT ★
> The hoatzin builds its nest over rainforest rivers, so that if its chicks are threatened, they can drop into the water to escape.

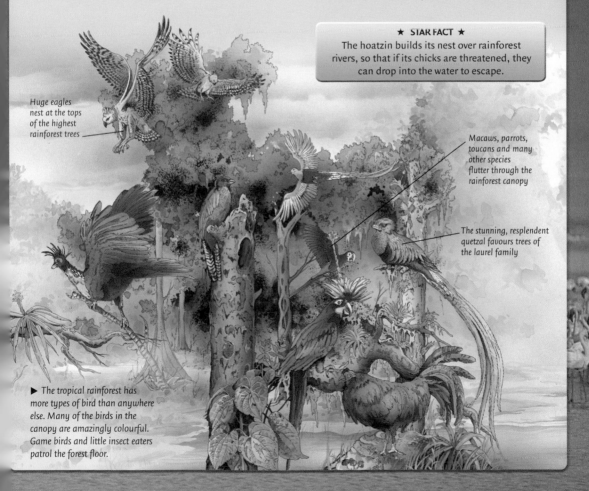

Huge eagles nest at the tops of the highest rainforest trees

Macaws, parrots, toucans and many other species flutter through the rainforest canopy

The stunning, resplendent quetzal favours trees of the laurel family

▶ The tropical rainforest has more types of bird than anywhere else. Many of the birds in the canopy are amazingly colourful. Game birds and little insect eaters patrol the forest floor.

# Larks and wagtails

- **The shore lark** has the widest distribution of any lark. Its habitats range from the icy Arctic to deserts.

- **The wagtail family** has about 60 species, most of which are small, insect-eating birds. They include pipits and longclaws.

- **The 75 species of lark** live in North America, parts of South America, Africa, Europe, Asia and Australia. The greatest number of species is found in Africa.

- **The female skylark** makes a shallow, grassy nest on the ground, and incubates 3–4 eggs.

- **The skylark** performs a beautiful song as it flutters up to a great height, hovers and descends again.

- **The thick-billed lark** has a larger, stronger beak than

most larks, and uses it to crush hard seeds and tough-shelled insects.

- **The shore or horned lark** is the only member of the family to live in the Americas.

- **The desert lark's coloration** varies according to where it lives – birds in areas of white sand have pale feathers, while those that live on dark laval sand are almost black.

- **Craneflies** are one of the favourite foods of the meadow pipit. Adults may feed their 3–5 chicks on craneflies for two weeks. The chicks develop in a nest of dry grass lined with hair.

◀ *The little pied wagtail bobs its tail up and down almost all the time as it searches for insects.*

> ★ STAR FACT ★
> The yellow-throated longclaw gets its name from the 5-cm long claw on each back toe.

# Kingfishers

- **The common kingfisher** nests at the end of a 60-cm long tunnel that it excavates in a river bank. The female lays 4–8 eggs.

- **The tiny African pygmy kingfisher** dives not into water, like the common kingfisher, but into grass, where it snatches grasshoppers and beetles.

- **The 86 or so species of kingfisher** are found all over the world, except parts of the far north.

- **The giant kingfisher** of Africa and

the Australian laughing kookaburra are the largest of the family, at about 45 cm long.

- **Common kingfishers** incubate their eggs for 19–21 days, and feed the young for up to four weeks.

- **The shovel-billed kingfisher** is armed with its own spade for digging in mud – it uses its large, heavy bill to dig up worms, shellfish and small reptiles.

- **A flash of iridescent turquoise feathers** streaking at high speed along a river bank indicates the presence of a common or European kingfisher.

- **In the forests of New Guinea**, the male paradise kingfisher shows off its very long tail feathers to females as part of its courtship display.

- **The laughing kookaburra** is named for its call, which sounds like noisy laughter. It makes its call to claim territory. Once one starts, others tend to join in!

- **In northern Australia**, termite mounds are adopted as nest sites by the buff-breasted kingfisher.

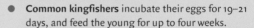

◀ *The kingfisher fiercely defends the stretch of river bank where it feeds and nests.*

# Thrushes and dippers

- **The wheatear** breeds in the Arctic, but in autumn flies some 3200 km to Africa, where it spends the winter.

- **The dipper** is the only type of songbird to live in and around water – it can swim underwater and even walk along streambeds as it searches for insect prey.

- **The familiar orange-red breast** of a robin indicates that the bird is at least two months old.

- **More than 300 species of thrush** are found nearly all over the world.

- **Best known for its beautiful song**, the nightingale sings during the day as well as at night.

- **The female blackbird** makes a cup-shaped nest of plant stems, grass, twigs and roots. The 4–5 eggs hatch after 11–17 days.

- **The five species of dipper** live in Europe, Asia and parts of North and South America.

- **The dome-shaped nests** of dippers usually have an entrance over running water.

- **The American robin** – the largest of the North American thrushes – lives both in cities and mountains.

- **Blackbirds** were taken to Australia and New Zealand in the 19th century, and their songs are now clearly different to blackbirds living in Europe.

◄ *The European robin is Britain's national bird.*

# Sandpipers

- **Coasts and marshes** are the home of the 88 or so species of sandpiper, which include curlews, snipe and phalaropes. Most have long beaks and long legs.

- **The western curlew** plunges its long, curved beak into soft coastal mud to find worms and clams.

- **As it dives** towards Earth, air rushing through the outermost tail feathers of the European snipe makes a sound called 'drumming'.

◄ *The curlew's long legs are ideal for wading through marshland.*

- **Sandpipers** range in size from the eastern curlew, at about 66 cm long, to the least sandpiper, at 11 cm.

- **Once the dowitcher's four eggs** have hatched, feeding the chicks is the responsibility of the male.

- **Unusually for birds**, female phalaropes are more brightly coloured than males. The female lays several clutches of eggs, leaving the male parent of each clutch to do all the caring for the young.

- **The turnstone** is so-named because it turns over stones on the beach in search of shellfish and worms.

- **In the breeding season**, male ruffs grow amazing feathers around the head and neck, and dance in groups to attract females.

> ★ STAR FACT ★
> The eskimo curlew is one of the world's rarest birds. With only 50 or so birds left in the world, it is on the brink of extinction.

# Large seabirds

- **The wandering albatross** has the longest wings of any bird – from tip to tip they are an incredible 3.4 m.

- **The white-tailed tropicbird** is noted for its amazing tail streamers, which measure up to 40 cm long.

- **The male frigatebird** has a bright red throat pouch that he inflates during courtship to attract females.

- **The wandering albatross** often flies 500 km in a day, soaring over the ocean in search of food.

- **The pirates of the bird world** are frigatebirds, which often chase other seabirds in the air and harass them into giving up their catches.

- **Frigatebird chicks** depend on their parents for longer than most birds. They start to fly at about six months, but continue to be fed until they are one year old.

- **The five species of frigatebird** fly over tropical areas of all oceans. They spend most of their lives in the air, rarely descending to land on water.

- **The three species of tropicbird** are all experts in the air and can dive into the sea to find prey, but cannot walk on land. With their legs set far back on their bodies, they can only drag themselves along.

- **The wandering albatross** can only breed every other year. It incubates its eggs for 11 weeks, and the chicks do not fly until they are about 40 weeks old.

▲ When courting a mate, the male frigatebird clatters his beak and flaps his wings, as well as inflating his red throat pouch into an eyecatching balloon. Also known as a 'man of war', the frigatebird is adept at stealing food and nest material from other birds in the colony. It builds its large nest in trees.

Long wings for gliding on the wind

★ STAR FACT ★
A wandering albatross chick may eat as much as 100 kg of food during the time it is being fed by its parents.

▶ Squid is the main food of the wandering albatross, but it will also snatch fish waste thrown from fishing boats. An expert glider, it can sail downwind from a height of about 15 m to just above the water's surface, before turning back into the wind to be blown upwards.

# Sunbirds and relatives

- **The 115 or so species of sunbirds** live in tropical parts of Africa, Asia and Australia.

- **The Kauai o-o**, a honeyeater, was thought to be extinct, but in 1960 some birds were found, and there is now a very small protected population.

- **The flowerpecker family** contains about 58 species living in parts of Asia, Southeast Asia and Australia.

- **At about 23 cm long**, the Sao Tomé giant sunbird is the largest of its family. It uses its hooked beak to dig into the bark of trees for insects.

- **Sunbirds** use their long, slender beaks and tubular tongues to extract sweet liquid nectar from flowers.

- **Female sunbirds** make purse-shaped nests for their

- 2–3 eggs, which hatch after 13–15 days.

- **Honeyeaters** are the most important flower pollinators in Australia. The brushlike tip on the honeyeater's tongue helps it to extract flower nectar.

- **The crested berrypecker** (flowerpecker family) has a habit of rubbing its plumage with crushed flower petals.

- **The tui** (honeyeater family) of New Zealand is also known as the parson bird, because of the bib of white feathers at its throat.

▶ *Sunbirds feed from tropical flowers. They often hover as they do so, but cannot fly backwards like hummingbirds.*

> ★ **STAR FACT** ★
> The mistletoe bird (flowerpecker family) swallows mistletoe berries whole, digesting only the flesh and not the seeds.

# Nests

- **The bald eagle** makes the biggest nest of any bird. It can be as large as 2.5 m across and 3.5 m deep – big enough for several people to hide inside!

- **The bee hummingbird's nest** is the smallest – only the size of a thimble.

- **The hammerkop**, a heronlike bird, makes a huge nest up to 2 m high and weighing 50 kg.

- **The hammerkop uses anything** from sticks to bits of bone and plastic to make its nest.

- **A cliff swallow's nest** is made up of about 1200 tiny balls of mud.

- **Nightjars** do not make a nest – they just lay their eggs on the ground.

- **The rufous-breasted castle builder** (woodcreeper family) makes a nest shaped like a dumb-bell, with two chambers – one for the chicks.

- **The turquoise-browed motmot** is a surprisingly efficient digger, excavating a 1.5-m-long burrow in just five days.

- **The European bee-eater** nests underground to keep cool. While the surface temperature may reach 50°C, the bee-eater's nest remains a pleasant 25°C.

- **Hummingbirds and honeyeaters** use spiders' webs to hold their nests together.

▼ *A bald eagle's nest is used and enlarged year after year.*

# Old World flycatchers

- **The spotted flycatcher** sits on a branch watching for insect prey, then darts out to catch it in mid-air – it has been seen catching one insect every 18 seconds.

- **The rufous-bellied niltava** lives and breeds in the Himalayas at altitudes of up to 2300 m.

- **The male pied flycatcher** may have two nests some distance apart, but he only helps rear the young in one of them.

- **There are 147 species of Old World flycatchers**. Some live in wooded parts of Europe, but they are more common in Asia, Africa and Australasia.

- **After a summer in Europe**, the red-breasted flycatcher flies to India and Southeast Asia for the winter.

- **The white-throated jungle flycatcher** is now very rare and lives only on two islands in the Philippines.

- **The female red-breasted flycatcher** makes a cup-shaped nest of moss, leaves, spiders' webs and plant down in which to lay her 5–6 eggs.

- **Male spotted flycatchers** bring all the food for their brood when they first hatch. Later, both parents feed the chicks.

- **Instead of catching all its food in the air**, the Australian flame robin often pounces onto its prey from a low perch.

- **In autumn and winter**, the pied flycatcher eats worms and berries as well as insects.

◀ *The spotted flycatcher lives in woodland, parks and gardens in Europe and parts of Asia and Africa.*

# Ovenbirds and relatives

- **The nest** of the firewood-gatherer (ovenbird family) looks like a bonfire. A group of birds make the nest together and sleep in it during the winter.

- **The red-billed scythebill** (a woodcreeper) has a long, curved beak for delving deep into rainforest plants such as ferns and bromeliads to find insects.

- **Ovenbirds** live in the forests, mountains and semideserts of Mexico, Central and South America.

- **Woodcreepers** often nest in old woodpecker nests.

- **The common miner** (an ovenbird) digs a 3 m long burrow with a nest chamber at the end, where it raises its chicks and roosts for the rest of the year.

> **★ STAR FACT ★**
> The rufous hornero's mud-and-straw nest is shaped like an old-fashioned clay oven.

- **Des Murs' wiretail** (an ovenbird) has six tail feathers, four of which may be three times the length of the body.

- **The 50 or so species of woodcreeper** live in forests and woodland in Mexico, Central and South America.

- **Insects and spiders** hiding among the densely packed leaves of bromeliads may be extracted by the long, probing beak of the long-billed woodcreeper.

- **The campo miner** (an ovenbird) nests in a very particular place – an old armadillo burrow.

◀ *The rufous hornero is the national bird of Argentina.*

# Polar and tundra birds

- **The willow ptarmigan** lives on the Arctic tundra. In winter it has white feathers that help to keep it hidden in the snow, but in summer it grows darker feathers again.

- **The ivory gull** of Arctic coasts and islands is the only all-white gull.

- **Adelie penguins** breed on coasts and islands around the Antarctic in huge colonies that return to the same site year after year.

- **Snowy owls** are among the fiercest Arctic birds. They soar over the tundra preying on other birds and small mammals such as lemmings.

- **Most birds leave Antarctica in winter**, but the southern black-backed gull stays all year round, feeding on fish, birds' eggs and carrion.

- **The emperor penguin** breeds in colder temperatures than any other bird. It survives temperatures of -40°C as it incubates its egg.

▲ In winter, the willow ptarmigan feeds mainly on the twigs and buds of dwarf willows.

- **The great skua** is the biggest flying bird in Antarctica, at up to 5 kg and 66 cm long.

- **Although only 10 cm long**, the little storm petrel may migrate 40,000 km a year between the poles.

- **The laysan albatross** breeds on central Pacific islands, but spends most of the year flying over the Arctic hunting for schools of fish to eat.

- **Tufted puffins** nest only on cliffs and islands in the Arctic North Pacific. One colony contained as many as 1 million nests.

# Avocets and relatives

- **Young jacanas** often hide underneath floating leaves if danger threatens.

- **The seven species of stilts and avocets** are all long-legged wading birds with long, slender beaks.

- **Female pheasant-tailed jacanas** mate with up to ten males in one breeding season. The males incubate the eggs and care for the young.

- **If a male pheasant-tailed jacana** thinks his eggs are in danger, he may move them one at a time, holding them between its breast and throat.

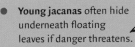

★ STAR FACT ★
The American jacana or lilytrotter has extremely long toes and claws allowing it to walk on floating waterlily leaves.

- **The long, curved beak** of the pied avocet turns up at the end. The bird sweeps this strange tool through mud or shallow water to find worms and shrimps.

- **The black-winged stilt** has extremely long, bright pink legs that allow it to wade in deeper water than other stilts as it searches for worms and shellfish.

- **Jacanas** range in size from 16–53 cm long.

- **Avocets** nest in a hollow in the ground, lined with dead leaves. Both partners incubate the 3–5 eggs.

- **Young avocets** can run soon after hatching, and can fend for themselves after six weeks.

◀ The African jacana is common around lakes and marshes, where it feeds on insects, fish and water plants.

# Lyrebirds and relatives

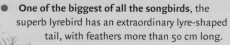

- **One of the biggest of all the songbirds**, the superb lyrebird has an extraordinary lyre-shaped tail, with feathers more than 50 cm long.

- **The rifleman**, one of the three species of New Zealand wren, lays eggs that are 20 percent of her body weight. She and the male recruit helpers to bring food to their young.

- **The two species of scrub-bird** live in Australia, where they feed on insects, lizards and frogs.

- **In its loud song**, the lyrebird may imitate other birds, barking dogs, chainsaws and even passing trains.

- **The female lyrebird** builds a domed nest, usually close to the ground. Her one chick stays with her for eight months or more.

- **The rufous scrub-bird** spends most of its time on the and rarely flies.

- **The two species of lyrebird** live in dense mountain forest in southeastern Australia.

- **Named after the small island** in Cook Strait where it lived, the Stephen Island wren was killed off by the lighthouse keeper's cat. It may have been the only flightless songbird.

- **A full-grown rufous scrub-bird** is 16–18 cm long and weighs about 30 g.

- **Young male superb lyrebirds** do not grow their lyre-shaped tails until they are three or four years old.

◀ *The lyrebird spends most of its life on the ground searching for insects.*

# Eggs

- **All bird species** lay eggs.

- **The biggest egg** is the ostrich egg. At 1.5 kg, it is 30 times heavier than an average hen's egg.

- **Incubation** is the process of keeping eggs warm while they develop. It can take from 10–80 days.

- **The yellow yolk** in an egg provides food for the growing embryo. The white provides food and moisture.

- **Gannets stand on their eggs** to keep them warm!

- **The shell of an egg** contains 50–100 tiny pores per sq cm, allowing oxygen to seep into the egg and carbon dioxide does the same outwards

- **Egg yolks** are not always yellow. The common tern's yolk is deep red, and the gentoo penguin's a pinky red.

★ STAR FACT ★
The bee hummingbird lays the smallest egg, at just 0.3 g. You could fit 4700 into one ostrich egg!

- **Eggshells** vary in thickness from 0.2 mm in the night heron's egg to 0.75 mm in the common murre's.

- **Not all eggs are oval** – those of owls and toucans are round, and auks lay pear-shaped eggs.

▲ *A bird's egg, though seemingly fragile, contains everything that the growing embryo inside needs to survive.*

# Crows

- **Members of the crow family** live on all continents of the world, except Antarctica. There are about 117 species, including jackdaws, rooks, ravens, nutcrackers, choughs and jays, as well as common crows.

- **Bold and aggressive**, a typical crow is a big bird with a strong body and legs, and a powerful beak that can deal with nuts, seeds and even small prey.

- **At 66 cm long**, the raven is the largest of the crow family, and the largest of the songbird group of birds.

- **Crows** are thought to be among the most intelligent of all birds. Studies on ravens have shown that they are able to count up to five or six.

- **When food is plentiful**, nutcrackers hide nuts and pine seeds in holes in the ground, and are able to find them again months later.

- **There are many superstitions** about ravens – the arrival of a raven is said to be an evil omen and a sign of an imminent death.

- **A species of crow** that lives on the Pacific island of New Caledonia uses tools such as hooked twigs and sharp-ended stems to extract grubs from the crowns of palm trees.

- **Breeding pairs** of Australian white-winged choughs use a team of up to eight other choughs to help them find food for their young.

- **Some crows in Japan** have learned how to get cars to crack nuts for them. They put the nuts in front of cars at traffic lights, wait for the cars to pass over them, and collect the kernels once the lights are red again!

★ STAR FACT ★
Magpies steal the eggs and young of other birds, as well as bright, shiny objects such as jewellery, which they hide in their nests.

▼ *The secret of the crows' success is their adaptability. They eat a wide range of foods and are intelligent enough to learn how to make use of new food sources. Shown here are: (1) the raven, (2) the rook, (3) the hooded crow,(4) the chough, (5) the jackdaw*

# Old World sparrows

- **The house sparrow** originally came from Southwest Asia, but has spread throughout the world. It feeds mainly on seeds, but also eats some insects and is happy to eat scraps put out on bird tables.

- **Chestnut sparrows** drive other birds from their nests and use the nests themselves, instead of making their own.

- **The snow finch** lives high in mountain ranges and makes its nest on mountain ledges at altitudes of 5000 m.

- **All the house sparrows in the USA** are descended from a few birds that were released in Central Park, New York, in 1850.

▶ *There may now be as many as 150 million house sparrows in the USA.*

> ★ **STAR FACT** ★
> Sparrows like to bathe and splash in water, and will even bathe in snow in winter.

- **House sparrows** generally have two broods a year of 4–7 eggs each.

- **The desert sparrow** makes a nest of dry grass and twigs, often in a wall, and lays 2–5 eggs.

- **Most sparrows** are about 14–18 cm long and have brownish or grey plumage.

- **The 40 or so species of Old World sparrow** live in Europe, Africa and parts of Asia, though some have been introduced elsewhere.

- **House sparrows** rarely nest away from human habitation.

# Auks

- **The Atlantic puffin's colourful beak** is striped red, yellow and grey blue, and can hold 12 or more fish.

- **The ancient murrelet** is so-named because it develops fine white feathers on its head in the breeding season, said to look like the white hairs of an elderly person.

- **The common guillemot** nests on narrow cliff ledges. Its eggs are pointed, so that if they get knocked, they roll in a circle and do not fall off.

- **The guillemot** can dive in water to a depth of 180 m as it hunts for fish.

- **The auk family** includes 22 species of diving birds, including auks, guillemots, puffins and razorbills. They live in and around the North Pacific, Atlantic and Arctic oceans.

- **The common guillemot** is the largest of the auks, at about 45 cm long and 1 kg in weight. The least auklet is the smallest auk, at 16 cm long and 90 g.

- **Common guillemots** nest in colonies of thousands, with as many as 70 pairs occupying 1 sq m.

- **The little auk** nests in a cliff crevice and lays 1–2 eggs, which both parents incubate.

- **Auk eggs** are reputed to taste good, and have long been collected and eaten by humans.

> ★ **STAR FACT** ★
> The puffin flies at up to 64 km/h, with its wings beating 300–400 times a minute.

▶ *The tufted puffin lives in the Arctic and North Pacific.*

# Bee-eaters and relatives

- **The five species of tody** are all insect-eating birds that live in the Caribbean islands.

- **Bee-eaters catch a bee or wasp** and kill it by striking it against a branch. Before eating it, the bird rubs the insect against the branch to expel its venom.

- **The blue-crowned motmot** has two long tail feathers with racquet-shaped tips. As the bird sits watching for prey, it swings its tail like a clock's pendulum.

- **Motmots** range in size from the 19-cm long tody motmot to the 53-cm long upland motmot.

- **Motmots lay their eggs** in a chamber at the end of a burrow dug in an earth bank. Both parents incubate the eggs and feed the chicks.

> ★ STAR FACT ★
> A European bee-eater eats about 200 bees a day.
> Its summer diet is mainly bumblebees, and in
> winter it eats honeybees and dragonflies.

- **The 16 species of bee-eater** are colourful birds that live in southern Europe, Africa, Asia and Australia.

◀ The white-fronted bee-eater lives in southern Africa.

- **The European bee-eater** flies some 16,000 km between Europe, where it breeds, and Africa, where it overwinters.

- **Todies** nest in 30-cm long tunnels, which they dig with their beaks.

- **The ten species of motmot** live only in forests from Mexico to northern Argentina.

# Warblers

- **The willow warbler** is only 11 cm long, but flies all the way from northern Europe and Siberia to Africa to spend the winter – a distance of some 12,000 km.

- **The rarely seen grasshopper warbler** has an extraordinary whirring song and can 'throw its voice' like a ventriloquist.

▶ At 19 cm long, the great reed warbler is larger than most European warblers.

- **The warbler family** has more than 380 species. Most live in Europe, Africa, Asia and Australasia, but there are a few species in North and South America.

- **Most warblers** are 9–16 cm long, but the two largest – the South African grassbird and the Australian songlarks – are up to 23 cm long.

- **The Aldabra warbler**, discovered in 1967, lives only on a small part of Aldabra Island in the Indian Ocean. It has not been seen since 1983, so may well be extinct.

- **Insects** are the main food of most warblers, but they also eat some fruits, berries and seeds.

- **The marsh warbler** can mimic about 80 other species.

- **Chiffchaffs and willow warblers** look almost exactly alike, but their songs are quite different.

- **The blackcap** lays 4–6 eggs in a neat, cup-shaped nest. Both parents incubate them for 10–15 days.

- **The tailorbird** makes a cradlelike nest from two leaves sewn together with plant fibres or spiders' webs.

# Pheasants and relatives

- **Domestic chickens** are descended from the red jungle fowl, which was first domesticated 5000 years ago. The jungle fowl still lives wild in Southeast Asia.

- **All 49 species of wild pheasant** are from Asia, except the Congo peafowl, which was first discovered in a Central African rainforest in 1936.

- **To attract females**, the male great argus pheasant dances and spreads out his enormously long wing feathers, like glittering fans.

- **The peacock's wonderful train** contains about 200 shimmering feathers, each one decorated with eyelike markings. When courting, he spreads the train and makes it 'shiver' to attract a female.

★ STAR FACT ★
The crested argus has the largest, longest tail feathers of any bird, at up to 170 cm long and 12 cm wide.

- **The Himalayan monal pheasant** spends some of the year above the tree line, where it has to dig in the snow with its beak to find insects and other food.

- **The male pheasant** mates with several females, each of which lays up to 15 eggs in a shallow scrape on the ground. The females incubate the eggs and care for the young by themselves, with no help from the male.

- **Most pheasants** nest on the ground, but the five species of tragopan, which live in tropical forests in Asia, nest in trees, often taking over the old nests of other birds.

- **The common pheasant** comes from Asia, but is now common in Australia, North America and Europe, where it is shot for sport.

- **In ancient Rome**, peacocks were roasted and served in their feathers as a great delicacy.

◀ The peacock is a native of India, Sri Lanka and Pakistan, but it has been introduced in many areas throughout the world. Only the male has the spectacular tail, which does not reach its full glory until the bird is about three years old. It may continue to grow for another 2–3 years.

▲ The male pheasant is a beautiful bird with iridescent plumage on his head and bright red wattles. Originally from Asia, this pheasant has been successfully introduced in Europe and North America, where it is very common.

# Manakins and cotingas

- **Manakins** are small birds that live in Central and South America. There are about 57 species.

- **Female manakins** do all the nesting work alone – they build the nest, incubate the eggs and care for the young.

- **The largest of the cotingas** is the Amazonian umbrellabird, which gets its name from the crest of feathers that hangs over its head.

- **The three-wattled bellbird** (cotinga family) is best known for its extremely loud call, which resounds through its jungle home.

- **Two of the most colourful South American birds** are the Guianan cock of the rock, which is bright orange, and the Andean cock of the rock, which is red (both cotinga family species).

- **Cocks of the rock** perform remarkable courtship displays – up to 25 male birds leap and dance together, fanning their feathers and making loud calls.

- **The 65 or so cotinga species live in** the forests of Mexico, some Caribbean islands and Central and South America.

- **Fruit and insects** are the main foods of both manakins and cotingas.

- **The female cock of the rock** makes a nest of mud and plants attached to a rock or cave wall, and incubates her eggs alone.

- **In his courtship display**, the male wire-tailed manakin brushes the female's chin with his long, wirelike tail feathers.

◀ The little wire-tailed manakin lives in the lower levels of the Amazonian rainforest.

# New World vultures

- **There are seven species of New World vultures** in North and South America. Like Old World vultures, their diet includes carrion.

- **New World vultures** lay their eggs on the ground or on a cliff ledge. The parent birds feed their young on regurgitated food.

- **Unusually colourful** for a bird of prey, the king vulture has bright red, orange and yellow bare skin and wattles on its head.

- **The king vulture** has a particularly good sense of smell, and can find carrion even in dense rainforest.

- **The turkey vulture** does not make a nest, but lays its 1–3 eggs on a cliff ledge or in a cave. Both parents help to incubate the eggs for up to 41 days.

- **Black vulture chicks** are looked after by both parents. They do not fly until they are 11 weeks old.

- **Vultures can go for weeks without food.** When they do find carrion, they eat as much as possible.

- **King vultures** have stronger beaks than other New World vultures, and are able to tear apart large animals.

- **The last wild California condors** were captured for captive breeding. By 1998 there were 170 birds, 50 of which were released into the wild.

- **The largest of all birds of prey** is the Andean condor, with a wingspan of more than 3 m.

◀ The Andean condor soars for hundreds of kilometres over the Andes mountains, searching for food such as dead deer.

# Shearwaters and petrels

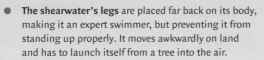

- **The shearwater's legs** are placed far back on its body, making it an expert swimmer, but preventing it from standing up properly. It moves awkwardly on land and has to launch itself from a tree into the air.

- **Unlike most birds**, shearwaters and petrels have a good sense of smell. They have long, tube-shaped nostrils on the tops of their beaks.

- **Shearwaters and petrels** are not tuneful birds, and at night the colonies make a very loud, harsh noise.

- **The 56 or more species** in the shearwater family include petrels, fulmars and prions. They range from the Antarctic to the Arctic.

- **Largest of the shearwater family** are the giant petrels, which at 99 cm long are almost the size of albatrosses.

▶ *Manx shearwaters nest in colonies of thousands of birds on offshore islands or isolated cliff tops.*

- **Fish and squid** are the main food of shearwaters, but giant petrels also feed on carrion, and can rip apart whales and seals with their powerful beaks.

- **The manx shearwater** lays one egg in a burrow. The male and female take turns at incubating it and feeding one another.

- **Young shearwaters** are fed on a rich mixture of regurgitated fish and squid, and may put on weight so quickly that they are soon heavier than their parents.

- **Prions** feed on tiny plankton, which they filter from the water through comblike structures at the sides of their beaks.

> ★ STAR FACT ★
> To defend themselves, shearwaters can spit out food and fish oil to a distance of 1 m.

# Cassowaries and kiwis

- **There are three species of kiwi**, found only in New Zealand. All are flightless birds that live in burrows.

- **The female dwarf cassowary**, or moruk, is an extremely dangerous bird and will attack anything that comes near its nest with its 10-cm-long claws.

- **The three species of cassowary** live in rainforests in New Zealand and northeastern Australia.

> ★ STAR FACT ★
> A kiwi lays the largest eggs for its size of any bird – each egg weighs 25 percent of its body weight. Females lay up to 100 in a lifetime.

- **Largest of its family is the brown kiwi**, which is about 55 cm long and weighs up to 3.5 kg.

- **Only the kiwi has nostrils** at the end of its beak.

- **The kiwi** is the national symbol of New Zealand, appearing on stamps, coins and banknotes.

- **Cassowaries in Australia** are known to eat the fruits of 75 different types of tree.

- **The female cassowary** mates with several males, laying 6–8 eggs each time. The males care for the young.

- **About 1200 years ago** there were probably 12 million kiwis in New Zealand. Today there are only 70,000.

◀ *The kiwi detects worms, insects and spiders using its sense of smell.*

# Storks

- **In tropical areas**, storks' nests perched high on buildings can get very warm, so parents cool their young by regurgitating a shower of water over them.

- **The huge beak** of the whale-billed stork, or shoebill, is 23 cm long and 10 cm wide. It uses it to catch lungfish, young crocodiles and turtles

- **The white stork** has long been a symbol of fertility in Europe. Parents used to tell their children that new babies were brought by a stork.

- **The 17 species of stork** live in North and South America, Europe, Africa, Asia and Australia.

- **Marabou storks** often scavenge on rubbish tips.

- **The openbill stork's beak** meets only at the tip. This helps it to hold its favourite food – large snails.

- **The tail feathers** of marabou storks were once used to trim hats and dresses.

- **When the wood stork's partly open beak** touches a fish under water, it snaps shut in 25 milliseconds – one of the fastest reactions of any animal.

- **Male and female white storks** take turns to incubate their clutch of 3–5 eggs. When the partners change shifts, they perform a special bill-clattering display.

- **The adjutant stork** is named after the adjutant army officer, because of its stiff, military-style walk.

▼ The saddlebill stork of southern Africa is easily recognized by its large red, yellow and black bill.

# Gulls and relatives

- **The great skua** is a pirate – it chases other birds and forces them to give up their prey in mid air.

- **The snowy sheathbill** scavenges for food on Antarctic research bases, and also steals eggs and chicks from penguin colonies.

- **There are about 48 species of gull** found on shores and islands all over the world.

- **Arctic glaucous and ivory gulls** sometimes feed on the faeces of marine mammals.

- **At up to 79 cm long**, the great black-backed gull is the giant of the group. The little gull is one of the smallest, at 28 cm long.

- **The Arctic explorer** James Clark Ross discovered Ross's gull in the 19th-century.

- **Skuas**, also called jaegers usually lay two eggs in a shallow, moss-lined nest on the ground. Both parents incubate the eggs and feed the young, which can fend for themselves by about seven weeks old.

- **The kittiwake** spends much more time at sea than other gulls, and usually only comes to land in the breeding season. It has very short legs and rarely walks.

- **Herring gulls** have learned that they can find food in seaside towns, and many now nest on roofs instead of cliff ledges.

- **The south polar skua** lays twotr eggs, but the first chick to hatch usually kills the second.

▲ Gulls eat a wide range of food, including fish, shellfish, the young of other seabirds and waste from fishing boats.

# Jacamars and relatives

● **Jacamars nest in tunnels** made in the ground or in
termite mounds. They lay 2–4 eggs, which they
incubate for 20–23 days.

● **Brightly coloured barbets** live in tropical forests and
woodlands in Africa, Asia and South America.

● **At 30 cm long**, the great jacamar is the largest of
the 17 species of jacamar. Its beak alone is
almost 5 cm long.

● **The white-fronted nunbird** (puffbird family) digs
a nesting burrow about 1 m long. The bird lays its
eggs in a chamber at the end of the burrow.

● **Biggest of the 75 species of barbet** is the

▶ *The crested barbet of southern Africa usually searches
for food on the ground.*

toucan barbet, at 20 cm long. It lives in mountain
forests in the northern part of South America.

● **The double-toothed barbet** lays 3–4
eggs, usually in a tree hole. Both
parents incubate the eggs and care
for the young.

● **A jacamar** snaps up an insect in
the air, then returns to its perch and
bangs the insect against a branch to
kill it before eating it.

● **There are about 33 species of
puffbird** living in Mexico and Central
and South America.

● **Barbet pairs** sing together to keep
their relationship close. One bird
starts to sing, then stops, and the
other bird continues the song within a
fraction of a second.

# Drongos and relatives

● **The huia**, a species of wattlebird, has not been seen
since 1907 and is probably extinct. It was noted for
having a different shaped beak in males and females
– the male's was straight and strong,
the female's slender and curved.

● **The greater racquet-tailed
drongo** has two long, wirelike tail
feathers with twisted tips that make a
humming noise as the bird flies.

● **The pied currawong** (Australian
butcherbird family) attacks other birds
and takes their young from their nests.

● **The 25 species of Old World oriole** live in Europe
and parts of Asia, Africa and Australia. They are
mainly tree-dwellers, feeding on insects and fruit.

● **There are two surviving species** of the wattlebird
family – the kokako and the wattlebird, both of which
live in New Zealand and rarely fly.

● **The golden oriole** makes a neat, cup-shaped nest that
it binds to two supporting twigs. It lays 3–4 eggs.

● **Australia and New Guinea** are home to the ten
species of insect-eating bell-magpies.

● **Australian mud-nesters** work together to build
nests of mud on the branches of trees.

● **The figbird** (oriole family) is a forest fruit-
eater, but is now also common in towns.

● **Wood swallows**, found in
Australasia and Southeast Asia,
feed mostly on insects, but also
drink nectar.

◀ *A common bird in southern
Africa, the fork-tailed
drongo has
distinctive
bright
red eyes.*

# Ibises and relatives

★ STAR FACT ★

Ibises and spoonbills are an ancient group of
birds – fossils of their ancestors have been
found that date back 60 million years.

- **The ibis** was a symbol of the god Thoth in ancient
  Egypt, and appears in many paintings and carvings.
  Mummified ibises have also been discovered
  – as many as 500,000 in one tomb.

- **The spoonbill's beak** has a spoon-shaped tip that it uses
  to search shallow water for fish and small creatures.

- **At 1.4 m long** and weighing about 4 kg, the greater
  flamingo is the largest of the five species of flamingo.

- **The flamingo feeds** by forcing mud and water through
  bristly plates at each side of its beak with its tongue.
  Tiny creatures, algae and other food particles are
  trapped and swallowed.

- **Until their beaks have developed fully**, young flamingos
  feed on a 'milky' substance from their parents' throats.

- **The 31 species of ibis and spoonbill** live in North and
  South America, southern Europe, Asia, Africa and
  Australia, often in wetlands.

- **The glossy ibis** makes its nest in a reedbed or tree,
  and lays 3–4 eggs. The female does most of the
  incubation, but the male helps to rear the young.

- **Young flamingos** have grey feathers at first. Adult
  birds get their pink colour from pigments in the
  algae that they eat.

- **The greater flamingo** has a wingspan of 140–165 cm.

Beak for
filtering food
from water

Long neck
allows the
bird to feed
in deep
water

▲ The ancient Egyptian moon god Thoth was sometimes shown in
paintings as an ibis, or as a human figure with the head of an ibis.

▶ The greater flamingo lives in huge flocks around lakes and
deltas in Europe, Asia, parts of Africa, the Caribbean and
Central America. It can live to be at least 50 years old.

# Rheas and tinamous

- **The largest bird in South America** is the greater rhea, which stands 1.5 m tall and weighs up to 25 kg.
- **The 45 or so species of tinamou** all live in South America.
- **Most tinamous can fly**, if only for short distances, but they tend to run or hide rather than take to the air.

> ★ STAR FACT ★
> Male rheas mate with as many as 15 females, all of which lay eggs in the male's large nest.

- **Female tinamous** lay eggs in the nests of more than one male. Males incubate the eggs and feed the chicks.
- **Rheas** feed mostly on plants, but will also eat insects and even lizards when they can.
- **Tinamous generally eat fruit**, seeds and other plant matter, but some species also gobble up insects.
- **Rheas live in flocks** of between 5–50 birds.
- **Rhea feathers** are used to make feather dusters, for sale mainly in the USA and Japan.
- **If threatened**, a rhea lies flat on the ground with its head stretched out in an attempt to hide.

◀ Flocks of rheas live on the pampas grasslands and in open woodland in southeastern South America.

# Gannets and boobies

- **The gannet plunges 30 m or so** through the air and dives into the water to catch prey such as herring and mackerel.
- **A specially strengthened skull** helps cushion the impact of the gannet's high-speed dive into water.
- **Boobies** were given their common name because they were so easy for sailors to catch and kill.
- **The male blue-footed booby** attracts a mate by dancing and holding up his brightly coloured feet as it struts about.
- **When a gannet** comes to take its turn

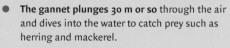

incubating the egg, it presents its mate with a piece of seaweed, which is added to the nest.

- **There are three species of gannet and six species of booby**. Boobies generally live in tropical and subtropical areas, while gannets live in cooler, temperate parts of the world.
- **The gannet** usually lays just one egg, which both partners help to incubate for 43–45 days. They feed their chick with regurgitated food for up to 13 weeks.
- **Young gannets and boobies** are kept warm on their mother's feet for their first few weeks.
- **Boobies** spend most of their time at sea, only landing to breed and rear their young.
- **At up to 86 cm long** and with a wingspan of 152 cm, the masked booby is the largest.

◀ Blue-footed boobies usually feed close to the seashore, while red-footed boobies venture further out to sea.

# Pelicans

- The great white pelican catches about 1.2 kg of fish a day in its large throat pouch.

- The brown pelican dives from a height of 15 m above the water to catch fish below the surface.

- Great white pelican breeding colonies may number as many as 30,000 pairs of birds.

- There are seven species of pelican. Most live and feed around fresh water, but the brown pelican is a seabird.

- One of the largest pelicans is the Australian pelican, which is up to 180 cm long and weighs about 15 kg.

- The white pelican lays 1–2 eggs in a nest mound on the ground. Both parents help to incubate the eggs and care for the young.

- Pelican chicks are able to stand at three weeks old and can fly at 7–10 weeks old.

- In heraldry, a pelican is often shown pecking its breast to feed its young on its blood. This myth may come from the bird's habit of resting its beak on its breast.

- White pelicans work as a group to herd fish into a shoal by swimming in a horseshoe formation. Then they scoop up pouchfuls of fish with their large beaks.

- When flying, a pelican flaps its wings 1.3 times a second.

◀ A great white pelican comes in to land on the water.

# Buzzards, kites and osprey

- Bees and wasps, their larvae and even their nests are the main food of honey buzzards, which remove the stings from adult insects before eating them.

- The snail kite's hook-tipped beak is perfectly shaped for extracting the soft flesh of snails from their shells.

- One of the most common of all birds of prey is the black kite, which lives throughout most of Europe, Africa, Asia and Australia.

- Osprey parents stop feeding their young when it is time for them to leave the nest.

- When fishing, the osprey plunges into water feet first and grasps its slithery prey with its spine-covered feet.

- The red kite often takes over the old nest of a raven.

- The rough-legged buzzard is common over open tundra in the far north. It preys on rodents and rabbits.

- A buzzard can spot a rabbit popping up out of its burrow from more than 3 km away.

- Male ospreys feed the whole family once the chicks have hatched.

★ STAR FACT ★
The osprey was described by Aristotle as early as 350 BC in his *Natural History*.

◀ The osprey's body measures 55–58 cm long, and it has an impressive 1.6-m wingspan. The females are slightly larger than the males.

# Toucans and honeyguides

- **At 61 cm long**, the toco toucan is the largest toucan. Its colourful beak alone is up to 20 cm long.

- **Although a toucan's beak is large**, it is not heavy. The beak is made of a lightweight material with a honeycomb structure.

- **The black-throated honeyguide** likes to feed on bees and their larvae. When it finds a bees' nest, it leads another creature, such as a honey badger, to the nest and waits while the animal breaks into the nest to feed on the honey. The honeyguide then has its share.

- **There are about 40 species of toucan.** They live in Mexico, Central and South America.

- **Toucans feed mostly on fruit**, which they pluck from

> ★ STAR FACT ★
>
> Honeyguides are the only birds that are able to feed on the wax from bees' nests, as well as on the insects themselves.

branches with their long beaks. They also eat some insects and small animals such as lizards.

- **Toucans** usually nest in tree holes. The female lays 2–4 eggs, and the male helps with the incubation, which takes about 15 days.

- **There are about 15 species of honeyguide.** Most live in forests and woodlands in Africa, but there are a few species resident in Asia.

- **Many honeyguides** lay their eggs in the nests of other birds, such as woodpeckers. When they hatch, the young honeyguides kill the young of the host bird.

- **Toucans are noisy creatures** – their loud squawks can be heard nearly 1 km away.

Beak is about 20 cm long and 7.5 cm deep at the base.

Strong claws for perching

◄ The toco toucan of Brazil is the largest and best-known of the toucans. It sometimes perches on a branch near another bird's nest to steal the eggs or chicks. Intimidated by the toucan's great beak, the parent bird will not generally attack. When it sleeps, the toucan turns its head to rest its long beak along its back, and folds its tail over its head.

► The black-throated honeyguide is usually a quiet little bird, but it chatters noisily when it wants to attract a helper, such as a honey badger, to a bees' nest, so it can have a share of the honey.

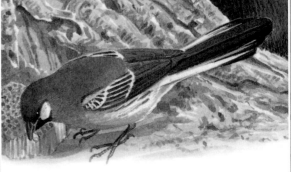

# Woodpeckers

- **The woodpecker feeds** by drilling into tree bark with its sharp beak and then inserting its long tongue into the hole to pick out insects living beneath the bark.

- **Woodpeckers drum** on tree trunks with their beaks to signal their ownership of territory or their readiness to mate. The greater spotted woodpecker has been timed making 20 strikes a second.

- **The 200 or so species of woodpecker** live all over the world, except in Antarctica and the far north.

- **The imperial woodpecker**, at 55 cm long, is the biggest of its family. The little scaled piculet, by contrast, is only 8 cm long.

- **Woodpeckers** nest in holes in trees. They may use a hole from a previous year, or dig out a new one for their 2–12 eggs.

- **The woodpecker's tongue** is well-adapted for catching insects. It is so long that the woodpecker can stick it out beyond the tip of its beak, and its sticky coating easily mops up its prey.

- **The sapsucker** (woodpecker family) feeds on sweet, sugary sap. It bores a hole in a tree and laps up the sap that oozes out.

- **As well as insects**, the great spotted woodpecker eats the eggs and young of other birds.

- **A woodpecker** may eat up as many as 1000 ants in one feeding session.

- **During autumn**, the acorn woodpecker of North America bores as many as 400 holes in tree trunks and puts an acorn in each one, to store for the winter.

◀ *This great spotted woodpecker is sharing a feeder with a siskin. It lives in Europe, parts of Asia and North Africa.*

# Grassland birds

- **The yellow-billed oxpecker** of the African grasslands sits on buffaloes' backs, pulling ticks from their skin.

- **Flocks of 1 million or more red-billed quelea** are seen moving like vast clouds over southern Africa.

- **The grasslands of South America** are home to the red-legged seriema, a long-legged, fast-running bird that eats anything it can find, including snakes.

- **Unlike most hornbills**, the southern ground hornbill of southern Africa spends most of its time on the ground.

- **One of the biggest creatures** on the South American pampas is the rhea, which feeds mainly on grass.

- **Cattle egrets** accompany large grassland mammals, feeding on the insects that live on or around them.

- **The crested oropendola** is a grassland bird of South America. It hunts insects and other small creatures.

- **North America's largest owl**, the great horned owl, includes other grassland birds such as quail in its diet.

- **The western meadowlark** makes a ground nest of grass and pine needles in prairie grasslands.

▼ *Secretary birds are often seen perching and nesting in acacia trees.*

# Monarchs and relatives

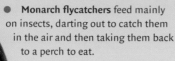

- **Monarch flycatchers** feed mainly on insects, darting out to catch them in the air and then taking them back to a perch to eat.

- **The male African paradise flycatcher's tail feathers** are up to 20 cm long – much longer than its body.

- **Only seven Chatham Island robins** (Australasian robin family) were thought to exist in 1976, but a breeding programme using the Chatham Island tit to foster eggs has helped increase the population.

- **There are about 90 species of monarch flycatchers.** They live

▲ The paradise flycatcher makes a neat nest of plant roots held together with spiders' webs on a slender branch or twig.

★ STAR FACT ★

Fantails are so-named because they continually fan their long tails from side to side.

in wooded areas in Africa, Southeast Asia, Australia and some Pacific islands.

- **The yellow-breasted boatbill**, a monarch flycatcher, has a broad beak with a hooked tip, which it uses to pick small insects off leaves.

- **Smallest of the Australasian robin family** is the rose robin, at 10 cm long and weighing only 10 g.

- **The black-naped blue monarch** lays 3–4 eggs in a nest of grass and bark bound together with spiders' webs. The nest is usually built on a forked branch.

- **In aboriginal folklore**, the willie wagtail (a fantail), was thought to be a gossipy bird that spread secrets.

- **The pied fantail's beak** is ringed with bristles that may help the bird to trap insect prey.

# Megapodes and guans

- **The 12 species of megapodes** are ground-living birds found in Australia and some Pacific islands.

- **The mallee fowl** (a megapode) lays her eggs in a huge mound of rotting leaves and sand, which acts as an incubator. The mound can be up to 11 m across and 5 m high.

- **The male mallee fowl** checks the temperature of his nest mound with its beak and keeps it a constant 33°C by adding or removing material.

- **Mallee fowl chicks** must dig their way out of their nest mound, and are able to fly a few hours later.

- **To attract females**, as it flies the male crested guan flaps his wings briefly at more than twice the normal speed, making a whirring sound.

- **One megapode in Tonga** makes a nest of hot volcanic ash, which keeps its eggs warm.

- **The 45 species of guan and curassow** live from the southern USA to northern Argentina.

- **The great curassow** is 95 cm long and weighs 4.8 kg.

- **True to its name**, the nocturnal curassow comes out at night to sing and feed on fruit.

- **The plain chachalaca** (curassow family) lays three eggs in a nest made of sticks, leaves and moss.

- **Now rare**, the white-winged guan lives in the Andean foothills, feeding on fruit, berries, leaves and insects.

▼ The male mallee fowl keeps a constant watch on its nest.

# Owls

- **Owls** range in size from the least pygmy owl, at only 12–14 cm long, to the Eurasian eagle owl, at 71 cm.

- **The burrowing owl** nests in burrows in the ground, either digging its own with its strong claws, or taking over the burrows of animals such as prairie dogs.

- **The soft, fluffy edges of an owl's feathers** help to reduce flight noise, so it can hunt almost silently.

- **Female owls** are usually larger than males.

- **Owls swallow prey**, such as mice and insects, whole.

- **The female barn owl** lays 4–7 eggs, often in a tree hole.

- **The brown fish owl** has bare legs and feet – feathers would get clogged with fish scales.

- **The 151 or so species of owl** live in most parts of the world except the far north, New Zealand and Antarctica.

- **About 80 species of owl** hunt mostly at night.

- **Some Native Americans** believed that owls were the souls of people, and so should never be harmed.

▼ *Pel's fishing owl lives along riverbanks in parts of southern Africa.*

# Buntings and tanagers

- **The little snow bunting** breeds in northern Greenland, further north than any other bird.

- **One tanager, the glossy flowerpiercer**, has a hooked, up-curved beak that it uses to pierce the bases of tubular flowers so it can feed on the nectar inside.

- **The 240 species in the tanager family** include flowerpiercers, honeycreepers and euphonias. All live in North and South America.

- **The male scarlet tanager** has bright red feathers in the breeding season, but in autumn his plumage changes to olive-green, similar to the female.

- **The western tanager** lines its nest of twigs and moss with fine roots and animal hair. The female incubates 3–5 eggs.

- **Some tanagers follow columns of army ants in** forests, and snap up the insects that flee the ants' path.

- **Seeds** are the main food of the dark-eyed junco (bunting family), although it does eat a few spiders.

- **The woodpecker finch** (a bunting) uses a fine twig or cactus spine as a tool to winkle out insects from holes.

- **The 13 species of finch** (bunting family) in the Galapagos Islands are probably all descended from the same ancestor, but have evolved different beak shapes and feeding habits depending on their environment.

- **The Galapagos finches** gave Charles Darwin important evidence for his theory of evolution.

◀ *The snow bunting spends summers in the Arctic, but flies south in winter.*

# Hornbills

- **There are about 45 species of hornbill**, 25 in Africa and 20 in Southeast Asia. Most live among trees.

- **Hornbills range in size** from 38–165 cm. The largest of the family is the great Indian hornbill, and the smallest is the dwarf red-billed hornbill.

- **The eastern yellow-billed hornbill and the dwarf mongoose** have an unusual relationship – they help each other find food and watch out for predators.

- **The female great Indian hornbill** incubates her eggs in a tree hole, the entrance of which is walled up with chewed bark and mud. Through a slit-like opening in the wall, the male passes her food.

- **Hornbills keep the nest clean** by pushing any food waste and droppings out through the slit opening.

- **In parts of South Africa**, the southern ground hornbill is traditionally considered sacred, and is protected.

- **Fruit** is the main food of most hornbills, but the two ground hornbills catch and eat small animals.

- **All hornbills have large beaks**. In many species the beak is topped with a casque made of keratin and bone.

- **A male hornbill** may carry more than 60 small fruits at a time to his nest to regurgitate for its young.

- **Hornbills are the only birds** in which two neck vertebrae are fused, possibly to help support the beak's weight.

◀ *The 50-cm long yellow-billed hornbill lives in southern Africa.*

# Bulbuls and relatives

- **The bearded greenbul** lives in African rainforests and has a beautiful whistling call that it uses to keep in touch with others of its species in the dense jungle.

- **Despite its small size**, the red-vented bulbul is an aggressive bird. In Asia, people sometimes bet on a male bird to win a fight against another male.

- **The yellow-vented bulbul** makes a nest of twigs, leaves and vine stems, often in a garden or on a balcony. Both parents incubate the 2–5 eggs and care for the young.

- **There are about 20 species of bulbul** found in Africa and southern Asia, usually in forests, although some bulbuls have adapted to built-up areas.

- **Bulbuls** range in size from 14–23 cm, and eat mainly insects and fruit.

- **The 2 species of fairy bluebirds** live in Asia, feeding on fruit, nectar and some insects.

- **Leafbirds** lay 2–3 eggs in a cup-shaped nest made in the trees.

- **The common iora** (a leafbird) scurries through trees searching the leaves for insects. It also sometimes eats mistletoe and other berries.

- **Male fairy bluebirds** have bright blue upperparts. Females are a dull greenish-blue with dark markings.

▲ *The fairy bluebird spends most of its time looking for ripe fruit, especially figs.*

★ STAR FACT ★
When courting, the male common iora fluffs up its feathers, leaps into the air and tumbles back to its perch again.

# Old World vultures

- **There are about 15 species of Old World vultures** living in southern Europe, Africa and Asia.

- **Unlike most birds of prey,** the palm-nut vulture is mostly vegetarian. Its main food is the husk of the oil palm fruit, although it also eats fish, frogs and other small creatures.

- **The Egyptian vulture** steals birds' eggs. It cracks the eggs by dropping them on the ground or throwing stones at them.

- **Most vultures are scavengers** rather than hunters – they feed on the carcasses of dead animals.

- **The lack of feathers** on a vulture's head means that it does not have to do lots of preening after it has plunged its beak deep into a carcass to feed.

- **Different species of vulture** eat different parts of a body – bearded vultures even eat the bones.

- **In hot weather,** some vultures cool down by squirting urine onto their legs – which can't smell nice!

> ★ STAR FACT ★
> The bearded vulture drops bones from a great height to smash them. It then swallows the bone fragments, which are broken down by powerful acids in its stomach.

- **The female white-backed vulture** lays one egg in a large stick nest made high in a tree. She incubates the egg for 56 days, being fed by the male. Both parents feed and care for the chick.

- **The lappet-faced vulture** is the largest vulture in Africa – it measures about 1 m long and has a huge 2.8 m wingspan. It also has a bigger beak than any other bird of prey.

▶ This Egyptian vulture is about to break open a thick-shelled ostrich egg with a stone so that it can eat the contents. The vulture also eats carrion – several birds may be seen circling above a dead or dying animal when they find one.

Hooked beak for pecking scraps of meat from bones

Stone raised to throw at egg to break it open

# Herons and bitterns

- **There are about 60 species of heron and bittern.**

- **The largest of the heron family** is the goliath heron of Africa and southwest Asia – it measures 1.5 m long.

- **The loud booming call** made by the male bittern in the breeding season can be heard up to 5 km away.

- **The great blue heron** makes a platform nest of twigs,

often high in a tree. The eggs take 25–29 days to hatch.

- **Special feathers** on the heron's breast and rump crumble into a powdery substance that the bird rubs into its plumage to help remove dirt and fish slime.

- **The white feathers of the great egret** were popular hat decorations in the late 1800s – more than 200,000 birds were killed for their feathers in a single year.

- **Like most herons**, the grey heron feeds on fish and frogs, which it catches with swift stabs of its beak.

- **Cattle egrets** nest in colonies – there may be more than 100 nests close together in one tree.

- **When hunting**, the black heron holds its wings over its head like a sunshade. This may help the bird spot fish, or the patch of shade may attract fish to the area.

▲ *The great egret catches fish and shellfish in shallow water.*

# Hummingbirds

- **The bee hummingbird** is not much bigger than a bumblebee and, at 6 cm long, is probably the smallest bird.

- **A hummingbird** hovers in front of flowers to collect nectar with its tongue, which has a brushlike tip.

- **When a bee hummingbird hovers**, it beats its wings 200 times a second.

- **The 320 or so species of hummingbird** live in North, Central and South America. Largest is the giant hummingbird, at about 20 cm long and weighing 20 g.

- **At 10.5 cm**, the beak of the sword-billed hummingbird is longer than the rest of its body.

- **Aztec kings** used to wear ceremonial cloaks made of hummingbird skins.

▲ *The tiny bee hummingbird lives on the island of Cuba in the Caribbean.*

- **Tiny ruby-throated hummingbirds** migrate each autumn from the USA across the Gulf of Mexico to Central America. Although only 9 cm long, the bird flies at a speed of about 44 km/h.

- **The female calliope hummingbird** lays two tiny eggs in a nest made of lichen, moss and spiders' webs. She incubates the eggs for 15 days, and feeds the young for about 20 days until they are able to fly and find food for themselves.

- **Hummingbirds** are the only birds able to fly backwards as well as forwards while they are hovering.

- **A hummingbird** must eat at least half its weight in food each day to fuel its energy needs.

# Nuthatches and relatives

- **The red-breasted nuthatch** paints the entrance of its tree hole nest with sticky pine resin. This may stop insects and other creatures getting into the nest, but the birds also have to take care not to get their own feathers stuck.

- **The wallcreeper** is an expert climber and can clamber up steep cliffs and walls in its search for insect prey. It lives high in mountains such as the Alps and Himalayas.

- **The treecreeper** supports itself with its stiff tail feathers as it moves up tree trunks feeding on insects and spiders.

- **The 24 or so species of nuthatch** live in North America, Europe, North

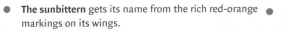

▲ The common treecreeper lives in woodland, parks and gardens in Europe and Asia.

Africa, Asia and Australasia.

- **The European nuthatch's 6–9 eggs** hatch after 14–18 days.

- **Insects and spiders are the main food of nuthatches**, but in autumn the birds store nuts and seeds for the winter.

- **There are 7 species** of treecreeper, seven species of Australian creeper and two species of Philippine creeper.

- **The largest nuthatch** is the giant nuthatch, at up to 20 cm long.

- **The Kabylie nuthatch** was only discovered in 1975, on an Algerian mountain.

> ★ STAR FACT ★
> Nuthatches are the only birds that can climb down trees head first, as well as up.

# Finfoots and relatives

- **The sunbittern** gets its name from the rich red-orange markings on its wings.

- **The sungrebe** (finfoot family) has an unusual way of caring for its young. The male bird carries his chicks in two skin pouches beneath his wings while they complete their development, even flying with them.

- **The only species in its family,** the sunbittern lives in jungles and swamps in Central and South America.

- **The kagu** is a flightless bird that lives only on the Pacific island of New Caledonia.

- **Finfoots are aquatic birds** that feed in the water on fish, frogs and shellfish. There is one species each in Africa, Southeast Asia and Central and South America.

- **The 2 species of seriema** live in South America. They eat snakes, banging their heads on the ground to kill them.

- **Seriemas can fly**, but prefer to escape danger by running fast over the grassy plains where they live.

- **Much of the kagu's habitat** on the island of New Caledonia has been destroyed by nickel mining, and the bird is now very rare.

- **The sunbittern lays two eggs** in a tree nest made of leaves and plant stems. Both parents take turns to incubate the eggs and care for the chicks.

- **The sungrebe and finfoots** have lobed feet, which help them swim.

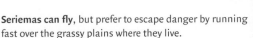

▶ A sunbittern shows off its beautiful plumage with its wings spread.

# Desert birds

- **The little cinnamon quail-thrush** of Australia hides in a burrow during the day to escape the hot sun.

- **The verdin** lives in the deserts of Mexico and the southwest of the USA, where it makes its nest on a cactus plant.

- **With few trees and bushes to sit in**, desert birds spend most of their lives on the ground.

- **The mourning dove** is a desert bird of the southwestern USA. A fast flier, it often travels great distances to find food and water.

- **Turkey vultures** soar over the American desert searching for carrion to eat.

- **Insects** are a favourite food of many desert birds, but some catch small mammals and others eat seeds.

★ **STAR FACT** ★
Desert-living bird species are usually smaller than those found elsewhere in the world.

- **Most desert birds** are active at dawn and towards sunset, resting in shade for much of the day.

- **Owls, poorwills and nightjars** cool down in the desert heat by opening their mouths wide and fluttering their throats.

- **The roadrunner** reabsorbs water from its faeces before it excretes them.

◄ *The greater roadrunner lives in the western USA, where it preys on snakes as well as insects and mice.*

# Mesites and relatives

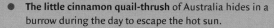

- **Mesites** are thrushlike birds that search for insects on the forest floor. They do have wings, but rarely fly.

- **There were 3 species of mesite in Madagascar**, but two have not been seen for years and may be extinct.

- **The 15 species of buttonquail** live in parts of Europe, Africa, Asia, Australia and some Pacific islands, usually on grassland. Although they look like quails, they are not related.

◄ *The little buttonquail lives in southern Europe, Africa and parts of Asia. It is 13–15 cm long.*

- **Shy little birds**, buttonquails lurk among low-growing plants feeding on seeds and insects.

- **The female buttonquail** is larger than the male. She mates with several males and leaves each to incubate the clutch of eggs and rear the young.

- **Buttonquails** are sometimes known as hemipode, or half-footed, quails, because they lack rear toes.

- **The plains-wanderer** lives on the dry plains of central Australia. If in danger, it stays very still.

- **Plains-wanderers** are now rare because so much of the grassland where they live and feed has been cleared for agriculture. There may be fewer than 8000 left in the wild.

- **The female plains-wanderer** lays four eggs, usually in a nest made in a hollow in the ground, but it is the male that incubates the eggs and rears the young.

- **Buttonquail young** can fly two weeks after hatching, and start to breed when only 4–5 months old.

# Cuckoos and hoatzin

- **The greater roadrunner,** a type of cuckoo, can move at a speed of 20 km/h or more on land.

- **The Eurasian cuckoo** is a 'brood parasite' – it lays its eggs in the nests of other birds.

- **Most birds take several minutes to lay an egg,** but the cuckoo lays one in just nine seconds, so it can quickly take advantage of any brief absence of the host bird.

- **Of the 129 or so species of cuckoo,** only about 50 lay their eggs in other birds' nests.

- **The 60-cm long hoatzin** (there is only one species) lives in South America's rainforest.

- **Hoatzin chicks** leave the nest soon after hatching. Two little claws on each wing help them clamber about.

- **The 22 species of turaco** live only in Africa. Largest is the 90-cm long great blue turaco, weighing 1 kg.

- **Turacos** feed mostly on fruit, leaves and flowers, but also catch some insects in the breeding season.

- **Amazingly, the eggs of brood parasite cuckoos** vary in colour and markings according to the host they use. A Eurasian cuckoo's eggs may resemble those of reed warblers, garden warblers or redstarts.

- **The Australian koel** prefers fruit to the caterpillars and other creatures eaten by other cuckoos.

▲ These flycatchers are busy feeding a cuckoo chick in their nest.

# Pittas and relatives

- **Bright red, green or yellow eyes** characterize the 15 colourful species of broadbill, which live in parts of tropical Africa and Southeast Asia.

- **The brightly coloured pittas** live in Africa, Southeast Asia and Australia. 'Pitta' is an Indian word meaning 'bird' – it was first used in the 1700s.

- **The four species of asity** are found only in Madagascar.

- **Most broadbills** feed on insects, which they catch in the air. Some also eat lizards and frogs.

- **The 24 or so species of pitta** range in size from 15–25 cm.

> ★ STAR FACT ★
> Rainbow pittas put wallaby droppings in and around their nests to disguise their own smell and keep tree snakes away from their eggs.

- **The Indian pitta** makes a nest of moss and twigs. Both parents incubate the 4–6 eggs.

- **The wattled false sunbird** (asity family) gets its name from its long, sunbird-like beak. Like the sunbirds, it takes nectar from flowers.

- **The green broadbill** hangs its nest from a vine and covers it with lichen and spiders' webs.

- **Pittas are said to have the best sense of smell** of any songbird. This may help them find worms and snails in the dim light of the forest floor.

◀ The hooded pitta (front) and red-bellied pitta live in tropical rainforests.

# Mousebirds and trogons

▶ *The beautiful quetzal is becoming rare because much of its forest habitat in Central America has been destroyed.*

● **The quetzal** is a species of trogon that lives in Central America. It was sacred to the ancient Maya and Aztec civilizations.

● **The male quetzal's beautiful tail feathers** are up to 1 m long.

● **Mousebirds** get their name from their habit of scurrying around on the ground like mice as they search for seeds and leaves to eat.

● **There are about 37 species of trogon** living in the forests and woodlands of Central America, the Caribbean islands and parts of Africa and Asia.

● **Trogons range in size** from the black-throated trogon, at 23 cm long, to the slightly larger resplendent quetzal, at 33 cm long not including the tail feathers.

● **The six species of mousebird** are all small, dull-coloured birds of about 10 cm in length. They live in Africa south of the Sahara.

● **Mousebirds are plant eaters**, feeding on a variety of leaves, buds, flowers and fruits.

● **Trogons nest in tree holes** or in old termite mounds or wasps' nests. Both parents incubate the 2 –4 eggs for 17–19 days, and both care for the young.

● **Insects** are the main food of the trogons, but some also eat fruit and catch creatures such as lizards.

> ★ **STAR FACT** ★
> The monetary unit of Guatemala is known as the quetzal, after the resplendent quetzal – the country's national bird.

# Wood warblers and icterids

● **The crested oropendola**, an icterid, weaves a hanging nest that may be up to 1 m long. The birds nest in colonies, and there may be as many as 100 large hanging nests in one tree.

● **Like the cuckoo**, the female brown-headed cowbird lays her eggs in the nests of other birds. She may lay as many as 40 eggs a year.

● **Kirtland's warbler** has very specialized breeding needs – it nests only around jack pine trees that are up to about 6 m tall.

● **The 114 species of wood warbler** live in North, Central and South America.

▶ *The yellow warbler can be found from chilly Alaska to tropical South America.*

● **The bobolink** breeds in southern Canada and the USA and migrates to South America for the winter – the longest migration journey of any icterid.

● **Great-tailed grackles** (icterid family) are big, noisy birds that scavenge on rubbish as well as feeding on insects, grain and fruit. They are common in towns and villages.

● **The Baltimore oriole** is the state bird of Maryland, USA. A song named after the bird was written by Hoagy Carmichael in the 1930s.

● **Male icterids** are generally much larger than females. The male great-tailed grackle is as much as 60 percent heavier than the female.

● **The yellow warbler** lays 4–5 eggs in a nest of bark and plant fibres made in a tree.

● **Largest of the 92 species of icterid** is the olive oropendola, at 52 cm long.

# Vireos and relatives

- **Plantcutters** get their name from their large, serrated beaks, used to chop leaves from plants.

- **The three species of plantcutter** live in southern South America. The birds are 17–20 cm long.

- **The sharpbill** of Central and South America picks tiny insects and spiders from leaves.

- **The 43 species of vireo** live in North, Central and South America, and range in size from 10–16 cm.

- **The black-capped vireo** usually attaches its nest to a forked twig. Both parents incubate the 3–5 eggs and feed the young.

- **Red-eyed vireo chicks** are naked and helpless when they hatch, but open their eyes after 4–5 days, and leave the nest after 12 days.

- **Insects** such as caterpillars and aphids are the main foods of vireos, but some species also eat fruit.

- **Vireos** take about a week to make their nest. The female makes a cup-shape of spiders' webs and silkworm threads around her body, and then adds plant material such as grass and moss to the nest.

- **When vireos were first named** in the 1800s, people thought they heard the word 'vireo', meaning 'I am green', in the birds' song. In fact most vireos are green.

- **The brown-headed cowbird** often lays its eggs in the nests of vireos, which sometimes throw out the cowbird's eggs.

◀ *The red-eyed vireo breeds in North America in the summer.*

# Endangered birds

- **More than 80 species of parrot**, such as the hyacinth macaw, are in danger of extinction or are very rare.

- **At least 1000 bird species** now face extinction – 30 or so became extinct in the 1900s.

- **The Hawaiian mamo** (Hawaiian honeycreeper family) became extinct in 1899, partly because more than 80,000 birds were killed to make a cloak for King Kamehameha I.

- **There are only about 600** black-faced spoonbills left.

★ **STAR FACT** ★
The bald eagle was threatened by the harmful effects of DDT on its eggs, but has recovered since the pesticide was banned in 1972.

- **The Fiji petrel** was first discovered on the island of Gau Fiji in 1855, and was not seen again until 1984. Numbers are thought to be low.

- **Possibly less than 1000** red siskins remain in the wild – it has been a popular cage-bird since the mid 1800s.

- **The Floreana mockingbird** disappeared from one of the Galapagos Islands because rats were introduced.

- **The short-tailed albatross** has long been exploited for its feathers, and has been extremely rare since 1930.

- **In New Zealand**, Hutton's shearwater is preyed on by introduced stoats, while deer trample its burrows.

◀ *The hyacinth macaw has suffered from illegal hunting for the pet trade and from habitat destruction. It is now bred in captivity.*

# MAMMALS

# Wild pigs and peccaries

- **To obtain fruit** that is out of reach, African bush pigs will lean against fruit trees, making them topple over.

- **The warthog** uses its huge tusks for fighting and impressing other warthogs, not for digging for food – it feeds almost exclusively on grass.

- **The fleshy 'warts'** on a male warthog's face protect its eyes from tusk blows when it is fighting.

- **The largest wild pig**, at over 2 m long, is the African giant forest hog, which weighs in at 275 kg or more.

- **Pigs** were first domesticated at least 7000 years ago in southwest Asia.

- **The babirusa**, or pig-deer, of the Indonesian islands has four tusks, two of which pierce its flesh and grow through the top of its muzzle.

- **Peccaries**, the wild pigs of South America, have complex stomachs for digesting tough plant fibres.

- **Unlike other wild pigs**, peccaries live in herds which includes the adult males.

- **When a herd of peccaries** is attacked by a predator, a single peccary may confront the attacker, allowing the rest of the herd to escape.

▲ Agile and powerful, the warthog forages across African woodlands and grasslands, often in family groups.

> ★ STAR FACT ★
> In 1975, the Chacoan peccary – known only from 10,000 year-old fossils – was found surviving in the forests of western Paraguay.

# Bison

- **Hunters** on the Great Plains of North America reduced the number of bison from 75 million to a few hundred between 1800 and 1900.

- **Bison bulls compete** for herd leadership by charging at each other, and have developed enormously thick skulls to withstand the blows.

- **Bison** have such bad tempers that they cannot be trained in captivity.

- **The European bison**, or wisent, browses on forest leaves of oak, willow and elm, unlike its American relations, which graze on grass.

- **Standing up to 2 m high** at the shoulder, the European bison is the continent's largest wild animal.

▲ Male bison compete by threats, which may develop into full scale battles.

- **The last truly wild** European bison was killed in 1919, but new herds – bred from zoo animals – have been established in reserves, in particular in the Bialowieza Forest in Poland.

- **In the 1800s,** the US Government approved the policy of killing bison in order to starve the Native Americans into submission.

- **The American plains bison** helped preserve the open prairies by eating the tree seedlings.

- **Saved by conservationists,** the American bison survives in small, managed herds in reservations and national parks.

- **Bison groom themselves** by rubbing their heads and bodies against tree trunks, and rolling in the dust.

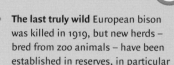

# Sea otters

- **Sea otters** live in the northeastern Pacific. They rarely come ashore, and sleep floating on their backs, wrapped in kelp seaweed to stop them drifting away.

- **The sea otter's thick fur** – the densest of any mammal in the world – keeps it warm in cold waters.

- **The heaviest** of all otters, the sea otter weighs up to 45 kg and reaches up to 1.4 m from nose to tail.

- **To maintain warmth and energy**, the sea otter eats up to 30 percent of its total weight each day, diving repeatedly for shellfish, sea urchins and octopi.

- **The sea otter** was the most recent mammal to evolve from a life on land to one in the sea.

- **In the 1700s and 1800s**, sea otters were hunted almost to extinction for their valuable fur, which was known as 'soft gold'.

- **To crack open shells**, the sea otter lies on its back and balances a rock on its stomach, using it like an anvil.

- **Sea otters** sleep, socialize and give birth on kelp beds.

- **Unique among otters**, sea otters can extend and contract the claws of their front feet, like a cat.

- **People have seen** sea otters bite open old drinks cans from the sea bed to get at octopi hiding inside.

▶ The sea otter uses both its front paws to hold food while floating on its back.

# Porcupines

- **When threatened**, some African porcupines erect their detachable quills and run backwards at their enemy.

- **African crested porcupines** warn off would-be predators by vigorously shaking their tail quills, producing a sound like the rattle of a rattlesnake.

- **The North American porcupine** has very poor eyesight.

★ STAR FACT ★
Some porcupines collect bones, which they gnaw on to sharpen their teeth. The bones provide them with phosphate.

- **Crested porcupines** are the longest lived of all rodents, the record being over 27 years.

- **American porcupines** are particularly vulnerable to attacks by fisher martens, which turn them over onto their backs to kill them, thus avoiding the quills.

- **The prehensile-tailed porcupines** of South America are active at night, and move to a new tree every 24 hours.

- **Baby porcupines** are born with soft quills to make the birth easier. Within a few hours the quills harden.

- **Some North American porcupines** have a craving for salt, and have been known to gnaw gloves, boots and saddles that are salty with sweat.

- **Old World porcupines** are not tree climbers.

▲ A porcupine's quills are soft when it is born, but harden within a few hours.

# Reindeer and caribou

- **Reindeer** (Europe and Asia) and caribou (North America) are basically the same animal.

- **Reindeer** were probably first tamed in the 5th century AD by hunters, who used them as decoys when hunting wild reindeer.

- **The broad hoofs** of reindeer and caribou help them to walk on snow.

- **In 1984**, 10,000 migrating caribou drowned in Canada when dam sluices were opened.

- **Reindeer** have a well developed homing instinct, and can find their way even in blinding snowstorms.

- **Reindeer bulls fight with their feet** and rarely with their antlers, which could become locked together, leading to the starvation of both animals.

> ★ STAR FACT ★
> The name 'caribou' means 'shoveller' in the language of one Canadian Indian people.

- **Reindeer are the best swimmers** of the deer family, due to the buoyancy of the hollow hairs of their coats.

- **Unlike other deer**, a reindeer's muzzle is covered in hair to help it forage in snow.

- **Reindeer dig** through the snow with their feet to find food.

▲ Caribou bulls rarely fight with their antlers, preferring to use their feet.

# Sloths

- **The sloths of South America** have a variable body temperature, and each morning need to bask in the sun above the forest canopy.

- **The sloth** has the most neck vertebrae of any mammal, and can look forwards when upside down.

- **Sloths even mate** and give birth while hanging upside down by their powerful, curved claws.

- **Sloths' fur** grows in the opposite direction to that of most mammals, pointing towards the ground so the rain runs off the body.

◄ The mother sloth carries her infant for up to 9 months on her belly, where it feeds on the leaves it can reach.

- **A sloth's large stomach** is divided into many compartments; the food inside can account for up to a third of the animal's weight.

- **A meal of leaves** may be retained in a sloth's digestive system for over a month.

- **The main predator** of the sloth is the harpy eagle.

- **Algae** grows in the grooves on a sloth's fur, helping to camouflage it in the forest greenery.

- **Sloths** have an amazing ability to heal themselves, and their wounds rarely become infected.

- **On land**, sloths can only move in an awkward, spread-eagled crawl, impeded by their curved claws.

# Walruses

- **A single walrus tusk** can measure up to 1 m long and weigh 5.4 kg.

- **Walruses swim** by sweeping their huge rear flippers from side to side, each one opening in turn like a 1 m wide fan.

- **The walrus is protected from the cold** by a thick layer of blubber – a third of its total weight.

- **In the summer,** basking walruses turn a deep pink as their blood vessels dilate to radiate heat away from the body.

- **Walruses** excavate shellfish from seabed mud by squirting a high-pressure blast of water from their mouths.

▶ *Walruses are very sociable, and like to gather in huge groups on coastal ice or rocks.*

★ STAR FACT ★
Walrus pups are born 15 months after the parents have mated – 4–5 months pass before the egg starts to grow in the mother's womb.

- **The walrus has 300 whiskers** on each side of its moustache, which it uses to help it find food in murky waters.

- **A walrus uses its long tusks** to help it clamber onto ice floes – its scientific name, *Odobenus*, means 'tooth walker'.

- **In water,** a walrus turns a pale grey colour as blood leaves its skin to maintain the temperature of its body core.

- **A walrus can eat** 3000 clams in one day.

# What are mammals?

- **Mammals have hairy bodies,** a large brain and special mammary glands for feeding their young with milk.

- **There are about 4500 species of mammal** in the world (and at least 1 million insect species!).

- **All mammals** except the duckbilled platypus and spiny anteater give birth to live young.

- **Mammals** evolved from reptiles, but are warm blooded.

- **The two main mammal groups** are the marsupials (whose young develop in the mother's pouch) and placentals.

- **All mammals** have three little bones in their ears that transfer sound vibrations to the inner ear from the eardrum.

- **Mammals** have a variety of teeth shapes: chisels for gnawing, long fangs for fighting and killing prey, sharp-edged slicers and flat-topped crushers.

- **The platypus and spiny anteater** are egg-laying mammals called monotremes.

- **Mammals** have a palate that enables them to breathe through their noses while chewing.

- **Mammals** give a level of maternal care beyond that of other animals.

▼ *Young mammals mature more slowly than other animal young, so they are looked after for longer.*

# Tigers

- **At over 3 m long** and weighing up to 360 kg, the rare Siberian tiger is the largest living member of the cat family. Tigers originated in Siberia.

- **Tigers need a very large hunting area**, and males in northern India often patrol an area of 130 sq km or more.

- **After feeding**, tigers sometimes save the remains of a kill for a later meal, burying it under branches to hide it from scavengers or other tigers.

- **In 1945** there were only 50 Siberian tigers left in the wild. Now there are 300 to 400 surviving in reserves.

- **Aggressive tigers** flash the distinctive white spots on their ears as a warning.

- **In India and Bangaladesh**, in the Sunderbans mangrove swamps, tigers keep cool in the water and ambush pigs, deer and monkeys.

- **In the early 1900s** there were probably at least 50,000 tigers. Now numbers have fallen to 6000 or less, half of them living in India.

- **A tiger's stripes** camouflage it as it hunts in the tall grasses by day. But tigers also hunt at night – their night vision is at least 6 times more acute than a human's.

- **Tiger cubs** depend entirely on their mothers for food until they are about 18 months old, when they begin to make their own first kills.

◄ The tiger uses its long canine teeth to bite the throat or neck of its prey as it brings it to the ground. Its sharp-edged rear teeth cut through the meat by sliding against each other like the blades of scissors.

> ★ STAR FACT ★
> Tigers eat a variety of foods, ranging from fish and turtles during times of flood to locusts during locust swarms.

Binocular vision allows the tiger accurately to judge distance

◄ To keep out the cold, the Siberian tiger has an outer coat of long, pale fur over a thick undercoat

Long rear legs help tigers to leap

Huge muscles in the front legs are used for holding and killing prey

# Orang-utans

- **Orang-utans** spend much more time in trees than the other great apes, and are the largest tree-dwelling mammals in the world.

- **Insatiable eaters**, orang-utans can spend an entire day feasting in one heavily laden fruit tree.

- **The name 'orang-utan'** means 'man of the forest' in the language of the local tribespeople of Southeast Asia.

- **A mature male orang-utan** makes his presence known to other orang-utans by breaking branches, bellowing and groaning. Local legends explain this as a sign of the ape's grief over losing a human bride.

- **In Sumatra**, the major predators of orang-utans are tigers at ground level, and clouded leopards in trees.

▲ *Orang-utans are slow breeders, and may only give birth to three or four babies in a lifetime.*

- **Once found all over Southeast Asia**, orang-utans now live only in tropical Borneo and Sumatra.

- **Like chimpanzees**, orang-utans use sticks as tools to retrieve food from crevices and to scratch themselves.

- **Male orang-utans** have large air sacs that extend from their throats, under their arms and over their shoulders, and increase the loudness and range of their calls.

- **To help her young** move from tree to tree, a mother orang-utan pulls the branches of two trees closer together and makes a bridge with her body.

- **Orang-utans make a nest** at night, building a roof to keep off the rain.

# Beavers

- **Beavers** are born with innate dam-building instincts. In zoos, they regularly 'repair' concrete dams with twigs.

- **It takes two adult beavers** about 15 minutes to gnaw their way through a tree-trunk with a 10 cm diameter.

- **Mother beavers** push tired youngsters ahead of them through the water, like swimming floats.

▼ *The beaver uses its huge incisor teeth to gnaw through branches and tree trunks.*

★ **STAR FACT** ★
European beavers took to living in burrows to avoid hunters. They are now protected by law.

- **Storing extra oxygen** in its lungs and body tissues, a beaver can remain under water for up to 15 minutes.

- **Beavers use the split claws** on their hind feet for grooming and spreading waterproof oil.

- **A beaver signals danger** by smacking the water with its tail. The noise carries over 1 km.

- **The territory-marking secretion** of the beaver contains the main ingredient in aspirin.

- **Beavers' dams** and lodges can help create environments for fish.

- **In some parts of the USA**, beavers are parachute-dropped into areas where remote rivers need damming to reduce erosion.

# Aardvarks

- **When in danger**, the aardvark can dig at great speed, and can outpace a team of men armed with spades.

- **An aardvark** has several burrows on its territory, often many kilometres apart.

- **Termites and ants** form the main food of the aardvark, which digs through concrete-hard termite mounds to reach them.

- **To stop termites and dust** entering its nose, the aardvark has stiff bristles on its muzzle, and can close its nostrils.

- **A moderate blow to the head** can kill an aardvark, which depends on its acute senses and digging abilities for survival.

- **If attacked**, the aardvark may roll onto its back and lash out with its feet .

- **The aardvark swallows** food without chewing, grinding it up in its stomach.

> ★ **STAR FACT** ★
> 'Aardvark' is Afrikaans for 'earth-pig' (but in fact aardvarks do not belong to the pig family).

- **Baby aardvarks** depend on their mothers for about 6 months, when they learn to dig burrows.

- **Some African peoples** who also eat termites keep an aardvark claw as a charm to increase the harvest.

◀ *The aardvark usually feeds at night, eating termites in the wet season and ants in the dry season.*

# Giraffes and okapis

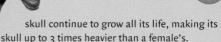

- **The giraffe's black tongue** is almost 0.5 m long. It uses it to grip vegetation and pull it into its mouth.

- **The giraffe is the world's tallest animal** – some males reach up to 6 m in height.

- **Male giraffes stretch** up to reach leaves high in the trees, while females bend their necks to take lower leaves, thus reducing food competition.

- **Bony growths** on a male giraffe's

▶ *A giraffe's front legs are longer than its rear legs.*

skull continue to grow all its life, making its skull up to 3 times heavier than a female's.

- **The extraordinarily long necks** of giraffes have only 7 neck vertebrae, just like other mammals, but they are greatly elongated.

- **From a few weeks old**, young giraffes spend much of their time in a 'crèche', looked after by a pair of adults.

- **Female giraffes with calves** have been seen to beat severely and drive off attacking lions, using their hoofs, necks and heads as weapons.

- **To reach water**, giraffes have to spread their front legs wide apart. Special valves stop the blood rushing to and from their heads as they raise and lower them.

- **Okapis**, which are related to giraffes, closely resemble fossils of the giraffe's most recent ancestor, *Paleotragus*, from about 12 million years ago.

- **Okapis live so deep in the forests** of the Congo that they were not discovered by Europeans until the 1900s.

# Wild dogs

- The South American bush dog pursues prey into the water, and, unlike most dogs, can swim underwater.

- African Cape hunting dogs live in packs in which only the dominant female has young.

- Cape hunting dog cubs are left in the den, protected by adult guardians, while the pack hunts, and are fed with disgorged meat when it returns.

- Cape hunting dogs do not creep up on prey, but approach a herd openly, selecting a single target to chase.

- Cape hunting dogs can run at 60 km/h for 5 km or more. They may travel 50 km a day while hunting, and patrol a range of 1500 to 2000 sq km.

▶ Cape hunting dogs are well camouflaged – no two individuals have the same markings.

★ STAR FACT ★
Cape hunting dog females may fight over possession of their puppies, often killing them.

- Indian wild dogs, or dholes, hunt in packs of up to 30, and can drive tigers and leopards from their kills.

- Dholes hunt in thick undergrowth, advancing in an extended line until they have flushed out their prey.

- The raccoon dog of east Asia eats insects, shellfish and fruit.

- Australian dingoes are probably descended from Indian wolves that were domesticated in Asia and taken by Aboriginal settlers to Australia, where they reverted to the wild.

# The first mammals

- Before true mammals emerged, some reptiles, such as the doglike Cynodonts, had developed mammalian characteristics such as hair and specialized teeth.

- The mammary glands with which mammals suckle their young evolved from sweat glands. Some mammal-like reptiles may have exuded a type of milk from sweat glands for their young.

- The earliest true mammals appeared more than 210 million years ago and were only 15 cm long.

- One of the best-known of the earliest fossil mammals was an insect eater named *Megazostrodon*.

- A major difference between mammals and reptiles was the development of the little bones linking the eardrum and inner ear, found only in mammals.

- During the Age of the Dinosaurs, which lasted 160 million years, mammals were small.

▶ The tiny Megazostrodon kept well-hidden from predatory reptiles, and was active at night.

★ STAR FACT ★
Within 10 million years of the extinction of the dinosaurs, most modern mammal orders, including horses and primates, had appeared.

- All known mammal fossils from 210 to 66 million years ago would fit into a normal-sized bucket!

- By the time the dinosaurs became extinct about 65 million years ago, marsupials, placentals and monotremes had all evolved.

- Fossils of very early mammals came from Europe, South Africa and China.

# Desert life

- **The American kangaroo rat** derives water from its food and by recycling its breath.

- **Prairie dogs** have air-conditioned homes. The air in their tunnels is renewed every 10 minutes by the suction effect of the entrances being at different heights.

- **Desert ground squirrels** have hairy feet to protect them from hot sand.

- **Desert bighorn sheep** let their body temperatures rise from 36.8°C to 40°C, re-radiating the excess heat at night.

- **Some desert-dwelling badgers and sheep** have a fatty layer that insulates their internal organs from heat.

▲ Living on dry plains, prairie dogs may inhabit extensive tunnel-and-nest 'towns' that cover up to 65 hectares.

- **The Australian fat-tailed mouse** has a carrot-shaped tail that stores fat, which it lives off during droughts.

- **Most desert mammals** rest in shade or burrows by day, emerging to seek food in the cool of night.

- **Collared peccaries,** or javelinas, are American desert pigs. In times of drought they eat cacti, spines and all.

- **The burrowing** Australian bilby licks seeds from the desert surface, and its dung pellets are 90 percent sand.

- **The long legs** of the Arabian camel raise its body to a height where air temperatures are up to 25°C cooler than ground temperatures.

# Sheep and goats

- **Despite their massive curled horns,** American bighorn rams fight predators with their feet.

- **The musk ox** of the Arctic tundra is more closely related to sheep and goats than to bison or oxen.

- **Sheep and goats** were domesticated as early as 7500 BC.

- **When young sheep and goats play,** they often leap onto their mothers' backs, practising for mountain life among the rocks.

- **Goats and sheep** have scent glands on their feet that mark mountain trails, helping herds stay together.

◀ Most domestic sheep have adapted to a life of migratory grazing, moving on as the grass is cropped.

- **Bighorn rams** only fight with one another if their horns are of a similar size, ignoring larger or smaller rivals.

- **Avalanches** are the main threat to Rocky Mountain goats.

- **Of the two,** only sheep have scent glands on their faces, and only male goats have beards and a strong odour.

- **Central Asian argalis** are the largest Eurasian wild sheep, weighing up to 200 kg.

- **In a fight,** a European chamois may feign death to avoid being killed, lying flat with its neck outstretched.

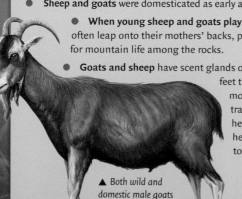

▲ Both wild and domestic male goats sport distinctive beards.

# Horses and asses

- **The earliest-known ancestor** of the horse, *Hyracotherium*, lived 50 million years ago, and was a forest dweller the size of a small dog.

- **Horses' earliest ancestors** evolved in America, and crossed land bridges to Asia and Europe, eventually becoming extinct in America.

- **A mule** is the offspring of a male ass and a female horse, while the rarer offspring of a male horse and female ass is called a hinny. Both mules and hinnies are unable to produce young.

- **Horses have very strong homing instincts**, and have been known to wander hundreds of kilometres to return to the place of their birth.

- **The domestic horse** is the only member of the horse family in which the mane falls to the side – in all others, including asses and zebras, it stands erect.

- **Horses' eyes** are set high in the head and far apart, giving almost all round vision. They can focus on near and far objects at the same time.

> ★ STAR FACT ★
> Horses were domesticated about 6000 years ago in Europe and Asia, mainly for their meat. They became transport animals from about 2000 BC.

- **The horse's large eyes** give it excellent night vision – almost as keen as that of owls.

- **Most horses sleep standing up** during the day, and at night sleep on the ground with their legs gathered under their bodies.

- **The earliest horses** had four toes per foot. These reduced as the horse moved from a forest to a plains life, and the modern horse has just a single toe.

▼ *The donkey evolved from African ass ancestors, and is capable of carrying heavy loads. All wild asses are desert dwellers, able to flourish on sparse vegetation, and survive burning hot days and icy cold nights.*

▼ *By nature horses are herd animals. In the wild a herd usually consists of one dominant stallion, accompanied by a number of mares and their young.*

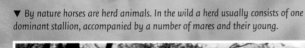

# Tasmanian wolf

- **The Tasmanian wolf** was a meat-eating Australian marsupial that became extinct in 1936.

- **Once common** throughout Australia and New Guinea, the Tasmanian wolf retreated to Tasmania some 3000 years ago, driven out by dingoes.

- **The Tasmanian wolf** had a pouch that opened to the rear, where the young spent their first 3 months.

- **Also called the Tasmanian tiger**, because of its stripes, the Tasmanian wolf was in fact neither a wolf nor a tiger.

- **The Tasmanian wolf** had a thick-based tail and hopped on its back legs if chased.

- **The jaws** of the Tasmanian wolf opened almost 180°, allowing it to kill an animal by crushing its skull.

- **With its immensely powerful jaws**, the Tasmanian wolf could kill a pursuing hunting dog with one bite.

- **Fossil remains** of an animal almost identical to the Tasmanian wolf were discovered in America.

- **Tasmanian wolves** may survive in the dense forest, but this remains to be proved.

> ★ STAR FACT ★
> Thousands of Tasmanian wolves were killed in the late 1800s, because they preyed on sheep.

▶ *Some people claim to have seen Tasmanian wolves still surviving in remote parts of Tasmania.*

# What are rodents?

▼ *The South American chinchilla has been hunted almost to extinction for its dense, soft fur, and is now sometimes raised on fur farms.*

- **Rodents**, which include mice, squirrels, beavers, porcupines and guinea pigs, have two incisor teeth in each jaw that never stop growing.

- **If a rodent's teeth** are not constantly worn down by gnawing, they can curve round into the animal's skull and kill it – the name 'rodent' means 'gnawer'.

- **Forty percent of mammal species are rodents**. They range in size from the 1.4 m-long capybara to the Baluchistan pygmy jerboa, at 4.7 cm (body length).

- **The earliest-known rodents** appeared in 57-million-year-old fossil beds in both Asia and North America.

- **The house mouse** and the brown rat occur more widely than any land mammal excepts humans, and are found in all continents, including Antartica.

- **Guinea pigs** in South America and edible dormice in Europe have both been bred to be eaten by humans.

- **Female Norway lemmings** can begin to breed when only 14 days old.

- **The fastest rodents** over the ground may be kangaroo mice and jerboas, which can bound along on their hind legs at speeds of up to 48 km/h.

- **In the Miocene period** (23 to 5 million years ago), some South American rodents were the size of rhinos!

- **A female house mouse** can produce 14 litters a year.

# Hippopotami

- **The lips of hippos** are up to 0.5 m wide, and contain strong muscles for grazing on short grasses.

- **Hippos feed** for 5 hours a night, and spend the next 19 hours resting in the water.

- **Hippos suckle** their young underwater and often sleep submerged, surfacing regularly to breath whilst still unconscious.

- **A pygmy hippo** is born on land in just 2 minutes, and has to be taught how to swim.

- **In dry air** the pygmy hippo loses water by evaporation at about 5 times the rate of human water loss.

- **Hippos travel** up to 30 km at night in search of food, but if frightened will run back to water to hide.

- **Hippos** are probably Africa's most dangerous animal. They kill a large number of humans each year.

- **Bull hippos** mark their territory by scattering dung with their whirling tails.

- **Aggressive hippos** warn off other hippos by opening their jaws to display their formidable tusks. They regularly fight to the death.

- **Male hippos** can weigh as much as 3200 kg.

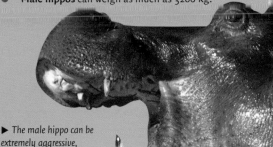

▶ The male hippo can be extremely aggressive, opening its huge mouth wide and displaying its tusks as a warning to other males.

# Rabbits and hares

- **Hares are born with fur**, their eyes open. Rabbits are born naked, their eyes shut.

- **Mother hares** visit their young for just 5 minutes a day to feed them on their milk.

- **Snowshoe hares** have broad, hairy hind feet for moving over snow.

- **If a hare sees it is being** stalked by a fox, it stands up to put the fox off a chase (which the hare would win).

- **The pikas** of Asia and western America 'sing' loudly.

- **Rabbits' incisors** grow constantly.

◀ Hares, like rabbits, can close and open their slit-like nostrils at will.

★ STAR FACT ★
Numbers of American snowshoe hares rise and fall in an 8–11 year cycle, affecting the numbers of lynxes, which depend on them as food.

- **Both sexes of hares 'box'** as part of the mating ritual.

- **Hares can reach speeds** of up to 60 km/h when running flat out.

- **Large-eared pika** is one of the highest-living mammal in the world, inhabiting mountain ranges in Asia at altitudes up to 6130 m.

▶ The snowshoe hare's large eyes help it see during dusk and after dark, when it is most active.

# Elephants

- **The name 'elephant'** means 'visible from afar'.

- **Elephants communicate** over great distances by making low frequency sounds (too low for humans to hear).

- **War elephants** were used by the Carthaginian general Hannibal against the Romans in the 3rd century BC, and by the Romans invading Britain in the 1st century AD.

- **Elephants sometimes enter caves** to excavate minerals such as sodium, needed as a supplement to their diet.

- **Elephants** spend up to 18 hours a day feeding.

> ★ STAR FACT ★
> Stone Age rock paintings in North Africa show that elephants once lived in the Sahara region, before it became desert.

▲ An elephant's trunk is a combination of upper lip and nose, and is used to place food into its mouth. It also doubles as a hose, squirting water down its throat and acting as a shower spray.

▶ The elephant's large ears help it to control its temperature, as well as aiding its acute sense of hearing. Movements of the ears are used to convey body language.

- **Elephants are good swimmers** – some Asian elephants have been seen to swim non-stop for as much as 10 km.

- **Asian elephants** are the world's longest-lived mammals after humans, and can live to be over 70 years.

- **An African elephant** needs to eat up to 6 percent of its bodyweight each day – 300 kg for a 5000 kg bull!

- **An elephant uses four grinding teeth** at any one time, and these are replaced as they wear out - it can get through 24 molars in its lifetime.

# Cheetahs

- **Cheetahs cannot** retract their claws. They grip the ground, like spikes on a sprinter's shoes.

- **A cheetah can accelerate** from 0 to 72 km/h in 2 seconds, and can reach a top speed of 120 km/h.

- **A silver vase** (c 2300 BC), found in the Caucasus, shows a cheetah in a collar, which suggests people used cheetahs then as hunting animals.

- **The 16th-century Mogul emperor Akbar** kept 1000 cheetahs, which he used to hunt blackbuck.

- **Cheetahs** have the same body length as leopards, but stand a good 35 cm taller on their long legs.

- **In the Kalahari Desert**, cheetahs can survive for 10 days without water by eating wild melons.

- **Young male cheetahs** often hunt in small groups (coalitions), and are healthier than solitary males.

- **A cheetah will chase a warthog** that runs, but will usually leave one that stands its ground.

- **If a cheetah does not catch its prey** in the first 300 to 400 m of the chase, it gives up and allows its heart beat to return to normal.

- **Cheetahs avoid lions**, which will kill them.

▶ *Cheetahs often sit on rocks or termite mounds to get a better all-round view when resting.*

# Gorillas

▲ *The male gorilla is far larger than the female, and is the largest of all the primates – big silverbacks can weigh as much as 200 kg.*

- **Male gorillas mostly walk on four limbs**, but will run on two legs, beating their chests, when showing off.

- **Adult gorillas** sleep in a new nest every night.

- **The mature male leader** of a gorilla group is called a 'silverback', after the saddle of white hair on its back.

- **Young male gorillas** form their own groups by kidnapping females from other groups.

- **Mountain gorillas** spend almost all their lives at 2800 to 3400 m above sea level, in damp, cloudy conditions.

- **Some gorillas supplement their plant diet** by eating handfuls of potassium- and calcium-rich soil.

- **If a gorilla cannot keep up** with the group because of a wound, the silverback slows down so it is not left behind.

- **When aggressive male gorillas** beat their chests and mock-charge one another, they give off an armpit odour powerful enough to be detected 25 m away by humans.

- **Despite their huge strength**, silverbacks are gentle with their offspring, allowing them to play on their backs.

★ STAR FACT ★
The 'nose-prints' of gorillas are as distinctive
as human fingerprints – no two are identical.

# Squirrels

- **Grey squirrels** have been known to kill and eat rabbits, rats, cockerels and stoats.

- **Flying squirrels** are nocturnal, and when gliding may emit high-pitched squeaks that help them to locate a landing place.

- **North American red squirrels** tap birch and maple trees for their sweet sap in spring.

- **Many squirrel species** spread woodland trees by burying nuts and then forgetting where they put them.

- **The North American red squirrel**, or chicaree, buries green pine cones in damp soil to delay their ripening until they are needed.

- **The largest member of the squirrel family** is the alpine marmot, at 73 cm long not including the tail.

- **Southeast Asian giant squirrels** prefer to hang upside down by their hind feet while eating.

- **Chipmunks**, or ground squirrels, store huge quantities of nuts in a single cache.

- **To prevent it slipping backwards** down a tree trunk, the scaly-tailed flying squirrel presses the horny scales of its tail against the trunk.

- **An adult red squirrel** can sniff out a pine cone buried 30 cm deep.

▶ The squirrel's bushy tail is a good balancing aid and rudder when climbing and leaping.

# Mammal senses

◀ Large cats have eyes on the front of their heads rather than at the sides, helping them to focus on their prey as they hunt.

- **Cheetahs** have a band of light-sensitive nerve cells across their retinas that give clear vision ahead and to the sides.

- **Desert mammals** such as the long-eared kit fox find sharp hearing more useful than a keen sense of smell in the dry air.

- **Polar bears can smell** seals up to 60 km away across the ice.

- **Cats have glands** between their toes that leave an identifying scent when they scratch trees.

- **Blue whales and fin whales** communicate by means of the loudest sounds produced by any living creature (up to 188 dB).

- **Baby wood-mice** emit ultrasonic distress calls in their first 10 days to summon their mother.

- **Many nocturnal mammals** have reflective areas in their eyes that help night vision.

- **Migrating whales** can sense the Earth's magnetic field, due to particles of the mineral magnetite in their bodies.

- **The exceptionally large ears** of fennec foxes can detect the sound of termites chewing beneath the ground.

- **Skunks use a powerful scent weapon** to deter their enemies.

# Rhinoceroses

- **The Sumatran rhino** is a relative of the woolly rhinoceros of the last Ice Age, and has reddish fur.

- **When black rhinos** are fleeing, the calf follows the mother, but when white rhinos are in flight, the mother runs behind the calf.

- **African ox-birds** ride aboard rhinos, cleaning out ticks from the folds in their hides.

- **Despite weighing 2 tonnes** or more, the rhino can run at 50 km/h, and make a 180° turn within its own body length.

- **If two rhinos feel threatened,** they stand back to back, confronting their enemies from different directions.

▶ *The rhino has excellent hearing.*

- **Rhinos can be heard** munching on plants from a distance of 400 m.

- **The upper lips** of the African white rhino are square, for grazing on grass. Those of the African black rhino are pointed, for plucking leaves.

- **Rhinos have poor eyesight,** and cannot locate a motionless object further than 30 m away.

- **A prehistoric relative** of the rhinoceros, *Indricotherium*, stood 5.4 m tall and weighed 20 tonnes.

- **Thicker skin** on a rhino's flanks protect it from horn wounds from rivals.

# Seals

- **When chasing penguins,** the leopard seal can leap 2 m high from the sea onto an ice floe.

- **Male southern elephant seals,** which weigh up to 3500 kg, have inflatable snouts used to impress females during mating displays.

- **In the four days after birth,** hooded seal pups double their weight from 25 kg to 50 kg.

- **The elephant seal** can dive 1500 m, and stay under water for 1–2 hours.

- **Leopard seals** are the only seals known to make unprovoked attacks on humans, lunging through ice to get at their feet.

- **Seals sleep** floating vertically in the water just beneath the surface, rising to breathe through their nostrils.

★ **STAR FACT** ★
The world's largest mammal herd consists of up to 1.5 million northern fur seals, which breed on two islands in the Pacific sub-Arctic region.

- **When a seal dives deep,** its heartbeat slows from 55–120 beats per minute to 4–15 beats per min.

- **Crab-eater seals** have special teeth that they use like strainers to catch the shrimp-like krill on which they feed.

- **The fur seals** of the North Pacific spend up to 8 months of the year continuously at sea, feeding.

◀ *The spotted seal frequents the icy waters of the North Pacific and Arctic Ocean.*

# Old World camels

- **Single-humped dromedaries** and twin-humped Bactrian camels can go for months without food and water, living on the fat in their humps.

- **A female dromedary** can produce 6 litres of milk a day for 9 to 18 months – the staple food for some camel-herding peoples.

- **After not drinking for many months**, a camel can drink up to 130 litres in just a few minutes.

- **Unlike other mammals**, camels have oval instead of round blood-cells. These prevent their blood thickening as their body temperature rises.

- **Evolving originally in North America**, some camel ancestors crossed land bridges to Asia to become today's Bactrian camels and dromedaries.

- **Introduced to Australia** as desert transport animals, dromedaries reverted to the wild there.

- **Domesticated in Arabia** some 6000 years ago, the dromedary, or Arabian camel, ceased to exist in the wild about 2000 years ago.

- **Camels do sweat**, but not until their body temperature has reached 40.5°C.

- **In the annual King's Camel Race** in Saudi Arabia, some 3000 camels are raced over a 23 km course.

- **Only about 1000** wild Bactrian camels survive, in Mongolia's Gobi Desert.

▶ *A camel's average laden speed is 3–8 km/h, which it can maintain for up to 18 hours without rest.*

# Otters

- **Otters enjoy playing** games, such as dropping pebbles into water and catching them on their heads!

- **The African clawless otter** can move its thumb across the other fingers to hold onto objects.

- **Clawless otters** gather freshwater mussels and then smash them on rocks.

- **When hunted by hounds**, otters have been known to drag their pursuers under water and drown them.

◀ *The otter's coat is made up of a dense layer of underfur, with an outer layer of long guard hairs.*

> ★ **STAR FACT** ★
> The Giant otter of Brazil is the longest of the otter family, at almost 2 m long .

- **Otters have special whiskers** on their muzzles and elbows that are sensitive to water disturbances and help them to locate prey.

- **Giant otters** clear a series of 7 m wide areas around their territories before scent-marking them.

- **Male Eurasian otters** patrols a territory of up to 50 km of river bank. Females' territory is 10 km.

- **The marine otter** of the west coast of South America is the smallest sea mammal in the world, weighing no more than 4.5 kg.

- **Some otters**, including the Cape clawless otter and the Oriental short-clawed otter, catch their prey in their paws rather than in their mouths.

# Hibernation and dormancy

- **The hibernating dormouse** does not attract the attention of predators because its body temperature is so low that it gives off no body odour.

- **The core body temperature** of some hibernating bats falls below freezing – in some cases as low as -5°C – without harming them.

- **Bears are not true hibernators**, but have a moderately reduced body temperature during their winter sleep, offset by the huge amounts of food that they eat before going to sleep.

- **The raccoon dog** is the only member of the dog family to hibernate.

- **The Eastern European dormouse** and the Canadian woodchuck may spend as much as 9 months of the year in hibernation.

- **Hibernators** such as ground squirrels have internal clocks that cause them to go into hibernation at the usual time of year, even if they are kept in warm conditions with plenty of food.

> ★ STAR FACT ★
> Hibernating mammals wake up by shivering violently, creating heat that passes to the brain, the vital organs and the rest of the body.

- **A hibernating bat's breathing rate** falls from about 200 breaths per minute to between 25 and 30 a minute for 3 minutes, followed by an 8 minute no-breathing break.

- **Alaskan ground squirrels**, born at the end of June, start to dig burrows 22 days later, and feed, fatten up and begin to hibernate by the end of August.

- **Brown fat,** found in high levels in hibernating mammals, creates heat as the temperature falls.

▼ *Many bat species are true hibernators, as is the dormouse, which may hibernate for up to 9 months, and the hedgehog, which usually sleeps through the winter. The grey squirrel is not a true hibernator, but is only active briefly on cold winter days. Eurasian badgers also become lethargic during cold spells.*

1 Bats
2 Grey squirrel
3 Dormouse
4 Eurasian badgers
5 Hedgehog

# Monotremes

- **Monotremes** are egg-laying mammals. There are only two groups: the duckbilled platypus of Australia and the echidna, or spiny anteater, of Australia and New Guinea.

- **If harassed** on soft ground by a predator, the echidna digs down until only an area of spines is showing.

- **The platypus** can detect the electric fields of its prey by means of electro-receptors in its muzzle.

- **Hunting underwater** with eyes and ears closed, the platypus eats up to 30 percent of its own weight each day.

- **The female echidna** has a pouch in which the young develop after hatching from their soft-shelled egg.

- **Poison** from the spurs on the male platypus's hind ankles can kill a dog within minutes.

- **Before the discovery** of fossil platypus teeth in Argentina, the animal was believed only to have existed in Australia and New Guinea.

- **The platypus loses its teeth** a few weeks after birth, and thereafter grinds its food with special mouth pads.

- **The platypus's burrow** can extend 30 m from the water's edge to the nest. It blocks the entrance to deter snakes.

> ★ **STAR FACT** ★
> The duckbilled platypus lives almost all its life either underwater or underground.

◄ *The duckbilled platypus swims mainly with its front legs, trailing its rear legs as a rudder.*

# Badgers

- **Successive generations** of Eurasian badgers use the same den or sett, sometimes for over a century.

- **The ferret badger** is the smallest member of the badger family, and the only badger to climb trees.

- **The honey badger** is led to bees' nests by the greater honey-guide bird, which attracts it with special calls. It feeds on beeswax once the badger has opened the nest.

- **The American badger** can burrow fast enough to catch a ground squirrel that is burrowing in the ground ahead of it trying to escape.

▶ *A Eurasian badger may eat several hundred earthworms in one night.*

- **A female European badger** sometimes has female helpers that baby-sit her cubs, often in their own nests, while she forages for food.

- **Despite a bear-like appearance**, badgers belong to the mammal group known as mustelids, and are related to otters and weasels.

- **The honey badger's** extremely tough skin protects it from all kinds of dangers, ranging from bee stings and porcupine quills to snake bites.

- **Badgers are enthusiastic housekeepers** – they regularly change their bedding, and also dig latrines some distance from their setts.

- **Earthworms** are one of the badger's favourite foods, and females suckling their young feed on little else.

- **Eurasian badgers** will enlarge their favourite setts. One ancient den consisted of 879 m of tunnels, with 178 entrances and 50 subterranean chambers.

# Hedgehogs

- **The Eurasian hedgehog** has between 5000 and 7000 spines on its back and sides, each erected by its own muscle, creating a defence difficult for predators to penetrate.

- **When a hedgehog rolls into a ball** at the approach of danger, a special muscle draws its loose skin together (like a drawstring on a bag) over its head and rump.

- **From Roman to medieval times** in Europe, it was believed that hedgehogs often carried a supply of fruit with them, impaled on their spines.

- **Over 150,000 hedgehogs** are killed every year on the roads of France alone.

- **The moonrats** of Southeast Asia and China are closely related to hedgehogs, but have no spines.

- **The long-eared and desert hedgehogs** of Asia and North Africa dig their own individual, short burrows.

- **Hedgehogs can go without water** for long periods, and if dehydrated will drink half their bodyweight in one go.

- **A western European male hedgehog** has a foraging territory of up to 35 hectares.

- **Lack of food** rather than cooling temperatures causes a hedgehog to hibernate.

> ★ STAR FACT ★
> The hedgehog keeps up a ceaseless whistling sound while hunting for food.

▲ Scent is important to hedgehogs, as they communicate and track food by smell.

# Domestic dogs

- **All modern domestic dogs**, from Chihuahuas to Great Danes, are direct descendants of grey wolves.

- **Grey wolves** were first domesticated over 12,000 years ago in Europe and Asia, for use as guards and herders.

- **Female domestic dogs** can have two litters of puppies a year; wild members of the dog family have only one.

- **The Portuguese water dog** can be trained to dive and retrieve fishing equipment in fresh or salt water.

- **Bloodhounds** can pick up a trail over two weeks old, and follow it for over 200 km.

- **The caffeine** compounds in a bar of dark chocolate can kill a dog weighing up to 5 kg.

- **St Bernard rescue dogs** work in teams of three – two to keep the victim warm, one to fetch their handler.

- **Some dogs can sense** when their owner is about to have an epileptic fit, and others can detect skin cancers before the recognized symptoms appear.

- **During World War II**, over 50,000 dogs were enlisted in the US forces, performing tasks from sentry duty to stealing enemy documents.

- **Native Americans** used dogs to drag a type of sledge.

▶ Male St Bernard dogs often weigh over 90 kg.

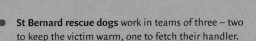

# Polar bears

▼ Apart from pregnant females, which spend the winter in dens where they give birth, polar bears are active all through the winter months, often travelling great distances in search of food.

● **The Polar bear** is the only bear which is almost exclusively a meat eater, other bears eat plants too.

● **While stalking a seal**, a polar bear will sometimes lie on its chest with its front legs trailing at its sides and its rump in the air, pushing itself forward with its rear legs.

● **Polar bears** can detect the scent of seal pups in dens buried 1 m deep in snow.

● **Lying in ambush** for a seal, a polar bear will sometimes cover its black nose with its paws to remain unseen against the snow and ice.

● **Polar bears** have a number of tiny protrusions and suction pads on the soles of their feet to give them a firm grip on the ice.

● **The most southerly place** that polar bears regularly visit is James Bay in Canada, which is on the same line of latitude as London.

● **Female polar bears** can put on as much as 400 kg in weight in the course of their summer feeding binge on seal cubs.

● **The polar bear** is a powerful swimmer, even though it uses only its front paws as paddles, letting its rear legs trail behind.

● **Beneath its thick white fur**, a polar bear's skin is black. Translucent hairs channel heat from the sun to the animal's skin, which absorbs the heat.

The heavy forelimbs are ideal for breaking through ice to get at seals' lairs beneath

The huge feet are used as paddles for swimming and snow shoes for crossing thin ice

# Manatees and dugongs

- **Manatees and dugongs**, known as sirenians, are the only vegetarian sea mammals in the world.

- **In the days of sail**, sailors sometimes mistook manatees, which can float upright in the water, for mermaids.

- **About 90 percent of Florida's manatees** carry scars on their bodies caused by power-boat propellers.

- **Manatees** are slow breeders, and currently more die each year than are born.

- **Manatees** have been used successfully to clear waterways of the fast-growing water hyacinth.

- **Stella's seacow** was a massive North Pacific sirenian, up to 9 m long and weighing 6400 kg. It was hunted to extinction in the 18th century.

- **Fossil evidence** shows that manatees and dugongs have existed for about 50 million years. They are probably related to elephants.

- **The teeth of manatees** are regularly replaced, being shed at the front as they wear out, and replaced by new ones moving forward.

- **Amazonian manatees**, found only in the Amazon River and its tributaries, fast during the 6-month dry season.

- **The dugong** of the Indian Ocean and South Pacific feeds on eel grass, the only flowering marine plant.

▲ *Manatees have rounded tails – dugongs' are more whale-like.*

# Tapirs

- **The forest-dwelling tapirs** of Asia and America are related to horses and rhinos, and probably resemble early horses.

- **Tapirs** moved across land bridges from North America to South America and Asia over 5 million years ago.

- **The Malayan tapir** has black-and-white colouring that breaks up its body outline in moonlit forests.

- **Tapirs use their long snouts as snorkels**, staying under water for several minutes to elude predators.

- **Newborn tapirs** have stripes and spots.

- **The South American mountain tapir** grazes at altitudes of over 5000 m.

- **The earliest-known tapir** lived some 55 million years ago.

- **Tapirs belong to** the *Perissodactyla* order of mammals, with an uneven number of toes per foot.

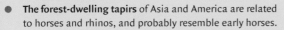

> **★ STAR FACT ★**
> The Malayan tapir walks along the bottom of rivers and lakes like a hippopotamus.

- **In South America**, engineers have built roads along ancient tapir trails, which accurately follow land contours.

▲ *The Malayan tapir eats the young shoots of rubber trees.*

# Llamas and their relatives

- **First domesticated some** 500 years ago, tame llamas and alpacas were important to the Inca empire (1400–1533 AD). The vicuña remained untameable.

- **Vicuña herds** defend two permanent territories, one where they feed, and a smaller one at a higher altitude where they sleep at night.

- **The Incas** used llamas to carry secret messages tied into their fur.

- **Vicuñas** can live at altitudes of 5486 m, where the air is too thin for most mammals.

- **Unlike** in other hoofed mammals, vicuñas' incisor teeth never stop growing.

◀ *Tame domestic llamas are usually mild-tempered, but still spit to show their anger.*

- **Fine vicuña wool** was reserved for the robes of the Inca royal family and their nobles.

- **When annoyed**, llamas spit at their opponents, sometimes including a pebble as a missile in with their saliva.

- **Llama herders** use the animals' fur for rugs and ropes, their hides for shoe leather, their fat for candles, their dung for fuel, and their milk and flesh for food.

- **Baby llamas** can get up and follow their mothers just 15–30 minutes after being born.

> ★ STAR FACT ★
> A llama can carry a 60-kg load up to 30 km a day across high mountainous terrain.

# Migration

- **Florida manatees** usually migrate south in winter, but recently they have moved instead into the warm water outlets of hydroelectric generating plants.

- **Hooded seals** usually migrate south from Greenland in the Atlantic Ocean, but in 1990 one seal ended up off California in the Pacific, having taken a wrong turn.

- **Migrating noctule bats** established themselves in Hawaii, after being blown 3000 km off course.

- **Migrating whales** travel huge distances with the aid of internal magnetic navigation.

> ★ STAR FACT ★
> Each year, grey whales migrate 20,000 km in all, going to and from their breeding grounds.

- **Oil pipe-lines** are serious obstacles to caribou, which follow traditional migratory routes every year.

- **Migrating European noctule bats** fly at high altitude, emitting loud, low-frequency sounds at one second intervals to keep in ground contact.

- **American grey squirrels** sometimes travel in their thousands, crossing roads, rivers and towns in their search for food.

- **Beluga whales** return to the estuaries where they were born to give birth.

- **Over 1 million wildebeest** take part in a circular seasonal migration in east Africa's Serengeti region.

▶ *The new-born grey whale calf accompanies its mother on the long journey from Mexican waters to the Arctic.*

# Rats

- **New World wood rats**, or pack rats, continually gather twigs and build them into mounds near their nests.

- **Polynesian voyagers** carried rats on their boats as a form of live meat.

- **One species** of the Southeast Asian bandicoot rat has a body and tail length of almost 1 m!

- **To stop the black rat** stowing away on ships, mooring ropes are sometimes fitted with metal cones, which the rats cannot get past.

- **Baby Norwegian rats** signal to playmates that their play-fights are not serious by occasionally flipping over onto their backs.

- **Rats** constantly investigate their environment, which makes them good problem-solvers in laboratories.

◀ Rats are among the world's most successful mammals.

- **Observers** have seen rats kick traps until they are sprung, before eating the bait in safety.

- **Norwegian or brown rats** are natural burrowers, and expert at colonizing human buildings.

- **Following heavy rains** in drought regions, 19th-century Australian settlers were subjected to plagues of long-haired rats.

★ STAR FACT ★
The black rat was indirectly responsible, via its fleas, for the death of 25 percent of the entire human population of Europe by bubonic plague between 1347 and 1352.

# Anteaters

- **To protect their long, curved digging claws**, giant anteaters have to walk awkwardly on the knuckles of their front feet.

- **Anteaters have no teeth.** They use their extremely long, sticky tongues to gather up termites after breaking into their concrete-hard mounds.

▼ The giant anteater sleeps up to 15 hours a day, and has one of the lowest mammal temperatures at 32.7°C.

- **The tamandua and pygmy anteaters** of South and Central America use their prehensile tails to climb trees, in search of termite and ant nests.

- **The Australian numbat** is the only marsupial adapted to feed exclusively on ants and termites. It has a long, sticky tongue but short, weak claws.

- **Giant anteaters**, over 2 m long from nose to tail tip, cover themselves with their bushy tails when sleeping.

- **Baby anteaters** ride clinging to their mother's backs until they are half her size.

- **Even jaguars are deterred** by the sharp, slashing claws of a giant anteater reared up on its hind legs.

- **The 15 cm long pygmy anteater** has jointed soles to its feet that help it to climb the trees in which it lives.

- **The mouth** of the giant anteater is so small that you could not insert a finger into it.

- **Fossils** found in Germany show that anteaters lived there over 50 million years ago.

# Pandas

- **In the late 1900s**, many pandas starved to death because the fountain bamboo they ate came to the end of its 100-year growth cycle and died back.

- **Giant pandas** often give birth to twins, but in the wild one cub is always left to die.

- **Pandas** have an inefficient digestive system – up to 50 percent of the plant material they eat passes out of the body intact within 10 hours.

- **Although bamboo** forms the bulk of its diet, the giant panda also eats fish, small birds and rodents.

▲ The giant panda eats sitting up, pushing bamboo canes into its mouth for 16 hours a day.

> ★ **STAR FACT** ★
> Giant and red pandas have an extra 'thumb' that enables them to grasp their food.

- **In ancient China**, pandas were believed to have magical powers, and people wore panda masks to ward off evil spirits.

- **Reduced in number** by hunting and deforestation, there are probably fewer than 1000 giant pandas left in the wild, in forest reserves in southeast China.

- **The giant panda** has an unsuccessful zoo breeding record, with about 20 successes in the last 50 years.

- **Much livelier** than the giant panda, the red panda is a nimble climber. It uses its long tail for balance, and when threatened rears up and hisses.

- **Giant pandas** reach a weight of up to 150 kg, but when new-born weigh only 100–150 g.

# Moles and shrews

- **Shrews** have to forage and eat almost continuously, day and night, to avoid dying of starvation.

- **The Namib golden mole** 'swims' through the desert sand, using its hypersensitive hearing to locate its insect prey.

- **The pygmy white-toothed shrew**, weighing about 2 g, is the smallest living land-based mammal on the planet.

- **European desmans** are aquatic members of the mole family, with long, flat tails, waterproof fur and webbed toes.

▶ Most of a mole's food comes from the creatures that fall into its tunnels.

- **The African armoured shrew** has such strong vertebrae that it can survive being stood on by a full-grown man.

- **After their milk teeth have gone**, shrews usually only have one set of teeth. When these wear out, the shrews die.

- **Some European water shrews** have stiff hairs on their feet and tail that trap air bubbles, enabling them to scurry across the surface of water.

- **Baby shrews** may follow their mother in a line, each one holding a mouthful of the rump of the one in front.

- **The star-nosed mole** has 22 mobile, pink tentacles around the end of its snout, which help it locate prey underground.

- **The American short-tailed shrew** has enough venom in its bite to kill 200 mice.

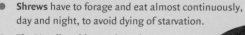
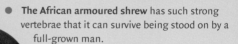

# Grizzly bears

- **The great hump** behind a grizzly's head is solid muscle, enabling it to overturn 50 kg rocks with its front paws, or kill an elk with a single blow.

- **During its winter sleep** the grizzly loses about 1 kg of bodyweight each day. Some grizzlies emerge from their sleep 50 percent lighter.

- **Grizzlies once ranged** across the USA, with numbers as high as 50,000–100,000. But as their terrain has been taken over by humans, their numbers have fallen to 6000–8000.

- **Most grizzlies are dark brown** in colour, but regional colouring ranges from black to very pale yellow.

- **Despite their great size**, grizzlies are nimble enough to catch squirrels and mice, and can reach a speed of over 55 km/h when charging.

▶ Grizzly mothers give birth to their cubs in their dens in winter, and go on to look after them for anything up to a further 4–5 years, teaching them to forage and hunt, and protecting them from predators.

- **Native Americans** had great respect for the grizzly, and apologized before killing it, sometimes laying out ceremonial clothes for it to wear in the spirit world.

- **Grizzlies are immensely strong**. They have been known to bite through cast iron, bend rifle barrels, and open up cars like sardine cans in search of food.

- **Originating in China**, the ancestors of the modern grizzly crossed land bridges from Asia to North America some 40,000 years ago.

- **Grizzlies** often enter their winter dens just ahead of a snowstorm, so that the snow covers up their fresh tracks and seals them in for their long winter sleep.

Guard hairs have light-coloured tips giving a 'grizzled' appearance this is how this bear gets its common name grizzly bear

★ STAR FACT ★
The huge Kodiak grizzly bear of the Alaskan coastal islands can reach a height of 3 m on its hind legs, and weigh up to 1 tonne.

Non-retractable claws

◀ Grizzlies sometimes dig huge holes to excavate food, using their powerful shoulder muscles and long, non-retractable claws.

# Arctic life

- **White fur** helps creatures such as Arctic hares to hide from predators in the snow, but also helps predators such as polar bears avoid detection as they hunt.

- **The ringed seal**, the most northerly of the seals, has been reported at the North Pole itself.

- **Polar bears** and Arctic foxes have tiny ears to reduce the loss of body heat in the icy Arctic.

- **Narwhals and belugas** migrate from the Arctic to warm estuaries and fjords to give birth, returning to the pack ice in late summer.

- **The bulky Arctic musk ox** has a double coat of dense wool overlaid with thick hair, and can stay in the Arctic all year, surviving temperatures of -70°C.

- **During blizzards**, musk oxen form a circle with the calves protected in the centre from the wind and snow.

- **The walrus** is a permanent inhabitant of the Arctic region, spending much of its life on the pack ice.

- **The ringed seal** gives birth in a snow cave, entered from the water through a hole in the ice.

- **Inuit hunters** fear a female walrus defending her calf more than they fear a polar bear.

- **In winter and spring**, Arctic foxes depend on scavenging from polar bear seal-kills – but can end up on the menu themselves!

◀ *A walrus's thick layer of blubber keeps it warm in sub-zero Arctic temperatures.*

# Lemurs

- **All lemurs** live on the island of Madagascar, where they evolved in isolation, separated from the African mainland by the 300 km wide Mozambique Channel.

- **In lemur groups** the females are the more aggressive protectors of territory than the males.

- **Early European travellers** to Madagascar described a giant lemur, now extinct, that was as large as a calf.

- **Contesting male lemurs** transfer scent from their wrist glands onto their tails, then use their tails to hurl scent 'bombs' over their heads at their rivals.

▶ *The ring-tailed lemur uses its distinctive tail to signal to others of its species. It may live in groups of up to 30 individuals.*

- **Lemurs were able to evolve** into their many species on Madagascar mainly because they had no competition from monkeys or other primates.

- **Long after Madagascar broke away** from Africa 65–50 million years ago, the lemurs' ancestors crossed the slowly widening channel on rafts of floating vegetation.

- **The aye-aye**, a close relative of the lemurs, has huge ears and can hear grubs chewing wood beneath bark. It extracts them with an elongated middle finger.

- **The indri** is the largest lemur, at up to 1 m from its nose tip to its almost tail-less rump.

- **Fat-tailed dwarf lemurs** sleep through the dry season in July and August, living on the fat stored in the thick bases of their tails.

- **Lemurs groom** using a special claw on one finger, and their front teeth, which resemble a comb.

# Capybaras and coypus

- **The South American capybara** is the world's largest rodent, a water-loving giant up to 134 cm long and 64 kg in weight.

- **Capybaras graze** in large groups on river banks. At the first sign of danger they dash into the water and the adults surround the babies.

▲ *The capybara spends much of its life in the water, and has webbed feet.*

- **South American coypu females** suckle their young while swimming, from rows of teats high on their sides.

- **Coypu** were hunted almost to extinction in the 1800s for their thick, soft fur, overlain with coarse hairs.

- **Captive farming of coypu** for what was called 'nutria' fur began in the 1920s. Many countries now have feral populations established by escaped captives.

- **The male capybara** has a hairless scent gland on its snout called the morillo (Spanish for 'small hill').

- **Capybaras mate in the water**, but give birth on land. All the females in a group feed the young if they have milk.

- **Catholic priests** once allowed capybaras to be eaten during Lent, because they considered them to be close relatives of fish (which were permitted to be eaten).

- **A capybara can stay under water** for up to 5 minutes, sleeping there with only its nose sticking out.

- **Some extinct capybara** weighed as much as a grizzly.

# The weasel family

- **In years of vole plagues**, the European common weasel may have up to three litters, because food is available.

- **Pest control** of American prairie dogs has led to the extinction of the black-footed ferret in much of its range.

- **Tribesmen in Burma** are reported to have used trained weasels to kill wild geese and the young of wild goats.

> ★ STAR FACT ★
> The American least weasel, at 15 cm long and weighing 30 g, is the world's smallest carnivore.

- **The 25 kg wolverine**, the largest weasel close relative, has large feet for hunting reindeer in deep snow.

- **Male weasels** are often twice the size of females.

- **Bred for the fur trade**, many American mink escaped into the European countryside, replacing European mink and depleting water vole populations.

- **Ferrets**, traditionally used in Europe to catch rabbits, are a domesticated form of the European polecat.

- **Black-footed ferret young** are cared for by their mother in a separate burrow until they are self-sufficient.

- **In New Zealand**, introduced weasels have almost wiped out some native birds by eating their eggs.

◄ *A mink's broad diet includes fish, bringing it into direct competition with otters.*

# Toothed whales

- **Beluga whales** are the only white whales. They were once called 'sea canaries' by seamen, because their bird-like calls can be heard above the water's surface.

- **Sperm whales** will form a defensive circle, heads to the centre, around young or wounded group members, and beat off predators with their tails.

- **Beaked whales** feed mainly on cuttlefish and squid – one bottle-nosed whale was found to have the remains of 10,000 cuttlefish in its stomach.

- **All dolphins are toothed whales.** The orca – the largest member of the dolphin family – sometimes half-beaches itself to catch seals at the water's edge.

- **Beaked whales will dive to 500 m** or more to escape orcas, staying in the depths for an hour or more until the danger has passed.

- **Spending 85 percent of the day** under the sea's surface, bottle-nosed whales have been recorded diving to well over 1500 m in their search for their squid prey.

- **Beluga whales** are frequently stranded in coastal shallows as the tide retreats, and wait patiently for the next tide to refloat them.

> **★ STAR FACT ★**
> The male strap-toothed whale has two teeth in its lower jaw that grow to wrap around its upper jaw, severely restricting its ability to open its beak-like mouth.

- **The massive sperm whale**, which weighs up to 70 tonnes, has the largest brain of any mammal on Earth. Fat deposits in its brain case help to focus the sounds the whale produces by echolocation.

- **Toothed whales** cooperate with one another far more than baleen whales do, often working together to herd prey into a tight mass for easy feeding.

▼ *Orcas are found throughout the world's oceans. They travel in close-knit social groups of up to 40 individuals, and hunt cooperatively, herding prey fish such as salmon into a close-packed mass before attacking them.*

*Extremely tall dorsal fin (straight and vertical in males, curved in females)*

*Pale markings help break up the body's outline*

# What are marsupials?

- **Marsupials** are born in a tiny, undeveloped form, and many spend months in a protective pouch, attached to a teat.

- **Marsupials** originated in America some 100 million years ago, at a time when America and Australia were still joined.

- **The red kangaroo** is the largest living marsupial today.

- **Marsupial mouse**, marsupial rat and marsupial mole are the popular names of some Australian marsupials.

- **Marsupials** have lower body temperatures than most other mammals, and have smaller brains than placentals of a similar size.

▲ *Opossums use their long toes and prehensile tails for grasping branches.*

- **Two-thirds of all marsupials** live in Australia and New Guinea. One-third are mainly South American opossums.

- **One marsupial**, the Australian numbat, eats only termites and ants

- **The wombat's pouch** faces backwards, so that the young are protected from pieces of flying earth when the mother is digging.

- **In Australia**, kangaroos fill the plains-grazing niche occupied elsewhere by antelopes and gazelles (placental mammals).

- **Many small marsupials**, including some opossums, do not have pouches.

# Leopards and jaguars

- **A leopard** can carry a prey animal three times its own weight up a tree, out of reach of scavengers.

- **Black panthers** are leopards with black pigmentation. Any leopard litter may include a black cub.

- **The South American jaguar** is America's only big cat.

- **A frozen leopard** carcase was found on Mount Kilimanjaro, Africa, at an altitude of 5692 m.

- **The jaguar** catches not only fish, but also otters, turtles, alligators and frogs.

- **Snow leopards**, which inhabit the mountains of Central Asia, have never been known to roar.

- **The snow leopard** has paws cushioned with hair to act as snow shoes. In the Himalayas it seldom goes below 2000 m, and sometimes goes as high as 5500 m.

- **Leopards** have survived successfully partly because they will eat almost anything, from crabs to baboons.

- **By far the best climber** of the big cats, the leopard sometimes drops straight out of a tree onto its victim.

- **The jaguar** was worshipped as a god by early South American cultures.

▶ *The leopard is by far the best climber of the big cats, and often sleeps in the branches, as well as storing food there and mounting a look out.*

# Armadillos and pangolins

- **The South American three-banded armadillo** can roll itself up into an impenetrable ball.
- **For swimming across rivers**, some armadillos increase their buoyancy by inflating their intestines with air.
- **The giant armadillo** has up to 100 small teeth.
- **The African giant pangolin** has a long tongue that extends internally as far as its pelvis.
- **The nine-banded armadillo** has four identical, same-sex young per litter, all developed from 1 egg.
- **The armadillo's armour** is made up of small bone plates covered in heavy skin. The pangolin's consists of overlapping plates of horn.

▶ *Armadillos walk mainly on their hind legs, with their forelegs just brushing the ground.*

> ★ STAR FACT ★
> Stone Age people used the 1.5 m high shell of the *Glyptodon*, an armadillo, as a shelter.

- **The long-tailed tree pangolin** and the white-bellied tree pangolin hardly ever leave the trees.
- **Pangolins** often use only their back legs when running.
- **The long-tailed tree pangolin** has 37–46 tail vertebrae – a mammal record for the most tail bones.

# Domestic cattle

- **European domestic cattle** are descended from the aurochs, a large wild ox seen in ancient cave drawings.
- **The wild auroch** was domesticated about 6500 BC.

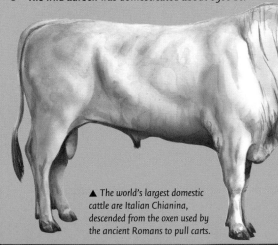

▲ *The world's largest domestic cattle are Italian Chianina, descended from the oxen used by the ancient Romans to pull carts.*

- **Humped zebu** are the main domestic cattle of Asia.
- **In India**, zebu are considered holy by Hindus, and are allowed to roam free, eat fruit off market stalls, and sleep in the roads.
- **Domesticated water buffalo** in Egypt, India and southeast Asia are powerful draught animals, and are also regularly milked.
- **India** is the country with the most domestic cattle: more than 270 million.
- **A large feral population** of domesticated water buffalo lives in northern Australia.
- **Masai cattle herders** in Kenya regularly take blood from the throats of their cattle and drink it.
- **In Tibet**, domesticated yaks thrive at altitudes well over 6000 m, providing meat, milk and transport.
- **Domestic cattle** sleep for up to 8 minutes at a time, for a maximum total of 60 minutes in 24 hours.

# Kangaroos

- **Female kangaroos** suckling young of different ages at the same time are able to produce milk of different concentrations for the individual youngsters.

- **Hopping** is a good way to travel fast, but to go slowly a kangaroo has to use its tail as a fifth supporting leg.

- **Some tree kangaroos** can leap to the ground from as high as 30 m without coming to harm.

- **New-born kangaroos** are deaf as well as naked and blind.

- **Flat out**, some kangaroos can reach a speed of almost 65 km/h, making huge hops of over 8 m in length.

- **When bounding**, most kangaroos can only move their hind

▼ A moving kangaroo uses its large, muscular tail as a counter-balance.

legs both at the same time, but when swimming can move them alternately.

- **Hare wallabies** are small members of the kangaroo family weighing only 1–4.5 kg.

- **Rock wallabies** live on rocky outcrops. Their rough-soled feet are fringed with stiff hairs, enabling them to climb steep rock faces.

- **When male kangaroos fight**, they support themselves on their tails and deliver slashing kicks with their hind legs.

long hind legs make the kangaroo the fastest marsupial

> ★ **STAR FACT** ★
> Prehistoric kangaroos in Australia included a giant that stood 2.4 m tall and weighed 270 kg, and at least one meat-eating species.

# Voles and lemmings

- **At up to 2 kg**, the American muskrat is 130 times heavier than most voles.

- **Every 3 or 4 years** some vole and lemming species undergo population explosions, followed by high numbers of deaths from stress and food shortages.

- **The mole-lemming** of the Central Asian steppes digs tunnels using its protruding incisor teeth.

- **Eurasian water voles** live in river bank burrows with entrances below the level of the water's surface.

- **At the peak** of a lemming population explosion, lemmings devastate the local vegetation – and the next summer predators can find them more easily.

- **At 1 m below the snow's surface**, a lemming's winter nest can be 10°C, while outside it is below freezing.

- **Some species of voles and lemmings** have their first litters when they are only 5 weeks old themselves.

- **The collared lemming** is the only rodent to change the colour of its coat to white in winter.

- **Lemmings** will swim across any water in their path as they migrate in search of new food sources. If the water is too wide to cross, they drown – hence the myth of lemmings committing mass suicide.

- **A fox can hear** and smell voles moving under the snow.

▼ The European water vole stores food for the winter.

# Communication

▲ Members of the dog family use ear positions as part of their language.

- **Whales' low frequency** calls travel thousands of km through the water.

- **Some whales** communicate with complex 'songs'. All the individuals in one ocean region sing the same song.

- **Some of the puppies** from the litter of a poodle bred with a jackal had the poodle's 'language'. Others had the jackal's. But the two groups could not communicate with one another.

- **Male chimps** establish their status by seeing who can make the most noise.

- **One chimp** learned to use 130 gestures of American Sign Language.

- **Cats and dogs** erect the hair on parts of their bodies to impress rivals and mates, or frighten off predators.

- **The gorilla groups** over 90 percent of all vocal signals and calls are made by the males.

- **A well-fed lion** can walk head-up through a herd of antelope without panicking them, but if its head is low, the antelope run, knowing it is hunting.

- **The sifaka lemur** has one alarm call to warn of birds of prey, and another to warn of snakes.

- **Many young mammals** have a 'play' body language just for mock fights.

◀ Chimps communicate with a wide range of facial expressions.

# Old World monkeys

- **Japanese macaques** sit in hot springs in winter to keep warm.

- **Some female red colobus monkeys** in Gambia gang up to attack, and even kill, strange males.

- **The Old World monkeys** of Africa and Asia rest by sitting down, and have tough pads on their bottoms to prevent sores developing.

- **Some colobus monkeys** gnaw on the charcoal of burned trees to help neutralize the toxins in some leaves.

◀ Old world monkeys forage for plant food during the day, and rest by night.

- **Red colobus monkeys** often travel in mixed groups with diana monkeys, as the diana monkeys are better at spotting the chimps that prey on colobus monkeys.

- **Talapoin monkeys** in Central Africa live in forests that are frequently flooded. Excellent swimmers, they often sleep on branches overhanging the water.

- **In Japan**, in areas where humans regularly feed macaques, the birth-rate of the animals rockets, leading to groups of up to 1000.

- **The Hanuman grey langur** of India is protected by religious law, in honour of Hanuman, the monkey god.

- **Some Japanese macaques** have learned to dip food in the sea to clean and salt it, and have become good swimmers in the process.

★ STAR FACT ★
The Barbary macaque is the only primate, apart from humans, living in Europe.

# Lions

- **The largest-known wild lion** was an African male man-eater, shot in 1936, and weighing 313 kg (the average male lion weighs 150–190 kg).

- **Male lions** have the job of protecting the pride, leaving the hunting to the females most of the time. But the males insist on eating first from any kills!

▲ Lion cubs suckle from their mother for the first six months of their lives, but begin to eat meat at three months old.

▶ Only male lions have a mane, which shows off their size, and also protects them during fights. The females are the main hunters in the pride.

★ STAR FACT ★
A male lion can eat up to 30 kg of meat at one sitting, and then will not need to eat again for several days.

- **Lions** are the only big cats that lead social lives, cooperating in hunting and sharing their prey.

- **Lions usually kill large prey** such as zebra by suffocating them, biting their throats and holding them around the neck with their paws.

- **When a foreign male** takes over a pride of lions by driving off its leading male, he kills cubs under about 6 months old and mates with their mothers.

- **Lions** spend most of their time sleeping, usually dozing for about 20 hours of the day.

- **Once widespread** throughout Southwest Asia and India, the only lions now surviving outside Africa are a few Asiatic lions in the Indian Gir Forest wildlife reserve.

- **The roar** of a male lion, used to intimidate rivals and locate pride members is audible 8 km away.

- **A male lion** will not usually allow other pride members to share a kill until he has had enough, though he may make an exception for small cubs.

# Parental care of mammals

- **Many mammals carry** their young around with them. Some bats even go hunting with a youngster aboard.

- **Mother whales** have to nudge and encourage newborn young up to the surface to take their first breath, often aided by 'aunts' from the same pod.

- **In wild dog packs**, several females may take turns to suckle and guard all the young in the group.

- **Sperm whale** offspring may suckle for up to 15 years.

- **Elephant young** are born after 22 months.

- **Mother cheetahs** teach their young how to hunt by bringing small live prey back for them to practice on.

- **A female big cat** carries her young by holding the entire head in her mouth, in a gap behind her teeth.

- **Young kangaroos** leave the pouch at 5–11 months, but continue to stick their head in to suckle for 6 months.

- **Many cats**, large and small, start to train their young by allowing them to attack their twitching tails.

◄ The baby baboon depends on its mother for food and transport, but is also protected from danger by certain males in the group.

> ★ STAR FACT ★
> Baby gorillas may only climb on the silver-back while they still have a white rump tuft.

# Dolphins

- **Groups of common dolphins**, travelling and feeding together, may number up to 2000 individuals.

- **Orcas**, or killer whales, are actually the largest species of dolphin, though they feed on other dolphin species.

- **There are five species** of freshwater dolphin living in Asian and South American rivers. Most catch fish by sound rather than sight.

- **Dolphins** have been known to aid humans by keeping them afloat and driving off attacking sharks.

- **Spinner dolphins** are named for the acrobatic leaps they perform, spinning up to 7 times in mid air.

- **The Atlantic hump-backed dolphin** helps fishermen in West Africa by driving shoals of mullet into their nets.

- **In Mexico's Baja California**, bottle-nosed dolphins chase fish up onto the shore, then roll up onto the beach, completely out of the water, to grab them.

- **Military observers** once recorded a group of dolphins swimming at 64 km/h in the bow wave of a warship.

- **The striped dolphin**, seen in ancient Greek paintings, leaps up to 7 m to perform somersaults and spins.

- **The Yangtse dolphin**, or baiji, is one of the world's rarest mammals – probably less than 300 survive.

◄ Many dolphin species 'spy-hop', holding their heads out of the water as they check on their surroundings for predators and potential food.

# Moose and elk

- **The world's largest deer** (called moose in North America and elk in Europe) stand up to 2 m tall at the shoulder.

- **Moose escape wolves** by retreating to marshes and lakes.

- **The prehistoric Irish elk**, which became extinct 10,000 years ago, had massive antlers up to 4.3 m across.

- **Moose** have reached Isle Royale in Lake Superior, USA, by swimming across 32 km of water.

- **To protect her calf** from wolves, the mother moose shepherds it into shallow water and stands between it and the wolves, which usually give up.

★ **STAR FACT** ★

The moose has been known to dive to 5.5 m, staying under water for 30 seconds, to reach water plants and roots.

- **A moose will use its great weight** to push over young trees to get at twigs and shoots.

- **A moose eats** the equivalent of 20,000 leaves a day.

- **The antlers** of a moose are 'palmate', with broad areas like hands.

- **A young moose** stays with its mother for almost a year, but she chases it away just before she is about to give birth to a new calf.

▶ Two male elk spar with their antlers, which they lose and regain every year.

# Australasian marsupials

- **The brush-tailed possum** is Australia's most common marsupial. It often moves into the lofts of houses.

- **Kangaroos** are not restricted to Australia – several tree-kangaroo species live in Papua New Guinea.

- **Australian marsupial moles** strongly resemble true moles, but have different ancestors.

★ **STAR FACT** ★

Kangaroos are serious competitors with sheep for grass, because with front teeth in both jaws instead of just one, they crop it much closer.

- **Wombats live in burrows** and weigh up to 40 kg (but one fossil wombat weighed in at a hefty 100 kg).

- **The Tasmanian devil** is the largest surviving marsupial carnivore, eating mainly carrion.

- **The Australian pygmy possum** sleeps so soundly that you can pick it up without it waking.

- **The muscular tail** of the long-tailed dunnart is up to 210 mm long (twice its body length).

- **Some bandicoots** (nocturnal, rat-like marsupials) have a gestation period of just 12.5 days – a mammal record.

- **The striped possum** digs for grubs in tree-bark with an elongated finger.

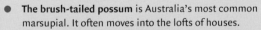

▶ The stocky wombat is related to the koala, but cannot climb trees and digs large burrows.

# Ice age mammals

- **Woolly mammoths** adapted to ice age conditions by developing a thick coat of dark hair, and using their enormous tusks to sweep snow off the grasses they ate.

- **The woolly rhinoceros** was up to 5 m long, and roamed the tundras of northern Europe and Asia. Like the mammoth, it featured in the cave drawings of hunters.

- **Several ice age mammals** became giant-sized to help them combat the cold, including aurochs – the giant ancestors of modern cattle.

- **Many mammoths** are so well preserved in the Siberian permafrost that their flesh is still edible, and their last meals remain in their stomachs.

- **On the tundra** at the edge of the ice sheets, some mammals migrated south in winter. Others, like the huge European cave bear, hibernated in their lairs.

- *Smilodon*, a large sabre-toothed cat, inhabited Ice Age North America, dying out along with many of the large animals it preyed on.

- **Many mammal species died out** between 12,000 and 10,000 years ago, as the last ice age ended. But some survived, including musk-oxen, horses, hyenas and saiga antelopes.

▲ Sabre-toothed *Smilodon* ranged from Canada to Argentina. It used its huge upper canine teeth to slice through the tough hides of large prey animals and bite out big chunks of flesh.

> ★ **STAR FACT** ★
> Cave bears used the same caves for many generations. One cave in Austria contained the bones of up to 50,000 individual bears.

- **The Ice Age bison** were similar to modern bison, but had 1-m long horns on either side of their heads.

- **The giant short-faced bear**, which inhabited North America until the end of the last ice age, was twice the size of the Kodiak bear, had long legs and weighed up to 1 tonne.

▲ The woolly mammoth had small ears to prevent heat-loss, and beneath its hairy skin was a thick layer of heat-preserving fat.

# Mongooses, civets and genets

- **African banded mongooses** gang up together to repel and attack predators such as jackals.

- **The Malaysian binturong** is related to civets, and is the only Old World mammal with a prehensile tail, which it uses as a brake when descending trees.

- **The palm civet** of Asia is known as the toddy cat, because it has a taste for a fermented alcoholic drink.

- **Civets** were once kept captive in Ethiopia and 'milked' of their strong-smelling musk, which was used in the perfume industry.

- **A mongoose will tire out a cobra** by making quick movements, then kill it.

- **The dwarf mongoose** marks its territory by doing a handstand to deposit a scent mark as high as possible on a rock or bush.

- **Common genets** are found in France and Spain. They may have been introduced in medieval times as pets and rat-catchers, by the Moors of North Africa.

▲ *The banded mongoose lives and forages in large groups, leaving a baby-sitting adult back in the den to guard the young.*

- **Otter civets**, like true otters, have webbed feet and closable nostrils. They catch fish and can climb trees.

- **Largest of the civet-mongoose family**, the fossa of Madagascar has a cat-like head and retractable claws.

- **In fights** against members of the same species, some mongooses curl over and present their posterior to their opponent, biting at him between their hindlegs.

# Camouflage

- **Stripes** benefit both predators and prey by breaking up the body shape, for example in tigers and zebras.

- **The simplest camouflage** makes an animal a similar colour to its surroundings, such as the white of a polar bear in snow.

- **Some whales and dolphins** are dark on top and light underneath, camouflaging them against the dark of deep water or the light of the sky.

- **Some camouflage** mimics the broken shapes of light shining through trees, as in the dappled markings of giraffes.

- **The young** of many mammal species, such as lions and pigs, have early camouflage markings that disappear as the animals grow older.

**★ STAR FACT ★**
Not all camouflage is visual – some mammals roll in dung to disguise their own scents.

- **The coats of Arctic foxes** and hares change from dark in summer to white in winter.

- **Bold markings**, such as the contrasting shapes of the oryx, camouflage by breaking up body outline.

- **The bobcat's spots** camouflage it in rocks, while the similar-shaped plain lynx merges with forest.

- **The elephant's huge grey form** disappears as it stands still in the shadows.

◀ *The orca's light underparts make it less visible from underneath against the water's surface in daytime.*

# New World marsupials

- **American marsupials** are nearly all from the opossum family, which has lived in America for 55 million years.

- **Opossums** have spread successfully northwards as far as Canada, but are vulnerable to frostbitten ears and tails.

- **When attacked**, the opossum goes into a death-like trance, called 'playing 'possum'.

- **Opossums entwine** their prehensile tails around those of their young when carrying them.

- **The Virginia opossum** usually has 13 teats in its pouch, but often gives birth to a higher number of young. Those that are not able to attach to a teat soon die.

- **The yapok**, or water opossum, is the only mainly aquatic marsupial. It has webbed rear feet.

- **The monito del monte** is a rat-sized marsupial unrelated

▲ Opossums eat fruit, flowers and nectar, as well as insects.

to opossums, and found in Chile's cool forests.

- **Once a baby opossum** has attached itself to a teat, it cannot let go until it is fully developed.

- **The newly born mouse opossum** is no larger than a grain of rice – the smallest new-born mammal.

> ★ STAR FACT ★
> The Maya civilization of Central America believed the opossum to be a magical animal.

# Mountain lions or pumas

- **The mountain lion**, or puma, is the widest-ranging American mammal, occurring from Canada in the north to southern Chile in the south.

- **Mountain lions** are the largest American desert carnivores.

▶ The puma is the largest of the so-called small cats, and its prey ranges from mice to full-grown deer.

- **The Patagonian puma** has a hunting territory of up to 100 sq km. Its main prey is the llama-like guanaco.

- **As a form of territorial marking**, pumas build little piles of soil or vegetation called scrapes.

- **Although the size of a leopard**, the mountain lion is classified as a small cat because it can purr.

- **In the Sierra Nevada**, the main prey of mountain lions is the mule deer, which can be twice the lion's weight.

- **High altitude varieties** of mountain lion may be much larger (113 kg) than those living lower down (45 kg).

- **Below the timber line**, the mountain lion hunts by night. At higher altitudes it may have to hunt by day.

- **There are few reports** of mountain lion attacks on humans, but attacks have increased as humans have taken over more of the mountain lion's territories.

- **Mountain lions** are solitary, avoiding one another except to mate. When the young leave their mother, they relocate at least 45 km away.

# Black bears

- **American black bears** vary in colour from black, brown, cinnamon, honey and grey, to white.

- **Beavers are a favourite food** of some black bears.

- **In autumn**, feeding up for the winter sleep, black bears put on up to 1.5 kg per day.

- **Black bears mate** in the summer, but the fertilized egg does not begin to develop until the autumn. The cubs are born in January.

- **'Nuisance' bears** that have learned to scavenge garbage in US national parks have to be tranquillized and moved to new areas.

▶ Black bears occasionally raid people's beehives and orchards, as well as city dumps.

- **The most northerly** Canadian black bears have a varied diet ranging from caribou and seals to birds' eggs and tiny shrimp.

- **The sun bear** of Southeast Asia is the world's smallest bear, at 27–65 kg. It specializes in gathering honey and insects with its long tongue.

- **South America's only bear** is the spectacled bear, which builds feeding and sleeping platforms in the branches of fruit trees.

- **The black sloth bear** of India has a mobile snout and closable nostrils for dealing with ants.

> ★ STAR FACT ★
> Asiatic black bears are constipated when they awake from their winter hibernation, and drink birch tree sap as a laxative.

# Mole rats

- **Unlike most rodents**, mole rats live for several years.

- **Mole rats** have extremely loose skin, which enables them to turn round in the tightest of tunnels.

- **Naked mole rats** have no fur. They live in colonies, like some insects, with a queen that bears all the young, and workers that dig the tunnels.

- **Mole rats**, unlike moles, dig with their protruding

▶ Naked mole rats enjoy stable temperatures of around 29°C in their humid burrows, when outside surface temperatures can be as high as 60°C.

front teeth. Lip folds prevent them swallowing earth.

- **Mole rats' eyes** are probably blind, but they may use the eye surface to detect air currents in the burrow.

- **Mole rats have been observed** biting off the growing sprouts of roots and tubers before storing them, thus preventing them losing nutritive value before use.

- **Blind mole rats** of the eastern Mediterranean have skin-covered eyes. They dig individual tunnel systems up to 350 m long.

- **Naked mole rats** cooperate to dig tunnels, several moving the soil to the surface and one kicking it out of the hole.

- **The 'queen'** of a naked mole rat colony suppresses the breeding ability of other females by means of chemical signals.

- **The Cape dune mole rat** moves up to half a tonne of soil in just 1 month.

# Prehistoric elephants

- **Platybelodon**, which lived up to 14 million years ago, had huge, shovel-like lower teeth for scooping up and cutting water plants, and a short, broad trunk.

- **Remains of 91-cm tall elephants** were found on Malta.

- **The last woolly mammoths** were a dwarf species that died out less than 7000 years ago.

- **Two million years ago**, *Deinotherium* may have used its curled tusks for scraping bark from trees.

- **The elephant *Gomphotheres*** had four straight tusks, and lived in Europe, Africa and Pakistan.

- **Forest-dwelling *Anancus*** had straight tusks up to 4 m long, which it used for digging up roots.

- **At one time**, more commercial ivory came from frozen mammoths in Siberia than from modern elephants.

- **Some Stone Age Siberian people** built huts from the tusks and long bones of the mammoths they hunted.

- **Mastodons** had smaller bodies and tusks than mammoths, and had a different diet.

> ★ STAR FACT ★
> One of the earliest-known elephant ancestors, *Moeritherium*, lived about 38 million years ago.

▲ Platybelodon *was a swamp elephant that devoured huge amounts of water plants, scooping them up with its lower jaw.*

# The mating game

- **In some species** of Australian marsupial mouse, the male dies after a two-week mating period.

- **A beaver** stays with its mate for many years, producing a new litter each year.

- **A male hedgehog** courts a female by circling her, sometimes wearing a deep groove in the soil, until she accepts him.

- **Male Californian sea-lions** bark to guard their mating territory. Underwater, the barks produce bursts of bubbles.

- **The hooded seal** impresses females by inflating a nostril lining into a red balloon.

- **The red markings** on a male mandrill's blue and red face become brighter during the mating season.

- **To attract potential mates**, orangutan males emit a series of loud roars that tail off into groans.

- **White rhino males** have strict territorial boundaries. They try to keep receptive females within the territory, but if a female strays outside, he will not follow her.

- **Hippos prefer to mate in the water**, with the female often completely submerged, and having to raise her head to breath every so often.

▶ A male narwhal's tusk can be up to 3 m long, and is actually one of its only two teeth.

> ★ STAR FACT ★
> Narwhal males compete for mates by 'fencing' with their long, spiral tusks.

# Bats

- **The earliest insect-eating bat fossil** is 50 million years old, and the earliest fruit bat fossil only 35 million years old, so they probably evolved from different ancestors.

- **The bumblebee bat** of Thailand is the world's smallest mammal. Its body is just 3 cm long, and it weighs only 2 g.

- **In one North American cave**, 10 million Mexican free-tailed bats give birth each year to 10 million young over a period of about a week.

- **Bat species** form 22 percent of the world's mammals, and are the most common rainforest mammal.

- **In some bat species**, males are known sometimes to produce milk, but it is not known if they ever suckle the young.

- **A resting bat** emits 10 sound pulses per second, rising to 30 per second as it flies, 60 per second when approaching an object, and 200 per second when approaching an insect.

- **Australia's ghost bat** is the continent's only meat-eating bat. It hunts and devours frogs, birds, lizards, small mammals, and even other bats.

- **The bulldog bat** feeds on fish, grabbing them from the surface of the water with its specially elongated toes.

- **Many tropical nectar- and pollen-eating bats** are important pollinators of plants, including some trees. They transfer the pollen from one plant to another as they feed inside the flowers.

▲ The only mammals capable of powered flight, bats come in a diverse range of shapes and sizes – but all have excellent hearing. Shown here are: (1) the red bat, (2) the Mexican fishing bat, (3) the African yellow-winged bat, (4) the noctule bat, (5) the long-eared bat, (6) the hoary bat, (7) the horse or hammer-headed bat, (8) the lesser horseshoe bat and (9) the spotted bat.

---

★ **STAR FACT** ★

The vampire bat uses razor-sharp teeth to make tiny cuts in the limbs of sleeping mammals, and then laps up the blood.

# Baleen whales

- **Baleen whales** include blue whales, the planet's largest mammals – the heaviest known weighed over 190 tonnes.
- **Blue whale calves** grow about 1000 times faster in the womb than human babies.

▼ Baleen whales' pleated lower jaws take in masses of water per gulp.

> ★ STAR FACT ★
> Humpback whales produce columns of air bubbles that force their prey into clusters.

- **Humpback whales** have been seen to leap out of the water as many as 100 times in quick succession.
- **Right whales** were so-named because they were the 'right' ones to hunt – heavy with oil, meat and baleen.
- **Despite being protected** since the 1940s, there are less than 320 northern right whales surviving.
- **The baleen plates** of modern baleen whales evolved about 30 million years ago.
- **Right whales** force a constant current of water through their baleen plates to trap their food – krill organisms.
- **Bowhead whales** are estimated to eat up to 1500 kg of filtered-out food organisms daily for 130 days at a time.
- **Women's corsets** were once made out of baleen plates.

# Buffaloes

- **The African buffalo** will stalk and attack a human even if unprovoked, and will mob lions and kill their cubs if it gets the chance.
- **The wild Asiatic buffalo** can weigh up to 1200 kg, and has the longest horns of any living animal, sometimes exceeding a 4-m spread.
- **African buffaloes** have a wide range of vocal communications, including signals for moving off, direction-changing, danger and aggressive intent.
- **In Australia in the dry season**, female feral water buffaloes leave their calves with a 'nursemaid' on the edge of the plains where they graze.
- **The African savannah buffalo** can weigh up to 875 kg, and herds can number several thousand.
- **A wounded African buffalo** will ambush its hunter, exploding out of cover in an unstoppable charge.
- **Needing to drink every day**, African buffaloes never stray more than 15 km from water.
- **Buffaloes rarely fight.** Contests consist of tossing the head, pawing the ground and circling, before one bull walks away.

- **Blind or crippled buffaloes** are sometimes observed living healthily in the herd, whereas loners would soon die.
- **In the rinderpest cattle epidemic** of the 1890s, up to 10,000 African buffaloes died for every one animal that survived.

▼ Swamp mud helps protect a water buffalo's skin from heat and insects.

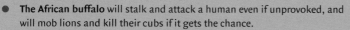

# Lynxes and bobcats

- **Bobcats and lynxes** are closely related, but the lynx inhabits northern conifer forests and swamps, and the bobcat prefers rocky regions with dense undergrowth.

- **Lynxes have shorter tails** than bobcats, and their longer legs help them to move through deep snow.

- **Chased by dogs**, the bobcat often takes to water, where it is a superior swimmer to its pursuers.

- **In experiments**, bobcats with clipped ear-tufts heard less well, suggesting the tufts aid their hearing.

- **Lynxes have thick fur** on the soles of their feet to keep them warm and help prevent slipping on icy surfaces.

- **The bobcat** is only found in America, but the lynx has populations across Europe and Asia.

> ★ STAR FACT ★
> Snow hares provide 70 percent of the North American lynx's diet. Lynx numbers fluctuate with the 10-year population cycle of the snow hare.

▲ Its long ear tufts help the lynx to hear its main prey, the snow hare, and long legs enable it to chase its prey through deep snow.

- **Bobcats** are taught to hunt by the age of 7 months. At 12 months the mother drives them away.

- **Unlike the lynx**, the bobcat flourishes in deserts.

- **The bobcat may live up to 20 years**, eating rabbits, prairie dogs, rattlesnakes and crayfish.

# Koalas

- **Koala numbers** started to rise after European settlers reduced the numbers of dingoes.

- **Male koalas mark their territories** by rubbing their large chest gland, which females lack, onto tree trunks.

- **The koala feeds** mainly on eucalyptus leaves.

> ★ STAR FACT ★
> A koala weighs less than 0.5 g at birth, and remains in its mother's pouch for 7 months.

- **Koalas** are the sole living representatives of their family, but are distantly related to wombats.

- **The koala grips branches** with its sharp-clawed hands by opposing the first 2 fingers to the other 3.

- **Koalas spend 80 percent of their day** asleep in trees.

- **When its body temperature** nears 37°C, the koala licks its paws and rubs cooling saliva onto its face.

- **The name 'koala'** comes from an Aboriginal word meaning 'no drink' – it gets most of the moisture it needs from the leaves it eats.

- **A giant koala**, twice the size of today's animals, existed over 40,000 years ago.

◄ Although resembling a bear, koalas are not related to the bear family.

# Chimpanzees

- **Chimps have a strict social ladder**, with dominant males at the top. These top males recognize property rights, and never steal food from their inferiors.

- **Observers** have noted chimpanzees carefully lifting a fellow chimp's eyelid to remove a speck of grit.

- **Chimps are the best tool-users** after humans. They use grass stems to fish for termites in their mounds, stones and anvils to crack nuts, and chewed leaves as sponges for gathering water.

- **Chimpanzees** actively hunt for meat, especially when plant food is scarce, and collaborate to catch colobus monkeys, young baboons, birds and rodents.

- **If a chimpanzee** finds a tree laden with fruit, it drums on a tree trunk and makes loud panting cries to summon other chimps from many kilometres away for a share of the feast.

- **Bands of male chimpanzees** have been observed attacking and killing all the males in a neighbouring band. Up to a third of adult male chimp deaths result from territorial disputes.

> ★ **STAR FACT** ★
> Chimpanzees reach puberty at about 10 years, give birth every four or five years, and may live into their 50s.

▲ Grooming is a very important activity amongst chimps. It helps to create strong bonds between individuals, and to establish the group's pecking order.

- **Bonobos**, or pygmy chimpanzees, are found in the dense forests along the Congo River. They are darker than other chimps, with longer legs and smaller heads, and walk upright more often.

- **A bonobo named Kanzi**, a very successful participant in language experiments, also learned how to light a barbecue and cook his own sausages.

- **Chimps eat** a range of plants as medicines, to get rid of conditions such as stomach aches and parasitic worms.

◀ With a large brain and intense curiosity, the chimp can absorb a considerable amount of information, and is also able to learn by imitation.

# Life on the plains

- **In the 1800s**, a vast springbok herd, 25 km wide and 160 km long, crossed the plains of southern Africa.

- **The Argentine maned wolf** has extremely long legs for hunting in the tall pampas grasses.

- **The African springhare** resembles a miniature kangaroo.

- **The world's biggest** grouping of large land mammals takes place every year on Africa's Serengeti plains, with the migration of 1.5 million wildebeest and 1 million other hoofed animals.

- **Savannah buffalo** graze on tall, grasses, reducing them to the height preferred by other grazers.

- Newborn wildebeest have a strong instinct to approach anything that moves – even, fatally, hyenas or lions.

- **As herds of wildebeest** trample and manure the ground, they stimulate the rapid regrowth of grasses.

- **If young wild dogs tire** while hunting on Africa's Okavango flood plain, the adults hide them and return for them later.

- **The American pronghorn antelope** can see the white warning patches on the rump of another pronghorn from several kilometres away.

- **The Bactrian camel** of Central Asia eats salty plants avoided by other grazers.

◀ *The pronghorn communicates over long distances.*

# New World monkeys

- **The howler monkey** has a special throat bone that enables it to produce its distinctive deep roar.

- **The pygmy marmoset** is the world's smallest monkey, weighing 125 g.

- **Unlike Old World monkeys**, most New World monkeys have prehensile tails, and can suspend their whole bodies from them when travelling or feeding.

- **New World monkeys** have broad noses with sideways-pointing nostrils. Old World monkeys' noses are narrow, with downward-pointing nostrils.

- **The pygmy marmoset** uses its teeth to gouge holes in tree bark so that it can extract the gum – a major part of its diet.

- **The South American night monkey** is the only truly nocturnal monkey.

- **The capuchin** is the brainiest New World monkey. In captivity, it soon learns to use tools to obtain food.

- **Marmosets and tamarins** always give birth to twins, carried mainly by the father.

- **Titi monkeys** live in small family groups, and all sleep together with their tails entwined.

▼ *The howler monkey makes ear-shattering calls to warn off rivals.*

★ STAR FACT ★
Spider monkeys hang by their tails from low branches over rivers to drink.

# Heat regulation

- **Fruit bats** are susceptible to heat stroke, so to keep themselves cool, some lick themselves all over and fan cool air at their bodies with their wings.

- **The oryx** has special blood vessels in its nose to keep its blood temperature low in the desert heat.

- **Large-eared desert species** such as fennec foxes use their ears as radiators to get rid of body heat.

- **The desert bighorn sheep** draws air over a thickly veined area of its throat to cool its blood.

- **Wallowing in mud** keeps pigs cool and protects their skin from the sun.

▶ Little kit foxes of the American prairies use their huge ears to help them cool down.

- **A hippos' skin** exudes a red, lacquer-like substance to protect it from sunburn.

- **During hot spells**, kangaroos lick their wrists a lot, so that the evaporation of the saliva causes cooling.

- **Indian zebu cattle** have more sweat glands than western cattle, and maintain a lower body temperature, making them common in China, Africa and South America.

- **The eland's temperature** can rise several degrees without causing sweating, allowing it to conserve 5 litres of water daily.

- **After feeding their young**, mother bats often leave them in the heat of the cave and perch near the cooler entrance.

# Fruit bats

- **In Southwest Asia**, some date farmers protect their fruit from fruit bat raiders by covering the dates with bags of woven palm leaves.

- **Island fruit bats** are vulnerable to tropical storms that can blow them far out to sea. This is how some species reached islands in the first place.

- **Fruit bats** enjoy eating fruit in mangrove forests, where sea-water minerals supplement their diet.

- **Large fruit bats** strip the leaves from the trees in which they roost to give them a clearer view.

- **Male hammer-headed bats** gather together in riverside trees called leks, so that the females can choose a mate from among them. As they hang, the males flap their wings and call out.

- **The Queensland tube-nosed bat** has tube-like nostrils projecting 5–6 mm from its face. These may act as snorkels as it feeds on pulpy fruit.

- **Fruit bats eat their own weight** in fruit each day, and are important seed-dispersers, spitting out seeds as they eat.

- **Australian black fruit bats** chew leaves to get protein, but spit them out after swallowing the juice to make flying easier.

- **Spectacled flying foxes** sometimes drink sea-water as they skim by, and have been snapped up by saltwater crocodiles.

> ★ STAR FACT ★
> The largest fruit bat is the Indian flying fox, which has a wingspan of up to 150 cm.

▶ Unlike echolocating bats, fruit bats, navigate visually, and live on a plant diet.

# Wolves

- **In wolf packs**, only the dominant female normally mates and has cubs. The female wolves sometimes fight to establish who is to be the pack mother.

- **Forest wolves stay all year** in their own territory, while tundra wolves are nomadic, following the migrations of prey such as caribou.

- **Wolves howl** to avoid territorial fights – if they know where another pack is, they usually steer clear of it.

- **Grey wolves** often go for a week without food. They only average one kill in every 10 hunting expeditions.

- **Although they normally hunt large prey** such as deer, wolves will also eat carrion, berries and even fish.

- **Wolf packs** may number 20 or so where moose are plentiful, but only 6 or 7 where deer are the main prey.

- **Tundra wolves** hunt larger prey than wolves further south, and tend to be larger themselves.

- **A pack's dominant pair** scent mark the home range (up to 1000 sq km) by urinating about every 3 mins.

▲ The grey wolf is the ancestor of the domestic dog, and still occasionally mates with dogs such as huskies.

- **Wolves** migrated into Europe, Asia and Africa from North America some 7 million years ago.

- **Wolves cull the old and weak** members in a herd of prey animals, improving the herd's overall health.

# Raccoons

- **In many suburban areas** of the USA, raccoons have moved into sheds and roof spaces, emerging at night to raid garbage cans.

- **Hunting raccoons** with 'coon dogs at night is popular in the southern states of the USA, but raccoons have been known to lure dogs into water and then drown them.

- **Raccoons** use their slender-fingered front paws to capture frogs and crayfish.

▲ The raccoon's distinctive 'mask' fits its reputation as a night-time bandit, thief and garbage raider.

★ STAR FACT ★
At one time raccoon skins were used as currency in parts of Tennessee, USA.

- **Raccoons have a weakness** for sweet corn, raiding crops just ahead of the farmer.

- **The crab-eating raccoon** of South America leads a semi-aquatic life, and is also a good tree climber.

- **Raccoons** belong to a family that includes long-tailed kinkajous, coatis and cacomistles in the Americas, and the red pandas in Asia.

- **In the northern part of their range**, raccoons may retire to their nests in winter for a month or two.

- **Captive raccoons** appear to wash food before eating it, but in the wild a raccoon's underwater manipulations are to locate food rather than to wash it.

- **In urban areas**, raccoons sometimes carry off garbage cans, even untying rope knots to remove lids.

# Gibbons

▲ From earliest infancy the gibbon spends nearly all its life above ground in the trees.

- **The gibbons of Southeast Asia** are the smallest and most agile of the apes. They pair for life, and each couple has its own song of whoops and wails.

- **Swinging by their long arms**, gibbons hurtle through the forest, flying up to 15 m between hand-holds.

- **With the longest arms**, relative to body size, of all the primates, gibbons often hang by just one arm.

- **No-one** has been able to keep up with gibbons to time how fast they swing arm over arm (brachiation).

- **Siamangs** are the largest gibbons, at up to 15 kg.

- **About 2 million years ago** there was only one gibbon species, but ice age changes in sea levels created forest islands, where separate species developed.

- **A gibbon sleeps** sitting up on a branch with its head between its bent knees, not in a nest like great apes.

- **Gibbons** are more closely related to orangutans than to the chimps and gorillas of Africa.

- **Gibbons have extremely flexible** shoulder joints, and can rotate through 360° while hanging from one arm.

> ★ STAR FACT ★
> In the black gibbon species, the male is all black, the female light cream with a black face.

# Hyenas

- **After making a successful kill**, the spotted ('laughing') hyena emits a blood-curdling, laugh-like cry.

- **The aardwolf** is a small, insect-eating member of the hyena family. One specimen was found to have over 40,000 termites in its stomach.

- **Often portrayed as a skulking scavenger**, the spotted hyena is in fact an aggressive hunter, and is also capable of driving lions from their kills at times.

- **The hyena's powerful jaws** can crush large bones, which its digestive system dissolves in a few hours.

- **Hyenas may suckle** their young for more than 1 year, compared to 2 months in the dog family.

- **All hyenas hide surplus food** for later – sometimes even underwater in the case of the spotted hyena.

- **Hyenas** are more closely related to mongooses than to members of the dog family.

- **In South Africa**, brown hyenas, or 'beach wolves', beachcomb for dead crabs, fish and sea mammals.

- **A female brown hyena** was once seen to take a springbok carcase from a leopard, and drive the leopard up a tree.

- **Brown and striped hyenas** erect their long manes to make them look larger when displaying aggression.

▶ The spotted hyena can chase a wildebeest for 5 km at up to 60 km/h.

# Gazelles and antelopes

- **The smallest antelope**, the West African royal antelope, is only the size of a brown hare, and weighs between 1.5 and 3 kg.

- **When the Indian blackbuck antelope** runs flat out, it reaches 80 km/h, making 8-m long strides. The Indian aristocracy once used trained cheetahs to hunt them.

- **When a dominant greater kudu bull lies down**, he suddenly loses all authority, and female and young bull kudus often harass and annoy him with impunity.

- **The giant eland** of West and Central Africa is the largest of all antelopes, reaching 3.5 m in length, 1.85 m at the shoulder, and weighing up to 940 kg.

- **The American pronghorn antelope** has been timed running at 56 km/h for 6 km, and up to 88.5 km/h over short distances less than 1 km.

- **When migrating** to new grazing grounds, herds of wildebeest sometimes number up to 1.3 million individuals, and the herd may measure as much as 40 km in length.

▶ A fleeing springbok may leap vertically in an activity known as 'pronking', confusing predators and giving the springbok a better view.

- **The Arabian oryx** is a desert specialist, with a pale, heat-reflecting coat and splayed hoofs for walking in soft sand. Its small size enables it to shelter in the shade of shrubby trees.

- **The spiral-horned antelopes**, which include elands, kudus and bongos, are found only in Africa, and are an offshoot of the ancestors of domestic cattle.

- **The springbok** is famous for its spectacular, leaps while running – a display activity known as 'pronking'.

> ★ STAR FACT ★
> The pronghorn is not a true antelope, and is more closely related to the deer family.

▶ The male pronghorn has several scent glands for marking territory, including glands beneath the ears, on the rump, above the tail and between the toes.

Large eyes give a 360° field of vision

▲ The Indian blackbuck is one of the world's fastest animals, with herds travelling at up to 80 km/h for 1 km at a time.

# Coyotes and jackals

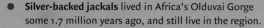

- **Silver-backed jackals** lived in Africa's Olduvai Gorge some 1.7 million years ago, and still live in the region.

- **The coyote** is probably the only predator whose range is increasing across North America.

- **Coyotes can live to be over 14 years old** in the wild, and over 21 years old in captivity.

- **Jackals are fearless defenders** of their family groups – a single jackal will attack a hyena five times its weight.

- **Farmers who poison coyotes** to reduce attacks on their livestock may be increasing the numbers of attacks, by killing the coyote's natural prey.

- **Native Americans** celebrated the cunning 'trickster' coyote, and told myths about its cleverness.

- **The golden jackal** of Eurasia and Africa is fond of fruit,

▶ A keen hunter, the coyote's prey ranges from mice to sheep.

eating figs, berries, grapes and desert dates, as well as animal prey.

- **When fighting** a predator or stealing a kill, pairs of jackals employ a 'yo-yo' technique, dashing in from each side alternately.

- **Without a 'helper'**, an average of one silver-backed jackal pup survives each litter, but with a helper three survive, and with three helpers an average of six survive.

> ★ STAR FACT ★
> Young coyotes may spend a year helping to raise their younger brothers and sisters.

# Gliders

- **Gliding mammals** include the flying squirrels of America and Asia, the scaly-tailed squirrels of Africa, and the marsupial gliding possums of Australia.

- **The Australian feather-tailed glider** is the smallest gliding mammal, weighing just 12 g.

> ★ STAR FACT ★
> The longest glide by a gliding mammal ever recorded was 450 m by a giant flying squirrel.

- **Gliding mammals** glide by means of a membrane called a patagium that joins the fore and hind limbs.

- **The Southeast Asian colugo's** glide membrane stretches from the neck to fingers, toes and tail-tip.

- **When flying squirrels** come to land on a tree, they brake by turning their tail and body under.

- **Africa's scaly-tailed flying squirrels** live in colonies of up to 100, and glide from tree to tree after dark.

- **Australia's gliders** feed on sap and gum, biting through tree bark and lapping up the sweet liquids.

- **Some flying squirrels,** when they land, quickly move to the opposite side of the tree trunk to avoid predators.

- **The colugo** is virtually helpless on the ground.

◀ The southern flying squirrel fluffs out its tail and uses it as a rudder in mid-air.

# Tenrecs and otter shrews

- **Tenrecs** live on the island of Madagascar. Their physical appearance ranges from hedgehog lookalikes to shrews and web-footed otters.

- **Otter shrews**, close relatives to tenrecs, evolved separately on the African mainland. One species features in folklore as half mammal and half fish.

- **The body temperature** of tenrecs and otter shrews falls close to the surrounding air temperature while they are resting, enabling them to save energy.

- **The common tenrec** rears more young than any other mammal on the planet, with litters of up to 24.

- **Some tenrecs** find their way around at night by using a form of echolocation, based on a series of fast clicking noises made with the tongue.

- **The web-footed** tenrec was thought to be extinct, but was recently re-discovered in Madagascar.

- **The insect-eating rice tenrec** resembles a mole, with its large front feet for digging and small eyes and ears.

- **The common tenrec**, weighing up to 1.5 kg, is the world's largest insectivore, and a ferocious fighter. It uses sharp neck spines to spike its attackers.

- **When alarmed**, baby common tenrecs rub together the quills on their backs to make a vibrating noise.

- **The aquatic otter shrews** of Africa use touch-sensitive whiskers to locate crabs and other prey.

◀ Long-tailed tenrecs live in the forests of Madagascar.

# Deer and chevrotains

- **The tiny Chinese water deer** is unique in the deer family in giving birth to as many as seven fawns at a time.

- **Chevrotains**, or mouse-deer, are in a separate family from true deer. They eat fish and meat as well as plants.

- **Reindeer** are the only deer species in which the females have antlers, using them to find moss under the snow.

> ★ STAR FACT ★
> In the Middle Ages, the kings of Europe planted royal forests specially for deer-hunting.

- **Male musk deer** use their long, down-curved canine teeth when fighting rival males in the mating season.

- **The antlers** that male deer use for fighting are shed each year, regrowing the following spring.

- **Indian chital deer** seek out langur monkeys, feeding on the leafy stems thrown down by the monkeys above.

- **When competing for females**, red deer stags prefer to roar at each other rather than fight and risk an injury.

- **Newly grown antlers** are covered with a protective skin known as 'velvet', which stags rub off against trees.

- **On the Scottish island of Rhum**, red deer supplement their plant diet by snacking on Manx shearwater chicks.

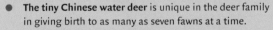

◀ Most deer have large, mobile ears that are constantly alert.

# The smaller cats

- **The fishing cat** of Southeast Asia and India inhabits marshes and swamps, and has slightly webbed paws. It preys on fish, crayfish, birds and small mammals.

- **The Iriomote cat** is probably the world's rarest cat. Less than 100 exist, on a remote, mountainous island off southern Japan.

- **The caracal** is a lynx-like African cat weighing up to 20 kg. It can kill antelopes twice its own weight.

- **The black-footed cat** of South Africa is the smallest wild cat. It spends the day in disused burrows, and eats spiders and beetles as well as small rodents.

▶ *The long-legged caracal is a good jumper and climber, and even takes sleeping birds, including eagles.*

- **The serval** is a cat of tall grasses, with very long legs and neck. It locates prey with its prominent ears, catching it with a high, fox-like pounce.

- **The secretive Andean mountain cat** lives at altitudes of up to 5000 m, protected from the cold by its fine fur and long, bushy tail.

- **The Central American margay** specializes in hunting birds high in the treetops, and is the best of all cat climbers, with flexible legs and ankles.

- **The sand cat** of Africa and Asia does not need to drink, and has hairy foot-pads for walking in hot sand.

- **Unlike most small cats**, the ocelot runs down its prey instead of ambushing it, and is an excellent swimmer.

- **The smaller cats purr**, but cannot roar.

# Baboons

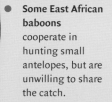

- **Baboons' feet** are suited to walking than grabbing branches.

- **Some East African baboons** cooperate in hunting small antelopes, but are unwilling to share the catch.

- **Male Hamadryas baboons** herd their females to keep them from other males.

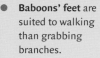

◀ *The male mandrill has a bright blue and red face for attracting females.*

★ STAR FACT ★
Olive baboon males fighting over females will enlist the help of a third male.

- **The olive baboons** of the East African highlands live in troops of up to 140 individuals.

- **When old male Hamadryas baboons** are defeated by younger males, they lose weight, and their distinctive grey mantle changes to the colour of the females' hair.

- **Chacma baboons**, found in the far south of Africa, often enter water to feed on water plants or shellfish.

- **For their first few weeks**, baby baboons hang upside down from their mother's chest, but by 4 or 5 months they are riding on her back, like jockeys.

- **The ancient Egyptians** sometimes trained Hamadryas baboons to harvest figs.

- **Baboons** in South Africa's Kruger National Park will risk electric fence shocks to steal food from tourists.

# Domestic cats

- **Domestic cats** probably evolved from African wild cats, which were domesticated as early as 4000 BC in Egypt.

- **The ancient Egyptians revered cats**, and believed they held the daylight in their eyes.

- **Clay tiles** in a Roman temple in Britain bear the imprint of cats' paws. It is likely that the Romans introduced domestic cats to the British Isles.

- **The long-haired Turkish Van cat** is sometimes called the swimming cat, and is known for its love of water.

- **Some 98 percent of the patched cats** known as tortoiseshells, or calico cats, are females.

- **The Maine Coon**, the oldest breed of domestic cat in the USA, may have Viking origins.

- **In 1950 a 4-month-old kitten** followed some climbers to the summit of the Matterhorn in the Swiss Alps.

- **Siamese cats** were once found only in Thailand's temples and palaces. One king's favourite cat was entombed with him, but it later escaped

- **In November 1939**, in Devon, a tabby cat called Puss celebrated its 36th birthday, and died the next day.

- **In the 10th-century**, a kitten was worth 2 pence before it caught its first mouse, and 4 pence afterwards.

▶ Domestic cats have retained their wild hunting instincts, and are major predators of garden birds.

# Skunks

- **The skunk squirts a sticky spray** at its enemy from glands under its tail. It can reach a target up to 6 m away, and is accurate up to 2 m.

- **The skunk's spray** can cause temporary blindness.

- **Before spraying**, a skunk stamps its feet as warning. The spotted skunk does a handstand and walks with its hind legs in the air.

- **Skunks** belong to the same family as weasels and polecats, all of which have smelly sprays.

- **Vets** recommend that dogs which have been sprayed by a skunk should be given a bath in tomato juice.

- **Most predators avoid skunks**, but it is a favourite prey of the great horned owl, which has a poor sense of smell.

- **In the USA**, skunks are major carriers of rabies

- **Skunks have little fear of humans** and are often sold as pets – after a de-scenting operation.

- **Skunks are great diggers**. They use their long, straight claws to rip apart rotten logs for grubs, and to dig in sand and mud for turtle eggs.

- **Skunks sleep in communal dens** when temperatures reach freezing, with up to 20 skunks in a den.

◀ The skunk eats mainly live prey, such as insects and small mammals, and also enjoys fruit and birds' eggs.

# Meerkats

- **Young meerkats** care for their younger brothers and sisters while their mother forages for food to maintain her milk supply.

- **Grey meerkats** often share their burrow systems with ground squirrels.

- **If surprised in open ground** by a hawk, the adults in a meerkat pack will cover the young with their bodies.

- **The grey meerkat** attacks intruders without warning or threats, and kills with an energetic shaking, followed by a neck bite.

▶ The meerkat lives in cooperative groups of up to 30 individuals in a complex warren system.

★ STAR FACT ★
Meerkat warrens can cover an area of up to 25 m by 32 m, with 90 separate entrances.

- **Meerkats** enthusiastically attack and eat scorpions, first rendering them harmless by biting off their tail stings.

- **Meerkats warm themselves up** in the morning sun, standing tall on their hind feet and tails, while constantly on the lookout for enemies.

- **Meerkats dig** for many food items, such as beetles, moth pupae, termites and spiders.

- **Living in the arid regions** of South Africa, the meerkat sometimes obtains moisture by chewing Tsama melons and digging up plant roots.

- **Faced with attack**, the normally slim meerkat becomes almost spherical, its hair bristling, tail up and back arched as it growls, spits and rocks to and fro.

# Mice

- **In the early 1940s**, a huge population of house mice in California had a density of about 200,000 per hectare.

- **The Andes fishing mouse** – only discovered in 1994 – fishes in streams at an altitude of at least 3600 m.

- **The Australian pebble mound mouse** builds large piles of rounded stones, and then takes up residence in them.

- **The Oldfield mouse** has an escape tunnel leading from its nest near to the surface, so it can escape intruders by breaking through the apparent 'dead end'.

- **The water mice** of Central America have webbed, hairy feet that help them dive for water snails and fish.

- **American grasshopper mice** defend their territory by standing on their hind legs, shrieking at rival mice.

- **Grasshopper mice** are sometimes kept as pets to clear a house of insect pests such as cockroaches.

- **An ancient Greek legend** tells how a Cretan army owed its success to divine mice, which gnawed through the shield straps of the enemy.

- **The Old World harvest mouse** climbs through tall grasses using its grasping tail and flexible feet.

- **American kangaroo mice** have long, hairy hind feet and a long tail, and often travel in a series of leaps.

◀ (1) Burrowing house mouse, (2) field mouse, (3) climbing harvest mouse.

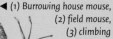

# Foxes

- **The larder of one Arctic fox** was found to contain 50 lemmings and 40 little auks, all lined up with tails pointing the same way and their heads bitten off.

- **African bat-eared foxes** have huge ears for radiating heat away from the body.

- **Arctic foxes** live only 480 km from the North Pole.

- **The grey fox** of North and Central America is the oldest surviving member of the dog family, first appearing up to 9 million years ago.

- **The African fennec fox's** 15-cm long ears are the largest of any carnivore.

- **The American grey fox** leaps with ease between tree branches.

- **Some foxes roll about** and chase their tails to 'charm' rabbits, which seem fascinated and come closer, allowing the fox to make a grab.

- **The red fox** has adapted with great success to urban life, even moving into houses via cat flaps.

- **When locating insects** beneath the ground, the bat-eared fox cups its large ears, gradually pinpointing the exact position of the prey before digging.

◀ Although basically a night hunter, the red fox is often seen during the day, and shows up sharply against winter snow.

# Zebras

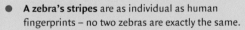

- **A zebra's stripes** are as individual as human fingerprints – no two zebras are exactly the same.

- **The quagga** was a South African zebra that only had stripes on the front part of its body.

- **The home range** of Grevy's zebra, which roams desert and savannah terrains in northeastern Kenya, sometimes exceeds 10,000 sq km.

- **The zebra** can be a formidable foe, driving off lions, and even killing humans to defend its foals.

- **The plains zebra** lived north of the Sahara, in Algeria and Tunisia, up until 10,000 years ago, when it was replaced by the African wild ass.

- **Grevy's zebra** is a large species with narrowly spaced stripes and very large, mule-like ears.

- **A plains zebra herd's stallion** will challenge any potential rival coming within 50–100 m of his herd.

- **The quagga** once existed in very large herds, but became extinct through over-hunting in the 1870s.

- **Mountain zebras** follow ancient trails to mountain springs and pools in the dry season, and dig for subsurface water in stream beds.

- **Chapman's zebra** has shadow stripes – light, greyish stripes that alternate with the dark main stripes.

▲ Zebras are sociable and like physical contact and mutual grooming.

MORAVI
MARCHIONATU
IN SEX CIRCULOS DIV
JUXTA RECENTISSIMAM DIMI
ET ACCURATISSIMAS OBSERV
ÆRI INCISUS ET VENUM EXPO
À
MATTH. SEUTTER. S.C.M.G
AUGUSTANO

# ANCIENT HISTORY

## THE AMERICAS AND PACIFIC

## CLASSICAL WORLD

## EUROPE

## AFRICA AND THE NEAR EAST

## ASIA AND THE FAR EAST

## PEOPLE AND LIFESTYLES

## SEARCH FOR THE PAST

# Origins of mankind

▼ Experts once thought humans evolved in a single line from australopiths, through Homo habilis (1), Homo erectus (2) and Neanderthal man (3) to humans (4). They now realize there were many branches.

- **Humans and apes** have so many similarities – such as long arms and fingers, and a big brain – most experts think they must have evolved from the same creature.

- **The common ancestor** may be four-legged orang-utan-like creatures called dryopithecines that lived in trees 22–10 million years ago (mya), like 'Proconsul' from E. Africa.

- **The break came when** 'hominids' (human-like apes) began to live on the ground and walk on two legs.

- **Footprints** of three bipedal (two-legged) creatures from 4 mya were found preserved in ash at Laetoli, Tanzania.

- **The oldest hominid** is called *Ardipithecus ramidus*, known from 4.4 mya bone fragments found in Aramis, Ethiopia.

- **Many very early** hominids are australopiths ('southern apes'), like the *Australopithecus anamensis* from 4.2 mya.

- **Australopiths** were only 1 m tall and their brain was about the same size as an ape's, but they were bipedal.

- **The best known** australopith is 'Lucy', a skeleton of *Australopithecus afarensis* of 3 mya, found in Kenya in 1974.

- **Lucy's discoverers** Don Johanson and Maurice Tieb called her Lucy because they were listening to the Beatles song 'Lucy in the Sky with Diamonds' at the time.

- **Many early hominid** remains are just skulls. Lucy was an almost complete skeleton. She showed that hominids learned to walk upright before their brains got bigger.

# Handy Man

- **2.5–1.8 million years ago** the first really human-like hominids appeared. These hominids are all given the genus (group) name *Homo*, and include us.

- **The best known** early Homos are *Homo rudolfensis* and *Homo habilis*.

- **The first Homos** were taller than australopiths and had bigger brains.

- **Unlike australopiths,** Homos ate meat. They may have been forced to eat meat by a drying of the climate that cut the amount of plant food available.

- **Brains need** a lot of food, and eating meat gave the extra nourishment needed for bigger brains.

▶ Skulls show that the first Homos, like Homo habilis, had brains of 650 cubic cm (cc) – twice as big as australopiths. Ours are about 1400 cc. But they had ape-like faces with protruding jaws and sloping foreheads.

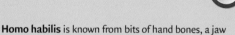

- **Homo habilis** is known from bits of hand bones, a jaw and a skull found in Tanzania's Olduvai Gorge in 1961.

- **Homo habilis** means Handy Man. He gets his name because he has a good grip for wielding tools – with a thumb that can be rotated to meet the tip of a finger. This is called an 'opposable thumb'.

- **The first Homos** used bones or stones to break open bones to get at the marrow. Later they sharpened stones to cut meat for eating and hides for clothing. They may even have built simple shelters to live in.

- **Some experts** think the bulge in 'Broca's area' of some Homo habilis skulls suggests they could speak in a crude way. Most think they could not.

- **The first Homos** lived for a million or more years alongside 'robust' (bigger) australopiths, such as *Paranthropus boisei*.

# Man the hunter

- **About 2 mya,** a much taller Homo called *Homo ergaster* appeared. Ergasters were the first creatures to have bodies much like ours, with long legs and straight backs.

- **Adult ergasters** were 1.6 m tall, weighed 65 kg and had brains of 850 cubic cm, well over half as big as ours.

- **Ergasters** did not just scavenge for meat like *Homo habilis*. They went hunting for large animals.

- **To hunt** and cut up meat, ergaster shaped stones, chipping flakes off to make proper double-edge blades or 'hand-axes'. Experts call this Acheulean tool-making.

- **To hunt effectively,** ergasters had to work together, so co-operation was the key to their success – and may have quickly led to the development of speech.

- **Ergasters** may have painted their bodies with red ochre.

▲ *Human development began when hominids learned to hunt together.*

- **Shortly after** ergaster came *Homo erectus* ('Upright Man').

- **Erectus** remains are found as far from Africa as Java. 700,000 year-old stone tools on the Indonesian island of Flores suggest they may have travelled by boat.

- **Erectus** learned to light fires, so they could live in colder places, and make a wider range of food edible by cooking.

> ★ STAR FACT ★
> Long legs and working together helped ergaster spread beyond Africa into Asia and maybe Europe.

# Neanderthals and others

- **Hominids** appeared in Europe much later. The oldest, called *Homo antecessor*, dates from 800,000 years ago. This may have been a kind of erectus, or another species.

- **800-600,000 years ago** *Homo Heidelbergensis* appeared in Europe, Asia and Africa.

- **Heidelbergensis** may be a single species that came from Africa – or various species that evolved in different places.

- **Heidelbergensis** has many features in common with erectus, but is a major step on the way to modern humans with, for the first time, a brain as big as ours.

▶ *Most early hominid remains have been found in Africa. Many species – including modern humans – may have emerged first in Africa, then migrated elsewhere. These are sites where remains were found.*

Swanscombe
Boxgrove
Les Eyzies
Grimaldi
Dolni Vestonice
Vindija, Croatia
Dmanisi
Shanidar
Skhul
Tabun
Bahr el Ghazal
Omo
Hadar
(Lucy)
Nariokotome
Olduvai
Laetoli
Kabwe
Sterkfontein
Taung
Swartkrans
Klasies River

✦Australopith, 1–4 mya
✦H. habilis, 2.5–1 mya
✦H. ergaster, 2–0.5 mya
✦H. H'berg, 500–100,000 yrs
✦N'thal 250–30,000 yrs
✦H. sapiens 30,000 yrs

- **Heidelbergensis** made good stone tools by making the core first, then shaping the blade with a single blow.

- **Heidelbergensis** was ancestor to Neanderthal Man, who lived in Europe from 250,000 to 30,000 years ago.

- **Neanderthals** were named after the Neander valley in Germany, where remains were found in 1856.

- **Neanderthals** were slightly shorter than modern humans but much stronger and with bigger brains. They must have been formidable hunters.

- **Neanderthals** buried their dead, often with tributes of flowers.

- **Neanderthals** lived in Croatia 28,000 years ago – long after modern humans. No one knows why they died out, leaving humans alone.

# Modern humans

- **The scientific name** for modern humans is *Homo Sapiens Sapiens*. The word *Sapiens* is used twice to distinguish us from *Homo Sapiens Neanderthalis* (Neanderthal Man).

- **Unlike Neanderthals,** modern humans have a prominent chin and a flat face with a high forehead.

- **Some scientists** think the similarity of DNA in our bodies means all humans are descended from a woman nicknamed 'Eve', who they calculate lived in Africa about 200,000 years ago. DNA is the special molecule in every body-cell that carries the body's instructions for life.

- **The oldest human skulls** are 130,000 years old and were found in the Omo Basin in Ethiopia and the Klasies river in South Africa.

- **About 30,000 years ago** modern humans began to spread out into Eurasia from Africa.

- **The earliest modern Europeans** are called Cro-Magnon Man, after the caves in France's Dordogne valley where skeletons from 35,000 years ago were found in 1868.

- **Modern humans** reached Australia by boat from Indonesia 50,000 years ago. They reached the Americas from Asia about the same time.

- **Modern humans** lived alongside Neanderthals for tens of thousands of years in the Middle East and Europe.

- **Modern humans** were probably the first creatures to speak what we would call language. Some scientists think language was a sudden genetic accident which gave humans a huge advantage.

- **With modern humans** came rapid advances in stone-tool technology, the building of wooden huts, a rise in population and a growing interest in art.

◀ *Both modern humans and Neanderthals used beautifully made spears for hunting.*

# Cave painters

- **Prehistoric people** sometimes lived in caves, but more often they went into caves to paint and draw.

- **The world's** most famous cave paintings, at Lascaux in France and Altamira in Spain, were found by children.

- **Carbon dating** shows the paintings in Lascaux are 31,000 years old. Those in Chauvet in the French Ardèche are nearly twice as old.

- **The pictures** at Cougnac in France were painted over a period of 10,000 years.

- **Most paintings** in caves show large animals such as bison, deer, horses and mammoths.

- **Caves** may have been the temples of prehistoric times, and the paintings linked to religious rituals.

- **Cave artists** often painted by spitting paint, just as Australian aboriginals do today.

- **To reach** the 14,000-year-old paintings in France's Pergouset, you must crawl through 150 m of passages.

- **In the caves** at Nerja in Spain there are rock formations that prehistoric people played like a xylophone.

- **The aboriginal paintings** on rocks in Arnhemland, Northern Territory, Australia may be over 50,000 years old.

◀ *The most famous cave paintings are those in the Hall of Bulls at Lascaux in France. These paintings show bison.*

# The Stone Ages

- **The Stone Ages** were the ages before humans discovered metals and so used mainly stones for making tools.

- **Stone tools** were made by chipping away stones to make hammers, spear and arrow heads, knives and scrapers.

- **People usually** used local stone, but sometimes good stones were imported from long distances.

- **Early Europeans** used mainly flint. Africans used quartz, chert, basalt and obsidian.

- **In Europe** there were three Stone Ages : Old (Palaeolithic), Middle (Mesolithic) and New (Neolithic).

- **The Palaeolithic** began 2 million years ago when various human ancestors gathered plants and hunted with stone weapons.

▶ *Mesolithic people hunted with bows and arrows and flint-tipped spears.*

- **The Mesolithic** was the transition from the Old to the New Stone Age – after the Last Ice Age ended around 12,000 years ago.

- **The Neolithic** was the time when people began to settle down and farm. This occurred first in the Near East, about 10,000 years ago.

- **In 1981,** a pebble shaped into a female form, half a million years old was found at Berekhat Ram in Israel's Golan Heights.

  - **Venus figurines** are plump stone female figures from *c.*25,000 years ago, found in Europe, e.g. the Czech Republic.

# The Bronze Age

- **The Bronze Age** is the period of prehistory when people first began to use the metal bronze.

- **Bronze** is an alloy (mix) of copper with about 10% tin.

- **The first metals used** were probably lumps of pure gold and copper, beaten into shape to make ornaments in Turkey and Iran about 6000BC.

- **Metal ores** (metals mixed with other minerals) were probably discovered when certain stones were found to melt when heated in a kiln.

- **Around 4000BC,** metal smiths in southeast Europe and Iran began making copper axeheads with a central hole to take a wooden shaft.

- **The Copper Age** is the period when people used copper before they learned to alloy it with tin to make bronze. Metalworking with copper was flourishing in the early cities of Mesopotamia, in the Middle East, about 3500BC.

- **The Bronze Age** began several times between 3500 and 3000BC in the Near East, Balkans and

SE Asia when smiths discovered that, by adding a small quantity of tin, they could make bronze. Bronze is harder than copper and easier to make into a sharp blade.

- **Knowledge of bronze** spread slowly across Eurasia, but by 1000BC it was in use all the way from Europe to India.

- **The rarity of tin** spurred long-distance trade links – and the first mines, like the tin mines in Cornwall, England.

- **Bronze** can be cast – shaped by melting it into a clay mould (itself shaped with a wax model). For the first time people could make things any shape they wanted. Skilled smiths across Eurasia began to cast bronze to make everything from weapons to cooking utensils.

◀ *By 1000BC, beautiful metal swords and other weapons with sharp blades like this were being made all over Europe and western Asia.*

# The Iron Age

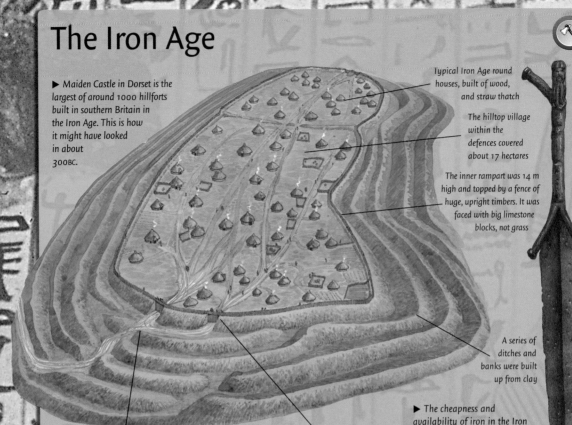

▶ Maiden Castle in Dorset is the largest of around 1000 hillforts built in southern Britain in the Iron Age. This is how it might have looked in about 300BC.

Typical Iron Age round houses, built of wood, and straw thatch

The hilltop village within the defences covered about 17 hectares

The inner rampart was 14 m high and topped by a fence of huge, upright timbers. It was faced with big limestone blocks, not grass

A series of ditches and banks were built up from clay

The entrance wound between ramparts to make life hard for attackers

The entrance through the inner ramparts had massive timber gates

▶ The cheapness and availability of iron in the Iron Age meant that even quite a poor man might have his own sword.

- **The Iron Age** is the time in prehistory when iron replaced bronze as the main metal.

- **The use of iron** was discovered by the Hittites in Anatolia, Turkey between 1500 and 1200BC. This discovery helped to make the Hittites immensely powerful for a few centuries.

- **Around 1200BC,** the Hittite Empire collapsed and the use of iron spread through Asia and central Europe. The Dorian Greeks became famous iron masters.

- **Tin is rare**, so bronze objects were made mostly for chieftains. Iron ore is common, so ordinary people could have metal objects such as cooking utensils.

- **Many ordinary farmers** could afford iron scythes and axes. With tough metal tools to clear fields and harvest crops quickly, farming developed much more rapidly.

- **Growth in population** put pressure on resources and warfare increased across Eurasia. Partly as a result, many northern Europe settlements developed into hillforts – hilltop sites protected by earth ramparts, ditches and stockades.

- **Around 650BC,** peoples skilled in iron working called Celts began to dominate northern Europe.

- **Iron working** reached China around 600BC. The Chinese used large bellows to boost furnace temperatures enough to melt ore in large quantities.

- **Iron tools** appearing in West Africa around 400BC were the basis of the Nok culture. Nok farmers speaking Bantu spread south and east all over Africa.

> ★ **STAR FACT** ★
> In 1950, an Iron Age man was found in a peatbog at Tollund in Jutland, Denmark, perfectly preserved over 2000 years.

# Megaliths

- **Megalith** means 'giant stone'.
- **Megaliths** are monuments such as tombs made from huge blocks of stone, built in western Europe in the Neolithic and Bronze Ages between 4000 and 1500BC.
- **It was once** thought megaliths began in one place. Now experts think they emerged in many areas.
- **Menhirs** are large standing stones. Sometimes they stand by themselves, sometimes in avenues or circles.
- **The largest** known menhir is the Grand Menhir Brisé at Locmariaquer near Carnac, France. This single stone once stood 20 m tall and weighed 280 tonnes.
- **The largest stone circle** is at Avebury in Wiltshire.
- **The most famous stone circle** is Stonehenge on Salisbury Plain, built between 2950 and 1600BC.

> ★ STAR FACT ★
> The Grand Menhir Brisé is seven times as heavy as the biggest stones at Stonehenge.

▲ *The most famous avenues of stone are at Carnac in Brittany, France, where thousands of stones stand in long lines.*

- **Some megaliths** align with amazing accuracy with astronomical events, such as sunrise at the solstice (midsummer day) and may have acted as calendars.
- **Erecting the stones** took huge teams of men working with wooden rollers, levers and ropes.

# Archaeology

- **Archaeology** is the scientific study of relics left by humans in the past, from old bones to ancient temples.
- **Most archeological relics** are buried beneath the ground or sunk beneath the sea.
- **Aerial photography** often shows places to dig. Crops and grass will grow differently if the soil is affected by a buried wall or filled-in ditch.
- **Geophysical surveys** involve using metal detectors and other electronic probes to pick up features underground.
- **Field walking** involves walking over the site, carefully scanning the ground by eye for tiny relics.

▶ *Archeological digging is a very painstaking process. Diggers must work with immense care to avoid missing or breaking tiny, fragile relics.*

- **During a dig,** archaeologists dig carefully down through the layers, noting exactly where every relic was found, in case their position helps to reveal the story.
- **Archaeologists** call on many different kinds of expert to help them interpret finds. Forensic scientists may help tell how a skeleton died, for instance.
- **The deeper** a relic is buried, the older it is likely to be.
- **Radio carbon dating** is a way of dating the remains of once-living things from their carbon content. This is accurate up to 50,000 years ago.
- **Potassium argon dating** helps to date the rocks in which relics were found from their potassium and argon content. Human remains in Africa were dated this way.

# The first farms

▲ *Farming began about 11,000 years ago as people began saving grass seed to grow, so they could grind new seed into flour.*

- **Starch marks** on stone implements found in Papua New Guinea suggest yams may have been grown there at least 30,000 years ago.

- **Water chestnuts** and beans may have been farmed near Spirit Cave in north Vietnam from 11,000 to 7,500BC.

- **About 9000BC,** some people abandoned the old way of life, hunting animals and gathering fruit, and settled down to farm in what is called the Neolithic Revolution.

- **Farming began** as people planted grasses for their seed (or grain) in the Near East, in Guangdong in China and in Latin America – and perhaps planted root vegetables in Peru and Indonesia too.

- **Emmer wheat and barley** were grown in the Near East c.8000BC. Sheep and goats were tamed here soon after.

- **The ox-drawn plough** was used from c.5000BC. The Chinese used hand ploughs even earlier.

- **Crop irrigation canals** were dug at Choya Mami, near Mandali in Iraq, between 5500 and 4750BC.

- **China,** the Indus, Egypt and Babylonia all had extensive irrigation systems by 3000BC.

- **The first farmers** reaped their grain with sickles of flint.

- **Farmers** soon learned to store food. Underground granaries at Ban-Po, Shansi, China, date from c.4800BC.

# The first cities

- **The walls** of the city of Jericho on the River Jordan are 11,000 years old, and the city has been continuously occupied longer than anywhere else in the world.

- **People began** to live in towns when farming produced enough extra food for people to specialize in crafts such as basket-making and for people to begin to trade.

- **Villages and towns** probably first developed in the Near East in the Neolithic, about 8000BC.

- **Tells** are mounds built up at ancient settlement sites in the Near and Middle East as mud-brick houses crumble.

- **The most famous** ancient town is Catal Hüyük in Anatolia, in Turkey, which was occupied from 7000 to 5500BC. 10,000 people may have lived here.

- **The houses** in Catal Hüyük were made from mud bricks covered with fine plaster. Some rooms were shrines, with bulls' heads and mother goddesses.

- **Asikli Hüyük** is a nearby forerunner of Catal Hüyük, dating from over a thousand years earlier.

- **The first big city** was Eridu in Mesopotamia (Iraq's Abu Shahrain Tell) which has a temple dating from 4900BC.

- **50,000 people** were living in Sumerian Uruk (modern Warka) on the banks of the Euphrates in Iraq in 3500BC.

- **Sumerian Ur** was the first city to have a population of a quarter of a million, by about 2500BC.

◄ *Houses in Catal Hüyük were so tightly packed people had to walk over flat roofs to get to them, then climb through a hole down ladders.*

# Mesopotamia and Sumer

- **Mesopotamia** lies between the Tigris and Euphrates Rivers in Turkey, Syria and Iraq. *Mesopotamia* is Greek for 'between rivers'.

- **Mesopotamia** is called the 'cradle of civilization' because many ancient civilizations arose here, including the Sumerian, Babylonian and Assyrian.

- **The first great civilization** was that of the Sumerians, who farmed irrigated land by the Euphrates c.5000BC and lived in mud-brick houses.

- **By 4000BC,** the settlements of Eridu, Uruk and Ur had grown into towns with water supplies and drainage systems, palaces and temple mounds called ziggurats.

- **Sumerians** devised the first writing system (cuneiform), made with wedge-shaped marks on clay tablets.

◄ No one knows when the wheel was invented. It probably developed from potters' wheels. But by 3200BC carts like this were used in Sumer.

- **Sumerians** made beautiful objects – first from copper, then, from 3500BC, in bronze.

- **The Sumerian** *Epic of Gilgamesh* tells of a flood similar to the biblical story of Noah's Ark.

- **The Sumerians** developed the first elaborate systems of government and law.

- **At first each city** or 'city-state' was run by a council of elders, but in wartime a *lugal* (leader) took charge. By 2900BC *lugals* were kings and ruled all the time.

- **In 2350BC** Sumer was overrun by Sargon of Akkad, but Sumerian power was re-established at Ur in 2150BC.

# Indus civilization

★ STAR FACT ★
Soapstone trading seals from the Indus have been found as far away as Bahrain and Ur.

▶ Seals like this were used by Indus merchants to stamp bales of goods.

- **About 3000BC** a civilization developed from small farming communities in the Indus valley in Pakistan.

- **The remains** of over 100 towns of the Indus civilization have been found. The main sites are Mohenjo-Daro, Harappa, Kalibangan and Lothal.

- **Indus cities** were carefully planned, with straight streets, bath-houses and big granaries.

- **At the centre** was a fortified citadel, built on a platform of bricks. The rulers probably lived here.

- **Indus houses** were built of brick around a central courtyard. They had several rooms, a toilet and a well.

- **The Indus civilization** had its own system of writing, which appears on objects such as carved seals – but no one has yet been able to decipher it.

- **Single-room** huts at all intersections are thought to be police-posts.

- **Mohenjo-Daro** and Harappa had 35,000 inhabitants each by about 2500BC.

- **By 1750BC** the Indus civilization had declined, perhaps because floods changed the course of the Indus River. War may also have played a part. It finally vanished with the arrival of the Aryans in India about 1500BC.

# Great migrations

- **The first migrations** occurred when human-like Homo *ergaster* walked out of Africa 750,000 years ago (ya).

- **Experts once** thought oceans blocked migrations but it now seems boats have been used since the earliest days.

- **100,000 ya** humans moved out of Africa into the Near East.

- **About 50,000 ya** humans began the great expansion that took them to every continent but Antarctica within 20,000 years – and wiped out the Neanderthals.

- **50–40,000 ya,** humans spread across Asia and Australasia. 40–35,000 ya, they moved into Europe. 30–25,000 ya, they trekked out of northeast Asia and crossed into the Americas.

- **Early humans** were mainly nomadic hunters, always on the move, following animals into empty lands.

- **Changes in climate** triggered many migrations. People moved north in warm times and retreated in Ice Ages. When the last Ice Age ended, 10,000 ya, hunters moved north through Europe as the weather warmed. Those left behind in the Middle East settled down to farm.

- **From 9000–7000 ya**, farming spread northwest through Europe – partly through people actually moving, partly by word of mouth.

- **4000 ya,** Indo-European peoples spread out from their home in southern Russia. They went south into Iran (as Mittanians) and India (Aryans), southwest into Turkey (Hittites) and Greece (Mycenaeans) and west (Celts).

- **About 3000 ya,** the Sahara began to dry up, and people living there moved to the fringes. Bantu people from Nigeria and the Congo spread south through Africa.

▶ Just like American pioneers in the 1800s, Aryans 4000 years ago moved their families and possessions in covered wagons, probably pulled by oxen.

# The beginnings of Egypt

▲ The Ancient Egyptians built great cities and monuments along the Nile Valley during the Old Kingdom.

- **While dozens** of cities were developing in Mesopotamia, in Egypt the foundations were being laid for the first great nation.

- **From 5000–3300BC** farmers by the River Nile banded together to dig canals to control the Nile's annual flooding and water their crops.

- **By 3300BC,** Nile farming villages had grown into towns. Rich and powerful kings were buried in big, box-like mud-brick tombs called *mastabas*.

- **Egyptian townspeople** began to work copper and stone, paint vases, weave baskets and use potters' wheels.

- **Early Egypt** was divided into two kingdoms: Upper Egypt, and Lower Egypt on the Nile delta. In 3100BC, King Menes of Upper Egypt conquered Lower Egypt to unite the two kingdoms, but a king of Egypt was always called King of Upper and Lower Egypt.

- **Menes** founded a capital for united Egypt at Memphis.

- **With Menes**, Egypt's Dynasty I – the first family of kings – began. The time of Dynasties I and II, which lasted until 2649BC, is known as the Archaic Period.

- **After the Archaic Period** came the Old Kingdom (2649–2134BC), the greatest era of Egyptian culture.

- **Craftsmen** made fine things, scholars developed writing and the calendar and studied astronomy and maths.

- **The greatest scholar** and priest was Imhotep, minister to King Zoser (2630–2611BC). Imhotep was architect of the first of the great pyramids, the Step Pyramid at Sakkara.

# Babylon

- **Babylon** was one of the greatest cities of the ancient world. It stood on the banks of the Euphrates River, near what is now Al Hillah in Iraq.

- **Babylon** reached its peak in two phases: the Old Babylonian Empire (1792–1234BC) and the New Babylonian Empire (626–539BC).

- **Babylon first** grew as a city from 2200BC, but only when Hammurabi became king in 1792 did it become powerful. In his 42-year reign, Hammurabi's conquests gave Babylon a huge empire in Mesopotamia.

- **Hammurabi** was a great law-maker, and some of his laws were enscribed on a stone pillar, or stele, now in the Louvre in Paris. One of his main laws was that 'the strong shall not oppress the weak'. There were also strong laws to punish crimes and protect people from poor workmanship by builders and doctors.

- **After Hammurabi died,** Babylonian power declined and the Assyrians gained the upper hand. After long Babylonian resistance, the Assyrians destroyed the city in 689BC, only to rebuild it 11 years later.

- **Just 60 years or so later,** Babylonian king Nabopolassar and his son Nebuchadnezzar II crushed the Assyrians and built the new Babylonian Empire.

- **Under Nebuchadnezzar II,** Babylon became a vast, magnificent city of 250,000 people, with grand palaces, temples and houses.

- **Babylon** was surrounded by walls 26 m thick – glazed with blue bricks, decorated with dragons, lions and bulls and pierced by eight huge bronze gates. The grandest gate was the Ishtar Gate, which opened on to a paved avenue called the Processional Street.

- **Babylonians** were so sure of their power that King Belshazzar was having a party when the Persians, led by Cyrus, attacked. Cyrus's men dug large canals to divert the Euphrates river, then slipped into the city along the river bed.

> ★ STAR FACT ★
> Dying of a fever, Alexander the Great found cool relief in the Hanging Gardens.

Gardens of lush trees and flowers filled rising brick terraces

The gardens were on a huge pyramid of brick and tar, 25 m high

▶ The Greeks described the Hanging Gardens of Babylon as one of the Seven Wonders of the ancient world. Nebuchadnezzar II was said to have had them built for his wife Amyitis, who missed the greenery of her mountain home.

Water for the plants was continually raised from the river by screw pumps wound by slaves

# First Chinese emperors

- **In China,** farming communities known as the Yanshao culture developed by the Huang He (Yellow River) 7000 years ago. By 5000BC, the region was ruled by emperors.

- **Early Chinese emperors** are known of only by legend. Huang-Ti, the Yellow Emperor, was said to have become emperor in 2697BC.

- **In about 2690BC,** Huang-Ti's wife, Hsi-Ling Shi, discovered how to use the cocoon of the silkworm (the caterpillar of the *Bombyx mori* moth) to make silk. Hsi-Ling was afterwards known as Seine-Than (the Silk Goddess).

- **By 2000BC,** the Chinese were making beautiful jade carvings.

▶ *The Shang emperors were warriors. Their soldiers fought in padded bamboo armour.*

- **The Hsias family** were said to be one of the earliest dynasties of Chinese emperors, ruling from 2000 to 1750BC.

- **The Shangs** were the first definitely known dynasty of emperors. They came to power in 1750BC.

- **Shang emperors** had their fortune told every few days from cracks on heated animal bones. Marks on these 'oracle' bones are the oldest examples of Chinese writing.

- **Under the Shangs,** the Chinese became skilled bronze casters.

- **In the Shang cities** of Anyang and Zengzhou, thick-walled palace temples were surrounded at a distance by villages of artisans.

- **Shang emperors** went to their tombs along with their servants and captives as well as entire chariots with their horses and drivers.

# Egyptian writing

- **Ancient Egyptian** writing developed between 3300 and 3100BC – perhaps inspired by Sumerian scripts.

- **Egyptian writing** is called hieroglyphic (Greek for 'holy writing'). The Egyptians called it the 'words of the gods', because they believed writing was given by the god Thoth.

- **The last known** hieroglyphs were written in AD394, long after anyone knew how to read them.

- **In AD1799,** the French soldiers of Napoleon's army found a stone slab at Rosetta in Egypt. It was covered in three identical texts.

- **In AD1822,** Jean François Champollion deciphered the Rosetta stone, realizing that hieroglyphs are pictures that stand for sounds and letters, not just for objects.

- **There are 700** hieroglyphs. Most are pictures and can be written from left to right, right to left or downwards.

- **Words inside** an oval shape called a *cartouche* are the names of pharaohs.

- **There were two short-hand** versions of hieroglyphs for everyday use – early hieratic script and later demotic script.

- **Egyptians** not only wrote on tomb walls but wrote everyday things with ink and brushes on papyrus (paper made from papyrus reeds) or ostraca (pottery fragments).

- **Only highly trained** scribes could write. Scribes were very well paid and often exempt from taxes.

◀ *The walls of Egyptian tombs are covered in hieroglyphs.*

# Egyptian lifestyles

▲ Egyptian girls were highly conscious of their looks, wearing make-up and jewellery and doing their hair carefully.

- **Egyptian women** painted their nails with henna and reddened their lips and cheeks with red ochre paste.
- **Egyptian fashions** changed little over thousands of years, and their clothes were usually white linen.
- **Men wrapped linen** round themselves in a kilt. Women wore long, light dresses. Children ran naked in summer.
- **Every Egyptian** wore jewellery. The rich wore gold inlaid with gems; the poor wore copper or faience (made by heating powdered quartz).
- **Egyptians** loved board games. The favourites were senet and 'hounds and jackals'.
- **Rich Egyptians** had lavish parties with food and drink, singers, musicians, acrobats and dancing girls.
- **Rich Egyptians** often went fishing or boating.

- **Egyptians** washed every day in the river or with a jug and basin. The rich were given showers by servants.
- **Instead of soap** they used a cleansing cream made from oil, lime and perfume. They also rubbed themselves all over with moisturizing oil.

# Ancient Crete

- **The Minoan civilization** of Crete – an island south of Greece – was the first civilization in Europe.
- **Minoan civilization** began about 3000BC, reached its height from 2200 to 1450BC, then mysteriously vanished – perhaps after the volcano on nearby Santorini erupted.
- **The name Minoan** comes from the Greek legend of King Minos. Minos was the son of Europa, the princess seduced by the god Zeus in the shape of a bull.
- **Greek stories** tell how Minos built a labyrinth (maze) in which he kept the Minotaur, a monster with a man's body and a bull's head.
- **Catching a bull** by the horns and leaping over it (bull-leaping) was an important Minoan religious rite.
- **Experts now think Minos** was a title, so every Cretan king was called Minos.
- **The Minoans** were great seafarers and traded all over the eastern Mediterranean.
- **At the centre** of each Minoan town was a palace, such as

those found at Knossos, Zakro, Phaestos and Mallia.

- **The largest Minoan palace** is at Knossos, which covered 20,000 square metres and housed over 30,000 people.
- **The walls** of the palace are decorated with frescoes (paintings), which reveal a great deal about the Minoans.

▶ Knossos had a very good water supply system via long clay pipes. This is the queen's bathroom.

# The pharaohs

Family shrine

Grand reception area where the official did his business for the pharaoh

Well

The central hall was where the official entertained friends

Bedrooms

Kitchen

Wine cellar

Servants' quarters

Stables

Grain stores

▶ The patronage of the pharaohs gave great power and prestige to their officials, who built houses like these around 1200BC.

★ STAR FACT ★
People thought the pharaoh could control the weather and make the land fertile.

● **Pharaohs** were the kings of Ancient Egypt. They were also High Priest, head judge and commander of the army.

● **Egyptians** thought of the pharaoh as both the god Horus and the son of the sun god Re. When he died he was transformed into the god Osiris, father of Horus. Since he was a god, anyone approaching him had to crawl.

● **The pharaoh was** thought to be so holy that he could not be addressed directly. Instead, people referred to him indirectly by talking of the pharaoh, which is Egyptian for 'great house'. Only after about 945BC was he addressed directly as the pharaoh.

● **In official documents** the pharaoh had five titles: Horus; Two Ladies; Golden Horus; King of Upper and Lower Egypt and Lord of the Double Land (Upper and Lower Egypt); and Son of Re and Lord of the Diadems.

● **The pharaoh's godlike** status gave him magical powers. His *uraeus* (the snake on his crown) was supposed to spit flames at his enemies and he could trample thousands.

● **There were 31 dynasties** (families) of pharaohs, beginning with Menes in c.3100BC and ending with the Persian kings in 323BC. Each dynasty is identified in order by a Roman numeral. So the fifth Dynasty is Dynasty V.

● **A pharaoh** usually married his eldest sister to keep the royal blood pure. She became queen and was known as the Royal Heiress, but the pharaoh had many other wives. If the pharaoh died while his eldest son was still a child, his queen became regent and ruled on his behalf.

● **To preserve their bodies for ever,** pharaohs were buried inside massive tombs. The first pharaohs were buried in huge pyramids. Because these were often robbed, later pharaohs were buried in tombs cut deep into cliffs.

● **One of the greatest pharaohs** was Ramses II, who ruled from 1290 to 1224BC. He left a legacy of many huge buildings including the rock temple of Abu Simbel.

# The Olmecs and Chavins

- **People** began farming in Meso America (Mexico and Central America) 9,000 years ago, almost as long ago as in the Middle East.

- **By 2000BC** there were permanent villages and large farms growing corn, beans, squash and other crops.

- **Between 1200 and 400BC,** a remarkable culture was developed by the Olmecs in western Mexico.

- **The Olmecs** had a counting system and calendar, but no writing system, so little is known about them.

- **Ruins of a huge** Olmec pyramid have been found at La Venta in Tabasco, Mexico.

- **The Olmecs** carved huge 'baby-face' heads from basalt with enormous skill – apparently with only stone chisels, since they had no metal.

- **By 2000BC,** huge religious sites were being built all over what is now Peru.

- **From 800 to 400BC,** the Chavin civilization spread from the religious centre of Chavin de Huantar in the Peruvian mountains.

- **From AD100 to 700,** America's first true city developed at Teotihuacan, with vast pyramids and palaces.

- **Teotihuacan** may have been the world's biggest city in AD300, with a population of over 250,000.

◀ The Olmec heads were carved from huge blocks of volcanic rock weighing up to 14 tonnes. No one knows how they were moved.

# Aryan India

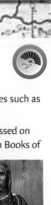

- **The Aryans** were a fair-skinned herding people from southern Russia, ancestors to both Greeks and Indians.

- **About 2000BC,** the Aryan people began to sweep through Persia and on into India, where they destroyed the Indus civilizations.

- **The Aryans** were tough warriors who loved music, dancing and chariot racing, but slowly adopted Dravidian gods and settled in villages as farmers.

- **Aryans** were originally split into three classes: Brahmins (priests) at the top, Kshatriya (warriors) in the middle and Vaisyas (merchants and farmers) at the bottom.

- **When they settled** in India, the Aryans added a fourth class, the conquered, dark-skinned Dravidians, who became their servants.

- **From the four Aryan classes,** the elaborate system of castes (classes) in today's India developed.

- **The Aryans** gave India Sanskrit, the ancestor of all India's languages today.

- **Sanskrit** is closely related to European languages such as English, German and Latin.

- **The Aryans** had no form of writing, but they passed on history and religion by word of mouth in spoken Books of Knowledge, or *Vedas*.

- **The Brahmins** created as *Vedas* the first Hindu scriptures, including the *Rig-Veda*, the *Sama-Veda* and *Yajur-Veda*.

▶ The dark-skinned Dravidian people who lived in India when the Aryans arrived became the servant class.

# Semites

- **Jewish people** and Arabs are Semitic people.

- **In 2500BC,** the Semites were farming peoples such as the Akkadians, Canaanites and Amorites, who lived in what is now Israel, Jordan and Syria.

- **In 2371BC,** an Akkadian called Sargon seized the throne of the Sumerian city of Kish. He soon conquered all Sumer and Akkad and created a great empire.

- **The Akkadian Empire** collapsed c.2230BC, under attacks from tribes of Gutians from the mountains.

- **From 3000 to 1500BC,** Canaanite Byblos was one of the world's great trading ports, famous for its purple cloth.

- **c.2000BC,** Amorites conquered Sumer, Akkad and Canaan. In 1792BC, the Amorite Hammurabi was ruler of Babylon.

◀ *The Dead Sea Scrolls, on display here, are ancient Hebrew manuscripts found by shepherds in 1947 in a cave near the Dead Sea. They include the oldest known texts of the Bible's Old Testament.*

- **The first Hebrews** were a Semitic tribe from southern Mesopotamia. Their name meant 'people of the other side' of the Euphrates River.

- **According** to the Bible, the first Hebrew was Abraham, a shepherd who lived in the Sumerian city of Ur, 4000 years ago. He led his family first to Syria, then to Canaan (now Palestine), where he settled.

- **Abraham's grandson** Jacob was also called Israel and the Hebrews were afterwards called Israelites.

- **About 1000BC,** the Israelites prospered under three kings – Saul, David and Solomon.

# The Assyrians

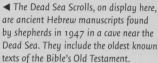

- **The Assyrians** came originally from the upper Tigris valley around the cities of Ashur, Nineveh and Arbela.

- **c.2000BC,** Assyria was invaded by Amorites. Under a line of Amorite kings, Assyria built up a huge empire. King Adadnirari I called himself 'King of Everything'.

- **The Old Assyrian Empire** lasted six centuries, until it was broken up by horsemen from a place called Mittani.

> **★ STAR FACT ★**
> King Assurbanipal's (668–627BC) palace was filled with books and plants from all over the world.

- **From 1114 to 1076BC,** King Tiglath Pileser I rebuilt Assyrian power by conquest, creating the New Assyrian Empire.

- **The New Assyrian Empire** reached its peak under Tiglath-Pileser III (744–727BC) and was finally overthrown by the Medes and Babylonians in 612BC.

- **The Assyrians** were ruthless warriors. They grew beards and fought with bows, iron swords, spears and chariots.

- **The Assyrians** built good roads all over their empire, so that the army could move fast to quell trouble.

- **The Assyrians** built magnificent palaces and cities such as Khorsabad and Nimrud.

- **Arab warriors** rode camels into battle for the Assyrians.

◀ Statues of winged bulls with human heads were found at Nimrud.

# Oceania

- **The people** of the Pacific may have been the greatest seafarers of the ancient world.

- **Up until 5000 years ago,** the sea was lower and Tasmania, Australia and New Guinea were all part of one big continent.

- **About 50,000 years ago,** bold, seafaring people crossed the ocean from Southeast Asia and settled in Australia.

- **Most early sites** are now lost offshore under the sea, which rose to cut off New Guinea and Australia c.5000BC.

- **The Australian** aboriginals are descendants of these original inhabitants.

- **The oldest settlement** in New Guinea is 40,000 years old.

- **c.4000BC,** domesticated plants and animals reached New Guinea from Asia, and farmers drained fields at Kuk Swamp. But many people remained hunters.

- **About 2000BC,** people sailed in canoes from Indonesia to colonize Melanesia and Micronesia – the islands of the western Pacific, such as Vanuatu.

▲ The people of Oceania crossed the oceans in canoes like these tens of thousands of years before the great European explorers.

- **Early Melanesians** are known by their 'Lapita' pottery, which originated in the Molucca Islands of Indonesia.

- **Rowing canoes** seen in a 50,000-year-old cave painting in Australia match those seen all over the Pacific – and in caves in the Amazon jungle.

# Dead Egyptians

- **Egyptians saw death** as a step on the way to a fuller life in the Next World.

- **Everyone was thought** to have three souls: the *ka, ba* and *akh*. For these to be well, the body must survive intact, so the Egyptians tried to preserve the body.

- **Gradually,** the Egyptians developed embalming techniques to preserve the bodies of kings and rich people who could afford it.

- **The organs** were cut out and stored in 'canopic jars' and the body dried with natron (salt).

- **The dried body** was filled with sawdust, resin and natron, then wrapped in bandages. The embalmed body is a 'mummy'.

- **A portrait** mask was put over the mummy's head, then it was put in a coffin.

- **Anthropoid (human-shaped)** coffins were used from about 2000BC onwards. Often, the mummy was put inside a nest of two or three coffins, each carved and painted and perhaps decorated with gold and gems.

- **The wooden coffin** was laid inside a stone coffin or sarcophagus inside the burial chamber.

- **At first,** the prayers said for a dead ruler were carved on pyramid walls as 'Pyramid Texts'. Later, they were put on coffins as 'Coffin Texts'. From 1500BC, they were written on papyrus in the *Book of the Dead*.

- **To help him** overcome various tests and make it to the Next World, a dead man needed amulets and a *Book of the Dead*, containing magic spells and a map.

◄ When placing the mask over the mummy, the chief embalmer wore a mask representing the jackal god Anubis.

# Persia

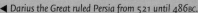

- **Iran** is named after the Aryan people who began settling there in c.15,000BC. Two Aryan tribes – the Medes and Persians – soon became dominant.

- **In 670BC,** the Medes under King Cyaxeres joined forces with the Babylonians to finally overthrow the Assyrians.

- **In 550BC,** the Medes themselves were overthrown by the Persians. The Persian king Cyrus II was the grandson of the king of the Medes, Astyages.

- **Cyrus II** had an army of horsemen and very skilled archers. He went on to establish a great Persian empire after conquering Lydia and Babylon.

- **The Persian Empire** was ruled by the Achaemenid family until it was destroyed by Alexander the Great in 330BC.

◀ *Darius the Great ruled Persia from 521 until 486BC.*

- **The Persian Empire** reached its greatest extent under Darius I, who called himself Shahanshah ('King of kings'). Darius introduced gold and silver coins, and also brought chickens to the Middle East.

- **Darius built** a famous road system and split his empire into 20 *satrapies* (regions), each ruled by a *satrap*.

- **'King's Ears'** were officials who travelled around and reported trouble back to the king.

- **The Persians** built luxurious cities and palaces, first at Susa, then in Darius's reign, at Persepolis.

- **Persian priests,** or magi, were known for their magic skills, and gave us the word 'magic'. A famous magus called Zarathustra, unusually, worshipped a single god: Ahuru Mazda. His god's evil enemy was Angra Mainyu.

# Weapons of war

- **Early stone axes and spears** may have been used both for hunting and as weapons. Remains of a half-a-million year-old wooden spear were found at Boxgrove, England.

- **A spear-thrower** was a stick with a notch in one end to take the end of a spear. With it, hunters (or fighters) could hurl a spear with tremendous force. Spear-throwers were the first ever machines made by humans, c.35,000BC.

▼ *The chariot was the airforce of the ancient civilizations, speeding archers and spear-throwers across the battlefield. Egyptians, Hittites and Assyrians fought huge battles with thousands of chariots.*

- **The first pictures** of bows come from North Africa, c.15,000-30,000BC. Bows could be devastatingly effective and were the main weapons of the earliest civilizations.

- **The invention** of bronze, c.3000BC, meant people could make metal swords, daggers, axes and spears.

- **A tiny bronze statue** of a chariot found at Tell Agrab, Iraq, dates from 3000BC. This is the first image of a chariot.

- **The Persian emperor** Cyrus (559–529BC) added scythes (long, sharp blades) poking out from chariot wheels to slice through the legs of enemy soldiers and horses.

- **The oldest helmet** (c.2500BC), made of a gold and silver alloy called electrum, was found in the royal tombs of Ur.

- **The crossbow** was invented in the Greek colony of Syracuse, about 400BC.

- **Alexander the Great** used giant crossbows firing 5 m arrows to win his empire between 340 and 323BC.

- **Around AD100,** Dionysius of Alexander in Egypt invented a rapid-firing crossbow, able to fire dozens of bolts a minute.

# Tutankhamun

- Tutankhamun was pharaoh (king) of Ancient Egypt from 1347 to 1339BC. He was a boy when he became pharaoh and only 18 when he died.

- Tutankhamun was the last of the great 18th dynasty (family) of pharaohs who ruled Egypt 1567–1339BC. They included the warrior queen Hatshepsut, and Thutmose III, who led Egypt to the peak of its power around 1400BC.

- Tutankhamun was the son of Akhenaten, who with his queen Nefertiti created a revolution in Egypt. Akhenaten replaced worship of the old Egyptian gods with worship of a single god, and moved the capital to Armarna.

- Tutankhamun's wife was his half-sister Ankhesenamun. When he died – perhaps murdered – Ankhesenamun was at the mercy of his enemies, Ay and general Horemheb. She wrote to the Hittite king asking for his son to marry, but the Hittite prince was murdered on the way to Egypt. Ankhesenamun was forced to marry Ay, who thus became pharaoh. She also died young.

> ★ STAR FACT ★
> Tutankhamun's third, inner coffin was made of over a tonne of solid gold.

- The Valley of the Kings near Luxor on the Nile in Egypt is the world's greatest archaeological site. It was the special burial place of the 18th dynasty pharaohs and contains the tombs of 62 pharaohs, and high officials.

- Tutankhamun's tomb was the only tomb in the Valley of the Kings not plundered over the centuries. When opened, it contained 5000 items, including many fabulous carved and gold items.

- Tutankhamun's tomb was discovered by the English archaeologist Howard Carter, in 1922.

- Rumours of a curse on those disturbing the tomb began when Carter's pet canary was eaten by a cobra – the pharaoh's symbol – at the moment the tomb was opened.

- Experts worked out the dates of Tutankhamun's reign from the date labels on wine-jars left in the tomb.

◀ A fabulous gold mask was found in the innermost coffin, over the badly mummified remains of the young king. The skull showed signs of a fracture from a hammer.

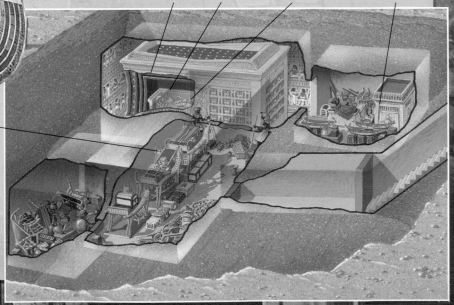

In the burial chamber were four shrines of gilded wood, one inside the other

Inside the shrines, there was a red sandstone sarcophagus (coffin)

Inside the sarcophagus, there were three gold coffins, one inside the other

Beyond the burial chamber was a treasury full of gold and other treasures

Fabulous beds, chests, gold chariot wheels, and carved animals in the anteroom were just a taste of the riches to come

▶ When Carter opened Tutankhamun's tomb, he came first to an anteroom. It took him three years to clear this room and enter the burial chamber, with its huge gold shrines containing the coffins.

# The Trojan Wars

- **From 1600 to 1100BC,** mainland Greece was dominated by tough warrior people called the Mycenaeans.
- **The Mycenaeans** fought with long bronze swords, long leather shields and bronze armour.
- **Mycenaeans** lived in small kingdoms, each with its own fortified hilltop city or *acropolis*.
- **A typical Mycenaean noble** was like a Viking chieftain. In the middle of his palace was a great hall with a central fireplace where warriors would sit around telling tales of heroic deeds.
- **After 1500BC** Mycenaean kings were buried in a beehive-shaped tomb called a *tholos*, with a long, corridor-shaped entrance.

▶ Troy fell when the Greeks pretended to give up and go home, leaving behind a huge wooden horse. The jubilant Trojans dragged this into the city – only to discover Greeks hiding inside it.

- **The Greek poet Homer** tells how a city called Troy was destroyed by the Mycenaeans after a ten-year siege. Historians once thought this was just a story, but now the remains of Troy have been discovered, they think there may be some truth in it.
- **The Trojan War** in Homer's tale is caused by the beautiful Helen of Sparta. She married Menalaus, brother of King Agamemnon of Mycenae, but she fell in love with Prince Paris of Troy.
- **Helen and Paris** eloped to Troy and Agamemnon and other Greeks laid siege to Troy to take her back.
- **The battle** featured many heroes – such as Hector, Achilles and Odysseus.
- **The Greeks** finally captured Troy when Greek soldiers hidden inside a wooden horse found their way into the city.

# Early Greece

- **Around 1200BC,** the Mycenaeans began to abandon their cities, and a people called the Dorians took over Greece.
- **Many Mycenaeans** fled overseas in a large battle fleet, and the Egyptians called them the Sea Peoples. Some ended up in Italy and may have been the ancestors of the Etruscan people there.
- **With the end** of Mycenaean civilization, Greece entered the Dark Ages as the art of writing was lost.

- **About 800BC,** the Greeks began to emerge from the Dark Ages as they re-learned writing from the Phoenicians, a people who traded in the eastern Mediterranean.
- **The period** of Greek history from 800 to 500BC is called the Archaic (Ancient) Period.
- **In the Archaic Period,** the Greek population grew rapidly. States were governed by a few rich aristocrats.
- **The early Greeks** loved athletics and held four major events. They were called the Panhellenic Games and drew competitors from all over the Greek world.
- **The four Panhellenic Games** were the Olympic, Pythian, Isthmian and Nemean Games.
- **The Olympic Games** started in 776BC and were the most important. They were held every four years at Olympia.
- **The Greek poet Homer** wrote his famous poems about the Trojan Wars around 700BC.

◀ A Greek house may have looked something like this 2,600 years ago, with first-floor bedrooms surrounding a courtyard.

# The Mayans

◄ The Mayan pyramid at Chichén Itzá in the Yucatán.

- **The Mayans** were a people who dominated Central America for 2500 years until AD1441.

- **The Mayans** began building large pyramids with small temples on top between 600BC and AD250.

- **Mayan civilization** peaked between AD250 and 900. This is called the Classic Period.

- **During the Classic Period,** Mayan civilization centred on great cities such as Tikal in the Guatemalan lowlands. They traded far and wide on foot and in dug-out canoes.

★ STAR FACT ★
The Mayans were brilliant astronomers and believed that the stars linked them to their gods.

- **Mayans in the Classic Period** developed a clever form of writing in symbols representing sounds and ideas. They recorded their history on stone monuments called *stelae*.

- **Mysteriously,** around AD800, the Mayans stopped making *stelae* and the Guatemalan cities were abandoned.

- **From AD800 to 1200,** the most powerful Mayan city was Chichén Itzá in the Yucatán region. From 1200 to 1440 another city, Mayapan, came to the fore. After 1440, Mayan civilization rapidly broke up, though no-one knows why.

- **The Mayans** were deeply religious. Deer, dogs, turkeys and even humans were often sacrificed to the gods in the temples on top of the pyramids.

- **Mayan farmers** grew mainly corn, beans and squash. From the corn, women made flat pancakes now called tortillas, and an alcoholic drink called *balche*.

# Confucius

- **Confucius** is the most famous thinker and teacher in Chinese history.

- **Confucius** is the name used by Europeans. Chinese people called him Kongzi or K'ung-Fu-Tzu.

- **Confucius was born** in Lu, now Shantung Province, in 551BC, traditionally on 28 September, and died in 479BC.

- **Confucius mastered** the six Chinese arts – ritual, music, archery, charioteering, calligraphy (writing) and arithmetic – and became a brilliant teacher.

- **Confucius** was the first person in China to argue that all men should be educated to make the world a better place, and that teaching could be a way of life.

- **In middle age,** Confucius served as a minister for the King of Lu. He had a highly moral approach to public service. He told statesmen this golden rule: 'Do not do to others what you would not have them do to you.'

- **The King of Lu** was not interested in Confucius's ideas, so Confucius went into exile, followed by his students.

- **After his death,** Confucius's ideas were developed by teachers like Mencius (390–305BC) and Xunzi (c.250BC) into a way of life called Confucianism. Until recently, this dominated Chinese life.

- **Living at the same** time as Confucius may have been a man called Lao-Tse. Lao-Tse wrote the *Tao Te Ching*, the basis of Taoist religion.

- **The *Tao Te Ching*** tells of the *Tao* (Way) – the underlying unity of nature that makes everything what it is.

► Confucius's belief was that court officials should not plot for power but study music, poetry and the history of their ancestors.

# Chinese technology

- **Western experts** have only recently realized that ancient Chinese technology was very advanced, and many of their early inventions only reached Europe thousands of years later.

- **In the early 1600s,** the great English thinker Francis Bacon said that three quite recent inventions had changed the world – printing, gunpowder and the ship's magnetic compass. All of these had been invented in China a thousand or more years earlier.

- **One of the oldest surviving** printed books is the *Diamond Sutra*, printed in China about AD868. But printing in China goes back to at least the 7th century AD.

- **The world's first robot** was an amazing ancient Chinese cart with gears from the wheels that turned a statue on top so that its finger always pointed south.

- **The Chinese** had alcoholic spirits 2000 years ago, over a thousand years before they came to Europe.

- **The horse stirrup** was invented in China in the 3rd century BC. This gave horse-soldiers a steady platform to fight from and allowed them to wear heavy armour.

- **The wheelbarrow** was invented by the Chinese c.100BC.

- **Cast-iron ploughs** were made in China around 200BC.

- **Football** was invented in China. About 200BC, they were playing a game called *t'su chu*. It involved kicking an inflated leather ball through a hole in a silk net.

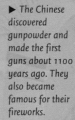

▶ The Chinese discovered gunpowder and made the first guns about 1100 years ago. They also became famous for their fireworks.

▶ The Chinese made a magnetic compass called a sinan over 2000 years ago. A ladle made of a magnetic stone called lodestone spins round on a shiny bronze plate to point south.

▲ One particularly nasty Chinese invention was the 'Heaven-Rumbling Thunderclap Fierce Fire Erupter'. This was a gunpowder-fired device that shot out shells of poisonous gas.

◀ In AD132, Chang Heng made the world's first earthquake detector with a special jar. When even a faint, distant quake occurred, a metal ball would fall with a clang from the dragon's mouth at the top of the jar into the toad's mouth.

▲ Acupuncture involves sticking pins in certain points on the body to treat illness. The Chinese used it 1800 years ago – but it may have been used earlier in Europe .

◀ The Chinese invented mechanical clocks in AD723 – 600 years earlier than Europe. This is Su Sung's 'Cosmic Engine', an amazing 10-m-high clock built at Khaifeng in AD1090.

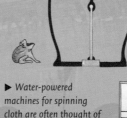

▶ Water-powered machines for spinning cloth are often thought of as inventions of the English Industrial Revolution in the 1700s. In fact, the Chinese were building them at least 500 years earlier, to spin a cloth called ramie.

# The search for Troy

- Troy is the city in the Ancient Greek poet Homer's famous epic, the *Iliad*. It was once thought to be entirely mythical.

- **In 1822,** British scholar Charles McClaren suggested that Homer's Troy might be in Turkey. He pinpointed a mound called Hisarlik near the Dardanelles – a narrow sea linking the Black Sea and the Aegean.

- **German archaeologist** Heinrich Schliemann began digging at Hisarlik mound in 1871.

- **In 1873,** Schliemann uncovered fortifications and remains of a very ancient city, which he believed to be Troy.

- **Schliemann** also found a treasure of gold and silver which he called Priam's treasure after the Trojan King Priam mentioned in the *Iliad*. He smuggled this out of Turkey to take to Europe.

- When Schliemann found this gold mask at Mycenae, in 1876, he thought it must be Agamemnon's. In fact, it dates from 300 years earlier.

- **In 1876,** Schliemann was digging at Mycenae in Greece. He found what he thought was the tomb of Agamemnon, king of the Trojans' enemies in the *Iliad*.

- **In the 1890s,** Wilhelm Dorpfield showed that Hisarlik mound is made of nine layers of city remains. This is because the city was destroyed by fire or earthquake nine times. Each time the survivors built on the rubble.

- **Schliemann** thought Homer's Troy was Troy II (2), second layer from the bottom. Dorpfield thought it was Troy VI.

- **Troy I to V** (1 to 5) are now thought to date from the early Bronze Age (c. 3000 to 1900BC).

- **Experts** now think Homer's Troy may be Troy VII, a layer of the seventh city, dating from about 1250BC.

# Greek city-states

- **Ancient Greece** was not a single country in its early days, but a collection of independent cities or city-states.

- **A Greek city-state** was called a *polis* (plural *poleis*).

- **Polis** gives us the words politics and police – and polite.

- **There were several hundred** *poleis* in Ancient Greece. The largest were Athens and Sparta.

- **Each city** typically had a mound called an *acropolis* with a temple on top, and a market place called an *agora*.

> ★ **STAR FACT** ★
> The laws of the Athenian oligarch Draco were so harsh that severe laws are still called draconian.

- **To start with** (from about 800 to 600BC), city-states were governed by oligarchs (a few powerful men) or a tyrant, but people gradually got more say.

- **People in Greek city-states** were either free or slaves. Free men (not women) were split into citizens (born in the city itself) and *metics* (immigrants).

- **In 508BC,** a man called Cleisthenes gave Athens a new system of government called democracy.

- **Democracy** comes from the Greek word *demos* (people) and *kratos* (rule). The idea was that every citizen (but not metics and slaves) had the right to speak and vote in the Assembly, held every ten days on a hill called the Pnyx.

◄ The most famous acropolis is the Acropolis in Athens with the Parthenon temple on top, but nearly every polis had one.

# Zhou and Qin dynasties

- *c.*1100BC, the Shang in China were conquered by a people called the Zhou.

- **The Zhou** extended the Shang's territory far across China, but the kingdom was divided into large estates, each with its own ruler.

- **In the time of the Zhou,** the Chinese began using iron, both for ploughs and weapons, and made many advances in technology.

- **Great thinkers** such as Laozi and Confucius came to the fore.

- **Confucius** believed morals were vital in government service, but a minister called Shang Yang (who died 338BC) thought the law must be strengthened by any means. This is called Legalism.

- **Shang Yang's** family – the Qin – overthrew the Zhou in 312BC.

▲ *Although today's brick and stone wall dates from the 1400s, the Great Wall of China was first built of earth bricks in 214BC, under Shi Huangdi.*

- **In 246BC,** Qin emperor Zheng expanded the empire and called himself Shi Huangdi, First Emperor. He had the 4000-km-long Great Wall built to protect his empire from nomads from the north.

- **Shi Huangdi** banned books and buried 460 Confucian scholars alive. His eldest son Fu Su was banished when he objected.

- **When Shi Huangdi** died, in 210BC, his body was taken secretly to the capital by minister Li Si with a fish cart to hide the smell of rotting flesh. Li Si sent a letter to Fu Su, pretending it was from his father, telling him to commit suicide. Fu Su did and so Li Si came to power.

- **Shi Huangdi** was buried with an army of 6000 life-size clay soldiers, called the Terracotta Army when found in 1974. Parts of the tomb are said to be booby-trapped.

# Famous generals

▶ *Hannibal's greatest feat was leading an army – with elephants – through Spain and then the Alps in winter to attack Rome from the north.*

- **In 2300BC** King Sargon of Akkadia led his soldiers to victory over much larger armies by using especially far-shooting bows.

- **Tuthmose III** (1479–1425BC) was perhaps the greatest of the warrior pharaohs, fighting 17 campaigns and taking Egypt to its greatest extent.

- **Assurbanipal** (669–627BC) was the great Assyrian leader whose chariots gave him a powerful empire from the Nile to the Caucasus Mountains.

- **Sun-Tzu** was the Chinese military genius who, in 500BC, wrote the first manual on the art of war.

- **Alexander the Great** was the Macedonian whose army of 35,000 was the most efficient yet seen – and who perfected the phalanx.

- **Hannibal** (247–182BC) was the greatest general of the powerful city of Carthage (now near Tunis in Africa).

- **Scipio** (237–183BC) was the Roman general who conquered Spain and broke Carthaginian power in Africa.

- **Julius Caesar** was the greatest Roman general.

- **Belisarius** (AD505–565) and Narses (AD478–573) were generals for Byzantine Emperor Justinian. Their mounted archers defeated the Vandals and Goths.

- **Charles Martel** (AD688–741), 'the Hammer', was the Frankish king who defeated the Moors at Tours in France in AD732 and turned back the Arab conquest of Europe.

# Buddha

- **Buddha** was the founder of the Buddhist religion, who lived in India c.563–483BC.

- **Buddha's** real name was Siddhartha Gautama.

- **Buddha** is not a name but a title (like the messiah) meaning 'enlightened one', so you should really say 'the Buddha'.

- **Archaeological excavations** finished in 1995 suggest that a man who may have been Siddhartha lived in the palace of his father Suddodhana on what is now the border of Nepal and India.

- **As a young prince,** Siddhartha lived a life of luxury. When he was 16 years old, he married his cousin the Princess Yasodhara, who was also 16 years old.

◄ Most statues of the Buddha show him sitting cross-legged deeply meditating (thinking).

- **The turning point** was when Siddhartha was 29 and he saw four visions: an old man, a sick man, a corpse and a wandering holy man.

- **The first three visions** told Siddhartha that life involved ageing, sickness and death. The fourth told him he must leave his wife and become a holy man.

- **After six years of** self-denial, Siddhartha sat down under a shady 'bo' tree to think – and after several hours the answer came to him.

- **The Buddha** spent the rest of his life preaching his message around India.

- **The Buddha** died at the age of 80. His bones became sacred relics.

# Greek thinkers

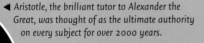

◄ Aristotle, the brilliant tutor to Alexander the Great, was thought of as the ultimate authority on every subject for over 2000 years.

- **The great thinkers** of Ancient Greece were called philosophers. Philosophy is Greek for 'love of wisdom'.

- **The key philosophers** were Socrates, Plato and Aristotle.

- **Socrates** (466–399BC) believed people would behave well if they knew what good behaviour was and challenged people to think about truth, good and evil.

- **Plato** (427–348BC) argued that, behind the messy chaos of everyday experience, there is a perfect and beautiful Idea or Form. He also tried to find the ideal way of governing a state.

- **Aristotle** (384–322BC) argued that, for true knowledge, you must find the 'final cause' – why something happens.

- **Aristotle** was the first great scientist, stressing the need to collect data, sort the results and interpret them.

- **Many of the basic** ideas in philosophy, even today, come from Socrates, Plato and Aristotle, and other Greek philosophers such as Epicurus and Diogenes.

- **Greek mathematicians** such as Euclid, Appolonius, Pythagoras and Archimedes worked out many of our basic rules of maths. Most school geometry still depends on the system devised by Euclid.

- **Greek astronomers** like Aristarchus and Anaxagoras made many brilliant deductions – but many of these were forgotten. Aristarchus realized that the Earth turned on its axis and circled the Sun. Yet it was almost 2,000 years before this idea was generally accepted.

★ STAR FACT ★
Archimedes showed how the effect of a lever could be worked out by maths.

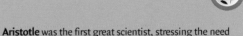

# Homer

- **Homer** is the Ancient Greek poet said to have written the ancient world's two greatest poems: the *Iliad* and the *Odyssey*.

- **Homer probably** lived in the 9th century BC in Ionia, on what is now the Aegean coast of Turkey, or on the island of Chios.

- **No one knows** for certain if Homer existed, or if he composed all of both poems. Most experts think he did.

- **In Homer's time** there was a great tradition of bards. These were poets who recited aloud great tales of heroic deeds. They knew the poems by heart and so never wrote them down.

- **The *Iliad* and the *Odyssey*** are the only poems from the times of the bards that were written down and so survive. They may have been written down at the time, or later.

- **After Homer's time** the two great poems were used in religious festivals in Greece.

◀ *Nothing is known for certain about Homer, but legend says he was blind.*

- **For centuries** after Homer's time, Greek children learned to read, and learned about the legends of the past, by studying Homer's two great poems.

- **In the 2nd century BC,** scholars at the Alexandrian Library in Egypt studied the poems. A few scholars came to the conclusion that they were so different in style they must have been written by two different poets.

- **The *Iliad*** is a long poem in lofty language about the Trojan Wars, in which the Greeks besiege the city of Troy to take back the kidnapped Helen.

- **The *Odyssey*** tells the amazing adventures of hero Odysseus on a great journey.

# Early Americans

▲ *Carving wooden duck decoys for hunting is a North American tradition dating back thousands of years.*

- **The Americas** were the last continents humans occupied.

- **The first Americans** may have been Australian aboriginals who arrived by boat 50,000 years ago.

- **Ancestors of today's Native Americans** probably came to the Americas 20–35,000 years ago, from Asia. They are thought to have walked across the strip of land that once joined Asia and North America across the Bering Strait.

> ★ STAR FACT ★
> A 50,000 year-old skull found in Colombia resembles the skulls of Australian aboriginals.

- **By 6000BC, the first Native Americans** had spread south from Alaska and far down into South America.

- **There is evidence** that humans were living in Mexico over 20,000 years ago. At El Jobo in Colombia, pendants dating back to 14,920BC have been found.

- **10,000 years ago,** groups of 'Paleo-Indians' on North America's Great Plains hunted now-extinct animals such as camels and mammoths. In the dry western mountains, Desert peoples planted wild grass-seed.

- **In Mexico,** people began to grow squash, peppers and beans at least 8500 years ago.

- **Corn was probably first** grown around 7000 years ago.

- **Corn, beans and squash** provided food for early American civilizations such as the Olmecs and Mayans.

# Greek art

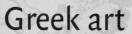

A chorus linked the scenes with verse and songs

The circular acting area was called the orchestra

A typical theatre, like the Theatre of Dionysus in Athens, seated 14,000 in stadium-like rows

Scenes were played by just two or three actors, each wearing a mask

Audiences took cushions to sit on and picnics to keep them going

Behind the orchestra was a house or 'skene' where the actors changed. Later this became a backdrop.

▶ Formal drama was developed in Ancient Greece in the 5th and 6th centuries BC. Huge audiences watched plays in open-air arenas.

In later Greek theatres, the skene developed side wings here called paraskinia

- **In the heyday of Ancient Greece,** thousands of sculptors, architects, painters, dramatists and poets were creating a fantastic wealth of beautiful works of art.

- **The Greeks** made graceful statues and friezes to decorate temples and homes. They were carved mostly from marble and limestone and then painted, though in surviving statues the paint has worn away.

- **The most famous sculptors** were Phidias (c.490–420BC), Praxiteles (c.330BC), Lysippus (c.380–306BC) and Myron (c.500–440BC). Phidias's huge gold and ivory statue of the god Zeus was famous throughout the ancient world.

- **Greek architects** such as Ictinus and Callicrates created beautiful marble and limestone temples fronted by graceful columns and elegant triangular friezes. The most famous is the Parthenon in Athens.

- **The Greeks** had three styles for columns: the simple Doric, the slender Ionic, topped by scrolls, and the ornate Corinthian, topped by sculpted acanthus leaves.

- **The style** created by the Greek temples is now called Classical and has influenced architects ever since.

- **The Greeks** believed each art was inspired by one of nine goddesses called Muses.

- **Ancient Greek writers** include the poets Homer, Sappho and Pindar. They created styles of writing including epic poetry.

- **The tragedy** is a grand drama doomed to end unhappily for the hero. Tragedy was created by Greek dramatists such as Aeschylus, Euripides and Sophocles, who wrote the tragedy King Oedipus.

> ★ STAR FACT ★
> The Colossus of Rhodes was a huge 37-m-high statue cast in bronze by Greek sculptor Chares. It stood near to the harbour of Rhodes, an island in the Aegean Sea.

▶ The famous Venus de Milo was found on the Aegean island of Milos in AD 1820. It was carved in Greek Antioch (now in Turkey) around 150BC and shows the goddess of love Aphrodite (Roman goddess Venus). The statue originally had arms.

# What people ate

- **1.5 million years ago,** people learned how to use fire to cook food. The oldest known cooking fire is at Swartkrans, South Africa.

- **The first ovens** were pits for hot coals, first used in the Ukraine about 20,000 years ago. The first real ovens were from Sumer and Egypt, c.2600BC.

- **Grain seeds** were cooked and mixed with water to make gruel (porridge). c.20,000 years ago, people learned to bake gruel on a hot stone to make flat bread, like pitta.

- **Pottery** meant liquids could be heated to make stews. The oldest pottery is 13,000-year-old pots from Odai-Yamomoto in Japan. The first pots from the Near East, from Iran, date back 11,000 years.

- **c.12,000 years ago,** people found how to make food last by letting it ferment, making cheese from milk and wine from grapes.

▶ *The earliest people simply ate what food they could find – either by hunting (like fish) or gathering (like berries).*

◀ *Bread was the first processed food, made by baking ground-up grass seeds mixed with water.*

- **c.8000BC,** people began to farm animals such as sheep and grow plants such as cereals for food. Diets became less varied than when people gathered food wild, but much more reliable.

- **c.4000BC** special farmers in Palestine were growing oil-rich olives to squeeze and make olive oil in huge amounts. Romans consumed vast quantities.

- **c.2600BC,** the Egyptians found that, by leaving gruel to ferment, they could make a dough. This they baked in ovens to make the first raised bread.

- **Honey** was the main sweetener. Egyptians kept bees for honey and also made sweet syrups from fruits.

- **The oldest recipe book** is an Assyrian stone tablet from 1700BC with 25 recipes, including a bird called a *tarru* cooked in onion, garlic, milk and spices.

# The Phoenicians

- **From about 3000BC,** Semitic peoples such as Canaanites lived on the eastern Mediterranean coast and built the great city of Byblos.

- **From about 1100BC,** the people living here became known as Phoenicians.

- **The word 'phoenicians'** comes from *phoinix*, the Greek word for a purple dye made famous by these people.

▶ *For long distance journeys, the Phoenicians used ships with both sails and oars.*

*Hull built from the famed cedars of Lebanon trees*

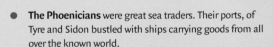

- **The Phoenicians** were great sea traders. Their ports, of Tyre and Sidon bustled with ships carrying goods from all over the known world.

- **The Phoenicians** used wool from Mesopotamia and flax and linen from Egypt to make cloth. They also made jewellery from imported gems, metals and ivory.

- **Phoenicians** invented the alphabet and gave us the word too. The Phoenician words *aleph* ('ox') and *beth* ('house') became the Greek letters *alpha* and *beta*. The word Bible and the prefix *bibli-* (meaning 'books') come from Byblos.

- **The dye** for which the Phoenicians were famous was made from the shells of murex snails.

- **c.600BC,** Phoenician sailors sailed from the Red Sea right round Africa and back into the Mediterranean.

- **Phoenicians** set up colonies across the Mediterranean as far west as Gades (now Cadiz, in Spain).

- **The greatest** Phoenician colony was the city of Carthage in what is now Tunisia.

# Polynesians

- **Polynesians** are the people who live on the islands in the middle of the Pacific Ocean, from Hawaii to Easter Island and New Zealand.

- **There are 10,000** islands in Polynesia and the rest of the eastern Pacific, with hundreds of different cultures and languages, each with its own history.

- **Many Polynesian islands** may well have been first settled 40,000 years ago by people from Southeast Asia.

- **2000 years ago,** a second wave of migrants moved east from Fiji, Samoa and Tonga to the Marquesas Islands.

- **The settlers** crossed the ocean in small double canoes and outriggers.

- **In their canoes** the settlers took crops (coconuts, yams, taros and breadfruit) and livestock (pigs and chickens).

▲ There are about 600 huge stone moai statues on Easter Island, on platforms called ahus. No one knows what they were for.

- **Every island** developed its own style of woodcarving.

- **About AD400,** the new Polynesians moved on to Hawaii and Easter Island.

- **Easter Islanders** created strange stone statues called *moais*, carved with stone tools since they had no metal.

> **★ STAR FACT ★**
> The biggest *moai* statues on Easter Island are up to 12 m tall and weigh 90 tonnes.

# Greek gods and myths

- **The Greeks** had a wealth of myths – stories about their gods, goddesses, heroes and villains.

- **We know** about the myths mainly from Homer's poems and Hesiod's book *Theogeny*, both from about 700BC.

- ***Theogeny*** tells how the Earth began, with the earth goddess Gaia emerging from chaos and giving birth to Uranus, the king of the sky.

- **The many children** of Gaia and Uranus were called the Titans, led by Cronos.

- **Cronos** married his sister Rhea. Their children, led by Zeus, rebelled against the Titans to become the new top gods, called the Olympians.

- **The Olympians** were said to live on Mt Olympus, and include the most famous Greek gods, such as Apollo the god of light, Demeter the goddess of crops, Artemis the goddess of the Moon and Dionysius the wine god.

◀ The Romans adopted many Greek gods. This is Venus (Greek goddess Aphrodite).

- **Greek heroes** were mostly heroes from the times of the Trojan Wars or earlier.

- **Early heroes** include Jason, who led his Argonauts (his crew) in search of the fabulous Golden Fleece, and Theseus, who killed the minotaur.

- **Trojan war heroes** included Achilles and Odysseus.

- **The greatest hero** was super-strong Heracles, whom the Romans later called Hercules.

# Alexander the Great

▶ In just nine years and a series of brilliant campaigns, Alexander created a vast empire. No one knows exactly what his plans were. However, the teachings of his tutor Aristotle were important to him, and he had his own vision of different peoples living together in friendship.

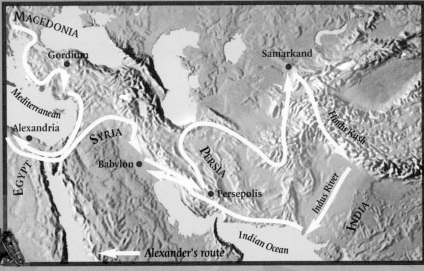

MACEDONIA

Gordium

Samarkand

Mediterranean

Alexandria

SYRIA

Babylon

PERSIA

Hindu Kush

EGYPT

Persepolis

Indus River

INDIA

Indian Ocean

← Alexander's route

● **Alexander the Great** was a young Macedonian king who was one of the greatest generals in history. He built an empire stretching from Greece to India.

● **Alexander** was born in 356BC in Pella, capital of Macedonia. His father King Phillip II was a tough fighter who conquered neighbouring Greece. His mother was the fiery Olympias, who told him that he was descended from Achilles, the hero of the *Iliad*.

● **As a boy,** he was tutored by the famous philosopher Aristotle. A story tells how he tamed the great unridable horse Bucephalus, which afterwards carried him as far as India.

● **When Alexander was 20,** his father was murdered by a bodyguard and he became king. Alexander quickly stamped out rebellion.

▶ The key to Macedonian success was the phalanx. In a phalanx, armoured soldiers stood in tightly packed rows bristling with long spears. Such a formation could withstand a cavalry attack, yet still move swiftly.

★ STAR FACT ★
An old legend said that anyone who untied a tricky knot in a town called Gordium would conquer Asia. Alexander instantly sliced through this Gordian knot with his sword.

● In 334BC, Alexander crossed the narrow neck of sea separating Europe from Asia with his army. Within a year, he had conquered the mighty Persian Empire.

● In 331BC, Alexander led his army on into Egypt where he was made pharaoh and founded the city of Alexandria. He trekked on to the desert oasis of Siwah where legend says an oracle proclaimed him son of the god Zeus.

● In 327BC, he married the lovely Bactrian princess, Roxane.

● **After capturing** the city of Babylon and finishing off Persian King Darius, Alexander led his conquering army into India. Here his homesick troops finally asked to go home.

● In 325BC, Alexander had ships built and carried his army down the Indus River and returned to Babylon. Within a year, he fell ill and died.

# The founding of Rome

- **People lived** in Italy long before Rome was founded and a people called the Etruscans created an advanced civilization in the northwest between 800 and 400BC.

- **According to legend,** Rome was founded in 753BC by the twins Romulus and Remus, who were said to have been brought up by a she-wolf.

- **By 550BC,** Rome was a big city ruled by Etruscan kings.

- **In 509BC,** the Roman people drove out the kings and made themselves an independent republic.

- **Republican Rome** was ruled by the Senate, an assembly made up of 100 patricians (men from leading families).

- **In theory,** Rome was governed by the people. But real power was in the hands of patricians; plebeians (ordinary citizens) had little. Slaves had no power or rights at all.

- **Plebeians** fought for power and, by 287BC, gained the right to stand as consuls, the highest official posts.

- **In the 400s** and 300s BC, Rome extended its power all over Italy by brute force and alliances.

▲ *Legend has it that Rome was founded by the twins Romulus and Remus, who were brought up by a she-wolf.*

- **By 264BC,** Rome rivalled Carthage, the North African city that dominated the western Mediterranean. In 164BC, Rome destroyed Carthage totally after the Punic Wars.

- **By 130BC** Rome had built a mighty empire stretching from Spain to Turkey and along the North African coast.

# Cleopatra

- **Cleopatra** (69–30BC) was the last Macedonian queen of Egypt. She was descended from Ptolemy, a general of Alexander the Great who made himself king after Alexander died.

- **Cleopatra may** have been beautiful. She was certainly intelligent, charming and highly determined.

- **Cleopatra** became queen in 51BC, when her father died. Her ten-year-old brother Ptolemy became king.

- **Ptolemy's guardians** seized power and drove Cleopatra out. She was restored to the throne by the Roman armies of Julius Caesar.

- **Legend has it** that Cleopatra had herself delivered to Caesar rolled up in a carpet. Whatever the truth, he fell in love with her, and she had a son, Caesarion, by him.

- **Caesar** invited Cleopatra and Caesarion to Rome, where she stayed until 44BC, when Caesar was assassinated.

◄ *Octavian described Cleopatra as a wicked temptress and the idea has stuck. But her people in Egypt thought of her as a great, just and much-loved queen.*

- **The Roman general** Mark Antony went to Cleopatra for her support in his bid for power in Rome. He too fell in love with her. They later married and had three children.

- **Mark Antony** returned to Rome to make a political marriage to Octavia, sister of Octavian. But he soon returned to Cleopatra.

- **Mark Antony and Cleopatra** were ambitious and strove to take over the eastern Roman Empire. But their armies were defeated at the Battle of Actium, off Greece, in 31BC by the forces of Octavian (later Augustus Caesar).

- **As Octavian** chased them to Alexandria, Cleopatra spread rumours that she was dead. In despair, Mark Antony stabbed himself. He died in her arms. Cleopatra tried to make peace with Octavian but failed. She took her life by placing an asp, a poisonous snake, on her breast.

# The rise of Rome

- **As Rome's** empire spread, the creation of plantations worked by slaves put small farmers out of work. The gap between rich and poor widened.

- **Many joined** the army to escape poverty and became more loyal to their generals than to the Senate.

- **Two popular generals,** Pompey and Julius Caesar, used their armies to take over Rome and suspend the Republic.

- **Caesar and Pompey** argued, and after battles right across the empire, Caesar gained the upper hand.

◀ Many Romans lived in comfortable two-storey townhouses (domi), with heated pools and underfloor heating.

- **Once in power,** Caesar restored order and passed laws to reduce people's debts.

- **Caesar** was made dictator and ruled Rome without the Senate.

- **In 44BC,** a man called Brutus killed Caesar to restore the Republic – but Caesar's place was taken by another general, Octavian, Caesar's adopted son.

- **By 27BC,** Octavian was so powerful he declared himself the first Roman Emperor and took the name Augustus.

- **Under Augustus,** rebellious parts of Spain and the Alps were brought under control and the empire was expanded along the Rhine and Danube Rivers.

- **By 1BC,** the days of strife were over and Rome presided over a vast, stable, prosperous empire.

# Jesus

- **Jesus Christ** was one of the world's great religious leaders. The religion of Christianity is based on his teachings.

- **Our knowledge** of Jesus's life comes almost entirely from four short books in the Bible's New Testament: the gospels of Matthew, Mark, Luke and John.

- **Roman writers** such as Pliny mention Jesus briefly.

- **Jesus** was born in Bethlehem in Palestine between 4 and 1BC.

◀ Jesus is his own name. Christ is a title that comes from the Greek word christos, which means 'anointed one'.

- **The Bible** tells how his poor young virgin mother Mary became miraculously pregnant after a visit by the archangel Gabriel, and that Jesus is the only Son of God.

- **Little** is known of Jesus's childhood. His teaching began after he was baptized by John the Baptist at the age of 30.

- **Jesus's mission** was to announce that the Kingdom of God was coming. From his many followers, he chose 12 'apostles' to help him spread the word.

- **Jesus performed** all kinds of miracles to convince people of the truth of his teachings.

- **Many Jews** felt Jesus was a troublemaker, especially after a triumphal entry into Jerusalem. They had the Roman governor Pontius Pilate put him to death by crucifixion (nailing to a cross).

> ★ STAR FACT ★
> After his death, Jesus was said to have been resurrected – brought to life again.

# The Han dynasty

- In 206BC, the Lman Han kingdom was ruled over by Liu Bang. Liu Bang was a poor villager who had come to power as the Qin Empire broke down.

- In 206BC, Liu Bang led an army on the Qin capital, Xiangyang. He looted Shi Huangdi's tomb, and burned the city and the library containing the books Shi Huangdi had banned – the only existing copies.

- In 202BC, Liu Bang proclaimed himself first Han emperor and took the name Gaozu.

- **Under the Han,** China became as large and powerful as the Roman Empire, and art and science thrived. Chinese people still sometimes call themselves Han.

- **Under Wudi** (141–87BC), Han China reached its peak.

- **Han cities** were huge, crowded and beautiful, and craftsmen made many exquisite things from wood, paint and silk – sadly destroyed when Han rule ended.

- **Silk, jade and horses** were traded along the Silk Route, through Asia as far as the Roman Empire.

▶ Beautiful objects like this bronze urn were traded between China and Europe along the famous Silk Route for thousands of years.

- **Han emperors** tried to recover the lost writings and revived the teachings of Confucius. Public officials became scholars and in 165BC the first exams for entry into public service were held.

- **About AD50,** Buddhist missionaries reached China.

- **By AD200,** the Han emperors were weakened by their ambitious wives and eunuchs (guardians). Rebellions by a group called the Yellow Turbans, combined with attacks by warriors from the north, brought the empire down.

# Roman towns

- **Roman towns** were the biggest and most sophisticated the world had seen. They were not built on rigid grids like Greek cities, but they all had common features.

- **Roman towns** had two main streets and many side streets with spaces in between called *insulae* (islands).

- **The *insulae*** were tightly packed with private houses – houses of the rich called *domi* and apartment blocks (also called *insulae*). The bigger houses had courtyards.

- **Traffic jams** were so common that many towns banned wheeled traffic from the streets during daylight.

- **Most towns** had numerous shops, inns (*tabernae*), cafés (*thermopilia*) and bakeries (*pistrina*).

- **The forum** was a large open market and meeting place surrounded on three sides by a covered walkway. The fourth side was the law courts and town hall (*basilica*).

- **Most towns** had many grand temples to Roman gods.

- **Most towns** had a large open-air theatre. There was also a games arena or stadium where warriors called gladiators fought and chariot races were held.

- **The bath houses** (*thermae*) were places where people came to sit around and dip into hot and cold baths in magnificent surroundings.

- **Towns** had very good water supplies and sewage systems.

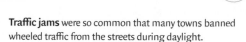

◀ The remains of the forum in Rome give a glimpse of just how magnificent Roman cities must have been.

# The Roman Empire

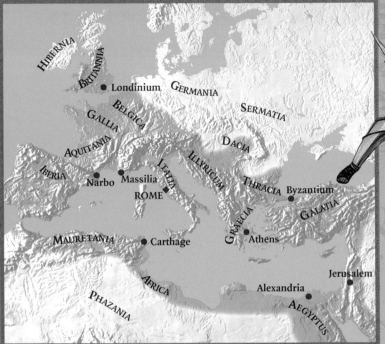

▲ Gladiators were prisoners and criminals who were made to fight in big arenas called amphitheatres to entertain people.

◄ This map shows the empire at its peak under the Emperor Trajan (AD98–117). It was divided into areas called provinces, such as Britannia (England and Wales) and Gallia (northern France). Each had its own Roman governor, often a retired consul (minister), who used his power to extort taxes.

- **For 200 years** after Augustus became emperor in 27BC, Roman emperors ruled over an empire so large and secure that citizens could talk of the *Pax Romana* (Roman Peace).

- **The Romans** built straight roads to move their troops about quickly. On the whole, they governed peacefully and also built hundreds of towns in the Roman manner.

- **After Augustus** died, in AD14, his stepson Tiberius succeeded him. Then came a succession of Augustus's descendants, including Gaius, Claudius and Nero.

- **Gaius** (AD37–41) was known as Caligula ('little boots') because of the soldiers' boots he wore as a child.

- **Soon after** Caligula became emperor, an illness left him mad. He spent wildly, had people whipped and killed, married and murdered his sister and elected his horse as a minister. Eventually he was murdered by soldiers.

- **Claudius** (AD41–54) replaced Caligula. People thought he was stupid because he stuttered and was crippled. But he proved the wisest and most humane of all emperors.

- **Claudius** was probably poisoned by his 4th wife Agrippina, who wanted power for her son Nero.

- **The power of Roman emperors** reached a peak under the 'Antonines' – Nerva, Trajan, Hadrian, Antoninus and Marcus Aurelius. They ruled AD96–180.

- **The empire** grew only a little after Augustus. Britain was conquered in AD43, and Trajan took Dacia (now Hungary and Romania).

★ STAR FACT ★
Roman historian Suetonius claimed Nero sang and played the lyre during Rome's great fire in AD64.

▶ Leading imperial officials wore distinctive flowing robes called togas, with a strip dyed in a rare purple called Tyrian purple. Laws were written on papyrus or parchment.

# The Roman army

- Rome owed its power to its highly efficient army.
- In a crisis, Rome could raise an army of 800,000 men.
- The Roman army fought mainly on foot, advancing in tight squares bristling with spears and protected by large shields called *scutari*. They often put shields over their heads to protect them from arrows. This formation was called a *testudo* or tortoise.
- Under the Republic, the army was divided into legions of 5,000 soldiers. Legions were made of 10 cohorts. Cohorts were made of centuries of 80-100 soldiers.
- Each legion was led by a *legatus*. A cohort was led by a *tribunus militum*. A century was led by a centurion.
- All Roman soldiers had a short sword (60 cm long) and carried two throwing spears. They also wore armour – first, vests of chain mail and a leather helmet; later, metal strips on a leather tunic and a metal helmet.
- Roman armies built huge siege engines and catapults called *ballistas* when they had to capture a town.

- After 100BC, most soldiers were professionals, who joined the army for life. Food took about a third of their wages.
- In training, soldiers went on forced 30 km marches three times a month. They moved at 8 km per hour, carrying very heavy packs.
- Soldiers were flogged for misbehaviour. Mutiny was punished by executing one in ten suspects. This was called decimation.

▶ The tough Roman soldier marched carrying all his weapons and armour, plus a heavy pack full of clothes, food and tools for digging and building.

# The Roman way of life

- In big cities, rich Romans had a comfortable way of life.
- For breakfast, Romans typically ate bread or wheat biscuits with honey, dates or olives, and water or wine.
- A Roman lunch (*prandium*) consisted of much the same things as breakfast.
- Romans had *cena* (the main meal) in the afternoon, after a visit to the baths. This became a very lavish affair with three main courses, each with many dishes.

> ★ STAR FACT ★
> The Circus Maximus chariot racetrack in Rome held up to 250,000 spectators.

- Rich Romans had a lot of free time, since slaves did all the work. Leisure activities included gambling by tossing coins (*capita et navia*) and knucklebones (*tali*).
- Public entertainments were called *ludi* (games). They included theatre, chariot races, and fights with gladiators (trained fighters) and animals.
- The Emperor Trajan went to a gladiator contest that lasted 117 days and involved 10,000 gladiators.
- Romans had more slaves than any empire in history. Many were treated cruelly, but some lived quite well.
- In 90BC, a man called Spartacus led a revolt of slaves that lasted two years, until crushed by Roman armies.

◀ Romans were very clean and often went to the public baths or bathed at home. These are the Roman baths at Bath, England.

# Famous disasters

▲ *The Greek island of Santorini was blown apart in 1500BC by a giant volcanic eruption, so ending the Minoan civilization.*

- **Many ancient civilizations** had legends of great floods.

- **In the Middle East,** a Sumerian named Ziusudra, the Babylonian Gilgamesh and the Jewish Noah all built an ark (boat) to ride out a flood that drowned all others.

- **In India,** Manu, the first man and first king, was warned by fish and survived the great flood by building a boat.

- **In the Americas,** the Aztecs believed four previous worlds had been destroyed by jaguars, hurricanes, thunder and lightning and a huge 52-year flood.

- **The huge eruption** of the Aegean island volcano of Thera (Santorini), in 1500BC, effectively destroyed Minoan civilization on Crete – and may have started legends of the lost civilization of Atlantis, drowned by a tidal wave.

- **While the Jews** were slaves there, Egypt was ruined by a flood of blood predicted by the Jew Moses – now thought to have been the Nile River in flood, stained by red algae.

- **In 464BC,** 10,000 were killed by an earthquake that rocked the Greek city of Sparta.

- **In 436BC,** a famine drove thousands of Romans to jump into the Tiber River to escape the pain of starvation.

- **In AD64,** the Rome of Emperor Nero was destroyed by a great fire. Angry people said that Nero had started it.

- **In AD79,** the Roman city of Pompeii was buried under ash from nearby volcano Vesuvius – and preserved to this day.

# Yamato

- **The oldest signs** of farming in Japan date back to 300BC, but Japan was inhabited long before that.

  - **The first known inhabitants** of Japan were the Ainu or Ezo, who were short, hairy, fair-skinned people. Some Ainu people still survive in northern Japan.

    - **About 250BC,** the Yayoi tribe became dominant in Japan. They used iron and bronze.

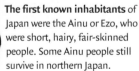

◄ *Shinto priests believe that all things that inspire awe – from twisted trees to dead warriors – have kami (spirits).*

- **In AD167,** priestess Himiko unified Japan under her rule.

- **Himiko** sent ambassadors to China for support, and imported many Chinese ideas.

- **From AD200–645,** the Yamato tribe dominated Japan. The Yamato conquered Korea and were the first emperors.

- **Right up to today,** Japanese emperors claim to be descended from the Yamato, who, in turn, claimed to be descended from the Shinto sun-goddess, Amaterasu.

- **Shotoku Taishi** (AD574–622) was a young regent for old Empress Suiko. He gave Japan organized Chinese-style government and promoted Buddhism and Confucianism.

- **Shinto** or 'way of the gods' has been Japan's religion since prehistoric times. It got its name in the 6th century to distinguish it from Buddhism and Confucianism.

> ★ STAR FACT ★
> In AD2000, the postholes of a round hut half a million years old were found in Japan.

# The Mauryan Empire

- **In 321BC,** the first great Indian empire was created by Chandragupta Maurya (c.325–297BC). Its capital was Pataliputra on the Ganges.

- **The Mauryan Empire** at its peak included most of modern Pakistan, Bangladesh and India – except for the very southern tip.

- **The most famous** Mauryan emperor was Chandragupta's grandson Asoka (c.265–238BC).

- **After witnessing** a horrific battle, Asoka was so appalled by the suffering that he resolved never to go to war. He devoted himself to improving the lot of his people.

- **Asoka** became a Buddhist and his government promoted the Dharma, or 'Universal Law'.

▲ During Asoka's reign, stupas (domed shrines) containing relics of the Buddha were built all over India.

- **The Universal Law** preached religious tolerance, non-violence and respect for the dignity of every single person.

- **Asoka's men** dug wells and built reservoirs all over India to help the poor. They also provided comfortable rest-houses and planted shady banyan trees for travellers along the new roads.

- **Asoka said** 'all men are my children', and sent officials out to deal with local problems.

- **A vast secret police force** and an army of 700,000 helped Asoka to run his empire.

- **Asoka's** Sarnath lion insignia is now India's national emblem.

# Early North Americans

- **Maize** was grown in southwestern USA c.2000–1000BC.

- **The first farming villages** in the southwest were those of the Anasazi, Mogollon and Hohokam peoples and dated from AD100. They lived either in caves or in underground 'pit houses' carved into the desert rock.

- **Anasazi** is Navajo Indian for 'Ancient Ones'.

- **The first Anasazi** are also known as Basket Makers because of their skill in weaving baskets.

- **About AD700,** the Anasazi began to build large stone villages called *pueblos*, which is why from this time they are also called Pueblo Indians.

- **In the 'Classic' Pueblo** period, from AD1050–1300, the Anasazi lived in huge apartments carved out of cliffs, like Pueblo Bonito. Pueblo culture began to fade c.AD1300.

> ★ STAR FACT ★
> Cliff Palace in Mesa Verde had space for
> 250 people in its 217 rooms.

▲ The most famous cliff pueblos are in Mesa Verde, Colorado.

- **In the east,** the first farming villages were those of the Hopewell peoples of the Illinois and Ohio valleys, between 100BC and AD200.

- **The Hopewell people** are known for their burial mounds. Things found in these mounds show they traded all over America.

- **About AD700,** farming villages with temple mounds developed near St Louis on the Mississippi.

# Early Ireland

- **Ireland** was settled late. The first proof of settlers are 8000-year-old flints left by hunters and fishers on beaches in the northeast, near the modern town Larne.

- **The New Stone Age** (Neolithic) began when the first farms and permanent homes appeared, 5000 years ago.

- **Neolithic people** honoured their dead with long mounds or barrows – called 'court graves' because they have a courtyard at the entrance. They also built barrows called portal graves with three huge stones set like a door.

- **The most dramatic remains** from earliest times are 'passage' graves. Inside an earth mound a long passage leads to a stone chamber. Of 150 in Ireland, the most famous is Newgrange in the Boyne valley near Dublin.

- **The Celts** invaded Ireland in the Iron Age, about 400BC, and many of Ireland's rich collection of heroic myths are probably based in this time.

★ STAR FACT ★
The passage tomb on Knocknarea in Sligo is said to be the burial-place of the legendary Queen Maeve.

- **Celtic Ireland** was split into 150 kingdoms or clans called *tuatha* and later into five provinces – Ulster, Meath, Leinster, Munster and Connaught. After AD500, there was a high king (*ard-ri*) ruling Ireland from Tara in Leinster.

- **Irish Celts** were both warriors and herdsmen who valued cows highly. They also revered poets (*file*), and their metalwork, revealed in items such as the Tara brooch and the Ardagh chalice, is extraordinarily beautiful.

- **Early Celtic priests** were druids, but in AD432, St Patrick, legend says, came to convert Ireland to Christianity.

- **Irish monasteries** became havens of art and learning in the Dark Ages, creating the famous *Book of Kells*.

▼▶ *The huge burial mound at Newgrange was built around 3100BC. A long, narrow passage leads to a burial chamber deep inside the mound. Above the entrance is an unusual 'roof-box' – a special slot through which the midwinter sun shines into the chamber.*

*Every year, at exactly 8.58 am on 21 December (the winter solstice), the rising sun shines through this roof-box and right down the passage to light up the burial chamber*

*One of Newgrange's most distinctive features is the rich ornamentation – especially the carved spirals, which must have had some ritual significance*

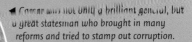

# Julius Caesar

- **Julius Caesar** (c.100–44BC) was Rome's most famous general and leader. He was also a great speaker who had the power to excite huge crowds.

- **Caesar's** individuality was clear from the start. At 17, he defied Sulla, the dictator of Rome and married Cornelia, the daughter of the rebel leader Cinna. Cornelia died when Caesar was about 30.

- **Caesar** began as a politician and made himself popular by spending his own money on public entertainments.

- **In 60BC,** he formed a powerful triumvirate (threesome) with Crassus and Pompey, which dominated Rome.

- **In 58BC,** Caesar led a brilliant campaign to conquer Gaul (now northern France), and invaded Britain.

- ◄ Caesar was not only a brilliant general, but a great statesman who brought in many reforms and tried to stamp out corruption.

- **Caesar** wrote an account of his campaigns in Gaul that is a classic of historical writing.

- **Pompey** was alarmed by the fame that Caesar's conquests brought him. The two began a war that lasted five years, ending in Egypt in 48BC, where Caesar met and fell in love with Cleopatra.

- **By 45BC,** Caesar was undisputed master of the Roman Empire. The people elected him dictator for life.

- **Caesar** was asked to become king, but he refused.

- **On 15 March 44BC** – called the Ides of March – Caesar was stabbed to death as he entered the Senate. His assassins were a group led by Brutus and Cassius, who felt that his ambitions were a threat to Rome.

# The Guptas

- **The Guptas** were a family of rulers who reigned in northern India from AD320–c.500. This is India's golden age, with writing, sculpture and other arts at their peak.

- **The Guptas** were originally a family of rich landowners, who took over control of the small kingdom of Magadha in the Ganges valley.

- **Chandragupta I** came to the throne in AD320. He widened his lands by marrying the right women.

- **Chandragupta's** son Samudragupta and his grandson Chandragupta II gained control over much of northern India by military conquests.

- **The Hindu and Buddhist** religions both began to flourish during the Gupta period.

- **Beautiful temples** and religious sculptures were created all over northern India.

- **About AD450,** Kalidása, India's greatest poet and dramatist, wrote his famous play *Sákuntala,* filled with romance and adventure.

- **Music and dance** developed their highest classical form.

- **Hindu mathematicians** developed the decimal system (counting in tens) that we use today.

- **Gupta power** collapsed by about AD500 under repeated attacks by Huns from the north.

▼ *The Hindu and Buddhist sculpture and painting of the Gupta period has been the model for Indian art down the centuries.*

# Gauls and Franks

- **The Gauls** were a Celtic people who lived in Western Europe, mainly in France.

- **The Gauls** could be brave warriors, and because the men had long hair and beards, the Romans thought them wild.

- **In 390BC,** Gauls crossed the Alps, swept down on Rome and sacked the city. They later withdrew, but they occupied northern Italy for almost 200 years.

- **In 278BC,** Gauls invaded what is now Turkey, settling the area called Galatia.

- **In the 50s BC,** Julius Caesar led a lightning Roman campaign to crush the Gauls. What is now France became Roman Gaul.

> ★ STAR FACT ★
> Franks were outnumbered 20 to 1 by Gallo-Romans – but France is named after them.

◀ In 52BC, the Gallic chief Vercingetorix led a last-ditch attempt to drive out the Romans. But he was beaten, taken to Rome as Caesar's prize and executed.

- **The Franks** were a German people split into two branches, the Salians and Ripurians.

- **In AD486,** Clovis, a king of the Salian Franks, invaded Roman Gaul to create a big kingdom covering modern France and Belgium.

- **The first period** of Frankish rule in Gaul is called Merovingian (from 486 to 751); the second is called Carolingian (751–987).

- **After Clovis's death** in 511, the Merovingian kingdom was divided and weakened. About 719, some Merovingian kings allowed a man called Charles Martel – *martel* means hammer – to take control in the north as 'Mayor of the Palace'. Martel soon controlled the whole of Gaul.

IN SEX CIRCULOS DIV

# Early African civilizations

- **The first civilizations** appeared in Africa along the Nile valley, in Egypt and further south in Nubia.

- **The first Nubian civilization,** called the A-group culture, appeared about 3200BC in the north of Nubia, known as Wawat. It was taken over by the Egyptians in 2950BC.

- **About 2000BC,** a new Nubian culture emerged in the then-fertile south, called Kush. Unlike the Wawat Nubians, who were Asian, the Kushites were black Africans.

◀ Africa was the birthplace of humanity, and rock paintings dating back 30,000 years are found all over Africa.

- **Egypt** conquered Kush in 1500BC, but the Kushites, led by King Shabaka, conquered Egypt in 715BC. For 50 years, the Kushites were pharaohs and their capital Napata was the centre of the ancient world.

- **In 666BC, Assyrians** drove the Kushites out of Egypt. But from the Assyrians, the Kushites learned iron-making.

- **Napata** had iron-ore, but little wood for smelting the ore. So the Kushites moved their capital to Meroe, where they built great palaces, temples, baths and pyramids.

- **From Kush,** iron-making spread west to Nigeria.

- **From AD100, the city of Axum** – now in northern Ethiopia – grew rich and powerful on ivory. About AD350, the Axumite king Aezanas invaded and overthrew Kush.

- **Kings of Axum** (later Ethiopia) were said to be descended from Jewish King Solomon and the Queen of Sheba. The Sheba were an Arab people who had settled in Axum.

- **King Aezanas** was converted to Christianity, but for 1500 years Axum/Ethiopia was Africa's only Christian country.

# The Celts

▶ Created in the early 800s in Iona and Ireland, the Book of Kells is one of the great treasures of Celtic art.

- **The Celts** are an ancient group of peoples who first appeared in the Danube valley in Germany about 3300 years ago.

- **The first Celts** are known as the Urnfield culture, because they put their cremated dead in urns.

- **From 800 to 400BC**, Celts spread across northern Europe, taking over what is now France as Gauls, England as Britons and Ireland as Gaels.

- **The first wave** of expansion is called Halstatt culture. With bronze, the Celts developed supreme metal-working skills.

- **c.500BC**, Celts learned to make iron and came into contact with Greeks and Etruscans. The 'La Tene' culture emerged.

- **In La Tene**, the distinctive Celtic swirls and spiral decoration appeared on weapons and ornaments.

- **After Gauls** sacked Rome, in 390, it seemed Celts might over-run Europe. But they were split into many tribes, and from 200BC they were pushed ever further west.

- **Some early Celts** used Greek letters to write in their own language, but our knowledge of them comes mostly from Greek and Roman authors.

- **The Celts** were fierce warriors who charged into battle shouting, naked and stained with blue woad dye. But they valued poets higher than warriors. Their poets' tales of heroes and magic tell us how rich their culture was.

- **Celtic clan society** was highly organized and revolved around a clan's chief, who made the laws.

# The first Britons

- **Britain** has been inhabited by human-like creatures for over 500,000 years. The oldest known settlement, at Star Carr in Yorkshire, dates back 10,000 years.

- **About 6–7,000 years ago**, Neolithic farmers arrived from Europe. They began to clear the island's thick woods to grow crops and build houses in stone.

- **The early farmers** created round monuments of stones and wooden posts called henges. The most famous is Stonehenge in Wiltshire.

- **c.2300BC**, new people from the Rhine arrived. They are called Beakerfolk, after their beaker-shaped pottery cups. They were Britain's first metal-workers.

- **Legend has it** that the name Britain came from Brutus, one of the sons of Aeneas, who fled from Troy.

- **c.700BC**, Celts arrived, often living in hillforts.

- **Iron axes** and ploughs enabled huge areas to be cleared and farmed, and the population rose.

- **When Julius Caesar** invaded, in 55 and 54BC, the Celtic people of England, called Britons, were divided into scores of tribes, such as the Catuvellauni and Atrebates.

- **Resistance** from tribal leaders such as Caratacus meant it took the Romans over a century to conquer the Britons.

- **The last resistance** was that of Queen Boudicca, in AD60.

▼ People of Bronze Age Britain lived in round houses like this, with thick stone walls and a steeply-pitched, thatched roof.

A central hearth kept the house remarkably warm

# The fall of Rome

- **After the death** of Marcus Aurelius, in AD180, Rome was beset by political struggles.

- **The Praetorian Guard** (the emperor's personal soldiers) chose or deposed emperors at will, and there were 60 emperors between AD235 and 284 alone.

- **The Empire fell** into anarchy and was beset by famine, plague and invasion.

- **Diocletian** (emperor from 284) tried to make the empire easier to govern by splitting it in two halves – East and West. He asked Maximian to rule the west.

- **Diocletian** retired 'to grow cabbages' at his palace in Dalmatia, and soldiers tried to choose a new emperor.

- **Constantine,** commander of the Roman armies in Britain, defeated his rivals to become emperor. It is said that before the main battle, he saw a Christian cross in the sky. After his victory, he became Christian.

- **In AD330,** Constantine made Byzantium (now Istanbul) his capital and called it Constantinople.

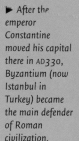

► After the emperor Constantine moved his capital there in AD330, Byzantium (now Istanbul in Turkey) became the main defender of Roman civilization.

- **After Constantine's death,** the empire fell into chaos again. It became split permanently into East and West.

- **The Western empire** suffered attacks from barbarians. Vandals invaded Spain and North Africa. Goths and Huns such as Attila attacked from the North.

- **In AD410,** Visigoths led by Alaric invaded Italy and sacked (burned and looted) Rome. In AD455, Vandals sacked Rome again. In AD476, the Western empire finally collapsed.

# The spread of Christianity

- **The first Christians** were Jews in Palestine, but followers like Paul soon spread the faith to gentiles (non-Jews) and countries beyond Palestine.

- **At first,** Roman rulers tolerated Christians, but after AD64, they saw Christians as a threat and persecuted them.

- **Persecution** strengthened Christianity by creating martyrs such as St Alban.

◄ Early Christian texts were manuscripts (handwritten) and monks spent years illuminating (decorating) them. The illuminated manuscripts of this time are among the most beautiful books ever made.

- **In 313,** Emperor Constantine gave Christians freedom of worship and called the first great ecumenical (general) church council in 325.

- **By 392,** Christianity was the official religion of the empire.

- **When the Roman Empire** split into East and West, so too did Christianity, with the West focused on Rome and the East on Constantinople.

- **The head of the Western church** was the pope; the head of the Eastern church was called the patriarch. The first pope was Jesus's apostle St Peter, and there has been an unbroken line of popes ever since. But the power of the popes really began with St Gregory, in 590.

- **To separate themselves** from the official religion, some Christians, such as St Benedict, began to live apart as monks in monasteries.

- **After AD500,** monks spread Christianity over NW Europe.

- **Monasteries** became the main havens for learning in the West in the Dark Ages, which followed the fall of Rome.

# The Byzantine Empire

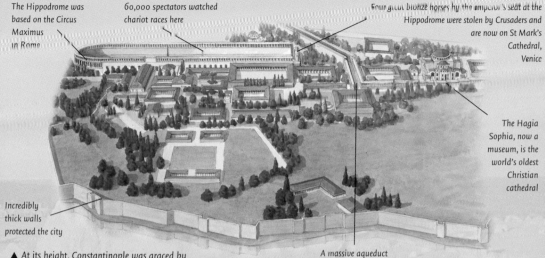

The Hippodrome was based on the Circus Maximus in Rome

60,000 spectators watched chariot races here

Four great bronze horses by the emperor's seat at the Hippodrome were stolen by Crusaders and are now on St Mark's Cathedral, Venice

The Hagia Sophia, now a museum, is the world's oldest Christian cathedral

Incredibly thick walls protected the city

A massive aqueduct (water channel) kept the city well supplied with water

▲ At its height, Constantinople was graced by some of the ancient world's most magnificent buildings – including the Hippodrome and the Hagia Sophia. This is the tranquil palace quarter. The rest of the city was noisy and crowded.

- **When Rome collapsed,** in 476, Constantinople (now Istanbul in Turkey) became the capital of what is now called the Byzantine Empire. It became the centre of Western civilization for the next thousand years.

- **In the six years** after Constantine made Byzantium his capital Constantinople, builders, architects and artists created one of the world's most magnificent cities.

- **Constantinople** was at the focus of trade routes between Asia and Europe. Silks, gems and ivories were traded for gold, grain, olives and wine. By charging ten per cent on all goods coming in and out, the city became fabulously rich.

- **When the great emperor Justinian I** came to the throne in 527, he tried to rebuild the Roman Empire. His general, Belisarius, reconquered Italy, and by 565 the Byzantine Empire stretched right round the Mediterranean.

- **Justinian** also built hundreds of churches, including the famous Hagia Sophia.

- **Justinian** modernized Roman law to create the basis of all western legal systems. This is called the Code of Justinian.

- **The Byzantine Empire** was under constant attack – from Goths, Huns, Persians, Avars, Bulgars, Slavs, Vikings, Arabs, Berbers, Turks, Crusaders and Normans. But it repelled attackers, often with its secret weapon 'Greek fire', invented in 650. This was a mix of quick-lime, petrol and sulphur, which burst into flames when it hit water.

- **In 1204,** Constantinople was ransacked by Crusader knights who were short of money. Almost every treasure in the city was stolen and it never recovered from this devastating blow. The city's population dwindled from 1 million to just 60,000 over the next 200 years.

- **Constantinople** was finally conquered by the Turkish Sultan Mehmet II in 1453.

▶ Justinian I was the greatest Byzantine emperor, although his general's secretary, Procopius, described him as 'a demon incarnate'. He ruled with his beautiful former actress wife, Theodora. Justinian relied on her for support and advice, and it was she who changed laws to improve the lives of women and the poor.

# The Sui, Tang and Song

▶ Gunpowder was invented in the Tang era. The Chinese used it first to make fabulous fireworks and later weapons.

- In AD581 Yang Chien seized the throne in the north of China, founding the Sui dynasty.

- **Yang Chien** conquered the south and reunited China for the first time since the fall of the Han in AD220.

- **Under the second** Sui emperor Yang Di, China's Grand Canal was rebuilt on an huge scale, linking China's main rivers. Other canals extended the network.

- **Yang Di** was betrayed by one of his 3,000 mistresses and strangled in 618. Li Yuan, an ambitious Sui minister, then seized the throne to found the Tang dynasty.

- **Under the Tang** trade grew, China became rich again and the arts and sciences flourished.

- **By AD751** China was the world's largest empire and the capital Chang'an was the world's largest city, with over a million inhabitants.

- **Chinese people** began to drink tea and sit on chairs.

- **Poets such** as Li Po (701–762) wrote of his love of wild mountains and the fleeting nature of happiness. China's tradition of great landscape painting began and the first printed book, *The Diamond Sutra*, was made in AD868.

- **By AD800,** the Tang dynasty was beginning to break up, Chang'an declined and China descended into turmoil.

- **Order was restored** in AD960 when the Song family began to rule from the city of Kaifeng. The Song lasted until AD1276, when the Mongol Kublai Khan conquered China.

*IN SEX* CIRCULOS DIV

# Barbarians

▶ Alaric was the great Gothic leader who took Rome in 410. He lies buried with the treasures he took from Rome in the bed of the Busentius River.

- **Barbarians** is what the Romans called all the peoples living outside the empire, who they thought of as uncivilized.

- **Barbarian** people rarely lived in large towns. Instead they lived in forts or small farming villages.

- **Many were brave warriors** but many too were skilled craftsmen, poets and humble farmers.

- **The Romans** thought barbarians wild and crude, but they survived and built a lasting civilization as the peoples of northern and western Europe.

- **They seemed** ill-disciplined in battle to the Romans, but rode horses and appeared in vast, wild, terrifying hordes.

- **The Goths** were German peoples who overran the western Roman empire in the 4th and 5th centuries. They were divided into Ostrogoths in the east near the Black Sea and Visigoths on the Danube. It was the Visigoths who under their king Alaric finally broke Rome in AD476.

- **Italians later** used the term *gothic* to sneer at what they saw as the ugly cathedrals of northern Europe and the term stuck.

- **The Vandals** were a German tribe who arrived in Europe from the east in the 1st century BC. When driven west by the Huns in c.AD380, they took over Spain and North Africa.

- **Vandals** swept down through Italy in AD455 to sack Rome and gave us the word 'vandal'.

- **The Huns** were nomadic Mongols from eastern Asia who arrived in Europe c.AD370, driving everyone before them, until finally defeated in AD455. The Huns were bogeymen for Romans. One Roman said, 'They have a sort of shapeless lump, not a face, and pinholes for eyes' – perhaps because Huns bandaged children's skulls to deform as they grew. The most feared Hun was Attila.

# Roman Britain

- **The Roman occupation** began in earnest when the armies of Claudius landed at Richborough in Kent in AD43. All of England and Wales was conquered by AD78.

- **Scotland** remained beyond Roman control. In AD122–130 the 118-km-long stone wall now called Hadrian's wall was built right across the country to act as a frontier.

- **The Roman army** in Britain was powerful. There were three legions (5,000 men each) at York, Chester and Caerleon, plus 40,000 auxiliaries.

- **Roman Britain** was ruled by a Roman governor, but the Romans co-opted local chiefs to help.

- **The Romans** built the first proper towns in Britain – like St Albans, Gloucester and Lincoln – with typical Roman features such as baths and theatres.

- **Demand** for food and leather from the army and new towns kept rising. Large estates centred on Roman-style villas grew rich, but even small farmers did well.

- **Most people** were bilingual, speaking and writing both Celtic and Latin, and many adopted Roman lifestyles.

- **When barbarians** attacked the empire on the continent in the AD300s, Roman Britain was left to fend for itself. Power fell into the hands of tyrants like the British king Vortigern (AD425–250).

- **Vortigern** invited Anglo-Saxons from Germany to settle in the east to help him against rebel Britons. But the Anglo-Saxons soon turned against him and invited in others of their kind to join them.

- **Villas** and towns were abandoned and Britons fled west or abroad as the Anglo-Saxons moved in.

◀ King Arthur became the greatest hero in British legend, but the real Arthur was probably a British chief who, for a while, turned the tide against the Anglo-Saxons with a victory at Mt Badon in 500.

# Muhammad

- **Muhammad** (c.570–632) was the Arab prophet whose teachings form the basis of the Islamic religion.

- **Muslims** believe Muhammad was the last and greatest prophet of God, who they called Allah.

- **Muhammad** was born in Mecca in Arabia.

- **His father** died before he was born and his mother died when he was a child. He was brought up by his grandfather and uncle, tending sheep and camels.

- **At the age of 25,** Muhammad entered the service of a rich widow of 40 called Khadija and later married her. They had two sons and four daughters.

- **When 35** Muhammad was asked to restore a sacred stone damaged in a flood. A vision told him to become a prophet and proclaim the word of God.

- **The people of Mecca** resented Muhammad's preaching, and in AD622 he fled to Medina.

- **In Medina** he attracted many followers. The Meccans went to war on Medina, but were driven back.

- **In AD630** Muhammad re-entered Mecca in triumph, pardoned the people and set up a mosque there.

▼ The Koran is Islam's holy book of Muhammad's teachings.

# What people wore

◄ Egyptians wore clothes made
mainly of white linen. At first,
men wore a short kilt, but later
they wore long, wrap-around
skirts. Egyptian women at first
wore sheath-like dresses. After
1500BC, men and women both
wore loose robes like these made
from rectangles of cloth instead.

▼ Roman clothing was quite
similar to the Greeks'. Men and
women wore tunics, called stola
(women) or tunica (men). Citizens of
Rome were allowed to wear a carefully
draped cloth called a toga
over their tunic.

◄ Greek clothes were very simple –
essentially just pieces of wool or linen wrapped
round to make a tunic, dress or cloak. Young Greek
men typically wore a short cloak called a
chlamys over a tunic sewn up at the side and
fastened at the shoulder. Women wore a dress
called a chiton, made from a rectangle of cloth.
They wore a longer cloak called a himation.

► In the north of Europe, Celtic
peoples wore warm clothes made
mainly of dyed wool and leather.
Women wore thick dresses and
headscarfs. Men wore long
tunics, leggings and a cloak.

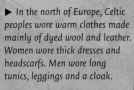

- **The earliest people** wore animal skins to keep warm.

- **The oldest signs** of woven cloth are marks in clay at Pavlov in Czechoslovakia, which date back 26,000 years.

- **Most of our knowledge** of ancient costumes comes from vases, statues and wall paintings. Colours have often faded, but we know from paintings such as those in the Roman city of Pompeii, preserved under volcanic ash, that ancient clothes were often colourful.

- **The oldest surviving clothes** come from Egyptian tombs dating back 5000 years.

- **The deep blue** dye indigo, from the indigo plant, has been found in Egyptian cloth from 4400 years ago.

- **Tyrian purple** was a purple dye, much-prized in ancient times. It came from Tyre (modern Lebanon) and was made from the Purpura and Murex snails.

- **People such as** the Ancient Egyptians often wore simple sandals or shoes of papyrus or leather. But the Greek dramatist Aeschylus is said to have invented the platform shoe, with 8-cm heels.

- **Minoan women** of 3500 years ago, unusually for ancient times, wore tight-waisted dresses. Their breasts were also left exposed.

- **Ordinary Roman citizens** wore an unbleached white toga. Coloured borders showed a particular status. Public officials at functions had togas with purple borders, called a toga praetexta. Early Roman generals wore togas dyed in Tyrian purple. From the time of Augustus, only the emperor wore a purple toga.

# Monks and monasteries

- **In religions** like Christianity and Buddhism, some devout people step out of ordinary life and live in a monastery, a community devoted wholly to religion.
- **The earliest Christian** monastery was that of the hermit St Anthony of Thebes, who went to live in the Egyptian desert about 271, and attracted followers.
- **Basil the Great** (c. 329–379) and his sister Macrina the Younger founded monasteries for men and women on their estate in Cappadocia in Turkey.
- **Monasticism** spread rapidly throughout the Byzantine Empire between the 4th and 7th centuries.
- **In the West,** monasticism grew more slowly, so St Martin of Tours (316–397) sent out monks to start new communities. They were very successful in Britain and Ireland.
- **British and Irish** monasteries such as Lindisfarne and Malmesbury were centres of learning in the Dark Ages.
- **The most famous** scholar monk was St Bede of Jarrow (c.672–735), known for his history of the English people.

▶ British and Irish monks laboured to create beautiful illustrated books by hand. This is the Lindisfarne Gospel.

- **The most famous** British monastery was the Scottish Isle of Iona, set up by St Columba in 563.
- **St Benedict** (c.480–547) developed a particular way of living for monks at Monte Cassino in Italy. By 1000, most monasteries followed Benedictine rules.
- **Monasteries** were very vulnerable to Viking raids. Monks were often killed and many treasures lost, and so the monastic life lost some of its attraction.

# The spread of Islam

- **Muslims** believe that their religion began the day a prophet named Muhammad left Mecca in AD622, but it was after his death in 632 that it really began to grow.
- **The spread of Islam** was led by caliphs (which means rightly guided).
- **Islam** expanded by conquest, and many peoples only

▼ The Dome of the Rock in Jerusalem, built by Abd al-Malik, was one of the first of many beautiful buildings created by Muslims.

became Muslims after they were conquered. But Muslim conquerors were tolerant of other religions.

- **The Muslims** regarded a conquest as a jihad (holy war) and this gave them a powerful zeal.
- **The Muslim Arabs** conquered Iraq (637), Syria (640), Egypt (641) and Persia (650).
- **By 661,** the Islamic Empire stretched from Tunisia to India. Its capital was Damascus.
- **The first Muslims** were Arabs, and as Islam spread, so did Arabs, but the empire contained many peoples.
- **Muhammad** commanded men to 'seek knowledge, even as far as China'. Many Muslims became great scholars.
- **Arts and sciences** flourished under Islam to make it the most cultured, advanced society in the world.

> ★ STAR FACT ★
> In just 100 years, the empire of Islam became bigger than the Roman Empire at its height.

# The Fujiwaras

▲ Life at the Fujiwara court was very cultured, with lots of poetry and music. But it was very formal too, with rules for everything.

- **The Fujiwaras** were the family who dominated Japan for five centuries from the 7th century.

- **The Fujiwaras' power** really began in 858, when Fujiwara Yoshifusa married the old emperor. When he died, Yoshifusa became regent to their young son.

- **The Fujiwaras** kept their position by marrying more daughters to emperors, and creating the role of all-powerful *kampaku* (chancellor).

- **The Fujiwara** *kampaku* or regent ran the country while the emperor dealt with religious matters.

- **Fujiwara power** peaked with Michinaga (966–1028).

- **Michinaga's mansions** were more splendid than palaces and filled with banquets, concerts, poetry and picnics.

- **Many women were** novelists and poets, and love affairs were conducted via cleverly poetic letters.

- **The brilliant** court life of Michinaga was captured in the famous novel *The Tale of Genji* by the lady Murasaki.

- **During Michinaga's** reign, warrior families gained the upper hand by quelling rural rebellions, so bringing about the Fujiwaras' downfall.

> ★ STAR FACT ★
> Sei Shonagon, a lady at Michinaga's court, wrote a famous *Pillow Book* – a diary about what she saw.

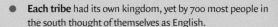

# Anglo-Saxons

- **The Angles, Saxons** and Jutes were peoples from Denmark and Germany who invaded Britain and settled there between AD45 and 600.

- **The Britons resisted** at first, but by 650, they were driven back into the west or made slaves.

- **The Angles** settled in East Anglia and the Midlands, the Saxons in Sussex, Essex and Wessex (Dorset and Hampshire).

◄ In 1939, the burial ship of the overlord Raedwald (died 625) was discovered at Sutton Hoo in East Anglia. This helmet is one of the treasures it held.

- **Each tribe** had its own kingdom, yet by 700 most people in the south thought of themselves as English.

- **Seven leading kingdoms** formed a heptarchy: Essex, Kent, Sussex, Wessex, East Anglia, Mercia and Northumbria.

- **One king** was *bretwalda* (overlord), but the kingdoms vied for power.

- **When Ethelbert of Kent** was *bretwalda*, in 597, St Augustine converted him to Christianity. Christianity spread rapidly throughout England. English monasteries became the universities of Europe. Masons from Gaul and Rome built stone churches.

- **Some Anglo-Saxons** were farmers. Others were warriors as their famous epic poem of heroism, *Beowulf*, shows.

- **In the 700s, Danish raiders** conquered all of England but Wessex. They were pushed back by King Alfred, but attacks resumed in the reign of Ethelred II (978-1016).

- **The last Anglo-Saxon king** was Ethelred II's son, Edward the Confessor (1042-1066).

# Bulgars

▶ In the 800s, the Bulgars were converted to Christianity and adopted the Eastern Orthodox church of the Byzantines. They began to create icons like this.

- **The Bulgars** were an Asian people who arrived in Europe on the Volga River c.AD370.

- **The Bulgars** were skilled horse warriors ruled by khans (chiefs) and boyars (noblemen).

- **The Bulgars** attacked the fringes of the Byzantine Empire until they were in turn attacked by another Asian people called the Avars.

- **After Kurt** became the Bulgar Khan in 605, the Bulgars re-established themselves on the steppes, but when Kurt died, the Bulgars split into five hordes.

- **Four of the five** Bulgar hordes vanished from history, but the fifth was led by Asparukh Khan, west into the Danube valley. Here they overpowered the Slavs living there to create a Bulgarian Empire.

- **Bulgarian Khans** were called caesars or czars after helping Byzantine Emperor Justinian II in 710.

- **The Bulgars** were more often at odds with the Byzantines. They were usually beaten, but after one victory, Krum Khan (803–814) lined Byzantine Emperor Nicephorus's skull with silver to make a drinking cup.

- **The Byzantines** sent St Cyril and his brother St Methodius to convert the Bulgars to Christianity. They succeeded when Czar Boris I was baptized in 864.

- **St Cyril** invented the Cyrillic alphabet, used by Russians and other eastern Europeans today.

- **The Bulgarian Empire** peaked under Simeon I (893–927). Its capital, Preslav, matched Constantinople in splendour.

# The caliphs

- **The caliphs** were the rulers of Islam. The word caliph means 'successor', and they were all meant to be successors of Muhammad after he died in AD632.

- **The first caliph** was Muhammad's father-in-law, Abu Bakr. After that came Umar, Uthman and Ali.

- **The first four caliphs** are called the Rashidun ('perfect') because they were the only caliphs accepted by everyone.

- **When Ali died,** in 661, Islam was torn apart by civil war. Some Muslims, called Shi'ites, saw only Ali's successors, the imams, as leaders. Most Muslims followed the Umayyad family, who became caliphs in Damascus.

- **The 14 Umayyad caliphs** expanded the Islamic Empire by conquest through North Africa and into Spain. But it proved too much for them to handle.

- **In 750** the last Umayyad caliph, Marwan II, was beaten at the Battle of the Great Zab by the rival Abbasids, who were descended from Muhammad's uncle.

- **The 38 Abbasid caliphs** turned their eyes eastwards and made a new capital at Baghdad, which soon became the richest city in the world.

- **Under the Abbasids,** Islam became famous for its science, learning and art, especially during the time of Harun al-Rashid.

- **One Umayyad** escaped to set up a rival caliphate in Spain (756–1031).

- **Descendants** of Muhammad's daughter Fatimah became caliphs in Egypt, creating the great city of Cairo.

▶ Under the Abbasid caliphs, Islamic artists made strikingly beautiful ceramic tiles and glassware.

# Alfred the Great

- **Alfred the Great** (AD849–899) was the greatest of the Anglo-Saxon kings.
- **Alfred** became king of Wessex in 871 at a time when the Danes had over-run East Anglia, Northumbria and Mercia.
- **In 878,** a series of ferocious Danish attacks drove Alfred to hide on the isle of Athelney in the Somerset marshes.
- **While on the run,** Alfred is said to have hidden in a pigherd's cottage. He was so tired he fell asleep by the fire, letting some cakes burn. Not realizing he was the king, the pigherd's wife scolded him.
- **From Athelney,** Alfred secretly assembled an army and emerged to score a decisive victory over the

> ★ STAR FACT ★
> Alfred translated many books from Latin into English so that his people could read them.

◄ This enamel and gold jewel was found near Athelney. It is inscribed with the words Aelfred me ech eh t gewyrcan – Old English for 'Alfred ordered me to be made'.

Danes at Edington. The Danes agreed to withdraw to East Anglia and their king Guthrum became a Christian.

- **In 886,** Alfred recaptured London and forced the Danes to stay within an area called Danelaw.
- **Alfred built forts,** reorganized his army and also created England's first navy to defend against invasions.
- **Alfred was a** wise and kindly king who created sound laws, protected the weak from corrupt judges and created laws to help the poor and needy.
- **Alfred was a scholar** who encouraged learning. He decreed that all young men should learn to read English, and made important books available in English.

# The Berbers

- **The Berbers** were the people who lived in North Africa before other peoples arrived.
- **'Berber'** comes from *barbara*, Roman for barbarians.
- **Numidian Berbers** allied themselves with Carthage (in what is now Tunisia), the city created when Phoenician traders from Lebanon settled there 3000 years ago.

- **The Berbers** lived with first Carthaginian, then Roman, Vandal and Byzantine invasions by withdrawing south into the desert, staying as bands of marauders.
- **In the 7th century,** Islamic Arabs invaded North Africa and many Berbers became Muslims.
- **The Berbers** kept their independence by changing Islam to their own tastes. They based their religion on marabouts, holy men who lived very frugally and morally.
- **After 740,** Berbers took back control of North Africa from the Umayyad caliphs.
- **The Berbers** built empires extending into Spain under the Almohads (1121–1269) and Almoravids (1061–1145).
- **Ibn Tumart** was the first Almohad leader, from c.1121. He claimed to be the Mahdi, the holy man whose coming was predicted by Muhammad.
- **The Berber empires** fell to the Arabs in the 12th century.

◄ When their empires fell, Berbers survived out in the Sahara desert.

# The Vikings

- **The Vikings** were daring raiders from Norway, Sweden and Denmark. Between AD800 and 1100, they swept in on the coasts of northwest Europe in their longships, searching for rich plunder to carry away.

- **People** were terrified by the lightning raids of the Vikings. A prayer of the time went, 'Deliver us, O Lord, from the fury of the Norsemen (Vikings). They ravage our lands. They kill our women and children.'

- **Vikings** prided themselves on their bravery in battle. Most fought on foot with swords, spears and axes. Rich Vikings rode on horseback.

- **Shock troops** called *berserkers* led the attack. Berserk is Norse for 'bare shirt' as they wore no armour. Before a battle, they became fighting mad through drink and drugs and trusted in their god Odin to keep them safe.

- **The word** 'Viking' was only used later. People of the time called them Norsemen. The word probably came from Vik, a pirate centre in Norway. When Norsemen went 'a-viking', they meant fighting as a pirate. Swedish Vikings who settled in eastern Europe may have been called Rus, and so Russia was named after them.

- **Not all Vikings** were pirates. At home, they were farmers and fishermen, merchants and craftworkers. Many went with the raiders and settled in the north of France, in northern England and in Dublin.

- The main Viking gods were Odin, Thor and Frey. The Anglo-Saxons had the same gods and their names have given us some days of the week: Odin's or Wodin's day (Wednesday), Thor's day (Thursday) and Frey's or Frigg's day (Friday). Thor's symbol was a hammer called Mjollnir, which caused thunder and lightning. A hammer like this one was used at many stages in a Viking's life – raised over the newborn, laid in the bride's lap at weddings, or carved on a gravestone.

- **The Vikings attacked** mainly Britain and Ireland, but raided as far as Gibraltar and into the Mediterranean.

- **In Eastern Europe,** the Vikings' ships carried them inland up various rivers. They ventured far through Russia and the Ukraine, sometimes marauding as far south as Constantinople, which they called 'Miklagard', the big city.

- **The Norsemen** who settled in northern France were called Normans. The Norman king William the Conqueror, who invaded England in 1066, was descended from their leader, Rollo.

> ★ **STAR FACT** ★
> In November 885, Count Odo and 200 knights fought heroically to defend Paris against Viking hordes but the city was reduced to ashes.

▼ The Vikings were master sailors, and their wooden sailing ships, called *longships*, are masterpieces of boat-building – light and flat-bottomed enough to sail up shallow rivers, yet seaworthy in the open ocean.

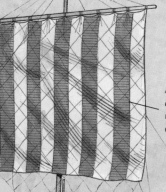

The ships often had a high prow, sometimes carved with a dragon's head

Shields were strapped in rows down each side

When the wind was still, they relied on banks of 20-30 rowers each side

At sea, ships were driven along by a large, square sail made from strips of woollen cloth stitched together

The ships were steered with a large paddle at the rear

# The first Russians

- **Little is known** of the earliest days of Russia, because it was inhabited mainly by nomadic peoples who left few records – such as the Cimmerians (1200–700BC) and later Huns and Khazars.

- **In the 800s AD,** Russia was on the major trade route from NW Europe to the world's richest cities – Constantinople and Baghdad.

- **Slavic peoples** set up trading towns such as Novgorod. They traded in amber, furs, honey, wax and wood.

- **From around 860,** Viking adventurers raided and traded in the region. They were known as the Varangian Rus. The most famous of them was Rurik of Jutland, who took over Novgorod.

- **The city of Kiev** grew up further south, on the Dnieper River.

◄ *Kiev, in the Ukraine, was the focus of the first Russian nation, from 900–1100.*

- **Soon** the Varangian 'grand prince' of Kiev ruled over a vast area historians call Kievan Rus. This covered what is now the Ukraine and eastern Russia.

- **In c.970,** the Slavs took over Kiev under Prince Svyatoslav and his son Vladimir.

- **Vladimir** made Kievan Rus the first Russian nation.

- **Legend says** Vladimir sent people to study different religions. Nothing impressed them until they reached the Hagia Sophia in Constantinople. They were so stunned 'they knew not whether they were in heaven or on earth'.

- **Kiev** quickly adopted Byzantine Christianity. Within 50 years it had 200 beautiful churches – including its own Hagia Sophia – and Vladimir was Russia's first saint.

# Harun al-Rashid

- **Harun al-Rashid** (766–809) was the most famous of all the caliphs.

- **In Harun's time,** Baghdad became the most glamorous city in the world, famed for its luxury as well as its poetry, music and learning.

- **Harun** was famous far and wide. He sent ambassadors to the Chinese emperor and an elephant to Charlemagne.

- **Harun's wife** Zubaydah would only drink from silver and gold cups studded with gems.

◄ *The magic and romance of Harun's Baghdad is captured in the tales of The Arabian Nights.*

- **Harun** was a great patron of the arts, and gave lavish gifts to poets and musicians. Yet he also enjoyed watching dogs fight – and often had people executed.

- **Stories tell** how Harun would wander in the moonlight with his friend Abu Nuwas, the brilliant poet, as well as Masrur the executioner.

- **Harun** has become famous because he features in the famous collection of 200-odd tales of *The Thousand and One Nights*, or *The Arabian Nights*.

- **The Arabian Nights** includes such famous characters as Aladdin and his genie, Ali Baba and Sinbad the Sailor.

- **The tales** begin with King Shahriyar of Samarkand distraught by his wife's unfaithfulness. He vows to marry a new girl each night and behead her in the morning.

- **The lovely princess Scheherazade** insists on marrying the king, then at night tells him a tale so entertaining that he lets her live another day to finish it. One story leads to another for 1001 nights, by which time the king has fallen completely in love with her.

# The Holy Roman Empire

- **The Holy Roman Empire** was a mostly German empire that lasted from 800 until 1806.
- **It began** when Pope Leo III tried to gain the protection of Charlemagne, the King of the Franks, by reviving the idea of the Roman Empire.
- **Pope Leo III** is said to have taken Charlemagne by surprise in St Peter's church in Rome on Christmas Day 800, and to have placed the crown on his head.
- **Charlemagne's Frankish Empire**, including France, Germany and Italy, became the Holy Roman Empire.
- **When Charlemagne died,** in 814, the newborn Holy Roman Empire fell apart.
- **150 years later,** in 962, the German King Otto I gained control of Italy as well as Germany and insisted the pope crown him Holy Roman Emperor.
- **Over the centuries** the empire was continually beset by conflicts with both powerful Germans and the pope.
- **In 1076,** Pope Gregory VII and Emperor Henry IV were

▲ Until 1531, all Holy Roman Emperors were crowned at Aachen in Germany, where Charlemagne built a cathedral and lies buried.

vying for control. Henry's subjects sided with the pope, so Henry had to give way.
- **Gregory** forced Henry to stand barefoot in snow for three days outside his castle in Tuscany to beg for a pardon.
- **The pope's Vatican** and other Italian cities gained almost complete independence from the emperor.

# The Toltecs

> ★ STAR FACT ★
> The name *Toltec* has many meanings: 'cultured person', 'city-type' and 'reed people'.

- **By 900,** the city of Teotihuacán was destroyed and much of Mexico was in the hands of warrior tribes from the north.
- **Legend says** that Teotihuacán was destroyed by one of these warrior tribes called the Toltecs, led by their ruler Mixcóatl. *Mixcóatl* means 'Cloud Serpent'.
- **Under Mixcóatl's son,** Topiltzin, the Toltec were said to have built an empire and also a capital at Tollan, now thought to be Tula, 45 km north of Mexico City.
- **Topiltzin** introduced the cult of the god *Quetzalcóatl* ('Feathered Serpent'), and took the name himself.
- **The Toltecs** were not only great warriors but fine builders and craftsmen. Tollan was full of pyramids, temples and other huge, impressive buildings.

- **Legend says** Tolpiltzin Quetzalcóatl was driven out of Tollan by jealous rivals – including the priests of the god Tezcatlipoca ('Smoking Mirror').
- **After leaving Tollan,** Quetzalcóatl sailed east into the Gulf of Mexico, vowing to return one day.
- **The Aztecs** were greatly influenced by the Toltecs. The Aztecs got the idea of human sacrifices from the priests of Tezcatlipoca. Some Aztecs believed that, when the Spanish arrived in 1519, it was Quetzalcóatl returning in vengeance.
- **The Toltec Empire** broke up in the 12th century and Tollan vanished.

▶ Toltec temples in Tollan were guarded by stone statues of warriors such as this.

# The Maoris

▲ The Maoris lived mostly near the coast or by rivers and travelled in light, swift canoes.

- **The early Polynesian** settlers came to New Zealand by canoe from islands in the Pacific.
- **In c.AD100,** Polynesians called the Morioris came here to settle from the Cook, Marquesas or Society Islands.
- **Maori** tradition tells how the Maoris arrived in waves of migration, beginning about 1150 and ending with the coming of a great fleet from the mythical land of Hawaiki 200 years later.
- **Hawaiki** is thought to be the Pacific island of Tahiti.
- **Archaeologists** have found signs of Maori settlement in New Zealand dating back to AD800 and earlier.
- **The first Maoris** lived mainly by hunting and fishing.
- **Maoris** were skilled woodworkers, building beautiful wooden houses covered in carvings.

- **No human** set foot on New Zealand before around 2000 years ago.
- **The first settlers** in New Zealand were Polynesians.

> ★ STAR FACT ★
> The first Maoris hunted gigantic, flightless birds called moas, which are now extinct.

# Charlemagne

- **In 732,** the Frankish (early French) leader Charles Martel halted the great Muslim invasion of Europe in battle at Tours in central France.
- **Martel's** son Pepin the Short made sure of his family's hold on power in the Frankish kingdom. In 768, Pepin's son Charlemagne became King of the Franks.
- **Charlemagne** (742–814) was the greatest European ruler for 1000 years after Rome's fall.
- **Charlemagne's** name means Charles the Great.
- **Charlemagne** was a great military leader, taking his armies on 53 successful campaigns. He scored victories against the Moors in Spain, and against Saxons and Avars in central Europe.

- **By 796,** Charlemagne had created an empire joining France, Germany, northern Italy and northern Spain.
- **Charlemagne** was a Christian, and in AD800 the pope made Charlemagne Holy Roman Emperor.
- **Charlemagne** was a great ruler who set up an effective law system and introduced the idea of juries in trials.
- **Charlemagne** knew Latin, German and Greek and encouraged scholarship, helped by the great teacher Alcuin.
- **The palace school** in Charlemagne's capital Aachen was the most important school in Europe.

◀ After his death, many legends grew up about Charlemagne. We know that he must have been a powerful personality. One eyewitness said: 'He had a broad and strong body of unusual height...and strode with a firm step and held himself like a man.'

# The Magyars

- The plains by the River Danube (an area now in Hungary) were settled early in the history of humankind, but little is known of the area before it formed the Roman provinces Dacia and Pannonia. At this time, it was home to Celts and Slavs.

- Roman Dacia and Pannonia fell early to the barbarian invaders – Goths, Huns and Avars.

- In 796, the Avars were crushed by Charlemagne.

- In 892, another Frankish king called Arnulf asked a people called the Magyars to help him against the Moravians, who now lived on the Danube plain.

- The Magyars were a people who lived from 3000BC to 800 on the steppes near Russia's River Don.

- In 889, the Magyars had been driven to the edge of their land by a people called the Pechenegs, so they were grateful for Arnulf's call.

- Led by the legendary Arpad, the Magyars swept into Hungary and made it their home.

- In 975, Arpad's great-grandson Géza became a Christian and began to form the Magyars into the Hungarian nation.

- Géza's son Stephen (997–1038) carried on his work and became the first king of Hungary.

- King Stephen, also called St Stephen, was crowned by the pope on Christmas Day, AD1000.

▲ *King Stephen is a famous figure in Hungarian history and his crown became the symbol of the nation.*

# Viking voyages

- The Vikings were great seafarers who made some of the most remarkable voyages of ancient times.

- The Vikings sailed east through the Baltic and up the Vistula and Dnieper Rivers.

- The Vikings sailed west around the British Isles, south round Spain into the Mediterranean.

- The most daring Viking voyages were out across the then-unknown open ocean of the North Atlantic.

- From 900, the Vikings sailed to and settled on remote islands to the far north – including Iceland, the Faroes and Greenland.

▶ *This map shows just some of the remarkable voyages made by the Vikings, and their approximate dates. Names in brackets are the Viking names.*

- About 800, Vikings led by Ohthere reached the remote Siberian islands of Novaya Zemlya in the Arctic.

- In 1000, Bjarni Herjulffson was blown off course sailing home from Greenland and saw an unknown shore.

- Leif Eriksson sailed west to find this unknown shore. Sagas tell how he found a new land. The Vikings called it Vinland because it was said to be abundant in 'wine berries'. The wine berries he found were probably cranberries.

- Most experts now think Vinland is North America, and Leif was the first European to reach it.

- In AD1004, the Viking Thorfinn took 130 people to settle in Vinland and stayed three years. Remains of Thorfinn's settlement were found in 1963 at L'Anse aux Meadows, on the northern tip of Newfoundland.

# Famous villains

- **Ancient history** has many famous villains – but most were called villains by their enemies, so we can never be sure just how bad they were.

- **Many of the best-known** villains are Roman, including the Emperors Caligula and Nero and Sejanus, Emperor Tiberius's minister, who is believed to have poisoned Drusus, Tiberius's son.

- **The Emperor Claudius's wife** Messalina (AD22–48) got Claudius to execute any man who resisted her advances. She once made love to hundreds of men in a night.

- **Claudius's fourth wife,** his niece Agrippina (AD15–59), probably poisoned him to make way for her son, Nero.

- **Many stories** are told of the Chinese emperor Shi Huangdi's cruelty, including killing 460 scholars.

- **Artaxerxes** (died 338BC) was the cruel Persian king who ravaged Egypt in 343BC.

- **Artaxerxes** and all his sons but Arses were murdered by his minister Bagoas in 338BC. Bagoas then killed Arses and tried to poison the next king, Darius III. Darius found out and made Bagoas drink the poison himself.

- **Herod the Great** (73BC–4BC) of Judea (modern Israel) was a strong king, but he is known best for the murder of his beloved wife Mariamne in a jealous rage and the Biblical tale of the Slaughter of the Innocents. This tale relates how Herod ordered soldiers to kill all babies in Bethlehem in order to get rid of the infant Jews, who prophets had said would be a threat to him.

- **Pontius Pilate** (AD36) was the Roman governor of Judea who let Jesus be crucified.

- **Theodora** was notorious for her secret police.

◀ History paints Nero (top) and Caligula (left) as real villains.

# Viking society

- **Vikings ate** beef, cheese, eggs and milk from their farms, meat from deer, elks and seals caught by hunters and fish such as cod, herring and salmon.

- **Vikings lived** in one-storey wooden houses with slanted roofs of turf or straw and no windows. At the centre was a hearth for warmth and cooking. The man of the house sat on a chair called the high seat; the rest sat on benches.

◀ Viking god Odin was said to ride on the eight-legged horse Sleipnir, accompanied by two ravens that brought him news of any battles.

> ★ STAR FACT ★
> Viking villages were ruled by a council called the *Thing* or *Folkmoot*.

- **Viking men wore** trousers and a long-sleeved smock shirt. Women wore long woollen or linen dresses.

- **Viking men** could have two or three wives, but marriages were arranged by parents.

- **A Viking woman,** unusually for the time, could own her own property and divorce her husband.

- *Skalds* (poets) went into battle to report on them in verse.

- **The Vikings** were great storytellers. They told of their adventures in long stories called *sagas*.

- **At first** the sagas were only spoken. From 1100–1300, they were written. The most famous is Njal's *saga*.

- **Vikings** were very religious and had several gods. They believed if they died fighting they would go to Valhalla, a special hall in Asgard, the gods' home.

# The first English kings

- **Egbert,** king of Wessex from 802 to 839, became in effect the first king of England when he conquered Mercia at Ellandun in 820. But his rule lasted just a year before the Mercian king Wiglaf claimed Mercia back.

- **For 100 years,** much of England was lost to the Danes, but Alfred the Great's son Edward and his daughter Aethelflaed gradually drove the Danes out by 918.

◀ The city of Winchester in southern England was Alfred the Great's capital, and in his time it became a great centre of learning. Canute also made it his capital, and his son Hardecanute is buried here, with Alfred.

- **England's kingship** really began with Athelstan, who was crowned 'king of all Britain' at Kingston on 4 Sept., 925.

- **Ethelred the Unready** was king of England from 978-1013 and 1014-1016. Rede was old English for advice, and his name meant he was always badly advised.

- **Ethelred** created so much distrust among his subjects that the Danes easily re-conquered England in 980.

- **In 1013** Dane Sweyn Forkbeard became king of England.

- **When Sweyn** died, Ethelred made a comeback until Sweyn's son Canute drove him out. Canute became king of England in 1016 by marrying Ethelred's widow, Emma.

- **Canute** ruled well. A story tells how he rebuked flatterers by showing how even he could not stop the tide coming in.

- **After Canute,** in 1035, came his son Hardecanute, who died in 1042. Ethelred's son Edward the Confessor then became king – but the Danes did not want a Saxon king.

- **The Danes** called on their Norwegian allies, led first by Magnus then Harold Hardraada, to win back the throne.

# Early Scots

- **The first settlers** came to Scotland around 7000 years ago, and the remains of their huts can be seen on Skara Brae in Orkney.

- **People called Picts** arrived here shortly before the times of the Romans, who failed to conquer Scotland.

- **The Picts** may have come from the Black Sea region. They got their name from the tattooed pictures on their bodies.

- **Brochs** are 15-m high stone towers built for defence around 100BC – perhaps by ancestors of the Picts.

- **Celts** called Scots came from Dalriada in Ireland in c.470. They soon conquered the west.

- **After St Columba** came to set up Iona monastery in 563, Scotland was slowly converted to Christianity.

- **In 563** Scotland was split into four kingdoms: the Scots' Dalriada in the west; the Picts in the north; the Britons' Strathclyde in the southwest; and Bernicia or Lothian of the Angles in the east.

- **In 685,** the Picts drove out the Angles, and in 863, the

Dalriada king Kenneth McAlpin conquered the Picts to create a country called Alba, the first Scotland.

- **In the 900s and 1000s,** many people fought to be king in Scotland. Kenneth III killed Constantine III to become king. Malcolm II killed Kenneth III and Duncan I who followed him was killed by his general Macbeth. Macbeth was killed by Malcolm III.

- **Malcolm III's** wife was Saint Margaret (1045–1093), brought up in Hungary where her father was in exile.

▶ Macbeth (died 1057) was the Scottish king who became the basis for Shakespeare's tragedy 'Macbeth'. The real Macbeth killed Duncan in battle, not in his bed as in Shakespeare's play.

# MODERN HISTORY

## PEOPLE

## WARS AND BATTLES

## EUROPE

## THE AMERICAS

## EVENTS

## THE WORLD

# The Norman invasion

- **On 5 January 1066**, the English king Edward the Confessor died. As he died, he named as his successor Harold Godwinson – the powerful earl of Wessex.

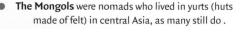

◀ *The Normans commemorated their victory at the Battle of Hastings with a famous tapestry, now in Bayeux in France.*

- **Harold's claim** to the English throne was challenged by William, the duke of Normandy in France, who claimed that Edward had already promised him the throne.

- **Harold's claim** was also challenged by Harold Hardraade (the Ruthless), the king of Norway.

- **In autumn 1066**, Hardraade invaded northern England with Harold Godwinson's brother Tostig. His army was routed by Harold's at Stamford Bridge on 25 September.

- **On 27 Sept**, William's Norman army of 7000 crossed from France and landed at Pevensey in S. England.

- **Harold marched** his army south to meet the Normans, walking over 300 km to London in just five days.

- **Harold's tired army** met the Normans at Hastings in Sussex on the 14th October, and took a stand by the Hoar Apple Tree on Caldbec Hill.

- **Harold's army** was mauled by William's archers, but axe-wielding English house-carles (infantry) put the Norman cavalry to flight. Harold was then killed – perhaps by an arrow. The English fought on for a while before fleeing.

- **After the battle** William moved on London, where he was crowned king in Westminster Abbey on 25 December.

- **Within** a few years, the Normans had conquered England.

# The great khans

- **The Mongols** were nomads who lived in yurts (huts made of felt) in central Asia, as many still do .

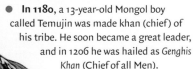

- **In 1180**, a 13-year-old Mongol boy called Temujin was made khan (chief) of his tribe. He soon became a great leader, and in 1206 he was hailed as *Genghis Khan* (Chief of all Men).

- **Genghis Khan** was a brilliant and ruthless soldier. His armies terrified their enemies, and butchered anyone they met.

◀ *Genghis Khan was a man of incredible physical strength and willpower. He could be tyrannical and cruel, yet philosophers would travel from far away to talk with him about religion.*

- **Genghis's horse archers** could kill at 180 m while riding at full gallop. They once rode 440 km in just three days.

- **In just four years (1210–14)**, Genghis Khan conquered northern China, much of India and Persia. His empire stretched right through Asia from Korea to the Caspian.

- **After Genghis Khan** died, his son Ogodai ravaged Armenia, Hungary and Poland.

- **Genghis Khan's grandson** – Kublai Khan – conquered the rest of China in 1265 and made himself the first of a line of Mongol emperors of China called Yuans. The Yuans lasted until 1368.

- **Kublai's** rule in China was harsh, but he was greatly admired by the Venetian traveller, Marco Polo.

- **Kublai Khan** created a grand new capital called Ta-tu ('the Great Capital') – now Beijing.

- **Kublai Khan** adopted Chinese ways of government and ruled with such efficiency that China became very rich.

# The Aztecs

- **In the 1200s,** a tribe called the Aztecs found that the only place to settle in crowded Mexico was on a lake.

- **By 1325,** the Aztecs were powerful and their lake home Tenochtitlán was a splendid city with canals and temples.

- **Aztec farmers** walked or rowed dugout canoes for hours to markets in cities like Tlateloco to sell farm produce in return for cocoa beans, which they used as money.

- **In Aztec society,** a powerful priest-king plus priests and nobles ruled ordinary folk and slaves with an iron hand.

- **The Aztecs** built vast pyramids topped by temples where priests made bloody human sacrifices on a huge scale.

- **The Aztecs** made human sacrifices because they believed that this gave their god Huitzilopochtli the strength to fight off the night and bring the morning.

▶ In battle, some Aztec warriors dressed as eagles, jaguars and other fierce animals.

- **In a special, sacred ball game** teams hit a rubber ball through a small ring in an I-shaped court – using their hips, knees and elbows. This very violent game caused serious injury, even death.

- **One of the ways** we know about the Aztecs is from folding books of picture-writing called codices, written by Aztec scribes. The most famous is the *Codex Mendoza*.

- **By 1521,** the Aztec Empire is finished. Spanish treasure-seekers led by Hernando Cortés defeat Montezuma II the Aztec emperor, and plunder their land and riches.

> ★ STAR FACT ★
> Every year Tenochtitlán took in 9000 tonnes of corn, beans and seeds in taxes.

# The Magna Carta

- **John I** was king of England from 1199 to 1216. He was one of the most unpopular kings in history.

- **John was nicknamed** 'Lackland' by his father Henry II because, unlike his older brothers Richard and Geoffrey, he did not inherit land to provide him an income.

- **John was hated** for his cruelty, for the demands he put on his barons for tax and military service and for trying to seize the crown while his popular brother King Richard the Lionheart was crusading.

- **On 15 June 1215,** rebellious barons compelled John to meet them at Runnymede on the Thames and agree to their demands by sealing the Magna Carta ('Great Charter').

▼ The barons compelled King John to put his seal (*wax stamp*) on the Magna Carta at Runnymede in 1215.

- **Ordinary people** gained little at the time from the Magna Carta but it is now seen as the world's first bill of rights and the start of fair government in England.

- **The Magna Carta** showed that even the king had to obey the law.

- **Magna Carta** contained 63 clauses, most relating to feudal customs.

- **Clause 39** gave every free man the right to a fair trial. Clause 40 gave everyone the right to instant justice.

- **Some parts of** the Magna Carta dealt with weights and measures, foreign merchants and catching fish.

- **John** got the pope to annul the document three days later, but it was reissued in 1225, after John's death.

# Saladin

- **Saladin** was perhaps the greatest Muslim (Islamic) leader of the Middle Ages. To his people he was a saintly hero. Even his Christian enemies were awed by his honour and bravery.

  - **Saladin is famed** as a brilliant soldier, but he was also deeply religious. He built many schools, mosques and canals.

  - **Saladin was a Kurd**, born in Tekrit, now in Iraq, in 1137, but he was brought up in Syria.

  - **He became** a soldier at the age of 14. Right from the start he had an intense belief in the idea of *jihad* – the holy war to defend the Islamic religion.

  ◀ *Saladin must have been a single-minded and ambitious man, but those who met him said he was the most humble, moral and generous of rulers. Strangely, he died virtually penniless.*

- **Saladin's leadership** brought him to prominence and in 1169 he was effectively made sultan (ruler) of Egypt.

- **By diplomacy and conquest**, he united the Muslim countries – torn apart by rivalries for the 88 years since the crusaders captured Jerusalem in 1099.

- **In 1187**, with Islam united, Saladin was able to turn his attentions to driving the crusaders out of the Near East.

- **On 4 July 1187** Saladin routed the Crusaders at Hattin in Palestine. This victory was so devastating to the Crusaders that within three months the Muslims had recaptured almost every bit of land they had lost.

- **Shocked by the fall** of Jerusalem, the Christian countries threw themselves into their last major Crusade, led in part by the great Richard the Lionheart.

- **Such was Saladin's** leadership that the Muslims fought off the crusaders' onslaught. Eventually, Richard and Saladin met up and, in a spirit of mutual admiration, drew up a truce that ended the Crusades.

# Bannockburn

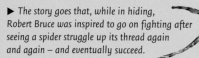

▶ *The story goes that, while in hiding, Robert Bruce was inspired to go on fighting after seeing a spider struggle up its thread again and again – and eventually succeed.*

- **In 1286, King Alexander III** of Scotland died. His grand-daughter – Margaret – 'Maid of Norway', died four years later. Their deaths left no obvious successor to the Scottish throne.

- **The Scottish lords** agreed to the suggestion of English king Edward I that he should decide between the 13 rival claimants, including John de Balliol and Robert Bruce.

- **Edward I** marched into Scotland, imprisoned the leading claimant John de Balliol and declared himself king. Some of Balliol's rivals, such as Robert, supported Edward.

- **The Scottish lords** did not react, but a small landowner called William Wallace began a heroic fight. With a band of just 30 men, he attacked Lanark, took the garrison and killed the English sheriff. Commoners flocked to his aid.

> ★ STAR FACT ★
> At Bannockburn, just 5000 Scots may have routed an English army of 23,000.

- **On 4 May 1297**, Wallace's small rebel army scored a stunning victory over the English at Stirling. He drove the English from Scotland and marched on into England. But the Scottish lords still gave him no support.

- **Wallace** was captured by the English in 1305. He was hanged, drawn (disembowelled) and quartered (cut in four pieces). His head was stuck on a pole on London Bridge.

- **Wallace's** heroism inspired Robert Bruce to lead a rebellion that finally included the Scottish lords.

- **Letting his enemies** think he was dead, Robert launched a campaign from Ireland in 1306. Within two years he had cleared the English from Scotland again.

- **Robert scored** a last decisive victory over the English under Edward II at Bannockburn on 23–24 June 1314. With this victory, the Scots regained their independence.

# African empires

- **From 1000 to 1500**, the interaction of black, Bantu-speaking Africans with Arab Muslims shaped African history.

- **In East Africa**, Bantu people and Arabs mixed to create the culture and language called Swahili.

- **Trade in gold and ivory** created thriving ports down the East African coast – such as Zanzibar and Kilwa.

- **Inland** the city of Great Zimbabwe flourished within its huge granite walls. It is now a ruin, but in the 1400s, gold made this city the heart of the Monomatapa Empire.

- **Further inland**, by the lakes of Uganda, were the extraordinary grass palaces of the Bugandan kings.

- **In West Africa**, trade across the Sahara made kingdoms like Ghana flourish. Two great empires grew up – first Mali (1240–1500) and then Songhai, which peaked in the 1500s.

- **The Mali** Empire centred on the city of Timbuktu.

- **Timbuktu's** glory began in 1324, when King Mansa Musa went on a grand trip to Mecca with camels laden with gold and brought back the best scholars and architects.

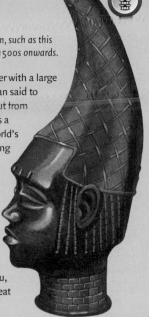

▶ *The brass sculptures of Benin, such as this head, were produced from the 1500s onwards.*

- **Timbuktu** means 'mother with a large navel', after an old woman said to have first settled here. But from 1324–1591 Timbuktu was a splendid city with the world's biggest university, catering for 25,000 students.

- **The Songhai Empire** in the 1400s stretched right across West Africa from what is now Nigeria to Gambia. It reached its peak under Sunni Ali (1464–92), who conquered Timbuktu, and his son Askia the Great (1493–1528).

# Serfs and lords

- **When the Roman** Empire collapsed, a new way of ordering society, called the feudal system, emerged.

- **In the feudal system**, a king or overlord gave a lord a *fief* (a grant of land). In return, the lord swore to train and fight for the king as a knight (horse warrior). Land was the security because it could not be moved. Any lord who got a fief was called his king's *vassal*.

- **In 732, Charles Martel**, ruler of the Franks (now France) drove back the invading Muslims at the Battle of Tours. But he was worried he might not beat the brilliant Muslim horsemen if they came back. So he developed one of the first feudal systems.

- **There were** different levels in the feudal system. The count of Champagne had 2017 vassal knights, but he himself was vassal to ten overlords, including the king of France.

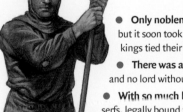

- **Only noblemen** could join the feudal system, but it soon took over most land in Europe, as kings tied their subjects by grants of land.

- **There was a saying**, 'No land without a lord; and no lord without a land'.

- **With so much land** in fiefs, most peasants were serfs, legally bound to their lords by the 'manorial' system, which centred on a lord's manor or castle.

- **Serfs** were given small plots of land to live off in return for working their lord's land.

- **Serfs** could not be evicted, but had few rights. They could not leave the village, marry or sell their possessions without their lord's permission.

- **The feudal and manorial systems** reached their peak in the 1100s but then began to decline.

◀ *Most people in medieval Europe were poor serfs tied to their lord. They lived in poor huts clustered round the lord's manor house and scraped a poor living.*

# Crusades

- **In the 11th century,** western Christian countries were feeling very threatened by the growing empire of the Muslim Seljuk Turks. In 1095, they were just a few miles outside Constantinople, capital of the Byzantine Empire and the main centre of Christianity in the east. The Byzantine emperor Alexander Comnenus appealed to the pope, Urban II, for help.

- **Urban II** held a meeting of church leaders at Clermont in France. He called for warriors to drive back the Turks and reclaim the Holy Land from the Muslims. This was not just a battle but a holy pilgrimage or Crusade. The word 'Crusade' comes from the Latin *crux*, meaning 'cross', the Christian symbol.

- **Before the armies** could set out, 50,000 peasants began marching from western Europe on their own 'People's Crusade' to free the Holy Land. They had been stirred by tales of Turkish atrocities, spread by a preacher called Peter the Hermit. Many peasants died or got lost on the way; the rest were killed by Turks.

- **In 1096,** armies of well-trained French and Norman knights set out on the First Crusade. At Constantinople, they joined up with the Byzantines. Despite a lot of quarrelling on the way, they captured Jerusalem in 1099 and then set about massacring Jews and Turks mercilessly.

- **After capturing** Jerusalem, the crusaders divided the Holy Land into four parts or Counties, together known as Outremer (said 'oot-rer-mare') which meant 'land beyond the seas'. The crusaders ruled Outremer for 200 years and built great castles like Krak des Chevaliers in Syria.

- **Two bands of soldier-monks** formed to protect pilgrims journeying to the Holy Land – the Knights Hospitallers of St John and the Knights Templars. The Hospitallers wore black with a white cross. The Templars wore a red cross on white, which became the symbol of all crusaders.

- **By 1144,** crusader control in Outremer weakened, and the Turks advanced. King Louis VII of France and King Conrad of Germany launched a Second Crusade. But by 1187, Saladin had retaken most of Outremer.

- **In 1190,** the three most powerful men in Europe – Richard I of England, Philip II of France and Frederick Barbarossa (Holy Roman Emperor) – set off on the Third Crusade. Barbarossa died on the way and Philip II gave up. Only Richard went on, and secured a truce with Saladin.

- **In 1212,** thousands of children set off on a Children's Crusade to take back Jerusalem, led by French farm boy Stephen of Cloyes. Sadly, most were lured on to ships in Marseilles and sold into slavery or prostitution.

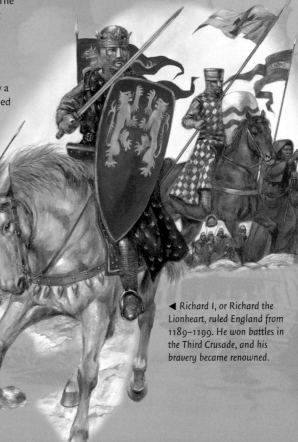

◀ Richard I, or Richard the Lionheart, ruled England from 1189–1199. He won battles in the Third Crusade, and his bravery became renowned.

# Marco Polo

- **Marco Polo** was a famous Italian traveller. Born c.1254 in Venice, he spent many years in the court of Kublai Khan, emperor of China.

- In the 1260s, most of Europe knew China only as the romantic land of 'Cathay'. But Marco's father Niccolo and uncle Maffeo were well-travelled merchants who had already been there.

- **In 1271**, Niccolo and Maffeo invited 17-year-old Marco to come with them to Cathay again.

- **The Polos took four years** to reach China, travelling on foot and horse along the 'Silk Road' – a route north of the Himalayan mountains. The Silk Road was the way merchants brought silk from China to Europe.

- **Kublai Khan** welcomed the Polos. Marco had a gift for languages and became one of the Khan's diplomats.

*(Map:)* Venice, Trebizond, Samarkand, Beijing, Balkh, Khotan, Quanzhou, Ayas, Hormuz

→ Outward journey 1271–75
← Return journey 1292–95

- ◀ *Marco Polo was one of the few Europeans to journey all the way to China and back in the Middle Ages.*

- **After 17 years**, the Polos decided to come back — but the Khan would only let them go if they took with them a princess who was to be wed to the Khan's grand-nephew in Persia.

- **The Polos** arrived back in Venice in 1295, laden with jewels, silks and spices.

- **Marco Polo** later wrote an account of his time in China while a prisoner of war in Genoa, dictating it to a man called Rustichello. It immediately became a best-seller.

- **Marco's** tales were so fantastic that some called the book *Il milione* ('The million lies'). Experts now think that he reported the truth as he saw it.

- **Christopher Columbus** was just one of many people inspired by Marco Polo's accounts.

# The Black Death

▲ *The Plague brought death so close to people that they began to think of death as a real person.*

- **The Black Death** was the terrible epidemic of bubonic plague and pneumonia that ravaged Europe between 1347 and 1351.

- **The Black Death** of the 1300s was perhaps the worst disaster ever to have struck humanity.

- **Worldwide,** the Black Death killed 40 million people.

- **The Black Death** killed 25 million people in Europe.

- **The disease** probably started in China. It was transmitted to Europeans when a Kipchak (Mongol) raiding party catapulted infected corpses into a Genoese trading centre in the Crimea.

- **The plague reached Genoa** in 1347 and spread west and north, reaching London and Paris in 1348.

- **The plague was** carried first by rat fleas that could also live on humans. It then changed to pneumonic plague which was spread through coughs and sneezes.

- **After the Black Death,** fields were littered with bodies. Houses, villages and towns stood silent and empty.

- **Afterwards** there was such a shortage of labour that wages soared and many serfs gained their freedom.

> ★ STAR FACT ★
> The Black Death killed more than one in every four Europeans in just four years.

# The Hundred Years War

▲ *The greatest knight of the war was Edward the Black Prince (1330–76), hero of the Battles of Crécy, Poitiers and Navarette.*

- **The Hundred Years War** was a long war between France and England, lasting from 1337 to 1453.

- **The war** was caused by disputes over Guyenne (English land in southwest France), English claims to the French throne, French support for the Scots and French efforts to block the English wool trade in Belgium.

- **1337:** French king Philip VI tried to take over Guyenne. English king Edward III, whose mother was sister to three French kings, retaliated by claiming the French throne.

- **1340:** Edward won a great naval battle off Sluis, Belgium.

- **1346:** Edward III's archers – outnumbered 3 to 1 – routed the greatest French knights at Crécy with their great 2-m-long yew bows – and so hastened the end of knighthood.

- **1347:** Edward III took the French port of Calais.

- **1356:** Edward III's son, the Black Prince, won a great victory over the French at Poitiers.

- **1415:** the last great English victory was Henry V's at Agincourt. 6000 English beat a French army of 30,000.

- **The English** won most battles, but the French won the war because they had three times the resources.

> ★ STAR FACT ★
> The tide turned for the French in 1429, when
> Joan of Arc led them to victory at Orléans.

# The Hanseatic League

▶ *Riches from the Hanseatic traders helped Hamburg build a great cathedral in the Middle Ages.*

- **By the 1400s,** the feudal system of knights fighting part-time in exchange for land was outmoded. Kings now relied on full-time armies.

- **Kings turned** to newly rich merchants to pay for their armies, so merchants gained power. The Italians invented banks to give loans.

- **From the 1300s,** many serfs gained freedom and became prosperous 'yeoman' farmers. They needed merchants to sell their produce.

- **After the Crusades,** silks, spices and riches from the east were traded in the Mediterranean for cloth, hides and iron. In northern Europe, the wool trade thrived.

- **Trading towns** began to thrive across western Europe in the 1300s and 1400s – Antwerp, Flanders, Bruges, Bristol, Norwich, York, Florence, Venice, Milan and many others.

- **Trading towns** grew powerful. In England, many became boroughs with charters giving them some self-rule.

- **Merchants and traders** organized guilds (like trade unions) to defend their rights.

- **In 1241,** the German ports of Hamburg and Lübeck set up a *hanse* (guild) to protect merchants against pirates. The hanse grew to a very powerful Hanseatic League that monopolized trade around the Baltic Sea.

- **The Hanseatic League** set up special areas in cities across north Europe and controlled most trading routes. The League also put financial pressure on kings and lords to keep them at peace, and not to disrupt trade.

- **Hanseatic merchants** brought raw materials, spices and silks from eastern Europe and traded them for cloth, linen, silverware and woollen clothes from the west.

# The Great Schism

- **In the Middle Ages**, kings and lords battled with the Church over who had the right to run people's lives.

- **The Church** was all-powerful but riddled with corruption. Men like John Wycliffe (1320–84) began to argue that it had too much power. He was supported by English kings.

- **In the 1200s**, scholars called 'scholastics' such as Roger Bacon tried to use reason to understand Christian ideas.

- **The French scholar** Peter Abelard argued that we should ask questions. 'By doubting, we come to inquiry, and by inquiry we come to truth.'

- **Churchmen** like Bernard of Clairvaux opposed scholastics: 'the faith of the righteous believes; it does not dispute.'

- **In 1302, Pope Boniface VIII** issued a decree called the *Unum sanctum* stating that everyone was subject to him.

- **French king** Philip IV said Boniface was trying to claim authority over the French king and French people.

- **In 1309**, Pope Clement V moved from Rome to Avignon in France. This became home to a series of French popes,

▶ The Palace of the Popes in Avignon in southern France was built between 1314 and 1370. It was the home of the French popes for 100 years at the time of the Great Schism.

until Pope Gregory XI went back to Rome in 1377.

- **When Gregory XI** died in 1378, there was a Great Schism (split) in the Church. Some claimed Italian Urban VI as pope. Others supported Robert from Switzerland. Urban stayed in Rome and Robert went back to Avignon. In 1409, some church leaders declared a third pope.

- **In 1417**, the Great Schism was ended when a council of all church leaders elected Martin V as pope in Rome. But the dispute had weakened the Church's authority fatally.

# The Ottoman Wars

- **In 1281**, a new power began to emerge in Turkey from a tiny state called Sögüt, led by a ruler called Osman.

- **Over 200 years** a huge Muslim empire was built up, called the Ottoman Empire after Osman's descendants. It stretched from the Euphrates River on the borders of Persia to the Danube in Hungary.

- **In 1453**, Christian Constantinople fell to the Ottoman Turks and became their capital, Istanbul.

- **For centuries**, the Christian countries of Europe were threatened by Turkish expansion.

▶ Lepanto was the last great battle between fleets of galleys – warships powered by huge banks of oarsmen.

- **Ottoman power** peaked in the 1520s under Suleiman, known as *Qanuni* ('law-giver') by Turks and 'the Magnificent' by Europeans because of his splendid court.

- **Suleiman** took all Hungary and attacked Vienna in 1529.

- **In 1522**, Suleiman took the island of Rhodes from his sworn enemies, the Knights of St John, who moved to Malta and built the fort of Valetta.

- **In the 1520s**, the Turkish pirate Khir or *Barbarossa* (Spanish for Redbeard) took most of North Africa and became an Ottoman admiral. Algeria and the Barbary coast (North Africa) became a feared base for pirates for 300 years.

- **In 1565**, Suleiman attacked the Knights of St John in Valetta, but they survived.

- **When the Turks** attacked Cyprus in 1571, Venetian, Spanish and Papal fleets combined to crush them at the crucial battle of Lepanto in Greece. Turkish power declined after this.

# The Wars of the Roses

- **The Wars of the Roses** were a series of civil wars fought in England in the 1400s as two branches of the Plantagenet family fought for the English throne.
- **On one side** was the house of York, with a white rose as its emblem. On the other was the house of Lancaster, with a red rose as its emblem.
- **The wars began** when Lancastrian king Henry VI became insane in 1453. With the country in chaos, Warwick the 'kingmaker' set up Richard, duke of York as Protector in Henry's place.
- **In 1455, Henry VI** seemed to recover and war broke out between Lancastrians and Yorkists.
- **Richard** was killed at the Battle of Wakefield in 1460, but Henry VI became insane again.

York

Lancaster

▶ The red rose and white rose were the emblems of the rival houses of Lancaster and York. When Henry VII wed Elizabeth of York, he combined the two to make the Tudor rose.

- **A crushing Yorkist victory** at Towton, near York, in 1461, put Richard's son on the throne as Edward IV.
- **Edward IV** made enemies of his brothers Clarence and Warwick, who invaded England from France in 1470 with Henry VI's queen Margaret of Anjou and drove Edward out.
- **Henry VI** was brought back for seven months before Edward's Yorkists defeated the Lancastrians at Barnet and Tewkesbury. Henry VI was murdered.
- **When Edward IV** died in 1483, his son Edward V was still a boy. When young Edward and his brother vanished – probably murdered in the Tower of London – their uncle Richard III seized the throne.
- **Richard III** made enemies among the Yorkists, who sided with Lancastrian Henry Tudor. Richard III was killed at Bosworth Field on 22 August 1485. Henry Tudor became Henry VII and married Elizabeth of York to end the wars.

# Monasteries

- **Monasteries** played a key role in medieval life in Europe, reaching a peak in the 1200s.
- **The most famous monastery** was Cluny in France, but there were thousands of others in France and England.
- **Most monasteries** had a church called an abbey, some of which are among the greatest medieval buildings.
- **Monasteries** were the places where the poor went for welfare and they were also the only hospitals.

- **Monasteries** were places for scholars to study. They were the only libraries. Most great works of medieval art, literature and scholarship came from monasteries.
- **Monasteries** were great landowners with immense power and wealth. In England, monasteries owned a third of the land and a quarter of the country's wealth. They were also Europe's biggest single employers.
- **Many monasteries** oppressed the poor by taking over land and taking a heavy toll in tithes (church taxes).
- **Many monasteries** became notorious for the indulgence of their monks in fine food and high living.
- **New orders** of monks tried every now and then to go back to a simpler life, like the Cistercians from Citeaux in France and the Premonstratensians from Laon in France.
- **Cistercians** founded monasteries in barren places like Fountains in Yorkshire. But even they grew rich and lazy.

◀ Like most English monasteries, the great 12th-century Cistercian monastery at Tintern in Wales was destroyed by Henry VIII.

# China

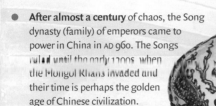

- **After almost a century** of chaos, the Song dynasty (family) of emperors came to power in China in AD 960. The Songs ruled until the early 1200s, when the Mongol Khans invaded and their time is perhaps the golden age of Chinese civilization.

- **The Song rulers** renounced the warlike policies that had kept China in strife, and brought peace by paying tribute money to the barbarian peoples in the north. They had a huge army, but this was partly to give jobs to hundreds of thousands of poor Chinese.

- **The Song slowly got rid** of soldiers from government and replaced them with civil servants.

- **In earlier times,** only aristocrats tended to hold key posts in government, but under the Song, anyone could enter for the civil service exams. Competition to do well in the exams was intense, and the main yearly exams became major events in the calendar.

- **The civil service exams** stressed not practical skills but the study of literature and the classic works of the thinker Confucius. So the Song civil service was full of learned, cultured men, known in the west as mandarins. Ou Yang-hsiu was a typical mandarin – statesman, historian, poet, philosopher, wine and music connoisseur and brilliant player of the chess-like game *wei-ch'i*.

◄ Chinese porcelain and pottery is famous for its beauty and delicacy, and the perfection of the covering glaze. It reached a peak in the Ming era (1368–1644).

- **Under the Song,** the Chinese population soared, trade prospered and all kinds of advances were made in science and technology – from the invention of gunpowder and the sailors' compass to paper and printing. Technologically, China was about 500 years ahead of Europe.

- **The Song period** is also known for its exquisite landscape paintings and fine porcelain, which is why good porcelain is called 'China'.

- **In 1126,** barbarian invasions forced the Song to move their capital from Kaifeng in the north to Hangzhou (modern Shanghai) in the south.

- **By 1275,** Hangzhou was the world's largest city, with a population of a million. Its warm climate encouraged a lively, leisurely lifestyle. The city was full of luxury shops, bars, restaurants, tea-houses and clubs where girls sang. Often, people went out to stroll in the gardens by the West Lake or lazed over long meals on the lake's scores of floating restaurants, pushed along by poles like Venetian gondolas. Marco Polo later complained that the people here were 'anything but warriors; all their delight was in women, nothing but women.'

> ★ STAR FACT ★
> The Song inventions gunpowder and printing had a huge influence on Europe when they arrived there centuries later.

▶ When the Mongol Khans seized China from the Song, they made a new capital in the north at Beijing. At its centre lies a walled area containing the emperor's palaces. It is called the Forbidden City because only the emperor and his servants could enter it.

# Joan of Arc

- **St Joan of Arc** (c.1412–31) was the peasant girl who led France from defeat in the Hundred Years' War and was burned at the stake for her beliefs.

- **Joan** was called Jeanne d'Arc in France. She called herself Jeanne la Pucelle (Joan the Maid).

- **Joan** was brought up in the village of Domrémy, near Nancy, northeastern France, as a shepherd girl.

- **By the age of 13**, Joan was having visions and believed that God had chosen her to help the French king Charles VII to beat the English.

- **Joan tried** to see the king but was laughed at until she was finally admitted to the king's court, in 1429.

- **To test Joan**, the king stood in disguise amongst his courtiers but Joan recognized him instantly – and also told him what he asked for in his secret prayers.

- **Joan was given** armour and an army to rescue the town of Orléans from the English and succeeded in just ten days.

- **Joan then** led Charles VII through enemy territory to be crowned at Rheims cathedral.

- **In May 1430**, Joan was captured by the English and accused of witchcraft.

- **Joan insisted that** her visions came from God, so a tribunal of French clergy condemned her as a heretic. She was burned at the stake in Rouen on 30 May 1431.

▶ Shortly after her death, the pope pronounced Joan innocent of all crimes. She was later made a saint.

# Knights

- **Knights** were the elite fighting men of the Middle Ages, highly trained for combat both on horseback and on foot.

- **Knights always wore** armour. At first, the armour was simply shirts of mail, made from linked rings of iron. By the 1400s, most knights wore full suits of plate armour.

- **Knights rode into battle** on a horse called a *destrier*, or warhorse, and usually had an easy-going horse called a *palfry* just for when he was travelling, plus a packhorse called a *sumpter*.

- **Knights had a strict** code of honour called chivalry – from *chevalier*, the French for 'horseman'.

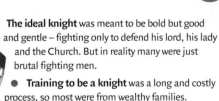

▶ A knight's armour often weighed 25 kg so he had to be very fit in order to ride and fight in it.

- **The ideal knight** was meant to be bold but good and gentle – fighting only to defend his lord, his lady and the Church. But in reality many were just brutal fighting men.

- **Training to be a knight** was a long and costly process, so most were from wealthy families.

- **A young boy** training to be a knight began at 7 as a page to a lord, then became a knight's squire (apprentice) at 14.

- **A squire's task** was to look after his master's armour, dress him for battle and serve his food.

- **A squire** who passed all the tests was dubbed a 'knight' at about 21 years old.

- **Knights took part** in mock battles called tournaments, often involving 'jousts', where two knights would charge at each other with lances.

# The Renaissance

- **The Renaissance** was the great revolution in arts and ideas in Italy between the 1300s and the 1500s.

- **Renaissance** is French for 'rebirth', because it was partly about a revival of interest in the works of the classical world of Greece and Rome.

- **The Renaissance began** when many people started to doubt that the Church had all the answers.

- **Scholars** gradually developed the idea of 'humanism' – the idea that man is the focus of things, not God.

- **A spur** to the Renaissance was the fall of Constantinople in 1453. This sent Greek scholars fleeing to Italy, where they set up academies in cities like Florence and Padua.

- **Artists** in the Renaissance, inspired by classical examples, began to try and put people at the centre of their work – and to portray people and nature realistically rather than as religious symbols.

- **In the 1400s** brilliant artists like Donatello created startlingly realistic paintings and sculptures.

▶ The ancient Italian city of Padua is full of masterpieces of Renaissance building and art, including paintings by Giotto and sculptures by Donatello.

- **The three greatest artists** of the Renaissance were Michaelangelo, Raphael and Leonardo da Vinci.

- **The Renaissance** saw some of the world's greatest artistic and architectural masterpieces being created in Italian cities such as Florence and Padua.

- **During the late 1400s**, Renaissance ideas spread to northern Europe.

# The Mogul Empire

- **The Moguls**, or Mughals, were a family who ruled most of northern India from 1526 to 1748.

- **The Moguls** were descended from the Mongol Ghengis Khan via Tamerlane – the great conqueror of the 1300s.

- **The first Mogul** emperor was Babur (1483–1530), who invaded India on swift horses that completely outran the Indians' slower elephants.

- **Babur** was a brave and brilliant leader, as well as a famous poet and diarist.

- **Babur** created gardens wherever he went and held garden parties there when they were finished.

▶ Jahangir's father Akbar (right) called his son plain Salim. He called himself Jahangir ('world beater').

- **After Babur** came a string of remarkable emperors: Humayun, Akbar, Jahangir, Shah Jahan and Aurangzeb.

- **Akbar** (1556–1605) was the greatest of the Mogul emperors – conquering most of India and setting up a highly efficient system of government.

  - **Jahangir** (1569–1627) was a great patron of the arts – but suffered from an addiction to drugs and alcohol. He was also attacked for being under the thumb of his Persian wife, Nur Jahan.

  - **The Mogul Empire** reached its peak under Shah Jahan (1592–1666), when many magnificent, luxurious buildings were built – most notably the Taj Mahal.

  - **Aurangzeb** (1618–1707) was the last great Mogul ruler. He inspired rebellion by raising taxes and insisting on a strict Muslim code.

# Voyages of exploration

- **In the late 1300s**, the Mongol Empire in Asia collapsed and Ottoman Turks grew powerful in the Near East. The roads to China and the east that brought silks and spices to Europe were cut off.

- **Italian merchant cities** like Genoa and Venice needed another route. So bold sailors set out from Portugal and Spain to find a way to the east by sea.

- **At first**, they tried to go round Africa, and voyages ventured down Africa's unknown west coast.

- **Many early voyages** were encouraged by Portugal's Prince Henry (1394–1460), called Henry the Navigator, who set up a school in navigation skills at Sagres.

- **In 1488**, Bartholomeu Dias sailed right round Africa's southern tip and into the Indian Ocean.

- **In 1497**, Vasco da Gama sailed round Africa to Calicut in India, and returned laden with spices and jewels.

- **Perhaps the greatest** voyage by a European was in 1492 when Genoese sailor Christopher Columbus set out across the open Atlantic. He hoped to reach China by travelling westwards around the world. Instead, he found the whole 'New World', North and South America.

- **Columbus** only landed on Caribbean islands at first. Even when he reached South America on his last voyage, he thought he was in Asia. The first to realize it was an unknown continent was the Florentine explorer Amerigo Vespucci who landed there in 1499. A map made in 1507 named North and South America after him.

- **In 1519–22**, Ferdinand Magellan's ship *Victoria* sailed across the Atlantic, round the southern tip of South America, across the Pacific and back round Africa to Spain. Although this Portuguese explorer was killed in the Philippines, his crew and ship went on to complete the first round-the-world voyage.

> ★ **STAR FACT** ★
> Venetian John Cabot set out from Bristol, England in 1497 – and 'discovered' North America when he landed in Labrador.

A lookout in the crow's nest often saw new land first

A triangular lateen sail on the mizzen (rear) mast helped the ship sail into the wind and manoeuvre along coasts

Big square sails on the fore and main masts filled like parachutes for high-speed sailing

A small poop (raised deck) held the captain's cabin

◀ Nearly all the great European explorers of the 1400s and 1500s – Dias, Columbus, da Gama, Vespucci, Cabot and others – sailed in a remarkable little ship called a caravel. Caravels were a revolutionary mix of European and Arab shipbuilding methods. They were rarely more than 20–30 m long and weighed under 150 tonnes. But they could cope with the roughest seas. More importantly, they could head almost into the wind, so they could sail in most directions. They were also very fast – vital for exploration when crossing vast oceans.

A raised section at the bow called the forecastle gave extra storm protection and extra accommodation

The caravel's strong deck was a platform for guns and made it very storm-proof

The caravel had a deep, narrow hull and a strong, straight keel for speed and stability

# The Medicis

- **The Medici family** of Florence in Italy were one of the richest and most powerful families in Europe between 1400 and 1700.

- **The Medicis' fortunes** began with the bank founded by Giovanni de' Medici in 1397. The bank was a success and the Medicis became staggeringly rich.

- **Giovanni's son**, Cosimo, built up the bank and there were soon branches in every major city in Europe.

- **By 1434**, Cosimo was so rich and powerful that he became ruler of Florence. Except for brief periods, the Medicis then ruled Florence for 300 years.

- **The Medicis** were famed for paying huge sums of money to commission works of art.

- **The artist** Michelangelo worked for the Medicis from 1515 to 1534 and created the fabulous Medici chapel for them.

- **The most famous Medici** was Lorenzo (1449–92), known as the Magnificent. Under him, Florence became Europe's most splendid city, full of great works of art.

▶ *Lorenzo de' Medici was a tough ruler who put down opposition brutally. But he was also a scholar and a fine poet.*

- **Lorenzo** may have been Magnificent, but he managed to bankrupt the Medici bank.

- **Three Medicis** became pope – Leo X (1513–21), Clement VII (1523–34) and then Leo XI (1605).

- **Two Medicis** became queens of France. One of these was Catherine de' Medici (1519–89), queen of Henry II .

# The Incas

★ **STAR FACT** ★
The Inca capital was called Cuzco, which means 'navel' because it was the centre of their world.

- **The Incas** were South American people who created a remarkable empire in the Americas in the 1400s.

- **The Incas** began as a tribe in highland Peru, but in 1438 Pachacuti Inca Yupanqui became their Sapa Inca (king) and they built a huge empire in an amazingly short time.

- **Pachacuti** and his son built a huge empire in just 50 years stretching 4000 km through what is now Peru and Chile.

- **Inca soldiers** were highly disciplined and deadly with slings, bronze axes and spears.

- **Inca engineers** swiftly built 30,000 km of paved roads across the empire, spanning deep ravines with dizzying suspension bridges.

- **The Incas** kept in close touch with local officials by relays of runners 2.5 km apart. A message could travel 250 km in under a day.

- **Inca builders** cut and fitted huge stones with astonishing precision to create massive buildings.

- **The royal palace** had a garden full of life-like corn stalks, animals and birds made of solid gold.

- **The Incas** worshipped the sun.

◀ *The Incas built a mountaintop city. Machu Picchu was a city high in the Andes Mountains, with gardens, a temple and a fortress.*

# Christopher Columbus

- **Christopher Columbus** (1451–1596) was the Genoese sailor who crossed the Atlantic and showed North and South America to Europe.

- **Columbus** was not the first European to cross the Atlantic. The Vikings, for instance, settled in Newfoundland in AD 1004. But it is Columbus's discovery that lasted.

- **Other sailors** were trying to find their way to China and the east by sailing south round Africa. Columbus, realizing the Earth is round, wanted to strike out west across the open Atlantic ocean and reach China that way.

- **After years spent trying** to get backing Columbus finally got support from Queen Isabella of Spain.

- **Columbus set sail** on 3 August 1492 in three caravels – the *Santa Maria*, the *Niña* and the *Pinta*.

- **They sailed west** into the unknown for three weeks, by which time the sailors were ready to mutiny with fear.

- **On 12 October**, a look-out spotted the Bahamas.

▶ *Columbus landing in the Bahamas.*

Columbus thought he was in the Indies (hence the 'West Indies'). He called the natives Indians.

- **Columbus** left 40 men on a large island that he called Hispaniola and went back to Spain a hero.

- **In 1493 and 1498**, he set off on two more trips with large fleets, as Viceroy of the Indies. He set up a colony on Hispaniola, but it was a disaster. Spaniards complained of his harsh rule and many Indians died from cruelty and disease. Columbus went back to Spain in chains.

- **Columbus** was pardoned, and began a fourth voyage in 1502. He died off Panama, still thinking it was India.

# The Reformation

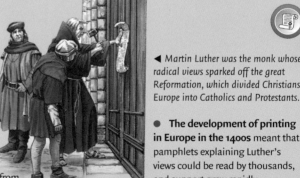

- **In the early 1500s**, many people were starting to question the teachings of the Catholic Church. They were angered by the excessive power of church leaders and the life of idleness that many monks seemed to lead.

- **Many critics were angered** by the huge amounts of money the Church made by selling 'indulgences' – a pardon for sin bought with cash.

- **Martin Luther** (1483–1546) was a poor miner's son from Saxony in Germany. As a monk at Wittenberg university, he earned a reputation for his great biblical knowledge.

- **Luther** attacked the sale of indulgences by Pope Leo X, who was selling them by the score to raise money to build St Peter's church in Rome.

- **In 1517**, Luther nailed a list of 95 grievances on the door of Wittenberg Castle's chapel, hoping to start a debate.

- **The pope** issued a bull (demand) that Luther go back on his views or face expulsion from the Church. Luther burned the bull – and the Church expelled him in 1521.

◀ *Martin Luther was the monk whose radical views sparked off the great Reformation, which divided Christians in Europe into Catholics and Protestants.*

- **The development of printing in Europe in the 1400s** meant that pamphlets explaining Luther's views could be read by thousands, and support grew rapidly.

- **Luther set up** his own church, whose members soon came to be called Protestants – because of their protests.

- **Other more extreme rebels** joined the cause, such as John Calvin (1509–64) and Ulrich Zwingli (1484–1531), and the movement gathered pace across northwest Europe.

- **Soon the Protestant** movement was so strong and widespread that the split with the Catholic Church seemed permanent. This is called the Reformation.

# The conquistadors

- **The conquistadors** ('conquerors') were Spaniards who landed in the 'New World' shortly after Columbus. They came to conquer the peoples there.
- **The most famous** conquistadors were Hernán Cortés (1485–1547) and Francisco Pizarro (c.1478–1541).
- **Cortés landed** in Mexico with just 500 men in 1519. The Indian girl Malintzin became his interpreter and lover.
- **Joining** with Indians rebelling against the Aztecs, he marched to Tenochtitlán, the Aztec capital.
- **Perhaps thinking** that Cortés was the god Quetzalcoatl, the Aztec leader Moctezuma let Cortés take him prisoner and become ruler in his place.
- **When Cortés** left Tenochtitlán six months later, the Aztecs rebelled. Cortés returned and destroyed the city.

▲ *A Spaniard's fanciful view of Cortés in Tenochtitlán.*

- **Pizarro** set off to find the Incas in 1524.
- **Pizarro** reached Peru when the Incas were hardly over a civil war between the Inca Atahualpa and his brother.
- **The Incas**, terrified of Pizarro's horses and guns, were easily slaughtered. Pizarro took Cuzco in 1533.

> ★ STAR FACT ★
> When Spaniards got off their horses, the Incas thought they were beasts splitting in two.

# Shoguns and samurai

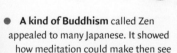

- **In the 12th century,** the civilized Japanese Fujiwara rulers were replaced by powerful warrior clans from country areas – notably the Taira and Minamoto.
- **In 1185,** the Minamoto Yoritomo crushed the Taira clan and made himself ruler of Japan as *sei-i-dai-shogun* which means 'barbarian conquering great general'.
- **Warrior shoguns** ruled Japan until the mid-1800s.
- **Japan** became dominated by *samurai*. The samurai warriors lived to fight and trained in fighting skills to a fanatical degree.
- **A samurai's prized possession** was his massive two-handed sword, which was sharpened and honed to such an extent that a skilled samurai could slice a man in half with a single stroke.
- **Samurai** means 'one who serves'.
- **The warrior culture** drove many to seek refuge in nature and men started to live for long periods in remote huts.

- **A kind of Buddhism** called Zen appealed to many Japanese. It showed how meditation could make then see beyond the material world.
- **In the 1300s** Samurai began to take a more Zen approach to their skills.
- **In the 1300s** these Zen Buddhists began to develop their own forms of elegant entertainment, like flower-arranging and tea-drinking.

◄ *The samurai practised with weapons and armour for long periods. They sometimes exercised with elaborate displays.*

# Henry VIII

- **Henry VIII** (1491–1547) was the Tudor king of England who separated the Church in England from Rome, and who married six wives, beheading two of them.

- **Henry's wives:** Catherine of Aragon (1509–33, divorced); Anne Boleyn (1533–36, beheaded); Jane Seymour (1536–38, died); Anne of Cleves (1540, annulled); Catherine Howard (1540–42, beheaded); and Catherine Parr (1543–47).

- **When Henry VIII** became king at 18, in 1509, he was handsome and athletic, spoke several languages, played the lute well and was keen on new 'humanist' ideas. As he grew old, he became grossly fat, riddled with sickness and inclined to terrible outbreaks of anger.

▲ *As a young man, Henry VIII was fit, handsome and keen on music and sport.*

- **Henry was served** by clever ministers like Wolsey and Cromwell. Many were executed when things went wrong.

- **Catherine of Aragon** bore Henry a daughter, Mary, but not the needed son. The pope refused a divorce, so Henry broke with Rome to become head of the English Church.

- **Split from Rome**, the Church of England moved towards Protestantism and the monasteries were destroyed.

- **Anne Boleyn** gave Henry a daughter, Elizabeth, but not the son he wanted, and her strong views made her enemies. She was beheaded on a charge of treason.

- **Jane Seymour** gave Henry a son, Edward, but died in childbirth in 1538.

- **Henry** found Anne of Cleves so ugly, he cancelled the marriage after five months.

- **Young Catherine Howard** was beheaded when she was found to have a lover. Only Henry's last wife, twice-widowed Catherine Parr, survived him when he died in 1547.

# Catholics versus Protestants

◀ *Thomas More (1478–1535) was executed in when he refused to acknowledge Henry VIII as head of the English Church.*

- **In the 1500s** the Roman Catholic church was determined to fight against the Protestant Reformation and other threats. Their fight is called the Counter-Reformation.

- **In 1534,** St Ignatius Loyola founded the Society of Jesus (Jesuits) to lead the Counter-Reformation.

- **Investigative bodies** called Inquisitions were set up to seek out and punish heretics – anyone who held views that did not agree with the Catholic Church's.

- **From 1483**, the Spanish Inquisition became a byword for terror, swooping on suspected heretics – Protestants and Jews alike – torturing them and burning them at the stake.

- **The battle between** Catholics and Protestants created many victims and many martyrs in the late 1500s.

- **In the St Bartholomew's Day massacre** in 1571, up to 70,000 French Protestants, called Huguenots, were killed on the orders of the Catholic queen Catherine de' Medici.

- **Many English Protestants** were burned in Catholic Queen Mary's reign, earning her the name 'Bloody Mary'.

- **English Catholics** such as Edmund Campion (1540–1581) were killed in Protestant Queen Elizabeth I's reign.

- **In Germany**, a terrible Thirty Years' War was started in 1618 as Catholic-Protestant rivalries flared up.

> ★ STAR FACT ★
> Catholic houses in England in the late 1500s had hiding places for priests called 'priest holes'.

# The Spanish Empire

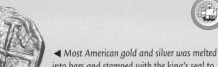

- **Within half a century** of Columbus's arrival in America in 1492, Spanish conquistadors had conquered all of what is now often called Latin America – from California to Argentina. This huge empire – the biggest yet seen in the world – became an immense source of wealth.

- **By the Treaty of Tordesillas (1494)** Portugal agreed to allow Spain to take any territory more than 370 leagues (about 2000 km) west of the Cape Verde islands – all of Latin America but Brazil.

- **Thousands of Spaniards** came to colonize Latin America in the 1500s, creating Spanish-style cities such as Cartagena in Colombia and Guayaqil in Ecuador.

- **The Spanish rulers** tried to deal with local people with the *encomienda*. Native Americans were assigned to Spaniards who were supposed to look after them in return for taxes and labour. In practice, many Spaniards were cruel to these people, and Spaniards now talk of how cruelly they abused the Native Americans. In 100 years, the number of Native Americans dropped from 50 million to 4 million, through cruelty, poverty and diseases brought by Spaniards.

- **Many Spanish Dominican friars** condemned the encomienda – especially Bartolomé de Las Casas – and fought unsuccessfully for better conditions for Native Americans.

◀ Most American gold and silver was melted into bars and stamped with the king's seal to go back to Spain. Some was minted into coins like these, such as the famous gold 'doubloon' (eight escudos) and silver 'pieces of eight' (eight reale).

- **Indians used** to mine silver, gold and gems in huge quantities in South America. The Muzo and Chivor mines in Colombia were famous for their emeralds.

- **Every year**, in the calm months between March and October, ships laden with treasure left the Americas bound for Spain.

- **Besides American** treasure, Spanish ships carried spices from the East Indies and silks from China. These were shipped across the Pacific from the Philippines to Mexico, then carried overland to be shipped from the Caribbean to Europe.

- **By the 1540s**, the Spanish ships were suffering pirate attacks, so the ships crossed the Atlantic every year in two great *flotas* (fleets) protected by an armada of galleons (warships).

> **★ STAR FACT ★**
> The Spanish brought new foods such as tomatoes, potatoes and chocolate back to Europe from their American empire.

*Hull and decking of winter-cut oak, cedar or cypress hardwood*

*Three masts with square sails – or, as here, with a triangular lateen on the mizzen (rear) mast*

*Banks of 20 or so cannon for 'broadsides' – firing together down one side*

▶ Late August every year, the two Spanish treasure fleets of 50 or so ships would leave together from Havana in Cuba guarded by the galleons of the Armada de la Guardia. Galleons (right) were the biggest, most powerful warships of the day, 35 m long and weighing around 500 tonnes.

# Elizabeth I

- **Elizabeth I** (1533–1603) was one of England's greatest rulers. The time of her reign is called the Elizabethan Age or England's Golden Age. Under her strong and intelligent rule, England became an enterprising, artistically rich and peaceful nation.

- **Elizabeth** was daughter of Henry VIII and his wife Anne Boleyn, who was beheaded when Elizabeth was three.

- **Elizabeth** was a brilliant scholar, fluent in many languages by the time she was 12.

- **When Henry VIII died**, Elizabeth's nine-year-old half-brother became King Edward VI, but he died in 1553. He was succeeded by her older sister 'Bloody' Mary.

- **Mary was** staunchly Catholic. For a while Elizabeth was locked up, suspected of involvement in a Protestant plot.

- **Elizabeth became queen** in 1558, when Mary died.

- **At once** Elizabeth strengthened the Protestant Church of England by the Act of Supremacy in 1559.

- **Elizabeth was expected** to marry, and she encouraged foreign suitors when it helped diplomacy. But she remained single, earning her the nickname 'The Virgin Queen'.

- **Elizabeth** sent troops to help Protestants in Holland against their Spanish rulers, and secretly urged Francis Drake to raid Spanish treasure ships. In 1588 Spain sent an Armada to invade England. Elizabeth proved an inspiring leader and the Armada was repulsed.

- **Elizabeth's reign** is famed for the poetry and plays of men like Spenser, Marlowe and Shakespeare.

◀ *Elizabeth I was greatly respected, and knew how to win public approval.*

# Colonization of America

- **In the 1580s,** English people tried unsuccessfully to set up colonies in North America.

- **The first successful English colony** was set up at Jamestown, Virginia on 24 May 1607, with 104 colonists.

- **Many of the Jamestown colony** died in 'the starving time' of winter 1609.

- **In 1610,** fighting broke out with the local Indians as the desperate colonists took the Indians' food supply.

> ★ **STAR FACT** ★
> Pocahontas died of influenza while in London trying to raise money for the colonists.

- **Colonist leader** John Smith was captured by the Indians, but the chief's daughter Pocahontas saved his life.

- **In 1612,** colonist John Rolfe introduced tobacco from the West Indies. It became the basis of Virginia's economy.

- **Pocahontas** was held hostage by the colonists in 1613. While captive she met, fell in love with and wed John Rolfe.

- **In 1620,** 102 'Pilgrims' arrived from Plymouth, England in the *Mayflower* and set up a new colony near Cape Cod. They survived thanks to help from Wampanoag Indians.

- **In November 1621** the Pilgrims invited the Wampanoags to celebrate their first harvest. This first Thanksgiving Day is now celebrated every year in the USA.

◀ *Some of the simple houses lived in by the Jamestown colonists have been recreated in this museum in Virginia.*

# Dutch independence

- **In 1500** there were 17 provinces making up what is now Belgium, the Netherlands and Luxembourg. The most important was Holland.

- **The provinces came** under Spanish rule in 1516, when their ruler Charles became the king of Spain.

▶ *In the 1400–1600s, Dutch artists like Steen, Vermeer and Rembrandt created vibrant, technically brilliant paintings, often of everyday scenes. This is by Van Eyck, who was said to have invented oil painting in the 1430s.*

- **In the 1500s,** Holland's capital Amsterdam became the leading commercial centre of Europe. With the growth of trade, Protestant ideas started taking hold.

- **Charles's son** Philip II and his deputy the duke of Alba tried to crush the Protestants by executing their leaders.

- **As Alba** became more ruthless, opposition spread.

- **In 1566,** William, prince of Orange, led the Dutch in revolt. Although the Dutch controlled the sea, they gradually gave way before the Spanish army.

- **In 1574,** the Dutch opened dikes holding back the sea to sail over the flood to Leiden and rescue the besieged.

- **Protestants** retreated to the northern provinces, and in 1581 declared themselves the independent Dutch Republic. The fighting ceased.

- **The 1600s** proved a Golden Age for the Dutch Republic.

- **The Dutch** merchant fleet became the biggest in Europe. Dutch banks and businesses thrived and Dutch scientists like Leeuwenhoek and Huygens made great discoveries.

# Toyotomi Hideyoshi

- **Toyotomi Hideyoshi** (1536–81) was the great Japanese shogun who unified Japan.

- **Hideyoshi** was the son of poor, hard-working peasants.

- **As a boy,** Hideyoshi believed that if he became a shogun, he'd make sure peasants wouldn't have to work so hard.

- **As a man,** Hideyoshi became a soldier for shogun Oda Nobunaga, who was trying to unify Japan through force.

- **One day,** legend says, Hideyoshi warmed Nobunaga's shoes for a winter walk. Nobunaga made him a general.

- **Hideyoshi** proved himself a brilliant general, and when Nobunaga was murdered, Hideyoshi carried on his work in unifying Japan – but by good rule as well as by arms.

- **By 1591,** Hideyoshi had unified Japan, but he kept warriors and peasants firmly separated as classes.

- **To establish** a mystique for his court, Hideyoshi had the Zen master Sen No Rikkyu perfect the tea ceremony.

- **Later, Hideyoshi** became paranoid. Suspecting his chief adviser Hidetsugu of plotting, he had

Hidetsugu's family killed – including the beautiful Princess Komahime.

- **Komahime's father** Yoshiaki sided decisively with Hideyoshi's enemy, the hero Tokugawa Ieyasu, in the great battle that led to Hideyoshi's downfall.

▶ *Great tea masters claim descent from Sen Rikyu, who Hideyoshi forced to commit suicide when he suspected a slight to him.*

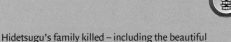

# Russia

- **In 1237**, savage Tatar hordes, the descendants of Genghis Khan, swept into Russia, burning cities and slaughtering huge numbers of people. The Tatars stayed there for 200 years, cutting Russia off from the Renaissance that was changing western Europe.

- **Some Russians** thrived under the Tatars and a trading post called Moscow grew into a powerful city at the centre of a province called Muscovy. In 1318, Prince Yuri of Moscow married the Tatar Khan's sister, and the Tatars helped Moscow ruthlessly suppress rivals. A later prince called Ivan began collecting taxes for the Tatars.

- **Moscow** grew stronger as the Tatars grew weaker. In 1453, Ivan III ('the Great'), Grand Prince of Muscovy, was strong enough to drive out the Tatars altogether.

- **Russians were Christians** of the Eastern Church ruled from Constantinople. Constantinople had become the second focus of Christianity when Rome fell to barbarians in the AD400s. When Constantinople fell to the Turks in 1453, Ivan III called for Moscow to be the Third Rome. He wed a Byzantine princess, and his grandson Ivan IV took the title czar after the Roman caesars.

- **Ivan's** ambitions left him in need of money and food, so he forced thousands of peasants into serfdom – at a time when peasants in western Europe were gaining their freedom. Those who would not submit to this yoke fled to the southern steppes, where they became known as Cossacks.

*▶ Ivan the Terrible was a clever man, notorious for his biting sarcasm as well as his rages. But no one really knows just how 'terrible' he was.*

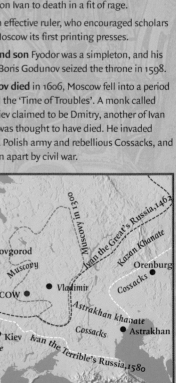

- **Ivan IV** (1544–84), the first czar, drove the Tatars out of Russia altogether, conquering Kazan, Astrakhan and much of Siberia – creating the first Russian Empire.

- **Ivan IV** was called 'the Terrible' for his brutality. He formed the *Oprichniki* – a police force to control people – and had hundreds of *boyars* (aristocrats) murdered. He even beat his son Ivan to death in a fit of rage.

- **Ivan IV was** an effective ruler, who encouraged scholars and brought Moscow its first printing presses.

- **Ivan IV's second son** Fyodor was a simpleton, and his wife's brother Boris Godunov seized the throne in 1598.

- **When Godunov died** in 1606, Moscow fell into a period of chaos called the 'Time of Troubles'. A monk called Gregory Otrepiev claimed to be Dmitry, another of Ivan IV's sons who was thought to have died. He invaded Moscow with a Polish army and rebellious Cossacks, and Russia was torn apart by civil war.

*▲▶ Under Ivan the Great and his grandson Ivan the Terrible, Moscow grew to become the centre of a vast Russian empire, which survived up until the time of the Russian Revolution in 1917. Ivan rebuilt Moscow's citadel, or Kremlin, as a vast walled complex of palaces and churches (above). It has remained the centre of Russian government ever since.*

# Mary Queen of Scots

◀ Mary was beheaded at Fotheringay Castle in 1587.

- **Mary Queen of Scots** (1542–87) was the Catholic queen of Scotland held captive in England by Elizabeth I for 19 years, then beheaded.
- **Mary became queen** when she was a baby but was brought up at the French court, where she enjoyed hunting and learned six languages.
- **Mary married** the French king Henry II's son Francis at 15 and was briefly queen of France, but Francis died in 1560.
- **In 1561**, Mary returned to Scotland to rule there. By this time, Scotland had become Protestant, while Mary was a Catholic.
- **In 1565**, Mary fell in love with her cousin Henry Stuart, Earl of Darnley. She married him and they had a child, but Darnley was only interested in power.
- **Led by Darnley**, Protestant nobles stabbed Mary's Catholic secretary David Rizzio to death before her.
- **The Earl of Bothwell** was in love with Mary and murdered Darnley. They married three months later.

The Scots were so outraged by the marriage that Mary had to flee to England.

- **Mary** was next in line to the English throne after Elizabeth. Many Catholics felt she was first in line, since they did not recognize Henry VIII's marriage to Anne Boleyn.
- **Mary** posed a danger to Elizabeth, so she was kept in captivity in English houses, where she became the focus for plots against Elizabeth.
- **Elizabeth's spy-master** Walsingham trapped Mary into going along with a plot by Babington. Mary was found guilty of treason and beheaded at Fotheringay in 1587.

# Native Americans

★ STAR FACT ★
Woodland tribes lived in wigwams, domes of sticks covered in hide and moss.

- **When the first European colonists** arrived in North America, there were one and a half million Native Americans living in North America.
- **There were hundreds** of tribes in North America, each with its own language.
- **There were six** kinds of tribal area: the Southwest, Great Plains, Far West Plateau, Northwest, Eastern Woodland and Northern.
- **Southwest** Native Americans like the Pueblo Indians lived by growing corn, beans and squash.
- **Plains** tribes like the Blackfoot, Comanche and Cheyenne hunted buffalo on foot.
- **With Woodland tribes** like the Delaware, the men hunted deer and fished while the women grew crops.

- **Plateau and Northwest** Native Americans like the Nez Percé and the Kwakiutl lived by fishing and gathering berries. They are famous for their baskets.
- **Northern** tribes like the Cree lived mainly by hunting caribou.
- **Until Europeans** arrived, Native Americans got around mainly on foot or by canoe. The Europeans introduced horses in the 1700s – and Indians quickly became skilled riders.

▶ North American Indians wore clothes of buckskin (tanned deer hide). They adorned the costume with eagle feathers, which had special significance.

# The Manchus

▲ Under the Qing, China remained as it had been for 3000 years, while much of the world was changing dramatically.

- **In the 1600s**, the Ming emperors of China were unpopular after three centuries in power. Rebellions became all too common.

- **In 1644**, the last Ming emperor hanged himself as the bandit Li Zicheng and his men overran Beijing.

- **Guarding the Great Wall** were Manchu troops, from Manchuria in the north. A desperate Ming general invited them to help get rid of Li Zicheng.

- **The Manchus** marched into Beijing and proclaimed their own child-emperor as the 'Son of Heaven' and set up the Qing dynasty of emperors.

- **Resistance** to the Manchu emperors went on in the south for 30 years, but was eventually suppressed.

- **At first, the Qing** forced Chinese men to put their hair in pigtails to show they were inferior to Manchus.

- **Manchus** and Chinese were also made to live separately and were not allowed to marry each other.

- **In time**, the Qing adopted Chinese ways, and even Manchu civil servants had to learn the classic works of Confucius, just like the Chinese.

- **Under the Qing**, China reached its greatest extent.

- **In the 1800s**, Qing power was weakened by rebellions, Muslim uprisings and growing European influence.

# Roundheads and Cavaliers

- **The English Civil War** (1642–49) was the struggle between 'Cavalier' supporters of King Charles I and 'Roundheads', who supported Parliament.

- **A key issue** was how much power the king should have. Charles wanted to be free to set taxes and his own brand of religion. Parliament demanded a say.

- **On the royalist side** were those who wanted the English Church more Catholic; on the other were Puritans.

- **Puritans** were extreme Protestants. They believed that churches (and people) should be stripped of the wasteful luxury they saw in the Catholic Church and the aristocrats at the court of Charles's French, Catholic wife.

◀▶ A Cavalier (royalist) soldier (left) and a Roundhead soldier from Parliament's army.

- **'Cavalier'** is from the French *chevalier* (horseman). It was meant as a term of abuse. Many Cavaliers were rich landowners.

- **Puritans** thought long hair indulgent, and the Roundheads got their name from their short-cropped hair. Many Roundheads were rich merchants and townspeople.

- **Many revolutionary groups** emerged among poorer people, such as the 'Diggers' and 'Levellers'.

- **The war** turned against the royalists when the parliamentarians formed the disciplined New Model Army.

- **Charles I** was beheaded in 1649.

- **Oliver Cromwell** (1599–1658) became Roundhead leader and signed Charles I's death warrant. In 1653, he made himself Lord Protector – England's dictator.

# The Sun King

- **Louis XIV** (1638–1715) was king of France for 72 years, a longer reign than any other European king in history.
- **Louis** became king in 1643, when he was five, and the first minister Cardinal Mazarin effectively ruled France.
- In 1648, heavy taxes and other grievances inspired a rebellion – the Fronde – against the hated Mazarin.
- **During the Fronde,** Louis was forced into hiding, and vowed never to let the same happen again.

- **Louis** said l'état c'est moi ('I am the State') and believed it was his God-given right to command his people totally.
- **When Mazarin died,** in 1661, Louis decided to run the country himself, and devoted huge energy to administering every detail of the nation's business.
- **Louis** made France the most efficiently run country in Europe. It hummed with new industries, road and canals.
- **Louis** used the finest artists to turn the French court into a glittering spectacle to distract nobles from rebellion. His palace was filled with banquets, plays and art.
- **Louis** got the nickname 'The Sun King' from his favourite dance role, that of Apollo the Sun God. He adopted the Sun as his emblem.

◀ Part of Louis's grand palace at Versailles, just outside Paris.

# Gustavus Adolphus

- **Gustavus Adolphus** (1594–1632) was Sweden's greatest king and military leader.
- **Gustavus** was a brilliant speaker and inspiring general who always led his men into battle from the front.
- **Gustavus** had a perfect ally in his chancellor Axel Oxenstierna (said 'erks'n'sherna'). Gustavus ran the foreign wars while Oxenstierna ran Sweden.
- **When Gustavus came** to the throne at the age of 17, Sweden was involved in three wars: with Denmark (1611–13), Russia (1611–17) and Poland.
- **Gustavus** quickly made peace with Denmark and Russia.
- **In skirmishes** with the Poles, Gustavus began to develop the first modern army – a large, highly mobile force combining foot soldiers and horsemen.
- **Gustavus** was a devout Protestant. When he saw the Protestants of Germany facing defeat in the Thirty Years' War against the Catholic Austrian emperor Ferdinand II, he decided to intervene.

- **In July 1630,** Gustavus's armies landed in Germany.
- **In 1631,** Gustavus won a great victory over Ferdinand's army at Breitenfeld near Leipzig.
- **On 6 Nov 1632,** the Swedes scored a crucial victory over Bohemian general Wallenstein, but Gustavus himself was killed leading a charge.

▶ Gustavus's great flagship, the Vasa, sank on its maiden voyage in 1628, but it has been recovered almost intact and can now be seen in Stockholm.

# Pirates

- **Barbary corsairs** were pirates from North Africa who raided ships in the Mediterranean between 1520 and 1830. Many corsairs were Muslims and regarded Christian merchant ships as fair game.

- **The most famous** corsairs were the Barbarossa brothers and Occhiali.

- **Sea dogs** were pirates like Sir Francis Drake, secretly encouraged by Queen Elizabeth I to raid the ships of her Spanish enemies in the Caribbean.

- **'Letters of marque'** from the monarch gave English raiders official blessing, so they were called privateers.

- **When King James I** withdrew letters of marque in 1603, privateers were replaced by lawless 'buccaneers' like Henry Morgan, who terrorized the Caribbean from bases on Jamaica like Port Royal.

◀ *The famous 'Jolly Roger' flag, flown from pirate ships.*

- **Buccaneer** comes from French *boucan* (barbeque) as many were poor hunters who grilled the meat of cows and pigs that they scavenged.

- **Piracy** reached its height between 1690 and 1720, preying on traders plying between Europe and its new colonies around the world.

- **In the Indian Ocean** were pirates like William Kidd from Madagascar. In the Bahamas, there were 'Calico Jack' Rackham and female pirates Anne Bonny and Mary Read.

- **The most notorious** pirate of this time was 'Blackbeard' (Edward Teach), who leaped into action with lighted firecrackers tied to his big black beard.

- **Piracy** diminished after 1720, when the British navy clamped down worldwide.

# The Restoration

- **For 11 years** after the execution of Charles I in 1649, England was without a king. It was ruled instead by the Commonwealth, run by the Puritans.

- **At first**, the Commonwealth consisted of Parliament and its Council of State, but its failure to make progress spurred general Oliver Cromwell to make himself Lord Protector and rule through army officers.

- **Cromwell's Protectorate** proved unpopular. When he died in 1658, the army removed his son Richard Cromwell as successor and called for Charles I's exiled son Charles II to be recalled as king.

◀ *The sedan chair was a popular way for the rich to get about in the years after the Restoration.*

★ **STAR FACT** ★
When London burned down, in 1666, Charles II personally organized the fire-fighting.

- **The Restoration** of Charles II as king was in May 1660.

- **Charles II** proved on the whole a skilful ruler, tactfully easing tensions between rival religious groups.

- **Charles II** was known as the Merry Monarch, because his love of partying, theatre, horse-racing and women was such a relief after years of grim Puritan rule.

- **Charles II** had many mistresses. The most famous was Nell Gwyn, an orange-seller who worked in the theatres.

- **The Restoration** saw the Puritan ban on Christmas and the theatre lifted. Plays like Congreve's *Way of the World* made Restoration theatre lively and outrageous.

- **Charles II** took a keen interest in science, encouraging great scientists like Isaac Newton, Edmund Halley and Robert Hooke to form the Royal Society.

# Slavery

- **Slaves** were used a great deal in the ancient world, as warring people put their captives to work. The pyramids of Egypt were probably built mostly by slaves. One in three people in Ancient Athens was likely to have been a slave.

- **Slavery** diminished in Europe when Rome collapsed, although in the Middle Ages Russian and African slaves were used on sugar plantations in the Mediterranean.

- **Slavery** grew hugely when Europeans established colonies in the Americas from the 1500s on.

- **At first,** the settlers used Native Americans as slaves, but as numbers dwindled, they took slaves from Africa to work on new sugar plantations. British and French sugar planters in the West Indies used African slaves too.

- **From 1500–1800,** Europeans shipped 10-12 million black slaves from Africa to the Americas. 40 percent went to Brazil, 30 percent to Cuba, Jamaica and Haiti, and 5 percent to the USA.

- **The slave trade** involved shipping several hundred thousand Africans across the Atlantic from the 'Slave Coast' of West Africa to the West Indies and the USA, or from Angola to Brazil. Once the slave ships had unloaded their slaves, they would return to Europe with a cargo of sugar, then sail for Africa with cotton goods and guns to exchange for slaves.

- **Slavery was rife** in the American south in the 1700s, where owners of large plantations needed cheap labour to grow first tobacco and then cotton.

- **In the West Indies** and Brazil, there were more blacks than whites and slaves often revolted. The greatest revolution was on French Haiti, where the slave Toussaint l'Ouverture (1743–1803) led 500,000 slaves to take over the country in 1791. For a while Haiti was black-governed – but Napoleon's troops reasserted control in 1802.

- **In the 1790s,** some Europeans began to speak out against slavery. Denmark banned the Atlantic slave trade in 1792. William Wilberforce got Britain to ban the trade in 1807. The USA banned the import of slaves in 1808. When Latin-American countries became independent in the early 1800s, they freed slaves. Britain abolished slavery in its empire in 1833, but the USA had to go through a civil war first.

◄▲ In southern USA many African slaves were field hands, picking cotton (left). Many tried to escape or protest, but they were in a minority – and there was no chance of a revolution like that led by Toussaint l'Ouverture (above) in Haiti.

# The Glorious Revolution

- **The Glorious Revolution** of 1688 was when the English parliament replaced James II with William III and Queen Mary.

- **James II** became king when his brother Charles II died in 1685.

- **James II** was Catholic. He upset people by giving Catholics key jobs in the army, the Church and the universities.

▶ *Mary sided with her Protestant husband, William, against her Catholic father James II.*

- **James II** jailed any bishops who refused to support his Declaration of Indulgence in favour of Catholics.

- **In 1688**, James II and his Catholic wife Mary had a son and it seemed that England was set to become Catholic.

- **Leading Protestants** met and decided to invite the Dutch prince William of Orange to help. William was married to James II's Protestant daughter Mary.

- **William landed** with his army at Brixham in Devon on 5 November 1688. James's army refused to obey its Catholic generals and so he was forced to flee to France.

- **Parliament** decided James's escape meant he had abdicated, and offered the throne to William and Mary.

- **James** tried a comeback, landing in Ireland with French troops. Defeat came at the Battle of the Boyne (July 1689).

> ★ **STAR FACT** ★
> Ulster Protestants are called Orangemen because they once helped William of Orange at the Boyne.

# The Age of Reason

- **The Age of Reason** is the time in the 1700s when many people began to believe that all-important questions about the world could be answered by reason.

- **The Age of Reason** is also called the Enlightenment.

- **The idea that human reason** has the answers was revolutionary. It meant that even the lowliest peasant was just as likely to be right as the highest lord. So why should a lord rule over a peasant?

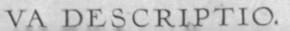

◀ *Newton outlined the principles of gravity and explained how the planets move through space.*

- **In earlier times**, kings had ruled by 'divine right' – and their power over other people was God's will. The Age of Reason questioned this right.

- **As the 1700s** progressed, the ideas of the Age of Reason turned into real revolutions in France and America.

- **The hero of the Age** was Isaac Newton. His discovery of the Laws of Motion proposed that every single event in the Universe could be worked out mathematically.

- **American revolutionary** leader Jefferson had a portrait of Newton before him as he wrote the Constitution.

- **In France**, the great ideas were worked out by philosophers like Rousseau and Voltaire. People discussed the ideas earnestly at fashionable 'salons' (supper parties).

- **In Britain**, thinkers like Hume showed how important it was to work things out for yourself – not just be told.

- **To sum up all** human knowledge, the first great encyclopedia was created – by Diderot in France.

VA DESCRIPTIO.

# Peter the Great

- **Peter the Great** (1672–1725) was the greatest of all the Russian czars (emperors). He built the city of St Petersburg and turned Russia from an inward-looking country to a major European power.

- **Peter was** well over 2 m tall, and towered above everyone else.

- **Peter had incredible** willpower and a burning interest in new ideas. But he was very impatient and often went into rages. When his son Alexei plotted against him, Peter had him put to death.

- **Peter became czar** at the age of ten. His step-sister Sophia ruled for him until 1689, when her enemies drove her out and Peter took charge.

- **In 1697–98** Peter travelled to Holland and England disguised as simple ship's carpenter in order to learn about western European technology and culture.

- **When Peter returned** from Europe, he brought with him many western European craftsmen and teachers.

▲ St Petersburg was founded as the capital of the Russian Empire by Peter the Great in 1703.

- **Peter** insisted on Russian men shaving off their old-fashioned, Russian-style beards.

- **Peter** was very keen on boats. He built the first Russian navy – on the Volga River. His wars later ensured that Russia had, for the first time, a sea port on the Baltic.

- **Peter** led the Russian armies to crucial victories in battle – notably against the Swedes at Poltava in 1709.

- **Peter** created the first Russian Academy of Sciences, started Russia's first newspaper, and founded many schools, technical institutions and art galleries.

# British India

- **Shortly after** Vasco da Gama reached India, in 1498, the Portuguese set up a trading base in Goa.

- **In 1600**, Elizabeth I of England gave a charter to the East India Co. to trade in India. It set up posts at Surat, Madras, Bombay and Calcutta.

- **The French** set up a base at Pondicherry, in 1668.

- **In the 1700s**, rebellions weakened the Mogul empire. The French and British vied to gain control.

- **In 1757**, 3000 British soldiers, led by the East India Co.'s Robert Clive, defeated an army of over 50,000 French and Indian troops at the battle of Plassey.

- **After Clive's victory**, the British gradually gained control over much of India through a combination of bribes, bullying and making well-placed allies.

- **In 1803**, the British captured the Mogul capital of Delhi – so completing their power base.

- **In 1857**, Indian soldiers revolted and other Indians joined them, but the 'mutiny' was crushed.

▲ British officials were sent to govern India during what is now called the Raj – the period of British imperial rule in India.

- **British rule** was resented by many Indians. Hindus felt that the British were undermining their religion.

- **In 1858**, the British decided to rule India directly. Their rule was called the Raj (which means 'rule'). In 1876, Queen Victoria of Britain was named empress of India.

# American independence

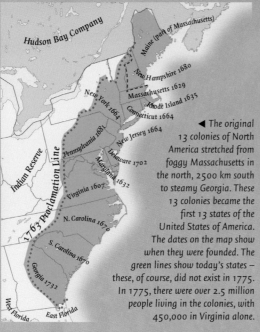

◀ The original 13 colonies of North America stretched from foggy Massachusetts in the north, 2500 km south to steamy Georgia. These 13 colonies became the first 13 states of the United States of America. The dates on the map show when they were founded. The green lines show today's states – these, of course, did not exist in 1775. In 1775, there were over 2.5 million people living in the colonies, with 450,000 in Virginia alone.

● **Colonists** tolerated sugar and quartering taxes, but the Stamp Tax provoked riots. Delegates from nine colonies met in New York to demand a say in how they were taxed, demanding 'No taxation without representation.'

● **As protests** escalated, Grenville was forced to withdraw all taxes but one, the tax on tea. Then, in 1773, a crowd of colonists disguised as Mohawk Indians marched on to the merchant ship *Dartmouth* in Boston harbour and threw its cargo of tea into the sea. After this 'Boston Tea Party', the British closed Boston and moved troops in.

● **A Congress** of delegates from all the colonies except Georgia met to demand independence, and appointed George Washington to lead an army to fight their cause.

● **In April 1775**, British troops seized military stores at Lexington and Concord near Boston and the war began.

● **At first** the British were successful, but the problems of fighting 5000 km from home told in the long run. In 1781, Washington defeated the British at Yorktown, Virginia and they surrendered.

● **In 1763**, Britain finally defeated the French in North America, adding Canada to its 13 colonies – but wanted the colonists to help pay for the cost. The colonists resented paying taxes to a government 5000 km away.

● **To avoid** costly wars with Native Americans, George III issued a Proclamation in 1763 reserving lands west of the Appalachians for native peoples and sent troops to keep settlers out, arousing the colonists' resentment.

● **In 1764–5**, British Prime Minister Grenville brought in three new taxes – the Sugar Tax on molasses, which affected rum producers in the colonies; the Quartering Tax, which obliged the colonists to supply British soldiers with living quarters; and the Stamp Tax on newspapers, playing cards and legal documents.

● **In 1776**, the colonists drew up a Declaration of Independence, written by Thomas Jefferson (1743–1826). The British recognized independence in 1783, and in 1787 the colonists drew up a Constitution to lay down how their Union should be run. In 1789, George Washington was elected as the first president of the United States of America.

◀ The American Declaration of Independence of 1776, written by Thomas Jefferson. The 'W' you can see is the first letter of the famous opening words 'We hold these truths...'

# The French Revolution

- **In 1789**, French people were divided among three 'Estates' – the nobles, clergy and middle class – plus the peasants. Nobles owned all the land, but were exempt from paying taxes, and the tax burden fell on the peasants.

- **In 1789**, France was bankrupt after many wars, and King Louis XVI was forced to summon Parliament, called the Estates General, for the first time in 175 years.

- **The three Estates** had met separately in the past, but now insisted on meeting in a National Assembly to debate how to limit the power of the king. The Assembly was dominated by the Third Estate, the middle class.

- **On 14 July 1789**, the poor people of Paris, tired of debates, stormed the prison fortress of the Bastille.

- **Fired by the fall** of the Bastille, peasants rose all over the country and refused to pay taxes. Parisian women marched to Versailles and dragged the king back to Paris.

- **The National Assembly** became more radical, ending serfdom and attacking the nobles and the Church. Many nobles fled the country in panic.

◀ The guillotine had a blade that dropped to cut victims' heads off instantly.

- **The Assembly** speakers who had the power to move the Paris mobs, like Georges Danton, came to the fore. The Assembly renamed itself the National Convention and set up the Committee of Public Safety to govern France by terror.

- **Many nobles** were sent to the guillotine and in 1793 Louis XVI and his queen, Marie Antoinette, were themselves guillotined.

- **This Reign of Terror** was presided over by Robespierre, who saw more and more of his rivals to the guillotine, including Danton. But in the end even Robespierre himself was guillotined, in July 1794.

- **With Robespierre gone,** conservatives regained control. Emphasis shifted to defending the revolution against foreign kings and to Napoleon's conquests.

# Agricultural Revolution

- **The Agricultural Revolution** refers to dramatic changes in farming in Britain in the 1700s and later in the USA.

- **Before the 1700s**, farmland was mostly wide open fields, cultivated in narrow strips by peasants growing food for themselves, using traditional methods.

- **The Agricultural Revolution** created large farms, growing food for profit in enclosed fields, using specialist techniques.

- **The most dramatic effect** was enclosure, in which peasants were evicted from open fields as they were parcelled up into small fields for rearing livestock.

- **Crop-growing** was improved by techniques such as the four-field rotation system.

- **The four-field system** of 'Turnip' Townshend and Thomas Coke meant growing turnips, clover, barley and wheat in successive years so land was used all the time.

- **Livestock farmers** found how to breed cattle, horses and sheep larger and fatter, like Bakewell's Leicester sheep.

- **New machines** were invented. Jethro Tull's drill, for example, made holes and planted seeds in them.

- **In 1793**, Eli Whitney invented a gin machine to separate cotton fibre from the seeds – so making large-scale cotton production profitable.

- **In 1834**, American Cyrus McCormick made the first mechanical harvester.

▼ Canals and new ways of farming changed the landscape of Britain in the 1700s.

# Industrial Revolution

▶ In 1764, Lancashire weaver James Hargreaves created the 'spinning jenny' to help cottage weavers spin wool or cotton fibres into yarn (thread) on lots of spindles, turned by a single handle.

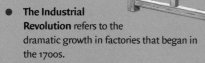

- **The Industrial Revolution** refers to the dramatic growth in factories that began in the 1700s.

- **Before the Industrial Revolution**, most ordinary people were farmers living in small villages. Afterwards, most were factory hands and foremen living in huge cities.

- **The Revolution** began in Britain in the late 1700s; in France, the USA and Germany in the early 1800s.

- **The Farming Revolution** created a pool of cheap labour, while the growth of European colonies created vast markets for things like clothing.

- **The Revolution** began with the invention of machines for making cloth, like the spinning jenny.

- **The turning point** was the change from hand-turned machines like the jenny to machines driven by big water wheels – like Arkwright's 'water [-powered spinning] frame' of 1766.

- **In 1771**, Arkwright installed water frames at Crompton Mill, Derby and created the world's first big factory.

- In the 1780s, James Watt developed a steam engine to drive machines – and steam engines quickly replaced water as the main source of power in factories.

- In 1713, Abraham Darby found how to use coke, rather than wood charcoal, to make huge amounts of iron.

- In 1784, Henry Cort found how to remove impurities from cast iron to make wrought iron – and iron became the key material of the Industrial Revolution.

# The Jacobites

▶ The Scottish Jacobites wore uniforms of plaid and carried swords and shields – but they were no match for the Redcoats.

- **After James II** was deposed as king of England and Scotland in 1688, many Scots still believed he and his Stuart descendants were rightful kings.

- **Supporters** of the Stuarts were called Jacobites after Jacobus, Latin for James.

- **James II's** son James was called the Old Pretender, because he pretended to (claimed) the English throne.

- **English Queen Anne** died childless in 1714, and the Scottish and English Jacobites rose in revolt in 1715. This revolution is called 'the Fifteen'.

- **The Old Pretender** arrived in Scotland only after the Fifteen and its leaders had been crushed.

- **The Scots hero** of the Fifteen was Rob Roy MacGregor (1671–1734), an outlaw who stole cattle from English-inclined Duke of Montrose, then joined the rebellion. His tale is told in Walter Scott's novel *Rob Roy* (1817).

- **The Old Pretender's** son Charles was Bonnie Prince Charlie, the Young Pretender.

- **In 1745**, Bonnie Prince Charlie led the Jacobites in a rebellion – called 'the Forty-Five' – against George II.

- **The Jacobites** defeated the English at Prestonpans, then invaded England, advancing as far as Derby before they lost their nerve and retreated.

- **In the sleet**, on bleak Culloden moor near Inverness on 16 April 1746, the Jacobites were routed by the English under the Duke of Cumberland. Cumberland came to be called Butcher, because of the way he ruthlessly hunted down and killed survivors.

# Napoleon

- **Napoleon Bonaparte** (1769–1821) was the greatest general of modern times, creating for a short while a French empire that covered most of Europe.

- **Napoleon** was quite short (157 cm) and was nicknamed *le Petit Caporal* ('the tiny corporal'). But he was an inspiring leader, with a genius for planning and an incredibly strong will.

- **Napoleon** was born on the island of Corsica. At the age of nine he went to army school and joined the French army at fourteen.

- **The Revolution** gave Napoleon the chance to shine and by 1794, at just 25, he was a brigadier general.

- **In 1796,** days after marrying Josephine de Beauharnais, Napoleon was sent with a small troop simply to hold up the invading Austrians. Instead, he drove them back as far as Vienna and conquered much of Austria.

◀ *Napoleon, with his right hand hidden, characteristically, inside his jacket.*

- By 1804, Napoleon's conquests had made him a hero in France, and he elected himself as Emperor Napoleon I.

- By 1812, Napoleon had defeated all the major countries in Europe but Britain and decided to invade Russia.

- **Napoleon's** invasion of Russia ended in such disaster that it broke his power in Europe. Soon afterwards, he was defeated at Leipzig, Paris was occupied by his enemies and he was sent into exile on the isle of Elba.

- **Napoleon escaped** from Elba in March 1815 to raise another army, but this was defeated by Wellington's armies at Waterloo, Belgium in June.

- **After Waterloo**, Napoleon was sent to the island of St Helena in the mid-Atlantic, where he died, aged 51.

# Ireland

- **When the Irish high king**, Turlough O'Connor, overthrew Dermot, the king of Leinster, c.1160, Dermot asked Henry II, the Norman king of England, for help.

- **When Dermot died**, the Norman baron Strongbow made himself king of Leinster. Henry II invaded and Normans slowly gained control of all Ireland.

- **Norman English power** in Ireland weakened as many people adopted Irish ways. By the 1400s, they controlled only a small area round Dublin called the Pale.

- **The phrase 'beyond the Pale'** originally meant the dark and wild Ireland outside the Pale.

- **To regain** control, the English began the 'plantation of Ireland' – giving English settlers land there.

- **In the late 1500s**, the English queen Elizabeth I tried to set up Protestantism in Ireland by force.

- **The Irish** in Ulster revolted, led first by Shane O'Neill and later his nephew Hugh O'Neill, but Elizabeth crushed the rebellion in 1603.

▲ *In July, 1690, William III of England fought the former King James II for the English crown at the Battle of the Boyne in Ireland.*

- **Oliver Cromwell** stamped out another Irish revolt in 1649.

- **After the defeat** of James II at the Boyne, Irish Catholics lost more land to English and Irish Protestants. By 1704, they owned just fifteen percent of Ireland.

- **In 1798**, Wolfe Tone led another Irish revolt – aided by a small French army – but the revolution was soon crushed.

# Industrial unrest

> ★ STAR FACT ★
> Thomas Paine's radical book *The Rights of Man*
> (1792) was the inspiration for many protesters.

- **Wages** in the new factories of the Industrial Revolution were low and working conditions were very poor.

- **Luddites** were English factory workers who, in 1811–12, smashed new machines that put people out of work.

- **High taxes** on imported corn meant that the poor were first to suffer in times of bad harvest, such as 1816–19.

- **The 'Peterloo' massacre** of 16 August 1819 was caused by a cavalry charge into a crowd gathered to hear radical leader Henry Hunt in Manchester's St Peter's field.

- **Welsh-born Robert Owen** (1771–1858) was the first great factory reformer and socialist.

- **Owen set up** 'ideal' communities at New Lanark in Scotland and New Harmony in Indiana, USA, where people might work together in good conditions.

▶ *GWM Reynolds was one of the leaders of the Chartists, the first great working class movement.*

- **Trade unions** were banned by British 'Combination' Acts. But these were partly removed in 1824.

- **Owen's** Grand National Consolidated Trades Union of 1833 – the first national union – was instantly repressed by the government.

- **The Tolpuddle martyrs** were six Dorset farmworkers who were deported to Australia for trying to form a trade union.

# Austria and Prussia

▶ *Maria Theresa's fight to become Holy Roman Emperor was crushed and Charles of Bavaria took the title. However, she rose to power once again as the wife of Charles's successor, Francis I.*

- **In 1711**, Austria, Hungary, Germany and parts of Italy were part of the Holy Roman Empire. The Emperor was Charles VI, the Archduke of Austria.

- **Charles VI** had no sons, but wanted his young daughter Maria Theresa to rule after him.

- **When Charles VI died, in 1740**, three non-Austrians claimed they should be Emperor. Maria Theresa rallied her Austrian people to defend her claim.

- **The War of the Austrian Succession** began with Britain, Hungary and the Netherlands backing Maria Theresa. Prussia, France, Bavaria, Saxony, Sardinia and Spain opposed her.

- **In 1742**, Maria Theresa was defeated and Charles of Bavaria became emperor. Charles, however, died in 1745. Maria Theresa's husband Francis I became emperor, though Maria was actually in charge.

- **The rise of Prussia** is linked to the rise of their ruling family the Hohenzollerns, and aristocratic landlords called junkers.

- **In 1417**, Frederick Hohenzollern became elector of Brandenburg. This meant he was one of the chosen few who could elect the Holy Roman Emperor.

- **By 1701**, Brandenburg expanded to become Prussia. Frederick I became its first king and built up his army.

- **Frederick I's son**, Frederick II or Frederick the Great (1712–86), was Prussia's greatest ruler. Frederick II was ambitious and manoeuvred Austria, France and Russia into wars that he used to gain land.

- **Austria and Prussia** lost much of their power after they were beaten by Napoleon's armies.

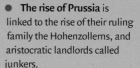

# Napoleonic Wars

▶ This map shows some of the major battles of the Napoleonic Wars.

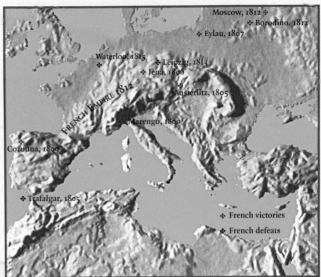

- **The Napoleonic Wars** were the long and bitter wars (1796–1815) between the France of Napoleon and other European countries, including Britain.

- **The wars began** with Napoleon scoring decisive victories over the Austrians in northern Italy in 1796 .

- **Napoleon** wanted to destroy British trade with the Middle East, and so attacked Egypt in 1798, defeating Egypt's rulers the Mamelukes – by the pyramids near Cairo. Napoleon's fleet was destroyed on the Nile by the British under Lord Nelson, but Napoleon then beat the Turks at Abuqir and went home in glory and triumph to be elected emperor.

- **The French Revolution** had introduced a conscript system, which meant that every Frenchman had to serve in the army – Napoleon's army was 750,000 in 1799. Two million more had joined up by 1815.

- **In 1805**, Britain, Russia and Austria allied against Napoleon. Napoleon crushed the Austrians and Russians at Austerlitz. When Prussia joined Russia the next year, Napoleon routed the Prussians at Jena and Auerstadt and the Russians at Friedland. But in 1805 Nelson's ships had destroyed the French and Spanish fleet at Trafalgar, off Spain. Nelson died at Trafalgar, but his victory ended Napoleon's chances of invading Britain.

> **★ STAR FACT ★**
> Napoleon won many victories by holding much of his army in reserve until he had opened up a carefully chosen weak point in enemy lines.

- **A key element** in the French success was the 'column'. Instead of advancing in a thin line, men marched almost up to the enemy in columns, then quickly spread out.

- **Napoleon** tried to destroy Britain with the 'Continental System', which banned any country from trading with it. This damaged British trade but cost Napoleon support.

- **In 1812**, Napoleon marched into Russia and captured Moscow, but the Russians burned everything as they fell back – leaving the French without food. Napoleon had to retreat from Moscow in the bitterest winter.

- **After the 1812 disaster**, Napoleon's enemies moved in swiftly. After a crushing defeat at Leipzig, Napoleon abdicated, his enemies occupied Paris and he went into exile on Elba. His brief comeback in 1815 ended in defeat at Waterloo.

◀ Napoleon's retreat from Moscow in 1812 was one of the worst of all military disasters. The winter trek was so cold and food so scarce that only 30,000 of the army of 695,000 that set out made it back to France.

# The Year of revolutions

▶ When rioters raged through Vienna, the feared Prince Metternich and many of his hated secret police were forced to flee.

- **The year 1848** saw revolutions break out right across Europe – in France, Germany, Italy, Austria and Hungary.

- **The revolutions** were not linked directly, but the revolutionaries had many of the same grievances.

- **Most revolutionaries** were also angry at repressive governments in which too few had a say.

- **Many revolutionaries** were angry too at the poverty suffered by ordinary people in the new industrial cities.

- **Many places**, like Hungary, Germany and Italy, were under the power of a foreign government, and revolutionaries were often nationalists who wanted freedom from foreign oppression for their country.

- **In Paris**, revolutionaries shouting 'bread or death' stormed government buildings, threw out the king and set up a republic.

- **In Vienna**, the powerful Prince Metternich and emperor were forced to flee as people created their own parliament and freed serfs.

- **In Hungary**, revolutionary leader Louis Kossuth set up a short-lived Hungarian republic.

- **In London**, the last and biggest Chartist rally took place. The Chartists had a charter demanding votes for all men and other political reforms. The rally dispersed peacefully.

- **All but the Paris Revolution** were quickly dealt with by armies – but the desire for change grew stronger over the century. The *Communist Manifesto*, written by Karl Marx and Friedrich Engels, was to become the basis of the great revolutions in Russia and China.

# Latin American revolts

- **By 1800**, Latin Americans were ready to revolt against the centuries of rule by Spain and Portugal.

- **When the Napoleonic Wars** turned Spain and Portugal into a battleground, Latin American revolutionaries seized their chance.

- **Mexicans** led by priests Hidalgo and Morelos revolted in 1810. The Spanish quelled the revolt and executed Hidalgo and Morelos. In 1821, however, Mexico gained independence.

- **In 1810**, José de San Martin led Argentina to independence. In 1816, San Martin made an epic march across the Andes to bring Chile freedom, too – with the help of Bernardo O'Higgins.

◀ Simon Bolivar (1783–1830) was South America's greatest revolutionary hero.

> ★ STAR FACT ★
> In 1824, San Martin left for Europe, saddened by disputes after independence and his wife's death.

- **In the north**, Venezuelans Francisco de Miranda, Simon Bolivar and Antonio de Sucre led a long fight against the Spanish in New Granada (now Colombia) and Peru. In 1819, after a great victory at Boyaca in Colombia, Bolivar proclaimed the Republic of Gran Colombia (now Venezuela, Colombia, Ecuador and Panama).

- **In 1824**, Sucre won a crucial victory at Ayacucho in Peru, freeing all of north South America from Spanish rule.

- **The Republic** of Bolivia was named after Bolivar, who wrote its constitution. Sucre became its first president.

- **Brazil** gained its freedom from Portugal without a fight when its ruler Prince John fled. His son became emperor.

- **Miranda** died in a Spanish jail after Bolivar handed him over. Sucre was assassinated in 1830. Bolivar died in 1830, shortly after a failed assassination attempt.

# Italian independence

► *Garibaldi was the hero who landed in Italy with just his thousand famous 'Red Shirts'. He went on to conquer all of southern Italy.*

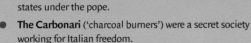

- **After the Napoleonic Wars**, Italy was split into various kingdoms – some, like Naples, under French Bourbon kings, some under Austrian rule and papal states under the pope.

- **The Carbonari** ('charcoal burners') were a secret society working for Italian freedom.

- **In 1820**, the Carbonari got the Bourbon king of Naples to agree to a constitution, but the Austrians stamped on it.

- **In 1831**, Giuseppe Mazzini founded 'Young Italy' to unite Italy. The drive to unite the country became known as the *Risorgimento* ('rising again').

- **In 1848**, revolutions broke out across Italy, but were put down.

- **In 1857**, Count Cavour, prime minister of Piedmont, asked France for help with evicting the Austrians.

- **In 1859**, France and Piedmont beat the Austrians at Magenta and Solferino. After political wrangling, northern Italy was joined to Piedmont under King Victor Emmanuel II.

- **Magenta** was such a bloody battle that a new purple-red colour was named after it.

- **In 1860**, the great hero Garibaldi led a rebellion and conquered all of southern Italy. Only Cavour's intervention stopped Garibaldi from taking Rome.

- **In 1861**, most of Italy was united under Victor Emmanuel. Venice was added in 1866 and Rome as capital in 1870.

# The Irish famine

- **The Irish potato famine** (1845–49) was one of the worst human disasters of the 1800s, when more than a million people in Ireland died of starvation.

- **In the 1800s**, most Irish were poor farmers, working tiny plots of land rented from Anglo-Irish landlords.

- **Potatoes were introduced** from America in the 1700s. They were such a successful crop that the Irish population grew to 8.4 million by 1844, but most were very poor.

- **Half the Irish** population depended entirely on potatoes for food, because English laws kept the price of bread too high for the poor Irish to buy.

- **In 1845**, much of the potato crop was ruined by blight, a disease caused by the fungus *Phytophthora*.

- **When the blight** ruined even more of the 1846-49 potato crops, millions of poor Irish farmers began to starve.

- **By August 1847**, three million were fed entirely on rations from soup kitchens set up by landlords and the British.

- **Many poor tenant farmers** were thrown off their land because they had no crop to sell in order to pay the rent.

- **Throughout the famine**, Irish farms exported grain, meat and vegetables too costly for the Irish to buy.

- **One and a half million** desperate Irish people packed up and left for America, leaving the country half-empty.

◄ *The potato famine devastated Ireland.*

# The British Empire

- **At its height**, in 1920, the British Empire covered a quarter of the world and ruled a quarter of the world's population.

- **The British** settled in more lands and ruled more peoples than any other nation in history.

- **The British Empire** began to build up in the 1600s, as British merchants started to extend their trading links throughout the world. The British won out over Dutch, Portuguese, French and Belgian rivals through the success of their navy and also their reasonably efficient colonial government.

- **The 13 American colonies** broke away in 1776, but Canada and many West Indian islands remained British.

- **Britain** gained control of India through the East India Company, between 1757 and 1858. In 1877, Queen Victoria was proclaimed Empress of India – the first time the word empire had been used in relation to the British possessions.

- **Many of the British possessions** had similar climates to Britain's – parts of Canada, South Africa, Australia and New Zealand – and British settlers moved to these places in huge numbers in the 1900s, pushing out the native inhabitants. These colonies were given more and more freedom to govern themselves and came to be called 'dominions'.

- **The Empire** reached its peak after World War I, when German and Turkish possessions were added.

- **After World War II**, more and more countries – especially in India and Africa – demanded independence. India and Pakistan became independent in 1947, Ceylon in 1948. By 1980, most African, West Indian and Pacific Island colonies also gained independence.

- **Most colonies** remained within the Commonwealth of Nations after independence. There are 54 Commonwealth nations, now linked essentially by agreed principles, but they all accept the British queen as head of the Commonwealth.

▲ The British Empire was kept under control both by the British Royal Navy, which commanded the seas, and the British army. The army, with its familiar red uniforms, were at work in every continent in the world, from India to Egypt, and Australia to Canada.

◄ This map shows the British Empire in the 1930s, when it was already beginning to shrink. Egypt was given some independence in 1922, when Sultan Ahmed became King Fuad I. Iraq gained a similar independence when amir Ahd Allah Faisal became King Faisal I.

- British Empire
- Semi-independent kingdoms

Canada
United Kingdom
Gibraltar    Malta    Iraq    Wei Hai Wei
Egypt    India    Hong Kong
Gambia    Nigeria    Aden
Sierra Leone    Br. Somaliland    Malay States    Brunei
British Guiana    Gold Coast
Br. East Africa    Br. New Guinea
N. & S. Rhodesia    Australia
Union of South Africa
New Zealand
Falklands

# The American Civil War

- **The American Civil War** (1861–65) was fought between northern states (the Union) and southern states (the Confederacy). It split friends and families and killed over 600,000 Americans.

- **The main cause** was slavery. In 1850, slavery was banned in the 18 northern states, but there were 4 million slaves in the 15 southern states, where they worked on huge plantations.

- **The conflicts developed** over whether new states, added as settlers pushed westward, should be 'slave' or 'free' states.

- **In 1854**, slavers gained legal victories with the Kansas-Nebraska Act, which let new states decide for themselves.

- **In 1860**, the Abolitionist (anti-slavery) Republican, Abraham Lincoln, was elected as president.

- **The southern states** immediately broke away from the Union in protest, to form their own Confederacy.

◀ *The Union flag had stars for all the 13 original states (top). The Confederates had their own version of the flag, also with 13 stars.*

- **As the war began**, the Confederates had the upper hand, fighting a defensive campaign.

- **The turning point** came in July 1863, when an invading southern army, commanded by Robert E Lee, was badly defeated at Gettysburg in Pennsylvania.

- **The extra** industrial resources of the north slowly began to tell and General Grant attacked the south from the north, while Sherman advanced ruthlessly from the west.

- **Lee surrendered** to Grant in Appomattox Court House, Virginia, on 9 April 1865. Slavery was abolished, but a few days later Lincoln was assassinated.

# Australia

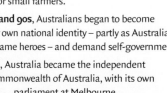

- **In 1788**, the British sent a fleet of 11 ships, carrying convicts, to start a prison colony in Australia.

- **The fleet landed** at Botany Bay, but the first governor, Arthur Phillip, settled in a new site that eventually became the city of Sydney.

- **160,000 convicts** were sent to Australia over the next 80 years, but by 1810 British settlers were arriving voluntarily.

- **After 1850**, settlers set up vast sheep farms in the interior. Many Aborigines were killed as they fought for their land.

- **In 1851**, gold was discovered in New South Wales and Victoria and many thousands of people came to Australia to seek their fortune, tripling the population to 1.1 million in just nine years.

- **After the gold rushes**, ex-miners campaigned to 'unlock the lands' – that is, free up land from squatters and landowners for small farmers.

- **In the 1880s and 90s**, Australians began to become aware of their own national identity – partly as Australian cricketers became heroes – and demand self-government.

- **In 1901**, Australia became the independent Commonwealth of Australia, with its own parliament at Melbourne.

- **In 1927**, the Australian government moved to a new capital in Canberra.

- **In 2000**, Australians voted to keep the British queen as head of state, rather than become a republic.

▼ *In 1770, Captain James Cook landed on the east coast of Australia and claimed it for Britain.*

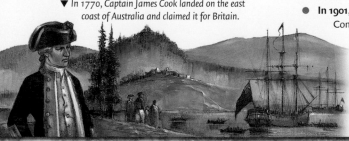

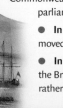

# The scramble for Africa

- **From 1500 to 1800**, Europeans were familiar only with the coast of Africa, from which slaves were taken.

- **After 1800**, many Europeans wanted to explore the interior in order to spread Christianity.

- **Some Europeans** wanted to develop trade in products like minerals and palm oil to help combat the slave trade.

- **Many European explorers**, such as David Livingstone and Richard Burton, went to Africa to find out more about its 'dark' (unknown) interior.

- **The wealth brought** to Britain by its colonies, such as India and North America, spurred the European powers to look for more lands to colonize.

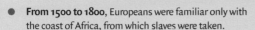

- **In the 1880s**, Europeans competed fiercely for African colonies. This feverish competition was called 'the scramble for Africa'.

- **By 1920**, Belgium, France, Germany, Great Britain, Italy, Portugal and Spain had divided all of Africa between them.

Belgian
French
Italian
German
Spanish
Portuguese
British
Independent

Rio de Oro
Libya (1912)
Egypt (1882)
French W.Africa (1876–98)
Sudan (1898)
Somaliland (1889–92)
Nigeria (1884–1900)
Liberia
Ethiopia
Br E. Africa (1886)
Congo (1885)
German E. Africa (1886)
Angola
Madagascar (1895–96)
SW Africa (1884)
SW Africa (1806)

▶ The European colonies in Africa in 1900, and the dates they were acquired.

- **In some parts** of Africa, colonial rule was established peacefully by agreement with the Africans.

- **In Nigeria** and Ghana, the Africans fought hard against British rule, and in Tanzania and Namibia, they fought against German rule.

- **Ethiopia and** Liberia were the only countries in Africa to hold on to their independence.

# The Oregon trail

- **After the USA** became independent, in 1783, waves of settlers began to move westward.

- **The first settlers** were fur traders. These were followed by cattle ranchers, then other farmers.

- **When cattle ranchers** moved to the Great Plains, they grazed huge herds on the open range and drove them to newly built rail depots for shipment east.

- **The cattle ranchers** of the Great Plains employed cowboys to herd the cattle and these cowboys became the symbol of the American west.

- **As the settlers** pushed west they came into conflict with Native Americans who already lived there.

- **The settlers** made many treaties with local peoples but broke almost all of them, and Native Americans were gradually driven from their lands or simply slaughtered.

- **In each decade**, new settlers struggled further west, facing great hardship in the hope of finding a new life.

- **Settlers** often set out with all their possessions in a covered wagon, often travelling with other wagons in a train (convoy) for safety.

- **The Oregon trail** was the longest of the routes to the west, winding over 3000 km from Independence, Missouri to the Pacific northwest.

- **The first group** of 900 wagons set out on the Oregon trail in the Great Migration of 1843.

◀ Would-be settlers packed everything they had in a covered wagon and joined a train heading west.

VA DESCRIPTIO.

# The Crimean War

- **The Crimean War** was fought in the Crimea – to the north of the Black Sea – between 1854 and 1856.

- **On one side** was Russia. On the other were Turkey, Britain, Piedmont/Sardinia and France.

- **The main cause** of the war was British, French and Turkish worries about Russian expansion in the Black Sea.

- **The war began** when Russia destroyed the Turkish fleet.

- **Armies on both sides** were badly organized. Many British soldiers died of cholera before they even reached the Crimea and wounded soldiers suffered badly from cold and disease.

- **During the Battle of Balaklava**, on 25 October 1854, a stupid mistake sent a gallant British cavalry charge straight on to the Russian guns. The heroic 'Charge of the Light Brigade' was made famous in a poem by Tennyson.

▶ More than 600 British soldiers charged into enemy fire and almost 250 of them were killed or wounded in the Battle of Balaclava.

- **Conditions** in the battle hospitals were reported in the first-ever war photographs and in the telegraphed news reports of W H Russell.

- **Nurses** like Florence Nightingale and Jamaican Mary Seacole went to the Crimea to help the wounded.

- **Lessons learned** in the Crimea helped to lay the foundations of modern nursing.

- **The war** finally ended in 1856 with the Treaty of Paris, with few gains on either side.

# Germany

- **In 1815**, Germany was divided among 38 different states of the German Confederation.

- **The most powerful** of the German states were Prussia and Austria, who sparred for dominance.

- **In 1862**, Otto von Bismarck (1815–98) became chancellor of Prussia. He was known as 'the Iron Chancellor 'and it was through his determination and skilful diplomacy that Germany was united.

- **In 1864**, Denmark tried to take over the disputed duchies of Schleswig and Holstein. The Austrians and Prussians sent an army to drive the Danes out.

- **Austria and Prussia** could not agree on what to do with Schleswig-Holstein.

- **Bismarck** proposed a new North German Confederation, excluding Austria.

- **Austria objected** to Bismarck's plan, but was defeated by Prussia in a very swift war in 1866.

- **To complete** Prussian control over Germany, Bismarck provoked a war against France, which had been the main opponent to German unity. He used the trick of the Ems telegram – a version of a telegram reporting a conversation between the Prussian king and the French ambassador, skilfully edited to imply an insult to France.

- **France** declared war on Prussia, but was swiftly beaten by the Prussians, who marched into Paris in January 1871.

- **After the defeat** of France, all the German states agreed to become part of a united Germany under Prussian leadership. On 18 January 1871, Wilhelm I was crowned kaiser (emperor).

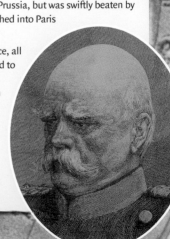

▶ Otto von Bismarck was the tough Prussian chancellor who engineered German unity.

# The rise of America

The President and Executive in the White House prepares laws and puts them into effect – and also conducts foreign affairs – but only Congress can make laws legal.

The Congress is the legislative body – the lawmakers. It meets in Washington's Capitol building and is split into two bodies: the House of Representatives and the Senate. There are 100 Senators (two from each state), elected for six years, and 435 Representatives or 'Congressmen', elected in batches every two years.

The Supreme Court is the judiciary, which decides how laws should be applied, and whether laws are acceptable by the Constitution. The nine judges meet in the Supreme Court building.

- **In the late 1800s,** the USA changed from a nation of farming pioneers and plantation owners to the world's biggest industrial powerhouse. American inventors and industrialists made products that changed the world – the typewriter (1867), the telephone (1876), the phonograph (1877) and electric light (1879). Then, in the early 1900s, Henry Ford pioneered the mass production of cars and made cars affordable for millions of ordinary people.

- **The writer** Mark Twain called the era of industrialization 'the Gilded Age', to describe the culture of the newly rich. Without any traditions of their own to draw on, they developed a showy culture aping that of European aristocrats – going to operas and building enormous European-style mansions filled with antiques, works by European painters and rare books.

◀ The Constitution of 1787 split the government of the USA into three arms, to prevent any part becoming too powerful: the President and Executive, Congress and the Supreme Court.

- **The less rich** enjoyed different kinds of show – circuses, vaudevilles and sport. By 1900, baseball was the national pastime. After 1920, motion pictures drew millions.

- **In the late 1800s,** many people started to realize that American progress was leaving many behind, and reformers called Progressives began to demand change. In 1891, farmers and labourers formed the Populist party.

- **In 1903,** Theodore Roosevelt was elected as president and promised Americans a 'square deal'. He tried to curb the power of monopolies like Standard Oil and supported striking miners.

- **Until 1900,** the USA played little part in world affairs. Bismarck said, 'A special Providence takes care of fools, drunkards and the USA'. But in 1898, the US battleship Maine was blown up off Cuba. Americans blamed the Spanish and in the war that followed, the USA easily defeated Spain.

- **From 1900 on,** the USA became more and more involved in world affairs, stepping in later in both World War 1 and World War II to play a decisive role. By the late 1900s, the USA saw itself to some extent as the world's policeman.

- **By the 1920s,** America was booming. The 1920s were known as the Roaring Twenties, because the pace of change was so exciting, and cars and loud jazz music made the new America so noisy and vibrant.

- **The confidence** of the 1920s spurred wild speculation on money markets, and in 1929 New York's Wall Street stock market crashed. US economic power was now so great that the crash plunged the world into the Great Depression of the 1930s, which saw businesses fold and millions unemployed.

▶ When Franklin D. Roosevelt (1882–1945) was elected President in 1932 one in four Americans were unemployed, many families too poor to eat and 5000 banks had failed. He promised a New Deal. Remarkably, it worked.

> ★ STAR FACT ★
> By 1930, Americans owned 23 million cars – three times as many as the rest of the world.

# Victorian England

- **In 1837**, 18-year-old Victoria became the queen of England and reigned for 63 years until 1901 – the longest reign in British history.

- **Victoria's reign** is called the Victorian Age.

- **In the Victorian Age**, Britain became the world's largest industrial and trading power and the British Empire reached its peak.

- **British factories and towns** mushroomed and railways were built throughout the country.

- **In 1851**, the Great Exhibition opened in a huge building of glass and iron, later called the Crystal Palace, to show British skills to the world.

- **In 1861**, Victoria's husband, Prince Albert, died and she went into mourning and wore black the rest of her life.

◄ Six million people visited the Great Exhibition in London in 1851.

- **The rapid expansion** of Victorian cities created vast slum areas where living conditions were appalling.

- **Social reformers** and writers such as Charles Dickens highlighted the problems of the slums. Slowly, parliament passed laws to improve conditions for working people and to provide education for all.

- **The two great** prime ministers of the Victorian Age were the flamboyant Benjamin Disraeli (1804–81) and the dour William Gladstone (1809–98).

- **Victorian middle-class life** cultivated cosy moral values, but there was also a seamy side, with widespread prostitution and crime.

# The Balkans

- **The Balkans** are the countries of southeastern Europe. The word *balkan* is Turkish for 'mountain'.

- **In 1800**, people of many nationalities lived in the Balkans – Slovenes, Croats, Serbs ,Bulgars, Greeks and Turks.

- **All the Balkan peoples** were ruled over by two old and weak empires – Austria-Hungary and Ottoman Turkey.

- **Through the 1800s**, many nationalities in the Balkans worked for independence.

- **European powers** like Russia and Germany encouraged independence movements for their own purposes.

- **Between 1829 and 1908**, Greece, Montenegro, Serbia, Romania and Bulgaria gained some independence, but many of their people were still in the old empires.

- **Austria refused** Slovenia and Croatia independence and held on to Bosnia-Herzegovina, which Serbia claimed.

- **In 1912**, various Balkan countries conspired to drive the Turks out of Europe in the First Balkan War, but rivalry between them led to a Second Balkan War in 1913, which

◄ Within just four weeks after the assassination of Archduke Franz Ferdinand, World War I had started.

let the Turks back in and left the Balkans highly unstable.

- **In June 1914**, Archduke Franz Ferdinand was assassinated in Sarajevo by Gavrilo Princip, a Serbian activist from Bosnia-Herzegovina.

- **Austria** believed Serbs were behind the assassination and declared war. Russia defended the Serbs as they had pledged by secret treaty. Soon all of Europe was engaged in World War I.

# The Opium Wars

▲ Opium extracted from poppies is highly addictive.

- **From 1759 to 1842**, Chinese emperors let European merchants trade only in the port of Guangzhou, and buy tea and silk only from the *cohong* (guild) of Chinese firms.

- **To pay for Chinese goods**, the East India Company used opium, the drug made from poppies. Huge loads of opium grown in India were sold to China.

- **All the silver** used to pay for opium upset the Chinese economy and opium-smuggling got out of hand.

- **In March 1839**, Chinese commissioner Lin Tse-hsü seized 20,000 crates of opium from British merchants.

- **Many ordinary** Chinese backed the British, because the British gave them opium and because the emperor's restrictive rule had brought poverty and hunger.

- **In 1840**, 16 British warships went to Guangzhou, starting the First Opium War.

- **Under the Treaty of Nanjing** in 1842, the Chinese gave Britain Hong Kong, abolished the cohong system and opened up trade to specially favoured nations.

- **In 1856**, Chinese police seized the *Arrow*, a ship flying a British flag, thus starting the Second Opium War.

- **British and French** armies invaded China and, after some wrangling, occupied Beijing in 1860.

- **At the Beijing Convention**, China opened more ports to western trade and allowed Europeans to travel inland.

# Abraham Lincoln

- **Abraham Lincoln** (1809–65) was America's 16th, and possibly greatest, president. He led the Union through the Civil War and the freeing of slaves.

- **He was born** in a backwoods log cabin in Kentucky, to a poor family.

- **He never went** to school but a relative said, "I never seen Abe after twelve 'at he didn't have a book in his hand or his pocket" – often the Bible.

- **He became a lawyer**, known for shrewd common sense and honesty. His defence of Rock Island Bridge (on the Mississippi River) against shipping interests made him famous.

- **Once elected** to Congress, he went on to win political fame as an opponent of slavery through debates over the Kansas-Nebraska Act, in the 1850s.

▲ Lincoln was a tall, lanky man. His razor-sharp mind, calm manner and resolutely moral attitudes made him a hero to many Americans.

- **In 1860**, just before the start of the Civil War ,between north and south, he was elected president – on the votes of the northern states alone.

- **On 1 January 1863**, Lincoln announced his Emancipation Proclamation, which freed all slaves.

- **In 1863**, after the terrible battle of Gettysburg, Lincoln made a famous speech called the Gettysburg Address, which summed up the spirit of democracy. In it he vowed that 'government of the people, by the people, for the people, shall not perish from the Earth.'

- **When the war** ended, in 1865, he made plans for peaceful reconciliation.

- **He was shot dead** at Ford's Theatre, Washington by John Wilkes Booth, a fanatical southerner.

# The Second Empire

- **In the 1840s**, the poverty of workers in French towns inspired men like Proudhon and Fourier to devise socialist ideas for solving various social problems.

- **Political meetings** were banned, so agitators held banquets to press their demands for liberal reforms.

- **On 22 February 1848**, the government banned a huge banquet in Paris, provoking such protest and rioting that King Louis-Philippe was forced to abdicate.

- **After much wrangling**, a new popular assembly set up the Second Republic and Louis-Napoleon Bonaparte was elected president in a vote by all French men.

- **Louis-Napoleon** (1808–73) was the son of Napoleon's brother and his step-daughter Hortense. In his youth, he had been active in the Italian Carbonari.

> ★ STAR FACT ★
> The famous boulevards of Paris, with their grand houses, were created on Napoleon III's orders.

- **The Assembly** proved conservative and, in 1852, Louis-Napoleon curbed their powers and had himself made Emperor Napoleon III by popular vote. His rule is called the Second Empire.

- **Napoleon III** gave state aid to industry, banks and railroads. Industry boomed and France grew rich. French engineers became world-famous.

- **Napoleon III's** Spanish wife, Eugenie, set the Empire Style for beautiful, lavish fashions and decoration that was mimicked across Europe.

- **Gradually**, Napoleon's rule provoked more and more hostility among radicals, and France's defeat by Germany in 1871 led to his downfall.

▶ Radical politicians came to the fore in the Empire.

# The Russian Revolution

- **In 1861**, Czar Alexander II freed Russian serfs, but they stayed poor. In towns, factory workers were just as poor.

- **Unrest among** factory workers and peasants grew and by 1901 there were two revolutionary parties: Socialist Revolutionary (SRP) and Socialist Democrat (SDP).

- **In 1903**, the SDP split into *Bolsheviks* (extremist majority), led by Lenin, and *Mensheviks* (moderate minority).

- **In 1905**, after Russia's disastrous war against Japan, workers and peasants rose in revolt and workers from arms factories set up the first *soviets* (workers' councils).

- **Czar Nicholas II** was forced to set up a *Duma* (parliament) but soon began to ignore it.

- **In March 1917**, terrible losses among Russian soldiers in World War 1, plus hardship at home, provoked a revolution.

- **The first 1917** revolution is called the February Revolution, because this was the month in the old Russian calendar.

- **Czar Nicholas** abdicated. Later, the Bolsheviks probably shot him and all his family at Ykaterinburg.

- **The SRP**, led by Kerensky, had the upper hand at first, but more soviets were set up and Bolseheviks gained support.

- **On 7 November** (25 October on the old calendar), the Bolsheviks seized the Winter Palace in St Petersburg. Lenin headed a new government, based in Moscow, and ended the war, while soviets took control of major cities.

▼ The Russian Revolution reached a climax when the Bolsheviks stormed the Winter Palace in St Petersburg.

# World War I

◀ Trenches were dug to protect troops from enemy gunfire, but soon became muddy hell-holes, filled with water, rats and disease. Soldiers had to eat, sleep and stand guard ankle-deep in mud. Every now and then, they were ordered by officers to 'go over the top' – climb out of their trenches and advance towards enemy lines. Once out of the trench, they were completely exposed to enemy fire, and quickly mown down. Millions of soldiers on both sides died this way. On 1 July 1916, 19,000 British soldiers were killed in just a few hours in the Battle of the Somme. The four-month Somme offensive killed 600,000 Germans, 400,000 British and 200,000 French – and advanced the Allies just 7 km. The horror of war in the trenches was conveyed in letters home and in poems by soldiers such as Siegfried Sassoon and Wilfred Owen.

- **World War I** (1914–18), the Great War, was the worst the world had seen (World War II would prove to be worse), killing ten million troops and involving many countries.

- **The war was caused** by the intense rivalry between European powers in the early 1900s. The trigger was the assassination of Franz Ferdinand in Sarajevo, Bosnia, on 28 June 1914. This made Austria start a war with Serbia and Russia came to Serbia's defence. Germany declared war on Russia and Russia's ally France on 3 August.

- **The Germans** had a secret plan (the 'Schlieffen plan') for invading France – and put it into action on 4 August. As well as tackling the French head-on, as expected, they swept round to the north through neutral Belgium. The outrage to Belgium drew Britain into the war.

- **As the Germans** moved on into France, they came up against the British and French (the Allies). The opposing armies dug defensive trenches – and stayed facing each other in much the same place for the whole four years of the war. The line of trenches, known as the Western front, soon stretched from the English Channel to Switzerland.

- **The war soon** developed an Eastern front, where the Central Powers (Austria and Germany) faced the Russians. This front, too, became bogged down. The deaths of millions of Russians provoked the 1917 Revolution, which took Russia out of the war.

- **In the Alps** the Central Powers were opposed by Italy, while at Gallipoli in Turkey, British and Anzac (Australia and New Zealand) troops fought the Turks.

- **The Allies** relied on supplies from N. America, so the Germans used U-boats (submarines) to attack ships in the Atlantic. The sinking of the liner Lusitania in May 1915, with 128 Americans out of 1198 casualties, helped bring the USA decisively into the war in 1917 against Germany.

- **In 1918** there were 3.5 million Germans on the Western front and in March they broke through towards Paris.

- **In July** British tanks broke the German line at Amiens.

- **An Allied naval blockade** meant many people were starving in Germany. As more US troops arrived, the Germans were pushed back. At 11 o'clock on 11 November 1918, the Germans signed an armistice (peace).

# The Ottoman Empire

- **In 1774**, the Turkish Ottoman Empire was defeated by the Russians after a six-year war, and was forced to allow Russian ships to pass through the Straits from the Black Sea to the Mediterranean.

- **During the 1800s**, the Ottoman Empire grew weaker and weaker and was called 'the Sick Man of Europe' by foreign statesmen.

- **In 1829**, the Greeks fought a successful war of independence against the Turks. Other Balkan states followed suit.

- **During the 1800s**, the Turks fought four wars against Russia and lost three. Russia gained Bessarabia (now Moldova and Ukraine) and control of the Black Sea.

▲ *Janissaries were the flamboyant elite soldiers of the Ottoman Empire. They were originally prisoners of war.*

- **Trying to stop** the empire's decline, Sultan Abdul-Hamid II crushed opposition violently in the 1890s.

- **The Young Turks** were students and army officers who, in 1908, revolted against Abdul-Hamid and then ruled through his brother Muhammad V.

- **The Turks** joined World War I on the German side to regain territory lost to the Russians and in the Balkans.

- **After World War I** ended, the Allies invaded Turkey and broke up the empire, leaving just modern Turkey.

- **The nationalist hero** Mustafa Kemal became first president of the Turkish republic, on 29 October 1923.

- **Kemal** became known as Ataturk (father of the Turks). He used his great power to weaken the hold of Islam.

# The rise of the Nazis

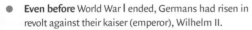

- **Even before** World War I ended, Germans had risen in revolt against their kaiser (emperor), Wilhelm II.

- **Wilhelm II** was driven out and in 1919 Germany became a republic, with a president elected by the people.

- **The republic** was called the Weimar Republic, because that was where the constitution was drafted.

- **Under the peace terms** for World War I, Germany was forced to pay huge amounts of money for war damage.

- **The cost of the war** ruined the German economy and rapidly rising prices made people poor overnight.

- **In 1923**, the National Socialist German Workers Party – Nazis – led by Adolf Hitler, tried a rebellion in Munich. The rebellion failed, but support for the Nazis grew.

- **The Great Depression** threw 6 million people out of work, and in 1933 enough people voted for the Nazis to make them the strongest party in parliament. Hitler became chancellor and at once set about destroying the opposition.

▶ *To boost their support, the Nazis held huge meetings called rallies, at which their cross symbol, the swastika, was prominently displayed.*

- **The Nazis** asserted German superiority over other races, including Jews and Slavs. They removed Jews from all government jobs and took away their rights.

- **On 9 Nov 1938**, Nazis broke windows and burned down synagogues and Jewish businesses. This night became known as *Kristallnacht* ('Night of the Broken Glass').

- **The Nazis** prepared for war to give Germans *Lebensraum* ('living space'). In 1936, they marched into the Rhineland. In 1938, they took Austria, followed by Czechoslovakia in 1939, and then Poland.

# Lenin and Stalin

- **Lenin** (1870–1924) was the leader of the Communist revolution in Russia.

- **Lenin's real name** was Vladimir Ilyich Ulyanov. He took the name Lenin from the River Lena in Siberia when he became a revolutionary.

- **Like Karl Marx** (1818–83), Lenin believed the world's workers would revolt and take over industry. Unlike Marx, he thought a small band of professionals like the Bolsheviks would need to lead the way.

- **After the 1905** revolution, Lenin lived in exile, but he returned to Russia when the czar fell, in 1917.

- **After the October Revolution**, Lenin ruled the country as head of the Bolsheviks (now the Communists). The Communists won the civil war that followed and in 1922 changed the Russian empire into a new nation, called

◀ *Lenin and Stalin in rare agreement.* the Union of Soviet Socialist Republics (USSR).

- **Joseph Stalin** (1879–1953) became dictator of the USSR after Lenin died in 1924, and remained so until he himself died, in 1953.

- **Stalin** was from Georgia and his real name was Joseph Vissarionovich Dzhugashvili.

- **Stalin used terror** to wipe out opposition and ensure the revolution survived. Russians lived in fear of the secret police NKVD (later the KGB), led by Beria, and millions went to their deaths in the *Gulags* (prison camps).

- **Millions of Russian peasants** starved in the 1930s as Stalin forced through government control of farms.

- **Stalin's** industrial programme transformed the USSR into one of the world's great industrial and military powers.

# Hitler

- **Adolf Hilter** (1889–1945) was the dictator who turned Germany into a war machine that started World War II and murdered 6 million Jews in the Holocaust.

- **Hitler** was born in Braunau-Am-Inn, Austria. He painted postcards before joining the German army in World War I.

- **Hitler** was so angry at the terms ending World War I that he joined the National Socialist (Nazi) party, becoming its leader.

▲*Hitler was a mesmerizing speaker, with the power to get the whole audience at his huge rallies shouting his praise.*

- **In 1923**, Hitler was put in prison after a failed Nazi coup, and there he wrote *Mein Kampf* ('My Struggle').

- **Mein Kampf** says Germany's problems were caused by Jews and communists and that it needed a strong *führer* (leader).

- **As the Depression** hit Germany in the early 1930s, Hitler's ideas gained support. In the 1933 elections, the Nazis got 37 percent of the vote and President Hindenburg asked Hitler to become chancellor (chief minister).

- **The Nazis** established the *Gestapo* (secret police) and used them to wipe out all opposition. When Hindenburg died in 1934, Hitler made himself führer.

- **Hitler** built up Germany's army, rigidly organized all workers and sent millions of Jews to concentration camps.

- **In 1938**, Hitler invaded Austria, then in 1939 Czechoslovkia and Poland too, and so began World War II.

- **Finally**, as Germany faced defeat in 1945, he married his mistress Eva Braun on 29 April, in their bomb shelter in Berlin. They shot themselves the next day.

# The Spanish Civil War

◀ A recruiting poster for the fascist Falange party.

- **In the 1920s**, a weak economy and political unrest led General de Rivera to run Spain as dictator, alongside King Alfonso XIII.

- **In 1930**, the army drove Rivera out. In 1931, a popular vote for a republic persuaded Alfonso to leave Spain.

- **Spain** was split. On the Left were socialists, communists and ordinary people who supported the republic. On the right were wealthy landowners, army officers, the Catholic Church, and the fascist Falange party, who wanted the king back.

- **Complicating the picture** were Catalonians and Basques, who wanted to break away from Spain.

- **In February 1936**, elections put the Popular Front, formed by all the left-wing groups, in power.

- **In July 1936**, a wave of army revolts started in Morocco and threatened to topple the Popular Front. The Popular Front supporters armed themselves and a bitter civil war began, with terrible atrocities on both sides.

- **The forces of the Right** were called the Nationalists and were led by General Franco. They were supported by fascist (very right-wing) Germany and Italy.

- **The forces of the Left** were called the Republicans or Loyalists and were supported by Soviet Russia. Liberals from other countries, like the writer Laurie Lee, formed an International Brigade to fight for the Loyalists.

- **At first**, Loyalists held the northeast and the big cities, but they gradually fell back. In March 1939, Franco's forces captured Madrid, the last Loyalist stronghold.

- **Franco** was dictator of Spain until he died in 1975.

# The Long March

- **In 1912**, the last Chinese emperor, six-year-old Pu-Yi, gave up his throne in the face of rebellion, and China became a republic, led by Sun Yat-sen.

- **When Sun died, in 1925, leadership of his Kuomintang** (Nationalist) party fell to Chiang Kai-shek, who allied with Communists to defeat warlords in the north.

- **In 1927**, Chiang Kai-shek turned on the Communists and forced their leaders to flee to the Jiangxi hills as he took control in Beijing.

- **By 1931**, the Communists had regrouped enough to set up a rival government in the south, called the Jiangxi soviet.

▶ The heroic Long March of the Red Army – to escape the Nationalists – became the stuff of Chinese legend.

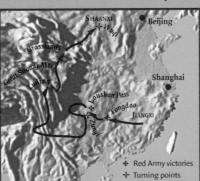

- **In 1934**, Chiang Kai-shek launched a massive attack on the Communist Red Army, forcing them to begin their famous Long March to the north to escape.

- **On the Long March**, the Red Army wound 10,000 km through the mountains, covering up to 100 km a day, until they reached Shaanxi in the north a year later.

- **Almost 95,000** of the 100,000 who set out on the Long March died of cold and hunger on the way. But, crucially, the Red Army survived.

- **During the March**, Mao Zedong became the Red Army leader.

- **Chiang** was forced to join with Mao to fight Japan in World War II, and Mao built up Red Army forces.

- **After the war**, Mao drove the weakened Kuomintang out and took control.

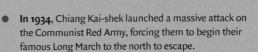

# World War II

▶ Winston Churchill (1874–1965) was the British prime minister whose courage and inspiring speeches helped the British withstand the German threat.

'Never in the field of human conflict have so many owed so much to so few' – Churchill on the British fighter pilots.

▲▶ In the crucial Battle of Britain, in 1940, heavily outnumbered British fighter planes eventually put a stop to massive German bombing raids on London and other English cities.

★ STAR FACT ★
The key to the early German successes was the *Blitzkrieg* ('lightning war') – a stunningly rapid attack with tanks and aeroplanes.

- **World War II** (1939–45) was the most terrible war ever fought. It not only killed 17 million soldiers – compared to 10 million in World War I – but also twice as many civilians, through starvation, bombings and massacres.

- **It was the first** truly global war – fought on the plains of Europe, in the jungles of Southeast Asia, on the deserts of Africa, among the islands of the Pacific, on (and under) the Atlantic Ocean, and in many other places.

- **It began** when Hitler's Germany invaded Poland on 1 Sept 1939. Great Britain thought the USSR would defend Poland but Hitler and Stalin made a pact. As Germany invaded Poland from the west, the USSR invaded from the east.

- **After a lull**, or 'Phoney War', in May–June 1940, the Germans quickly overran Norway and Denmark, then

▶ There were two main areas of war. 1. Europe, where Britain and the USSR, and later the USA, were fighting Germany and Italy. 2. The Pacific and SE Asia, where the US and Britain were fighting Japan.

Luxembourg, the Netherlands, Belgium and France.

- **The British army** was trapped by the Channel coast, but the Germans held back, and 338,000 British troops got away from Dunkirk, France, on an armada of little boats.

- **By August 1940**, Italy joined the war on the German side, and Germany launched air raids on England to prepare for an invasion. This was the Battle of Britain (above).

- **Fearing the USSR** would turn against him, Hitler launched a sudden invasion of the USSR on 22 June 1941. The USA joined the war when Japan bombed its fleet without warning in Pearl Harbor, Hawaii, on 7 Dec 1941.

- **Germany, Italy, Japan** and six other nations joined forces as the 'Axis'. Britain, the USA, USSR, China and 50 other nations were together called the Allies. In 1942, the Allies halted the Axis in Africa, invading Italy in 1943 and France in 1944. In 1945, the Allies drove into Germany from east and west. Germany surrendered on 7 May 1945. The terrible Pacific conflict ended when the USA dropped atom bombs on the Japanese cities Hiroshima and Nagasaki. Japan surrendered on 2 Sept 1945.

- **As the Allies** moved into Germany, they found the horror of Nazi death camps like Auschwitz and Buchenwald, where millions of Jews and others had been slaughtered by starvation and in gas chambers.

Battle of Britain
Stalingrad
North Atlantic
El Alamein
Iwo Jima
Burma
Philippines

➤ Early Axis advances,1939–41
✳ Crucial campaigns
◀ Allied advances in the Pacific, 1943–45

# India

- **Indian discontent** with British rule began to boil after the British killed 379 protestors at Amritsar, in 1920.

- **In 1920,** Mahatma Gandhi became the leader of a movement demanding independence for India.

- **Gandhi** led a series of non-violent protests against the British, such as boycotting British goods and refusing to pay taxes. He gained millions of supporters.

- **In 1930,** Gandhi marched to the sea to make salt from seawater in protest against a tax on salt.

- **In 1935,** the British gave India a new constitution that allowed Indians more power. For the Muslims, however, led by Mohammed Ali Jinnah, this was not enough.

- **Jinnah** demanded a new country for Muslims called Pakistan, separate from the Hindus.

- **In World War II,** Indians said they would only fight on the British side if they were given independence.

- **In 1942,** Gandhi launched his 'Quit India' campaign to get rid of the British, who then jailed Indian leaders.

▲ *The Indian government building in Delhi.*

- **In 1946,** Britain offered independence to all of India, but Muslims did not want to live under a Hindu majority and terrible riots broke out in Calcutta.

- **Indian and British** leaders agreed to partition (split) India and Pakistan. Pakistan became independent on 14 August 1947, India the next day. 7.5 million Muslims immediately fled to Pakistan and 10 million Hindus to India.

# Mao

▶ *Mao Zedong gained worldwide fame after the communist victory in 1949.*

- **Mao Zedong** (1893–1976) led China's struggle towards communism and was China's leader for 27 years.

- **Mao was** born in 1893 to a peasant family in Shaoshan in Hunan.

- **In 1921,** he and 11 others formed the Chinese Communist Party. He led the Red Army on the Long March.

- **Mao** led the communist takeover of China in 1949 and then ruled China as Chairman of the Republic.

- **Mao** ordered the redistribution of land and the elimination of rural landlords. He spurred peasants to work together on collective farms.

- **Mao's** ideas were stated in a little red book – *The Thoughts of Chairman Mao* – learnt by heart by Chinese children.

- **In 1957,** Mao's 'Great Leap Forward' forced his people to work on communes to develop farming and industry.

- **In 1959,** Mao retired as Chairman, but stayed in control.

- **In 1966,** Mao launched a 'Cultural Revolution'. Led by Mao's wife Jiang Qing and friends (the Gang of Four).

- **Mao died** in 1976.

# Gandhi

◀ *Gandhi always dressed with extreme simplicity, wearing just a plain robe and shorts, his feet bare or in sandals.*

- **Mohandas Gandhi** (1869–1948) was the inspirational leader who led India's fight for independence in a remarkable campaign of non-violent protest.

- **Gandhi** is often called *Mahatma*, which means 'Great Soul'. He believed truth could only be known through tolerance and concern for others.

- **He was born** in Probander in India. At 13, he married a girl of 13 called Kasturba. They later had four children. At 19, he went to study law in London.

- **Gandhi** went to work as a lawyer in South Africa in 1893, but soon after arriving was thrown out of a railway carriage because of the colour of his skin. He then stayed in South Africa for 21 years to fight for Indian rights.

- **Gandhi** emphasized non-violent protest. By imposing hardship on himself and showing no anger or hatred, he believed he could persuade his opponents he was right. This method of action was called *Satyagraha*.

- **Gandhi** returned to India in 1915, and after the Amritsar massacre led India's fight for independence.

- **In 1920**, Gandhi began a programme of hand-spinning and weaving that he believed would give Indians economic independence, so challenging the British.

- **Gandhi** was jailed again and again for his protests, both in South Africa and India, and spent seven years in jail.

- **Gandhi** was assassinated on 30 January 1948, by a Hindu who hated his tolerance of Muslims and others.

> **★ STAR FACT ★**
> In 1948, Gandhi persuaded Hindus and Muslims to stop fighting by going on a fast.

# Israel

- **In the 1920s**, Palestine was under British rule, and the British encouraged Jews to settle there.

- **In the aftermath** of the Holocaust, when Hitler killed six million Jews, most countries supported the idea of a homeland where Jews would be free from persecution.

- **In 1948**, the United Nations split Palestine between Arabs and Jews. Arabs saw this as a theft of Arab land.

- **Arabs immediately** invaded Israel (Jewish Palestine), but were defeated. Israel took over all of Palestine except the Gaza strip (to Egypt) and the West Bank (to Jordan).

- **In 1956–57**, Arab Egypt took control of the Suez Canal.

- **In 1967**, Egypt closed the Gulf of Aqaba, Israel's only way to the Red Sea. Israel declared war on the Arab states.

- **Israel** won the war in just six days, and calls it the 'Six Day War'. Arabs call it the June War. Afterwards, Israel controlled Sinai, the Gaza strip and the West Bank.

- **In 1973**, Egypt attacked the Israelis in Sinai, starting the Yom Kippur War. With US help, the Israelis repulsed them.

- **By the Camp David Accords** of 1978, Egypt recognized Israel's right to exist and Israel returned Sinai to Egypt. US president Jimmy Carter set up the agreement.

- **The PLO**, led by Yasser Arafat, began to fight for Palestinian independence after the Six Day War. Fighting and negotiation continue to this day.

▼ *An Israeli tank taking part in 1967's Six Day War.*

# The Cold War

▲ For many, the tearing down of the Berlin Wall, in 1989, marked the end of the Cold War. Berliners had a huge party on the ruins.

- **The Cold War** was the rivalry between communist and non-communist countries after World War II – between the USSR and USA in particular.

- **It was called** the Cold War because the USSR and USA did not fight directly. But both supported countries that did – like the USA in Vietnam and the USSR in Korea.

- **The Iron Curtain** was the barrier between western Europe and communist eastern Europe.

- **The name Iron Curtain** was used by German propagandist Goebbels and adopted by Churchill.

- **The Berlin Wall** dividing communist East Berlin from the West was a powerful Cold War symbol. Dozens were shot trying to escape from the East over the wall.

- **The Cold War** was fought using both propaganda and art and by secret means such as spies and secret agents.

- **The USA and USSR** waged an arms race to build up nuclear bombs and missiles one step ahead of their rival.

- **Real war** loomed when US president Kennedy threatened the USSR as it tried to build missile bases on Cuba in 1962.

- **The Cold War** thawed after 1985, when Soviet leader Mikhail Gorbachev introduced reforms in the USSR and began to co-operate with the West.

- **In 1989**, the Berlin Wall came down. In 1989–90, many eastern European countries broke away from Soviet control.

# Scandinavia

- **In 1397**, Sweden, Norway and Denmark had joined together as one kingdom to combat the threat of German influence.

- **In 1523**, a Swedish noble called Gustavus Vasa took Sweden out of the Union. Under Gustavus Adolphus (ruled 1611–32), and later Charles XII (ruled 1697–1718), Sweden became a powerful nation in its own right, and gained possession of Finland.

- **After the Napoleonic Wars**, Sweden lost Finland, but gained Norway from Denmark, which had sided with defeated France.

- **In the 1800s**, Norwegians began to revive national traditions – like the Viking language and 'Hardanger' fiddle music – and demand independence from Sweden. This was finally granted in September 1905.

◄ Copenhagen's most famous landmark is the 1913 statue of the Little Mermaid, from the famous tale by Danish 19th-century children's writer, Hans Christian Andersen.

- **In World War II**, Norway tried to remain neutral, but Germany invaded.

- **The Germans** made a Norwegian who helped them, Vidkun Quisling, prime minister. *Quisling* is now a word for traitor.

- **Since 1932**, Sweden has been governed mostly by the socialist SDP, who have spread Sweden's high standard of living to all levels of society.

- **In 1966**, the National Insurance Act passed by Norway's *Storting* (parliament) gave Norwegians one of the world's best welfare systems.

- **In 1986**, Swedish PM Olof Palme was assassinated.

- **Sweden and Denmark** joined the European Union in the 1990s; Norwegians voted against joining in 1994.

# Japan

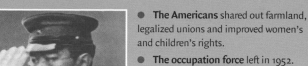
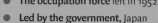

▶ *Emperor Hirohito (1901–89) was the first Japanese emperor to give up his god-like status, ruling after 1945 as a figurehead only.*

- **In 1942,** Japanese conquests in World War II gave it a huge empire across SE Asia, but after they lost the decisive naval battle of Midway to the USA, the tide turned against Japan.

- **The final blow** for the Japanese was the devastating atomic bombs dropped on the cities of Hiroshima (6 Aug 1945) and Nagasaki (9 Aug).

- **The Japanese** surrendered to the USA on 2 September 1945.

- **The surrender** brought a foreign occupying force to Japan, led by US general, Douglas MacArthur.

- **MacArthur** drew up a new constitution for Japan. Under this, Emperor Hirohito lost all real power.

- **The Americans** shared out farmland, legalized unions and improved women's and children's rights.

- **The occupation force** left in 1952.

- **Led by the government,** Japan recovered from the ruin of the war and launched itself on an amazing industrial boom which turned Japan into the world's healthiest economy in barely 25 years.

- **Japanese** society changed as people moved to the cities and the young began to behave independently.

- **In the 1980s,** the government was rocked by corruption scandals. The economy suffered too, as exports declined, and the country experienced a crisis of confidence.

# South Africa

- **In 1910,** four British colonies – Transvaal, Orange Free State, Cape Colony and Natal – joined to make the self-governing Union of South Africa.

- **White people** had almost complete power in the Union, and blacks had virtually no legal rights.

- **Gandhi** campaigned for Indian rights in South Africa and had limited success.

◀ *Many blacks were tortured, imprisoned or killed in the long and bitter struggle against apartheid. 600 died here at Soweto in 1976.*

- **When Gandhi** returned to India, black South Africans set up their own campaign in 1912 with the movement later called the ANC (African National Congress).

- **Afrikaners** – descended from the Dutch Boer people – began to fight for control. Their National Party made headway and in 1948 came to power. It enacted 'apartheid' laws to keep all the races firmly apart.

- **The ANC** fought against apartheid – and especially against 'pass' laws that meant blacks had to carry passes.

- **In 1960,** police opened fire on protesting blacks at Sharpeville, killing 69. The government banned the ANC.

- **In the 1970s and 80s,** opposition to apartheid grew both in and outside South Africa, with many countries applying sanctions (trade restrictions).

- **In 1990,** President de Klerk released Nelson Mandela, an activist jailed since 1962, and repealed apartheid laws.

- **In 1994,** the ANC won the first open elections and Nelson Mandela became South Africa's first black president.

# United Nations

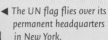

- **In the aftermath** of World War I, the great powers had set up a League of Nations – a forum for nations to come together, discuss world problems and so avoid war.
- **In 1942**, the Allies pledged to fight against the Axis powers with a statement called the Declaration by United Nations.
- **In 1944**, the same nations – including Britain, the USA, USSR and China – got together at Dumbarton Oaks in Washington DC to try and set up a peacekeeping organization.
- **The key to the** Dumbarton Oaks plan was a Security Council in which Britain, the USA, USSR and China would be permanent members.
- **In February 1945**, US president Roosevelt, British PM Churchill and Soviet leader Stalin met at Yalta in the Crimea and announced that a UN conference would meet in San Francisco. The three introduced the idea of them having a special veto (right to reject UN measures).

◄ The UN flag flies over its permanent headquarters in New York.

- **50 nations** met at San Francisco in April 1945 to draw up the Charter for the United Nations.
- **The Big Three** – Britain, the USA and USSR – gave themselves veto power over the Security Council, but the smaller nations gave the UN a General Assembly to help make it a truly global organization.
- **The UN Charter** came into effect on 24 October 1945.
- **In 1971**, the UN expelled Taiwan and admitted Communist China instead.
- **In recent years**, the UN peacekeeping force has been involved in keeping the peace in many places, including Haiti, the Congo, Kosovo, Sierra Leone and E.Timor.

# Vietnam

- **From 1883**, Vietnam, along with Cambodia and Laos, was ruled by France as French Indochina or *Indochine*.
- **As Germany** invaded France in World War II, Japan took over Vietnam.
- **When Japan lost**, in 1945, Vietnamese communists – the Vietminh – led by Ho Chi Minh, took over Vietnam.
- **British and Chinese** troops reclaimed Vietnam for the French, but the Vietminh fought back. The French set up a State of Vietnam under Bao Dai to oppose the Vietminh.
- **In 1954**, the warring parties agreed to split Vietnam into the North under Ho Chi Minh and South under Bao Dai.
- **The Vietminh-backed** Viet Cong started a rebellion in the South. In 1965, the USA began to bomb North Vietnam, while the USSR and China gave them arms.

▲ US helicopters proved highly effective in the Vietnam jungles.

- **As fighting escalated**, Americans began to protest against US involvement and in 1973, the US withdrew.
- **In 1975**, the Viet Cong captured Saigon, the capital of the South, and the next year united North and South.
- **One million** Vietnamese left as refugees, but by 2000, Vietnam was developing quietly and some returned.

> ★ STAR FACT ★
> The Vietnamese war was the first war that was widely televised as it happened.

# Iraq and Iran

- **Iran** used to be called Persia, which, 2500 years ago, ruled over one of the great ancient empires.
- **The last shah** (king) of Iran fled the country in 1979. The *ayatollah* (religious teacher) Khomeini became leader.
- **Iraq** used to be called Mesopotamia and was part of the Turkish Ottoman Empire until 1920 when it came under British control.
- **In 1930,** Iraq became independent as a kingdom. But British influence was strong until the last king, Faisal II, was killed and Iraq became a republic in 1958.
- **Saddam Hussein** became Iraqi president in 1979.
- **Saddam Hussein** was worried by the unsettling effects of the Islamic revolution in Iran and was also eager to seize some disputed territory.

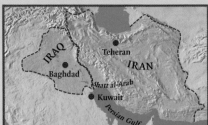

◀ Iran and Iraq have a long and disputed common border.

- **In September 1980,** Iraq invaded Iran to begin the eight-year-long Iran-Iraq War.
- **The war** devastated both countries and killed 1.5 million people. Iraq launched bombing raids and Iran replied with missile attacks on Baghdad.
- **In 1988,** careful negotiations by the UN leader Perez de Cuéllar arranged a peace settlement.
- **In 2003,** accusing Saddam of possessing 'weapons of mass destruction', a US-led force invaded Iraq, ousting Saddam. The country collapsed in anarchy, as they fought each other and the foreign troops.
- **Saddam was captured in 2003,** tried in 2005–2006, and executed in 2006.

# The break-up of Russia

- **After Stalin died,** in 1953, many people were released from the Siberian prison camps, but the USSR, under its new leader Khrushchev, stayed restrictive and secretive.
- **The KGB** was a secret police force. It dealt harshly with anyone who did not toe the communist line.
- **In the 1980s,** cracks began to appear in the communist machine.
- **In 1985,** Mikhail Gorbachev became Soviet leader and introduced policies of *perestroika* (economic reform), *glasnost* (government openness) and *demokratizatsiya* (increased democracy).
- **Gorbachev** also made cuts in army spending and improved relationships with the West.

◀ *Mikhail Gorbachev.*

- **In 1989,** a McDonalds restaurant opened in Moscow.
- **As people** in the USSR gained freedom, so people in communist eastern Europe demanded freedom. New democratic governments were elected in Hungary, Poland, Czechoslovakia, Romania and Bulgaria.
- **The republics** within the USSR demanded independence too, and in 1991 the USSR was dissolved and replaced by a Commonwealth of Independent States (CIS).
- **Gorbachev's reforms** angered Communist Party leaders, who staged a coup and imprisoned Gorbachev, but he was freed and the coup was brought down by Boris Yeltsin, who became Russia's first president.
- **Under Yeltsin,** the state industries of the Soviet era were gradually broken up and Russia seemed to be moving towards Western-style capitalism. But the collapse of the Communist Party structure led to chaos, lawlessness and economic problems. In 2000, the Russians elected Vladimir Putin as president, a strong leader who they hoped would see them out of the crisis.

# The European Union

◀ The European Commission building is in Brussels. The Parliament is in Strasbourg. The Court of Justice is in Luxembourg.

- **The European Union** is an organization of 27 European countries, including France, Germany and the UK.
- **After World War II** ended in 1945, Jean Monnet promoted the idea of uniting Europe economically and politically.
- **In 1952,** six countries formed the European Coal and Steel Community (ECSC), to trade in coal and steel.
- **The success of the ECSC** led the member countries to break down all trade barriers between them as part of the European Community (EC), in 1967.

- **1973–81:** six new countries join the EC, including the UK.
- **In 1992,** the 12 EC members signed a treaty at Maastricht in the Netherlands to form the European Union (EU).
- **The EU** added cooperation on justice and police matters and cooperation in foreign and security affairs to the economic links of the EC. These three links are called the 'Three Pillars' of the EU.
- **The EU** has five governing bodies: the Commission, Council of Ministers, Court of Justice, Parliament and the European Council. The 27 Commissioners submit laws for the Council to make and put into effect. Parliament has very limited powers but is gaining more each year.
- **In 1999,** the EU launched the Euro, which is intended to become a single European currency.

> ★ STAR FACT ★
> The EU has 27 members. Eight more have applied or have stated their intention to apply.

# Latin America

- **In the 1950s,** many Latin American governments sought to break their dependence on single farm products such as sugar and beef through major industrialization programmes.
- **'Populist' alliances** between workers and industrialists came to the fore.
- **In Argentina,** Juan Perón came to power and tried to build up industry at the expense of agriculture.
- **Landowners** suffering from the emphasis on industry began to form alliances with the army. Army coups took place in Argentina (1955), Brazil (1964) and Chile (1973).
- **Many** of the military regimes were secretly backed by foreign powers such as the USA.

▲ Che Guevara became a hero to political activists throughout the world.

- **In the 1960s,** some Latin American groups resorted to guerrilla warfare to bring down the military dictatorships.
- **In 1959,** an Argentinian communist called Che Guevara helped overthrow the dictator of Cuba and bring Fidel Castro to power.
- **In 1965,** Che Guevara was killed leading a guerrilla band trying to overthrow the dictator of Bolivia.
- **Under the dictators,** opposition was suppressed and many people were tortured, imprisoned or 'disappeared', as 20,000 did in Argentina.
- **In the 1980s and 90s,** economic failure brought down most Latin American dictators, including Pinochet in Chile (1990) and Galtieri in Argentina (1983).

# Acknowledgements

**The publishers would like to thank the following sources
for the photographs used in this book:**

Page 57 Kobal Collection/Amblin/Universal;
p179 Universal/pictorialpress.com; p188 Warner/pictorialpress.com;
p368 (B/C) Illustrated London News; p373 (B/C) Lowell Georgia/CORBIS;
p379 (B/R) Vanni Archive/CORBIS; p381 (B/R) Lindsay Hebberd/CORBIS;
p382 (B/L) Michael Nicholson/CORBIS; p402 (T/L) Staffan Widstrand/CORBIS;
p409 (B/R) Christel Gerstenberg/CORBIS; p411 (B/R) Bojan Brecelj/CORBIS;
p419 (T/R) Aachen Tourist Board; p427 (T/R) Gianni Dagli Orti/CORBIS;
p427 (B/R) Bettmann/CORBIS; p429 (T/R) Burstein Collection/CORBIS;
p432 (T/L) Angelo Hornak/CORBIS; p432 (B/C) Michael Maslan Historic Photographs/CORBIS;
p437 (T/R) Yann Arthus-Bertrand/CORBIS; p437 (B/C) Yann Arthus-Bertrand/CORBIS;
p439 (C/B) Gianni Dagli Orti/CORBIS; p441 CORBIS; p442 (B/L) Dave G. Houser/CORBIS;
p446 (T/R) Bettmann/CORBIS; p449 (B/R) Macduff Everton/CORBIS;
p451 (B/R) Gianni Dagli Orti/CORBIS; p454 (B/R) Reuters NewMedia Inc./CORBIS;
p458 (T/R) Hulton-Deutsch Collection/CORBIS; p460 (T/C) Archivo Iconografico;
p465 (T/C) Bettmann/CORBIS; p467 (T/C) Historical Picture Archive/CORBIS;
p468 (T/L) Sean Sexton Collection/CORBIS; p469 (B/R) Bettmann/CORBIS;
p471 (T/C) Historical Picture Archive/CORBIS; p472 (T/L) CORBIS;
p474 (T/L) Museum of Flight/CORBIS; p475 (T/R) Angelo Hornak/CORBIS;
p476 (B/L) Vittoriano Rastelli/CORBIS; p478 (B/L) Hulton-Deutsch Collection/CORBIS;
p479 (B/R) Bettmann/CORBIS; p481 (B/R) Tom Bean/CORBIS.

All other photographs are from MKP Archives, Castrol, CMCD, Corbis, Corel,
digitalSTOCK, digitalvision, Flat Earth, Hemera, ILN, John Foxx, PhotoAlto, PhotoDisc,
PhotoEssentials, PhotoPro, Stockbyte